ZAGATSURVEY®

2002

NEW YORK CITY RESTAURANTS

Editors: Curt Gathje and Carol Diuguid

Coordinator: Larry Cohn

Published and distributed by
ZAGAT SURVEY, LLC
4 Columbus Circle
New York, New York 10019
Tel: 212 977 6000
E-mail: newyork@zagat.com
Web site: www.zagat.com

Acknowledgments

Thanks to the following, each of whom edited sections of this guide: Olga Boikess, Daphne Dennis, Peter Gambacchini, Katie Hottinger, Gwen Hyman, Bernard Onken, Tanya Wenman Steel and Reece Wilson.

This guide would not have been possible without the hard work of our staff, especially Betsy Andrews, Erika Boudreau-Harris, Deirdre Bourdet, Phil Cardone, Reni Chin, Jamie Clark, Anne Cole, Erica Curtis, Liz Daleske, Jessica Fields, Jeff Freier, Shelley Gallagher, Randi Gollin, Jessica Gonzalez, Diane Karlin, Natalie Lebert, Charles Levine, Mike Liao, Dave Makulec, Lorraine Mead, Andrew O'Neill, Rob Poole, Brooke Rein, Benjamin Schmerler, Troy Segal, Robert Seixas, Christy Stabin, Danny Vera, Wei Wu and Kyle Zolner.

The reviews published in this guide are based on public opinion surveys, with numerical ratings reflecting the average scores given by all survey participants who voted on each establishment and text based on direct quotes from, or fair paraphrasings of, participants' comments. Phone numbers, addresses, and other factual information were correct to the best of our knowledge when published in this guide; any subsequent changes may not be reflected.

© 2001 Zagat Survey, LLC
ISBN 1-57006-322-2

Contents

What's New	4
About This Survey	6
Key to Ratings and Symbols	7
Most Popular and Most Visited Places	9
Top Ratings: By Food, Decor and Service	12
Best Buys and Prix Fixes	20
RESTAURANT DIRECTORY	
Names, Addresses, Phones, Ratings and Reviews	23
INDEXES	
Cuisines	218
Locations	238
Special Features	256
All You Can Eat	256
Bathrooms to Visit	256
Breakfast	256
Brunch	257
Buffet Served	257
Business Dining	257
Celebrity Chefs	258
Cheese Trays	259
Child-Friendly	259
Delivery/Takeout	260
Dining Alone	260
Entertainment/Dancing	261
Family-Style	262
Fireplaces	262
Game in Season	262
Historic Places	263
Hotel Dining	264
"In" Places	265
Jacket Required	265
Jury Duty	266
Kosher	266
Late Dining	266
Meet for a Drink	267
Natural/Organic	268
Noteworthy Newcomers	268
Noteworthy Closings	270
Outdoor Dining	271
Parkside Views	271
People-Watching	272
Power Scenes	272
Pre-Theater/Prix Fixe Menus	273
Private Rooms for Parties	273
Pubs/Bars/Microbreweries	274
Quick Bites	274
Quiet Conversation	275
Raw Bars	275
Romantic Places	275
Saturday & Sunday – Best Bets	276
Senior Appeal	278
Singles Scenes	279
Sleepers & Teflons	279
Tasting Menus	280
Tea Service	280
Theme Restaurants	280
Transporting Experiences	280
Visitors on Expense Account	281
Winning Wine Lists	281
Wine Chart	283

What's New

Here are the most significant trends of the past year:

- **Continuing Growth:** Despite the national economic downturn and the destruction of the World Trade Center, there were 221 noteworthy restaurant openings in New York this year, compared with a mere 80 closings. This remarkable resiliency corresponds to the record of openings versus closings during the 1988–1992 recession. The fact is that the underlying forces that have been driving the restaurant revolution in America for more than a generation remain in place. We predict that whatever trials the industry may currently face, it will emerge stronger than ever.

- **Important Arrivals:** Openings over the past year include a number of first-rate venues that would be the envy of any city in the world: Arezzo, Artisanal, Beppe, Bid, Citarella, Craft, Danzón, D'Artagnan, db Bistro Moderne, Fleur de Sel, Ilo, Man Ray, MarkJoseph, Mary's Fish Camp, Medi, 92, Olives, Ouest, Pico, Tamarind, Town and Virot.

- **Works in Progress:** A number of prominent projects are due to open in the coming months. Among the most important are: Blue Fin, a 400-seat Times Square seafooder from Steve Hanson's B.R. Guest Restaurant Group; Blue Smoke, Danny Meyer's ambitious take on BBQ near Madison Park; Catch, a Flatiron seafood house via chef/TV personality Bobby Flay; Fiamma Osteria, Steve Hanson's first venture into Italian dining, in SoHo; Marseille and Pigalle, two massive Midtown French brasseries, with chef Alex Urena (ex Blue Hill) running the former; Opia, an international entry to an underdeveloped part of East 57th Street; R.S.V.P., an East Side spin-off of Swifty's; Spice Market, an Asian addition to the Meatpacking District from Jean-Georges Vongerichten; and Washington Park, a Village American that marks the return of chef-owner Jonathan Waxman (ex Jams).

- **Taking a BATH:** The principal effect of this present economic slowdown has been a tendency by diners to choose less expensive restaurants. Thus, casual, homey and inexpensive BATH (Better Alternative to Home) restaurants, mostly in neighborhoods near to home, are doing better than ever. Although seldom mentioned in the press, these usually simple places make up the vast majority of our city's restaurants. At the other end of the spectrum, top-of-the-line places may be easier to reserve but remain generally full. It's the middling "expense-account" specialists, concentrated near our business districts, that are being hardest hit.

- **Inflation Continues:** During the past year, the price of an average meal rose 6.1% to $37.29, and at the 20 most expensive places, there was a 4.3% increase to $80.01 per dinner, excluding the Alain Ducasse restaurant. Despite this inflation, the availability of special promotions, especially the expansion of the $20 prix fixe lunch menu, have kept even the most renowned restaurants easily affordable.

- **Comparative Dining Cost:** Though NY's average meal cost remains above the national average of $27.38 for the 40 other major U.S. markets that we survey, travelers are well aware that NY dining is a relative bargain compared with Paris ($41.48), London ($44.88) or Tokyo ($61.56).

- **Moving on Up:** Besides seizing the Top Food ranking, Daniel moved up from No. 7 to No. 3 in popularity. Other surveyor favorites include Jean Georges (up from No. 10 to No. 7), Danube (28 to 21), Eleven Madison Park (26 to 22), La Grenouille (30 to 26), Union Pacific (36 to 32), Oceana (38 to 34), La Caravelle (42 to 36) and Cello (debuting at 38).

- **Say Cheese:** The cheese course was revived as an important aspect of fine dining in a number of high-end restaurants, most notably Terry Brennan's new entry, Artisanal, offering over 100 choices. His Picholine really started the trend.

- **Name Game:** What does "AZ 92 db NL" signify? It's not a radio station's call letters or Morse code, but rather a string of monikers for New York's new breed of abbreviated restaurant names. Perhaps '21' started it all over 70 years ago, but now the city has a long list of very short names, including A, 57 57, Ñ, Q, 1492, 3333, 212 and 222.

- **Neighborhood Watch:** Location is everything in the restaurant game, and yesterday's red-hot Flatiron District remains just that, accounting for at least a half-dozen of this year's most noteworthy (and highly rated) newcomers. In the outer boroughs, Brooklyn forged ahead with significant activity on Carroll Gardens' Smith Street, Park Slope's Fifth Avenue, the DUMBO area off Brooklyn Heights, as well as in Fort Greene and Williamsburg. Even the Upper West Side, long a culinary desert, has discovered new oases, particularly Tom Valenti's Ouest.

- **Boutique Hotels:** A rash of new boutique hotels has made fine dining and drinking part of their marketing plan. Most notable are db Bistro Moderne (City Club Hotel), Ilo (Bryant Park Hotel), Olives (W Union Square), Thom (60 Thompson), Town (Chambers) and Virot (Dylan).

- **Looking Ahead:** Despite the uncertainties of the moment, NY's restaurant scene continues to hold its own, and its best practitioners can be found in this guide. Of course, a number of restaurants in TriBeCa were seriously affected by the World Trade Center tragedy, but have managed to stay open. However, other restaurants in the nearby World Financial Center and Battery Park City remain at risk, namely American Park, Au Mandarin, Coco Marina, Grill Room, Hudson River Club and Roy's. Though they are temporarily closed at press time, it is our fervent hope that they – and this great city of ours – will be back, stronger than ever, before long.

New York, NY
October 1, 2001

Nina and Tim Zagat

About This Survey

For 23 years, Zagat Survey has reported on the shared experiences of diners like you. Here are the results of our *2002 New York City Restaurant Survey,* covering some 1,951 restaurants.

By regularly surveying large numbers of avid local restaurant-goers, we hope to have achieved a uniquely current and reliable guide. For this book, 29,116 people participated. Since the participants dined out an average of 3.7 times per week, this *Survey* is based on roughly 15,400 meals per day. In addition, 13,112 people provided comments on their PDAs, bringing our total participation up to a record 42,228 people.

Of our surveyors, 51% are women, 49% men; the breakdown by age is 21% in their 20s, 26% in their 30s, 18% in their 40s, 19% in their 50s and 16% in their 60s or above. We thank each of these surveyors – this book is really theirs. In producing this guide, our editors have tried to synopsize our participants' opinions, with their exact comments shown in quotation marks.

To help guide our readers to NYC's best meals and best buys, we have prepared a number of lists. See Most Popular (page 9), Most Visited (page 11), Top Ratings (pages 12–19), Best Buys (page 20) and bargain Prix Fixe Menus (pages 21–22). To assist the user in finding just the right restaurant for any occasion, without wasting time, we have also provided 52 handy indexes and have tried to be concise.

As companions to this guide, we also publish *New York City Nightlife* and *Marketplace Surveys,* and a NYC Restaurant Map, as well as *Zagat Surveys* and Maps to more than 70 other markets around the world. Most of these guides are also available on mobile devices and at **www.zagat.com,** where you can also vote and shop.

To join our next *New York City Restaurant Survey* or any of our other upcoming dining or hotel *Surveys,* and to receive a free copy of the resulting guides, e-mail customerservice@zagat.com or use the pull-out card that's in this book.

Your comments, suggestions and even criticisms of this *Survey* are also solicited. There is always room for improvement with your help. You can contact us at newyork@zagat.com or by mail at Zagat Survey, 4 Columbus Circle, New York, NY 10019. We look forward to hearing from you.

New York, NY
October 1, 2001

Nina and Tim Zagat

Key to Ratings/Symbols

Name, Address & Phone Number

Zagat Ratings

Hours & Credit Cards

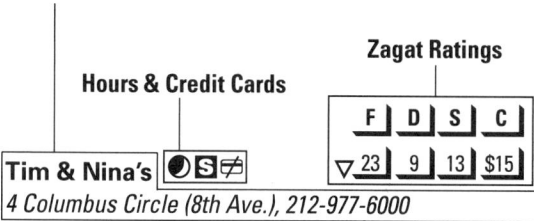

Tim & Nina's ◐ 🆂 ⌀

F	D	S	C
▽ 23	9	13	$15

4 Columbus Circle (8th Ave.), 212-977-6000

◪ Open 24/7, this "literal dive" is located in the IND station under Columbus Circle; as NY's first subway "soul pizza" stand, it offers "suculent" slices with toppings of BBQ sauce, pork or fried chicken to harried strap-hangers "for little dough"; but for the "cost of your MetroCard" and the "need to shout your order" when the A train comes in, this would be "some trip."

Review, with surveyors' comments in quotes

Restaurants with the highest overall ratings and greatest popularity and importance are printed in CAPITAL LETTERS.

Before each review a symbol indicates whether responses were uniform ■ or mixed ◪.

Hours: ◐ serves after 11 PM
🆂 open on Sunday

Credit Cards: ⌀ no credit cards accepted

Ratings: Food, Decor and Service are rated on a scale of **0** to **30**. The Cost (C) column reflects our surveyors' estimate of the price of dinner including one drink and tip.

F	Food	D	Decor	S	Service	C	Cost
23		9		13		$15	

0–9 poor to fair   **20–25** very good to excellent
10–15 fair to good   **26–30** extraordinary to perfection
16–19 good to very good   ▽ low response/less reliable

For places listed without ratings or a cost estimate, such as an important **newcomer** or a popular **write-in,** the estimated cost is indicated by the following symbols.

I $15 and below   **E** $31 to $50
M $16 to $30   **VE** $51 or more

www.zagat.com

Most Popular

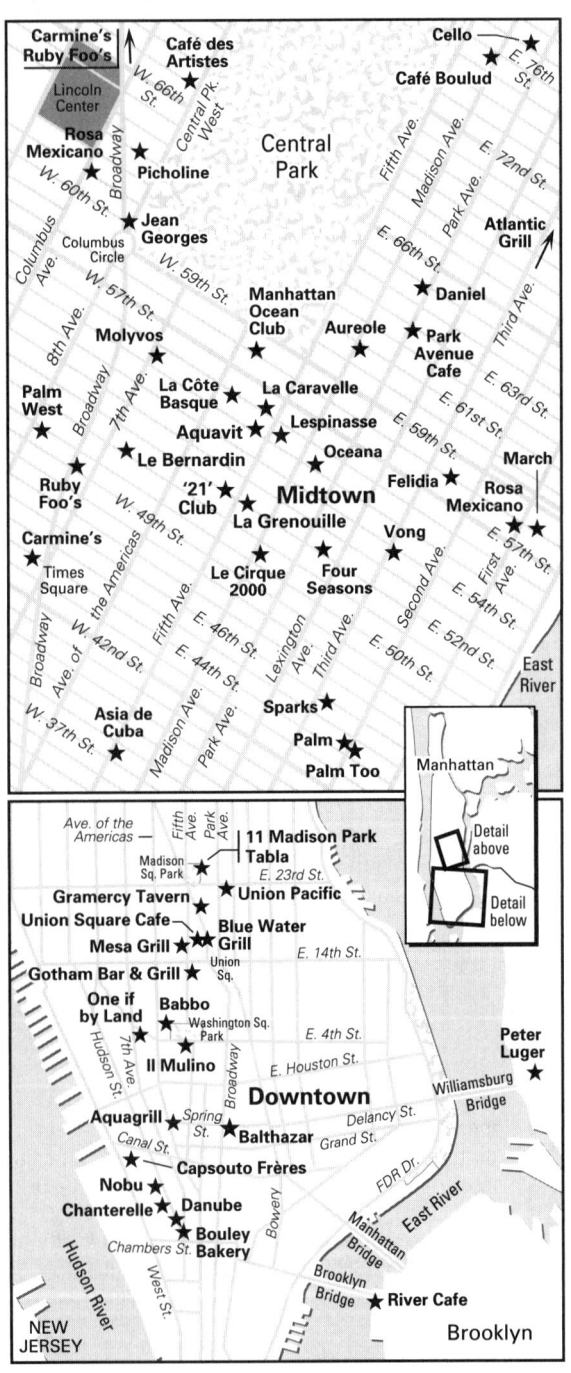

Most Popular

Each of our reviewers has been asked to name his or her five favorite restaurants. The 50 spots most frequently named, in order of their popularity and followed in parentheses by the year they opened, are:

1. Union Square Cafe ('85)
2. Gramercy Tavern ('94)
3. Daniel ('93)
4. Gotham Bar & Grill ('84)
5. Peter Luger (1887)
6. Le Bernardin ('86)
7. Jean Georges ('97)
8. Aureole ('88)
9. Bouley Bakery ('97)
10. Four Seasons ('59)
11. Nobu ('94)
12. Café des Artistes ('17)
13. Chanterelle ('79)
14. Babbo ('98)
15. Le Cirque 2000 ('74)
16. La Côte Basque ('58)
17. Blue Water Grill ('96)
18. Aquavit ('87)
19. Picholine ('93)
20. Balthazar ('97)
21. Danube ('99)
22. Eleven Madison Park ('98)
23. Il Mulino ('80)*
24. Lespinasse ('91)
25. Tabla ('98)
26. La Grenouille ('62)
27. One if by Land, TIBS ('72)
28. Asia de Cuba ('97)
29. Carmine's ('90)
30. Aquagrill ('96)
31. Atlantic Grill ('98)
32. Union Pacific ('97)
33. Café Boulud ('98)
34. Oceana ('92)
35. Vong ('92)
36. La Caravelle ('60)
37. Palm ('26)
38. Cello ('99)
39. Mesa Grill ('91)
40. River Cafe ('77)
41. Sparks Steak House ('69)
42. Park Avenue Cafe ('92)
43. Molyvos ('97)
44. Capsouto Frères ('80)
45. March ('90)
46. Ruby Foo's ('99)
47. '21' Club ('29)
48. Felidia ('81)
49. Rosa Mexicano ('84)
50. Manhattan Ocean Club ('84)

It's obvious that many of the restaurants on the above list are among the city's most expensive, but New Yorkers also love a bargain. Fortunately, our city has an abundance of wonderful ethnic restaurants and other inexpensive spots that fill the bill. Thus, we have listed 100 Best Buys on page 20 and both Prix Fixe and Pre-Theater Bargains on pages 21–22. In fact, despite New York's reputation as an expensive place to live, due to its vast size and its less-pricey outer boroughs, the city offers far more affordable and diverse dining options than any other U.S. city.

---

* Tied with the restaurant listed directly above it

NYC Neighborhoods

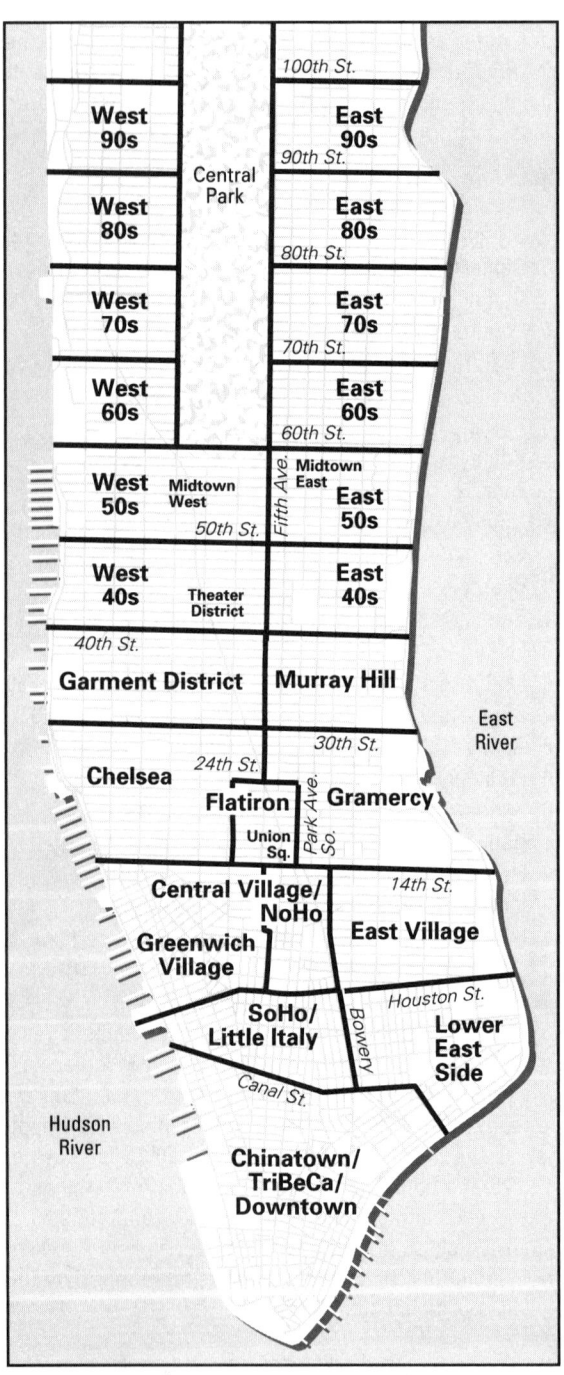

Most Visited

This list reflects a different measure of popularity. It indicates the 50 spots most often visited and the number of surveyors who went to each place in the past year.

4,454	Union Square Cafe	2,453	Le Cirque 2000
3,957	Blue Water Grill	2,436	Babbo
3,941	Peter Luger	2,420	Krispy Kreme
3,849	Balthazar	2,371	Second Avenue Deli
3,681	Gotham Bar & Grill	2,366	Redeye Grill
3,661	Gramercy Tavern	2,362	Smith & Wollensky
3,636	Café des Artistes	2,335	Jackson Hole
3,604	Carmine's	2,289	Palm
3,482	Ruby Foo's	2,232	Sarabeth's
3,258	Cosi	2,209	Rosa Mexicano
3,008	Carnegie Deli	2,148	Picholine
2,909	Aquavit	2,128	Mesa Grill
2,908	Aureole	2,121	Docks Oyster Bar
2,864	Bouley Bakery	2,093	La Côte Basque
2,861	Starbucks	2,072	Vong
2,835	Nobu	2,069	Molyvos
2,776	John's Pizzeria	2,067	Katz's Delicatessen
2,766	Atlantic Grill	2,058	Eleven Madison Park
2,673	Tavern on the Green	1,994	Zen Palate
2,659	Le Bernardin	1,973	Angelo & Maxie's
2,592	Daniel	1,941	Oyster Bar (Gr. Cent.)
2,513	Jean Georges	1,897	Aquagrill
2,483	Asia de Cuba	1,850	Ollie's
2,468	Four Seasons	1,778	Cafe Un Deux Trois
2,458	EJ's Luncheonette	1,743	T.G.I. Friday's

Since each surveyor visited each restaurant in our *Survey* 7 times annually on average, the number of meals eaten in the above restaurants is enormous – for example, 31,178 meals at Union Square Cafe, or quite probably over 85 surveyors eating there every day!

In reviewing the above list, it's clear that some of these restaurants are high-traffic spots for reasons other than their food. Indeed, they often get short shrift from professional food critics. What the above report reflects is that other features – such as ambiance, convenience and value – frequently determine where people elect to eat. Our Teflons index (page 279), which shows restaurants with low food ratings but extremely high customer traffic, confirms this.

For this reason we have always felt it was important to rate food, decor, service and cost separately so that you can choose the elements that best suit your plans for any occasion.

www.zagat.com

Top Ratings

Top lists exclude restaurants with low voting.

Top Food Ranking

28 Daniel
Chanterelle
Le Bernardin
Nobu
Jean Georges
27 Gramercy Tavern
Aureole
Peter Luger
Gotham Bar & Grill
Il Mulino
Lespinasse
La Grenouille
Kuruma Zushi
Bouley Bakery
Union Square Cafe
Oceana
Four Seasons
Tomoe Sushi
Café Boulud
Soup Kitchen Int'l
Sushi Yasuda
Picholine
71 Clinton Fresh Food
Veritas
26 La Côte Basque
Montrachet
March
Cello
La Caravelle
Scalini Fedeli
Babbo
Union Pacific
Blue Ribbon Sushi
Sushi of Gari
Danube
Milos Estiatorio
Alain Ducasse
Grimaldi's
Sugiyama
Le Cirque 2000
Pearl Oyster Bar
Aquavit
25 Aquagrill
Eleven Madison Park
Taka
Yama
Felidia
Tabla
Canton
Lutèce

Top Food by Cuisine

American
27 Gramercy Tavern
Aureole
Gotham Bar & Grill
Union Square Cafe
71 Clinton Fresh Food
Veritas

American (Regional)
26 Pearl Oyster Bar/NE
24 Cooking with Jazz/Cajun
Mesa Grill/SW
23 Hudson River Club/NY
22 Michael's/CAL
Tropica/FL

Barbecue
24 Pearson's
22 Kum Gang San
21 Kang Suh
20 Virgil's
19 Green Field Chur.
18 Master Grill Int'l

Brasseries
23 Balthazar
Artisanal
22 L'Absinthe
21 City Hall
Redeye Grill
Les Halles

Caviar & Champagne
25 Caviar Russe
24 Petrossian
22 Caviarteria
21 FireBird
Russian Samovar
20 King Cole Bar

Chinese
25 Canton
24 Tse Yang
Shun Lee Palace
Mr. K's
Shun Lee
23 Chin Chin

Top Food

Coffeehouses
- 20 Grey Dog's Coffee
 Once Upon a Tart
 Cafe Lalo
 Ferrara
- 19 Omonia Cafe
- 18 Edgar's Cafe

Continental
- 27 Four Seasons
- 24 Petrossian
 Carlyle
- 23 Two Two Two
- 21 Kings' Carriage House
 Parsonage

Dessert
- 24 Emack & Bolio's
- 23 Veniero's
- 22 Cupcake Cafe
 Sweet Melissa
 Lady Mendl's
- 21 Sant Ambroeus

Delis
- 23 Second Avenue Deli
 Barney Greengrass
- 21 Ess-a-Bagel
 Katz's Deli
 Carnegie Deli
- 19 Stage Deli

French
- 28 Daniel
 Chanterelle
 Le Bernardin
 Jean Georges
- 27 Lespinasse
 La Grenouille

French (Bistro)
- 26 Montrachet
- 25 Jo Jo
- 24 Payard Bistro
 Capsouto Frères
 Alison on Dominick
- 23 Chez Michallet

Greek
- 26 Milos
- 25 Periyali
- 24 Elias Corner
- 23 Molyvos
 Telly's Taverna
 Ithaka

Hamburgers
- 23 Corner Bistro
- 22 Wollensky's Grill
 '21' Club
- 21 City Hall
 Island Burgers
- 19 Cal's

Indian
- 25 Tabla
- 24 Tamarind
- 23 Dawat
 Bukhara Grill
 Jackson Diner
- 22 Shaan

Italian
- 27 Il Mulino/Aquila
- 26 Scalini Fedeli/multi
 Babbo/multi
- 25 Felidia/Trieste
 Il Giglio/Rome
 Pic. Venezia/Venice
 Gennaro/Lipari
 Roberto's/Naples
- 24 Il Tinello/Florence
 Piccolo Angolo/Genoa
 Erminia/Rome
 Pó/Pistoia
 Don Peppe/multi

Japanese
- 28 Nobu & Nobu, Next Door
- 27 Kuruma Zushi
 Tomoe Sushi
 Sushi Yasuda
- 26 Blue Ribbon Sushi
 Sushi of Gari

Korean
- 24 Hangawi
- 22 Woo Lae Oak
 Kum Gang San
- 21 Dok Suni's
 Do Hwa
 Won Jo

Mediterranean
- 27 Picholine
- 24 Verbena
- 23 Terrace in the Sky
 Savoy
 Olives
 Mignon

Mexican/Tex-Mex
- 25 Maya
- 23 Mexicana Mama
 Rosa Mexicano
 Hell's Kitchen
- 22 Mi Cocina
 Zarela

Middle Eastern
- 22 Oznot's Dish
 Moustache
- 21 Sahara
 Cafe Mogador
- 19 Layla
 Al Bustan

Top Food

Noodle Shops
- 25 Honmura An
- 23 Soba-ya
- 22 Great NY Noodle Town
- 21 Big Wong
- 20 Sweet-n-Tart
- Bo-Ky

Pizza
- 26 Grimaldi's
- 24 Lombardi's
- Nick's
- 22 Joe's Pizza
- Totonno
- 21 John's Pizzeria

Seafood
- 28 Le Bernardin
- 27 Oceana
- 26 Cello
- Milos
- 25 Aquagrill
- Manhattan Ocean Club

South American
- 24 Patria/Nuevo Latino
- 22 Calle Ocho/Latin Amer.
- Chicama/Pan-Latin
- Chur. Plataforma/Brazilian
- 21 Coco Roco/Peru
- Cabana/Nuevo Latino

Southern/Soul
- 21 Amy Ruth's
- Mardi Gras
- 20 Jezebel
- Shark Bar
- 19 Soul Cafe
- 18 Sylvia's

Spanish
- 24 Meigas
- 23 Bolo
- Marichu (Basque)
- 22 Solera
- Francisco's Centro
- Sevilla

Steakhouses
- 27 Peter Luger
- 25 Sparks
- Palm
- 24 Morton's of Chicago
- 23 Post House
- Smith & Wollensky

Tapas
- 22 Solera
- El Cid
- 21 La Paella
- Pipa
- 20 Oliva
- Xunta

Thai
- 25 Vong
- 23 Thailand Rest.
- Planet Thailand
- Q, a Thai Bistro
- 22 Holy Basil
- Elephant, The

Vegetarian
- 24 Hangawi
- 22 Vatan
- Mavalli Palace
- Josie's
- 21 Angelica Kitchen
- 20 Pongal

Vietnamese
- 23 Nha Trang
- 22 Vietnam
- Saigon Grill
- Le Colonial
- Pho Viet Huong
- 21 Indochine

Wild Cards
- 26 Danube/Austrian
- Aquavit/Scandinavian
- 24 Asia de Cuba/Asian-Cuban
- 23 Nyonya/Malaysian
- Sushi Samba/Jap.–S.A.
- Zum Stammtisch/German

Top Food by Special Feature

Breakfast
- 24 Payard Bistro
- 23 Balthazar
- Second Avenue Deli
- 22 Michael's
- Tartine
- 21 Sarabeth's

Brunch
- 25 Park Avenue Cafe
- River Cafe
- 24 Café des Artistes
- Capsouto Frères
- 22 Café Botanica
- 20 Lola

Hotel Dining
- 28 Jean Georges/Trump Int'l
- 27 Lespinasse/St. Regis
- 26 Alain Ducasse/Essex House
- Le Cirque 2000/NY Palace
- 25 Town/Chambers
- 24 Norma's/Parker Meridien

Improved
- 23 Shaffer City
- Tommaso's (Bklyn)
- 22 Diner (Bklyn)
- 21 Carino
- 20 Walker's
- 19 Jimmy's Bronx Cafe

Top Food

Kosher
- *23* Tevere
  Second Avenue Deli
- *22* Va Bene
- *21* Levana
  Haikara Grill
  Le Marais

Late Dining
- *28* Nobu, Next Door
- *25* Blue Ribbon
- *23* Planet Thailand
  Balthazar
  Raoul's
- *22* Wollensky's Grill

Lunch ($20)
- *28* Nobu
  Jean Georges
- *27* Gotham Bar & Grill
- *26* Union Pacific
  Aquavit
- *24* L'Ecole

Newcomers/Rated
- *26* Alain Ducasse
- *25* Annisa
  Town
  Craft
  Mary's Fish Camp
- *24* Tamarind

Newcomers/Unrated
- Arezzo
- Bid
- Citarella
- Convivium*
- Danzón
- db Bistro Moderne
- Ilo
- Man Ray
- MarkJoseph*
- Medi
- 92
- Ouest*
- Virot*

Party Sites
- *26* Le Cirque 2000
- *23* Terrace in the Sky
- *22* Water Club
  Rainbow Room
- *21* Guastavino, Upstairs
- *17* Tavern on the Green

People-Watching
- *27* La Grenouille
- *25* Bond Street
- *23* Fresco by Scotto
  Mercer Kitchen
- *22* Da Silvano
- *19* Park, The

Power Scenes
- *27* Four Seasons (lunch)
- *26* Le Cirque 2000
- *24* Rao's
- *23* Gabriel's
- *22* '21' Club
- *20* Regency (breakfast)

Private Rooms
- *28* Daniel
  Le Bernardin
- *27* Gramercy Tavern
  La Grenouille
  Oceana
  Four Seasons

Pub Dining
- *23* Corner Bistro
- *22* Wollensky's Grill
- *21* Keens Steakhouse
- *20* Walker's
- *19* Moran's Chelsea
  Tír na nóg

Quick Fixes
- *27* Soup Kitchen Int'l
- *23* Mexicana Mama
  Second Avenue Deli
- *22* Oyster Bar (counter)
- *21* Bereket
- *18* Cosi

Sleepers*
- *27* Charles' Southern
- *24* Nadaman Hakubai
  Kam Chueh
- *23* Casa
  Jarnac
- *22* 26 Seats

Tasting Menus
- *28* Daniel ($110 & up)
  Chanterelle ($95)
  Le Bernardin ($125)
  Nobu ($80 & up)
  Jean Georges ($115)
  Gramercy Tavern ($90)

Trips to the Country
- *29* Xaviar's/NY
- *28* Jean Louis/CT
  Thomas Henkelmann/CT
  Ryland Inn/NJ
  La Panetière/NY
  Mill River Inn/LI

24-Hour
- *21* Bereket
- *20* Wo Hop
- *19* Veselka
  Florent
- *18* L'Express
- *17* Cafeteria

---

* Low votes

Top Food
Top Food by Neighborhood

Chelsea
- 24 Da Umberto
- 23 Sandro's
  - Daniella
- 22 Red Cat
  - Tonic, The
  - Francisco's Centro

Chinatown
- 25 Canton
- 23 Thailand Rest.
  - Nha Trang
  - Grand Sichuan
  - Wong Kee
- 22 Great NY Noodle Town

East 40s
- 27 Kuruma Zushi
  - Sushi Yasuda
- 25 Hatsuhana
  - Sparks
  - Palm
- 24 Inagiku

East 50s
- 27 Lespinasse
  - La Grenouille
  - Oceana
  - Four Seasons
- 26 March
  - Le Cirque 2000

East 60s
- 28 Daniel
- 27 Aureole
- 25 Jo Jo
  - Park Avenue Cafe
  - Maya
- 24 Sushihatsu

East 70s
- 27 Café Boulud
- 26 Cello
  - Sushi of Gari
- 24 Campagnola
  - Mark's
  - Lusardi's

East 80s
- 24 Erminia
  - Primavera
- 23 Etats-Unis
  - Sistina
  - Tevere
  - Paola's

East 90s & Up (below Harlem)
- 22 Sharz Cafe & Wine Bar
- 21 Pascalou
  - Table d'Hôte
  - Sarabeth's
- 20 Vico
  - Eli's Vinegar Factory

East Village/Lower East Side
- 27 71 Clinton Fresh Food
- 25 Hasaki
- 24 Iso
  - Tasting Room
- 23 Veniero's
  - Il Bagatto

Flatiron/Union Square
- 27 Gramercy Tavern
  - Union Square Cafe
  - Veritas
- 25 Craft
  - Periyali
- 24 Tamarind

Garment District/West 30s
- 22 Kum Gang San
- 21 Keens Steakhouse
  - Won Jo
  - Nick & Stef's
  - Kang Suh
  - Woo Chon

Gramercy/Madison Park
- 26 Union Pacific
- 25 Eleven Madison Park
  - Yama
  - Tabla & Bread Bar
- 24 Verbena
- 23 I Trulli

Greenwich Village
- 27 Gotham Bar & Grill
  - Il Mulino
  - Tomoe Sushi
- 26 Babbo
  - Pearl Oyster Bar
- 25 Taka

Harlem
- 24 Rao's
- 21 Amy Ruth's
  - Patsy's Pizza
  - Bayou
- 19 Copeland's*
- 18 Sylvia's

---

* Low vote

Top Food

Meatpacking District
- 21 Old Homestead
- Frank's
- 20 Pastis
- 19 Fressen
- Markt
- Lotus

Murray Hill/East 30s
- 25 Sushi Sen-nin
- 24 Hangawi
- Asia de Cuba
- 23 Artisanal
- 22 Water Club
- Villa Berulia

SoHo/Little Italy
- 26 Blue Ribbon Sushi
- 25 Aquagrill
- Honmura An
- Blue Ribbon
- 24 Omen
- L'Ecole

TriBeCa/Downtown
- 28 Chanterelle
- Nobu & Nobu, Next Door
- 27 Bouley Bakery
- 26 Montrachet
- Scalini Fedeli
- Danube

West 40s
- 25 Sushi Zen
- 24 Triomphe
- Sushiden
- 23 Sea Grill
- Esca
- 44 & X Hell's Kitchen

West 50s
- 28 Le Bernardin
- 26 La Côte Basque
- La Caravelle
- Milos
- Alain Ducasse
- Sugiyama

West 60s
- 28 Jean Georges
- 27 Picholine
- 24 Café des Artistes
- Shun Lee
- 23 Rosa Mexicano
- Gabriel's

West 70s
- 23 Ocean Grill
- Two Two Two
- 22 Josie's
- 21 Pasha
- Pomodoro Rosso
- Scaletta

West 80s
- 23 Haru
- Barney Greengrass
- 22 Calle Ocho
- Saigon Grill
- Nëo
- La Mirabelle

West 90s/100s/Columbia
- 25 Gennaro
- 23 Terrace in the Sky
- 22 Métisse
- 21 Mamá Mexico
- Alouette
- 20 Pampa

Outer Boroughs

Bronx
- 25 Roberto's
- 23 Le Refuge Inn*
- 22 Dominick's
- 20 Mario's
- 19 Jimmy's Bronx Cafe
- 18 Lobster Box

Brooklyn
- 27 Peter Luger
- 25 Garden Cafe
- River Cafe
- Grocery
- 24 Cucina
- Areo

Queens
- 25 Pic. Venezia
- 24 Don Peppe
- Cooking with Jazz
- Elias Corner
- Park Side
- 23 Telly's Taverna

Staten Island
- 25 Carol's Cafe
- Trattoria Romana*
- 23 Denino's
- 22 Aesop's Tables
- Angelina's
- 21 Parsonage

---

* Low vote

Top Decor Ranking

- **28** Four Seasons
  - Daniel
  - Danube
  - La Grenouille
  - Lespinasse
- **27** River Cafe
  - King Cole Bar
  - One if by Land, TIBS
  - Le Bernardin
  - Rainbow Room
  - Chanterelle
  - Le Cirque 2000
  - Café des Artistes
- **26** Café Botanica
  - Jean Georges
  - FireBird
  - Aureole
  - Carlyle
  - La Côte Basque
  - Water's Edge
  - Gramercy Tavern
  - View, The
  - Union Pacific
  - Lady Mendl's
  - Terrace in the Sky
  - Tao
  - Town
  - Hudson River Club
  - Box Tree
  - Cello
  - Eleven Madison Park
  - Tabla
  - Craft
  - Top of the Tower
  - Guastavino, Upstairs
- **25** Aquavit
  - Alain Ducasse
  - Russian Tea Room
  - Chez Es Saada
  - Kings' Carriage House
  - Café Pierre
  - March
  - La Caravelle
  - Gotham Bar & Grill
  - Scalini Fedeli
  - Casa La Femme
  - Palm Court, The
  - Mark's
  - Oceana
  - Tavern on the Green

Gardens*

- **25** Tavern on the Green
  - Park, The
  - AZ
- **24** Guastavino, Downstairs
- **23** Barbetta
  - Sea Grill
- **22** Verbena
  - I Trulli
- **21** Bryant Park Grill
  - Barolo
  - Dolphins
  - I Coppi
  - Gascogne
- **20** Le Jardin Bistro
- **19** Bottino
- **18** Va Tutto!
  - Grove
- **16** Metropolitan Cafe

Old NY

- 1726 One if by Land, TIBS
- 1794 Bridge Cafe
- 1864 Pete's Tavern
- 1868 Landmark Tavern
- 1868 Old Homestead
- 1879 Gage & Tollner
- 1880 White Horse Tavern
- 1888 Katz's Delicatessen
- 1890 P.J. Clarke's
- 1890 Walker's
- 1900 Bamonte's
- 1908 John's of 12th St.
- 1913 Oyster Bar (Gr. Cent.)
- 1917 Café des Artistes
- 1921 Sardi's
- 1929 '21' Club

Romance*

- **28** Danube
  - La Grenouille
- **27** River Cafe
  - King Cole Bar
  - One if by Land, TIBS
  - Rainbow Room
  - Café des Artistes
- **26** FireBird
  - Water's Edge
  - Terrace in the Sky
  - Box Tree
- **25** Chez Es Saada
  - March
  - Mark's
- **24** Erminia
  - Jezebel
- **23** Barbetta
  - Temple Bar
- **21** Rafaella
- **19** Chez Michallet

---

* By Decor rating

Spectacular Rooms*

- **28** Four Seasons
  Danube
  La Grenouille
  Lespinasse
- **27** Le Bernardin
  Rainbow Room
  Le Cirque 2000
- **26** Jean Georges
  FireBird
  Carlyle
  La Côte Basque
  Gramercy Tavern
  Union Pacific
  Town
  Hudson River Club
  Craft
- **25** Aquavit
  Russian Tea Room
  March
  Gotham Bar & Grill
  Scalini Fedeli
  Palio
- **24** Milos Estiatorio
  Brasserie 8½
  Gage & Tollner
  Circo, Osteria del
- **23** Balthazar
  Brasserie
- **22** Monkey Bar
- **18** Zen Palate

Views*

- **27** River Cafe
  Rainbow Room
- **26** Water's Edge
  View, The
  Terrace in the Sky
  Top of the Tower
- **25** Tavern on the Green
  Water Club
- **24** Nirvana
  Boat House
- **23** Foley's Fish House
  Harbour Lights
  American Park
- **22** World Yacht
  Métrazur
- **21** Bryant Park Grill
  Michael Jordan's
  14 Wall Street
  Harry Cipriani
  Spirit Cruises

Top Service Ranking

- **27** Le Bernardin
  Daniel
  Lespinasse
  Chanterelle
  Four Seasons
  Jean Georges
  La Grenouille
  Alain Ducasse
  Gramercy Tavern
- **26** Union Square Cafe
  Aureole
  La Côte Basque
  March
  Danube
  Le Cirque 2000
  La Caravelle
  Gotham Bar & Grill
  Café Boulud
  Oceana
- **25** Scalini Fedeli
  Cello
  Veritas
  Lutèce
  Carlyle
  Eleven Madison Park
  Picholine
  Union Pacific
  Tabla
  Nobu
  One if by Land, TIBS
  Montrachet
  Aquavit
  Bouley Bakery
  Le Perigord
  Mr. K's
- **24** Sugiyama
  Mark's
  Café Pierre
  Adrienne
  Atlas
  Babbo
  River Cafe
  Il Tinello
  Il Mulino
  Garden Cafe
  Annisa
  Tasting Room
  Sono
  Erminia
  Box Tree

---

* By Decor rating

www.zagat.com

Best Buys

Top Bangs for the Buck

List derived by dividing cost of a meal into its ratings.

Full-Menu Restaurants

1. Mama's Food Shop/*American*
2. Bereket/*Turkish*
3. Pump Energy Food/*Health Food*
4. La Taza de Oro/*Puerto Rican*
5. Big Wong/*Chinese*
6. Pepe Giallo To Go/*Italian*
7. Bo-Ky/*Vietnamese*
8. Rice/*Asian-Eclectic*
9. Planet Thailand/*Thai*
10. New Pasteur/*Vietnamese*
11. Angelica Kitchen/*Vegetarian*
12. Nha Trang/*Vietnamese*
13. Pho Viet Huong/*Vietnamese*
14. Fresco on the Go/*Italian*
15. Flor's Kitchen/*Venezuelan*
16. Excellent Dumpling/*Chinese*
17. Nyonya/*Malaysian*
18. Amy Ruth's/*Soul Food*
19. Thali Vegetarian/*Vegetarian*
20. Vegetarian Paradise/*Chinese*
21. Dojo/*Health Food*
22. Wong Kee/*Chinese*
23. Veselka/*Ukrainian*
24. Pho Bang/*Vietnamese*
25. Chez Brigitte/*French*
26. Great NY Noodle/*Chinese*
27. Vynl/*American-Thai*
28. L'Annam/*Vietnamese*
29. Flor de Mayo/*Peruvian*
30. Jackson Diner/*Indian*
31. Sweet-n-Tart/*Chinese*
32. Coco Roco/*Peruvian*
33. Sam's Noodle Shop/*Chinese*
34. Cafe Mogador/*Moroccan*
35. Mangia/*Mediterranean*
36. Tsampa/*Tibetan*
37. Wo Hop/*Chinese*
38. Thailand Rest./*Thai*
39. Rice 'n' Beans/*Brazilian*
40. Cambodian Cuisine/*Cambodian*
41. Vietnam/*Vietnamese*
42. Chanpen Thai/*Thai*
43. Kitchenette/*American*
44. Tea Box/*Japanese*
45. Katz's/*Deli*
46. Moustache/*Middle Eastern*
47. Sammy's Asian Grill/*Chinese*
48. Bendix Diner/*American*
49. Old Town Bar/*American*
50. Saigon Grill/*Vietnamese*

Specialty Shops

1. Krispy Kreme/*doughnuts*
2. Emack & Bolio's/*ice cream*
3. F & B/*European hot dogs*
4. Papaya King/*hot dogs*
5. Amy's Bread/*baked goods*
6. Little Italy Pizza/*pizza*
7. Ess-a-Bagel/*deli*
8. Vinnie's Pizza/*pizza*
9. Gray's Papaya/*hot dogs*
10. Eisenberg/*sandwiches*
11. DT•UT/*coffehse.*
12. Daily Soup/*soup*
13. Joe's Pizza/*pizza*
14. Peanut Butter & Co./*s'wiches*
15. Hale & Hearty Soups/*soup*
16. Grey Dog's Coffee/*coffehse.*
17. Sweet Melissa/*pastry*
18. Soma Soup/*soup*
19. Veniero's/*Italian pastry*
20. Emerald Planet/*wraps*
21. Cupcake Cafe/*pastry*
22. Cosi/*sandwiches*
23. Dishes/*salad & s'wiches*
24. Johnny Rockets/*burgers*
25. Soup Kitchen Int'l/*soup*
26. Corner Bistro/*burgers*
27. City Bakery/*American*
28. Caffe Reggio/*coffehse.*
29. Once Upon a Tart/*pastry*
30. Island Burgers/*burgers*
31. Burritoville/*Mexican*
32. Tossed/*salads*
33. Two Boots/*pizza*
34. Ferrara/*Italian pastry*
35. Cafe Lalo/*coffehse.*
36. Denino's Pizzeria/*pizza*
37. Grimaldi's/*pizza*
38. 'ino/*Italian sandwiches*
39. Edgar's Cafe/*coffehse.*
40. Pintaile's Pizza/*pizza*
41. Big Nick's/*burgers*
42. Columbus Bakery/*American*
43. Nick's Pizza/*pizza*
44. Benny's Burritos/*Mexican*
45. Lombardi's/*pizza*
46. Omonia Cafe/*desserts*
47. John's Pizzeria/*pizza*
48. Burger Heaven/*burgers*
49. Le Pain Quotidien/*baked goods*
50. Angelo's Pizzeria/*pizza*

Under $40 Prix Fixe Menus*
Lunch

Restaurant	Price	Restaurant	Price
Adrienne	32.00	Jean Georges	35.00
Aleutia	20.00	L'Absinthe	29.50
Ambassador Grill	24.99	La Caravelle	38.00
Aquavit	20.00	La Côte Basque	36.00
Arqua	20.00	La Mangeoire	21.00
Au Mandarin	18.95	La Petite Auberge	15.75
Aureole (2–2:30)	20.00	L'Ecole	20.00
Avra Estiatorio	22.95	Leopard, The	39.00
Becco	16.99	Le Perigord	28.00
Bistro du Nord	13.95	Lumi	21.00
Bouley Bakery	35.00	Lutèce	38.00
Brasserie 8½	20.00	Madison Bistro	19.99
Café Botanica	29.00	Manhattan Grille	19.95
Café des Artistes	23.00	Manhattan Ocean Club	21.50
Cafe Luxembourg	20.00	Mark's	21.00
Cafe Nosidam	21.95	Mercer Kitchen	20.00
Capsouto Frères	20.00	Métrazur	20.00
Castellano	25.95	Milos	32.95
Cello	35.00	Montrachet (Fri. only)	20.00
Chanterelle	38.00	Mr. K's	25.00
Charlotte	31.50	Nick & Stef's Steak	20.00
Christer's	25.00	Nobu	20.00
Chur. Plataforma	27.95	Park Bistro	22.00
Cibo	24.95	Pasticcio	12.50
Circo, Osteria del	29.00	Patria	20.00
Commune	20.00	Payard Bistro	28.00
Danube	21.00	Petrossian	24.00
D'Artagnan Rotisserie	20.00	Picholine	24.00
Delegates' Dining Room	21.50	Quatorze Bis	16.00
Destinée	20.00	Quilty's	20.95
Duane Park Cafe	22.00	Rive Gauche	14.99
Eleven Madison Park	25.00	Russian Tea Room	28.00
Felidia	29.50	San Domenico	20.00
Ferrier Bistro	20.95	Sardi's	19.50
FireBird	20.00	Strip House	20.00
Fleur de Sel	30.00	Tabla	20.00
Frère Jacques	22.00	Terrace in the Sky	20.00
Gage & Tollner	20.00	Thalia	20.00
Gascogne	17.50	Tocqueville	20.00
Gigino Trattoria	20.00	Tribeca Grill	20.00
Gotham Bar & Grill	20.00	Ulrika's	22.00
Halcyon	25.00	Union Pacific	22.00
Hangawi	18.95	ViceVersa	20.00
Heartbeat	20.00	Virot	29.00
Icon	20.00	Vong	28.00
Il Menestrello	29.95	Water Club	20.00
Inagiku	35.00	Water's Edge	29.00
Independent	19.95	Zoë	20.00

* This list shows the lowest prix fixe menus available; there may be higher-priced options. Since prix fixe prices may change or be canceled at any time, check on them when reserving. Nearly all Indians serve an all-you-can-eat buffet lunch for $15 or less.

www.zagat.com

Dinner*

Abajour**	25.00	La Mediterranée	20/32
Above**	34.00	La Nonna	25.00
Adrienne**	36.00	La Petite Auberge	23.95
Algonquin Hotel**	30.00	L'Ardoise**	14.95
Ambassador Grill**	28.00	Le Boeuf à la Mode	35.00
Aquavit	32.00	L'Ecole	29.95
Arqua	25.00	Le Colonial**	24.00
Atlantic Grill**	21.95	Le Garrick**	29.95
Avra Estiatorio**	34.95	Lenox**	25.00
Beacon**	35.00	Le Refuge	19/33
Becco	21.99	Levana	27.99
Bistro du Nord**	19.95	Madison Bistro	31.50
Bistro Les Amis**	21.95	Manhattan Grille**	19.95
Brasserie 8½**	29.00	Manhattan Ocean Club**	37.50
Bryant Park Grill**	25.00	Marchi's	36.90
Café Botanica**	38.00	Marika**	39.00
Cafe Centro	28.00	Mark's**	34.00
Café des Artistes	39.00	Merge**	20.00
Cafe Greco	21/26	Métrazur	29/39
Cafe Luxembourg	38.50	Metronome**	28.00
Cafe Nosidam**	21.95	Michael's**	32.50
Candela**	19.99	Milos, Estiatorio**	32.00
Captain's Table	24.95	Montrachet	36.00
Castellano	28.95	O'Neals**	28.95
Charlotte	39.50	Park Bistro**	22.00
Chelsea Bistro & Bar**	28.50	Pasha**	22.95
Chez Michallet**	22.95	Payard Bistro**	32.00
Christer's**	36.00	Pershing Square**	29.95
Chur. Plataforma	38.95	Pisces**	14.95
Cibo	29.95	Red/Bar	25.00
Circo, Osteria del**	39.00	Rive Gauche**	19.99
Commune**	35.00	Rock Center Café	35.00
Dolphins**	20.00	Russian Samovar**	25.00
Ferrier Bistro**	21.95	Russian Tea Room**	32.00
FireBird**	30.00	Sal Anthony's**	21.95
Florent	19/21	Sal Anthony's S.P.Q.R.**	21.95
Frère Jacques**	27.00	San Domenico**	32.00
Gaby Brasserie**	35.00	Screening Room**	35.00
Gage & Tollner**	23.00	Supper Club, The**	34.00
Garden Cafe (Bkyn)	25.00	Table d'Hôte**	22.50
Gascogne**	27.00	Thalia**	28.00
Hangawi	29.95	Top of the Tower	35.00
Il Menestrello	39.95	Trattoria Chianti**	25.00
Indochine**	25.00	Tropica	29.00
Joanna's**	24.75	Two Two Two	29/39
Josephina**	25.95	ViceVersa**	29.50
Kings' Carriage House	39.00	Vivolo**	21.95
La Boite en Bois**	29.00	Vong**	38.00
L'Acajou**	29.50	Water Club	38.00
La Mangeoire	21/27	Willow**	22.50

---

* Prices divided by a slash are for pre-theater and normal hours.
** Pre-theater only

Restaurant Directory

			F	D	S	C

A ⓈØ
| – | – | – | M |

947 Columbus Ave. (bet. 106th & 107th Sts.), 212-531-1643
Subway-themed, Metrocard-size Morningside Heights cafe that turns out impeccable French-Caribbean edibles from a tiny kitchen outfitted as sparely as a pioneer's mess kit; its hipster following touts the low tabs but wishes it had more than 20 seats.

Abajour Ⓢ
| 18 | 21 | 19 | $42 |

1134 First Ave. (bet. 62nd & 63rd Sts.), 212-644-9757
■ "Sunny" and "cheery", this East Side American bistro "should be more crowded" given its "satisfying" cooking and "lovely" upstairs lounge; but picky eaters say the "overpriced" fare needs "more pep."

Abigael's Ⓢ
| 19 | 17 | 19 | $39 |

1407 Broadway (bet. 38th & 39th Sts.), 212-575-1407
◪ "If you've got to go kosher", this "safe" but "solid" Garment District New American is the "way to go", providing some "style" on the plate, even if some say you'll be paying "a lot of money to eat in a basement" setting that "needs help" decor-wise.

Above Ⓢ
| 20 | 21 | 21 | $46 |

Hilton Times Square, 234 W. 42nd St., 21st fl. (bet. 7th & 8th Aves.), 212-642-2626
■ Perched "above the fray of 42nd Street", this "serene" New American is a "cut above" its Times Square competition thanks to an "interesting", midpriced menu jazzed up with "Asian touches"; its "downsides" include a "hotel lobby" location and a "view that's not as spectacular" as advertised.

Acappella
| 23 | 21 | 23 | $57 |

1 Hudson St. (Chambers St.), 212-240-0163
■ Warblers have "something to sing about" at this "underrated" TriBeCa Northern Italian renowned for its "over-the-top" service and high-"quality" meals polished off with "potent" "homemade grappa"; sure, you'll "feel like royalty", but be ready to "spend a bundle."

Acme Bar & Grill ●Ⓢ
| 15 | 13 | 14 | $23 |

9 Great Jones St. (bet. B'way & Lafayette St.), 212-420-1934
◪ "Hog wild" habitués insist "it's all about the sweet potato fries" at this "grungy" NoHo Cajun dishing out "authentically fake Southern" eats that make for "inexpensive", "messy fun"; as for that "faux roadhouse" decor, let's just say it's not to everyone's taste.

Acquario ●Ⓢ
| 20 | 17 | 19 | $35 |

5 Bleecker St. (bet. Bowery & Elizabeth St.), 212-260-4666
◪ "Cramped yet cozy", this "shabby chic" NoHo Mediterranean is a good bet if you're trawling for "earthy" cooking along the lines of a very "authentic Portuguese fish stew"; still, the "smoking-allowed" policy is "a little *too* authentic" for fresh-air fanatics.

Adä Ⓢ
| ▽ 20 | 22 | 22 | $57 |

208 E. 58th St. (bet. 2nd & 3rd Aves.), 212-371-6060
◪ The name of this "upscale" "interpretive Indian" near the Queensboro Bridge means "flair" in Urdu, and its "grace notes" include a "very Uptown" "silky" setting and "bend-over-backward" staff; but foes fuss you "pay a fortune" for the "same old, same old" chow with "fancier names."

Adrienne Ⓢ
| 23 | 25 | 24 | $65 |

Peninsula Hotel, 700 Fifth Ave. (55th St.), 212-903-3918
■ "Civility" rules at this "wonderfully calm" Midtown hotel New French where the "beautifully done" fare is dispatched "with elan" in "posh" mezzanine environs that often "seem rather empty"; ok, the "price may be a stretch", but given the location it's not so bad.

	F	D	S	C

Adulis ●🅢   20 | 19 | 19 | $38
39 E. 19th St. (bet. B'way & Park Ave. S.), 212-358-7775
■ "Jaded NY palates" find "new sophistication" in the "complex" cuisine of this "upscale" Flatiron Eritrean with Med influences; if a few complain that flavors have been "dulled down" in the move from New Haven, devotees demur that the "subtle" spicing will "make converts of even conservative eaters."

Aesop's Tables (Staten Island) 🅢   22 | 19 | 20 | $39
1233 Bay St. (Maryland Ave.), 718-720-2005
■ You won't "believe you're in Staten Island" at this petite New American–Med "charmer" that's "very sophisticated" for its "rural" environs; equally hard to believe, its "pleasantly unusual" menu and "tranquil garden" (aka "Martha Stewart's backyard") are "just a ferry ride away."

Afghan Kebab House 🅢   17 | 10 | 16 | $20
1345 Second Ave. (bet. 70th & 71st Sts.), 212-517-2776
2680 Broadway (102nd St.), 212-280-3500
764 Ninth Ave. (bet. 51st & 52nd Sts.), 212-307-1612
155 W. 46th St. (bet. 6th & 7th Aves.), 212-768-3875
74-16 37th Ave. (bet. 74th & 75th Sts.), Queens, 718-565-0471
◪ For a "bargain" "quickie dinner", you can't go wrong at these Afghan BYOs where the "fantastic" grub is so "solid" that it "survives takeout"; just be prepared for "zero" ambiance except for the "Z-100 radio music in the backroom."

Ajisen Noodle 🅢⌀   – | – | – | I
14 Mott St. (bet. Chatham Sq. & Pell St.), 212-267-9680
A wall lined with bowls leaves little doubt about the concept at this new, inexpensive slurpeteria bringing Japanese flavor to the heart of Chinatown; expect a limited menu – several varieties of Ramen noodles, a number of small plates.

AKA Cafe ●   – | – | – | M
49 Clinton St. (bet. Rivington & Stanton Sts.), 212-979-6096
This blithe Lower East Side American-Latino newcomer from the owners of 71 Clinton offers a quirky, midpriced tapas-style menu that includes seviche, empanadas and matzos in non-kosher oyster soup; its moodily lit mod interior makes even the nonhip feel hip.

Aki Sushi 🅢   ▽ 18 | 13 | 18 | $32
1425 York Ave. (bet. 75th & 76th Sts.), 212-628-8885
◪ "The Far East comes to the far East Side" at this "intimate" Japanese doling out "delicious sushi" at "decent prices"; mutes find "nothing to speak of" here, but at least "you can bring your own wine."

ALAIN DUCASSE   26 | 25 | 27 | $162
Essex House, 155 W. 58th St. (bet. 6th & 7th Aves.), 212-265-7300
◪ After a bumpy start, Michelin eight-star chef Alain Ducasse has turned what threatened to be a "bomb into fireworks" with "superb" French food, "elegant" decor and "impeccable service", all of which make it the *Survey*'s highest-rated newcomer; despite top-of-the-market prices (the dinner prix fixe menus start at $160, although as a sign of the times, it's now offering a "bargain" $65 lunch), fans report it's "extraordinary in every way" and "eating doesn't get any better than this"; skeptics quip "when you're robbed by Willie Sutton, acknowledge perfection and pay up."

Al Baraka ●🅢   ▽ 19 | 21 | 19 | $38
1613 Second Ave. (bet. 83rd & 84th Sts.), 212-744-2122
■ Have a "taste of Marrakech without the sand" at this "worthy" Upper East Side Moroccan newcomer with an "over-the-top" "jewel box of a

dining room", "authentic" dishes and "friendly if amateurish service"; occasional "belly dancers" keep it shaking.

Al Bustan S
19 | 17 | 19 | $38

827 Third Ave. (bet. 50th & 51st Sts.), 212-759-5933

◪ "About the only choice left for Lebanese food in NY", this Midtown Middle Eastern offers enough "classic" appetizers to make into a meal without needing an entree; foes deplore the "stale atmosphere" and "obnoxious minimum" but salute the "friendly service."

Al Di La (Brooklyn) S
23 | 17 | 20 | $36

248 Fifth Ave. (Carroll St.), 718-783-4565

■ "There's a reason for the crowds" at this "cramped" Park Slope "neighborhood asset": "lip-smacking", "boldly flavored" Venetian cooking at "Brooklyn prices"; the "no-reservations policy" (except for large groups) is a "pain", so "come early or wait forever."

Aleutia ●S
19 | 21 | 18 | $50

220 Park Ave. S. (18th St.), 212-529-3111

◪ "If you can get past the bar scene" at this "sleek" New American near Union Square, you'll uncover "cutting-edge", Asian-inflected fare that's as "pretty" as the "hip" clientele; for the unhip, there's the "quieter upstairs" space, but there's no escaping the staff's "amateur" service.

Alfama S
20 | 22 | 21 | $40

551 Hudson St. (Perry St.), 212-645-2500

■ It "feels like Lisbon" at this "small but attractive" West Village Portuguese where the "unique" dishes are "more refined than what you'll find in Newark"; waiters in "sailor boy outfits" and "live fado music Wednesdays" add to the ambiance.

Alfredo of Rome S
▽ 18 | 17 | 19 | $43

4 W. 49th St. (bet. 5th & 6th Aves.), 212-397-0100

◪ After a five-year hiatus, this ex–Citicorp Building Italian has resurfaced near Rock Center, and if "not quite the original", it still serves its "deliciously fattening" signature dish, fettuccine Alfredo; though its setting is "lovely" enough, some find the crowd "too touristy."

Algonquin Hotel S
16 | 21 | 19 | $48

59 W. 44th St. (bet. 5th & 6th Aves.), 212-840-6800

◪ "History is the best feature" of this Midtown hotel "literary landmark" – not the "boring, expensive" American menu; still, it works when you're in the mood to "hang out in the lobby with a drink" or catch "excellent performers" in its Oak Room cabaret.

Alison on Dominick Street S
24 | 21 | 23 | $57

38 Dominick St. (bet. Hudson & Varick Sts.), 212-727-1188

■ "Harder to find than *Producers* tickets", this "heart-of-nowhere" SW SoHo Country French "labor of love" "hits the mark on all counts" with its "foodie heaven" cooking, "flawless service" and "less-is-more decor" that's so "romantic" it inspires "stolen kisses."

Alley's End S
19 | 20 | 19 | $37

311 W. 17th St. (bet. 8th & 9th Aves.), 212-627-8899

■ With its "easy-to-miss entrance", this "grotto-like" Chelsea "hideaway" has an "old speakeasy" feel enhanced by a "serene" "glassed-in garden" and "startling bathrooms" reminiscent of an "LSD" trip; sure, the midpriced New American chow could be "a little better", but the "escape factor" alone makes this one "worth sleuthing out."

Allioli (Brooklyn) ●S
– | – | – | M

291 Grand St. (bet. Havemeyer & Roebling Sts.), 718-218-7338

The open kitchen of this spunky new Williamsburg Spaniard puts out a wide range of modestly priced tapas and *raciones* served either

F	D	S	C

indoors (with no frills) or in its tree-covered backyard; its refreshing sangria cools the heat of weekly flamenco shows and live rumba.

Alouette ⓢ   21 | 17 | 17 | $41
2588 Broadway (bet. 97th & 98th Sts.), 212-222-6808
■ "So out of place and so welcome", this double-decker West Side French bistro presents "well-thought-out" fare that "rivals" that of "far costlier" establishments; just ignore "your neighbor's elbows", the "awkward space" and somewhat "scatterbrained service."

Alphabet Kitchen ●ⓢ   ▽ 21 | 20 | 18 | $33
171 Ave. A (bet. 10th & 11th Sts.), 212-982-3838
■ This affordable new East Village Iberian "beats the odds" with a "varied", "tasty" menu from which you can "make a meal on its delicious appetizers" alone; an "open kitchen" and "nice outdoor garden" complete with a waterfall add to its breezy allure.

Alva ●   19 | 16 | 18 | $40
36 E. 22nd St. (bet. B'way & Park Ave. S.), 212-228-4399
■ In the Flatiron "sea of trendy hot spots", this "reliable" New American named after Thomas Alva Edison provides "solid", if "not electrifying", fare amidst low-rheostat, "light bulb–themed" decor; those who feel it could use some "rewiring" insist the up-front "bar scene is better."

Amaranth ●ⓢ   16 | 17 | 15 | $49
21 E. 62nd St. (bet. 5th & Madison Aves.), 212-980-6700
◪ "St. Tropez comes to Manhattan" at this "sexy" East Side Mediterranean "total scene" known more for its "Euro-trendy", "face-lift crowd" with "no visible income" than for its "pedestrian" kitchen; but who cares about eating "when you can table-hop instead"?

Amarone ●ⓢ   19 | 15 | 18 | $35
686 Ninth Ave. (bet. 47th & 48th Sts.), 212-245-6060
■ "Absolutely fresh pasta" at "half the price" of the high-end competition makes this Hell's Kitchen Italian an "excellent pre-theater" choice; sure, it could stand an "interior decorator", but its "namesake wines" are fine as is.

Ambassador Grill ●ⓢ   20 | 20 | 20 | $49
UN Plaza Hotel, 1 UN Plaza (44th St., bet. 1st & 2nd Aves.), 212-702-5014
◪ "Out of the way unless you're a diplomat", this New American across from the UN works best for folks with "deep pockets and conservative palates" or "nostalgia buffs" fond of "tacky '70s decor."

America ●ⓢ   14 | 15 | 14 | $28
9 E. 18th St. (bet. B'way & 5th Ave.), 212-505-2110
◪ Sure, this "cavernous" Flatiron American birthday venue can get "rowdy" but compensates with "cheap", "Kate Smith"–size portions of "Midwestern" "comfort food"; it's so "kid friendly" that "Shirley Temples are the drink of choice."

American Grill, The   – | – | – | E
(Staten Island) ⓢ
420 Forest Ave. (bet. Bard Ave. & Hart Blvd.), 718-442-4742
This Traditional American Staten Island yearling already has a loyal following thanks to its crowd-pleasing, if pricey, fare like double-cut pork chops and Key lime pie; keeping folks equally amused are the caricatures of local notables (à la Sardi's) that line the walls.

American Park at The Battery ⓢ   19 | 23 | 18 | $48
Battery Park (opp. 17 State St.), 212-809-5508
◪ "Inspired views" of the "glorious harbor" and "Miss Liberty" "make up for any shortcomings" on the seafood-accented menu at this Battery

| F | D | S | C |

Park American; sure, it's a bit "pricey" and "touristy", yet a "sorely needed" option for "amazing sunsets"; N.B. closed at press time.

Amici Amore I (Queens) S ▽ 21 | 18 | 20 | $38
29-35 Newtown Ave. (30th St.), 718-267-2771
■ This "charming" little Astoria "oasis" courtesy of the maître d'hôtel of the James Beard House features "passionate" Northern Italian fare and "extremely accommodating" service and exudes enough "romance" that nonlocals "wish it had a Manhattan location."

Amy Ruth's S 21 | 13 | 17 | $21
113 W. 116th St. (bet. Lenox & Seventh Aves.), 212-280-8779
■ "When cholesterol isn't an issue", come Uptown for "the best Southern food north of the Mason-Dixon line"; look for "huge portions" of "great" "down-home" eats served at "bargain prices" in a "friendly", "laidback atmosphere" that's "like eating Sunday dinner with your family"; P.S. save room for the layer cakes, and come early for the old-time breakfasts.

Amy's Bread S 23 | 12 | 16 | $12
972 Lexington Ave. (bet. 70th & 71st Sts.), 212-537-0270
672 Ninth Ave. (bet. 46th & 47th Sts.), 212-977-2670 ⌿
Chelsea Mkt., 75 Ninth Ave. (bet. 15th & 16th Sts.), 212-462-4338
■ "No matter how you slice it", you'll find "awesome treats" ranging from the "staff of life" to sandwiches and sweets at these easily affordable bakery/cafes – though their "tiny teacup"–size settings aren't really "designed for on-site dining."

An American Place S 21 | 20 | 20 | $53
Benjamin Hotel, 565 Lexington Ave. (bet. 50th & 51st Sts.), 212-888-5650
◪ "Master chef" Larry Forgione "hasn't lost his touch" at this Midtown American where the fare has "flair" and most diners by necessity have "expense accounts"; still, some say it runs "hot and cold" and "lost some character in its move Uptown."

Anche Vivolo ● 19 | 17 | 19 | $38
222 E. 58th St. (bet. 2nd & 3rd Aves.), 212-308-0112
■ "Respectable old standby" near Bloomingdale's that "tries hard to please" with its "attractively presented" Italian dishes, "pleasant" service and "bargain prix fixes"; though it's popular with the "long-in-the-tooth" set, younger folks request a "zest infusion."

Angelica Kitchen S⌿ 21 | 16 | 17 | $21
300 E. 12th St. (bet. 1st & 2nd Aves.), 212-228-2909
■ "Common tubers" morph into something "delectable" at this "earnest" East Village Vegan "hippie haunt" where the setting's a cross between a "Zen commune" and a "food court" and the grub's either "love-infused" or "monotonous", depending on who's talking.

Angelina's (Staten Island) S 22 | 18 | 19 | $51
26 Jefferson Blvd. (Annadale Rd.), 718-227-7100
◪ Granted, the "prices are a bit steep", but the "money crowd" at this Staten Island Italian says it's "worth it" in return for "superb" dining and "impeccable service"; still, some of its "captive audience" warn that "outdoor dining" means a table overlooking a "strip-mall parking lot."

Angelo & Maxie's S 21 | 19 | 19 | $46
233 Park Ave. S. (19th St.), 212-220-9200
1285 Sixth Ave. (52nd St.), 212-459-1222
◪ "Young" dudes and "bada-bing"–worthy gals comprise the "hot crowd" at these chop-shop twins known for their "value"-priced, "caveman-size" hunks of beef; unfortunately, "big egos", "unbearable noise" and "thick smoke" come with the territory.

		F	D	S	C

Angelo's of Mulberry Street ●S 20 | 14 | 17 | $38
146 Mulberry St. (bet. Grand & Hester Sts.), 212-966-1277
🔳 This "Little Italy favorite" has been dishing out "big portions" of "zesty" Italian "red-sauce" fare for a century now and still enjoys a brisk trade of both natives and "throngs of tourists" despite "no decor to speak of" and "Grand Central"-like bustle.

Angelo's Pizzeria S 20 | 13 | 15 | $20
117 W. 57th St. (bet. 6th & 7th Aves.), 212-333-4333
🔳 For an "affordable option" along the "57th Street strip mall" corridor, the parsimonious praise this pizza purveyor for its "delicate", thin-crusted pies straight from a "coal oven"; the trade-offs are "less-than-perfect" surroundings and service.

Angels ●S 17 | 12 | 16 | $25
1135 First Ave. (bet. 62nd & 63rd Sts.), 212-980-3131
🔳 "Large portions" at "low prices" are a winning combination at this "humble" East Side Italian that's often "elbow-to-elbow", even though picky eaters find the "generic" grub "not heavenly."

Anglers & Writers ●S 16 | 19 | 17 | $26
420 Hudson St. (St. Luke's Pl.), 212-675-0810
🔳 "Relaxed" West Village American providing comfort food for the "homesick" (plus a mighty "great brunch") in "rustic", "very Vermonty" environs; but the "food could be better" and you'll "need an angler's patience" to cope with the "chatty, kooky service."

Annie's S 16 | 15 | 16 | $27
1381 Third Ave. (bet. 78th & 79th Sts.), 212-327-4853
🔳 The "carriage trade" at Jim McMullen's Upper East Side American means "babies in strollers" not bon tons in limos; though the fare is "solid" but "unspectacular", the price is right, so gird yourself for a "brunch mob scene."

Annisa 25 | 23 | 24 | $57
13 Barrow St. (bet. 7th Ave. S. & W. 4th St.), 212-741-6699
🔳 From "brilliant" chef Anita Lo comes this "calming" West Village New American, a "charming little haven" where you can anticipate a "warm welcome in a cool setting" followed up by "perfect, clean flavors" on your plate; granted, it's "pricey" and portions run on the "small" side, but for "civilized, grown-up dining", this one's hard to top.

Anton's S ∇ 20 | 16 | 20 | $38
259 W. Fourth St. (Perry St.), 212-675-5059
🔳 "What a West Village restaurant should be", this "below-the-radar" Italian-Eclectic is a "simple, old-world eatery" featuring "quality dishes" and "no-pressure service"; other than the "smoke" problem, you'll "feel like you're at home."

AQUAGRILL S 25 | 20 | 22 | $49
210 Spring St. (6th Ave.), 212-274-0505
🔳 "So many oysters, so little time" sigh "hooked" addicts in the "recurring crowd" at this SoHo "pearl" where "pristine seafood" served by "waiters who really know what they're talking about" delights deep-sea diners; no surprise, there are "people everywhere" "packed in like sardines" and you must "book way ahead."

AQUAVIT S 26 | 25 | 25 | $61
13 W. 54th St. (bet. 5th & 6th Aves.), 212-307-7311
🔳 From its "sublime" Scandinavian fare to the "therapeutic" waterfall, this "flawless" Midtown "Modernist classic" from "culinary magician" Marcus Samuelsson celebrates the "joys of salmon" and "just gets better" with time; though the prices are "as high as the [atrium]

F	D	S	C

ceiling", its "wonderful selection of aquavits" numbs the sting and the casual upstairs "cafe remains a bargain."

Arabelle ▣

– | – | – | E

Hotel Plaza Athénée, 37 E. 64th St. (bet. Madison & Park Aves.), 212-606-4647

Formerly the opulent Le Régence, this East Side hotel dining room has undergone a redo, turning its color scheme from robin's-egg blue to buttercup, though the lighter look belies the serious intentions of chef Raymond Saja's ambitious global French menu; although it's quiet, its alluring, adjacent bar/lounge gives this belle a boost.

Archer's ◐▣

23 | 18 | 20 | $32

1643 First Ave. (bet. 85th & 86th Sts.), 212-628-6266

■ Since this Yorkville yearling "aims to please", it's popular with locals "tired of takeout" who meander by for affordable American "dishes made with lots of heart"; while most agree the "cute backyard" and occasional live jazz hit the "bull's-eye", others feel it just misses.

Archives (Brooklyn) ▣

∇ 18 | 20 | 21 | $36

NY Marriott Brooklyn, 333 Adams St. (Willoughby St.), 718-222-6543

■ You can "learn about Brooklyn" while you dine at this historical ephemera–bedecked hotel New American; maybe it's "not one for the ages", but the "solid" buffet lunches are "so satisfying."

Areo (Brooklyn) ◐▣

24 | 19 | 19 | $44

8424 Third Ave. (85th St.), 718-238-0079

■ Perpetually "crowded" Bay Ridge Italian offering "scrumptious food" in "big portions" that match the "big hair" of the *Saturday Night Fever* eye candy" crowd; though there's "service with a smile", you may get "preferential treatment" if you're sporting a "pinky ring."

Arezzo

– | – | – | E

46 W. 22nd St. (bet. 5th & 6th Aves.), 212-206-0555

Chef Margherita Aloi (ex Le Madri) returns with a flourish at this Flatiron Italian where the spare but elegant design allows diners to concentrate on her seasonally inspired menu; it's named after the town featured in *Life Is Beautiful*, and early eaters echo that sentiment.

Arizona 206 ▣

18 | 17 | 17 | $38

206 E. 60th St. (bet. 2nd & 3rd Aves.), 212-838-0440

☑ "An old friend in Bloomingdale's Country", this "safe" East Side Southwestern offers "decent" grub and a "cozy ambiance" reminiscent of "Tucson on a good day"; critics sigh "long past its heyday."

Arqua ▣

23 | 20 | 21 | $48

281 Church St. (White St.), 212-334-1888

■ When hankering for a "quick trip to Italy", nomads migrate to this "discreet little Northern Italian in TriBeCa" as much for its "generous portions of delicate cuisine" as for the way "they let you linger" in the "airy, welcoming room" straight out of a "Merchant Ivory movie."

Arté ▣

18 | 18 | 19 | $39

21 E. Ninth St. (bet. 5th Ave. & University Pl.), 212-473-0077

■ "Cute and neighborhoodish", this "solid" Village Northern Italian "sleeper" charms with a "comfortable fireplace in winter" and a "romantic garden" in warmer months; "pleasant", if "nothing memorable", cooking completes the picture.

Artie's Deli ▣

15 | 12 | 15 | $19

2290 Broadway (bet. 82nd & 83rd Sts.), 212-579-5959

☑ "A much-needed kosher-style deli", this Upper Westsider dishes out "lean pastrami" and "matzo balls as big as baseballs", but kvetchers sigh it's so "dumbed down" that it would "embarrass my bubbe."

	F	D	S	C

ARTISANAL ●S
2 Park Ave. (32nd St.), 212-725-8585 — 23 | 22 | 21 | $52

■ Terry Brennan's Murray Hill brasserie-meets-fromagerie is "Disney World for cheese lovers", with lactophiles and oenophiles alike pouring in for its "stunning variety of offerings" (especially those "phenomenal fondues"), not to mention over 180 wines by the glass; look for neo-"deco" (wanna-be La Coupole) decor by Adam Tihany, a "fun, noisy" ambiance and food that's worthy of the inevitable "expensive price tag."

Arturo's Pizzeria ●S
106 W. Houston St. (Thompson St.), 212-677-3820 — 20 | 12 | 15 | $20

■ "Village staple"–cum–"down-home pizza joint" with "what-you-see-is-what-you-get" decor that lures "NYU trendoids" with its "coal-fired" pies, "carafes of inexpensive wine" and nightly jazz.

Artusi
36 W. 52nd St. (bet. 5th & 6th Aves.), 212-582-6900 — 19 | 18 | 20 | $45

■ If you have to "talk business", this "reliable", "high-end" Midtown Italian provides "perfectly spaced tables" for tête-à-têtes; illicit rendezvousers report it gets nice and "quiet at dinner."

ASIA DE CUBA ●S
Morgans Hotel, 237 Madison Ave. (bet. 37th & 38th Sts.), 212-726-7755 — 24 | 25 | 20 | $51

■ "Glam" Murray Hill Asian-Cuban "air-kiss scene" where the "prettiest of the pretty" sip cocktails and fiddle with their "dark glasses" amidst "drop-dead gorgeous", "white-hot" decor by Philippe Starck; expect "unusually delicious", "underrated food" served by a "staff that thinks the world revolves around them" – if you want the royal treatment, "bring Elizabeth Hurley."

Assaggio ●S
473 Columbus Ave. (bet. 82nd & 83rd Sts.), 212-877-0170 — – | – | – | M

The name means 'tasty', and locals find this new Italian a delightful option given its daily changing menu; a few more like this and we'll put to rest the notion that the West Side is the graveyard of fine dining.

À Table (Brooklyn) S
171 Lafayette Ave. (Adelphi St.), 718-935-9121 — 19 | 18 | 18 | $31

■ "Petite" French bistro in "up-and-coming" Fort Greene that's a "must" for outgoing locals, who tout its pair of communal tables; adherents say it "would be mobbed if it were in Manhattan", though *au contraire*–ians fear the "Parisian vibe" extends to its "attitude."

ATLANTIC GRILL ●S
1341 Third Ave. (bet. 76th & 77th Sts.), 212-988-9200 — 22 | 20 | 20 | $44

■ For "swimmingly great" seafood "with spunk" served by a staff that "can read your mind", check out Steve Hanson's "handsome", "bustling" Upper East Side yearling where the "price is right" and the "Hamptons-like atmosphere" makes for "quite the bar scene"; even though the "fad phase is over", it remains "always busy."

Atlas ●S
40 Central Park S. (bet. 5th & 6th Aves.), 212-759-9191 — 24 | 24 | 24 | $73

■ "Adventurous palates" avow this CPS "jewel by the park" is a "really different" dining experience, offering "perfecto" New American meals with global tweaking via chef David Coleman; though a few fret about its "awkward room", most salute this "brilliant" "contender" for its "wonderful wine list" and less expensive "outdoor cafe."

Au Mandarin S
World Financial Ctr., 200 Vesey St. (West St.), 212-385-0313 — 20 | 17 | 18 | $32

■ "You'll be in and out" of this WFC "chichi Chinese" "before you can finish reading your fortune cookie", which is fine with regulars who find "taking out better than eating in"; no wonder it's a "working lunch" "staple"; N.B. closed at press time.

AUREOLE | 27 | 26 | 26 | $73 |
34 E. 61st St. (bet. Madison & Park Aves.), 212-319-1660
■ There's a new chef, Gerry Hayden, at this "fine dining" "benchmark" owned by Charlie Palmer that still remains a "last-meal-of-your-life" kind of place (despite the 'Grimes Effect'), featuring "precise" New American cuisine and desserts resembling "MOMA's sculpture garden"; romeos report that its "timeless" duplex townhouse (complete with "perfect flowers" and "better lighting than Barbara Walters gets") will "sweep your lady away"; for bargain hunters, there's a $20 three-course prix fixe lunch available at 2 PM.

Avalon Bar-Grill ●S | 20 | 20 | 19 | $42 |
Hotel Avalon, 16 E. 32nd St. (bet. 5th & Madison Aves.), 212-696-1800
■ With its "great contemporary menu" and "strong drinks", this Murray Hill New American is a young-"people magnet", though some post-adolescents find the overall experience "not memorable."

Avenue S | 20 | 15 | 16 | $36 |
520 Columbus Ave. (85th St.), 212-579-3194
■ Scott Campbell's "consistent" Upper West Side French-American bistro is "kid-friendly during the day, adult-friendly at night" and "oh so busy" most of the time; the "best-bet brunch" and "chocoholic's dream hot chocolate" make up for "invisible waiters."

Avra Estiatorio ●S | 23 | 22 | 20 | $50 |
141 E. 48th St. (bet. Lexington & 3rd Aves.), 212-759-8550
■ For the most "engaging taverna-like atmosphere" this side of the "Greek Islands" (or Astoria), join the "feeding frenzy" at this "airy, whitewashed" Midtown Hellenic where the "melt-in-your-mouth fish" has fans "dancing on the tables"; word is it's "as good as Milos but cheaper", though the "by-the-pound" pricing still "adds up."

AZ S | 23 | 25 | 22 | $60 |
21 W. 17th St. (bet. 5th & 6th Aves.), 212-691-8888
■ Dining at this Flatiron New American can be an "adventure", since each Asian-accented dish from chef Patricia Yeo's kitchen is a "new discovery", while the "gorgeous cocktails" in the "cool", "Zen"-like lounge and "glass elevator" ride to the "skylit" dining room ice the cake; but traditionalists find it "too faddish" and "snobby", suggesting it be renamed "EA – as in Expense Account."

Azuri Cafe S≠ | ▽ 23 | 6 | 11 | $13 |
465 W. 51st St. (bet. 9th & 10th Aves.), 212-262-2920
■ The "lifted-out-of-a-souk" "authenticity" of this low-budget West Midtown Mideastern is apparent in its ultra-funky setting, but the trade-off is some of the "best falafel on the continent."

Babalu | 20 | 20 | 19 | $43 |
327 W. 44th St. (bet. 8th & 9th Aves.), 212-262-1111
■ Things get "lively after dark" at this Theater District Nuevo Latino when nightclubbers fill its "deep cobalt interior" for dancing; though the "food's better than you'd expect", some aficionados find it "less Ricky Ricardo" and more "Fred Mertz."

Ba Ba Malaysian ●S≠ | ▽ 21 | 15 | 14 | $20 |
53 Bayard St. (bet. Bowery & Mott St.), 212-766-1318
■ For a "delicious" meal "at the price of a martini Uptown", fans flock to this "heart-of-Chinatown Malaysian" that's "light on decor but heavy on flavor" ("the peanut pancakes will take you to heaven"); a "real sleeper", it works well whether on "jury duty" or "with a group."

BABBO ◐[S] 26 | 23 | 24 | $63

110 Waverly Pl. (bet. MacDougal St. & 6th Ave.), 212-777-0303

■ "Everything you've heard is true" about this "mind-boggling" Village "crowd-pleaser" from the Batali-Bastianich team, where the "lusty" "modern Italian" cooking and "beautiful bi-level" townhouse setting are equally "fabbo"; even though this "red-hot" celeb spot is "crazy busy", it still "runs like a Swiss watch" – except for a "reservation hassle" that may leave you with a "blister from hitting redial."

Baby Bo's Burritos [S] – | – | – | I

627 Second Ave. (bet. 34th & 35th Sts.), 212-779-2656

"Terrific, little-known Tex-Mex" hiding out in Murray Hill, despite "addictive" burritos served in a "cozy" space; though prices are low in general, its "fabulous lunch specials" are especially noteworthy.

Bacco ◐[S] ▽ 20 | 18 | 19 | $42

150 Spring St. (bet. W. B'way & Wooster St.), 212-334-2338

◪ "Cozy" SoHo Italian offering "fresh, original entrees" and a stellar wine cellar that are both "nicely priced"; but dissenters say "early success went to their heads" and aren't sure they'll be back-o.

Baci [S] 18 | 15 | 17 | $33

Lucerne Hotel, 412 Amsterdam Ave. (bet. 79th & 80th Sts.), 212-496-1550

■ Amici send a "smooch" to this "smooth" West Side trattoria known for its "hearty", moderately priced Italian fare and tables "so close together you can [save money by] eating your neighbor's food."

Baci Italian Restaurant (Bklyn) **[S]** ▽ 22 | 16 | 19 | $36

7107 Third Ave. (bet. 71st & 72nd Sts.), 718-836-5536

■ Folks up for dinner and a show come to this Bay Ridge Italian whose "opera-singing" chef "loves to serenade" his patrons; food-wise, expect "pasta aplenty" served by a "friendly" crew, though the "small", "tight" setting vexes claustrophobes.

Baldoria [S] 20 | 17 | 19 | $54

249 W. 49th St. (bet. B'way & 8th Ave.), 212-582-0460

◪ "Rao's for beginners", this bi-level Theater District Italian from Frank Pellegrino Jr. (son of Rao's owner) dishes out good, hearty food in a "boisterous", "Damon Runyon"–esque setting; though grousers say the service is sometimes "so slow, the kitchen could be in Italy", it's "over its opening-night jitters" – and in contrast to dad's place, "at least you can get in."

Bali Nusa Indah [S] 18 | 12 | 16 | $23

651 Ninth Ave. (bet. 45th & 46th Sts.), 212-265-2200

◪ There's "exotic flair" to spare at this "fragrant" Theater District Indonesian, though it all goes into the "far-out dishes" like the "delicious" rijsttafel and not the "uninspiring decor"; calculators figure the "serving size is inversely proportional to the [low] cost."

BALTHAZAR ◐[S] 23 | 23 | 20 | $50

80 Spring St. (bet. B'way & Crosby St.), 212-965-1414

■ Keith McNally's "archetypal French brasserie" in SoHo is "as close to Paris as you can get" without paying airfare; "bustling, noisy and crowded", it's a "real happening" with "consistently good food" and "surprisingly good service", and rather than fight for a reservation at night, go for a more laid-back lunch or after 10 PM; if not everyone is a fan ("overpriced", "overhyped", "overrated"), they're a distinct minority.

Baluchi's [S] 18 | 16 | 16 | $26

1565 Second Ave. (bet. 81st & 82nd Sts.), 212-288-4810

1149 First Ave. (63rd St.), 212-371-3535

(continued)

(continued)
Baluchi's
283 Columbus Ave. (bet. 73rd & 74th Sts.), 212-579-3900
240 W. 56th St. (bet. B'way & 8th Ave.), 212-397-0707
361 Sixth Ave. (bet. Washington Pl. & W. 4th St.), 212-929-2441 ●
104 Second Ave. (bet. 6th & 7th Sts.), 212-780-6000
193 Spring St. (bet. Sullivan & Thompson Sts.), 212-226-2828
113-30 Queens Blvd. (76th Rd.), Queens, 718-520-8600

■ For a "little bit of Sixth Street all over the city", try this burgeoning Indian chain whose Italian-sounding "name makes no sense", yet it delivers "tastefully nuanced flavors" that are a "cut above" the rest.

Bambou S | 20 | 22 | 19 | $44
243 E. 14th St. (bet. 2nd & 3rd Aves.), 212-358-0012

■ You take a "trip to the islands by taxi" when you visit this "laid-back" East Village Caribbean – the "creative fare" and "old-school waiters" make it feel like "Kingston, Jamaica on 14th Street."

Bamonte's (Brooklyn) S | 22 | 15 | 20 | $38
32 Withers St. (bet. Lorimer St. & Union Ave.), 718-384-8831

■ It's "no wonder" that this "101-year-old" Williamsburg Southern Italian "time capsule" "has been around forever" – it "never disappoints" when it comes to "red-sauce" "food for the soul"; despite a "gruff" staff that's "older than the furniture", it's always "mobbed."

Banania Cafe (Brooklyn) S⌀ | 20 | 17 | 17 | $31
241 Smith St. (Douglass St.), 718-237-9100

■ "Plate-wiping good" French bistro fare "wows" Carroll Gardens at this "storefront" that's "fast becoming a Smith Street institution"; credit the "incredible bargain prices" for the "lines that are getting longer" and "tables as tight as a seat on the Métro."

Bandol Bistro S | 19 | 16 | 19 | $43
181 E. 78th St. (bet. Lexington & 3rd Aves.), 212-744-1800

◪ The "wine list is the main attraction" at this "hidden" Upper East Side French bistro, and though the vino "emphasis keeps the menu small", there are some "*extraordinaire*" choices to be had; still, the sharp-tongued find it "rather dull", even if it's "trying very hard."

Bangkok Cafe S | 18 | 14 | 17 | $25
27 E. 20th St. (bet. B'way & Park Ave. S.), 212-228-7681

◪ "Great ginger dishes" and "face-lift"–alert decor collide at this Flatiron Thai that's "easy on the mouth, but hard on the eyes"; though "affordable" and "fine for what it is", some yawn "nothing special."

Bangkok Cuisine ●S | 19 | 15 | 18 | $27
885 Eighth Ave. (bet. 52nd & 53rd Sts.), 212-581-6370

■ "Always good and spicy", this Theater District "Thai diehard" is a "real bargain", especially for its $8.95 Wednesday–Friday AYCE lunch buffet; despite "bare-bones decor" and dishes that don't deviate much from "standard issue", it's just the thing for showgoers "in a pinch."

Banjara ●S | ▽ 23 | 19 | 21 | $30
97 First Ave. (6th St.), 212-477-5956

■ New East Village Indian that, except for price, is "many cuts above its cookie-cutter" Curry Row neighbors, owing to a kitchen stressing "subtlety and novelty"; its "distinctly modern" look distinguishes it from the rest of the "Sixth Street conveyor belt."

Bann Thai (Queens) S | ▽ 19 | 20 | 20 | $31
68-12 Austin St. (Yellowstone Blvd.), 718-544-9999

◪ This "welcome addition to Forest Hills" turns out "authentic tasting" Thai at prices that may be a bit more "expensive" than the local

| F | D | S | C |

competition, but deservedly so; aesthetes adore the "charming decor", though some say it "looks more exotic than it tastes."

Baraonda ⦿🆂   17 | 18 | 15 | $39
1439 Second Ave. (75th St.), 212-288-8555

◪ It's a "constant party" at this "lively" Northern Italian Eastsider where "beautiful" "wild Euros" "table-hop" and "table dance" the night away; even so, the "food's acceptable in relation to the prices."

Barbaresco 🆂   ▽ 18 | 17 | 19 | $44
843 Lexington Ave. (bet. 64th & 65th Sts.), 212-517-2288

■ Its "unpretentious", "cramped" setting doesn't prepare East Side types for the "surprisingly good food" at this "honest" Northern Italian "keeper" that's on its way to "neighborhood favorite" status; "enthusiastic" service makes it all the more "welcoming."

Barbetta ⦿🆂   20 | 23 | 21 | $55
321 W. 46th St. (bet. 8th & 9th Aves.), 212-246-9171

■ "Best in spring or summer in the romantic garden", this "elegant" Restaurant Row Classic Italian, founded in 1906, is a good bet any time with its "lovely" "old-world" setting, "very good food" and sure-footed, black-tie service.

Bardolino ⦿🆂   18 | 13 | 17 | $27
1496 Second Ave. (bet. 77th & 78th Sts.), 212-734-9050

■ "You can't do better than the $8.95 prix fixe dinner" at this Upper East Side Italian famed for "average food" at "pittance" prices; indeed, its "bowling alley"–esque layout is so "busy" that the "sidewalk seating" has been "expanded."

Bar 89 ⦿🆂   16 | 22 | 15 | $28
89 Mercer St. (bet. Broome & Spring Sts.), 212-274-0989

■ "See-through bathrooms" with "glass doors that fog up when you close them" (make sure they're tightly shut) are conversation starters at this SoHo American that's more popular for its "fabulous" cocktails than for the "standard" bar chow and service.

Barking Dog 🆂⌀   16 | 14 | 15 | $21
1678 Third Ave. (94th St.), 212-831-1800 ⦿
1453 York Ave. (77th St.), 212-861-3600

◪ Parents are as "loyal as puppies" to these affordable East Side "Ivy League diners" with "doggone" "decent" grub served amidst "ruff" "canine decor"; family-unfriendly types growl both the menu and the ambiance "need some grooming."

Barney Greengrass 🆂⌀   23 | 8 | 14 | $23
541 Amsterdam Ave. (bet. 86th & 87th Sts.), 212-724-4707

■ There's nova and "chopped liver to write home about" at this "lovable" West Side Jewish deli–cum–"sturgeon king" that's been packing 'em in since 1908 despite a "know-it-all staff" and "cramped quarters" that "could use a can of paint"; still, it's a "Sunday morning staple, if you can stand the wait."

Bar Odeon ⦿🆂   18 | 17 | 17 | $35
136 W. Broadway (bet. Duane & Thomas Sts.), 212-233-6436

■ A "simpler alternative" to its "parent across the street", this "cool" and "casual" TriBeCa American bistro remains "faithful to the original" – except that there's "less room", a "more relaxed" vibe and a "shorter wait" to get a seat.

Barolo ⦿🆂   19 | 21 | 17 | $49
398 W. Broadway (bet. Broome & Spring Sts.), 212-226-1102

◪ The very "Eden"-esque "garden is where it's at" say fans of this SoHo Northern Italian that might be on the "pricey" side but is "worth every penny" if you sit out back; but the "pretty food" and "pretty" patrons don't jibe with the "laughable" service out of a "Roberto Benigni farce."

Bar Pitti ●S⌀   21 | 15 | 17 | $32
268 Sixth Ave. (bet. Bleecker & Houston Sts.), 212-982-3300
■ Abutting "the widest sidewalk in NY", this West Village Northern Italian offers lots of square footage for amusing "people-watching" from its "fantastic outdoor seats"; a variety of "sturdy" entrees at "reasonable prices" seals the deal, yet "'tis a pity it's so packed."

Barrio ●S   ▽ 21 | 19 | 19 | $35
99 Stanton St. (bet. Ludlow & Orchard Sts.), 212-533-9212
■ Adding "even more creativity" to the "Lower East Side scene", this "minimalist" 24/7 Eclectic with a "funky vibe" turns out "dashing, modern dishes" in a "super-sketchy" nabe; though it's "way too loud", word is the chow is "much better than expected."

Bar Six ●S   16 | 17 | 15 | $31
502 Sixth Ave. (bet. 12th & 13th Sts.), 212-691-1363
■ A very "hip bar scene" is the raison d'être of this West Village French-Moroccan bistro despite its "tasty", "honest cooking"; of course, as the late-night "crowds come in, service goes out", but morning persons rise and shine for brunch served "under the skylight in the back."

BarTabac (Brooklyn) ●S   ▽ 17 | 18 | 16 | $31
128 Smith St. (Dean St.), 718-923-0918
■ Think "Balthazar in Brooklyn" to get the sense of this "tasty" new French bistro; though critics complain of "noise and smoke", the kitchen's "extended hours" have night owls hooting "finally!"

Basta Pasta S   19 | 15 | 18 | $34
37 W. 17th St. (bet. 5th & 6th Aves.), 212-366-0888
■ "Flair" heats up the Flatiron at this one-of-a-kind fusion of Italian and Japanese cooking, a "strange mix" that "works" for many; yet even those who find the "food average", the portions "spare" and the decor "sterile" agree that the staff's "graciousness is abundant."

Bateaux New York S   ▽ 18 | 25 | 19 | VE
Chelsea Piers, Pier 61, W. 23rd St. & Hudson River, 212-352-9009
■ "Dine alongside Lady Liberty" on this three-hour cruise around lower Manhattan set on a glass-topped yacht offering dinner and dancing; despite scattered gripes about "unimaginative" New American fare, most remember it as a "wonderful evening."

Bayard's   24 | 24 | 24 | $59
1 Hanover Sq. (bet. Pearl & Stone Sts.), 212-514-9454
■ "Like your rich uncle's club", this Financial District French-American presents "civilized food in a civilized atmosphere" fitted out with a fine wine cellar as well as "relics of NY's maritime past"; though you'll contend with "bull-market prices", the payoffs are "dishes bursting with flavor", thanks to the "golden touch" of chef Eberhard Mueller (ex Lutèce, Le Bernardin).

Bay Leaf S   21 | 18 | 19 | $35
49 W. 56th St. (bet. 5th & 6th Aves.), 212-957-1818
■ "Upscale" Midtown Indian that's consistently well "above par", offering "imaginative dishes" "suited to American tastes"; outside of the $15 "great-deal buffet lunch", it gets more "high priced" at the dinner hour, but then again, "you get what you pay for."

Bayou S   21 | 18 | 18 | $34
308 Lenox Ave. (bet. 125th & 126th Sts.), 212-426-3800
■ "Harlem's lucky" to host this Cajun-Creole "bit of New Orleans" that's proving it's not "too far north" after all; revelers trumpet its "fun" feel,

while stargazers hope for the possibility of "rubbing shoulders with Bill Clinton at a power lunch."

B Bar & Grill ◐S
F	D	S	C
14	16	12	$32

40 E. Fourth St. (bet. Bowery & Lafayette St.), 212-475-2220

■ In summer, "there's nothing quite like lounging in the backyard" under the trees at this NoHo American grill; however, aside from the mimosa brunch, "everything's gone downhill" and the scene has moved west to owner Eric Goode's new Chelsea hot spot, The Park.

Beacon
F	D	S	C
23	22	21	$55

25 W. 56th St. (bet. 5th & 6th Aves.), 212-332-0500

■ Fans consider chef Waldy Malouf's "classy" New American grill a "winner on all counts", citing its "open kitchen" complete with a "wood-burning oven" producing "hearty", flavorsome food; its "dramatic" "tri-level" space and excellent party rooms are equally noteworthy.

Becco ◐S
F	D	S	C
20	18	20	$39

355 W. 46th St. (bet. 8th & 9th Aves.), 212-397-7597

■ The $21.95 "all-you-can-eat homemade pasta" at this Restaurant Row Northern Italian might be an "invitation to overeat" but is "such a bargain", it almost "makes getting to the show on time less important"; no surprise, "it fills up fast", so "reserve early" or come after 8 PM.

Bella Blu ◐S
F	D	S	C
18	18	18	$39

967 Lexington Ave. (bet. 70th & 71st Sts.), 212-988-4624

■ Throngs of "singles" show up "to be fed and seen" at this "frenetic" Upper East Side Northern Italian; though the wild decor almost overwhelms its "terrific pizzas", most people are having too good a time to notice.

Bella Donna
F	D	S	C
17	11	16	$24

1663 First Ave. (bet. 86th & 87th Sts.), 212-534-3261 S
307 E. 77th St. (bet. 1st & 2nd Aves.), 212-535-2866 ◐S
18 E. 23rd St. (Madison Ave.), 212-505-3678

◪ "No-frills" pasta in mighty "big portions" makes this "dependable" Italian trio popular with "poor-but-in-love" folks who "can handle being shoehorned into a table" in settings that "need work" in exchange for some "amazingly inexpensive" grub.

Bella Luna S
F	D	S	C
17	16	17	$32

584 Columbus Ave. (bet. 88th & 89th Sts.), 212-877-2267

◪ Locals looking for a "quick neighborhood dinner" stand by this Upper West Side Northern Italian that's "friendly" and "affordable"; but trendoids say that despite a decor "renovation", "they haven't changed the menu in years."

Bellavista Cafe (Bronx) S
F	D	S	C
▽ 19	18	20	$31

554 W. 235th St. (Johnson Ave.), 718-548-2354

■ "Damn good for Riverdale", this "dependable" Italian is a "Manhattan-like" gem in a "restaurant wasteland"; it's best known for its "wood-burning brick oven" that turns out "totally excellent pizza."

Bellini
F	D	S	C
22	21	22	$51

208 E. 52nd St. (bet. 2nd & 3rd Aves.), 212-308-0830

■ "Lovely" manager/co-owner Donatella Arpaia "certainly adds to the decor" at this "elegant" "piece of Venice in Midtown" that caters to an "older", "designer handbag"–toting crowd; expect "great variety" on its Italian menu and tabs on the "pricey" side.

Bello
F	D	S	C
21	18	20	$40

863 Ninth Ave. (56th St.), 212-246-6773

■ "Perfect for pre-theater" given a location convenient to both Broadway and Lincoln Center, this Hell's Kitchen Northern Italian rises to the occasion with "solid" cooking, "charming" service and an unbeatable bonus: "free parking" with dinner.

Belluno
▽ 22 | 21 | 23 | $41

340 Lexington Ave. (bet. 39th & 40th Sts.), 212-953-3282
■ "Hidden" in Murray Hill and thus "rarely busy", this "warm, brick-walled" Italian is worth seeking out for "home cooking at its best", "service to match" and a "comfortable atmosphere" that's "quiet enough" to actually have a conversation.

Belmondo ●◐S
– | – | – | M

98 Ave. B (bet. 6th & 7th Sts.), 212-358-1166
Named after matinee idol Jean-Paul Belmondo, this hip, new East Village French bistro leaves diners breathless with its combo of cheap, tasty vittles and clouds of cigarette smoke; a tiny zinc bar adds to the Paris-circa-1959 vibe.

Ben Benson's S
23 | 18 | 21 | $56

123 W. 52nd St. (bet. 6th & 7th Aves.), 212-581-8888
■ Midtown "manly man" "meat mecca" where "no-nonsense" chops accompanied by selections from an "exhausting wine list" arrive in "noisy, bustling" environs; maybe it's "not the best", but fans insist "old dependable Ben" still "kicks ass" – and if the "high-end" pricing is a problem, "bring someone else's credit card."

Bendix Diner S
15 | 11 | 14 | $18

219 Eighth Ave. (21st St.), 212-366-0560
167 First Ave. (bet. 10th & 11th Sts.), 212-260-4220
■ "Believe it or not", there's a "weird amalgam of pad Thai and pancakes" on the "cheap" "Asian/diner" menu of these "kitschy" crosstown "truck stops"; foes call them "last resorts."

Benihana of Tokyo S
17 | 16 | 19 | $36

120 E. 56th St. (bet. Lexington & Park Aves.), 212-593-1627
47 W. 56th St. (bet. 5th & 6th Aves.), 212-581-0930
■ Small fry "ooh and ahh" over these "interactive" Midtown teppanyaki steakhouses when the blade-wielding samurai chefs "put on a show" as they "cook at your table", but most adults label them the "Siegfried and Roy of Japanese cuisine."

Benny's Burritos S
17 | 10 | 13 | $16

113 Greenwich Ave. (Jane St.), 212-727-0584
93 Ave. A (6th St.), 212-254-2054 ●
■ "Hindenburg-size burritos" at "rock-bottom prices" draw "big-bellied" folk to these Downtown Mexican "shrines" that double as "solutions to the gas shortage"; those who can't stomach the "thrift shop" decor rely on their "great delivery."

Ben's Kosher Deli S
18 | 12 | 15 | $22

Bay Terrace, 211-37 26th Ave. (Bell Blvd.), Queens, 718-229-2367
209 W. 38th St. (7th Ave.), 212-398-2367
■ For a "dependable nosh", these "no-frills" kosher transplants of the Long Island chain dole out "mouthwatering" "Jewish soul food" in "'50s dinette" settings; "waist-watchers" say that despite the "he-man" portions, you'll "lose weight running after the waiter."

Beppe ●
21 | 21 | 20 | $52

45 E. 22nd St. (bet. B'way & Park Ave. S.), 212-982-8422
■ Though its "opening was much delayed", this Flatiron Tuscan "lives up to its advance notices" with "intoxicatingly flavorful dishes" served by a "knowledgeable staff" in "rustic" environs reminiscent of "being in Luca" (chef Cesare Casella's hometown); while there may be some "kinks to work out", overall "Beppe is *bene*."

Bereket ●🆂≠
21 | 7 | 14 | $14

187 E. Houston St. (Orchard St.), 212-475-7700
■ 24/7 Lower East Side über-"dive" offering "cheap Turkish" eats to "taxicab drivers" and "pub crawlers" who don't want the night to end; despite a "zero-decor" "cafeteria setting", it's "kebab heaven" for folks "on the run."

Beso (Brooklyn) 🆂
∇ 20 | 14 | 18 | $26

210 Fifth Ave. (Union St.), 718-783-4902
■ "Brunch is a scene" but "dinner is relaxing" at this Park Slope Nuevo Latino yearling that's such a "good find" that even "Manhattanites happily make the trip"; although brainy types tout its "interesting menu", aesthetes moan the "basic" digs still "need to be decorated."

Bice ●🆂
20 | 20 | 18 | $52

7 E. 54th St. (bet. 5th & Madison Aves.), 212-688-1999
◪ There's "lots of action" at this ever "bustling" Midtown Northern Italian full of "the best Eurotrash" "jangling their jewels" (even "the waiters wear Rolexes") while nibbling on above-"average pasta" at well-above-average prices; though clearly "more for the scene than the food", that appears to be enough to satisfy most customers.

Bid 🆂
– | – | – | E

1334 York Ave. (71st St.), 212-988-7730
It's no surprise that Sotheby's in-house restaurant would be artfully designed, but this luxurious new Yorkville American also features a rotating series of soon-to-be-auctioned artworks; given the scarcity of local dining options, you should book early before reservations are going-going-gone.

Bienvenue
19 | 15 | 19 | $36

21 E. 36th St. (bet. 5th & Madison Aves.), 212-684-0215
■ Nostalgics yearning for the "good old days" frequent this longtime "Murray Hill treasure" that offers "inexpensive", "quality bistro cuisine" in a "1940s French restaurant" setting; though modernists say it "needs updating", most find it "appealingly authentic."

Big Nick's ●🆂
17 | 7 | 13 | $14

2175 Broadway (bet. 76th & 77th Sts.), 212-362-9238
■ Ok, it's a "quintessential dump" with service that verges on "wham, bam, thank you ma'am", but folks still like this 24-hour Upper West Side burger joint where "grease is the word" and takeout is preferred.

Big Wong 🆂≠
21 | 5 | 10 | $13

67 Mott St. (bet. Bayard & Canal Sts.), 212-964-0540
◪ Despite "cafeteria-like" looks and "surly" service, this Chinatown Cantonese noodle nook is "very popular" for "delicious" eats that you can cover "with the change in your pocket" – just "keep your eyes closed and your taste buds open."

Bill Hong's 🆂
21 | 14 | 19 | $40

227 E. 56th St. (bet. 2nd & 3rd Aves.), 212-751-4048
◪ While the "Charlie Chan atmosphere" and the "above-average" food at this Midtown Chinese "bring you back to your childhood", its "too pricey" tabs are definitely "today"; fans who "have been going here for years" show up for a reason: that "must-have lobster roll."

Billy's ●🆂
16 | 13 | 18 | $39

948 First Ave. (bet. 52nd & 53rd Sts.), 212-753-1870
■ This circa 1870 "basic chophouse" near Sutton Place is so "old school that the vegetable with your steak is the olive in your martini"; although both its "menu and clientele are geriatric", "nostalgia" buffs insist that "it hasn't changed in years – that's what's good about it."

	F	D	S	C

Biricchino   20 | 13 | 18 | $34
260 W. 29th St. (8th Ave.), 212-695-6690
■ "Top-of-the-link sausages", plenty of pasta and a "poetry-in-motion" staff combine to make this Chelsea Northern Italian "more reliable than the Knicks" for getting MSG ticket-holders to the "game on time"; while some find it "small and crowded", optimists call it "cozy."

Bistro du Nord S   19 | 16 | 17 | $42
1312 Madison Ave. (93rd St.), 212-289-0997
■ Whether it's a "shoebox" or a "jewel box", this "elbow-to-elbow" Carnegie Hill charmer delivers "authentic French bistro" fare "without the attitude"; a few find it "costly", but not for the "bargain prix fixes."

Bistro Latino   18 | 17 | 18 | $41
1711 Broadway, 2nd fl. (54th St.), 212-956-1000
☑ "Sassy salsa dancing" enlivens this "MGM"-esque Midtown mezzanine supper club where the "creative Latin fare" and "great beat" make for a "win-win situation"; still, you have to "shout over the music" to be heard.

Bistro Les Amis ●S   20 | 19 | 21 | $37
180 Spring St. (Thompson St.), 212-226-8645
■ "Sweet" SoHo bistro with a "convivial" "French feel" that draws passersby in to sample its "downright good" cooking; some propose "spiffing" things up, yet its overall "solid" performance is fine as is.

Bistro Le Steak ●S   18 | 15 | 17 | $39
1309 Third Ave. (75th St.), 212-517-3800
■ Juicy "steak and all the trimmings at fair prices" keep this East Side neighborhood French bistro bopping, even though finicky diners find the "cramped", "Frankie-on-the-stereo" ambiance a bit "boring."

Bistro St. Mark's (Brooklyn) S   – | – | – | M
76 St. Mark's Ave. (6th & Flatbush Aves.), 718-857-8600
Chef Johannes Sanzin (ex Bouley) has resurfaced in Park Slope at this airy French bistro on an unlikely corner off Flatbush Avenue; moderately priced, impeccably prepared dishes have diners digging in for dinner, lunch and brunch.

Bistrot Margot S   19 | 16 | 17 | $31
26 Prince St. (bet. Elizabeth & Mott Sts.), 212-274-1027
■ Romantics seeking a "slice of French life" swoon over this modestly priced SoHo bistro, even if others quip it's "just a very thin slice"; no question, the "quiet back garden" is a fine brunch getaway, particularly for puffers looking for a "Gauloises scene."

B.K. Sweeney's (Queens) S   17 | 16 | 17 | $28
42-15 235th St. (R.R. Station), 718-225-1866
☑ Old-fashioned "bang for the buck" is the secret behind this popular Queens American newcomer where "upscale" ambitions meet "downscale crowds"; but insiders say it's a "bar masquerading as a restaurant" and suggest you "stick to the tap."

Blue Elephant ●S   – | – | – | M
1409 Second Ave. (bet. 73rd & 74th Sts.), 212-327-0400
Serving 'American bistro' fare, this stylish new Upper Eastsider sports an eclectic menu including everything from shepherd's pie to spice-crusted tuna to a raw bar; there's also a lively bar scene.

BLUE HILL S   25 | 22 | 23 | $56
75 Washington Pl. (bet. 6th Ave. & Washington Sq. W.), 212-539-1776
■ "Ethereal" modern American food that's "delicious every time" is how surveyors describe this "friendly" yearling just West of Washington

Square; "sleek, modern" with "a touch of class", this is certainly "one of NYC's best newcomers"; N.B. although chef-owner Daniel Barber still presides, respected sous-chef Alex Urena has recently departed.

BLUE RIBBON ●S 25 | 18 | 21 | $47
97 Sullivan St. (bet. Prince & Spring Sts.), 212-274-0404
280 Fifth Ave. (bet. 1st Ave. & Garfield Pl.), Brooklyn, 718-840-0404
■ Whether you "go early" (to "get a seat") or "late" (to eyeball celeb chefs), there's "always a buzz" at this "trendy" Bromberg brothers SoHo Eclectic with a "cool crowd" and "scrumptious" menu; although they don't take reservations, the "good-looking" servers and "funny" barkeeps will "keep you amused while you wait" – even at the bustling new Brooklyn outpost.

Blue Ribbon Bakery ●S 23 | 19 | 21 | $38
33 Downing St. (Bedford St.), 212-337-0404
■ Francophile "grazers" love foraging at this charming West Village corner bistro with "something for everyone" on its "tapas-style menu"; besides "amazing breads, cheeses, meats and wine", there's a "fab brunch" and "private wine cellar party room"; now, if they just accepted reservations and were less "cramped!"

BLUE RIBBON SUSHI ●S 26 | 18 | 20 | $47
119 Sullivan St. (bet. Prince & Spring Sts.), 212-343-0404
■ "Phenomenal", "magic-on-a-wooden-platter" sushi rivals the oh-so-"watchable" scene at this petite SoHo spot that's "hardly bigger than the cell phone they call you on when your table's ready" – but plan on "waiting a long time" to get in and "spending a lot" to get out.

Blue Velvet ●S 20 | 14 | 17 | $30
227 First Ave. (bet. 13th & 14th Sts.), 212-260-9808
☑ "Delicately handled Vietnamese" fare is the forte of this East Villager that offers "surprising civility" at "inexpensive" tabs; but some say the "ordinary setting" needs a shake-up, ditto the "staff on another planet."

BLUE WATER GRILL ●S 24 | 22 | 21 | $47
31 Union Sq. W. (16th St.), 212-675-9500
■ Perennially one of NYC's most popular restaurants, this "vibrant", "high-ceilinged" former bank on Union Square was converted by Steve Hanson into a "sensational", yet "affordable" "date place" cafe with standout grilled fish, pasta, raw bar and brunch; street-side balcony tables, a downstairs jazz room, frequent celebrity sightings and friendly laid-back service all help explain why this is such a "crowd-pleaser"; call ahead!

Boat House, The S 17 | 24 | 17 | $44
Central Park, enter on E. 72nd St. (Central Park Dr. N.), 212-517-2233
☑ Like being "in a Renoir painting", this "idyllic" Central Park New American offers a bucolic "view like no other" in town; though its "thoughtful menu" is "interesting" (and "pricey"), many say "who cares about the food" when you can watch a "gondola sailing by"?

Bobby Van's Steakhouse 22 | 18 | 20 | $55
230 Park Ave. (46th St.), 212-867-5490
☑ "Bring bucks" to this big-time "boys' club" of a steakhouse where Midtown "broker types" do biz in a "macho", "testosterone madhouse" setting; yes, it's "cattle-car crowded" and there are "better choices" around, but for sure "nobody leaves hungry."

Boca Chica S 19 | 15 | 16 | $27
13 First Ave. (1st St.), 212-473-0108
☑ "Tasty" South American dishes, "colorful" trappings and "killer" cocktails add up to a "fun, inexpensive" evening at this "festive" East

| F | D | S | C |

Villager "jam-packed" with "young, hungry, thirsty" types; though "nothing will blow you away" on the menu, the acoustics may.

Boerum Hill Food (Brooklyn) S ▽ 21 | 15 | 17 | $18
134 Smith St. (bet. Bergen & Dean Sts.), 718-222-0140

☑ "Ultra-casual" Boerum Hill neighborhood American cafe specializing in "fresh", "wholesome" takeout; when the "waits get long at the other Smith Street places", savvy sorts come here to "pack a picnic" to go.

Bo-Ky S≠ 20 | 7 | 12 | $14
80 Bayard St. (bet. Mott & Mulberry Sts.), 212-406-2292

☑ "Affordable on a jury duty stipend", this Chinatown noodle shop is just right for a "quick", "yummy" fill-up, offering "one-bowl" meals that could "cure the common cold"; but the jurors' verdict on service and decor isn't so warm: "not the best."

Bolo S 23 | 20 | 21 | $51
23 E. 22nd St. (bet. B'way & Park Ave. S.), 212-228-2200

■ Contemporary Spanish fare "packed with a wallop of flavor" and presented in "hip, hopping" digs makes for a "bol-me-over terrific" experience at Bobby Flay's Flatiron "hit"; but when a chef achieves "rock star" fame (and charges accordingly), soaring expectations are bound to be occasionally "disappointed."

Bombay Palace S 19 | 18 | 19 | $35
30 W. 52nd St. (bet. 5th & 6th Aves.), 212-541-7777

☑ For a "reasonable" AYCE lunch buffet in "pleasant" Midtown environs, try this "upscale" Indian; it's "reliable" enough for a "fine" meal, even though a few connoisseurs protest it's "not very exotic."

Bondi Ristorante S 21 | 18 | 19 | $41
7 W. 20th St. (bet. 5th & 6th Aves.), 212-691-8136

■ Savoring "well-prepared" Sicilian specialties in this Flatiron Italian's "delightful" rear garden is "like being in Palermo for a few hours"; even better, it "tastes authentic."

Bond Street ●S 25 | 23 | 19 | $54
6 Bond St. (bet. B'way & Lafayette St.), 212-777-2500

■ "Matisse meets sashimi" at this "ultra-cool" NoHo Japanese where the "artfully done", sushi-centric menu is as "delicious" as the "rail-thin", "leggy" crowd; no surprise, you can count on "high-octane attitude" and "prices that aren't as anorexic as the waitresses", but in return there's that "sexy", "sleek" setting and "downstairs bar that's quite the scene."

Bonnie's Grill (Brooklyn) S ▽ 20 | 16 | 20 | $20
278 Fifth Ave. (bet. 1st St. & Garfield Pl.), 718-369-9527

■ For "great bar food without the bar", try this "small" Park Slope diner; night owls crow about its late hours (till 1 AM on weekends), a rarity in this otherwise "revitalized" neighborhood.

Borgo Antico ●S 18 | 19 | 19 | $39
22 E. 13th St. (bet. 5th Ave. & University Pl.), 212-807-1313

■ "Inviting" Villager that "captures the atmosphere of Italy" with "comforting" fare (including game) served in a "relaxed" upstairs dining room; though trendoids shrug "nothing special", "dollar for dollar", it adds up to "great value."

Bot S ▽ 17 | 20 | 18 | $38
231 Mott St. (bet. Prince & Spring Sts.), 646-613-1312

☑ "Groovy mod" plastic decor is the conversation starter at this NoLita offshoot of Bottino, where hepcats tuck into "light, flavorful" Tuscan fare; though critics yawn "all style and no substance", those unwinding in its "awesome" garden are confident they'll "hammer out the kinks."

Bottino ◐ [S] 19 | 19 | 18 | $43

246 10th Ave. (bet. 24th & 25th Sts.), 212-206-6766

■ Radiating Way West "Chelsea cool", this "modernist" Northern Italian is where "arty" locals and "fashion" followers show up to "see everyone" and toy with "solid food" in the "stunning garden"; though a few snub it as "self-impressed", most say it's "totally hip", "adult and interesting" – if a "tad pricey."

Bouchon [S] 22 | 16 | 19 | $36

41 Greenwich Ave. (bet. Charles & Perry Sts.), 212-255-5972

■ "Petite, sweet" West Village French bistro that's "worthy of a cult following" given its "deft" cooking, "genuinely caring" staff and "great bang for the buck"; though "no elbow room" detracts, it's "worth being cramped" here.

Boughalem, Restaurant ◐ 21 | 18 | 19 | $45

14 Bedford St. (bet. Downing & Houston Sts.), 212-414-4764

■ "No one can pronounce the name", but some linguists say this "unsung" New American storefront "defines a Village bistro" thanks to its "top-notch", "creative" food presented in "cozy, romantic" quarters; regulars are delighted that it now "accepts reservations."

BOULEY BAKERY ◐ [S] 27 | 23 | 25 | $66

120 W. Broadway (Duane St.), 212-964-2525

■ For repasts that "transcend expectations", foodies cheer David Bouley's TriBeCa New French where "heaven on a plate" awaits either in its "relaxing", vaulted dining room or the "more casual" cafe, backed up by "polished", "not stuffy" service; if "no match for the original" Bouley, it's "excellent" by any other standard and the $35 prix fixe lunch is a "steal."

Bouterin [S] 22 | 24 | 22 | $58

420 E. 59th St. (bet. 1st Ave. & Sutton Pl.), 212-758-0323

■ A "delightful" "profusion of plants, flowers" and "knickknacks" nearly "steals the show" at chef Antoine Bouterin's regional French near the Queensboro Bridge, but its "touch of Provence" menu holds its own; fans say it just gets "better and better" and wish it "would open for lunch."

Box Tree [S] 23 | 26 | 24 | $73

250 E. 49th St. (bet. 2nd & 3rd Aves.), 212-758-8320

◪ "Opulent" "art nouveau" decor sets the "fantasy" mood at this Midtown French hideaway where "superior" cooking and "celebrity" treatment reinforce its "be in love, fall in love" ambiance; though the hard-hearted say it's "too pretentious by half" and "quite expensive", the majority insists it's "everything a restaurant should be."

Brasserie ◐ [S] 20 | 23 | 19 | $45

100 E. 53rd St. (bet. Lexington & Park Aves.), 212-751-4840

◪ Imagine you're a "model on a catwalk" as you descend the "entrance ramp" of this "eye-popping" Midtown brasserie "revival" offering "futuristic", "beam-me-up-Scotty" decor that nearly overwhelms the "surprisingly good" grub; but cynics nix "cold service" and "brassy", "noisy" environs, saying that it "doesn't come close to the original", with the exception of "those bathrooms."

Brasserie 8½ ◐ [S] 20 | 24 | 20 | $51

9 W. 57th St. (bet. 5th & 6th Aves.), 212-829-0812

■ With its "flashy", "über-hip" looks, chef Julian Alonzo's "surprisingly good food" and a "high drama" grand staircase entrance ("à la Loretta Young"), this Midtown brasserie somehow manages to make "you feel rich and famous even if you're not"; but despite "nicely spaced tables" and "no noise", killjoys lament "couture prices."

	F	D	S	C

Brasserie Julien ☒ 19 | 16 | 18 | $39
1422 Third Ave. (bet. 80th & 81st Sts.), 212-744-6327
■ "French charm" warms the Upper East Side at this "appealing" brasserie with some "interesting" choices on the menu (like ostrich and buffalo burgers); some say "more effort should be placed on ambiance", and a new lounge and sidewalk terrace are attempting to do just that.

Bravo Gianni ●☒ 22 | 17 | 20 | $58
230 E. 63rd St. (bet. 2nd & 3rd Aves.), 212-752-7272
■ The "food never fails, nor does the welcome" at this Italian Eastsider where "irrepressible" chef-owner Gianni Garavelli "runs the place like a ringmaster"; though the decor and pricing may need "a little refurbishing", there's nothing wrong with the portion sizes – you "won't leave hungry."

Brawta Caribbean Café (Bklyn) ☒ 19 | 13 | 14 | $22
347 Atlantic Ave. (Hoyt St.), 718-855-5515
■ "If Carribean's your thing", this "funky" Boerum Hill spot provides a "little slice of Jamaica in Brooklyn"; the only thing more authentic than the "zesty" chow, "exotic drinks" and "cheap" tabs is the "West Indian welcome" – "friendly" but "unbelievably slow."

Bread Bar at Tabla ☒ 24 | 23 | 22 | $39
11 Madison Ave. (25th St.), 212-889-0667
■ "Only Danny Meyer could make a bread bar a destination", and this "sleek, sexy" Madison Square space (below Tabla) lures "chic" young things with "wacky drinks" and a "wonderful sampling menu" of Indian-inspired small plates and native breads; in addition, there's easygoing outdoor seating in summer.

Briam ●☒ 20 | 16 | 19 | $34
322 E. 14th St. (bet. 1st & 2nd Aves.), 212-253-6360
■ "You don't have to go to Astoria" for "fresh", "flavorful" Greek cooking so long as you have this "folksy" East Villager's address; its "solid" "wine list won't bankrupt you", and they're "child-friendly" too.

Bricco ☒ 19 | 17 | 18 | $37
304 W. 56th St. (bet. 8th & 9th Aves.), 212-245-7160
■ West Midtown "neighborhood resource" for "first-rate" brick-oven pizza and "light" Southern Italian fare; when in "pre-theater friendly" mode, it can be "noisy", so it works better as an "out-of-the-way lunch spot"; P.S. watch out for "Nino, the kissing host."

Bridge Cafe ☒ 21 | 18 | 19 | $41
279 Water St. (Dover St.), 212-227-3344
■ "If you can find it", this "real gem" under the Brooklyn Bridge puts out "consistently good" New American cooking in a brick-walled "old saloon" setting; though what's "cozy" for some is "cramped" for others, there's no question it's one of "NY's oldest" eateries.

Bright Food Shop ☒ 19 | 11 | 16 | $24
216 Eighth Ave. (21st St.), 212-243-4433
◪ "Kinda tiny" Chelsea diner that surprises with a "vibrant" Mex-Asian menu that particularly shines at brunchtime; sure, the decor "couldn't be more drab" and service careens from "cheery" to "shabby", but "for the price" it's hard to find anything better.

Brio ☒ 19 | 15 | 19 | $37
786 Lexington Ave. (61st St.), 212-980-2300
■ They're "serious about serving all Italiano" at this "unassuming" spot near Bloomie's that whips up "carefully prepared old classics"; its "less formal" annex (Brio Forno) supplies wood oven–fired pizzas that are "killer."

Broadway Diner [S] — 14 | 11 | 14 | $21
590 Lexington Ave. (52nd St.), 212-486-8838 ⊄
1726 Broadway (55th St.), 212-765-0909
◪ "Convenient", if "unmemorable", Midtown pit stops specializing in "el cheapo" diner grub; despite separate ownerships, both locations suffer from overall "hustle-bustle" and "plodding service."

Brooklyn Diner USA [S] — 16 | 15 | 16 | $28
1081 Third Ave. (bet. 63rd & 64th Sts.), 212-838-7570
212 W. 57th St. (bet. B'way & 7th Ave.), 212-977-2280 ◐
■ Shelly Fireman's "finer diners" recreate the "stick-to-your-ribs" food of your "Brooklyn childhood" in mega-serving sizes; despite quibbles about "noise", "tourists" and "2001 prices", in general "everything rocks" here.

Brooklyn Grill (Brooklyn) [S] — 21 | 18 | 19 | $34
320 Atlantic Ave. (bet. Hoyt & Smith Sts.), 718-797-3324
■ "Manhattan quality" at "Brooklyn prices" lures nomads to this Boerum Hill New American "sleeper"; you "can actually hear" yourself eat here, and its "patio bar is a big draw in warm weather."

Broome Street Bar ◐ [S] — 16 | 14 | 15 | $23
363 W. Broadway (Broome St.), 212-925-2086
■ "Thank heaven" this "low-rent" SoHo beer-and-burger "joint is still jumping", supplying "adequate nutrition" in a "comfy old shoe atmosphere" at cheap tabs.

Brother Jimmy's BBQ ◐ [S] — 15 | 11 | 13 | $22
1644 Third Ave. (92nd St.), 212-426-2020
1485 Second Ave. (bet. 77th & 78th Sts.), 212-288-0999
428 Amsterdam Ave. (bet. 80th & 81st Sts.), 212-501-7515
◪ "Low-down" Southern BBQ hangouts where "eternal" frat boys "put on bibs" and dig into "darn good ribs" and "heavenly wings" in "homecoming party" atmospheres; old-timers (those "over 24") grumble about "earsplitting" "decibel levels", "messy" settings and high-octane "heartburn."

Brothers BBQ [S] — 16 | 13 | 14 | $24
225 Varick St. (Clarkson St.), 212-727-2775
◪ For "Southern fun in the big city", this "bare-bones" West Village barbecue is known for "terrific dry rub" ribs that fans insist are the "real thing"; however, purists posit that this "dump" specializes in "pseudo", "greasy" grub and "clueless" service.

Brunelli [S] — 19 | 17 | 20 | $37
1409 York Ave. (75th St.), 212-744-8899
■ "Family-owned, old-style Italian" that's a little bit of "Arthur Avenue" transplanted to "desolate" Yorkville; kudos abound for its "big portions" of "reliable", midpriced food (especially the "standout artichokes") and its "warm", "gracious" staff.

Bruno Ristorante — 23 | 20 | 23 | $53
240 E. 58th St. (bet. 2nd & 3rd Aves.), 212-688-4190
■ There's "no shame in being mature" at this "sophisticated", high-end Italian near the Queensboro Bridge where "older men and their nieces" savor "traditional" fare "cooked with care and served with grace"; the "upstairs piano bar makes it especially fun."

Bryant Park Grill/Cafe [S] — 17 | 21 | 17 | $38
25 W. 40th St. (behind NY Public Library), 212-840-6500
◪ It's "scenery first, food second" at these "glorious" Bryant Park Americans where the less expensive alfresco Cafe is a "breath of fresh air amid the skyscrapers", while the more upscale Grill provides a

| F | D | S | C |

"spacious" indoor setting with "big picture windows" that "bring the outdoors in"; "impossible" "hordes" and "erratic" service by "actor/waiters" are the only downsides.

B. Smith's Restaurant Row S | 19 | 19 | 18 | $43 |
320 W. 46th St. (bet. 8th & 9th Aves.), 212-315-1100

As "glamorous as its owner", TV host Barbara Smith, this Restaurant Row Eclectic "with soul" is a "congenial" place that "gets you to the theater well-fed"; but naysayers sigh the "menu fails to deliver."

Bubby's S | 19 | 15 | 16 | $26 |
120 Hudson St. (N. Moore St.), 212-219-0666

"Venerable" "TriBeCa original" that dishes out American "comfort food to the max" – including biscuits as "flaky" as its staff – and is noted for "celeb sightings"; those who can't handle the "weekend zoo" crowds say there are "better places to stargaze – like the planetarium."

Bukhara Grill S | 23 | 18 | 20 | $36 |
217 E. 49th St. (bet. 2nd & 3rd Aves.), 212-888-2839

"Strong, flavorful" aromas signal the authenticity of this Midtown Northern Indian's "excellent" cuisine, while its "always interesting" $13.95 lunch buffet pleases both gourmands and penny-pinchers; "doting service" and "pleasant" decor complete with a "serene waterfall" make for an "agreeable" repast.

Bull & Bear ●S | 19 | 19 | 19 | $49 |
Waldorf-Astoria, 570 Lexington Ave. (49th St.), 212-872-4900

"Well-made drinks make life worth living" at this Waldorf-Astoria steakhouse-cum-"unrepentant capitalist temple" frequented by "high-powered" guys and dolls; financiers warn "make sure your wallet is going through a bull period" before chowing down.

Burger Heaven | 15 | 10 | 13 | $16 |
536 Madison Ave. (bet. 54th & 55th Sts.), 212-753-4214 S
9 E. 53rd St. (bet. 5th & Madison Aves.), 212-752-0340 S
20 E. 49th St. (bet. 5th & Madison Aves.), 212-755-2166
291 Madison Ave. (bet. 40th & 41st Sts.), 212-685-6250

"Cheerful coffee shops" that "do the job" for "pretty consistent" burgers at "heavenly prices"; foes yawn "McBland" and avoid them "except during heavy rain."

Burritoville S | 16 | 8 | 12 | $12 |
1606 Third Ave. (bet. 90th & 91st Sts.), 212-410-2255
1489 First Ave. (bet. 77th & 78th Sts.), 212-472-8800
866 Third Ave. (52nd St.), 212-980-4111
451 Amsterdam Ave. (bet. 81st & 82nd Sts.), 212-787-8181
166 W. 72nd St. (bet. Amsterdam & Columbus Aves.), 212-580-7700 ●
625 Ninth Ave. (44th St.), 212-333-5352 ●
352 W. 39th St. (9th Ave.), 212-563-9088
264 W. 23rd St. (bet. 7th & 8th Aves.), 212-367-9844 ●
298 Bleecker St. (7th Ave. S.), 212-633-9249 ●
141 Second Ave. (bet. 8th & 9th Sts.), 212-260-3300 ●
Plus other locations in the NY area

For "cheap, addicting" fill-ups, this "omnipresent" Tex-Mex chain supplies "sombrero"-size burritos and "fire extinguisher"–worthy salsas; given the "ornery" service, "take it home or have it delivered."

Bussola Ristorante ● | ∇ 20 | 15 | 18 | $49 |
65 Fourth Ave. (bet. 9th & 10th Sts.), 212-254-1940

"Thoughtful" Southern Italian cooking makes this Central Villager "outstanding" to followers, though others say it's "overpriced" and "needs an injection of energy"; an upcoming rehab may just do the trick.

	F	D	S	C

Butterfield 81   21 | 19 | 20 | $53
170 E. 81st St. (bet. Lexington & 3rd Aves.), 212-288-2700
◪ Although the "chefs keep coming and going", this "intimate" "clubhouse" still provides "provocative takes on American classics" and works especially well for "trysts", since it has the "best lighting on the East Side"; solo diners head for the "secret back bar" and "drink their dinner."

Cabana Carioca S   17 | 11 | 15 | $28
123 W. 45th St. (bet. 6th & 7th Aves.), 212-581-8088
◪ "Hungry" folk "put up with the decor" in exchange for "mountains" of "earthy" chow at this Times Square–area Brazilian; but despite "el cheapo" tabs, some say it's only a deal "if you're not picky."

Cabana Nuevo Latino S   21 | 19 | 18 | $32
1022 Third Ave. (bet. 60th & 61st Sts.), 212-980-5678 ●
South Street Seaport, 89 South St., Pier 17, 3rd fl. (bet. Fulton & John Sts.), 212-406-1155
107-10 70th Rd. (bet. Austin St. & Queens Blvd.), Queens, 718-263-3600 ●
■ "Life's a party" at these "jumping" Cuban-Caribbeans where "delicioso" dishes, "sexy" atmospheres and "rowdy crowds" add up to a "lotta bang for your pesos"; sun 'n' sea savvy surveyors single out the Seaport outpost for its "sway-your-hips, gaze-at-ships" scene.

Cafe Alyss S   ▽ 19 | 17 | 19 | $38
222 Thompson St. (bet. Bleecker & W. 3rd Sts.), 212-387-8239
■ "Cute" Village side-street yearling that works "marvels" in a "cramped" setting, whipping up a "creative", if "limited", French-American menu; nearby NYU students show up for its "pleasant" pricing and "European charm."

Cafe Asean S⊘   20 | 16 | 18 | $24
117 W. 10th St. (bet. Greenwich & 6th Aves.), 212-633-0348
■ The "low-rent glamour" of this West Village SE Asian cafe "couldn't be more charming"; though its "spiciness varies like the weather", "inexpensive, reliable" dining is the prevailing forecast.

CAFÉ BOTANICA S   22 | 26 | 23 | $52
Essex House, 160 Central Park S. (bet. 6th & 7th Aves.), 212-484-5120
■ "Breakfast is bliss" amidst the flowers and greenery that "mirror" this "delightful" Med-French's "lush" Central Park views; though the cooking's typically "delicious", its "good value" prix fixe deals and buffet "brunches fit for a king" are standouts.

CAFÉ BOULUD S   27 | 24 | 26 | $68
Surrey Hotel, 20 E. 76th St. (bet. 5th & Madison Aves.), 212-772-2600
■ "Everyone wears black" but the "food is in Technicolor" at Daniel Boulud's "less formal" yet still "divine" East Side French-Eclectic where "dynamite" cuisine and "lovely service" are "on a par" with that of his eponymous flagship; though seating may be "close" and tabs indubitably "pricey", "nobody does it better" when it comes to "sophisticated, comfortable" dining.

Cafe Centro   19 | 18 | 18 | $42
MetLife Bldg., 200 Park Ave. (45th St. & Vanderbilt Ave.), 212-818-1222
■ "You'll run into everyone in your Rolodex" at this "aptly named" Mediterranean brasserie centro-ly located just north of Grand Central; a "crazy-busy" "lunch headquarters" by day, it's quieter at night.

Cafe Colonial ●S   20 | 20 | 17 | $40
276 Elizabeth St. (Houston St.), 212-274-0044
■ A "cool" colonial setting straight out of "Graham Greene" and "fine food" keep this "hip" yet "relaxing" SoHo Brazilian-American hopping;

diehards say they'd "like to be buried" with a dish of their "heavenly chocolate bread pudding."

Cafe Con Leche 🅂   17 | 12 | 14 | $21
726 Amsterdam Ave. (bet. 95th & 96th Sts.), 212-678-7000
424 Amsterdam Ave. (bet. 80th & 81st Sts.), 212-595-7000

◪ It costs "next to nothing" to "gorge" on the "flavorful" Cuban-Dominican specialties at these "lively" Upper West Side storefronts; just ignore the "run-down" digs and "erratic" service.

Café Crocodile   21 | 19 | 21 | $48
354 E. 74th St. (bet. 1st & 2nd Aves.), 212-249-6619

■ You "feel like family" at Andrée and Charles Abramoff's East Side standby featuring "straightforward" French-Med fare along with loads of "charm" and "kitsch"; though some of its "older" crowd could "use more elbow room", most call it "cozy", even "homey."

Café de Bruxelles ●🅂   21 | 17 | 18 | $39
118 Greenwich Ave. (W. 13th St.), 212-206-1830

■ "Faux Belgians come and go", but this "faithful" West Villager "endures" thanks to "irresistible mussels", "*les frites magnifiques*" and an "encyclopedic" beer selection served from a "real zinc bar."

Café de Paris 🅂   19 | 18 | 19 | $40
924 Second Ave. (49th St.), 212-486-1411

◪ For "instant Paris", this Midtown French bistro supplies a "warm" ambiance, "honest" cooking and sidewalk seating that's "nice in summer"; still, Francophobes protest its "smoking-permitted" area and "too limited" menu.

CAFÉ DES ARTISTES ●🅂   24 | 27 | 23 | $60
1 W. 67th St. (bet. Columbus Ave. & CPW), 212-877-3500

■ "Everything glows" at this "famously romantic" Lincoln Center–area "grande dame" via George and Jenifer Lang, where "glorious" French fare, "truly courteous" service, bowers of flowers and lovely Howard Christy Chandler murals combine to produce an incredibly "seductive" experience that "makes one thankful to be a NYer"; though a meal here can be "expensive", the prix fixe menus are bona fide "deals."

Cafe Deville ●🅂   ∇ 23 | 21 | 20 | $46
103 3rd Ave. (13th St.), 212-477-4500

◪ "Ambitious" new East Village bistro offering "better-than-expected" Classic French fare along the lines of frogs' legs and escargots; easygoing early visitors find the menu a bit "pretentious", but the "dimly lit" bar is more appealing.

Cafe du Pont 🅂   19 | 16 | 18 | $38
1038 First Ave. (bet. 56th & 57th Sts.), 212-223-1133

◪ "Tiny storefront" French-Continental supplying "secluded charm" and "pleasant" fare to the Sutton Place set; though it's "not very inventive", the early-bird dinner is an indisputable "bargain."

Cafe Español ●🅂   19 | 14 | 18 | $30
172 Bleecker St. (bet. MacDougal & Sullivan Sts.), 212-505-0657
63 Carmine St. (7th Ave. S.), 212-675-3312

◪ "Deadly sangria" makes it "hard to leave sober" from these reasonably priced, separately owned Village Spaniards, though plentiful portions ("lobsters as big as Spain", "truckloads of paella") work well for absorption; fussy folks fume "predictable" and "unexciting."

Cafe Fiorello ●🅂   20 | 17 | 19 | $42
1900 Broadway (bet. 63rd & 64th Sts.), 212-595-5330

■ A "justly famous", "in-depth" antipasto bar and a choice of hearty pastas are the headliners at this Italian "godsend" that's a "stone's

		F	D	S	C

throw from Lincoln Center"; though the place can get "frenzied", "zippy service" "gets you out fast" when there's a curtain to catch.

Café Frida S | 18 | 16 | 16 | $33 |
368 Columbus Ave. (bet. 77th & 78th Sts.), 212-712-2929
� "Not your basic boring Mexican", this Upper Westsider has "flair" to spare; though "blue-collar service at white-tablecloth prices" can be a bummer, the overall "good vibes" leave most in the pink.

Cafe Greco S | 18 | 16 | 18 | $33 |
1390 Second Ave. (bet. 71st & 72nd Sts.), 212-737-4300
■ "Lots of grandparents" patronize this East Side Greek-Med, drawn by "delicious, well-prepared" food at "supersaver" prices; though a minority finds "not much zing", the "so-friendly" ambiance and "waiters with the patience of saints" make it "not just for seniors."

Café Habana ●S | 20 | 14 | 15 | $23 |
17 Prince St. (Elizabeth St.), 212-625-2001
■ Following its appearance in a "Lenny Kravitz video", this SoHo Cuban-Mexican has been "overrun with trendoids", but even non-scenesters enjoy its *mucho delicioso* chow; P.S. to beat the crowds try the "take-out shop" around the corner.

Cafe Joul S | 21 | 15 | 18 | $39 |
1070 First Ave. (bet. 58th & 59th Sts.), 212-759-3131
■ At their "modest" Sutton Place storefront, Bertrand and Heidi Vernejoul – perhaps the "most casual French folk on the planet" – have "charmed" the locals with their "affordable", "refined bistro" cuisine (including an "outstanding" $22 dinner prix fixe).

Cafe Lalo ●S | 20 | 18 | 13 | $18 |
201 W. 83rd St. (bet. Amsterdam Ave. & B'way), 212-496-6031
▰ It's "wall-to-wall calories" at this West Side "dessert dynamo" coffeehouse that's often packed (especially since *You've Got Mail* put it on the map"); it's a "great first-date place" too, since there are no awkward "silences" at this "noisy" "zoo."

Cafe Loup ●S | 19 | 18 | 19 | $39 |
105 W. 13th St. (bet. 6th & 7th Aves.), 212-255-4746
■ After a quarter-century, this "laid-back", "versatile" Village French bistro is "the same as it ever was" (i.e. "welcoming" and "mercifully untrendy"); the dishes on its "esoteric", midpriced menu are "reliably" "pleasant", if "not exciting."

Cafe Luluc (Brooklyn) ●S⊄ | – | – | – | – |
214 Smith St. (Baltic St.), 718-625-3815
Breakfast service distinguishes this casual Carroll Gardens French bistro from the rest of the Smith Street pack; recession-proof prices, an open-air front entrance and a dandy patio suggest it's here to stay.

Cafe Luxembourg ●S | 21 | 19 | 19 | $47 |
200 W. 70th St. (bet. Amsterdam & West End Aves.), 212-873-7411
■ "Still packed" "after all these years", this "low-lit" West Side "retro" deco French bistro's "close tables" teem with "Downtown-moves-Uptown" types as well as "some celebs"; aficionados advise it's "worth the extra few blocks" and bucks for a "civilized" Lincoln Center meal.

Cafe Mogador ●S | 21 | 16 | 16 | $22 |
101 St. Marks Pl. (bet. Ave. A & 1st Ave.), 212-677-2226
■ "Impoverished hipsters" living *la vie bohème* seek "cheap" Med–Middle Eastern fixes "served with style" at this "comfortable" East Village fixture; given the "tasty" tagines, "great people-watching" and belly dancing, no one minds that "space is tight."

www.zagat.com

			F	D	S	C

Cafe Noir ◐ⓢ 17 | 18 | 14 | $32
32 Grand St. (Thompson St.), 212-431-7910
■ "Hipsters" "drink and nibble" on tapas and other "tasty" fare at this SoHo Med manned by an occasionally "surly" staff; to avoid the "dim" interior's "cigarette" haze, fresh-air fans "snag tables on the patio."

Cafe Nosidam ◐ⓢ 18 | 17 | 18 | $43
768 Madison Ave. (66th St.), 212-717-5633
■ An East Side shoppers' "respite", this "upscale", up-price Italo-American's "very Euro" crowd strikes friends as "classy" and foes as "stuffy"; all agree, however, that its "sidewalk tables" make a fine spot for munching while watching the chic Madison Avenue parade.

Cafe Petite Crevette (Brooklyn) ∌ ▽ 20 | 9 | 18 | $26
127 Atlantic Ave. (bet. Clinton & Henry Sts.), 718-858-6660
■ "It's about the fish, not the furniture" at this "no-nonsense" BYO Brooklyn Heights French cafe – despite "zero atmosphere", there's plenty of "wonderfully" "fresh, simply prepared" seafood that's a "real bargain."

Cafe Picasso ⓢ 20 | 17 | 16 | $25
359 Bleecker St. (bet. Charles & W. 10th Sts.), 212-929-4774
■ Priceless pizza from a wood-burning oven is an art form at this Village Italian, whose back patio is a "hidden" masterpiece; though the interior packed with Picasso memorabilia may "need a paint job", the clientele finds it "charming" nonetheless.

Café Pierre ⓢ 23 | 25 | 24 | $62
Pierre Hotel, 2 E. 61st St. (5th Ave.), 212-940-8195
■ A haven for "upper-crust NY", this "genteel" French Eastsider is all about "elegant" traditional decor, "superior" classic cuisine and "formal" service; music from the Kathleen Landis Trio is the crowning touch that makes it well "worth the expense."

Cafe S.F.A. ⓢ 19 | 18 | 18 | $28
Saks Fifth Ave., 611 Fifth Ave., 8th fl. (bet. 49th & 50th Sts.), 212-940-4080
■ "High atop Saks", this New American "favorite" of the "shop-till-you-drop crowd" offers "restorative" light lunches along with a "glorious" "view of St. Patrick's"; it makes for a "civilized" "pick-me-up", but you must "go early" to avoid "a long wait."

Cafe Spice ⓢ 20 | 17 | 16 | $28
72 University Pl. (bet. 10th & 11th Sts.), 212-253-6999
Grand Central Terminal, lower level (42nd St. & Lexington Ave.), 646-227-1300
■ "Hip Indians" combine "cheap" cuisine with "Pottery Barn decor" and get "cool" results at this Village "twentysomething hangout"; but they're "not kidding about that spice thing" – "in a word: hot"; as for the Grand Central kiosk, it's takeout only.

Cafe Steinhof (Brooklyn) ⓢ – | – | – | M
422 Seventh Ave. (14th St.), 718-369-7776
Don your dirndl and head to Park Slope for a hearty Austrian *wilkomenn* of goulash, sauerbraten and Wiener schnitzel at budget prices; the Klaus Kinski posters on the wall are chef-owner Paul Goebert's postmodern nod to things Viennese.

Cafeteria ◐ⓢ 17 | 17 | 14 | $29
119 Seventh Ave. (17th St.), 212-414-1717
◪ This 24/7 "South Beach on Seventh" "scene" brims with "Chelsea boys" and "fashionistas" toying with above-average American "comfort" classics; however, the "slow", "distracted" service leads some to conclude "models shouldn't be waiters."

			F	**D**	**S**	**C**

Cafe Trevi ◐
			23	18	23	$48

1570 First Ave. (bet. 81st & 82nd Sts.), 212-249-0040

◼ "Primo is primo" cheer devotees of owner Primo Laurenti and his "romantic", "comfortable", "old-school" Upper East Side Italian, where seemingly every customer receives "special attention" and the classic dishes are always "excellently prepared"; for such "wonderful" experiences, it's no surprise that it's on the "expensive" side.

Cafe Un Deux Trois ◐S
			16	15	16	$38

123 W. 44th St. (bet. B'way & 6th Ave.), 212-354-4148

◼ "One, two, three and you're done" at this "huge", "hectic" Theater District "standby" with "formulaic" French bistro eats and "deafening" acoustics; still, it "gets you to the theater on time" and even provides "crayons for the child in all of us."

Caffe Cielo ◐S
			19	17	19	$37

881 Eighth Ave. (bet. 52nd & 53rd Sts.), 212-246-9555

◼ "Cute" painted clouds float across the ceiling of this affordable, "old-school" Clinton Italian whose "interested owner" watches over proceedings to ensure that both food and service work well; though it may not win any Tonys, it's still a "solid" "pre-theater" choice.

Caffe Grazie S
			19	17	19	$41

26 E. 84th St. (bet. 5th & Madison Aves.), 212-717-4407

◼ Upper Eastsiders say *grazie* for this "civilized" Italian just off the Museum Mile in a "charming" "townhouse you wish you could afford"; its "dependable" fare, "good manners" and "reasonable" tabs make it "one of the best choices near the Met."

Caffe Linda
		▽	21	16	19	$26

145 E. 49th St. (bet. Lexington & 3rd Aves.), 646-497-1818

◼ "Click your heels and you're in Florence" at this sleek, new banquette-clad Midtown trattoria; the "decor's a bit cold" compared with the "delicious cooking" and "charming" hosts, but "amazing quality for the price" warms most hearts.

Caffé on the Green (Queens) S
			22	22	22	$44

201-10 Cross Island Pkwy. (bet. Clearview Expy. & Utopia Pkwy.), 718-423-7272

◼ Once "Rudolph Valentino's summer home", this "picturesque" Bayside Italian is "an outer-borough Tavern on the Green" where there's always a "special" "celebration" going on; its "high-class" cuisine, "attractive setting" (especially the "great garden") and "efficiency" hit all the right notes, despite the "catering-hall" feel.

Caffe Rafaella ◐S≠
			18	19	16	$23

134 Seventh Ave. S. (bet. Charles & W. 10th Sts.), 212-929-7247

◼ Recently expanded, this Village Italian has more room than ever for locals to "nurse their cappuccinos" and "luscious desserts"; given the easygoing, "loungey" atmosphere, denizens shrug off the "unspectacular service."

Caffe Reggio ◐S≠
			17	19	15	$17

119 MacDougal St. (bet. Bleecker & W. 3rd Sts.), 212-475-9557

◼ At "the original Greenwich Village Italian coffeehouse", seemingly nothing – from the "antique cappuccino machine" to the "rich pastries" and "bargain" red-sauce classics – has changed in 75 years; it may need a "scrubbing", but still it's one of the last "existentialists."

Caffe Rosso ◐S
		▽	20	18	19	$36

284 W. 12th St. (W. 4th St.), 212-633-9277

◼ "They get it right" at this West Village Italian "charmer" whose "tasty" pastas, "romantic" ambiance and "reasonable prices" add up to a "great" "date place"; still, a few gripe "service is not on the menu."

	F	D	S	C

California Pizza Kitchen S   15 | 12 | 15 | $20
201 E. 60th St. (bet. 2nd & 3rd Aves.), 212-755-7773
42nd St. Food Court, 234 W. 42nd St. (bet. 7th & 8th Aves.), 212-869-8231
◪ "Cheap" designer pizzas and salads draw the masses to these "family-friendly" links of the Left Coast chain known for "varieties galore" of toppings; purists ask "with all the great pies in NY – why?"

Calle Ocho S   22 | 23 | 20 | $44
446 Columbus Ave. (bet. 81st & 82nd Sts.), 212-873-5025
■ "Grab a mojito" and "forget you're in NY" at this "slick", "cavernous" West Side Pan-Latino that "bursts with creative energy and youth"; be forewarned, though, that the kitchen sends out "more flavor than you'll know what to do with", while the "hot" bar action may make you "glad" (or sad) "you're not single."

Cal's ◐S   19 | 19 | 19 | $39
55 W. 21st St. (bet. 5th & 6th Aves.), 212-929-0740
■ Few Flatiron spaces are as suited to "private conversation" as this "roomy" Med-Continental, and just as few achieve its balance of "solidly good" food (including the "best gourmet burgers") and "accommodating" service.

Cambodian Cuisine (Brooklyn) S   21 | 7 | 14 | $18
87 S. Elliot Pl. (bet. Fulton St. & Lafayette Ave.), 718-858-3262
◪ While most "would be happy" eating this Fort Greene Cambodian's "cheap, strange and delicious" dishes anywhere, a more timid minority objects to the "dingy" decor and "grumpy" staff.

Campagna ◐S   24 | 21 | 21 | $53
24 E. 21st St. (bet. B'way & Park Ave. S.), 212-460-0900
■ Mark Strausman's "phenomenal", "pricey" Flatiron Northern Italian seldom disappoints its "who's who" clientele thanks to the kitchen's "earthy", "rousingly fine" cuisine and the interior's "true rustic" feel; as the "limo lineup" outside attests, it's as popular as ever.

Campagnola ◐S   24 | 20 | 22 | $55
1382 First Ave. (bet. 73rd & 74th Sts.), 212-861-1102
■ "Great for business, or with a classy babe", this "old-school" East Side Italian is hard to beat with its "fantastic" classic dishes and pro waiters who "practically wipe your chin"; of course, it helps to be a "regular" – and to have deep pockets.

Campo S   ▽ 18 | 14 | 18 | $29
502 Amsterdam Ave. (bet. 84th & 85th Sts.), 212-874-4559
■ "It isn't Buenos Aires", but when the urge for Pampas-style beef strikes, this "friendly" Upper West Side Argentinean fills the bill with its "decent", "inexpensive" mixed grill specialties; interesting South American wines and live Latin jazz are further enticements.

Canaletto S   22 | 17 | 21 | $46
208 E. 60th St. (bet. 2nd & 3rd Aves.), 212-317-9192
■ An "ingratiating" recovery zone for Bloomie's shoppers and moviegoers, this "gracious" Italian "cooks to please", and it shows; it's a rare-for-the-area oasis of "calm" with "pleasant, warm" decor, though sticklers suggest a little "more light."

Canal House ◐S   ▽ 20 | 20 | 19 | $48
SoHo Grand Hotel, 310 W. Broadway, 2nd fl. (bet. Canal & Grand Sts.), 212-519-6500
◪ Though the trendoids who populate this "elegant", "austere" New American come mostly for the "hip" scene, the "sophisticated" food is "very impressive" too; however, those more interested in "people-watching" than eating "go straight to" the "jumping" bar.

Candela [S] — 19 | 22 | 18 | $38

116 E. 16th St. (bet. Irving Pl. & Park Ave. S.), 212-254-1600

◪ "A little spooky", this Union Square New American's "dark", "medieval" interior has "lots of candles" to shed flattering light on the "cell-phone vampires" who flock here; while the Asian-accented cuisine's "appealing", it's secondary to the "fierce" "bar scene."

Candido Coal Brick Oven Pizza ◐ [S] ≠ — 20 | 10 | 13 | $19

1606 First Ave. (bet. 83rd & 84th Sts.), 212-396-9401

■ Fans feel "fortunate" with each bite of the coal-oven pizza created by "one of the true masters", Joe Candido, at his Upper East Side Italian; for these "thin-crusted wonders", it's "worth sacrificing decor" ("dim", "sparse") and service ("neglectful").

Candle Cafe [S] — 20 | 13 | 18 | $25

1307 Third Ave. (bet. 74th & 75th Sts.), 212-472-0970

◪ "Pretty damn" "delicious" cooking proves there's "no taste penalty" for "healthy" eating at this East Side vegan mecca – nor a pocket penalty (it's "not expensive"); still, it would help if the staff was less "holier-than-thou" and management "fixed the place up" a bit.

Canteen ◐ [S] — 18 | 21 | 16 | $42

142 Mercer St., downstairs (Prince St.), 212-431-7676

◪ Matthew Kenney's "retro-futuristic" SoHo New American is quite "a scene" where "beautiful" types nibble on "gourmet mac 'n' cheese" and other updated "comfort" classics while sitting on "fashion-forward orange chairs"; however, it won't be seen long unless he upgrades the "unfriendly" service and downgrades prices.

CANTON ◐ [S] ≠ — 25 | 14 | 21 | $43

45 Division St. (bet. Bowery & Market St.), 212-226-4441

■ NYers have been engaged in a "longtime love affair" with this "civilized" Chinatown Cantonese "classic", the *Survey*'s top-rated Chinese; don't bother "looking at the menu", just ask "charming" manager Eileen to guide you to the "superb" "seasonal specialties" that make meals here "worth the high cost" (for C-town).

Canyon Road Grill [S] — 20 | 18 | 17 | $33

1470 First Ave. (bet. 76th & 77th Sts.), 212-734-1600

■ "Like a Ralph Lauren ad" for Santa Fe, this "handsome", "adobe" East Side SW watering hole offers "upscale" eats in exchange for "annoying waits" and "incredible noise" levels; just "beware" the "killer margaritas" or "you won't remember the meal."

CAPSOUTO FRÈRES [S] — 24 | 23 | 23 | $53

451 Washington St. (Watts St.), 212-966-4900

■ Your "taxi driver's nightmare" is finding this "out-of-the-way" ("Capsouto where?") TriBeCa "treasure" whose "imaginatively prepared" French meals, "romantic" setting and "welcoming" spirit merit a few "wrong turns"; luckily there are "no parking hassles", in case you drive yourself.

Captain's Table, The [S] — 18 | 16 | 19 | $44

860 Second Ave. (46th St.), 212-697-9538

◪ "Huge portions of very fresh" seafood keep locals coming back to this East Midtown "fish emporium"; despite generally "smooth sailing", "overpriced, inadequate" eats and "tired" quarters kick up a squall.

Cara Mia [S] — 20 | 15 | 17 | $31

654 Ninth Ave. (bet. 45th & 46th Sts.), 212-262-6767

◪ "Bargain"-seeking ticket-holders hit this "cozy" Hell's Kitchen Italian "find" for "good", "homestyle" Italian fare served by a staff that

| F | D | S | C |

"rushes" to get everyone "to the theater on time"; given the "small" space, it's no surprise it can be "loud" and "cramped."

Carino ꜱ | 21 | 13 | 21 | $31
1710 Second Ave. (bet. 88th & 89th Sts.), 212-860-0566
■ Mama Carino's "sturdy" Southern Italian cooking and "friendly", "take-care-of-you" attitude keep this "tiny", low-budget Upper East Side storefront popular; needless to say, it's "best when Mama is in."

CARLYLE RESTAURANT ꜱ | 24 | 26 | 25 | $68
Carlyle Hotel, 35 E. 76th St. (Madison Ave.), 212-744-1600
■ The "Social Register" set basks in "glorious civility" at this "grand luxe", "quintessential Upper East Side" dining room famed for its "old-world grace", with "glorious" French-Continental cuisine and silky service "to match"; in sum, it's ideal for an "elegant", "refined" dining experience — with an appropriately lofty tab.

Carmaya (Brooklyn) ●ꜱ≠ | – | – | – | M
139 N. Sixth St. (Bedford Ave.), 718-302-4441
High-tech Williamsburg newcomer offering a reasonably priced Italian menu that's just as tasty as its garden, one of the prettiest around; given the piped-in house music, slick decor and CD jewel box menus, some say it's more about the scene than the food.

CARMINE'S ꜱ | 20 | 15 | 17 | $33
2450 Broadway (bet. 90th & 91st Sts.), 212-362-2200
200 W. 44th St. (bet. B'way & 8th Ave.), 212-221-3800 ●
◪ "Take a group", "a big appetite", a "megaphone" and "breath mints" and "be prepared to wait" at these "crowded", "garlic"-fueled Italians where the "family-style" service is "slow" and the volume loud; but *paesanos* happily overlook any flaws for *Flintstones*-size portions of "mama mia" classics.

Carnegie Deli ●ꜱ≠ | 21 | 10 | 13 | $24
854 Seventh Ave. (55th St.), 212-757-2245
■ This "bustling", "crowded" Midtown deli is an "institution" that "even jaded NYers enjoy"; plan to sit elbow-to-elbow at communal tables, eat "impossibly large" sandwiches followed by "mountains" of cheesecake and try to forget what your cardiologist would say; besides the tourists, diners are a cast of characters right out of *Broadway Danny Rose* (which was filmed here).

Carol's Cafe (Staten Island) | 25 | 19 | 20 | $49
1571 Richmond Rd. (bet. Four Corners Rd. & Seaview Ave.), 718-979-5600
◪ Chef-owner Carol Frazetta's "masterful" "touch" is evident in her Staten Island Eclectic's "lovingly prepared", "innovative" cuisine, "engaging" service and "Greenwich Village–like" ambiance; it's "one of SI's better restaurants", even if a few dissenters complain of "Manhattan prices."

Casa ●ꜱ | ▽ 23 | 20 | 21 | $37
72 Bedford St. (Commerce St.), 212-366-9410
■ "Small, delightful", "quaint and quiet" West Village Brazilian "near the Cherry Lane Theater" that has a "romantic" feel that's "charming for a first date"; in addition to "yummy" standards, its "wonderfully tasty" "home cooking" ventures "outside of Rio" to encompass specialties "from the countryside."

Casa La Femme ●ꜱ | 17 | 25 | 17 | $54
150 Wooster St. (bet. Houston & Prince Sts.), 212-505-0005
◪ At this "transporting" SoHo *Arabian Nights* fantasy, "hookahs", "belly dancers" and "sexy" "private tent" Egyptian dining inspire "French kisses galore"; just don't let the "arrogant" service and "large bill" break the "magical" mood.

			F	D	S	C

Casa Mexicana ●S   20 | 17 | 17 | $33
133 Ludlow St. (bet. Rivington & Stanton Sts.), 212-473-4100
■ A "genuine effort to upgrade" the "quality" of Lower East Side Mexican dining, this "lively" "surprise" specializes in "authentic" regional dishes and prices as well; most consider it a "classy" operation, though a few call it "over-yuppified."

Casa Mia S   20 | 19 | 20 | $30
225 E. 24th St. (bet. 2nd & 3rd Aves.), 212-679-5606
■ "Your home away from home" is hidden on a "quiet" Gramercy side street where "down-to-earth" Italian food is served in what could be "your grandmother's" "cozy" dining room; the prices are so "reasonable", it's no surprise complaints are few.

Cascina ●   – | – | – | E
647 Ninth Ave. (bet. 45th & 46th Sts.), 212-245-4422
A wood-burning oven anchors the rustic dining room of this new Hell's Kitchen Italian that appeals to locals and theatergoers alike; specials are announced via blackboard, and the owner's family vineyard supplies the wine list.

Casimir ●S   21 | 19 | 16 | $33
103-105 Ave. B (bet. 6th & 7th Sts.), 212-358-9683
■ The "Left Bank" comes to Alphabet City via this "terrific" Gallic bistro that's good enough and priced low enough to stay "stuffed with more French people than the RER"; there are often "maddeningly" long waits, but overlook the staff's "attitude" and pass the time in the "cool lounge."

Castellano S   20 | 18 | 21 | $49
138 W. 55th St. (bet. 6th & 7th Aves.), 212-664-1975
◪ Patrons still get the "white-glove treatment" at this "classic, correct" Midtown Northern Italian appreciated for its "reliable" cuisine and "quiet" ambiance; it's also "handy to City Center", but tightwads note "what you save in cab fare you spend here."

Caviar Russe S   25 | 23 | 23 | $74
538 Madison Ave., 2nd fl. (bet. 54th & 55th Sts.), 212-980-5908
■ "A spoonful of caviar helps everything go down" at this "decadent" Midtown New American "aerie" where "extravagance" rules; "you can go through money like water or vodka" in this "romantic" setting, and it's fun to guess who's "having an illicit affair."

Caviarteria S   22 | 14 | 17 | $51
Delmonico Hotel, 502 Park Ave. (59th St.), 212-759-7410
■ "Casual indulgence is good for the soul" say gourmands who satisfy their "caviar and champagne" cravings "on the run" at this quickie Midtowner where prices range from "affordable to Donald Trump."

Cellini   22 | 20 | 22 | $47
65 E. 54th St. (bet. Madison & Park Aves.), 212-751-1555
■ The "corporate-card" crowd gravitates toward this "pretty", Tuscan-style Midtown Northern Italian trattoria boasting "interesting" specials; "quiet" and "friendly", it's a "solid" choice for both "nononsense" business lunches and "dining with friends."

CELLO   26 | 26 | 25 | $82
53 E. 77th St. (bet. Madison & Park Aves.), 212-517-1200
■ "Truly a well-tuned instrument", this "magnificent" East Side French seafooder produces meals in which "every note is perfect": chef Laurent Tourondel's "unerring", "classical preparations", the "exquisite" townhouse setting and smoothly "orchestrated" service; for such "divine" experiences, fans settle the "expensive" tabs "with a smile"; prix fixe only: $35 lunch, $75 dinner.

Cendrillon [S] — 21 | 19 | 19 | $38

45 Mercer St. (bet. Broome & Grand Sts.), 212-343-9012

■ "Challenging but delicious" cuisine comes out of the SoHo kitchen of this "worldly" Filipino–Pan-Asian with a vaguely "French colonial" air; given the "warm hospitality", this "serene" spot is a "great de-stresser."

Cent'Anni [S] — 22 | 15 | 20 | $47

50 Carmine St. (bet. Bedford & Bleecker Sts.), 212-989-9494

■ "May it last 100 years": this forever-"unchanged" Village Northern Italian wins kudos for its "commitment" to keeping "old-world culinary values alive"; even if it's "cramped" and could "use a paint job", it's a neighborhood "shining star."

Centolire [S] — ▽ 19 | 23 | 19 | $56

1167 Madison Ave. (bet. 85th & 86th Sts.), 212-734-7711

◪ "Pino Luongo's done it again" rave admirers of his "beautiful" new Eastsider whose "solid" retro Italian menu includes "hard-to find" timpano (the grand dish "featured in *Big Night*"); skeptics suspect it "needs more time" to hit its stride and "justify the prices."

Chadwick's (Brooklyn) [S] — 20 | 18 | 20 | $38

8822 Third Ave. (89th St.), 718-833-9855

■ "A-1 steaks" and other "real American food" come in "warm surroundings" at this Bay Ridge "favorite", which "Brooklyn locals" appreciate especially for its "great bar" "staffed by gentlemen."

Chameleon — ▽ 21 | 21 | 20 | $43

125 E. 39th St. (bet. Lexington & Park Aves.), 212-983-4949

■ "Playing footsie" by the fire comes naturally at this Asian-inflected New American "date place" "in a lovely Murray Hill brownstone"; the prix fixe "bargain" is a "good lure for trying" its "luscious" fare, but when it comes to seating, request the "front" room.

Chanpen Thai [S] — 20 | 16 | 19 | $24

761 Ninth Ave. (51st St.), 212-586-6808

◪ Theatergoers say this "little piece" of Thailand "holds its own" for a "flavorful", "efficient" and "cheap" pre-show meal, especially the "delicious vegetarian selections" and "superb fake duck"; however, some find the "artificial" decor less than "convincing."

CHANTERELLE — 28 | 27 | 27 | VE

2 Harrison St. (Hudson St.), 212-966-6960

■ "Beyond cloud nine and past seventh heaven" floats David and Karen Waltuck's TriBeCa French "classic that continues to impress" after more than two decades; this "sustained champion's" "sumptuous" cuisine ranks No. 2 this year, though with a "beautifully appointed dining room" and "divine service", "it's about the total experience, not just one element"; "if you can afford it", it's "absolutely essential" for any serious food lover; dinner is $84, prix fixe only.

Charles' Southern-Style Kitchen [S] — ▽ 27 | 11 | 19 | $17

2839 Eighth Ave. (bet. 151st & 152nd Sts.), 212-926-4313

■ It's "worth the hike" to eat "like a king for pennies" at this no-frills "Harlem heaven"; fortunately, you'll have cash left over for a taxi home because the buffet of "crisp, juicy" fried chicken and other "hearty" "joys" can land you in a "coma."

Charley O's ◐ [S] — 13 | 13 | 14 | $33

218 W. 45th St. (bet. B'way & 8th Ave.), 212-626-7300

◪ "Decent" for a "pre-theater" meal, this Shubert Alley "pub-style" "hamburger joint" is a tourist staple and "quick when in a rush", just "don't expect anything" beyond "run-of-the-mill."

			F	D	S	C

Charlotte S
Millennium Broadway Hotel, 145 W. 44th St. (bet. B'way & 6th Ave.), 212-789-7508
19 | 19 | 20 | $48

■ "Attractive, convenient" and "usually not crowded", this New American "oasis" near Times Square is "pleasant" for "bargain prix-fixe" dining before a show; biz types also tout its "power lunches."

Chat n' Chew S
10 E. 16th St. (bet. 5th Ave. & Union Sq. W.), 212-243-1616
17 | 14 | 15 | $21

■ For "good ol' homestyle cookin'" amidst "Americana" "clutter", you'll be "comforted" at this Flatiron "dive"; "non-dieters" dub both service and decor "shabby" but will "endure anything for that mac 'n' cheese."

Chazal Bistro ●S
41 Madison Ave. (26th St.), 212-545-8555
19 | 18 | 16 | $46

■ At this French "yuppieville" bistro near Madison Square Park, it's like "a *Sex and the City* episode" where the gals get it on with "jet-set" "Eurotrash"; despite "blasting dance music" and a "club"-like "late-night party scene", the pricey fare is "surprisingly good."

Chef Ho's Peking Duck Grill S
1720 Second Ave. (bet. 89th & 90th Sts.), 212-348-9444
19 | 15 | 18 | $27

■ Most Upper Eastsiders are "glad to have" these "one-notch-above-ordinary" Hunan eats close to home; still, a few snipers say "all the linen tablecloths in the world won't make the food any better", but they do make this "gracious" place a bit chic for the price.

Chelsea Bistro & Bar S
358 W. 23rd St. (bet. 8th & 9th Aves.), 212-727-2026
22 | 19 | 20 | $46

■ For "delicious" bistro "classics", this "romantic" French with an "Edenic" garden and a "cozy fireplace" is the "real deal", at least until the bill arrives; some feel it's fitting that this "old-fashioned" "charmer" is in Chelsea, because it feels like "gay Paris."

Chelsea Grill S
135 Eighth Ave. (bet. 16th & 17th Sts.), 212-242-5336
18 | 15 | 16 | M

■ It's "the kind of bar and grill that you thought high rents had made extinct", and this "best-buy" Chelsea American-Eclectic's "huge burgers and spicy fries" taste best in its heated "year-round garden."

Chelsea Ristorante S
108 Eighth Ave. (bet. 15th & 16th Sts.), 212-924-7786
20 | 17 | 20 | $35

■ "A delicious" and affordable pre-"Joyce choice", this "family-run" Chelsea "Tuscan treasure" has "excellent" brick-oven pizza and signature artichokes that "bring tears to your eyes"; possibly "the only thing with bad taste here is the decor."

Chez Bernard S
323 W. Broadway (bet. Canal & Grand Sts.), 212-343-2583
▽ 19 | 17 | 18 | $41

■ With his "kisses good-bye", owner Bernard Eloy adds "an authentic touch" to his SoHo French bistro; the decor is a bit "dated", but the "food's tasty" and there's an added French accent – "smoking."

Chez Brigitte S⊄
77 Greenwich Ave. (bet. Bank St. & 7th Ave. S.), 212-929-6736
18 | 10 | 18 | $19

■ "Good, cheap" French bistro fare is "prepared before your eyes" at this West Village "lunch-counter" "landmark"; with only 11 stools, you can't help getting "up close and personal" with your fellow diners.

Chez Es Saada ●S
42 E. First St. (bet. 1st & 2nd Aves.), 212-777-5617
19 | 25 | 17 | $43

■ If you "follow the rose petal"–strewn stairwell, you'll discover an "out-of-this-world scene" in this "beautiful" East Village basement "casbah"; replete with "hot belly dancers" and not-so-hot Moroccan-French fare, it's so romantic, you may even excuse the "rude service."

Chez Jacqueline [S] 21 | 18 | 20 | $45

72 MacDougal St. (bet. Bleecker & W. Houston Sts.), 212-505-0727

■ If they ignore "the constant traffic passing by", diners sitting in this "old-faithful" French bistro "on a spring day" may "feel like they're in Provence" instead of the Village; though the menu's somewhat predictable, the "traditional" dishes are "reliably good."

Chez Josephine 🌙 20 | 21 | 20 | $46

414 W. 42nd St. (bet. 9th & 10th Aves.), 212-594-1925

■ "As wonderful and dramatic as Josephine Baker herself", owner Jean-Claude's "quirky" Times Square paean to his mother "gets you in the mood for the theater"; its recently redone "decadent" decor and "tasty" French fare also add to the "ooh-la-la" factor.

Chez Ma Tante 🌙[S] 19 | 18 | 18 | $41

189 W. 10th St. (bet. Bleecker & W. 4th Sts.), 212-620-0223

◪ This tiny, "quaint", "*très Parisien*" New French bistro has "been around a long time", yet Villagers still favor it as a "friendly" place to "sit for hours" along the sidewalk and watch the "street theater."

Chez Michallet [S] 23 | 19 | 22 | $50

90 Bedford St. (Grove St.), 212-242-8309

■ Seeking the perfect venue for "Valentine's Day", you can't do better than this "sweet", "romantic" West Village corner bistro; when you "squeeze" in for a "delicious French" meal, "do you feel sorry for those people waiting outside for your table?" – "nah."

Chez Napoléon 20 | 15 | 21 | $38

365 W. 50th St. (bet. 8th & 9th Aves.), 212-265-6980

■ At this "quintessentially '50s" "little Normandy" Theater District bistro, a French "*grand-mère*" "serves you with a smile"; "faithful" fare and decor from "the beginning of the world" ensure it remains "an oldie but a goodie."

Chez Oskar (Brooklyn) 🌙[S] ▽ 20 | 18 | 18 | $35

211 DeKalb Ave. (Adelphi St.), 718-852-6250

■ A "funky", "hand-painted" facade, "velvety red" banquettes and a free-range "roast chicken you'll happily cross the river for" have Fort Greene scenesters saying this "French-hippie" "fixture" is "better for the money" and "way cooler than anything in Manhattan."

Chez Suzette 🌙[S] 17 | 15 | 19 | $35

675B Ninth Ave. (bet. 46th & 47th Sts.), 212-581-9717

◪ "Reliable" and "friendly", this "old-fashioned", "bare-bones" Theater District French joint serves meals "without pretension"; if the "chef could use more practice", at least the place is "inexpensive."

Chiam Chinese Cuisine 🌙[S] 22 | 20 | 21 | $42

160 E. 48th St. (bet. Lexington & 3rd Aves.), 212-371-2323

■ "When you don't want crowds and are willing to part with some money", try this handsome, modern East Midtown Chinese with a "tasty" American "spin" and "delicious dim sum" at weekend brunch; "popular for business lunches", its service is so "polished", "they do everything except eat for you."

Chianti (Brooklyn) 🌙[S] 20 | 17 | 19 | $36

8530 Third Ave. (86th St.), 718-921-6300

■ One "mama-style portion" of "authentic" eats "feeds two" at this Bay Ridge Italian where "share, share, share" is the way to go; "loud" and "annoying" to some, it's like eating pasta with a large, noisy family, but boy, is that "zesty tomato sauce" "delicious."

Chicama [S] 22 22 19 $48

ABC Carpet & Home, 35 E. 18th St. (bet. B'way & Park Ave. S.), 212-505-2233

■ "You feel like you're in a piñata" "partying away" on "wham-bam drinks" and "dazzling" cuisine at Douglas Rodriguez's pricey South American "sensation" just north of Union Square; it's always "filled to the gills", but "service keeps on top of things despite the lunacy."

Chikubu ∇ 22 15 19 $42

12 E. 44th St. (bet. 5th & Madison Aves.), 212-818-0715

■ "One of the few restaurants in NY that actually feels like one in Tokyo", this Midtowner is a refreshing "change of pace from the usual sushi routine"; here, "Japanese businessmen start lining up before noon" to lunch on "authentic" specialties.

Chimichurri Grill [S] 21 15 18 $42

606 Ninth Ave. (bet. 43rd & 44th Sts.), 212-586-8655

■ "Big-league carnivores" come to this "little" Argentinean "gem" in the Theater District for "kick-ass" meat "so good that they must be rolled out the door"; "it doesn't have the glitz of the fancier steakhouses", but "the aroma of their signature chimichurri sauce could convert a vegetarian."

China Fun ◐ [S] 15 9 12 $20

1221 Second Ave. (64th St.), 212-752-0810
246 Columbus Ave. (bet. 71st & 72nd Sts.), 212-580-1516
1653 Broadway (bet. 51st & 52nd Sts.), 212-333-2622

◪ The "decor isn't fun", but there"s "dim sum all day" at these "chaotic" Chinese joints where the "cheap", "voluminous menu" lures fans; critics counter "General Tso needs a demotion."

China Grill [S] 23 21 19 $47

CBS Bldg., 60 W. 53rd St. (bet. 5th & 6th Aves.), 212-333-7788

■ "Cell phone–talking" types have Midtown "meetings" at this "soaring", "expensive" Asian-Eclectic eatery; it's often "too loud to hear yourself chew", but the flavors are so "explosive" you wouldn't want to pay attention to conversation anyway.

Chinam 28 [S] 19 15 19 $25

1643 Second Ave. (bet. 85th & 86th Sts.), 212-717-6688

■ Regulars "order the dumplings for an appetizer, for a main course and then again for dessert" at this "friendly", easily affordable East Side Vietnamese-Mandarin where those little Asian pillows are considered "exceptional" but everything else is just "ordinary."

Chin Chin ◐ [S] 23 19 21 $45

216 E. 49th St. (bet. 2nd & 3rd Aves.), 212-888-4555

◪ At this stylish, modern East Midtown Chinese that could be renamed "Chic Chic", both "beautiful people" and business folk praise the kitchen's "very delicious, non-mainstream" cuisine; with superior service under the direction of Jimmy Chin, you could hardly do better for your "top-dollar" tab.

Chinghalle ◐ [S] 18 19 16 $45

50 Gansevoort St. (bet. Greenwich & Washington Sts.), 212-242-3200

◪ After a bumpy start, this much-"hyped" Meatpacking District Italian should rally now that owner Mark Strausman is manning the burners; given the nearby competition, this yearling had better improve!

Chinoiserie ◐ [S] 17 21 17 $44

Hotel Giraffe, 365 Park Ave. S. (26th St.), 212-213-3125

◪ "It may be a good thing it's too dark to see the meal" at this "sexy" new Chinese-French Gramercy basement boîte; however, the "velvet-rope crowd" doesn't mind groping for its "yummy" cocktails.

	F	D	S	C

Chip Shop (Brooklyn) S⌀ ▽ 19 | 14 | 17 | $18
383 Fifth Ave. (bet. 6th & 7th Sts.), 718-832-7701
■ The "wee tastes of the British Isles" are mostly "deep-fried" at this Park Slope "kitsch cutie", but "don't watch your weight" – just revel in "lovely fish 'n' chips", "delectable mushy peas" and the like.

Cho Dang Gol S ▽ 23 | 16 | 18 | $24
55 W. 35th St. (bet. 5th & 6th Aves.), 212-695-8222
■ "A tasty tofu odyssey" awaits culinary "adventurers" at this Midtown Korean where soybean curd is the "homemade specialty"; "from mild to spicy, from soft to firm", "everything tastes delicious."

Chola S 22 | 17 | 19 | $38
232 E. 58th St. (bet. 2nd & 3rd Aves.), 212-688-4619
■ This East Side Indian's "eclectic menu" offers "fascinating flavors", and the "staff truly tries to explain" its "different finds"; the lunch buffet is a "great" intro, but be warned: "for once, hot means hot!"

Chop't Creative Salad ▽ 21 | 14 | 16 | $14
24 E. 17th St. (bet. B'way & 5th Ave.), 646-336-5523
■ "Count on it being fresh" at this Flatiron salad place that "serves mean greens" and "endless" toppings; just lunch "early or you'll have to wait on line longer than at the Kate Spade sample sale."

Choshi S 19 | 13 | 15 | $29
77 Irving Pl. (E. 19th St.), 212-420-1419
■ "Big rolls" stuffed with "the freshest of fish" "make you grateful for the ocean" at this Gramercy Japanese that "gives Yama a run for its money"; insiders say "you're better off not seeing the interior", so savor your sushi "alfresco" at a sidewalk table.

Chow Bar S 21 | 19 | 18 | $36
230 W. Fourth St. (W. 10th St.), 212-633-2212
■ "Everything hits the spot" at this West Village "winner" that's "one of the few places where Asian fusion actually works"; with "reasonable" prices, a "nice", "funky staff" and "festive" decor "straight out of a Wong Kar-wai movie", it's becoming "very popular."

Christer's 22 | 20 | 21 | $49
145 W. 55th St. (bet. 6th & 7th Aves.), 212-974-7224
■ "Salmon enchanted evening" you may meet a stranger restaurant than this Scandinavian fish and game "standout" near City Center; its "funky neo-hunting lodge" interior is "so cozy" that you'll be looking around for a "pillow and afghan to snuggle with" "by the fire."

Christine's S⌀ 16 | 8 | 13 | $18
208 First Ave. (bet. 12th & 13th Sts.), 212-254-2474
■ "Why cook?" – you can grow "fat cheaper than at home" polishing off pierogi at this East Village Polish coffee shop; it's "dumpy", but its "solid" fare induces "recurring dreams" of the "old country."

Christos Hasapo-Taverna (Queens) ●S ▽ 21 | 16 | 20 | $34
41-08 23rd Ave. (41st St.), 718-726-5195
■ You can dine on "top-quality meat in-house" and then "buy some" to take home at this Greek butcher shop that's a restaurant at night; "the best steak and lamb in town for the price" "demand a trip" to Astoria, though the "cigarette smoke is thicker than the taramasalata."

Churrascaria Plataforma ●S 22 | 18 | 20 | $47
Belvedere Hotel, 316 W. 49th St. (bet. 8th & 9th Aves.), 212-245-0505
■ "Holy cow!" – herds of "gluttons, gourmands" and "tourists" "belly up" to the "all-you-can-eat parade of meats" at this "lively" Theater

			F	D	S	C

District Brazilian rodizio; the "salad bar is groaning" and so will you, especially after a few of their "amazing" caipirinhas.

Ciao ●S — | — | — | M
185 Bleecker St. (MacDougal St.), 212-673-8901
On a well-traveled Village corner, this new Italian is producing classic dishes from Campagna for a walk-in crowd lured by the sidewalk seating and charmingly rustic interior; its succinct menu is bolstered by interesting daily specials.

Ciao Europa ●S 19 | 19 | 18 | $42
Warwick Hotel, 63 W. 54th St. (bet. 5th & 6th Aves.), 212-247-1200
■ There's "nothing extraordinary" at this "relaxing" Midtown Italian that has a prix fixe that's "a steal" before or after the theater; as a "pleasant spot where you can carry on a conversation", it's also popular for "business lunches."

Cibi Cibi/Yellowfingers S 15 | 13 | 14 | $30
200 E. 60th St. (3rd Ave.), 212-751-8615
◪ After shopping, the "Bloomingdale's crowd" refuels on Italian-accented American sandwiches, salads and such at this "casual" East Side cafe; "service is slow", but the "hopping bar" works "after work."

Cibo S 21 | 20 | 20 | $42
767 Second Ave. (41st St.), 212-681-1616
◪ Loyal locals say this "lovely" Tuscan–New American "really uplifts Tudor City's sagging scene" with a "gorgeous space" and food that just "keeps getting better"; a few may say it's "ho-hum", but in this "wasteland" it's more than just a "neighborhood joint."

Cilantro ●S 18 | 17 | 17 | $27
1712 Second Ave. (bet. 88th & 89th Sts.), 212-722-4242
1321 First Ave. (71st St.), 212-537-4040
◪ Since it produces "mega-margaritas" and "tasty", "cheap" eats, it's no surprise that these Upper East Side Southwesterners "skew young"; nonetheless, "the food's surprisingly authentic", and the "great little garden" is a neighborhood "oasis."

Cinquanta ●S ▽ 22 | 18 | 21 | $43
50 E. 50th St. (bet. Madison & Park Aves.), 212-759-5050
■ While there must be *cinquanta* Italian restaurants in its section of Midtown, this "amiable" "standby" sets itself apart with "delicious" classic dishes, "dependable", "friendly" service and moderate prices.

Cinque Terre S 21 | 17 | 18 | $45
22 E. 38th St. (bet. Madison & Park Aves.), 212-213-0910
■ In Murray Hill, this "charming, hidden" Italian "transports" diners to Liguria, a coastal province known for its "fabulous" seafood and "fine" regional wines; here, "authentic" culinary and gustatory "delights" aid "client entertaining" in a "quiet", "comfortable setting."

Circo, Osteria del ●S 22 | 24 | 21 | $54
120 W. 55th St. (bet. 6th & 7th Aves.), 212-265-3636
■ The Maccioni family's Le Cirque spin-off "wakens all the senses" with its "whimsically beautiful", recently revamped "circus" decor, "non-stop action at the bar" and Mama Eggi's "terrific" Tuscan cuisine; in short, "Sirio's boys" know how to deliver "a fun, fine meal."

Circus ●S 20 | 19 | 19 | $43
808 Lexington Ave. (bet. 62nd & 63rd Sts.), 212-223-2965
■ "Everyone's having fun" at this "little", "action-packed" East Side Brazilian, "especially as the caipirinhas kick in" and folks dig into the "deliciously" "different" cuisine; it's a "delightful place for lunch" too.

	F	D	S	C

Citarella — | — | — | VE
1240 Sixth Ave. (49th St.), 212-332-1515
Long one of NY's top retail seafood purveyors, this gourmet food store now cooks it for you at this triplex Midtown newcomer where chef Brian Young (ex Le Bernardin) offers delicious dishes for deep-pocketed diners and pastry chef Bill Yosses (ex Bouley) does his sweet things; with designer David Rockwell completing the team, this has to be one to watch.

Cité ●S 22 | 20 | 21 | $55
120 W. 51st St. (bet. 6th & 7th Aves.), 212-956-7100
■ "Hang with the suits" at this "classy" Midtowner where "top-notch steaks", "even better fries" and "free-flowing" vino make for "evenings you won't forget – or perhaps can't remember"; insiders say it's best "when the company's picking up" the tab.

Cité Grill ●S 21 | 19 | 19 | $44
120 W. 51st St. (bet. 6th & 7th Aves.), 212-956-7262
■ "Cheaper" and "more casual" than the "big room" next door, this "Cité lite" lures "young" Midtowners with its "cool bar scene" and grill "staples", as well as the same "fabulous wine specials" as its parent.

Citrus Bar & Grill ●S 18 | 18 | 16 | $34
320 Amsterdam Ave. (75th St.), 212-595-0500
◪ Known for its "lethal but yummy margs", this West Side "watering hole for the under-40 crowd" also turns out "fun spins" on Southwestern cooking at "moderate" prices; by consensus the "drinks are better than the food."

City Bakery ●S 23 | — | 15 | $17
3 W. 18th St. (bet. 5th & 6th Aves.), 212-366-1414
■ Now that "king of tarts" Maury Rubin has relocated his cafe/bakery to new, bigger Flatiron digs, there's lots more room for his "divine baked goods" and "sophisticated", "market fresh" salads, sandwiches and soups; as a bonus, it's now open till midnight.

City Crab & Seafood Co. ●S 19 | 15 | 16 | $38
235 Park Ave. S. (19th St.), 212-529-3800
◪ "What's more fun than a hammer + crabs + beer?" – figure in a "young" "after-work pickup" scene at the bar and a "decent" shore-fare menu, and you've cracked this "frenetic" Flatiron "seafood gymnasium's" equation, even if it does feel like "you're in the suburbs."

City Eatery ●S ∇ 19 | 16 | 17 | $42
316 Bowery (Bleecker St.), 212-253-8644
■ "An exciting mix of old and new" marks this "ambitious" NoHo newcomer featuring Italian-influenced New American food; so far it's something of a "sleeper", with early fans wondering "why isn't it full?"

City Grill ●S 16 | 14 | 16 | $27
269 Columbus Ave. (bet. 72nd & 73rd Sts.), 212-873-9400
■ This "casual" West Side American offers "simple" but "well-prepared" eats in a "cozy" pub-like space; good for a "bargain" pre–Lincoln Center meal, it's "no big deal", but "every neighborhood could use" one.

City Hall 21 | 22 | 21 | $49
131 Duane St. (bet. Church St. & W. B'way), 212-227-7777
■ The "City Hall you shouldn't fight", this "spacious, elegant" TriBeCa American brasserie hung with "wonderful photos of old NY" has "city politicians" and the "courthouse crowd" crowing over its "delicious" fare, overall "smooth operation" and ability to tax without complaint.

		F	D	S	C

Clay ◐S
▽ 19 | 19 | 17 | $31

202 Mott St. (bet. Kenmare & Spring Sts.), 212-625-1105
■ It's "off-the-beaten-track", but Downtown types call this "hip" NoLita Korean as "good as its Koreatown" compatriots; if the fare's only "quasi"-authentic, it's authentically cheap, and the "casual but chic" ambiance is genuinely a "scene."

Clove S
– | – | – | E

24 E. 80th St. (bet. 5th & Madison Aves.), 212-249-6500
Fka the Lobster Club, this bi-level townhouse lures Eastsiders out of their own townhouses for its tony renditions of regional New American fare at tony prices; N.B. insiders opt for the airier upper level over the more closed-in ground floor.

Cocina Cuzco S
▽ 20 | 17 | 19 | $27

55 Ave. A (4th St.), 212-529-3469 ◐
222 Seventh Ave. (3rd St.), Brooklyn, 718-788-5036
■ "True-blue Peru" meets Manhattan at this "friendly" East Village corner spot brimming with music, murals and "budget"-priced "homemade dishes"; service can take a while, but it's a "charming" place to linger; the Park Slope branch is new and unrated.

Coco Marina S
17 | 18 | 16 | $40

2 World Financial Ctr. at the winter garden (bet. Liberty & Vesey Sts.), 212-385-8080
◪ "Thrillingly located" in the WFC's airy Winter Garden, Pino Luongo's Coco Pazzo offshoot offers a familiar Tuscan menu that draws mostly "business" types on "expense accounts"; a "disappointed" contingent calls it "complacent" and "overpriced"; N.B. closed at press time.

Coconut Grill ◐S
16 | 14 | 16 | $30

1481 Second Ave. (77th St.), 212-772-6262
◪ "Average American food" meets "above-average singles" at this popular Upper Eastsider; there's "often a long wait" for its "basic brunch", and at lunchtime "watch out for the strollers."

Coco Pazzo S
21 | 20 | 20 | $54

23 E. 74th St. (bet. 5th & Madison Aves.), 212-794-0205 ◐
Time Hotel, 224 W. 49th St. (bet. B'way & 8th Ave.), 212-320-2929
■ "You can cozy up next to Ron Perelman" and other "captains of industry" while savoring "tasty" Tuscan cuisine at this "elegant" Pino Luongo–owned pair; while the Café has closed, the East Side original and the relocated Teatro remain as "good to impress" as ever.

Coco Roco (Brooklyn) S
21 | 16 | 18 | $23

392 Fifth Ave. (bet. 6th & 7th Sts.), 718-965-3376
■ Though the rotisserie chicken is "divine", any of the "reasonably priced" "delicacies" are worth trying at this "popular" Park Slope Peruvian; just "prepare to be stuffed."

Coffee Shop ◐S
16 | 14 | 12 | $27

29 Union Sq. W. (16th St.), 212-243-7969
◪ "By day a regular coffee shop" "with a South American twist", this Union Square "staple" becomes an increasingly "sizzling scene" in the evening; aside from low prices, its "main attraction is the beauty" of its patrons and "attitudinous" staff.

Cola's S
▽ 19 | 15 | 17 | $28

148 Eighth Ave. (bet. 17th & 18th Sts.), 212-633-8020
■ "Having a bowl of pasta and watching the boys go by" are the main activities at this "honest" Chelsea Mediterranean; after several years in business, the fact that it's "still there and still inexpensive" shows that this "little restaurant that could" does things "right."

			F	D	S	C

Col Legno ◐S   20 | 13 | 18 | $32
231 E. Ninth St. (bet. 2nd & 3rd Aves.), 212-777-4650
■ East Villagers are "charmed" by the "reliable Tuscan" fare and "warm" vibe at this "sweet little place"; though local "artists' work" is the "simple" room's "only distinction", "you can't beat the aroma of the wood-burning oven" or the "old-world service."

Columbus Bakery S   19 | 13 | 11 | $17
957 First Ave. (bet. 52nd & 53rd Sts.), 212-421-0334
474 Columbus Ave. (bet. 82nd & 83rd Sts.), 212-724-6880
■ "Self-serving" "yuppies with kids" hungry for pastries, salads and sandwiches crowd these "cheerful" crosstown "carbohydrate heavens"; though "you need roller-derby manners to get a table", you can always opt for a "picnic in the park."

Comfort Diner, The S   15 | 12 | 14 | $20
142 E. 86th St. (Lexington Ave.), 212-426-8600 ◐
214 E. 45th St. (bet. 2nd & 3rd Aves.), 212-867-4555
■ After eating the "greasy good burgers" at this "retro-cool" East Side duo, you'll "feel like a high schooler again", though the "enormous portions" will remind you that "your jeans aren't as comfortable" as they were in the "'50s."

Commune ◐S   18 | 21 | 17 | $44
12 E. 22nd St. (bet. B'way & Park Ave. S.), 212-777-2600
■ "If you're 25, solo" and crave "comfort food", "you'll love" Matthew Kenney's "cool and sexy" Flatiron American boasting bevies of "vixens, mixin's and fixin's" – "if you can stand the cell phones" and "noise."

Convivium Osteria (Brooklyn) S   ▽ 25 | 22 | 24 | $41
68 Fifth Ave. (bet. Bergen St. & St. Mark's Ave.), 718-857-1833
■ "You'll need a translator" to read the menu of "delicious Portuguese, Italian and Spanish" dishes at this "fantastic addition" to Park Slope; with its communal tables and "old-farmhouse" decor, this newcomer is as "uncompromisingly authentic" as the "scrumptious" fare.

Cooke's Corner S   ▽ 21 | 16 | 21 | $37
618 Amsterdam Ave. (90th St.), 212-712-2872
■ "Thank God!" exclaim Westsiders celebrating the arrival of this "friendly" "boon" to a "neighborhood starved" for "tasty, creative" cuisine; it's "small", but the midpriced New American–European eats are "worth the squeeze."

Cookies & Couscous S⌀   19 | 11 | 16 | $23
230 Thompson St. (bet. Bleecker & W. 4th Sts.), 212-477-6562
◪ The "passionate" chef-owner at this "tiny" Village Moroccan is "eager to show what his food can do"; though fans tout the tagines, unimpressed patrons suggest "skip the couscous and go straight to the cookies" and "off-the-wall sorbets."

Cooking with Jazz (Queens) S   24 | 14 | 20 | $37
1201 154th St. (12th Ave.), 718-767-6979
■ "The Big Easy comes north" to Queens at this "little dynamo of Cajun cooking" and "N'Awlins-funky" jazz; the "spicy", moderately priced meals aren't "for the faint of heart", but for those who like it "hot, hot, hot", "it's Fat Tuesday all year round."

Copeland's S   ▽ 19 | 15 | 17 | $26
547 W. 145th St. (bet. Amsterdam Ave. & B'way), 212-234-2357
■ "Lip-smackingly good" grub, "great history" and "gospel brunch for tourists" are the hallmarks of this inexpensive "real down-home Soul Food" "classic" in Harlem; the clientele isn't all camera-toting – Uptown's "movers and shakers" also chow down here.

F	D	S	C

Coppola's ⓈⒶ   19 | 15 | 18 | $31
206 W. 79th St. (bet. Amsterdam Ave. & B'way), 212-877-3840
378 Third Ave. (bet. 27th & 28th Sts.), 212-679-0070 ◐

■ Murray Hillers and Westsiders slurp "delicious spaghetti" at these "neighborhood favorites" where everyone's "squished" "elbow-to-elbow"; but "when you crave the Italian basics", these bargain "red-sauce" joints make you "an offer you can't refuse."

Coq Hardi (Brooklyn) Ⓢ   ▽ 20 | 17 | 21 | $30
142 Montague St. (bet. Clinton & Henry Sts.), 718-246-5577

◪ In a second-floor space above Montague Street, this new French-Med "find" "looks promising"; it's "trying hard, with partial success", to deliver "imaginative" meals, like its signature couscous royal, but many come at lunch "just for the burgers."

Cornelia Street Cafe ◐Ⓢ   19 | 16 | 17 | $30
29 Cornelia St. (bet. Bleecker & W. 4th Sts.), 212-989-9319

■ In the mind of every NY romantic, "a quaint cafe on a luscious street" awaits "in the heart of the Village"; this "darling" "old staple" fits the bill, with "no-risk" French-American fare, "good wines" and "seats by the fire."

Corner Bistro ◐Ⓢ⇌   23 | 11 | 13 | $16
331 W. Fourth St. (Jane St.), 212-242-9502

■ Designed so you can "indulge your cholesterol, smoking and liquor" habits, this "dingy" West Village "dive" has long waits, "paper plates" and "noise beyond belief", but the "big, fat, juicy, fall-apart, packed-with-everything burgers" could "convert a vegetarian" (and are rated tops in this *Survey*).

Cosi   18 | 12 | 13 | $13
60 E. 56th St. (bet. Madison & Park Aves.), 212-588-0888
165 E. 52nd St. (bet. Lexington & 3rd Aves.), 212-758-7800
38 E. 45th St. (bet. Madison & Vanderbilt Aves.), 212-949-7400
685 Third Ave. (bet. 43rd & 44th Sts.), 212-697-8449 Ⓢ
Paramount Plaza, 1633 Broadway (51st St.), 212-397-2674 Ⓢ
11 W. 42nd St. (bet. 5th & 6th Aves.), 212-398-6660
61 W. 48th St. (bet. 5th & 6th Aves.), 212-265-2674
202 W. 36th St. (bet. 7th & 8th Aves.), 212-967-9444
3 E. 17th St. (bet. B'way & 5th Ave.), 212-414-8468 Ⓢ
841 Broadway (13th St.), 212-614-8544 ◐Ⓢ
Plus other locations in the NY area

■ Conspiracy theorists say "they must put something in the bread" at these sandwich shops "because it's amazing how the suits dive for the stuff when it comes out of the oven"; more and more NYers create lunches between their "addictive" slices.

Cosmic Cantina ◐Ⓢ⇌   – | – | – | I
201 Third Ave. (13th St.), 212-420-0975

In the heart of NYU territory comes this new Mexican with a healthy spin, turning out fare made strictly from organic ingredients; even better, prices are right and it's open daily till 5 AM.

Country Cafe Ⓢ   21 | 18 | 19 | $33
69 Thompson St. (bet. Broome & Spring Sts.), 212-966-5417

■ "Just plain adorable" SoHo bistro offering "delightful" Gallic fare with Moroccan "flair" in "miniscule" but "atmospheric" digs; though it's hard to "avoid the smoke", the "reasonable" prices are easier to take.

Coup   21 | 21 | 19 | $44
509 E. Sixth St. (bet. Aves. A & B), 212-979-2815

■ As its ratings suggest, this "stylish" New American is a "hit", with "top-grade" cooking, "friendly" service and "sleek", "lounge-like"

www.zagat.com

ambiance capped by a "pretty garden"; still, some of its hipster crowd consider it "*un peu cher*" for the East Village."

Cowgirl Hall of Fame S
15 | 18 | 15 | $25

519 Hudson St. (W. 10th St.), 212-633-1133

🗹 "Corn dogs and tequila shots" make an interesting meal at this West Village Southwesterner known for its "trailer park" eats served in "campy" digs, though the ultra-"cheap" tabs are no joke.

CRAFT S
25 | 26 | 23 | $67

43 E. 19th St. (bet. B'way & Park Ave. S.), 212-780-0880

■ "A la carte" dining rises to the next level at this handsome, "groundbreaking" Flatiron New American from Gramercy Tavern's "crafty" Tom Colicchio, whose "design-your-own-meal" concept features a menu emphasizing "purity" and broken down by food type and cooking method; sure, it "gets pricey fast" and a few find the process of ordering "too much work", but fervent foodies say it's "worth the extra thought."

Cuba Libre S
20 | 17 | 16 | $34

200 Eighth Ave. (bet. 20th & 21st Sts.), 212-206-0038

🗹 "Busy, buzzy" Chelsea Cuban that has comrades "swearing fidelity" to its "delicious Latin fusion" cooking and "*muy bueno*" mojitos; though "spotty service" and a major "acoustics problem" make some scream, the "sexy bar scene" leaves most swooning.

Cub Room ●◐ S
21 | 20 | 19 | $46

131 Sullivan St. (Prince St.), 212-677-4100

■ The "swinging bar" up-front contrasts with the "quiet dining room" in back at this "trendy" SoHo New American where the "Frank Lloyd Wright"–esque decor is the "stunning backdrop" for "wonderful" cooking; the cafe adjunct serves "simpler, cheaper" fare.

Cucina (Brooklyn) S
24 | 21 | 21 | $45

256 Fifth Ave. (bet. Carroll St. & Garfield Pl.), 718-230-0711

🗹 Park Slope's "trailblazer" evokes "love at first sight" for those enthralled with its "lusty" Italian cooking and "attentive service" "without Manhattan attitude"; still, some hedge that the departure of chef Michael Ayoub puts its food rating in question.

Cucina di Pesce ●◐ S ⌿
19 | 15 | 18 | $26

87 E. Fourth St. (bet. 2nd Ave. & Bowery), 212-260-6800

■ "High-class food at low prices" draws "young", frugal types to this Alphabet City Italian known for its "can't-be-beat" $9.95 early-bird special; it can be a "mob scene", but a "beautiful garden" and a new fireplace and skylight-equipped back room ease the crush.

Cupcake Cafe S ⌿
22 | 9 | 13 | $14

522 Ninth Ave. (39th St.), 212-465-1530

■ For "buttercream bliss", you can't beat this bakery behind the Port Authority that turns out "sinfully luscious" confections "so beautiful it's a shame to eat them"; though it also serves breakfast and lunch, it's really "all about the cupcakes" here.

Cupping Room Cafe ●◐ S
17 | 16 | 15 | $26

359 W. Broadway (bet. Broome & Grand Sts.), 212-925-2898

🗹 Granted, it's "been the same for years", but this SoHo Eclectic is still dispensing "pretty good food" in a "tight", "living room–like" setting; the "bohemian" air extends to the "discombobulated" service.

Curry Leaf S
∇ 19 | 15 | 19 | $25

99 Lexington Ave. (27th St.), 212-725-5558

■ This "solid" new "addition to Curry Hill" from the owners of the nearby Kalustyan's spice shop is a "real up-and-comer", offering "better-than-average" Indian fare and "accommodating service"; just turn a blind eye to the "dreary decor" and think how cheap everything is here.

Cyclo [S] — 20 | 15 | 17 | $29

203 First Ave. (bet. 12th & 13th Sts.), 212-673-3975

◪ "Inventive" Vietnamese cooking at "most reasonable prices" makes this "funky" East Villager "quite a find"; still, some say it "skimps on portion sizes" and there are "too many tables" crammed into "close quarters."

Da Andrea [S] — ▽ 22 | 17 | 22 | $31

557 Hudson St. (bet. Perry & W. 11th Sts.), 212-367-1979

■ Maybe the "atmosphere isn't superfancy", but this "dependable", "neighborhoody" West Village Italian remains a "wonderful little" nexus where the "chef knows his food" and the staff excels at "personal attention", all for "almost-bargain" prices.

Da Antonio Ristorante — 21 | 18 | 21 | $52

157 E. 55th St. (bet. Lexington & 3rd Aves.), 212-588-1545

◪ A "congenial host" makes first-timers "feel like regulars" at this "upscale" but "homey" Midtown Italian that's "like eating at a friend's"; maybe it's a "little overpriced", but high and low rollers alike call it a "safe bet" for "civilized" dining and "outstanding" service.

Da Ciro — 21 | 17 | 19 | $38

229 Lexington Ave. (bet. 33rd & 34th Sts.), 212-532-1636

■ Take a "Roman holiday in NY" via this Murray Hill Italian that's renowned for its "sublime" focaccia robiola straight out of a "fantastic" brick oven; since this "neighborhood secret's been let out of the bag", a quieter "upstairs dining room" has been added to handle the "crowds."

Da Filippo [S] — 21 | 18 | 21 | $47

1315 Second Ave. (bet. 69th & 70th Sts.), 212-472-6688

■ There's "never a misstep" from the "assertive" kitchen of this East Side Northern Italian, and the service is "impeccable"; that's lucky, since its neighborhood is loaded with tough Italian competitors.

Daily Chow [S] — 18 | 17 | 16 | $26

2 E. Second St. (Bowery), 212-254-7887

◪ Part of the "Bowery's revival", this bi-level Pan-Asian's gimmick is a "delicious Mongolian barbecue" where you can customize "your own stir-fry"; critics feel it "sacrifices authenticity for trendiness" and, although it's "cheap", "you get what you pay for."

Daily Soup — 18 | 9 | 13 | $10

134 E. 43rd St. (bet. Lexington & 3rd Aves.), 212-949-7687
780 Third Ave. (bet. 48th & 49th Sts.), 212-828-7687 🚫💳
241 W. 54th St. (bet. B'way & 8th Ave.), 212-765-7687
325 Park Ave. S. (bet. 24th & 25th Sts.), 212-531-7687 🚫💳
41 John St. (bet. Dutch & Nassau Sts.), 212-791-7687
55 Broad St. (Beaver St.), 212-222-7687 🚫💳

◪ A "wide variety" of "homemade tastes" makes this cheap soup chain "worthwhile" for "quick lunches"; still, some suggest that the "stainless steel" "assembly-line" ambiance and daily pricing mean "Campbell's need not worry."

Dakshin Indian Bistro — ▽ 20 | 14 | 19 | $25

1713 First Ave. (bet. 88th & 89th Sts.), 212-987-9839 🚫💳
741 Ninth Ave. (50th St.), 212-757-4545 [S]

■ Those needing proof that Ninth Avenue is becoming a "more reasonably priced restaurant row" need look no further than this Indian

F D S C

"find" featuring flavorsome fare at "inexpensive" tabs; the East Side branch is new and unrated.

Dalga Seafood Grill S ▽ 23 | 15 | 19 | $43
401 E. 62nd St. (bet. First & York Aves.), 212-813-1790
■ The name translates as 'wave', and this "small" Turkish newcomer near the Queensboro Bridge is making a big splash stressing a "wonderful selection" of sensational seafood rather than the conventional kebabs; the "soothing", marine-blue decor may get modest ratings, but the "pleasant" service does better.

Dallas BBQ ●S 15 | 9 | 13 | $19
3956 Broadway (166th St.), 212-568-3700
1265 Third Ave. (bet. 72nd & 73rd Sts.), 212-772-9393
27 W. 72nd St. (bet. Columbus Ave. & CPW), 212-873-2004
132 W. 43rd St. (bet. B'way & 6th Ave.), 212-221-9000
21 University Pl. (8th St.), 212-674-4450
132 Second Ave. (St. Marks Pl.), 212-777-5574
☑ "Dee-licious" BBQ chicken-and-ribs "filling stations" that are "true friends of the working man" (and family) thanks to ultra-"cheap" tabs; foes cite quality akin to a "Vegas buffet" and "food court" decor, but happy fans "bring a bib" and dig in.

Danal S 21 | 21 | 18 | $36
90 E. 10th St. (bet. 3rd & 4th Aves.), 212-982-6930
■ Urbanites go "rustic" at this "quaint" Central Village "retreat" for "yummy" "Country French cooking" in "homey" quarters adorned with "kitschy" "knickknacks" right out of *Antiques Roadshow*; it's "great for a date" or "take-your-parents-to-brunch day", but beware the "bohemian" pace.

Da Nico S 21 | 16 | 19 | $33
164 Mulberry St. (bet. Broome & Grand Sts.), 212-343-1212
☑ "Old-fashioned" types, "tourists" and even "Rudy" sate their "Little Italy cravings" at this "charming" "Mulberry Street favorite" purveying "big portions" of *molto bene* "red-sauce" standards; "lovely" "garden seating" and "good value" add appeal, though a few skeptics shrug "hit-or-miss."

DANIEL 28 | 28 | 27 | $87
60 E. 65th St. (bet. Madison & Park Aves.), 212-288-0033
■ "Oh, to be rich" sigh wanna-be regulars "swooning" over "main man" Daniel Boulud's "truly deserving" East Side "stunner", a "heavenly" "feast for the eyes and palate" featuring "flawless" French food (rated No. 1 in this *Survey*) and "exquisite wines", "impeccably" decanted in ultra-"luxe", colonnaded quarters; though a tad "haughty", it's a "sensual", "crème de la crème" experience – so long as you don't forget to "bring at least *one* Amex."

Daniella Ristorante S 23 | 17 | 22 | $46
320 Eighth Ave. (26th St.), 212-807-0977
■ Despite its "shoebox" dimensions and non-shoebox tabs, this "unpretentious" Italian "standby" wins big cheers for its "pleasing" pastas and "service with a smile"; ticket-holders up for a "quick" bite rate it "one of the better finds" on this "out-of-the-way" turf "near MSG."

Dan Maxwell's Grill S 18 | 15 | 18 | $41
1708 Second Ave. (bet. 88th & 89th Sts.), 212-426-7688
☑ Maybe it's "not top tier", but this "straight-shootin'" Upper East Side red meatery is a "friendly" enough "joint", but even with a new, more "diverse menu", critics call the "plain fare" and "mall-like" setting a "disappointment."

	F	D	S	C

Danube ◐Ⓢ
26 | 28 | 26 | $80

30 Hudson St. (bet. Duane & Reade Sts.), 212-791-3771
■ A Tyrolean "feather in the cap" for David Bouley, this "amazing" TriBeCa "dreamworld" transports diners with "heavenly, not heavy" Austrian cooking showcasing "spectacular" takes on schnitzel and other Viennese "classics"; set in a "gorgeous" "temple to Klimt" ("vat a room!") with "exemplary service" worthy of the "Hapsburg dynasty", it's way über the top but "hits every note" in Straussian style – "*ach, du liebe!*"

Danzón
– | – | – | E

126 E. 28th St. (Lexington Ave. & Park Ave. S.), 212-252-1345
Mexican regional cooking gets a boost at this latest entry from talented chef Zarela Martinez that brings Veracruz coastal cuisine to the hot Madison Park area; downstairs, there's a bar scene, with a narrow dining room above decorated with a collection of high heels, since Danzón is a ballroom dance.

Darna Ⓢ
∇ 22 | 22 | 20 | $36

600 Columbus Ave. (89th St.), 212-721-9123
■ "Best of its kind" proclaim partisans of this West Side kosher Moroccan "phenom", hailed for its "surprisingly good" glatt "delicacies" and unexpectedly "charming" Tangier-tinged decor; "pleasant service" is a plus, and it's darn "well-priced" too.

D'Artagnan Rotisserie
21 | 19 | 21 | $49

152 E. 46th St. (bet. Lexington & Third Aves.), 212-687-0300
■ Foie gras fanciers raise "four crossed swords" to Ariane Daguin's "welcoming" new Midtown bistro, home to "tasty", "artery-clogging" "comfort food" via Southwest France's Gascony; the "knowingly prepared specialties" and "plain" "country" decor make it "one for all" who appreciate "authenticity."

Da Silvano ◐Ⓢ
22 | 17 | 19 | $52

260 Sixth Ave. (bet. Bleecker & Houston Sts.), 212-982-2343
◪ A "trip to Tuscany" by way of *Vanity Fair*, this ever-"trendy" Villager draws a "chic", "celeb-sprinkled" crowd ("Uma", "Gwyneth", "Calvin") with "delicious", "upper-class" versions of "standard" Italian fare; though some cede the "brusque" scene to "Hollywood hopefuls", the coveted "sidewalk seating" is a "consistently good" spot to whip out the shades and "stargaze."

Da Tommaso ◐Ⓢ
21 | 15 | 19 | $42

903 Eighth Ave. (bet. 53rd & 54th Sts.), 212-265-1890
◪ This "traditional" Italian on the "edge of the Theater District" is a "reliable" curtain-raiser (though "later is better") for "fresh" pastas and "professional" service; knockers rap its "lackluster" looks, but the overall "warm" feel makes it a "local favorite."

Da Umberto
24 | 18 | 21 | $55

107 W. 17th St. (bet. 6th & 7th Aves.), 212-989-0303
■ "Better than mama's" declare devotees of the "authentic" cooking at this attractive Chelsea Tuscan where "delicious" dishes from antipasti to tiramisu are matched with "excellent" wines and "attentive" service; despite upside pricing, it's a proven "class act" that "still delivers" dependably.

Dawat Ⓢ
23 | 19 | 20 | $42

210 E. 58th St. (bet. 2nd & 3rd Aves.), 212-355-7555
■ Enriched by actress/cookbook creator Madhur Jaffrey's "subtlety of spice", the "fabulous" food at this "upscale" East Side Indian ranks among the "best in town", while "attractive decor" and a "most

helpful" staff also curry favor; though it may not please picky Punjab purists, this place has "winner" written all over it.

DB BISTRO MODERNE S — | — | — | E

City Club Hotel, 55 W. 44th St. (bet. 5th & 6th Aves.), 212-391-2400
Star chef Daniel Boulud has just opened this new Midtown French eatery offering refined, modern bistro cooking that includes an already famous $27 burger; divided into two sections, the fiery-red room is livelier up-front, while the banquette-lined back is more formal – but either way, the prices are lower than at Boulud's other outlets.

DeGrezia 23 | 22 | 23 | $55

231 E. 50th St. (bet. 2nd & 3rd Aves.), 212-750-5353
■ Something of an "undiscovered" "treasure", and priced accordingly, this "charming" Midtowner offers a "quality" menu of "terrific" Northern Italian specialties served in a "fancy" "downstairs" space by an "attentive" staff; even better, it's a "subdued" spot with plenty of privacy to "conduct business" or maybe pitch some woo.

Delegates' Dining Room 21 | 23 | 21 | $39

United Nations, 4th fl. (1st Ave. & 45th St.), 212-963-7626
■ Ground zero for weekday "diplomat-watching", this lunch-only UN dining room purveys a "wonderful" "international buffet" that's a "high-quality" showcase of "diverse tastes" allied with a "beautiful" East River view; the "civilized" atmosphere (enforced by a "security check") "wows out-of-towners", while the $21.50 prix fixe "value" needs no translation.

Del Frisco's ● 22 | 23 | 20 | $62

1221 Sixth Ave. (49th St.), 212-575-5129
■ Midtown does Dallas at this "bold" Lone Star claim on the "NY steak scene" (and after-work bar scene), where the "melt-in-your-mouth" beef arrives in "Texas-size portions" that befit the "grand", block-long bank space; the prime cuts and "stunning" cattle-baron interior lasso a "lively" crowd of big-spending "suits", though anyone cowed by "bull-market prices" may want to steer clear.

Delhi Palace (Queens) S ▽ 21 | 16 | 18 | $23

37-33 74th St. (bet. Roosevelt & 37th Aves.), 718-507-0666
■ A "quiet", "friendly" Jackson Heights Indian that offers an "above-average" mix of "really good" food and "pleasant" surroundings for below-average prices; for those on a tight budget, the "incredible" lunchtime "buffet deal" is the way to go.

Della Femina 20 | 20 | 20 | $56

135 E. 54th St. (bet. Lexington & Park Aves.), 212-752-0111
◪ Socialites skip the jitney and take a "quick", albeit imaginary, trip to East Hampton via ad exec Jerry Della Femina's "refreshing" Midtown replica of his Long Island beachhead; most maintain "it sells itself" with a "bright, airy room" and "flavorful" New American menu, though tougher customers shrug "sterile" and "expensive for what it is."

Delmonico's 20 | 21 | 20 | $52

56 Beaver St. (S. William St.), 212-509-1144
◪ The Street's "Gordon Gekko" stand-ins wheel and deal at this latter-day incarnation of the "historic" Downtown steakhouse where the "rich" woodwork, "staid service" and "perfectly charred" beef still "recall yesteryear"; though dismissed by some as "stodgy" and surviving "purely on its rep", all agree it works best "if it's on the firm."

Delta Grill, The S 19 | 16 | 17 | $29

700 Ninth Ave. (48th St.), 212-956-0934
■ Jambalaya junkies fix on cheap, "calorific" "Southern comfort" food at this Hell's Kitchen "rajun Cajun" where the "spicy" eats

| | | | F | D | S | C |

and "enjoyable" "bayou atmosphere" make up for the "down-and-dirty" digs.

Demarchelier S 17 | 17 | 17 | $44
50 E. 86th St. (bet. Madison & Park Aves.), 212-249-6300
■ An "easy" option for Eastsiders with "few choices", this "agreeable" "neighborhood" bistro offers "solid" Gallic grub in "lively" quarters; locals label it a "decent" enough "Left Bank" knockoff, though the "snobby" service strikes some as a tad "too French."

Denino's Pizzeria & Tavern 23 | 10 | 17 | $18
(Staten Island) S∌
524 Port Richmond Ave. (bet. Hooker Pl. & Walker St.), 718-442-9401
■ This "family" pizza joint is "Staten Island's finest" source of "fabulous" thin-crust pies, "excellent fried calamari" and "old-time Islander" camaraderie; a perpetually packed "favorite", it's the "last of a breed", right down to the "paper plates" and frill-free decor.

Dervish Turkish ●S 21 | 17 | 20 | $33
146 W. 47th St. (bet. 6th & 7th Aves.), 212-997-0070
■ "Up-and-coming" Theater District Turk that's reputedly a "real find" for "ample" portions of "authentic" food at "fair prices"; followers tip their fezzes to the "courteous", "unpretentious" staff.

Destinée 23 | 21 | 23 | $61
134 E. 61st St. (bet. Lexington & Park Aves.), 212-888-1220
■ A "civilized", if *cher*, East Side "destination" for "top-drawer" dining, this "charming" "miniature" near Bloomie's caters to a "genteel" clientele with "delectable" French fare and "gracious" service; its "rare", "no-airs" style "sets it apart" from the "snooty" competition.

Deux Amis S ▽ 19 | 16 | 20 | $41
356 E. 51st St. (bet. 1st & 2nd Aves.), 212-230-1117
■ Friends and sweethearts "meet and linger" over "flavorful" bistro dishes topped with "to-die-for" chocolate soufflé at this "cozy" Midtowner; fans of the "comfortable" room and "friendly staff" call it a "much-needed addition" to this restaurant-deprived neighborhood.

Dim Sum Go Go S 19 | 13 | 15 | $23
5 E. Broadway (Chatham Sq.), 212-732-0797
■ Run in part by epicure-on-the-go Colette Rossant, this newish Chatham Square dim sum parlor is an "instant favorite" among dollar-conscious dumpling devotees delighted with its "fresh", "artful" offerings and "innovative" "East-meets-West" approach (i.e. no carts); but a few take a dim view of service lapses and "garish decor."

Diner (Brooklyn) ●S 22 | 17 | 18 | $27
85 Broadway (Berry St.), 718-486-3077
■ Williamsburg's "hippest" share booths at this refurbished road-stop to chow down on "surprisingly good" "mainstream" American fare in "funky" digs; low prices and the "out-of-the-way" locale attract a "scruffy" crowd, causing some to "feel self-conscious without a tattoo."

Dinerbar ●S – | – | – | I
1569 Lexington Ave. (bet. 100th & 101st Sts.), 212-348-0200
A pioneer on an underpopulated stretch of the Way Upper East Side, this stylish neo-diner offers an eclectic comfort food menu that's available all day; come nighttime, it morphs into a more loungey scene.

Dining Room, The S 22 | 19 | 19 | $54
154 E. 79th St. (bet. Lexington & 3rd Aves.), 212-327-2500
■ The "promising" sequel to The Screening Room, this East Side New American premieres with "delicious" "homestyle cooking" in a "low-

F | D | S | C

key", "inviting" duplex space that blends a "Downtown feel" with an "Uptown address" and prices; it "plays nicely" with area "swells" who keep the "close quarters" (especially upstairs) "crowded."

Dishes ⊅
21 | 11 | 13 | $15

47 E. 44th St. (bet. Madison & Vanderbilt Aves.), 212-687-5511
☒ Just "follow the crowds" to this Midtown eat-in/take-out cafe for "top-tier" breakfast and lunch bites that "elevate" a workday slump; but given the "long lines" and haphazard service, don't expect fast food.

Dish of Salt ⓿
20 | 21 | 20 | $43

133 W. 47th St. (bet. 6th & 7th Aves.), 212-921-4242
☒ This "classy" Theater District Chinese standby plays to "out-of-town" and "expense-account" crowds with "elegant" dishes served in a "cavernous" setting; though its performance is peppered with praise, critics contend "you pay for its looks", since the food is no great shakes.

District S
20 | 21 | 20 | $50

Muse Hotel, 130 W. 46th St. (bet. 6th & 7th Aves.), 212-485-2999
■ A "welcome" debut in "Theaterland", this New American is a "stylish" "oasis of calm" with a playhouse theme; applause for the "inviting atmosphere" and chef Sam DeMarco's "excellent", "creative" menu suggests that it "has its act together."

Divino Restaurant ⓿S
19 | 15 | 18 | $39

1556 Second Ave. (bet. 80th & 81st Sts.), 212-861-1096
■ "That's Italian" note locals who divine the obvious at this East Side "neighborhood drop-in" for "hearty" cooking "at fair prices"; believers call it "comfortable" and "welcoming" with "no pretenses", though nothing out of the "ordinary."

Diwan Grill S
21 | 17 | 18 | $32

148 E. 48th St. (bet. Lexington & 3rd Aves.), 212-593-5425
■ Rising "a step above" Jackson Diner (its famed Queens sibling), this Midtown Indian lays out a "great buffet lunch" for a hard-to-beat $13.95; it also offers a dinner menu that's "delicious", if "a bit pricey."

Diwan's Curry House ⓿S
20 | 12 | 16 | $28

302 Columbus Ave. (bet. 74th & 75th Sts.), 212-721-3400
■ Westsiders attest this "funky" Indian is the one for "exotic" spices that hold "unexpected pleasures" for the daring; many also think a "great deal" of the $7.95 lunch buffet, while the "bizarre zebra-print surroundings" are either a "conversation" starter or a takeout inducer.

Dizzy's (Brooklyn) S⊅
— | — | — | M

511 Ninth St. (8th Ave.), 718-499-1966
This chrome-and-linoleum-lined Park Slope diner lures locals with homey, just-like-mom-used-to-make cooking with an urban twang; in a nod to a famous Dizzy (Gillespie), there's piped-in jazz on the soundtrack and the real live thing on weekend nights.

Docks Oyster Bar S
21 | 17 | 18 | $43

633 Third Ave. (40th St.), 212-986-8080
2427 Broadway (bet. 89th & 90th Sts.), 212-724-5588
■ These "big", "brash" seafooders hold their own as "steady" landings for "solid", "fresh fish" and raw-bar bites; they stay "busy and noisy", and if a few harbor doubts about "impersonal" service, most dive in with a "full wallet" and "stick to the basics."

Do Hwa ⓿S
21 | 20 | 18 | $36

55 Carmine St. (bet. Bedford St. & 7th Ave. S.), 212-414-1224
■ You can actually "use 'trendy' and 'Korean' in the same sentence" at this "hip" West Villager (a Dok Suni's spin-off) where the "stylish"

setting complements a first-rate "mainstream" menu; grill-your-own "barbecue tables" offer "something different" for seen-it-all types.

Dojo ◐ S ⌿ | 15 | 8 | 12 | $14 |
14 W. Fourth St. (Mercer St.), 212-505-8934
24-26 St. Marks Pl. (bet. 2nd & 3rd Aves.), 212-674-9821
■ "Healthier than McDonald's", the "filling" "cheap eats" at these "hippie-esque" Village veggie outlets are a "salvation" for "tattooed 19-year-olds" who can "tolerate" "no-frills" digs and "aimless service"; they're "convenient" "grub hubs", but be ready to "rough it."

Dok Suni's ◐ S ⌿ | 21 | 16 | 15 | $28 |
119 First Ave. (bet. 7th St. & St. Marks Pl.), 212-477-9506
■ It's "challenging to get in", but this "casual", itty-bitty East Village Korean rewards persistence with "spicy", "delish" fare "like your mama-san used to make"; though a bit "Americanized", it passes muster with a "painfully cool" clientele that gladly endures the "cramped" conditions and "long waits."

Dolphins ◐ S | 19 | 21 | 19 | $34 |
35 Cooper Sq. (bet. 5th & 6th Sts.), 212-375-9195
■ Thirsting for a "quiet" "oasis" in the Cooper Square dining "desert", nomads turn to this "swell" seafooder, which continues to "surprise" first-timers with its "lovely garden seating" and "good selection" of fin fare; it's also priced for "value", with a certified "steal" of a $20 pre-theater prix fixe.

Domani Ristorante S | ▽ 23 | 21 | 22 | $46 |
1590 First Ave. (bet. 82nd & 83rd Sts.), 212-717-7575
■ Though kosher Italian sounds more "interesting" than inviting, this dinner-only Eastsider "gets away with it" by offering "personal service" and "fantastic food" that's "authentic" enough to "match up" with The Boot's best.

Dominick's (Bronx) S ⌿ | 22 | 10 | 16 | $33 |
2335 Arthur Ave. (bet. Crescent Ave. & E. 187th St.), 718-733-2807
■ Show up "willing to share" at this cheap, family-style Arthur Avenue Italian where the "waiter tells you what you'll have" (there's no menu) and the "no-nonsense" cooking is "excellent"; despite elbow-to-elbow seating at "long communal tables" and often "lengthy" waits, this is the "real deal" and "a must – at least once."

Don Giovanni Ristorante ◐ S | 18 | 13 | 15 | $24 |
358 W. 44th St. (bet. 8th & 9th Aves.), 212-581-4939
214 10th Ave. (bet. 22nd & 23rd Sts.), 212-242-9054
■ "Thin-crust" connoisseurs sing the praises of the "excellent brick-oven pizza" at this "unpretentious" West Side duet, "dependable" and "cheap" places where it pays to "keep it simple"; hedgers warn of "so-so pastas" and oh-so-"slow service."

Donguri S | ▽ 26 | 17 | 24 | $46 |
309 E. 83rd St. (bet. 1st & 2nd Aves.), 212-737-5656
■ Patrons feel like "honored guests" at this "tranquil" East Side Japanese "gem", home to "dainty", "beautifully prepared" dishes that echo its "tiny" space; the "different" menu and "attentive" service via a "warm" "husband-and-wife team" make it a "real treat" if you're not treating.

Don Luca (Brooklyn) S | – | – | – | M |
221 Smith St. (bet. Baltic & Butler Sts.), 718-222-8723
Tapas finally arrive on Smith Street at this new Carroll Gardens Spaniard; its backyard patio is just the spot to sip sangria and think of all the money you're saving by not dining in Manhattan.

F	D	S	C

Don Peppe (Queens) S⌀ — 24 | 13 | 18 | $41
135-58 Lefferts Blvd. (149th Ave.), 718-845-7587
■ The white clam sauce sets off a "feeding frenzy" at this old-school Italian in Ozone Park, a "favorite" "garlic blast" where the "family-style" fare is "fabulous" and the "crowded", "boisterous" room is definitely "not for romance"; "don't eat for a week" ahead of time, "bring cash" and "expect to wait in line."

Druids ●S — 18 | 15 | 18 | $31
736 Tenth Ave. (bet. 50th & 51st Sts.), 212-307-6410
■ "Pub grub" gets some "inventive" twists at this "quaint" Celtic Westsider, a "cheerful" "neighborhood spot" that "satisfies" with "above-average" Eclectic–New American fare; the "dark" interior is offset by a "lovely courtyard", and admirers hoist their pints to the all-around "value."

DT·UT ●S — 17 | 19 | 14 | $13
1626 Second Ave. (bet. 84th & 85th Sts.), 212-327-1327
■ "Starbucks feels like McDonald's" compared with this Upper East Side Gen Y coffee bar, beloved for its "supersized sweets"; it's an ideal "date place" or "rainy-day" chat room, though seats on the "flea market furniture" can be "hard to come by."

Duane Park Cafe — 24 | 20 | 22 | $49
157 Duane St. (bet. Hudson St. & W. B'way), 212-732-5555
■ Behind a "calm, quiet" exterior, this "unsung" TriBeCa New American squares off against its "flashier neighbors" with "delightful", "innovative" fare, a "refined" setting and "hospitality plus"; for "upscale" style at "downright reasonable" prices, alert types deem it a "real sleeper."

Due ●S⌀ — 21 | 18 | 20 | $39
1396 Third Ave. (bet. 79th & 80th Sts.), 212-772-3331
■ Locals give this "small, friendly" East Side Italian its due for serving "solid" "home-cooked" fare at low prices; thanks to a "charming" staff, it wins many a "bravo" for "dependable" dining, though "it would be nice if they took credit cards."

Duke's S — 17 | 14 | 15 | $23
99 E. 19th St. (bet. Irving Pl. & Park Ave. S.), 212-260-2922
■ Everything's fried and true at this "laid-back", "down-home" Southern BBQ "comfort-grub joint" with kitschy decor; although the beer-fueled, "fratty" after-work scene is a bit much, this Gramercy spot is "kid-friendly" and boasts good delivery.

DuMont (Brooklyn) S — – | – | – | M
432 Union Ave. (bet. Devoe St. & Metropolitan Ave.), 718-486-7717
In an uncharted section of Williamsburg, this welcoming new American cafe turns out a small selection of big plates, with half of its menu as daily specials; the tin ceiling, tile floor and dark-wood counter enhance the old-fashioned feel of the fare.

Dylan Prime — 22 | 23 | 21 | $53
62 Laight St. (Greenwich St.), 212-334-4783
■ The times they are a-changin' at this TriBeCa outpost of "carnivorous pleasures", a "cool" "alternative" to the old "boys' club" "slab-of-meat" specialists; it offers "tasty" steaks, "oversized martinis" and "great sauces and sides" amid "sexy, dark" decor, which help compensate for a locale that's a ways "off the beaten trail."

East S — – | – | – | M
354 E. 66th St. (bet. 1st & 2nd Aves.), 212-734-5270
210 E. 44th St. (bet. 2nd & 3rd Aves.), 212-687-5075

(continued)
East
253 W. 55th St. (bet. B'way & 8th Ave.), 212-581-2240 ◐
9 E. 38th St. (bet. 5th & Madison Aves.), 212-685-5205
366 Third Ave. (bet. 26th & 27th Sts.), 212-889-2326
Some outlets of this "dependable" chain of sushi specialists offer a "conveyor-belt revolving sushi bar", while others feature the "traditional Japanese" shoes-off approach to dining; either way, expect "bargain" tabs.

East Lake (Queens) ◐ S ≠ ▽ | 20 | 11 | 14 | $24 |
42-33 Main St. (Franklin Ave.), 718-539-8532
■ Chinatown has nothing on this "converted diner" in Flushing, noted for its "addictive" dim sum "variety" and "delicious" "fresh seafood"; the "authentic", "inexpensive" chow reels in "major crowds" that can live with the perfunctory service and "rather common" digs.

East of Eighth ◐ S | 17 | 16 | 17 | $29 |
254 W. 23rd St. (bet. 7th & 8th Aves.), 212-352-0075
◢ A "lively" Chelsea "staple", this "boys' hangout" is known for its "basic" Eclectic eats (especially brunch), "modest prices", "charming garden" and staff of "interesting characters"; the "friendly", "unpretentious" ambiance "makes up for the fair food."

East Post ◐ S ▽ | 22 | 21 | 21 | $29 |
92 Second Ave. (bet. 5th & 6th Sts.), 212-387-0065
■ "Rustic" is the word at this "very Italian" East Village newcomer, from the "wonderful" "home cooking" and "charming old-world" decor to the "great prices"; no wonder it's sometimes hard to get a seat.

East River Cafe S | 19 | 19 | 20 | $44 |
1111 First Ave. (61st St.), 212-980-3144
■ "Romantic" enough for a "special affair", this "comfortable" East Side Italian–cum–"active piano bar" is favored by "loyal regulars" who appreciate "well-prepared pastas" and prix fixes that "won't break the bank."

E.A.T. S | 20 | 12 | 14 | $35 |
1064 Madison Ave. (bet. 80th & 81st Sts.), 212-772-0022
◢ Aka P.A.Y., this "high-rent" purveyor of "awesome" sandwiches, desserts and deli bites comes with the renowned Eli Zabar "pedigree"; though East Side society finds it "top-notch", mere mortals are overcome by "attitude" overdoses and "gimme-a-break" pricing.

Eatery ◐ S | 18 | 19 | 16 | $30 |
798 Ninth Ave. (53rd St.), 212-765-7080
◢ At least for "15 minutes" the "coolest place in Hell's Kitchen" is this "trendy" New American where the "slick", "austere" room and overall "hip urbanity" nearly steal the show from the "decent" (if "somewhat limited") menu; early odds are the "South Beach" vibe and "busy bar" will keep the "people in black" coming back.

Ecco | 21 | 18 | 19 | $45 |
124 Chambers St. (bet. Church St. & W. B'way), 212-227-7074
■ "Unhip" it may be, but this Downtowner satisfies its white-collar clientele with "superior" "old-world Italian food" served in an "elegant" barroom left over from the Gilded Age; regulars declare it a "real find" for "genuine" cooking, "comfortable surroundings" and "good service."

Ecco-la S | 18 | 15 | 16 | $26 |
1660 Third Ave. (93rd St.), 212-860-5609
◢ This "Upper East Side hideaway" is an "affordable" "neighborhood joint" plating up "pre-marathon portions" of "basic pasta" with "real

homemade taste"; but nonfans shrug this "very average" effort is only "ok in a pinch" and can get so "noisy" that you hear the echo.

Edgar's Cafe ◐[S]≠ 18 | 17 | 15 | $19

255 W. 84th St. (bet. B'way & West End Ave.), 212-496-6126

■ The "ghost of Poe" presides over this "relaxed" West Side cafe "sanctuary", a favorite "evermore" for its "elaborate" desserts and "crumbling villa decor"; service may be nevermore, but to "indulge" either a sweet tooth or "bohemian longings", it's always a "pleasure."

Edison Cafe [S]≠ 16 | 10 | 15 | $20

Hotel Edison, 228 W. 47th St. (bet. B'way & 8th Ave.), 212-840-5000

◪ "When you crave deli before a matinee", this "cheap", "one-of-a-kind" Times Square coffee shop awaits with "blintzes like mama's" and the "best matzo ball soup in the biz"; the "vaudevillian" "charm" of its "oy-vey" "surly" staff and "dumpy" decor is "soon to be featured in [Neil Simon's new] show", *45 Seconds From Broadway.*

Eighteenth & Eighth ◐[S] 17 | 15 | 16 | $27

159 Eighth Ave. (18th St.), 212-242-5000

◪ Chelsea "hunks" "squeeze in" to this "busy" "telephone booth–size" coffee shop for "wholesome", affordable "home cooking"; nobody minds that the food's just "ok", since it's such a "fun" scene and the "pumped waiters" are such a "feast" for the eyes.

Eight Mile Creek [S] 21 | 16 | 20 | $46

240 Mulberry St. (bet. Prince & Spring Sts.), 212-431-4635

◪ An "unusual" "treat from Down Under", this surprisingly good SoHo Australian lets "adventurers" "'ave some grilled" kangaroo or "amazing" emu carpaccio; despite a heartily "sociable staff", we hear gripes about "cramped space" and cramp-causing prices.

Eisenberg Sandwich Shop ≠ 19 | 11 | 16 | $12

174 Fifth Ave. (bet. 22nd & 23rd Sts.), 212-675-5096

■ It's a "totally authentic" "trip back to 1930" (even cost-wise) at this Flatiron luncheonette, with counter "characters" out of "Damon Runyon" and "fine and dandy" egg creams; the "timeless" dingy digs reinforce its "gritty charm."

EJ's Luncheonette [S] 16 | 12 | 15 | $20

1271 Third Ave. (73rd St.), 212-472-0600 ≠

447 Amsterdam Ave. (bet. 81st & 82nd Sts.), 212-873-3444 ≠

432 Sixth Ave. (bet. 9th & 10th Sts.), 212-473-5555

◪ The "stroller" set rolls out in force at this way "popular" all-American trio, home to "hearty" helpings of "blue-plate" "'50s diner" fare served in "simple", "retro" surroundings; during prime times, they're "rushed" "mob scenes", but the counter-recessionary eating is "really good" for those who "can bear the wait."

Elaine's ◐[S] 14 | 14 | 14 | $46

1703 Second Ave. (bet. 88th & 89th Sts.), 212-534-8103

■ Despite extravagant media reports and occasional celeb sightings, most normal folks simply "don't see why people keep going" to this Upper East Side watering hole–cum–Italian restaurant: "only for a drink", "infuriating", "a total waste of time and money" – unless Elaine likes you.

El Charro Español [S] 20 | 15 | 19 | $35

4 Charles St. (bet. Greenwich Ave. & 7th Ave. S.), 212-242-9547

■ This "solid Spaniard" in the West Village wins olés the "old-fashioned" way, with "friendly service" and "*excelente*" specialties; in spite of the "tight space" and "basement feel", it's "always crowded" with sangria-sipping stalwarts.

El Cid [S] 22 | 14 | 18 | $33

322 W. 15th St. (bet. 8th & 9th Aves.), 212-929-9332

◪ It's so "cramped" that you're bound to "get to know your neighbors" at this "tiny", "festive" Chelsea Spanish "hideaway"; despite "cheesy decor", "delicious" "garlicky tapas" and other "authentic" nibbles that can be had "for a song" keep 'em coming.

Elephant, The ◐[S] 22 | 18 | 16 | $33

58 E. First St. (bet. 1st & 2nd Aves.), 212-505-7739

■ Always "packed", this East Village "hot spot" serves "innovative" Thai-French fusion in "claustrophobic" digs with a faux "tropical" motif; its "young crowd" is undaunted by the "din" and "long waits."

Elephant & Castle ◐[S] 18 | 15 | 16 | $24

68 Greenwich Ave. (bet. 6th & 7th Aves.), 212-243-1400

■ "Nothing ever changes" at this "relaxing" West Village American "hangout" where it's fine to "dine single" on breakfast, Sunday brunch or an "mmm good" burger; though it's "unremarkable", "you can't beat the quality for the price", which explains its "longevity."

ELEVEN MADISON PARK [S] 25 | 26 | 25 | $61

11 Madison Ave. (24th St.), 212-889-0905

■ "Danny Meyer does it again" at this Madison Park New American where "grand", "airy" deco-rations, pleasing private party rooms and "superb" hospitality are backdrops to an "exciting menu" from "top chef" Kerry Heffernan and a typically well-balanced, well-priced wine list; in sum, "everything works" here – "modern" "sophistication" "never felt so sexy", nor so "warm and friendly."

El Faro [S] 21 | 12 | 17 | $35

823 Greenwich St. (Horatio St.), 212-929-8210

■ "Make sure your date has garlic too" at this West Village "Spanish treasure", the "standard" "for many decades" when it comes to "mouthwatering" paella, green sauce and sangria; with food this "reliable" and affordable, aesthetes don't mind that the "gloomy" "relic" of a room "could stand a little brightening."

Eliá (Brooklyn) [S] ▽ 25 | 18 | 22 | $45

8611 Third Ave. (bet. 86th & 87th Sts.), 718-748-9891

■ "Ulysses would stop wandering" if he discovered the "serious cooking" at this Bay Ridge Greek "delight"; the "excellent grilled fish", though pricey by outer-borough standards, offers "Manhattan-caliber" quality, and the "amiable staff" "always tries to please."

Elias Corner (Queens) ◐[S]🚫 24 | 10 | 15 | $32

24-02 31st St. (24th Ave.), 718-932-1510

■ Call it "Athens by the El": this Greek seafarer just across the Triboro in Astoria features "fish of all kinds", "fresh off the boat" and "perfectly prepared" in "simple", "grill-to-order" style; though a "no-frills" vessel with "spotty service", it's the "real deal" at "affordable" prices.

Elio's ◐[S] 23 | 18 | 20 | $52

1621 Second Ave. (bet. 84th & 85th Sts.), 212-772-2242

■ This "clubby", "high-end" Yorkville Italian "celeb scene" for the "over-45" set "packs them in" with its "terrific", "robust" food and "powerhouse" ambiance; it's "hard to go wrong" with the "top-quality" dishes and "courteous" service, though outsiders observe "regulars get better treatment" (and "more elbow room").

Eli's [S] 20 | 15 | 17 | $37

Eli's Manhattan, 1411 Third Ave. (80th St.), 212-717-9798

◪ Although "not for the faint of purse", this East Side Eclectic via the talented Mr. Zabar delivers "wonderful", "straight-on" cooking employing "superfresh" ingredients from the market; it's somewhat "more formal" than its siblings, though few forget they're dining "in a grocery store."

Eli's Vinegar Factory

20 | 14 | 15 | $27

431 E. 91st St., 2nd fl. (bet. 1st & York Aves.), 212-987-0885
🔳 A magnet for "kids and cell phones", the upstairs "loft" at this Upper East Side gourmet market morphs into a "yuppieland" "mob scene" on weekends, when there's a "fabulous", "creative" brunch; "go early to beat the lines" and "hectic" "*Romper Room*" crowds.

Ellen's Stardust Diner ●S

13 | 16 | 14 | $23

1650 Broadway (51st St.), 212-956-5151
🔳 The "singing-waiter show" is as "cheesy" as the cheap, "retro" grub at this "noisy", "kitschy" Theater District diner, a "kid-friendly", mock-"'50s" setup that invariably wows "out-of-towners"; for others, one glance at the "basic" menu suggests "greasy" is the word.

El Parador Cafe

20 | 17 | 20 | $37

325 E. 34th St. (bet. 1st & 2nd Aves.), 212-679-6812
🔳 Though "getting on in years", this moderately priced Murray Hill Mexican is still aces with amigos for "awesome, authentic" chow and an "old-world feel" defined by "welcoming", "first-rate" service and atmospheric "dim lighting"; contras contend it's "seen better days."

El Pote

22 | 13 | 20 | $34

718 Second Ave. (bet. 38th & 39th Sts.), 212-889-6680
◼ Maybe this Murray Hill "standby" is "not much to look at", but it steps beyond its "old-shoe" decor to offer "tasty" Spanish fare (e.g. "simply delicious" paella) and "pro" service; on top of that, it's a real value.

El Quijote ●S

20 | 14 | 17 | $36

226 W. 23rd St. (bet. 7th & 8th Aves.), 212-929-1855
◼ Ignore that "tacky decor" and focus instead on the "abundance" at this Chelsea Spaniard, famed for its "unbelievable" "lobsterama" deal; it's an "old reliable" for a sangria and "garlic fixes", but steel yourself for a windmill-like "noisy" "crush", except at off-hours.

El Rio Grande ●S

17 | 15 | 15 | $30

160 E. 38th St. (bet. Lexington & 3rd Aves.), 212-867-0922
🔳 Ai-yi-yi, it's a "drinks-and-singles" "madhouse" at this Murray Hill Tex-Mex cantina, site of an "after-work" party-hearty scene fueled by "fab margaritas" and "decent", "generic" grub; given the "potent" potables, "who cares what the food tastes like?"

El Teddy's S

17 | 19 | 16 | $35

219 W. Broadway (bet. Franklin & White Sts.), 212-941-7071
🔳 Still a "staple" in TriBeCa, this "funky" Mexican serves "fair" if "unamazing" food; the "fiesta" bar scene offers "killer margs" that "should be on the DEA's controlled substance list."

Emack & Bolio's S

24 | 9 | 14 | $8

389 Amsterdam Ave. (bet. 78th & 79th Sts.), 212-362-2747
56 Seventh Ave. (bet. 13th & 14th Sts.), 212-727-1198 ●
Macy's, 151 W. 34th St., 4th fl. (Herald Sq.), 212-494-5853
◼ Purveying "heavenly" ice cream and frozen yogurt in "radical flavors", these local outlets of a Boston-based chain may produce "long lines", but that doesn't deter committed coneheads from enjoying a "sinful" "splurge."

Embers (Brooklyn) S

22 | 15 | 18 | $40

9519 Third Ave. (bet. 95th & 96th Sts.), 718-745-3700
🔳 The "poor man's Peter Luger", this "hospitable" Bay Ridge meat-eater's "mainstay" is a great place to "come hungry" and gorge on

| F | D | S | C |

"affordable" "prime" cuts; notwithstanding beefs about the "tight seating" and endless "waits", it's a surefire "cholesterol high" amid "big hair" and "gold chains."

Emerald Planet   17 | 10 | 12 | $12
30 Rockefeller Plaza, concourse level (bet. 49th & 50th Sts.), 212-218-1133
2 Great Jones St. (bet. B'way & Lafayette St.), 212-353-9727 S
■ At these New Age sandwich shops you can see how they're lunching "back in California" by trying the "hearty", "innovative" wraps plus stellar smoothies that make for "sweet and healthy" sipping "after your workout."

Emily's ●S   ▽ 18 | 16 | 15 | $27
1325 Fifth Ave. (bet. 111th & 112th Sts.), 212-996-1212
☒ BBQ lovers "let their belts out and enjoy" this Harlem tribute to "quality" Southern cooking where ribs reign supreme; a "pleasant atmosphere" accompanies the spread, though a few pick a bone with the "spotty service."

Emo's S   ▽ 19 | 17 | 17 | $31
1564 Second Ave. (bet. 81st & 82nd Sts.), 212-628-8699
■ "Thank God for more variety" exclaim Upper Eastsiders who turn to this "attractive" Korean newcomer for "authentic", "sophisticated" food that's a welcome respite from the "usual" Italian options.

Empire Diner ●S   15 | 16 | 14 | $23
210 10th Ave. (22nd St.), 212-243-2736
☒ 24/7 "film noir" stainless steel diner car in West Chelsea dishing out "good", "basic" grub and rich desserts that "stick to the ribs"; it may be "kind of pricey" and the staff needs a "casting director", but who's complaining at 4 AM?

Empire Szechuan ●S   16 | 10 | 14 | $21
4041 Broadway (bet. 170th & 171st Sts.), 212-568-1600
2642 Broadway (100th St.), 212-662-9404
2574 Broadway (97th St.), 212-663-6004
251 W. 72nd St. (bet. B'way & West End Ave.), 212-873-2151
193 Columbus Ave. (bet. 68th & 69th Sts.), 212-496-8778
381 Third Ave. (bet. 27th & 28th Sts.), 212-685-6215
173 Seventh Ave. S. (bet. Perry & W. 11th Sts.), 212-243-6046
15 Greenwich Ave. (bet. 6th Ave. & W. 10th St.), 212-691-1535
☒ When your "wallet is thin", this "cookie-cutter" chain offers a fat menu of "reliable" Chinese eats (plus sushi); though "generic", it's "efficient" and "easy", with the "fastest delivery" men on wheels.

Ennio & Michael S   21 | 18 | 22 | $40
539 La Guardia Pl. (bet. Bleecker & W. 3rd Sts.), 212-677-8577
■ Even nonregulars "feel at home" at this "little-known" Central Village "gem", a "solid old-school Italian" with an "upscale" menu and "comfy" surroundings, a "most congenial" staff keeps up the "warmth" day after day, "year after year."

Enoteca i Trulli   23 | 20 | 22 | $43
124 E. 27th St. (bet. Lexington Ave. & Park Ave. S.), 212-481-7372
■ The selection of "superlative Italian wines" is "truly the best" at this "cozy" vino bar annex of Gramercy's I Trulli; oenophiles salute the "charming" matchup of "heavenly" vintages and "lovely light" "nibbles" – "what more could you want?"

Enzo's (Bronx) S   ▽ 23 | 15 | 21 | $32
1998 Williamsbridge Rd. (Neill Ave.), 718-409-3828
■ Though "nothing fancy", this "traditional" Bronx Italian is hailed as a "find" for "fabulous" fare and "friendly" service starting with chef-

	F	D	S	C

owner Enzo DiRende himself; tabs are "reasonable" for the "quality and quantity", while "tight quarters" make it all the more neighborly.

Epices du Traiteur S   19 | 16 | 19 | $34
103 W. 70th St. (bet. B'way & Columbus Ave.), 212-579-5904
■ Lauded for its "delicate flavors", this moderately priced West Side Med-Tunisian is a "pleasant" "change of pace"; the "intimate", "hole-in-the-wall" space is "crowded" enough to cast doubt on its "local secret" status.

Erminia   24 | 24 | 24 | $55
250 E. 83rd St. (bet. 2nd & 3rd Aves.), 212-879-4284
■ "Intimate" and "incredibly romantic", this "quiet" Eastsider offers a "tiny" candlelit room where would-be Valentinos "gaze into the eyes" of their paramours over "first-class" Northern Italian cooking; service is suitably "unobtrusive", and if it's "expensive", the overall ambiance cries out "serious date."

Ernie's S   16 | 15 | 16 | $33
2150 Broadway (bet. 75th & 76th Sts.), 212-496-1588
◪ "Grab anything Italian" from the "colossal menu" at this "popular" Westsider, a "reliable" "standby" for "enormous" bowls of pasta; despite "predictable" "family fare" and a "noisy", sprawling setting, "good value" keeps it "bustling."

Esca ●   23 | 19 | 20 | $56
402 W. 43rd St. (9th Ave.), 212-564-7272
■ Pasta and seafood lovers casting about for something new are "jumping at the bait" at this "come hither" Southern Italian in the Theater District, "another coup" from Babbo impresarios Batali and Bastianich; the "fabulous" fin fare is "so fresh you can taste the sea" and, combined with the "stylish" space and outdoor summer seating, "worth every cent."

Esperanto ● S   ▽ 21 | 17 | 18 | $28
145 Ave. C (9th St.), 212-505-6559
◪ "Happening" vibes and modest prices attract the intrepid to this way "out-of-the-way" East Village "discovery" for "exciting" Nuevo Latino eating; it speaks to the "young and hip" with a "cool atmosphere" and "strong mojitos" – despite "lots of attitude" from the staff.

Esperides (Queens) ● S   ▽ 22 | 17 | 20 | $32
37-01 30th Ave. (37th St.), 718-545-1494
■ Rising "a cut above" its Astoria rivals, this Hellenic "standout" is "worth the trek" to Queens for "tasty", "creative" specialties that verge on being "aphrodisiacs"; its "excellent" seafood, "airy room" and "friendly staff" are as agreeable as the "Greek isles."

ESPN Zone ● S   13 | 19 | 14 | $27
1472 Broadway (42nd St.), 212-921-3776
◪ "Size matters", and this Times Square sports bar "on steroids" delivers big-time amusement for "teenagers and overgrown teenagers" thanks to "more TVs than a Sony warehouse"; suds flow freely to wash down the "satisfactory" all-American "fried food", but athletic supporters "get pumped" on the "testosterone" alone.

Ess-a-Bagel S   21 | 8 | 13 | $10
831 Third Ave. (bet. 50th & 51st Sts.), 212-980-1010
359 First Ave. (21st St.), 212-260-2252
■ "Highly ess-teemed" East Side delis supplying "awesome", "hubcap"-size bagels paired with a "superior" selection of spreads; just "guard your place in line" and beware that "wiseass" remarks are the staff's idea of "fawning service."

Essex Restaurant ◐ [S] ▽ 21 | 19 | 20 | $40

120 Essex St. (Rivington St.), 212-533-9616

■ This upstart in the Lower East Side's Essex Street Market offers a mid-priced melting pot of New American food enlivened by Jewish and Latin accents; though the room's "big", much of the limited, "creative" menu is of the small-plate variety.

Estia [S] ▽ 21 | 18 | 20 | $37

308 E. 86th St. (bet. 1st & 2nd Aves.), 212-628-9100

■ Adherents hep to this East Side Greek "secret" stick to the "delicious fish" and stick around for the "live Greek music"; regulars are apt to "join the musicians in song and dance" in spite of the "crowded" conditions – "turn me loose, Zeus!"

Etats-Unis [S] 23 | 17 | 22 | $55

242 E. 81st St. (bet. 2nd & 3rd Aves.), 212-517-8826

■ It's literally "hard to get in" to the "tiny", "not-for-claustrophobes" space at this "wonderful" East Side New American where the "brilliant food" is "expensive for the surroundings" yet high prices are "justifiable" given the "sublime" results; N.B. there's a lighter, cheaper version of the menu at their wine bar across the street.

Eugene ◐ 17 | 22 | 16 | $49

27 W. 24th St. (bet. 5th & 6th Aves.), 212-462-0999

◪ "Impress a date" at the Flatiron's swingingest "chichi supper club" where "oh so trendy" types sip martinis in "gorgeous" surroundings; the menu's comprised of "pricey" but "tasty" New American fare in "itsy-bitsy portions", but the dining room seems "dull" compared with the "ultra-swank lounge" and dance floor.

Evergreen Shanghai [S] 18 | 12 | 16 | $26

1378 Third Ave. (bet. 78th & 79th Sts.), 212-585-3388
10 E. 38th St. (bet. 5th & Madison Aves.), 212-448-1199
785 Broadway (10th St.), 212-473-2777
63 Mott St. (bet. Bayard & Canal Sts.), 212-571-3339 ◐ 🚫💳

■ Not your "run-of-the-mill Chinese", this "convenient", if basic, quartet pleases those who pine for "above-average", "genuine Shanghai" specialties and "attentive service"; greenhorns are intrigued by the "interesting" chow on the "cheap."

Excellent Dumpling House [S] 🚫💳 19 | 6 | 11 | $15

111 Lafayette St. (bet. Canal & Walker Sts.), 212-219-0212

■ Go back to "basics" at this Chinatown "dive" where there's "no decor whatsoever" to distract from the "mouthwatering" potstickers; it's a "must" for blowing a "jury duty" stipend, since it's really cheap and there's "no point in lingering."

Faan (Brooklyn) [S] – | – | – | M

209 Smith St. (Baltic St.), 718-694-2277

Asian fusion comes to Smith Street at this quirky Carroll Gardens newcomer offering Thai, Vietnamese and sushi in a colorful, funky setting; a bare-bones streetside patio absorbs the overflow crowds.

Fairway Cafe [S] 18 | 9 | 11 | $17

Fairway, 2127 Broadway, 2nd fl. (74th St.), 212-595-1888

■ For a "real treat" "above the din" of the "landmark" West Side grocer, check out this "casual" "respite" where Mitchel London offers "serious" American food at prices in sync with the "low-budget decor."

F & B [S] 19 | 14 | 16 | $11

269 W. 23rd St. (bet. 7th & 8th Aves.), 646-486-4441

■ The "best wurst" ushers in a hot dog "renaissance" at this "cute" Chelsea yearling, a Euro-style street-food vendor with "really interesting" red hots, frites and beignets, plus Belgian beer and champagne splits for refreshment; "Gray's Papaya it ain't."

Fanelli Cafe ●S
15	15	14	$23

94 Prince St. (Mercer St.), 212-226-9412
■ An "honest joint" that predates SoHo's "Prada mobs", this "gruff and lovable" 1872 saloon provides "well-priced" "bar food" in a "smoky", "checkered-tablecloth" setting; a "crowded", "convivial" "landmark" for beer, "burgers and bourbon", it's the "only plain eating" in the area.

FELIDIA
25	22	23	$64

243 E. 58th St. (bet. 2nd & 3rd Aves.), 212-758-1479
■ PBS cooking show host Lidia Bastianich "excels on TV and in person" at her East Midtown Italian namesake, a temple of "innovative" "culinary delights", effortlessly matched by an "elegant" "townhouse" setting, seamless black-tie service and "adventurous" "high-end" wines; fans say forget the expense and "just go."

Félix S
17	18	14	$40

340 W. Broadway (Grand St.), 212-431-0021
■ Thanks to a "smoke-blowing" "Euro" clientele and "snooty" service, this midpriced SoHo bistro is "ground zero" for a bona fide Parisian experience; first-timers join the "lively" crowd for steak frites and other "solid", "simple" fare while trying to separate the "hip" from the "pretentious."

Ferdinando's Focacceria (Brooklyn) ⊄
▽	21	12	16	$22

151 Union St. (bet. Columbia & Hicks Sts.), 718-855-1545
■ Only in Palermo does it get more "authentic" than this Carroll Gardens Sicilian, which has fed "real old-world" specialties to everyone "from longshoremen to yuppies" for nearly a century; if you like spleen sandwiches served in very "down-to-earth" digs, "this is your place."

Ferrara S
20	14	14	$17

195 Grand St. (bet. Mott & Mulberry Sts.), 212-226-6150
Roosevelt Hotel, 363 Madison Ave. (bet. 45th & 46th Sts.), 212-599-7800
■ Sure, it's "busy and touristy", but this circa 1892 "classic Italian patisserie" "keeps up the traditional quality" of its "delicious sweets" and coffees, and it's hard to refuse the "invitation to indulge" that cannoli craving; loyalists of the Little Italy original "don't bother" with the modern-day Midtown spin-off.

Ferrier Bistro ●S
19	16	16	$44

29 E. 65th St. (bet. Madison & Park Aves.), 212-772-9000
■ Given the "minimal space", it's a good thing "everyone's beautiful" at this "happening", "noisy" East Side Euro-filled bistro where the "quite good" French fare is secondary to the "flashy 'new money'" scene; here's a chance to "wear your Manolos" and chat up the "flirty" folks.

Fifth Ave. Seafood S
–	–	–	E

2014 Fifth Ave. (125th St.), 212-987-6030
Harlem hangs at this popular bare-bones joint where Soul Food and seafood meet cute in the fishnet-festooned upstairs dining room; downstairs, tasty takeout leaves customers as happy as clams.

55 Wall ●S
20	21	21	$53

Regent Wall St., 55 Wall St. (bet. Hanover & William Sts.), 212-699-5555
■ Its Wall Street site is a "virtue" for "impressing a client", and this "high-class" hotel New American follows through with "beautifully presented" food and "classic service"; insiders say this "power place" "deserves its reputation" for "civilized" dining and "insane prices" – "J.P." would approve.

	F	D	S	C

Fifty Seven Fifty Seven S   24 | 25 | 24 | $61
Four Seasons Hotel, 57 E. 57th St. (bet. Madison & Park Aves.), 212-758-5757
■ "Few do it better" than this "very posh" Eastsider that raises the "standard" for "superior hotel dining" with I.M. Pei's "sleek", "austere" design and the "delicious" "textures and flavors" on its New American menu; despite all the "celebs" and "big deals" going down, you can count on plenty of "TLC" from the "polished" staff.

Figs (Queens) S   ▽ 19 | 15 | 16 | $27
LaGuardia Airport, Central Terminal Bldg., 718-446-7600
■ Frequent fliers hail the arrival of "gourmet airport food" at this Mediterranean "sleeper" grounded at LaGuardia, the latest hub for Boston chef Todd English's chain; the pizza, pasta and panini are all "worth eating", ergo airport "delays were never so painless."

F.illi Ponte   22 | 21 | 21 | $55
39 Desbrosses St. (West Side Hwy.), 212-226-4621
■ Get "away from everything" and "relax" at this "beautiful", if pricey, Downtown Italian purveying "terrific", "hearty" food and a "spectacular view" of the Hudson; though it's now refurbished and living a "new life", traces of its former "*Sopranos*" days linger on.

Fine & Schapiro S   16 | 9 | 12 | $22
138 W. 72nd St. (bet. B'way & Columbus Ave.), 212-877-2721
◪ A "true kosher deli" since 1927, this Westsider is "affordable and convenient", but it's less than fine for foes who "expected more" than "surly" service and "unexciting food."

Fino   20 | 17 | 20 | $45
4 E. 36th St. (bet. 5th & Madison Aves.), 212-689-8040
■ One of Murray Hill's more "consistent" performers, this "solid" "neighborhood spot" pampers partisans with "tasty", "traditional" Northern Italian fare and "smooth service"; it offers "quality" in a "dining wasteland", even if many hint its "tired", "mid-'80s" look "needs sprucing up."

Fiorentino's (Brooklyn) S   20 | 14 | 18 | $31
311 Ave. U (bet. McDonald Ave. & West St.), 718-372-1445
■ "Brooklynese" dining thrives at this Gravesend Italian "throwback" where "everyone goes" for Neapolitan "homestyle cooking" smothered in "superb" red gravy; "jammed" but "exuberant", it has the "fair prices" and "long waits" that come with the territory.

FireBird S   21 | 26 | 22 | $57
365 W. 46th St. (bet. 8th & 9th Aves.), 212-586-0244
■ A "back to St. Petersburg" experience, this "glitzy" Restaurant Row Russian is where "hedonists" "indulge their inner czar" with "opulent" food, "wonderful vodkas" and "imperial" service; the "enchanting" townhouse rooms have enough artwork to rival a "trip to the Hermitage", and for a "lavish" pre-theater "treat" or "that special occasion", this one's "worth every ruble."

Firenze ●S   21 | 18 | 21 | $43
1594 Second Ave. (bet. 82nd & 83rd Sts.), 212-861-9368
■ "Small" but "comfy" East Side Northern Italian that "delivers" with "reliable", "old-school" cooking and a "warm", "inviting" ambiance; the "personal" yet "understated" style makes this "romantic" storefront "great for a first date."

First ●S   21 | 19 | 18 | $39
87 First Ave. (bet. 5th & 6th Sts.), 212-674-3823
■ A "leather jacket's more appropriate than a dinner jacket" at this East Village New American that "surprises" with "yummy" food that's

| F | D | S | C |

best enjoyed with friends in one of the comfortable circular booths; the "dark, cozy" room exudes a "good vibe", and "those tiny 'tinis" (mini-martinis) sure "get the party started right."

Fish ●S
21 | 15 | 18 | $37

280 Bleecker St. (Jones St.), 212-727-2879

■ Make that "Excellent Fish" say supporters of this "unassuming", anchovy-size Villager, a "swimming" spot for "fresh, appetizing" seafood and "wonderful raw bar" trawling; "once a hidden treasure", it's more "crowded" now, though still anchored by "friendly" service and net pricing.

Fish Restaurant S
19 | 13 | 17 | $29

2799 Broadway (108th St.), 212-864-5000

☑ The generic name's in keeping with the "simple cooking" at this "low-key" Uptown island of "flavorful" seafaring; the "varied selection" and "relaxed" mood make up for "not-so-great decor" and the schools of "Columbia kids" lured in by the "low cost."

Five Points ●S
21 | 22 | 20 | $43

31 Great Jones St. (bet. Bowery & Lafayette St.), 212-253-5700

■ "Young upscale" types in search of "hip" dining "without the fuss" put out an "all-points bulletin" on this NoHo Med-American where "accessible", "well-executed dishes" are presented in "peaceful", modern "Zen-like" digs.

Flea Market Cafe ●S
19 | 17 | 16 | $30

131 Ave. A (bet. 9th St. & St. Marks Pl.), 212-358-9282

■ This "cute" East Village "favorite" is a "mellow", "reasonably cheap" place to "kick back" with "basic" French bistro fare and "smoke all you want"; it's debatable whether the garage-sale "schlock" decor is supposed to be "shabby chic" or "avant-garde."

Fleur de Sel S
24 | 20 | 22 | $61

5 E. 20th St. (bet. B'way & 5th Ave.), 212-460-9100

■ Now blooming in the Flatiron, this welcoming French "charmer" has made a "stellar" debut with "pedigreed" chef-owner Cyril Renaud's "inventive" seasonal menu, a "revelation" that's wholly "worth its salt"; the "peaceful", understated setting is decorated with Renaud's own paintings, though "once you're eating you don't notice the room" – or the premium prices.

Flor de Mayo ●S
19 | 9 | 16 | $19

2651 Broadway (101st St.), 212-663-5520
484 Amsterdam Ave. (bet. 83rd & 84th Sts.), 212-787-3388

■ "Nothing to look at" but "always satisfying", these Peruvian-Chinese Upper Westsiders have "no competition" when it comes to cross-cultural dining on "incredible" rotisserie chicken and "uncommonly good" plantains; their "unbelievable" "value" would keep even Fidel and Zhu "appreciative."

Flor de Sol ●
20 | 22 | 19 | $38

361 Greenwich St. (bet. Franklin & Harrison Sts.), 212-334-6411

■ Let the "romantic" "good times" roll at this TriBeCa Spaniard where the "sexy scene" is easily as delightful as the "fab sangria", "tasty" tapas and plentiful paellas; add "flattering candlelight, "mysterious" "castle decor" and "dreamy" Don Juan waiters and it's no surprise surveyors shout "olé."

Florent S⌿
19 | 15 | 15 | $29

69 Gansevoort St. (bet. Greenwich & Washington Sts.), 212-989-5779

■ Post-party revelers of all sorts stumble into this Meatpacking District landmark that's a quirky after-hours "godsend at 4 AM" for "solid" Paris-meets-diner fare; though perhaps not as "funky" as during its

| F | D | S | C |

former frontier days, it's "still the king" of "drag queens" ("pardon me, is that an Adam's apple?").

Flor's Kitchen S | 19 | 10 | 16 | $18
149 First Ave. (bet. 9th & 10th Sts.), 212-387-8949
■ The "*arepas* taste like Caracas" at this "teeny-tiny" East Villager that whips up "delicious", "satisfying" Venezuelan "home cooking" for "*pequeño* prices"; followers are eager to "wait" for a chance to "squish in."

Foley's Fish House S | 20 | 23 | 20 | $49
Renaissance NY Hotel, 714 Seventh Ave. (bet. 47th & 48th Sts.), 212-261-5200
■ Though "a little touristy", you "can't beat" the "showstopper" views down the middle of Times Square offered by this Boston-based seafooder's mezzanine perch; a "surprisingly good" menu starring New England crab cakes makes it an "all-around enjoyable" prelude to "theatergoing", or even a stage for breakfast.

Forbidden City ●S | ▽ 21 | 23 | 20 | $40
212 Ave. A (bet. 13th & 14th Sts.), 212-598-0500
■ New to the East Village, this Pan-Asian dim summer complements its "wonderful food" with solid service and "amazing" East-meets-West decor focused around a "huge oval bar" up-front; pricey for the neighborhood but not for the quality, it's a favorite of insomniacs who "love the late-night hours."

44 & X Hell's Kitchen ●S | 23 | 20 | 21 | $39
622 10th Ave. (44th St.), 212-977-1170
■ A "welcome addition" to a "tough" dining area, this Way West Theater District American unites a "home-cooking sensibility" with "creative" touches to produce "excellent" "updates" of the "basics"; the style is "hip but friendly", with "stark", "bright" decor that's more "Hamptons" than Hell's Kitchen.

FOUR SEASONS | 27 | 28 | 27 | $76
99 E. 52nd St. (bet. Lexington & Park Aves.), 212-754-9494
■ "Oh to be a regular" at this "classic" "for all seasons", a Midtown "experience" that "still lives up to its rep" for "consistently glorious" Continental dining framed by "sensational service" and the "grandeur" of Philip Johnson's "timeless" design (voted No. 1 for Decor in this *Survey*); from "fabulous" lunching among the bold-faced "elite" in the Grill Room to the "sheer elegance" of the Pool Room, it's "tops" among NY's "best places to splurge."

1492 Food ●S | ▽ 21 | 20 | 21 | $36
60 Clinton St. (bet. Rivington & Stanton Sts.), 646-654-1114
■ This "welcoming" new Lower East Side Spaniard mixes "traditions", offering "good" Iberian fare jazzed up with "inventive" Mideastern flourishes; it's a way to explore multicultural possibilities over tapas and wine in a "warm", unpretentious setting.

14 Wall Street Restaurant, The | 20 | 21 | 20 | $47
14 Wall St., 31st fl. (bet. Broad St. & B'way), 212-233-2780
☑ Once "J.P. Morgan's brownstone in the sky", this "elegant" Wall Street French aerie is still on the money with a "beautiful" "high-altitude" view, "discreet service" and food worthy of a robber baron", but "a little expensive" if you're off the "corporate" tab.

Francisco's Centro Vasco S | 22 | 14 | 18 | $40
159 W. 23rd St. (bet. 6th & 7th Aves.), 212-645-6224
■ Shellfishionados say "put on your bib" at this "informal" Chelsea Spaniard where the "large portions" are "claws down" the "best lobster buy" around; paella and free-flowing sangria round out the "reliable" menu, and it's a "loud, fun" time for those willing to "wait."

| F | D | S | C |

Frank ●🆂
23 | 14 | 16 | $28
88 Second Ave. (bet. 5th & 6th Sts.), 212-420-0202

■ Now "discovered" and perpetually "jammed", this "tiny" East Villager is a "staple" for "fabulous" "country Italian" doused with "savory" sauces and served to an "elbow-to-elbow" crowd; those prepared to "wait forever" for a "rickety table" or communal seating are rewarded with "great value" – "whatta deal!"

Frankie & Johnnie's Steakhouse ●
21 | 15 | 19 | $48
269 W. 45th St. (bet. B'way & 8th Ave.), 212-997-9494

◪ There's "history" aplenty at this Theater District walk-up, which plays to the "nostalgia"-prone with its "mammoth", "satisfying" steaks" delivered by a "colorful" staff of "old pros"; many note it's "noisy" and "rushed" before showtime – "just like it always was."

Frank's Restaurant 🆂
21 | 17 | 20 | $50
85 Tenth Ave. (15th St.), 212-243-1349

■ Visit "cholesterol city" at this "no-nonsense" Meatpacking District steakhouse where "quality" beef is served in a "handsome", "huge open space" that doubles as a "cigar-friendly" "old boys'" "hangout"; a vet with a "manly" style and hungry traders on the floor, it has lots of private party space available since the markets headed south.

Fred's 🆂
18 | 16 | 17 | $29
1649 Third Ave. (bet. 92nd & 93rd Sts.), 212-289-2700
476 Amsterdam Ave. (83rd St.), 212-579-3076

■ Decor goes to the dogs at these "lively" canine-themed joints, serving affordable but solid Americana for master and mastiff alike; with the unleashing of the East Side branch, now you "can actually get a seat."

Fred's at Barneys NY 🆂
19 | 18 | 16 | $40
660 Madison Ave., 9th fl. (60th St.), 212-833-2200

■ Perhaps the "best deal in the store", this Tuscan now on Barneys ninth floor is a "luncheon treat" offering "tasty" "light" fare along with frock star "celeb watching" and "major attitude"; it can be "fast-paced" but is ultimately an "upscale time-saver."

French Roast ●🆂
15 | 14 | 12 | $23
2340 Broadway (85th St.), 212-799-1533
78 W. 11th St. (6th Ave.), 212-533-2233

◪ "Youngish" neighbors make up the "hopping" caffeinated scene at these 24/7 "ersatz" French bistros that are also "reliable" for "late-night munchies"; despite "dippy service" and a "generic" approach, they're an "easy" option "any time."

Frère Jacques
18 | 16 | 18 | $43
13 E. 37th St. (bet. 5th & Madison Aves.), 212-679-9355

■ Murray Hill Francophiles praise this "charming" "hideaway", a "true French bistro" serving "satisfying" dishes in "cozy" environs; for an "evening of conversation with friends", it's suitably "quiet."

Fresco by Scotto
23 | 20 | 21 | $52
34 E. 52nd St. (bet. Madison & Park Aves.), 212-935-3434

■ "Forget the diet" and get to "know the family" at the Scotto clan's "festive" Midtown Italian where the "rustic" food is "fantastic" and the ever-"accommodating" staff radiates "personality plus"; "packing in" the "chic" "corporate set" and "media celebs", it's a big-bucks "power" scene where, amazingly, everyone "feels special."

Fresco on the Go
20 | 12 | 14 | $18
40 E. 52nd St. (bet. Madison & Park Aves.), 212-754-2700

■ For lunchers sans expense account, this "speedy" Midtown eat-in/take-out operation up the block from Fresco is a "delicious" "blessing";

| F | D | S | C |

the "hearty" Italian specialties are nearly "as good" as (but much less expensive than) the famed flagship's.

Fressen   19 | 23 | 17 | $48
421 W. 13th St. (bet. 9th Ave. & Washington St.), 212-645-7775
⚐ A "standout" in the über-cool Meatpacking District, this "unmarked" New American serves "palatable" fare in a "stylish" layout that attracts "outrageous" scene-makers; it's easy to "feel hip" dining with the "hot yuppies" and "model-looking" size zeroes – "even if you aren't" one yourself.

Friend House ●S   – | – | – | I
99 Third Ave. (bet. 12th & 13th Sts.), 212-388-1838
A self-described 'Asian bistro', this East Village neophyte is creating a stir with a full Chinese-Japanese menu at really low prices; it also draws applause for its sparely minimal dining room complete with a waterfall and a very Zen garden.

Friend of a Farmer S   17 | 18 | 16 | $27
77 Irving Pl. (bet. 18th & 19th Sts.), 212-477-2188
⚐ "Old McDonald" goes to Gramercy at this "quaint" American, which lays on the "homespun charm" with "hearty" "New England" "country food" and "grandma's kitchen decor"; the "precious" "B&B" feel wins hearts, though some say the eating's "just ok" and the "ridiculous" line for brunch is "no picnic."

Frutti di Mare ●S⇌   18 | 14 | 17 | $27
84 E. Fourth St. (2nd Ave.), 212-979-2034
⚐ A "standby" supplier of "good" seafood-heavy "Italian for the younger set"; this "consistent" East Villager's "low prices" and "big portions" ensure there's "always a full house" – which is fine for a "first date", but potentially "too close for comfort" for less romantic groupings.

Fujiyama Mama ●S   20 | 19 | 17 | $37
467 Columbus Ave. (bet. 82nd & 83rd Sts.), 212-769-1144
■ "Eat up and disco down" at this "wild" West Side Japanese where the glaring "neon" and DJ-spun "dance music" delight the "loud crowd" just as much as the "pretty good sushi"; although a "tacky", "so '80s" scene with "killer decibel levels", it makes "birthdays special" and every day a "celebration."

Funky Broome ●S   19 | 14 | 15 | $24
176 Mott St. (Broome St.), 212-941-8628
■ "Change of pace" mavens turn to this Little Italy Chinese, a "bright", "modern" venue trimmed with "retro hip" neon lighting; its "huge menu" of "tasty", "above-average" eats, at below-average tabs, offers a mix of "classics" and "interesting choices."

Gabriela's S   18 | 14 | 16 | $26
685 Amsterdam Ave. (93rd St.), 212-961-0574
311 Amsterdam Ave. (75th St.), 212-875-8532
■ "Irreplaceable" West Side "favorites", these "welcoming" cantinas are the "real deal" for "plentiful", "honest" "Mexican home cooking" at "fair prices"; the younger sister near Lincoln Center is as of yet "less crowded" but less "colorful", lacking the original's "kitschy decor" and "circus" ambiance.

Gabriel's   23 | 19 | 21 | $51
11 W. 60th St. (bet. B'way & Columbus Ave.), 212-956-4600
■ It "feels like Sinatra might walk in" to this "earthy yet elegant" Lincoln Center–area Tuscan, which inspires arias for its "splendid food" and "gracious" service; it's known for "dependable" "fine dining", and

| F | D | S | C |

owner Gabriel Aiello "works the room" to make everyone from concertgoers to the frequent "celebs" "feel at home."

Gaby Brasserie Francaise ●S ▽ 20 | 21 | 17 | $45
Sofitel, 44 W. 45th St. (bet. 5th & 6th Aves.), 212-354-3460

☒ Putting on the Ritz in a Midtown hotel, this deco brasserie serves "authentic" French standards in a "very pretty" Jazz Age setting complete with a pianist; but given the up-to-date prices, critics suggest the staff and kitchen "need more rehearsals."

Gage & Tollner (Brooklyn) 22 | 24 | 22 | $47
372 Fulton St. (Jay St.), 718-875-5181

☒ "Step back" into "old NY as it was" at this "venerable", vintage-1879 Brooklyn "tradition" for stellar steaks and seafood, a "staid", "gaslit" "classic" known for its "professional" service; though "hanging tough" in a "tacky" area costs it some luster, there's plenty of "character" left over from the "horse-and-buggy" days.

Gallagher's Steak House ●S 21 | 17 | 18 | $52
228 W. 52nd St. (bet. B'way & 8th Ave.), 212-245-5336

■ A "landmark" "guys' place" "convenient" to the Theater District, this "loud", "fast-paced" circa 1927 steakhouse is famed for "perfect dry-aged beef", "masculine sports-theme decor" and "waiters who don't aspire to be actors"; though some say this meatery is "past its prime", most maintain it "holds up pretty well."

Gam Mee Ok ●S ▽ 21 | 14 | 16 | $20
43 W. 32nd St. (bet. B'way & 5th Ave.), 212-695-4113

■ Providing "Korean food for the purist" in non-purist quarters, this 24/7 "secret" bargain in the Garment District "hits the spot" with its specialty *sullongtang* (beef soup) providing both "delicious" flavor and "medicinal" properties ("cures hangovers and colds"); the rest of the menu is "limited" but still "as authentic as you can get."

Garage Restaurant ●S 19 | 19 | 19 | $30
99 Seventh Ave. S. (bet. Barrow & Grove Sts.), 212-645-0600

☒ West Villagers pull in to this "roomy" New American for "solid food" "jazzed up" by a "cool" onstage band; though the music's "din" may curb conversation, it's a "lively", "casual" scene and the "jazz brunch" is a hep, reasonably priced place to park by the hour.

Garden Cafe (Brooklyn) 25 | 22 | 24 | $41
620 Vanderbilt Ave. (Prospect Pl.), 718-857-8863

■ "Who needs Manhattan?" ask Brooklynites at this "quiet" Prospect Heights "miniature", an "unexpected" place to find "spectacular" New American food; the "warm" staff "charms in a low-key way", though regulars want to "keep it a secret" until they "knock out a wall."

Gargiulo's (Brooklyn) S 22 | 18 | 20 | $42
2911 W. 15th St. (bet. Mermaid & Surf Aves.), 718-266-4891

■ The nearly "100-year history speaks for itself" at this Coney Island "classic", an "old-line" Neapolitan the size of a "catering hall", where patrons out of "central casting" "pig out" on "hearty" favorites; with "courtly service right out of *The Godfather*", there "ain't nothing like the real thing, baby."

Gascogne S 22 | 21 | 20 | $46
158 Eighth Ave. (bet. 17th & 18th Sts.), 212-675-6564

■ Stick to Gascony specialties or "go for the Armagnacs" at this "date-worthy" "Southern French oasis" in Chelsea, home to "rich", "wonderful" "country" fare and "charm-your-socks-off" service; the "beautiful summer garden" is made for a "secret" rendezvous.

| | F | D | S | C |

Gebhardt's (Queens) S ▽ 20 | 16 | 19 | $32
65-06 Myrtle Ave. (bet. 65th Pl. & 65th St.), 718-821-5567
🗷 A rare source of "hearty German" "home-cooked meals", this Glendale "family" favorite is the place to "meet locals" who come for its "authentic", "stick-to-the-ribs-and-waist" chow; it's "been there forever", and the "retro" welcome extends from the menu to the "expected Bavarian atmosphere."

Gene's S 19 | 14 | 19 | $35
73 W. 11th St. (bet. 5th & 6th Aves.), 212-675-2048
■ "Among the last of the traditionalists", this "comfortable Villager" keeps loyalists loyal with "good-and-plenty" Italian food at "painless prices"; it's "not trendy but definitely reliable", and that "back-to-the-'50s" decor is "unintentionally kitschy."

Gennaro S⊅ 25 | 12 | 17 | $35
665 Amsterdam Ave. (bet. 92nd & 93rd Sts.), 212-665-5348
■ There's "no better Italian for the price" than this Upper West Side "hole-in-the-wall" where fans endure "interminable" waits to tuck into "mouthwatering" "real food" on the "cheap"; seating is "shoehorned" and service "pressured", but make no mistake – "this place is hot."

Ghenet S 20 | 15 | 18 | $25
284 Mulberry St. (bet. Houston & Prince Sts.), 212-343-1888
🗷 Adventurers are "rewarded" with "succulent" specialties at this "easygoing" SoHo Ethiopian where no-utensils dining makes for a hands-on "experience" using injera bread as a scoop spoon; with a "simple" setting and "sweet" staff, it's a "cheap and different" way to walk out "stuffed."

Giambelli ●S 21 | 18 | 21 | $54
46 E. 50th St. (bet. Madison & Park Aves.), 212-688-2760
🗷 It "seems like time stands still" at this Midtown Italian townhouse, an ever-"dependable" "business lunch" locus that delivers "solid" food and "old-school" tuxedoed service; in spite of "expensive" prices and "signs of wear", it's as "comfortable" as ever.

Gigino at Wagner Park S ▽ 19 | 22 | 17 | $35
20 Battery Pl. (West St.), 212-528-2228
■ Given the "million-dollar" harbor view, it's an effort to "notice the food" at this Battery Park City Italian; though the menu is less impressive than the original Gigino's, there's "more atmosphere" – after all, "sunset over the Statue is hard to beat."

Gigino Trattoria S 21 | 19 | 20 | $38
323 Greenwich St. (bet. Duane & Reade Sts.), 212-431-1112
■ "Popular" with "neighborhood" types for its "homey atmosphere", this TriBeCa Tuscan is a "consistent" performer with "simple yet noteworthy" food, "efficient service" and a "rustic", "barn-like" setting; all in all, a pleasant "peasant" night out.

Gingko Leaf Cafe (Brooklyn) S – | – | – | M
788-A Union St. (bet. 6th & 7th Aves.), 718-399-9876
Hidden behind a curio shop, this tiny Park Slope Japanese delivers a serious shot of serenity with a spare, blond-wood dining room that opens onto a lovely courtyard; it's an oasis where you can sip sake and dine on a bento box in utter peace.

Gino S⊅ 20 | 15 | 19 | $42
780 Lexington Ave. (bet. 60th & 61st Sts.), 212-758-4466
■ "Frozen" in the "'40s", this "clubby" East Side "institution" with a loyal once-a-week crowd is a "sentimental" "favorite" for "satisfying" Southern Italian dishes slathered with the "best tomato sauce" in town.

www.zagat.com

Giorgio's of Gramercy [S] 21 | 20 | 20 | $40

27 E. 21st St. (bet. B'way & Park Ave. S.), 212-477-0007

■ "Shhh": this "intimate" Flatiron New American "secret" is slowly being "discovered" by folks seeking "creative cuisine" "on a par with the city's finest" at "great prices"; the "cushy" surroundings are ideal for a "romantic interlude."

Giovanni ◐ [S] 20 | 18 | 20 | $48

47 W. 55th St. (bet. 5th & 6th Aves.), 212-262-2828

■ "Quiet" and "congenial", this attractive, modern Midtown Italian turns out "very good" versions of the "usual" suspects matched by an unusually "impressive wine list"; for "business entertaining" or a "non-rushed" "pre-theater dinner", it's "well worth" the upscale cost.

Giovanni Venticinque [S] ▽ 21 | 19 | 21 | $50

25 E. 83rd St. (bet. 5th & Madison Aves.), 212-988-7300

■ Diners in search of "excellent" ("rather than trendy") Italian cooking find this "small" Eastsider a "hospitable" "hideaway" with "consistently fine food" and a "low noise level"; it also keeps museumgoers "fortified" after a marathon "visit to the nearby Met."

Girasole ◐ [S] 21 | 18 | 20 | $52

151 E. 82nd St. (bet. Lexington & 3rd Aves.), 212-772-6690

■ This Upper East Side "local haunt" maintains a "steady clientele" that "expects the expected": "consistently good" Italian fare, a "pretty townhouse" setting and "courteous" service; for a "relaxing lunch" or "sophisticated" (if "noisy") dinner, it's a "real sleeper" of a keeper.

Global 33 ◐ [S] 19 | 20 | 16 | $32

99 Second Ave. (bet. 5th & 6th Sts.), 212-477-8427

■ "Remarkably hip considering no one there has any hips", this "upbeat", down-priced East Village Eclectic is now installed in a "sleek" new space following a fire and still lures the "young" and "chic" with globe-trotting tapas and other "swanky snacking."

Globe, The [S] – | – | – | E

373 Park Ave. S. (bet. 26th & 27th Sts.), 212-545-8800

Following a complete remodeling, this American brasserie is back with a new steel, aluminum and glass design and two squares a day (no more breakfast, though); its ultra-trendy Park Avenue South site suggests it will continue to be patronized as much for the scene as the food.

Gnocco Caffe [S] ⌀ ▽ 21 | 17 | 18 | $33

337 E. 10th St. (bet. Aves. A & B), 212-677-1913

■ "East Village Italian funk" makes this recently arrived "gem" a "find"; it keeps things "simple" with affordable "fresh pasta" and the "amazing" fried dough it's named for, while the "tight" layout is redeemed by a "lovely garden" out back.

Golden Unicorn [S] 20 | 11 | 13 | $25

18 E. Broadway, 3rd fl. (Catherine St.), 212-941-0911

◪ At this Chinatown standout, the "superior dim sum" defines the "essence" of Hong Kong; despite "mayhem", "third-rate" service and a third-floor setting, you must expect "long weekend waits" for its "cheap", "classic" eats.

good [S] 20 | 16 | 19 | $30

89 Greenwich Ave. (bet. Bank & W. 12th Sts.), 212-691-8080

■ The name's an "understatement" say admirers of the "inventive", Latin-accented food at this Village New American; given the "sunny" decor, "friendly neighborhood" ambiance and modest prices, it's fast becoming a local "staple" and a "brunch favorite."

F	D	S	C

Good Enough to Eat ⓢ | 20 | 15 | 16 | $24 |
483 Amsterdam Ave. (bet. 83rd & 84th Sts.), 212-496-0163
■ Go ahead, "bust your buttons" at this "wholesome" West Side "taste of Vermont" where the American fare comes in "big portions" of "high quality", especially at the "exceptional" "country breakfasts."

Good Health Cafe ⓢ | – | – | – | I |
324 E. 86th St. (bet. 1st & 2nd Aves), 212-439-9680
Upper East Side Vegetarian that also doubles as a health food store, serving soul- and stomach-satisfying eats, including fish for the less fully committed; surroundings are plain but pleasant, while service is of the accommodating, sit-as-long-as-you-like variety.

Good World Bar & Grill ●ⓢ | ▽ 19 | 16 | 16 | $27 |
3 Orchard St. (bet. Canal & Division Sts.), 212-925-9975
◪ Sited far "off the beaten path", this easily affordable Lower East Side "hideout" offers "great-tasting plates" of "pure Swedish" food washed down by Scandinavian beer and cocktails; it's frequented by the "coolest hipsters", who mainly "go there to drink."

Goody's ⓢ | 20 | 8 | 14 | $20 |
1 E. Broadway (bet. Catherine & Oliver Sts.), 212-577-2922
■ This "reliable" Chinatown Shanghainese boasts "rock-bottom prices" that make it easy to "indulge" in their "divine soup dumplings" and "heavenly" steamed buns; aesthetes insist the "tacky decor" is a good match for the "tacky name."

Googie's ●ⓢ | 16 | 12 | 14 | $22 |
1491 Second Ave. (78th St.), 212-717-1122
◪ "Yuppies" with kids in tow show up at this East Side diner featuring a "vast menu" highlighted by "must-have shoestring fries"; it's a "lovable", "affordable" spot for "brunch madness", though dissenters deem the "greasy" grub and those who serve it merely "passable."

Go Sushi ⓢ | – | – | – | I |
982 Second Ave. (52nd St.), 212-593-3883 ●
756 Ninth Ave. (50th St.), 212-459-2288
511 Third Ave. (bet. 34th & 35th Sts.), 212-672-1999 ●
3 Greenwich Ave. (6th Ave.), 212-366-9272 ●
Go-getting local Japanese chainlet that's winning favor, having grown to four locations after just five years of operation; partisans praise the "reasonably priced fresh sushi", despite "no decor at all."

GOTHAM BAR & GRILL ⓢ | 27 | 25 | 26 | $63 |
12 E. 12th St. (bet. 5th Ave. & University Pl.), 212-620-4020
■ "Quintessential NY dining" finds a "benchmark" at this "resplendent" Village New American that generates enough "electricity" to be ranked No. 4 for Popularity this year; Alfred Portale's "exquisite" "architectural food" still "towers above most", and the "elegant", "soaring space" and "impeccable service" "hit the mark" whether the occasion is a "lovely evening" or the "bargain" $20 prix fixe lunch.

Grace ●ⓢ | 18 | 18 | 17 | $33 |
114 Franklin St. (bet. Church St. & W. B'way), 212-343-4200
■ Graced with a "big, long bar" and "wonderful woodwork", this modestly priced New American is a "sceney" spot to share "tasty" tapas-style dishes and sip "swell" cocktails with the "TriBeCa crowd"; adherents advise "go with a group" but "don't go hungry."

Grace's Trattoria ⓢ | 18 | 17 | 17 | $36 |
201 E. 71st St. (bet. 2nd & 3rd Aves.), 212-452-2323
◪ This extension of the well-known gourmeteria is "a bit of Italy" in an "inviting" East Side setting that rises "above expectations" with

"upscale eats" and ambiance; though perhaps "not as good as the market", it works for "light, ladylike lunches."

Gradisca ●S⊄ ▽ 19 | 15 | 16 | $34

126 W. 13th St. (bet. 6th & 7th Aves.), 212-691-4886
■ Following the "cheerful" lead of its siblings Piadina and Malatesta, this "welcome addition" to the Village pleases pastaphiles with "pretty decent" Northern Italian fare served in "dark", "loud" digs; its attractions include the "infectious energy" of the youthful staff and "totally reasonable" prices.

GRAMERCY TAVERN S | 27 | 26 | 27 | $66

42 E. 20th St. (bet. B'way & Park Ave. S.), 212-477-0777
■ Still "as good as it gets", Danny Meyer's "brilliant" Flatiron/Gramercy "tavern for our time" (rated No. 2 for Popularity) "continues to amaze" with Tom Colicchio's "intensely delicious" American cuisine and "out-of-this-world" desserts from pastry chef Claudia Fleming; the "tasteful" "modern colonial" decor and "wonderful service" are a "sheer delight", and while it's a "so-civilized" way to "blow the budget", the "front tavern room" is "more relaxed" (no reservations necessary) and easier on the wallet.

Grand Sichuan S⊄ | 23 | 10 | 16 | $24

125 Canal St. (Bowery), 212-625-9212

Grand Sichuan Int'l

745 Ninth Ave. (bet. 50th & 51st Sts.), 212-582-2288
229 Ninth Ave. (24th St.), 212-620-5200 S
■ As "authentic as Szechuan can get" beyond the Chinese mainland, this threesome (not all related) lays out a "banquet" of "spicy, flavorful food" that's a perfect "escape from run-of-the-mill" dining; "cheap" tabs compensate for "hopeless decor."

Grange Hall S | 20 | 19 | 18 | $35

50 Commerce St. (Barrow St.), 212-924-5246
■ A "convivial" scene in a "quiet" corner of the West Village, this "comfortable" "Midwestern outpost" American plates up always-"enjoyable", "homestyle" chow from the "heartland" amid wall-to-wall "'30s" "Americana"; "massive crowds" attest to its success, and there's a "handsome bar" too.

Grano Trattoria ●S ▽ 18 | 16 | 18 | $32

21 Greenwich Ave. (W. 10th St.), 212-645-2121
■ The "attention to detail" is apparent in this "homey" West Villager's "accommodating service" and "interesting", "very Italian" menu (highlighted by wild game and other "seasonal" dishes); for "authentic" dining with "no pretensions", it's "a cut above" the pack.

Grappa Café (Brooklyn) S ▽ 20 | 18 | 19 | $34

112 Court St. (State St.), 718-237-4024
■ Grab a pre- or post-movie bite at this "much-needed" addition to Brooklyn Heights that's noted for its "quality Italian" fare, "well-designed space" and "efficient staff"; despite the "quiet" vibe, it's "trying hard" to "rival the good ones" across the river.

Gray's Papaya ●S⊄ | 19 | 6 | 12 | I

2090 Broadway (72nd St.), 212-799-0243
402 Sixth Ave. (8th St.), 212-260-3532
535 Eighth Ave. (37th St.), 212-904-1588
☒ Downturn victims "low on funds" "go to the dogs" at these 24/7 "mainstay" juice stands where the "cheapest and best franks" are washed down with foamy fruit drinks; though they're notorious for their "messy" housekeeping (and clientele), you'll save enough to "go to Krispy Kreme for dessert."

		F	D	S	C

Great Jones Cafe ●S⊉ — 19 | 15 | 16 | $23
54 Great Jones St. (bet. Bowery & Lafayette St.), 212-674-9304
■ "N'Awlins" goes NoHo at this "funky" home to "killer" Cajun-Southern eats served in "smoky", "divey" digs brimming with down-home "personality" and a jumpin' jukebox; gird yourself for a "small" space crawling with cool cats, but "if you can fit in", the gumbo, beer and "good tunes" are a surefire "hoot."

Great NY Noodle Town ●S⊉ — 22 | 7 | 12 | $18
28½ Bowery (Bayard St.), 212-349-0923
■ At this Chinatown noodle specialist, the "fabulous" chow and "late-late" hours make "real food" available even at 3 AM; the shared tables stay "crowded", and if it's "unimpressive to look at", the "authentic" fare and "dirt-cheap prices" more than compensate.

Green Field Churrascaria (Queens) S — 19 | 14 | 18 | $32
108-01 Northern Blvd. (108th St.), 718-672-5202
◪ Arrive "*really* hungry" and "bring cholesterol pills" to this Corona all-you-can-eat Brazilian BBQ, a soccer field–size arena in which to "pig out" on "all kinds of meat" until it's time to let out a "few belt notches"; a "bountiful" salad bar is the only nod to variety.

Grey Dog's Coffee S⊉ — 20 | 16 | 17 | $15
33 Carmine St. (bet. Bedford & Bleecker Sts.), 212-462-0041
■ "What Starbuck's wishes it was", this "laid-back" West Village cafe is – a "usually packed" "urban boho" scene for relaxing chitchat over "coffee and huge sandwiches"; the "charming" space reeks of "cute", so "bring your dog" and dream of a seven-day "weekend."

Grifone — 23 | 19 | 23 | $55
244 E. 46th St. (bet. 2nd & 3rd Aves.), 212-490-7275
■ "Not everyone knows" this "subdued" Eastsider, a "hideaway" for "excellent" Northern Italian cooking and suitably "dignified" service; despite "somewhat close" seating and a slightly "dated" ambiance, it's a "class operation" that's made for treating a "client to lunch" or dinner.

Grilled Cheese NYC S⊉ — ∇ 23 | 12 | 19 | $12
168 Ludlow St. (bet. Houston & Stanton Sts.), 212-982-6600
■ You feel like a "kid" when clutching the "ultimate sandwich" at this Lower East Side storefront, which "upgrades" snacktime with a "fresh", "dee-lish" selection spotlighting its "melt-in-your-mouth" namesake; a "perky" staff and "happy wallet" pricing are bonuses.

Grill Room, The — ∇ 21 | 23 | 19 | $53
World Financial Ctr., 225 Liberty St. (West St.), 212-945-9400
◪ With a commanding view of the Hudson, this Downtowner draws Wall Streeters for "pretty good", pretty pricey meat-and-potatoes American fare; though some say the service "falls short", it remains a "classy setting" for "entertaining new prospects"; N.B. closed at press time.

GRIMALDI'S (Brooklyn) — 26 | 12 | 16 | $20
19 Old Fulton St. (bet. Front & Water Sts.), 718-858-4300
■ "Mama mia", this Brooklyn Heights simple venue is once again the No. 1 rated pizzeria in this *Survey* based on the "perfection" of its "world-class" coal-oven pies, "done right" with a "light", crisp crust and "Ol' Blue Eyes on the juke"; enthusiasts say "the long wait only makes you want it more."

Grocery, The (Brooklyn) — 25 | 17 | 21 | $42
288 Smith St. (bet. Sackett & Union Sts.), 718-596-3335
■ One of Carroll Gardens' "creative" yardsticks blossoms with "excellent", "ambitious" New American fare in "detail-oriented"

preparations courtesy of chef-owners Sharon Pachter and Charles Kiely; despite "tight tables" and a "nondescript" space, the "warm welcome" and "hip haute cuisine" keep its "yuppish" devotees happy.

Grove S
| 19 | 18 | 18 | $37 |

314 Bleecker St. (Grove St.), 212-675-9463

■ A "popular neighborhood" bistro "to fit all occasions", this West Villager offers "well-prepared" French-American fare, but what "makes the place" is the "quiet, lovely garden" out back – it's among the "most romantic" around.

Guastavino, Downstairs S
| 18 | 24 | 17 | $49 |

409 E. 59th St. (bet. 1st & York Aves.), 212-980-2455

◪ The base of the Queensboro Bridge is the "epic" setting for Sir Terence Conran's "busy", "beautiful" and "not afraid to flaunt it" brasserie where the "clever" Eclectic menu is somewhat "overshadowed" by the "very dramatic" "Gothic-arched" space.

GUASTAVINO, UPSTAIRS S
| 21 | 26 | 20 | VE |

409 E. 59th St. (bet. 1st & York Aves.), 212-421-6644

■ "Serene", "top-echelon" dining is yours at this Eastsider where the "breathtaking" tile-"vaulted" underside of the Queensboro Bridge serves as a backdrop for Daniel Orr's "superb" French cuisine; a "haven" from the "madhouse" downstairs, it's a "special occasion" nexus that's well "worth the extra" bucks; dinner is prix fixe only at $65.

Gus' Figs Bistro S
| 20 | 16 | 19 | $35 |

250 W. 27th St. (bet. 7th & 8th Aves.), 212-352-8822

■ This Chelsea Mediterranean "retreat" serves up "surprisingly good dishes" in "pleasant", "relaxed" surroundings; fans figure the "unusual" menu and "good value" are a "much-needed" "find" in the eatery-starved area around FIT.

Gus' Place S
| 21 | 18 | 20 | $36 |

149 Waverly Pl. (6th Ave.), 212-645-8511

■ Village "locals" know this "casual", "convivial" Greek-Med as a "sweet spot" for "satisfying food and service" executed by a "great staff" and an always "warm" proprietor – "Gus is the man."

Haikara Grill S
| 21 | 19 | 18 | $46 |

1016 Second Ave. (bet. 53rd & 54th Sts.), 212-355-7000

◪ Sushi goes kosher at this East Midtown Japanese that's "a bit of a novelty" but "elegant" nonetheless; though it takes a grilling for being "expensive" and "uneven" servicewise, "if one needs to do kosher", many say it's up there with the "best."

Hakata Grill ●S
| – | – | – | M |

230 W. 48th St. (bet. B'way & 8th Ave.), 212-245-1020

More tables and comfortable banquettes are the most obvious improvements to this recently renovated, contemporary looking Theater District Japanese, which has also added some Pacific Rim dishes to supplement its midpriced sushi and noodle offerings.

Halcyon ●S
| 21 | 24 | 22 | $51 |

Rihga Royal Hotel, 151 W. 54th St. (bet. 6th & 7th Aves.), 212-468-8888

■ For a "grown-up meal", this Midtown New American maintains a "quiet", "classy ambiance" to complement its "satisfying" menu and "capable" service; it's ideal for "leisurely" dining near the theaters.

Hale & Hearty Soups ⌀
| 20 | 9 | 12 | $11 |

849 Lexington Ave. (bet. 64th & 65th Sts.), 212-517-7600 S
22 E. 47th St. (bet. 5th & Madison Aves.), 212-557-1900
685 Third Ave. (bet. 43rd & 44th Sts.), 212-681-6460

(continued)
Hale & Hearty Soups
55 W. 56th St. (bet. 5th & 6th Aves.), 212-245-9200
49 W. 42nd St. (bet. 5th & 6th Aves.), 212-575-9090
462 Seventh Ave. (bet. 35th & 36th Sts.), 212-971-0605
Chelsea Mkt., 75 Ninth Ave. (bet. 15th & 16th Sts.), 212-255-2400 S
32 Court St. (Remsen St.), Brooklyn, 718-596-5600
☑ Supporters hail the "big variety" of "fresh", "original" options at this chain of "soup"-and-sandwich scenes, even if prices are "a bit steep" for a cuppa; given the "quality", the lunch-hour "mobs" hardly mind that there's "no decor" and service is "lacking."

Hallo Berlin S | 18 | 9 | 14 | $19 |
402 W. 51st St. (9th Ave.), 212-541-6248
626 10th Ave. (bet. 44th & 45th Sts.), 212-977-1944
■ Say "goodbye, diet" at this Hell's Kitchen German pair where the "tasty wursts" and "great selection" of suds make for a "hearty", "bargain-basement" "sausagefest"; just be prepared for a suitably "grungy" "beer hall" setting.

Hamachi | 21 | 12 | 17 | $34 |
34 E. 20th St. (bet. B'way & Park Ave. S.), 212-420-8608
☑ Well-prepared "fresh fish", "inventive rolls" and fair prices are the main draw at this "hole-in-the-wall" Flatiron Japanese standby; given the "dim waiters" and "nonexistent decor", some "stick to takeout."

Hampton Chutney Co. S | – | – | – | I |
68 Prince St. (bet. B'way & Lafayette St.), 212-226-9996
Savory dosas are the specialty of this inexpensive, Indian-inflected SoHo American that's a clone of the popular Amagansett original; look for chutneys, of course, plus refreshing homemade drinks and some American-style sandwiches, all served at counters so slim you may want to opt for takeout.

Hangawi S | 24 | 25 | 23 | $42 |
12 E. 32nd St. (bet. 5th & Madison Aves.), 212-213-0077
■ "Better than meditation" and "cheaper than a day spa", the "Zen-like setting" of this Murray Hill Korean Vegetarian "could mellow out Jesse Ventura", while its "outstanding" fare is equally "inspired" (though presented in "tiny portions"); just "don't have holes in your socks" – you'll be going "shoeless" here.

Harbour Lights ●S | 17 | 23 | 18 | $45 |
South Street Seaport, Pier 17, 3rd fl. (bet. Fulton & South Sts.), 212-227-2800
☑ The "lovely" harbor vistas and good bar make this "waterfront" South Street Seaport New American "not too shabby for a date"; however, some take a "dim" view of the "pricey", "passable", seafood-heavy menu.

Hard Rock Cafe ●S | 13 | 18 | 14 | $28 |
221 W. 57th St. (bet. B'way & 7th Ave.), 212-489-6565
☑ Ok, the "burgers really rock" at this music memorabilia–strewn Midtown American theme joint, and it works as a "bribe for kids after museums", but otherwise this "tourist"-clogged, "T-shirt"–vending institution might be better on Napster.

Harley Davidson Cafe S | 12 | 16 | 13 | $28 |
1370 Sixth Ave. (56th St.), 212-245-6000
☑ Even "cycle enthusiasts" detect "very little vroom" at this Midtown American themer better known for its "born to be wild" decor than its "uninspired" grub and stalled service; many opt to drive "right past it."

	F	D	S	C

Harry Cipriani S — 22 | 21 | 21 | $69
Sherry Netherland, 781 Fifth Ave. (bet. 59th & 60th Sts.), 212-753-5566
☑ You might want to "call your publicist" before venturing into this "celebrity-laden", "high-brow" East Side Venetian where the "fab food" is almost as good as the "stargazing", but some complain of "ridiculous" tariffs and a "fawning atmosphere" that "lost something in the transit from Venice."

Harry's at Hanover Square — 18 | 16 | 18 | $43
1 Hanover Sq. (bet. Pearl & Stone Sts.), 212-425-3412
☑ There's a "new" surf 'n' turf menu at this wood-paneled "Wall Street tradition" and though it may need to "work out the kinks", it's still "dependable" as a "clubby, all-guys" nexus made for "making deals" over "three-martini lunches"; for optimum enjoyment, use "someone else's credit card."

Haru — 23 | 16 | 17 | $35
1329 Third Ave. (76th St.), 212-452-2230 ◐ S
1327 Third Ave. (76th St.), 212-452-1028 ◐ S
280 Park Ave. (enter on 48th St., bet. Madison & Park Aves.), 212-490-9680
433 Amsterdam Ave. (bet. 80th & 81st Sts.), 212-579-5655 ◐ S
205 W. 43rd St. (bet. B'way & 8th Ave.), 212-398-9810 ◐ S
■ "Can't-go-wrong", "always mobbed" Japanese mini-chain "popping up in every neighborhood" that's far from "serene" but compensates with "sexy sushi" in "Texas"-size "pieces as big as the actual fish"; N.B. the wait might be less painful at the new, relatively unknown Times Square and Park Avenue outposts.

Harvest (Brooklyn) S — 17 | 14 | 16 | $25
218 Court St. (Warren St.), 718-624-9267
☑ "Brunch is a revelation" at this Southern-accented Cobble Hill American, though otherwise the "dressed-up, down-home" cheap comfort food is "ordinary" and the decor "homely, not homey" (save for the "great garden"); still, there's "no portion-control problem", making it very "family- and kid-friendly."

Hasaki ◐ S — 25 | 16 | 18 | $37
210 E. Ninth St. (bet. 2nd & 3rd Aves.), 212-473-3327
■ "Superfresh sushi", modest prices and "no reservations" equal "interminable waits" at this "crowded" "little" East Village Japanese where "variety makes up for the small portions"; once inside, "sit in the garden" and "be rewarded" with some "amazing" grazing.

Hatsuhana — 25 | 17 | 20 | $48
17 E. 48th St. (bet. 5th & Madison Aves.), 212-355-3345
237 Park Ave. (enter on 46th St., bet. Lexington & Park Aves.), 212-661-3400
■ "They "might not have Nobu's atmosphere", but these "modest" Midtown Japanese standbys have sushi "masters" who slice up some of the "best bait in town"; but even though the raw fish is so "fresh" that it "melts in your mouth", your "wallet may melt down" too.

Havana Chelsea S⌀ — ▽ 20 | 10 | 14 | $20
190 Eighth Ave. (bet. 19th & 20th Sts.), 212-243-9421
■ "Dynamite Cuban sandwiches" and "soul-satisfying rice 'n' beans" lure Latin lovers to this Chelsea "lunch counter" that "really does justice" to "good home cooking" on the "cheap"; given the funky "Little Havana decor", some insist "don't even think of eating in."

Haveli ◐ S — 21 | 17 | 19 | $29
100 Second Ave. (bet. 5th & 6th Sts.), 212-982-0533
■ A "step above the tacky" joints on nearby Sixth Street, this "reliable" East Village Indian beats the competition with "better food",

| F | D | S | C |

"nicer decor" and bonus "outdoor seating"; true, it's a "bit more expensive", but "you won't go back to Curry Row after this."

Heartbeat S | 20 | 21 | 20 | $49
W New York, 149 E. 49th St. (bet. Lexington & 3rd Aves.), 212-407-2900
◼ Fond hearts go "pitter patter" about the New American "spa food" (and "fabulous tea selection") at this "guilt-free" Midtowner with a menu that's butterless, creamless and sans saturated fat; but some "blood pressures rise" over the "bland", "expensive" offerings, even though the room "sure is pretty."

Heartland Brewery S | 14 | 14 | 14 | $25
1285 Sixth Ave. (on 51st St. bet 6th & 7th Aves.), 212-582-8244
127 W. 43rd St. (bet. B'way & 6th Ave.), 646-366-0235
35 Union Sq. W. (bet. 16th & 17th Sts.), 212-645-3400
◼ Made-on-premises brews and "glorified bar food" are "good for what ales you" at these "deafening", "post-college drinking halls" where "eat, drink and be merry" gets the idea right, but the order of importance reversed.

Heidelberg S | 18 | 15 | 17 | $32
1648 Second Ave. (bet. 85th & 86th Sts.), 212-628-2332
◼ The "last of a dying breed", Yorkville's remaining "temple to things Teutonic" serves "hardy", "hearty" grub that's just right "when you don't care about your waistline"; if detractors decry its "Chef Boyardee German" cooking and "musty, dusty" digs, staunch supporters want to "landmark it."

Heights Cafe (Brooklyn) ◐S | 17 | 17 | 16 | $29
84 Montague St. (Hicks St.), 718-625-5555
◼ Brooklyn Heights "home away from home" for locals looking for an "agreeable", affordable repast in a "pseudo-Manhattan" setting; though "nothing's inspiring", there's "something for everyone" on the menu and the Promenade's nearby, begging for an after-dinner stroll.

Hell's Kitchen S | 23 | 18 | 18 | $36
679 Ninth Ave. (bet. 46th & 47th Sts.), 212-977-1588
◼ Look for "limited seating, not limited taste" at this "creative nouveau Mexican" in the Theater District courtesy of Sue Torres, a "chef on fire with new ideas" whose "knockout" cooking "excites the palate"; just "don't expect to linger with these crowds."

Henry's ◐S | 18 | 19 | 18 | $31
2745 Broadway (105th St.), 212-866-0600
◼ Way "Upper West Side charmer" that's "desperately needed" on this "underserved stretch" of Broadway; fans fall for its "family-friendly" feel, fair fares, spacious sidewalk seating and "just-right brunch", but knockers shrug it's "easier than cooking at home – but not much."

Henry's End (Brooklyn) S | 23 | 15 | 21 | $38
44 Henry St. (Cranberry St.), 718-834-1776
◼ "Game" diners "go on safari" to this Brooklyn Heights New American known for its "spectacular" seasonal wild fare ("delicious elk", "the best ostrich") and "superb wine list"; despite "uncomfortable" "shoehorn seating", many "would kill for a Manhattan branch", especially at these prices.

Henry's Evergreen S | 22 | 15 | 20 | $32
1288 First Ave. (bet. 69th & 70th Sts.), 212-744-3266
◼ "You won't believe the wine list" at this East Side Hong Kong–style Chinese also renowned for "terrific dim sum"; sure, the digs could stand some "fancying up", but there's "no need to go to Chinatown anymore" for "reasonably priced", "damn good" eating.

	F	D	S	C

Herban Kitchen | 20 | 15 | 17 | $28 |
290 Hudson St. (bet. Dominick & Spring Sts.), 212-627-2257
☑ "Cooking with a conscience" comes cheap at this SoHo organic American that leaves novices gasping "I can't believe it's tofu" the "fresh, straightforward preparations" are polished by a "nice candlelit vibe" and "great garden", but tarnished by a "spacey staff that needs more protein in their diet."

Historic Old Bermuda Inn | ▽ 18 | 23 | 18 | $43 |
(Staten Island) **S**
2512 Arthur Kill Rd. (St. Lukes Ave.), 718-948-7600
☑ Granted, Staten Island might be a "step back in time already", but this "newly renovated" "old mansion" "brings you even further back" to 1716, when it was built; though it's reputedly "haunted" by a bona fide ghost, only the "sentimental" are possessed by its "just-ok" Continental cooking.

Hog Pit BBQ **S** | 17 | 11 | 13 | $22 |
22 Ninth Ave. (13th St.), 212-604-0092
■ "Manhattan rednecks" "close their eyes" and channel "Texas" at this Meatpacking District BBQ joint that supplies cheap, "lurid fun with greasy food"; there's agreement it looks like a "rickety shack", but debate over "what's saucier – the ribs or the barmaids?"

Holy Basil **S** | 22 | 17 | 18 | $29 |
149 Second Ave. (bet. 9th & 10th Sts.), 212-460-5557
■ "Ask for it hot" at this "cool" East Village Thai with an "exceptional", "upscale menu" (that only comes "spicy at your request"); though some bemoan the "incredibly shrinking portions" and "dark", "palm reader–like" digs, kudos abound for its "great big bang for the buck."

Home **S** | 21 | 17 | 19 | $36 |
20 Cornelia St. (bet. Bleecker & W. 4th Sts.), 212-243-9579
■ "Home away from home" for homebodies, this "unpretentious" West Village American is known for "Julia Child–style comfort food" "cooked with love"; the "heated outdoor garden" is the preferred locus, since inside is "like being in a [narrow] studio apartment."

Home Sweet Harlem Café **S** | – | – | – | I |
270 W. 135th St. (bet. 7th & 8th Aves.), 212-926-9616
As Harlem revitalizes, dining does too, and one of the latest entries is this tin-ceilinged coffee shop that lays out breakfast and lunch for a song in a funky, country-kitchen setting with mismatched furniture; there's also dinner, but on Fridays only, and with reservations required.

HONMURA AN **S** | 25 | 24 | 23 | $49 |
170 Mercer St. (bet. Houston & Prince Sts.), 212-334-5253
■ For a "little Zen in SoHo", try this "soothing" Japanese that's as "elegantly understated as a pearl" and yields "brilliant" "hand-pulled soba noodles" in "Iron Chef–style" creations; it's "better than psychotherapy" (and about as "pricey") when you're dreaming about "true serenity in dining."

Houlihan's | 11 | 11 | 12 | $25 |
677 Lexington Ave. (56th St.), 212-339-8858 ●**S**
380 Lexington Ave. (42nd St.), 212-681-8409 **S**
1900 Broadway (63rd St.), 212-339-8862 ●**S**
729 Seventh Ave. (49th St.), 212-626-7312 ●**S**
Empire State Bldg., 350 Fifth Ave. (34th St.), 212-630-0339 **S**
Penn Station, 2 Penn Plaza (33rd St.), 212-630-0348 **S**
196 Broadway (bet. Fulton & John Sts.), 212-240-1280
■ Perhaps "better in Indiana than NY", this burger-and-booze chain is "adequate" for "office farewell luncheons", provided your coworkers

can abide "mass-produced" grub "masquerading as food" served in "frat-boy settings."

Hourglass Tavern S | 17 | 17 | 18 | $28
373 W. 46th St. (bet. 8th & 9th Aves.), 212-265-2060
■ "Quick" is the idea behind this Restaurant Row American whose "timely concept" is "in and out" in under an hour; while the cooking is "pleasant" and "inexpensive" enough, folks with hourglass figures "may have trouble squeezing into" the "packed-tight" triangular space.

Houston's S | 20 | 18 | 18 | $31
CitiCorp Ctr., 153 E. 53rd St. (enter at 54th St. & 3rd Ave.), 212-888-3828
NY Life Bldg., 378 Park Ave. S. (27th St.), 212-689-1090
■ "Too good to be a franchise" and "too busy" to be any kind of secret, this surprisingly talented American duo is touted for its "famous spinach dip" that's so "amazing" some would like to "bathe in it"; the "lounge-lizard spawning ground" scene at the bar is equally invigorating, though the "no-rezzies" policy "bugs" many.

HSF ●S⊄ | 19 | 12 | 13 | $26
46 Bowery (bet. Bayard & Canal Sts.), 212-374-1319
■ "Meals of many courses" are wheeled out at this Chinatown dim summer where there's a "large variety" of "tiny dishes" for patrons to "point" to; though the "recent renovations" are a "vast improvement", that "stadium fluorescent lighting" isn't.

Hudson Cafeteria ●S | 17 | 23 | 17 | $43
Hudson Hotel, 356 W. 58th St. (bet. 8th & 9th Aves.), 212-554-6000
◪ It's obvious why this "trendy" American in Ian Schrager's Hudson Hotel is "all the rage": Philippe Starck's "dramatic", high-ceilinged design, which looks like a "monastery" by way of "Harry Potter"; an open kitchen, "communal tables" and Gothic chairs are the backdrop to haute comfort chow that's somehow "better than expected."

Hudson River Club S | 23 | 26 | 23 | $60
4 World Financial Ctr., 250 Vesey St. (West St.), 212-786-1500
■ "Keep an eye on your yacht" from windows overlooking the "captivating" harbor at this WFC American "class act" that works for both "power lunches" and "romantic" tête-à-têtes; "impressive" dishes inspired by the Hudson Valley and "attentive service" make the "memories linger", though your "platinum card" bill will jog your memory too; N.B. closed at press time.

Hunan Park ●S | 17 | 11 | 15 | $22
721 Columbus Ave. (95th St.), 212-222-6511
235 Columbus Ave. (bet. 70th & 71st Sts.), 212-724-4411
■ "Better-than-average", "cheap" West Side Chinese duo where the "decor won't keep you coming back, but the food will"; service is so darn "speedy" "you'll be in and out before you realize you've eaten."

Icon S | 22 | 21 | 20 | $48
W Court Hotel, 130 E. 39th St. (Lexington Ave.), 212-592-8888
◪ "Atmosphere is everything" at this Murray Hill New American via Drew Nieporent, from the "stylish crowd" to the "slinky" design with "tunnel-of-love lighting"; cynics, contradicted by the menu's high ratings, say the kitchen's "creativity" plays second fiddle to the "scene", adding "you have to be young to stand the noise level."

I Coppi S | 22 | 21 | 20 | $44
432 E. Ninth St. (bet. Ave. A & 1st Ave.), 212-254-2263
■ "Bucolic" East Village Tuscan that caters to an "adult crowd" "without tattoos" owing to its "Uptown feel" and pricing; many say it's "getting better with age", crediting "honest", "top-notch" cooking

and the "peaceful ambiance" of its "glorious garden", complete with "resident cat."

Ideya ●S
▽ 20 | 16 | 16 | $35

349 W. Broadway (bet. Broome & Grand Sts.), 212-625-1441
🔲 Regulars "try not to get soused" too quickly and "miss the amazing food" at this "bustling", reasonably priced SoHo South American, but it's not easy given the "lively party atmosphere" and "potent" tropical drinks; "confused service" fits in with the overall "chaos."

ike ●S
– | – | – | M

103 Second Ave. (6th St.), 212-388-0388
Cooking à la Betty Crocker gets a postmodern spin at this East Village American that dishes out '50s classics like deviled eggs and shrimp cocktail, but is best known as the only place in town serving TV dinners; the slickly retro digs also host a bar/lounge that easily upstages the food.

Ikeno Hana S
▽ 20 | 12 | 18 | $34

1016 Lexington Ave. (bet. 72nd & 73rd Sts.), 212-737-6639
■ The sushi's "so fresh it practically swims" to the table at this "tight" East Side Japanese beachhead; it could stand a "face-lift", but otherwise, it's the "next best thing when you can't get into Haru."

Il Bagatto ●S∅
23 | 17 | 16 | $31

192 E. Second St. (bet. Aves. A & B), 212-228-0977
🔲 "Don't tell your friends" – this "adorable" Alphabet City Italian is already "crowded" enough, thanks to its "affordable" pasta; but killjoys complain those "low prices don't compensate" for the "daunting" waits and "public shaming" from the "struggling rock star" staff.

Il Buco ●S
22 | 22 | 19 | $48

47 Bond St. (bet. Bowery & Lafayette St.), 212-533-1932
■ "Antiques everywhere" lend a transporting "old Italian country kitchen" feel to this NoHo Mediterranean, and "fabulous food" prepared with housemade olive oils helps maintain the illusion (though "attitude" somewhat detracts).

Il Cantinori ●S
23 | 21 | 21 | $56

32 E. 10th St. (bet. B'way & University Pl.), 212-673-6044
■ This Village Northern Italian standby continues to exude enough "romance" via "gorgeous flowers" and "lighting that makes everyone look good" to attract both "celebrities" and "normal people" alike; while the "thoughtful" Tuscan cooking blends well with the "calming atmosphere", "high prices" tend to jolt one back to reality.

Il Corallo Trattoria S
21 | 14 | 18 | $24

176 Prince St. (bet. Sullivan & Thompson Sts.), 212-941-7119
■ There could possibly be more kinds of "pastas than tables" at this "outstanding" Italian that's "sanely priced for trendy SoHo", so be "patient" when faced with "long waits" to get in.

Il Cortile ●S
23 | 21 | 20 | $45

125 Mulberry St. (bet. Canal & Hester Sts.), 212-226-6060
■ "Eating in the courtyard" Garden Room of this Little Italy Italian makes the "surprisingly good" fare "taste even more *bella*"; though prices may be "expensive for the area", a groundswell says it's the "best on Mulberry Street" – as well as the "prettiest."

Il Covo dell'Est S
20 | 18 | 21 | $37

210 Ave. A (13th St.), 212-253-0777
■ "It's hard to believe you're in the East Village" at this "beautifully appointed" Northern Italian that's more "reminiscent of Tuscany" than

Avenue A; "more people should discover it", as the "food's a cut above" the competition at prices that are a cut below.

Il Fornaio S | 22 | 14 | 18 | $30

132A Mulberry St. (bet. Grand & Hester Sts.), 212-226-8306
■ Sample the "flavors of Little Italy" at this "homey" Mulberry Street Italian that's "good for a quick bite" of "tasty" red-sauce fare; despite the "plain atmosphere", there are "nice-size portions for the price" and service is "superfriendly."

Il Gatto & La Volpe S | ▽ 21 | 16 | 19 | $40

1154 First Ave. (bet. 63rd & 64th Sts.), 212-688-8444
■ Although "not well-known", this "tiny" East Side trattoria "exceeds expectations" with "well-prepared" Italian dishes and "warm" service; sure, the quarters may be "close", but surveyors seeking "intimate" dining find it "comfortable" enough.

Il Giglio | 25 | 20 | 23 | $59

81 Warren St. (bet. Greenwich St. & W. B'way), 212-571-5555
■ "Zesty food", a "great wine list" and "attentive service" keep this "expense-account" Italian almost as popular as its highly regarded cousin, Il Mulino, while its Downtown location works equally well for "jury duty" and "romantic dinners"; those who "wish it was open on weekends" will be cheered to learn that it has added Saturdays to its repertoire.

Il Menestrello | 21 | 19 | 22 | $55

14 E. 52nd St. (bet. 5th & Madison Aves.), 212-421-7588
■ Credit its "highly professional" service, "quietly elegant" ambiance and "consistently good" food for this Midtown Italian's being "always dependable for a business lunch"; granted, many "go on an expense account", though some belt-tighteners say "for the price there are better" alternatives.

Il Monello S | – | – | – | VE

1460 Second Ave. (bet. 76th & 77th Sts.), 212-535-9310
This venerable East Side Italian, on the scene since 1974, is back in action after a temporary hiatus; if its past is any indicator, you should expect tasty, pricey dishes with an emphasis on tableside preparation.

IL MULINO ◐ | 27 | 20 | 24 | $68

86 W. Third St. (bet. Sullivan & Thompson Sts.), 212-673-3783
■ NYC's No.1 Italian for the 18th straight year, this "dark", "crowded" Villager serves "huge amounts" of "gutsy", "garlicky" food that's so good it "makes you feel you died and went to *Sopranos* heaven"; although owner/maitre d' Fernando and his family "run a tight ship", enormous popularity can mean "waiting even with reservations" – to beat the lines, go for lunch or at off-hours.

Il Nido | 24 | 20 | 22 | $58

251 E. 53rd St. (bet. 2nd & 3rd Aves.), 212-753-8450
■ This East Midtown Northern Italian "old-timer" is "still holding up" and "deserves respect" for its "refined retro" dishes and "top-drawer" service from "waiters who really care"; though perhaps a "shade too expensive", many say they're "never disappointed" – so long as "someone else pays."

ILO ◐S | – | – | – | VE

Bryant Park Hotel, 40 W. 40th St. (bet. 5th & 6th Aves.), 212-642-2255
Only the name of this Midtown newcomer (meaning "joyous" in Finnish) reflects chef-owner Rick Laakkonen's Scandinavian roots, since his ambitious, modern American menu emphasizes market freshness; set in a slick yet serene space, this is serious destination dining, from the

F	D	S	C

cheese and wine selections to the table settings to the skillful servers; naturally, the price tags are just as serious.

Il Palazzo S ▽ 23 | 19 | 21 | $38
151 Mulberry St. (bet. Grand & Hester Sts.), 212-343-7000

■ "Not touristy" Little Italy Italian known for "food that takes you to Rome" backed up by truly "friendly" service; besides, there's a "lovely outdoor garden", complete with "cute waterfall", so "for the price" it's hard to do better – just "leave room" for the "unbelievable desserts."

Il Postino ●S 23 | 19 | 21 | $58
337 E. 49th St. (bet. 1st & 2nd Aves.), 212-688-0033

◪ "Amazing waiters" with "exceptional memories" reel off the "longest list of specials" in town (as if "reciting the Holy Grail") at this "exceptional" East Side Italian; some find the procedure "gimmicky", but the food's "fabulous", even if it comes at an "ungodly price."

Il Riccio ●S 21 | 16 | 20 | $45
152 E. 79th St. (bet. Lexington & 3rd Aves.), 212-639-9111

◪ "Another reason to stay on the Upper East Side for dinner", this "cozy" Southern Italian is a "cut above the typical neighborhood" pasta palace with "well-prepared" fare, "friendly" service and a "garden room in back"; the biggest drawbacks are its "small", "uncomfortable" setup and not-so-small tabs.

Il Tinello 24 | 20 | 24 | $57
16 W. 56th St. (bet. 5th & 6th Aves.), 212-245-4388

■ Maybe this "underappreciated" Midtown Northern Italian is a "throwback", but it's "old-fashioned in a nice way", with "refined" cooking and "gracious" service led by "maitre d' Mario"; though prices may soar, most everything is "first class" here.

Il Vagabondo ●S 18 | 15 | 17 | $37
351 E. 62nd St. (bet. 1st & 2nd Aves.), 212-832-9221

◪ "No-frills" East Side Italian that's the "godfather of red sauce" and a "bargain" to boot; it's also renowned for its very "cool indoor bocce court" (reserved for more serious players, so "kids can't use it"), although the "family-friendly" vibe is otherwise strong.

Il Valentino S 21 | 20 | 20 | $52
Sutton Hotel, 330 E. 56th St. (bet. 1st & 2nd Aves.), 212-355-0001

◪ Return to a "less-rushed era" at this "quiet" Sutton Place Northern Italian where the food's "delicious", the setting "somewhat formal" and "conversation can be had"; its "older" crowd asserts "you can't go wrong here", despite the rather "expensive" tabs.

Inagiku S 24 | 21 | 22 | $55
Waldorf-Astoria, 111 E. 49th St. (bet. Lexington & Park Aves.), 212-355-0440

■ "Japanese diplomats" patronize this "highly civilized" Midtowner for its "real taste of Tokyo" cuisine ("close-to-perfect tempura", "gorgeous sushi"); the only jarring note in this otherwise "Zen" experience comes when the check arrives.

Independent, The ●S 18 | 17 | 17 | $41
179 W. Broadway (bet. Leonard & Worth Sts.), 212-219-2010

◪ "Quintessentially TriBeCa" American duplex with a "quiet upstairs", "lively downstairs" and sidewalk cafe made for people-watching; some say it has "lost its spark", citing a kitchen that "needs to turn up the flavors a notch."

India Grill S ▽ 19 | 13 | 17 | $31
240 E. 81st St. (bet. 2nd & 3rd Aves.), 212-988-4646

◪ "Tranquil" to some, "deadsville" to others, this Upper East Side Indian "secret" offers "succulent" chicken tikka, "responsive" (if "slow")

| F | D | S | C |

service and "price-is-right" tabs – making it all the more difficult to figure out "why there isn't anyone there."

Indochine ●S
| 21 | 21 | 19 | $47 |

430 Lafayette St. (bet. Astor Pl. & 4th St.), 212-505-5111

■ "Indoscene!"; this crowd-pleasing Astor Place French-Vietnamese, where the "dining room is like a [fashion] runway", remains hot after all these years thanks to "very good", "exotic" food, sexy black-clad servers and jungle-style, "palm frond" wallpaper and "rattan furniture"; the main problem is getting past the "exceedingly rude reservations staff" – but perhaps that's part of the experience.

'ino ●S≠
| 22 | 16 | 18 | $21 |

21 Bedford St. (bet. Downing St. & 6th Ave.), 212-989-5769

■ "Teeny-tiny", "phone booth"–size West Village wine bar that enjoys a "cult following" for its "authentic panini" and other "satisfyingly light" Italian snacks; though "guys may leave hungry" and service can be "uneven", it's "totally adorable" and "always packed."

Inside S
| ▽ 20 | 16 | 18 | $42 |

9 Jones St. (bet. Bleecker & W. 4th Sts.), 212-229-9999

■ Anne Rosenzweig (ex Lobster Club, Arcadia) has a "secret" in the West Village: a "creative", midpriced New American serving "delicious" "comfort food" courtesy of chef Charleen Badman in an "unpretentious" setting; early fans hope it will "work out the kinks."

Intermezzo S
| 19 | 16 | 17 | $30 |

202 Eighth Ave. (bet. 20th & 21st Sts.), 212-929-3433

■ This Chelsea Italian "standby" near the Joyce Theater supplies "truthful", "not expensive" cooking "without a fuss"; still, some decry "patchy service", "ordinary" food and an "unexciting" ambiance.

Ipanema S
| 19 | 15 | 20 | $33 |

13 W. 46th St. (bet. 5th & 6th Aves.), 212-730-5848

■ With a "sturdy", modestly priced, "meat galore" menu supplying some "va-va-voom", this Midtown Brazilian grill remains "one of the better choices" on Brazilian Row; a "helpful" staff and "strong caipirinhas" supply the "welcome-to-Rio vibe."

Irving on Irving S
| 19 | 16 | 17 | $29 |

52 Irving Pl. (17th St.), 212-358-1300

■ "Like eating at a B&B", this "small" Gramercy New American offers "counter service" by day and waiter service at night; its "bargain", "retro" menu and "cafeteria"-esque setup are "perfect for quick bites", though claustrophobes complain it's "cramped for dinner."

Isabella's ●S
| 20 | 19 | 18 | $37 |

359 Columbus Ave. (77th St.), 212-724-2100

■ Be prepared for a "hopping scene" at this "electric" Med-American that's *the* place for Sunday brunch on the Upper West Side; in spite of all the "hustle-bustle", the food's "imaginative", the "staff keeps its cool" and the "sunglasses-at-night" crowd stays engrossed in serious "people-watching" from its coveted outdoor tables.

Isla S
| 19 | 19 | 16 | $46 |

39 Downing St. (bet. Bedford & Varick Sts.), 212-352-2822

■ "Don't plan to converse" at this "noisy" West Village Cuban with "pounding music" and "Jetsons-in-Havana" decor; the "swell" drinks outshine the "hip" menu, making "what food?" a common refrain.

Island Burgers & Shakes S≠
| 21 | 10 | 14 | $15 |

766 Ninth Ave. (bet. 51st & 52nd Sts.), 212-307-7934

■ "Awesome burgers, dude" say fans of this low-budget Hell's Kitchen diner where the "lack of french fries is a downer" but "sassy shakes" and the "best chicken sandwich on earth" are uppers; don't mind the "narrow", "run-down" space – "delivery is fast, hot and accurate."

Island Spice 20 | 14 | 18 | $29
402 W. 44th St. (bet. 9th & 10th Aves.), 212-765-1737
■ Though service verges on "quiet and sleepy", the grub's "hot and cheap" at this Hell's Kitchen Caribbean that's such a "tight fit" that many "wish it were bigger"; still, the "low-key" atmosphere and "flavorful" cooking make it a swell "theater find."

Iso ◐ 24 | 14 | 18 | $37
175 Second Ave. (11th St.), 212-777-0361
■ For the "upper echelon of sushi", top feeders head for this East Village Japanese where the "succulent", "swimmingly fresh" fare is "iso good"; although the digs are "not fancy" and "waits can be awful", "Nobu-on-a-budget" pricing is the payoff.

Isola ◐S 19 | 15 | 17 | $31
485 Columbus Ave. (bet. 83rd & 84th Sts.), 212-362-7400
☑ "Comforting pastas and pizzas" fill out the menu of this West Side Italian "neighborhood" "drop-in" that's "great for families" 'cause it's so "mellow"; still, some feel it "just misses a beat."

Ithaka ◐S 23 | 20 | 21 | $40
48 Barrow St. (bet. Bedford & Bleecker Sts.), 212-727-8886
■ "Ulysses would approve" of this "attractive" West Village Greek where "light, classic" cooking that works "magic with fish" combines with a "taverna"-like ambiance that makes many "nostalgic for the islands"; sure, it's a "bit overcrowded, but it's easy to taste why."

I Tre Merli ◐S 17 | 18 | 15 | $42
463 W. Broadway (bet. Houston & Prince Sts.), 212-254-8699
☑ "You truly feel you're in SoHo" at this "fashionable" Northern Italian "scene" where you can "mingle with Euros" while nibbling on "ok pasta"; the "wine bottle–lined" digs and "models smoking cigars" provide distraction from the "aloof", "indifferent" waitrons.

I Trulli 23 | 22 | 22 | $53
122 E. 27th St. (bet. Lexington Ave. & Park Ave. S.), 212-481-7372
■ "Delectable" Southern Italian dishes, "polished" service and the choice of dining in a "soothing garden" or the "romantic", fireplace-equipped interior make this Gramercy "favorite" "trulli memorable"; although "it doesn't come cheap", "magical experiences" seldom do.

It's Greek to Me S – | – | – | I
128 E. Seventh St. (bet. Ave. A & 1st Ave.), 212-473-0220
The latest (and first NY) link of the North Jersey chain, this East Village Greek specializes in souvlaki, accompanied by a host of Hellenic usual suspects at good-to-go prices; given the clichéd blue-and-white decor, aesthetes have it delivered.

Ivy's Bistro S ▽ 21 | 16 | 18 | $37
385 Greenwich St. (N. Moore St.), 212-343-1139
■ For "mom's cooking away from home" in a "small" setting that has eluded TriBeCa's "attitude epidemic", this off-the-beaten-path Eclectic remains a "best-kept secret"; given the "reasonable" prices and "attentive" service, it's hard to understand why.

Ivy's Cafe ◐S ▽ 19 | 11 | 18 | $24
154 W. 72nd St. (bet. B'way & Columbus Ave.), 212-787-3333
■ A "welcome" Upper West Side addition, this "surprisingly good" yearling has "raised the quality of Chinese/Japanese takeout" with its "carefully prepared" food and "amazingly fast delivery"; on-premises diners attribute the low prices to its having spent so little on decor.

Jack Rose [S] 17 | 17 | 17 | $43

771 Eighth Ave. (47th St.), 212-247-7518

◪ Most have "nothing to beef about" at this Theater District surf 'n' turfer–cum–active bar where "above-average" grub comes in a spacious, airy, "leather-and-wood"–lined setting; however, critics find it merely "serviceable."

Jackson Ave. Steakhouse (Queens) [S] ▽ 21 | 17 | 20 | $38

12-23 Jackson Ave. (47th Rd.), 718-784-1412

◪ "Full-flavored steaks" at "decent prices" are served by "friendly" folks at this "Long Island City treasure" that some rank as a "super find"; others say its "plain atmosphere" makes it "second-level."

Jackson Diner (Queens) [S] ≠ 23 | 12 | 16 | $21

37-47 74th St. (bet. Roosevelt & 37th Aves.), 718-672-1232

■ One of the "best bargains this side of Bombay" is just a "quick F train trip" away at this Jackson Heights Indian where "you won't be sari" after sampling the "fresh, pungent" dishes; just ignore the "Formica" decor and "minimal service" – there's "nowhere else you'll find food this good, this cheap."

Jackson Hole [S] 16 | 10 | 13 | $19

1270 Madison Ave. (91st St.), 212-427-2820
1611 Second Ave. (bet. 83rd & 84th Sts.), 212-737-8788 ◐
232 E. 64th St. (bet. 2nd & 3rd Aves.), 212-371-7187 ◐
517 Columbus Ave. (85th St.), 212-362-5177 ◐
521 Third Ave. (35th St.), 212-679-3264 ◐
35-01 Bell Blvd. (35th Ave.), Queens, 718-281-0330 ◐
69-35 Astoria Blvd. (70th St.), Queens, 718-204-7070 ◐

◪ "Holy cow!" – "obscenely large" "burgers too big to eat" attract the "masses" to this "cheap" chainlet where only "growing boys" are "up to the challenge"; as for the decor and service, ratings tell the story.

Jacques [S] 19 | 16 | 18 | $41

204-206 E. 85th St. (bet. 2nd & 3rd Aves.), 212-327-2272

■ "Dependable" Upper East Side brasserie with a "chummy" Gallic ambiance, "genuine" "home cooking" and "reasonable" tabs; it's a "great little escape", though its year-old expansion leaves loyalists lamenting the loss of its original "cozy boîte" feel.

Jade Palace (Queens) ◐ [S] ▽ 21 | 13 | 15 | $25

136-14 38th Ave. (Main St.), 718-353-3366

■ The "unusual variety of dim sum" is the draw at this Flushing Chinese, a "big barn" of a place that "beats the ride to Chinatown" (not to mention the "trip to Hong Kong"); a "broad menu" of "authentic" goodies makes "getting there early on weekends" essential.

Jade Plaza (Brooklyn) ▽ 22 | 13 | 15 | $24

6022 Eighth Ave. (bet. 60th & 61st Sts.), 718-492-6888

■ On weekends, the "lines are longer than the Great Wall" at this happy (as in "noisy") Hong Kong–style Sunset Park Chinese where "inexpensive", "mind-blowing dim sum" and "excellent seafood" are the lures.

Jai Ya Thai [S] 21 | 12 | 15 | $27

396 Third Ave. (bet. 28th and 29th Sts.), 212-889-1330 ◐
81-11 Broadway (bet. 81st & 82nd Sts.), Elmhurst, 718-651-1330

◪ "Hot means hot" at this tasty Thai twosome that those with tender tummies think is "a trifle too authentic"; by consensus, "Elmhurst is better" than the Gramercy offshoot, yet both share "dingy" looks and "substandard service."

			F	D	S	C

Jane ●S
– | – | – | M

100 W. Houston St. (bet. La Guardia Pl. & Thompson St.), 212-254-7000
Like the name says, this Village newcomer is all about simplicity, from its solid, get-to-the-point Americana to its large space done in neutral colors that are as pleasing as the menu; it's already attracting a lively Downtown crowd on the merits of its modest pricing alone.

Japonica S
23 | 16 | 19 | $39

100 University Pl. (12th St.), 212-243-7752
■ "No reservations" equals "killer lines" at this Village "Japanese standby" whose "trademarks" include "whale-size" pieces of "grade-A sushi" from a "menu longer than *Shogun*", but bring your "black card" because all those pieces can mount up.

Jarnac S
∇ 23 | 20 | 23 | $44

328 W. 12th St. (Greenwich St.), 212-924-3413
■ This new French-Med "entry in the West Village foodstakes" has quickly found a following thanks to a frequently changing, "top-quality" menu with "service to match"; a "schmoozing chef" (Maryann Terillo) and "charming", "cozy" digs ice the cake.

Jasmine S
21 | 17 | 17 | $26

1619 Second Ave. (84th St.), 212-517-8854
☑ "Tasty dishes" at "incredibly reasonable prices" can cause crowding and service meltdowns at this "Thai-riffic" Upper Eastsider, but regulars always "leave with a smile"; irregulars cite "run-of-the-mill" cooking that may "lack spicing."

Jean Claude S⇗
23 | 17 | 19 | $47

137 Sullivan St. (bet. Houston & Prince Sts.), 212-475-9232
☑ Infrequent fliers "save on airfare to France" and head to this SoHo "bargain" for a "near-perfect bistro experience"; despite sometimes "snobby" service and a crowd that "eats and smokes at the same time", the "absolutely delicious" cooking still "packs them in."

JEAN GEORGES S
28 | 26 | 27 | $86

Trump Int'l Hotel, 1 Central Park W. (bet. 60th & 61st Sts.), 212-299-3900
■ "As good as it gets", "A+", "food as good as sex", "better each time" typify the reactions to "innovative" chef Jean-Georges Vongerichten's Contemporary French flagship on the north side of Columbus Circle; with a choice of eating in the more formal (and more expensive) dining room, the more casual Nougatine Room or terrace dining in summer, there's something for everyone – and the regularly changing $20.01 three-course lunch may be "NY's best dining buy."

Jean-Luc ●S
– | – | – | E

507 Columbus Ave. (bet. 84th & 85th Sts.), 212-712-1700
This ambitious new West Side French bistro's decidedly upscale cuisine from chef Eric Le Dily (ex Raoul's) should leave diners breathless; if that doesn't do it, high prices, plush banquettes, antique mosaics and a communal table in the bar should complete the task.

Jekyll & Hyde Club ●S
12 | 21 | 14 | $29

1409 Sixth Ave. (bet. 57th & 58th Sts.), 212-541-9517
☑ "Great special effects" and "costumed waitresses who love to ham it up" leave kids "howling" at this "ghoulish" Midtown American themer, but those spooked by "long lines of tourists" and "not relevant food" groan "don't scare me – spare me."

Jeollado ●S⇗
20 | 12 | 13 | $23

116 E. Fourth St. (bet. 1st & 2nd Aves.), 212-260-7696
☑ "Sushi for the punk generation" surfaces at this "garagelike" East Village Japanese offering "mass-produced" raw fish (plus a dab

	F	D	S	C

Jerry's S — 17 | 14 | 15 | $29
101 Prince St. (bet. Greene & Mercer Sts.), 212-966-9464

☑ "Art world chic meets great french fries" at this "highbrow SoHo diner" popular for "simple, inexpensive" American grub; despite "nonchalant service" that's "as variable as Bush's environmental policy", it's refreshingly "unpretentious."

Jewel Bako — – | – | – | E
239 E. Fifth St. (bet. 2nd & 3rd Aves.), 212-979-1012

The buzz is out on this, well, jewel box–size East Village sushi newcomer, whose appeal is matched only by its incredible fresh fish and chef Tatsuya Nagata's talent for deploying it; owners Jack and Grace Lamb run the front of the house with equal finesse.

Jewel of India S — 21 | 20 | 21 | $36
15 W. 44th St. (bet. 5th & 6th Aves.), 212-869-5544

■ "Superb" prix fixes let diners "eat like a raja" on a beggar's budget at this aptly named Midtown Indian; while most report "mouthwatering Mogul meals" and "handsome surroundings", a few scribes write it off as slightly "faded."

Jezebel S — 20 | 24 | 19 | $47
630 Ninth Ave. (45th St.), 212-582-1045

☑ "You only live once", so "damn the cholesterol" and dig in at this "tasty", theatrical Theater District Southerner with "down-home" eats and "fiddle-dee-dee" decor; though tightwads tag it "pricey" for "poor folks' Soul Food", most find it kinda "sexy" on the "porch swings."

J.G. Melon ●S≠ — 18 | 13 | 16 | $25
1291 Third Ave. (74th St.), 212-744-0585

■ "Some things never change", as this "classic" 1960s-era East Side pub demonstrates; purveying "hamburgers anytime" and "amazing cottage fries" to "aging boomers", it still has a "happening bar scene" into the wee hours.

Jimmy's Bronx Cafe (Bronx) ●S — 19 | 16 | 18 | $32
281 W. Fordham Rd. (Major Deegan Expwy.), 718-329-2000

■ "Good" Nuevo Latino eats, "salsa music", a "pumping bar" and charming owner Jimmy Rodriguez are the irresistible draws that attract "Bronx politicos" and "NY Yankees" to this sprawling cafe "just off the Deegan"; its "not typical" menu arrives in portions as "large" as the setting, while the "flesh market" crowd provides the "atmosphere."

Jimmy Sung's S — 19 | 20 | 20 | $36
219 E. 44th St. (bet. 2nd & 3rd Aves.), 212-682-5678

■ Hardly "unsung", this East Midtown Chinese is "always reliable" for "authentic" dishes and simply "beautiful" after a redo; its "classy charm" extends to a staff that "couldn't be more helpful."

Jimmy's Uptown ●S — ∇ 21 | 23 | 20 | $41
2207 Seventh Ave. (bet. 130th & 131st Sts.), 212-491-4000

☑ "What a surprise!" – this spacious, super-"swanky" eatery and très "trendy" upstairs club help highlight Harlem's historic renaissance; while the "gourmet" Latino – Soul Food wows most, it leaves others "unimpressed" and thinking it still has "some kinks" in the kitchen.

Joanna's S — 18 | 17 | 20 | $44
30 E. 92nd St. (bet. 5th & Madison Aves.), 212-360-1103

■ A "gracious welcome" from an "owner who remembers everyone" gives this Carnegie Hill Northern Italian an edge; though it's "pricey", the "cozy townhouse" setting, "delicious" fare and "aim-to-please service" make it a neighborhood natural.

Joe Allen ◐ S — 17 | 16 | 17 | $38

326 W. 46th St. (bet. 8th & 9th Aves.), 212-581-6464

◪ "Stargazing potential" reaches celestial heights at this reasonable Restaurant Row respite where "celebrity watching over meat loaf" is par for the course; as for the American menu, it's "nothing remarkable" but good enough to keep the place perennially packed.

Joe's Pizza S — 22 | 8 | 14 | $12

233 Bleecker St. (Carmine St.), 212-366-1182
7 Carmine St. (6th Ave.), 212-255-3946

◪ The "slices of heaven" at this pair of Village pizza places are "close to the best in NY", "thin, crispy and mmm-good"; though the decor's as "cheesy" as the pies and there's "no seating" at the Bleecker branch, most agree it's "worth standing for."

Joe's Shanghai S — 22 | 9 | 13 | $23

24 W. 56th St. (bet. 5th & 6th Aves.), 212-333-3868
9 Pell St. (bet. Bowery & Mott St.), 212-233-8888 ◐ ≠$
82-74 Broadway (bet. 45th & Whitney Aves.), Queens, 718-639-6888 ≠$
136-21 37th Ave. (bet. Main & Union Sts.), Queens, 718-539-3838 ≠$

◪ "Soup dumplings beyond compare" keep this Chinese quartet "famous", even if you must abide "no ambiance", "rushed" service and "eating with strangers" at "communal tables"; since the Midtown outpost has "higher tabs" and "more attitude", many "stay Downtown."

Johnny Rockets ◐ S — 15 | 16 | 15 | $15

42 E. Eighth St. (bet. B'way & University Pl.), 212-253-8175

◪ A "babysitter's best friend", this Village "burger joint" dishes out "'50s food" at "'50s prices"; despite an all-"singing", all-"dancing" staff and "free nickels for the jukebox", cynics sigh "you can't eat nostalgia."

John's of 12th Street S ≠$ — 20 | 15 | 18 | $29

302 E. 12th St. (2nd Ave.), 212-475-9531

■ East Village Italian "local legend" (since 1908) known for its "price-is-right", "epic-proportion portions" of "garlicky" "red-sauce" fare; true, there's "nothing chichi" about its "old-world", "tacky" interior, but "candles everywhere" have made it a "first-date" magnet for decades.

John's Pizzeria ◐ S — 21 | 13 | 15 | $20

278 Bleecker St. (bet. 6th Ave. & 7th Ave. S.), 212-243-1680 ≠$
408 E. 64th St. (bet. 1st & York Aves.), 212-935-2895
48 W. 65th St. (bet. Columbus Ave. & CPW), 212-721-7001
260 W. 44th St. (bet. B'way & 8th Ave.), 212-391-7560

■ The "perfect pies" from the brick ovens of this Village "institution" and its three offspring "could be the prototype for the perfect American pizza"; but the "whole-pie-only" policy means you "can't buy slices."

Jo Jo — 25 | 21 | 23 | $61

160 E. 64th St. (bet. Lexington & 3rd Aves.), 212-223-5656

■ Surveyors await chef-owner Jean-Georges Vongerichten's reopening (after a thorough renovation and menu revamp) of his Eastside townhouse bistro that some say was growing "tired"; elements they hope "don't change" are the "high-quality food" that "recreates his Alsatian roots", delivered by "friendly servers" in a "cozy, elegant" room.

Josephina ◐ S — 19 | 17 | 18 | $38

1900 Broadway (bet. 63rd & 64th Sts.), 212-799-1000

■ For a "feeling of well-being" at an affordable price, folks head for this Lincoln Center–facing New American where the "guiltless" menu boasts healthy items "for veggies, carnivores and anyone who just likes good food"; a few find "not enough zip", but showgoers say it's "trusty."

Josie's ◐S | 22 | 16 | 18 | $29 |
300 Amsterdam Ave. (74th St.), 212-769-1212
565 Third Ave. (37th St.), 212-490-1558
■ "Blissfully healthy" West Side Eclectic where "crunchy" crowds convene for "lip-smacking", "wholesome" fare; the new Murray Hill offspring is "just as good", "much trendier" and "chick city", according to our bird-watchers.

Joya (Brooklyn) ◐S∄ | ▽ 23 | 19 | 18 | $21 |
215 Court St. (Warren St.), 718-222-3484
■ "One of the best newcomers" in Cobble Hill, this "chic-looking", cash-only Thai is most "en-joya-ble" given its "outstanding" food at "amazing prices"; sure, it can be "noisy", "what with the DJ at dinner" and the "mobbed singles scene", but that's the trade-off when you're a "true original."

Jubilee S | 23 | 17 | 19 | $43 |
347 E. 54th St. (bet. 1st & 2nd Aves.), 212-888-3569
■ "Mussels are a must" (and the house specialty) at this service-centric, "sophisticated" Sutton Place–area neighborhood bistro that often "feels like a party" thanks to its explosive mix of "well-dressed" types in "tight quarters"; local fans feel it's "underestimated" and deserves more attention.

JUdson Grill | 23 | 22 | 21 | $55 |
152 W. 52nd St. (bet. 6th & 7th Aves.), 212-582-5252
■ Chef "Bill Telepan has hit his stride" at this "smart" Midtown New American, an "airy", "luxury liner" of a room where "beautifully choreographed" seasonal menus are "flawlessly presented" by a "knowledgeable" staff and supplemented by a "terrific wine list"; an "active" "expense-account power lunch" locus by day, its bar morphs into a major after-work "suit pickup scene."

Judy's Chelsea ◐S | ▽ 17 | 16 | 17 | $37 |
169 Eighth Ave. (bet. 18th & 19th Sts.), 212-929-5410
☒ "Music is the point" of this "fun" Chelsea American supper club with a "wonderful cabaret in the rear" that's a must-visit when David Lahm is tickling the ivories and owner Judy Kreston is singing; the "fair food" at fair prices comes courtesy of a "friendly" staff.

Jules ◐S | 19 | 18 | 16 | $35 |
65 St. Marks Pl. (bet. 1st & 2nd Aves.), 212-477-5560
☒ "St. Marks Place meets the Left Bank" at this "smoky" "bohemian" bistro that's "so French even the French go"; despite "inattentive service" and "loud" acoustics, its "interesting food", "romantic" air and weekend live jazz make for one "hip" "neighborhood haunt."

Julian's ◐S | 20 | 18 | 18 | $36 |
802 Ninth Ave. (bet. 53rd & 54th Sts.), 212-262-4800
■ Part of the Hell's Kitchen restaurant renaissance, this Mediterranean "sleeper" provides "consistently good food" in "pretty" environs complete with a "romantic" "enclosed garden" that's "comfortable even in winter."

Junior's S | 18 | 11 | 15 | $22 |
386 Flatbush Ave. Ext. (DeKalb Ave.), Brooklyn, 718-852-5257 ◐
Grand Central Terminal, Grand Central Dining Concourse (42nd St. at Park Ave.), 212-983-5257
☒ "Serious cheesecake" is the main appeal of this "enduring" Brooklyn "institution" (and its Grand Central offshoot) that's otherwise a "diner"

| F | D | S | C |

serving "ok but ordinary" eats; the interior is done in a color scheme so "orange that it could cure scurvy", but so what!

Juniper Café ●S ▽ 20 | 16 | 17 | $32
185 Duane St. (bet. Greenwich & Hudson Sts.), 212-965-1201
■ "TriBeCa's secret gem" may not be so secret anymore, since guests from nearby "boutique hotels have found it", but despite "vague" service, it still "charms" with "original" New American fare and a "mellow", "low-lit" setting.

Junno's S ▽ 21 | 20 | 20 | $33
64 Downing St. (bet. Bedford & Varick Sts.), 212-627-7995
☒ "Hip and happening" West Villager that may be more about "vibe" than food, given its "über-trendy" bar scene; those who do dine applaud its reasonably priced, artfully prepared Japanese menu, but note it's "limited" ("no sushi") and arrives in "scrawny", "model"-size portions.

Justin's ●S 17 | 19 | 16 | $38
31 W. 21st St. (bet. 5th & 6th Aves.), 212-352-0599
☒ "Where's Puffy?" is the question of the hour at this Flatiron Southern-Caribbean owned by the renowned rapper, but since "his Puffness" is easier to find in court, his buppie followers settle for "ordinary" vittles and "good people-watching" instead; critics suggest he needs to "remix the menu."

J. W.'s Steakhouse S ▽ 21 | 21 | 21 | $52
Marriott Marquis Hotel, 1535 Broadway, 8th fl. (bet. 45th & 46th Sts.), 212-704-8900
■ "Underappreciated" steakhouse in the Marriott Marquis that sports a "great view" of Times Square given its eighth-floor perch; look for "delicious", albeit "pricey", chops, a "nice atmosphere" and excellent time-sensitivity for theatergoers.

Kabul Cafe S ▽ 19 | 13 | 16 | $25
265 W. 54th St. (bet. B'way & 8th Ave.), 212-757-2037
■ "Often overlooked", this Afghan "secret" in Hell's Kitchen supplies "reliable" cooking at "bargain tabs"; though there's "no decor to speak of", there are no crowds either, making it a canny pre-theater option.

Kam Chueh ●S≠ ▽ 24 | 8 | 16 | $25
40 Bowery (bet. Bayard & Canal Sts.), 212-791-6868
■ "Meet what you eat" at this Chinatown "temple of seafood" where the still-swimming fare goes "straight from the tanks" to the kitchen; the resulting "dynamite" dishes and low prices compensate for the "Vegas"-meets-"Asia" decor and crapshoot service.

Kang Suh ●S 21 | 10 | 13 | $28
1250 Broadway (32nd St.), 212-564-6845
☒ The chance to "barbecue right at your table" provides some "interactive fun" at this round-the-clock Garment District Korean; it's "consistently busy" despite "feeble" looks, "rushed service" and the likelihood that "you'll smell like smoke when you leave."

Karyatis (Queens) ●S 23 | 18 | 21 | $36
35-03 Broadway (bet. 35th & 36th Sts.), 718-204-0666
■ "Head and shoulders above most Astoria Greeks", this "pleasing", if formal, Hellenic offers "dining instead of eating", with "fantastic" cooking "served with a flourish" and enlivened by occasional "live music"; if you're looking for a lively Greek taverna, this ain't it.

Katsuhama S ▽ 21 | 13 | 16 | $29
11 E. 47th St. (bet. 5th & Madison Aves.), 212-758-5909
■ "Indulge yourself" at this modestly priced Midtown Japanese specializing in "deep-fried" delights; regulars warn "don't look for

sushi" (and "don't look for the waiter either"), though the lunch boxes are worth a look.

Katz's Delicatessen S | 21 | 10 | 12 | $19
205 E. Houston St. (Ludlow St.), 212-254-2246
■ This vast Lower East Side "Jewish deli theme park" is a standard bearer for "sandwiches no human can get their mouth around" and still remembered for the "I'll-have-what-she's-having" scene in *When Harry Met Sally*; it's "not for the dainty", but the "drab" decor, "barking waiters" and sea-of-humanity crowd are all "part of the experience."

Kazan Turkish Cuisine (Queens) S ▽ | 21 | 13 | 18 | $25
95-36 Queens Blvd. (bet. 63rd Ave. & 63rd Dr.), 718-897-1509
■ Folks feel they're in the "Middle East, not the middle of Queens" at this "unhurried", "pleasant" Rego Park Turkish BYO where "good" "homey" cooking comes with weekend belly dancers; the bargain pricing offsets the bargain-basement decor.

Kazusa S | – | – | – | M
1400 Second Ave. (bet. 72nd & 73rd Sts.), 212-472-1700
Clean and well-lit, this moderately priced Upper East Side Japanese offers an extensive takeout menu that includes lunch specials; a friendly staff serves up the sushi and other standard dishes.

K.B. Garden (Queens) S | 20 | 12 | 13 | $24
136-28 39th Ave. (bet. Main & Union Sts.), 718-961-9088
■ For "some of the best dim sum outside Hong Kong", try this colossal Flushing Chinese with "excellent variety" and a "zoo"-like ambiance at prime feeding times; vets warn there's "lots of staff, not lots of attention" and add the "cart pushers speak zero English."

Keens Steakhouse | 21 | 21 | 20 | $50
72 W. 36th St. (bet. 5th & 6th Aves.), 212-947-3636
■ "It's not a pipe dream" – there are thousands of clay pipes on display at this wonderful 1885 Garment District chop shop that exudes so much history you'll "feel like you're in a Caleb Carr novel"; so "gnaw on mutton chops", "sip a scotch" (from the over 190 single-malts available) and check out the amazing bar.

Keewah Yen ●S | 20 | 16 | 20 | $35
50 W. 56th St. (bet. 5th & 6th Aves.), 212-246-0770
◪ If it "seems a bit dated", there's good reason: this Midtown Chinese is celebrating its 30th anniversary of serving "food as good as any in China"; yet despite a "partial face-lift", it's often underused.

Kelley & Ping S | 18 | 16 | 14 | $24
127 Greene St. (bet. Houston & Prince Sts.), 212-228-1212
◪ "Trendy types" frequent this "quirky" SoHo noodle shop/tearoom/ emporium for "inexpensive" Pan-Asian nibbles in a très "cool" setting that's one part "Shanghai movie set", one part "Asian bazaar" and one part lounge; but cynics nix "spotty service" and less-than-stellar eats.

Kiiroi-Hana S | 19 | 11 | 16 | $32
23 W. 56th St. (bet. 5th & 6th Aves.), 212-582-7499
◪ "Steady Midtown Japanese option" for "tasty sushi" at "very fair prices"; though "dreary decor" and "impersonal service" detract, it supplies a "solid business lunch" for nearby wage slaves.

Killmeyer's Old Bavaria Inn (Staten Island) S ▽ | 21 | 19 | 19 | $32
4254 Arthur Kill Rd. (Sharrotts Rd.), 718-984-1202
■ The "beer selection's almost as large as the portions" at this "little taste of Germany in Staten Island" rolling out a surprisingly good "stick-

to-your-ribs" menu of "homey" Deutschland favorites in a beirgarten setting; "Sunday is fun day" when the oompah band blows in.

KING COLE BAR ●S | 20 | 27 | 22 | $45 |

St. Regis Hotel, 2 E. 55th St. (bet. 5th & Madison Aves.), 212-339-6721

■ There's "no more elegant setting for a drink" than this "marvelous" Midtown hotel bar where "old pro bartenders" shake "smart cocktails" for a "very grown-up crowd"; though its "tasty" American menu is "expensive", the "priceless" Maxfield Parrish mural and swell people-watching balance the books.

Kings' Carriage House S | 21 | 25 | 22 | $50 |

251 E. 82nd St. (bet. 2nd & 3rd Aves.), 212-734-5490

■ Think "English country manor" to get the mood of this Upper East Side Continental nestled in a converted carriage house that goes beyond its "beautiful setting" to provide "traditional" fare "fit for a king"; whether it's "lunch with the girls", "tea with grandma" or a "romantic" dinner with whomever, this "hideaway" will surely "impress."

Kin Khao ●S | 21 | 18 | 16 | $32 |

171 Spring St. (bet. Thompson St. & W. B'way), 212-966-3939

■ "Sticky rice" adherents tout the "terrific Thai" treats at this "trendy", tight SoHo scene frequented by a "too beautiful" "Downtown" crowd; to see in the "pitch-black" room, bring your "infrared glasses", and plan for a wait that's "longer than the meal itself."

Kitchen Club S | ▽ 22 | 19 | 21 | $44 |

30 Prince St. (Mott St.), 212-274-0025

■ Despite some "kooky combos", chef-owner Marja Samson's "inventive" NoLita Japanese-Eclectic generally serves "delicious" food with a "personal touch"; "say hello" to her dog (who will "visit your table"), and don't miss Chibi's, the adjacent sake bar.

Kitchenette S | 20 | 11 | 13 | $19 |

80 W. Broadway (Warren St.), 212-267-6740

■ "Fattening" "comfort food at its best" is served at this TriBeCa American that draws such "huge lines" for brunch that "by the time you get a table, it's time for dinner"; but diehards downplay the service snafus and "cafeteria"-like setting, since tabs are dirt "cheap" and the cooking darn "good."

Knickerbocker Bar & Grill ●S | 20 | 18 | 19 | $40 |

33 University Pl. (9th St.), 212-228-8490

■ A "blast from the past", this Central Village steakhouse is "like eating at home, only the food's better" and there's "fab jazz at night" too; though it strikes some as "a bit stodgy", this "wonderfully informal" place appeals to both "old school" and new school NYers.

Kodama Sushi S | 19 | 12 | 17 | $30 |

1465 Third Ave. (bet. 82nd & 83rd Sts.), 212-535-9661
301 W. 45th St. (bet. 8th & 9th Aves.), 212-582-8065 ●

■ Thanks to "always-fresh" sushi at "best-buy" prices, this Hell's Kitchen Japanese is a "real pre-theater find"; though "undiscovered and underdecorated", it's "reliable" and "satisfying"; N.B. the Yorkville offshoot is new and unrated.

Komodo ●S | ▽ 23 | 18 | 23 | $33 |

186 Ave. A (12th St.), 212-529-2658

■ The union of Asian and Mexican cooking at this "offbeat" East Villager makes for some "clever" "new tastes to wake up your mouth"; though some snipe at "fusion confusion", modest prices and "caring" service led by a "personable owner" make this a must-try.

Korea Palace [S] 18 | 15 | 17 | $32

127 E. 54th St. (bet. Lexington & Park Aves.), 212-832-2350

■ Credit its "bright", "unintimidating" ambiance, "helpful" staff and affordable prices for the popularity of this "big" Midtown Korean; "great choices from barbecue to sushi" cap off the "enjoyable" experience.

Kori [S] ▽ 19 | 19 | 19 | $33

253 Church St. (bet. Franklin & Leonard Sts.), 212-334-4598

■ "TriBeCa savvy meets Korean cuisine" at this "serene oasis" on a "bleak stretch of Church Street"; it "holds its own" with "creative creations" and "super-value lunchboxes" served by a "friendly, discreet" staff.

Kotobuki Bistro (Brooklyn) [S] – | – | – | M

142 Columbia St. (bet. DeGraw & Sackett Sts.), 718-246-7980

Polaroids of smiling customers cover the exterior of this new midpriced West Carroll Gardens Japanese boasting a broad sushi, sashimi and hand-roll selection as well as cooked dishes (including some Thai offerings); though out of the way, it delivers as far as Brooklyn Heights.

Krispy Kreme 22 | 8 | 12 | $7

1497 Third Ave. (bet. 84th & 85th Sts.), 212-879-9111 [S]
141 W. 72nd St. (bet. B'way & Columbus Ave.), 212-724-1100 [S]
Port Authority, 625 Eighth Ave. (bet. 40th & 41st Sts.), no phone ≠
265 W. 23rd St. (bet. 7th & 8th Aves.), 212-620-0111 [S]
2 Penn Plaza (33rd St. on Amtrak rotunda level), 212-947-7175 [S]
280 W. 125th St. (Frederick Douglass Blvd.), 212-531-0111 [S]

◪ "Even the holes are tasty" at this bright-green-and-white doughnut shop chain purveying "warm sugar clouds" that "melt in your mouth" with "no chewing necessary"; though a "workout's worst nightmare" to some, they're a "life-altering experience" to others; P.S. "get your coffee elsewhere."

Kum Gang San ◑ [S] 22 | 18 | 17 | $29

138-28 Northern Blvd. (bet. Main & Union Sts.), Queens, 718-461-0909
49 W. 32nd St. (bet. B'way & 5th Ave.), 212-967-0909

■ "Bring your appetite" to these 24-hour Koreans with "encyclopedia"-size menus to match the "big flavors" and spacious settings; expect "loud", "hopping" atmospheres at both branches, though cognoscenti claim the huge handsome original in "Flushing is better than [the offspring in] Manhattan."

KURUMA ZUSHI 27 | 17 | 23 | $77

7 E. 47th St., 2nd fl. (bet. 5th & Madison Aves.), 212-317-2802

■ What may be NY's "ultimate sushi" turns up at this "hidden", second-floor Japanese Midtowner that takes you to a "whole other level" with "phenomenal" "fish prepared to perfection"; the only catch is the cost, which can be "staggering", but in the end "worth every yen."

Kyma ◑ [S] ▽ 21 | 17 | 18 | $39

300 W. 46th St. (8th Ave.), 212-957-8830

■ From the owner of Ithika comes this "engaging" new Theater District Greek where the "wonderful" food is like taking "a flight to Athens" but a lot "cheaper"; though "still finding its footing", it's already got the "great location" part down pat.

La Baraka (Queens) [S] 22 | 18 | 23 | $38

255-09 Northern Blvd. (Little Neck Pkwy.), 718-428-1461

■ They "pack 'em in" at this "little" Little Neck French-Tunisian, but with good reason – the "down-to-earth cooking" seems to "get better all the time"; the notably "impeccable service" begins with a greeting from "hostess Lucette", who adds some "kiss-kiss" to the couscous.

	F	D	S	C

La Belle Epoque ◐ S   17 | 23 | 17 | $39
827 Broadway (bet. 12th & 13th Sts.), 212-254-6436
◪ This "charming" Central Village French-Creole "transports you" to a "different era" with its "stylized" take on "19th-century Paris"; it's "most fun on tango nights", but ratings show you "could do better."

La Belle Vie S   ▽ 19 | 18 | 18 | $34
184 Eighth Ave. (bet. 19th & 20th Sts.), 212-929-4320
◼ Formerly Trois Canards, this "solid, modest bistro" remains "exactly the same", with "enjoyable" food at price tags that "don't break the bank"; service veers from "iffy" to "friendly", but the sidewalk-seat view of the "Chelsea parade" is an amusing distraction.

La Bergamote S⇗   ▽ 22 | 14 | 15 | $14
169 Ninth Ave. (20th St.), 212-627-9010
◼ Like a "gift from France", this "casual", moderately priced Chelsea bakery/cafe produces "pastries that taste as good as they look" along with sandwiches and "desserts to die for"; however, the "like-you're-in-Paris" experience extends to service that "could be friendlier."

La Bicyclette S   17 | 17 | 16 | $38
519 Columbus Ave. (85th St.), 212-579-1145
◪ "Low-key" Upper West Side brasserie offering "casual" grazing on "standard" fare in a "white tablecloth" setting; phobes find "two flat tires" here: the "not memorable" grub and a "staff that needs training."

La Boite en Bois S⇗   21 | 17 | 20 | $47
75 W. 68th St. (bet. Columbus Ave. & CPW), 212-874-2705
◼ "Tantalizing" food trumps "snug" seating at this truly "tiny" French bistro near Lincoln Center that's a better fit for "short, thin" folks; regulars yearning for "*un peu de Paris*" "reserve waaay ahead" for its *petit prix fixe* but still find the "no-credit-card" policy "annoying."

La Bonne Soupe ◐ S   17 | 13 | 15 | $27
48 W. 55th St. (bet. 5th & 6th Aves.), 212-586-7650
◪ A "Midtown rarity", this "old reliable" French bistro satisfies "champagne tastes on a beer budget"; skeptics say the "frumpy" menu and even frumpier decor need "revamping."

La Bouchée (Brooklyn) S   ▽ 17 | 16 | 18 | $34
136 Montague St. (bet. Clinton & Henry Sts.), 718-222-3550
◼ Brooklyn Heights surveyors report that this new French bistro has a "very good chef", solid service and "reasonable prices" that total up to a "fine addition" to the area.

La Bouillabaisse (Brooklyn) S⇗   23 | 13 | 18 | $35
145 Atlantic Ave. (bet. Clinton & Henry Sts.), 718-522-8275
◼ Its "amazing" (and eponymous) signature dish is the raison d'être of this Heights seafood bistro where "all senses are engaged"; modest pricing makes the "cramped" room fill up fast, so show up "early before the blackboard menus get smudged."

L'Absinthe S   22 | 23 | 20 | $57
227 E. 67th St. (bet. 2nd & 3rd Aves.), 212-794-4950
◼ "Like a Toulouse-Lautrec painting", this "posh" Eastsider supplies "lots of flash" via its "superb" brasserie offerings, "great wine list" and "gorgeous", flower-filled interior; granted, tabs are "steep", but in exchange you're transported to "fin de siècle Paris."

L'Acajou ◐ S   20 | 15 | 18 | $41
53 W. 19th St. (bet. 5th & 6th Aves.), 212-645-1706
◼ Though "not much to look at", this "unpretentious", moderately priced Flatiron Alsatian bistro features "hearty" cooking ("some

nouvelle choices, some traditional") abetted by a "superb wine list"; still, "cigarette smoke" casts a cloud over the proceedings for some.

La Cantina S ▽ 25 | 20 | 24 | $43
(fka Trattoria Cantina)
38 Eighth Ave. (Jane St.), 212-727-8787
■ The "hands-on owner" of this West Village Southern Italian "jewel" is "always there to greet you" and "help you decide what to order"; given such "cozy warmth", it "feels like it's been around longer than it has."

LA CARAVELLE 26 | 25 | 26 | $75
33 W. 55th St. (bet. 5th & 6th Aves.), 212-586-4252
■ "One of the last bastions of civilization", André and Rita Jammet's "elegant" Midtown French, after 40 years, continues to set the "gold standard" for "luxury dining"; credit the "flawless cuisine" of new chef Troy Dupuy, a setting that melds "luxury and comfort" seamlessly and service more "gracious" than "the average 'La Restaurant'"; though not inexpensive (prix fixe only, $68 dinner, $38 lunch), an "extraordinary" meal is the payoff – "if only real life could be this good."

La Caridad 78 ●S⊄ 16 | 6 | 11 | $16
2197-2199 Broadway (78th St.), 212-874-2780
◪ Maybe their "English isn't great", but the "food's just right" at this cheap West Side Sino-Cuban "dive" that's a "taxi driver" magnet; "depressing decor" and "abysmal service" are the downsides.

La Cocina S 19 | 14 | 17 | $25
2608 Broadway (bet. 98th & 99th Sts.), 212-865-7333
217 W. 85th St. (bet. Amsterdam Ave. & B'way), 212-874-0770
762 Eighth Ave. (bet. 46th & 47th Sts.), 212-730-1860
430 Third Ave. (30th St.), 212-532-1887
■ "Loud, lively and likable", these four amigos may "look like dives" but whip up "cheap", "surprisingly good Mexican" grub that results in "long waits for tables"; impatient types opt for "extra-speedy takeout."

La Corniche ●S – | – | – | M
156 E. 64th St. (bet. Lexington & 3rd Aves.), 212-421-7899
Moroccan brothers Kalilil and Said Hraiche have opened this elegant Mediterranean in an airy Upper East Side townhouse with a sleek upstairs bar; the moderately priced menu features seafood and, naturally, tagines and other couscous dishes; if the economy keeps heading south, you can spend your vacation here instead of Marrakech.

LA CÔTE BASQUE S 26 | 26 | 26 | $74
60 W. 55th St. (bet. 5th & 6th Aves.), 212-688-6525
■ An "age-old favorite that never ages", this "perennial" French Midtown "star" still "twinkles" thanks to Jean-Jacques Rachou's "heavenly" creations, service that's "formal and friendly at the same time" and a "glamorous" setting highlighted by murals of the Basque coast; be prepared for "upper-crusty" tabs (prix fixe $36 lunch, $68 dinner), but then again it will save you the "bother of going to France."

L'Actuel ●S 19 | 18 | 18 | $49
145 E. 50th St. (bet. Lexington & 3rd Aves.), 212-583-0001
◪ "As up to date as its name", this "spiffy" brasserie "fills a void" in Turtle Bay's dining "purgatory" by providing "pricey", "pretty food" to "pretty people"; wafflers say its "modern design doesn't feel French."

Lady Mendl's S 22 | 26 | 21 | $36
The Inn at Irving Place, 56 Irving Pl. (bet. 17th & 18th Sts.), 212-533-4466
■ Imagine you're "Edith Wharton" and "wear a hat" at this "daintily elegant" "Victorian" Gramercy tearoom where you can nibble "crumpets" with the "ladies who lunch" or host a "bridal shower";

| F | D | S | C |

though some tea-party poopers protest "overpricing", most counter "worth every penny" – Indian heads, we suppose.

La Flor Bakery & Cafe (Queens) S ⊄ | – | – | – | I |
53-02 Roosevelt Ave. (bet. 53rd St. & 43rd Ave.), 718-426-8023
Bargain-hunting Woodsiders flock to this cheery corner Mexican all day for everything from tacos and takeout to Mediterranean-influenced appetizers and entrees; the *muy rica* selection of sweets is baked on premises by chef Viko Ortega.

La Giara S | 19 | 17 | 20 | $34 |
501 Third Ave. (bet. 33rd & 34th Sts.), 212-726-9855
■ The moderately priced "creative fare" and "ultra-attentive service" at this Murray Hill Italian please patrons who call it their "favorite neighborhood place"; dissenters deem it "one of the best in the area, which isn't saying much."

La Gioconda | ▽ 21 | 16 | 20 | $36 |
226 E. 53rd St. (bet. 2nd & 3rd Aves.), 212-371-3536
■ Its "carefully prepared menu", casual "exposed-brick setting" and "lite prices" make this "tiny" East Midtown Italian a "terrific neighborhood" option; ok, it's a "tight squeeze", but gracious service makes it bearable.

La Goulue ●S | 20 | 20 | 18 | $53 |
746 Madison Ave. (bet. 64th & 65th Sts.), 212-988-8169
■ "Air kissing should be on the menu" of this "chichi", wood-paneled East Side bistro, patronized by a mix of "Park Avenue" ladies and "smoking" "Euros"; expect "rude attitude" and high prices – and, unless you're Anne Bass, expect to sit in Siberia."

LA GRENOUILLE ● | 27 | 28 | 27 | VE |
3 E. 52nd St. (bet. 5th & Madison Aves.), 212-752-1495
■ "A perennial favorite", this dressy East Side French "classic", run by the Masson family, combines "elegance" and "glamour" with "great food and service"; many consider it "NY's most beautiful restaurant" given its "breathtaking flowers" and "*magnifique*" atelier private room; for an affordable intro, try the $45 prix fixe lunch and sit with Henry Kissinger; for dinner, you have the choice of wearing your jewels or pawning them.

La Grolla Café S | 20 | 14 | 18 | $42 |
411-A Amsterdam Ave. (bet. 79th & 80th Sts.), 212-579-9200

La Grolla, Ristorante S
413 Amsterdam Ave. (bet. 79th & 80th Sts.), 212-496-0890
■ The "unique" cooking of Northern Italy's Val d'Aosta region is showcased at this West Side "pleasure" that's a "giant leap" forward for the area, even if the decor could stand a "feng shui expert"; those who find it too "hectic" head for the adjacent, "better value" cafe.

La Houppa ●S | 18 | 18 | 18 | $46 |
26 E. 64th St. (bet. 5th & Madison Aves.), 212-317-1999
■ "Uncrowded" yet "groovy", this East Side Med-Italian turns out "fast pizzas" and an "eclectic range" of dishes that run on the "expensive" side; its right-"off-Madison" address provides swell "sidewalk" dining "after Barneys" without all the Avenue "traffic."

La Lanterna di Vittorio ●S | ▽ 18 | 21 | 16 | $19 |
129 MacDougal St. (bet. W. 3rd & W. 4th Sts.), 212-529-5945
■ "Warm, fuzzy" types swear this "cozy" Village coffeehouse is the "best place to wrap up a date when you mean business", while those through with love say it works equally well for affordable desserts by the fireplace; but beyond that, the "food's forgettable."

				F	D	S	C

La Locanda dei Vini ●S ▽ 20 | 16 | 20 | $37
737 Ninth Ave. (bet. 49th & 50th Sts.), 212-258-2900
■ Those looking for a "real Italian experience" seek out this "unpretentious" Ninth Avenue "storefront" that offers "enough interesting dishes to differentiate it from competitors" in the "blossoming" Clinton area; although "cramped", "concerned service" and fair prices mean it's more than "worth a detour."

La Lunchonette S 21 | 15 | 19 | $39
130 10th Ave. (18th St.), 212-675-0342
■ Despite its "bistro-meets-greasy-spoon" moniker, this "funky French" bistro serves "excellent", relatively "inexpensive" food that goes down easy "after Chelsea gallery gawking"; it's no longer a "pioneer" now that this "once forgotten" neighborhood has turned "hip."

La Mangeoire S 20 | 20 | 20 | $44
1008 Second Ave. (bet. 53rd & 54th Sts.), 212-759-7086
■ "Wonderful Provençal food" fills out the menu of this "solid" Midtown bistro that's pleasantly "old-style" (i.e. "you're not hungry when you leave"); a "reasonable prix fixe" and "rustic" "French country" decor lead many to say it's "underrated."

La Méditerranée S 19 | 17 | 20 | $41
947 Second Ave. (bet. 50th & 51st Sts.), 212-755-4155
■ This "low-key" "neighborhood secret" is something of a "time warp" that caters to "mostly seniors" who enthuse about its "extensive menu" of satisfying French bistro classics; while "warm service" and "good values" are pleasing, the nightly pianist "makes it even better."

La Mela S 19 | 12 | 17 | $34
167 Mulberry St. (bet. Broome & Grand Sts.), 212-431-9493
❏ "Little Italy meets *Animal House*" at this "rowdy", "off-the-wall" Italian where there's "no menu", meaning the "crazy waiters" will "just keep bringing you food" till you "explode"; though some revelers might find it "funny", it's not for "picky eaters", aesthetes ("do-it-yourself decor") or native NYers ("they treat everyone like tourists").

La Metairie S 21 | 19 | 20 | $50
189 W. 10th St. (W. 4th St.), 212-989-0343
■ "Utterly charming", this French West Villager is "reminiscent of a Provençal inn" to many thanks to its *magnifique plats du jour* and "outrageous wine list"; if it's a "bit snug" and verging on "overpriced", no one minds much considering that they treat you like a "long-lost friend."

La Mirabelle S 22 | 19 | 23 | $46
102 W. 86th St. (bet. Amsterdam & Columbus Aves.), 212-496-0458
■ "You're part of the family" at this "pleasant" "plum" of an Upper West Side bistro offering "Classic French fare" in a theatrically "old-fashioned" setting that fawning fans say is "like Sunday dinner at mom's – without the aggravation"; the less-enthralled shrug "dependable if not brilliant."

Lan ●S 23 | 18 | 19 | $34
56 Third Ave. (bet. 10th & 11th Sts.), 212-254-1959
■ The "sushi rolls are out-lan-dish" (ditto the "awesome shabu-shabu") at this East Village "do-it-all Japanese" where the portions and the prices are equally diminutive; it's naturally "getting more crowded" now that the "word's out", so reservations are essential unless you relish "long waits."

	F	D	S	C

Landmark Tavern S | 16 | 18 | 17 | $34
626 11th Ave. (46th St.), 212-757-8595
■ "It's all about the history" at this circa 1868 Way West Midtown tavern where fans warm themselves in front of the fire or with the "wide variety" of single-malt scotches; the "hearty" Irish-English chow may be just "average", but the "free soda bread" is a "gift from the gods."

L'Annam ●S | 20 | 14 | 17 | $21
393 Third Ave. (28th St.), 212-686-5168
■ Gramercy Parkers suffering from "Chinese takeout burnout" check out this "winning" Vietnamese "neighborhood staple" that dispenses "enormous portions" of "yummy" eats at super-"cheap" tabs.

La Nonna S | 19 | 19 | 18 | $44
133 W. 13th St. (bet. 6th & 7th Aves.), 212-741-3663
◪ Florence alights in the West Village at this "unsung" "sleeper" with a "terrific" Tuscan menu that tastes even better in the "pleasant" covered garden; nonfans cite "erratic" service.

Lansky Lounge & Grill S | 18 | 20 | 17 | $37
104 Norfolk St. (bet. Delancey & Rivington Sts.), 212-677-9489
■ They just "put up a sign", but you still feel "like a gangster or street urchin" slipping in through the "back-alley entrance" of this moderately tabbed Lower East Side surf 'n' turfer, which once housed a speakeasy and recently expanded by annexing most of the "old Ratners" space; night owls hoot it's a "better bar than grill."

Lanza Restaurant S | 17 | 14 | 17 | $31
168 First Ave. (bet. 10th & 11th Sts.), 212-674-7014
■ "You can't go wrong with the basics" at this "red-sauce" East Village Italian featuring "old-school" cooking at "il cheapo" prices and a "quiet" garden to boot; on the scene since 1904, it's "holding up well."

La Paella ●S | 21 | 18 | 18 | $31
214 E. Ninth St. (bet. 2nd & 3rd Aves.), 212-598-4321
◪ "There's something sexy" about this "dimly lit" East Village Spaniard where a "noisy young crowd" gobbles up tasty tapas and pleasing paella chock-full of seafood; after enough of the "unbelievable sangria", you'll hardly notice the "squeeze" or "spotty service."

La Palapa Cocina Mexicana ●S | ▽ 23 | 20 | 21 | $35
77 St. Marks Pl. (bet. 1st & 2nd Aves.), 212-777-2537
■ For "real deal" Mexican fare, you can't do much better than this "bustling" new East Village taqueria with a "sophisticated", "ambitious menu", "friendly staff" and "flatteringly lit" digs adorned with pre-Columbian pottery; besides having plenty of "potential", it's a bargain.

La Petite Auberge S | 20 | 17 | 20 | $43
116 Lexington Ave. (bet. 27th & 28th Sts.), 212-689-5003
■ "Every neighborhood should have a French bistro" like this "low-key" Gramercy veteran that draws "older" types with "reliable" classics like frogs' legs and "ooh-la-la soufflés"; though a "face-lift" may be in order, its "gracious" service is a sufficient distraction.

La Pizza Fresca Ristorante S | 21 | 16 | 16 | $30
31 E. 20th St. (bet. B'way & Park Ave. S.), 212-598-0141
■ "Authentic" Neapolitan brick-oven pizza topped with San Marzano tomatoes and "great buffalo mozzarella" is the must-try item at this rustic Flatiron Italian; nifty salads, "decent" pastas and an "ambitious" wine list make up the supporting cast.

		F	D	S	C

L'Ardoise
18 | 12 | 18 | $37

1207 First Ave. (bet. 65th & 66th Sts.), 212-744-4752

■ "Tiny" East Side French bistro purveying a "limited menu" of "solid" dishes at penny-pinchin' prices; despite "no ambiance", the "hyper", "omnipresent owner" adds color to the proceedings.

La Ripaille ●S
20 | 17 | 18 | $45

605 Hudson St. (bet. Bethune & W. 12th Sts.), 212-255-4406

■ "As comfortable as your favorite slippers", this "dark" West Village "quintessential bistro" reeks of "old-world charm" and its "courteous" staff serves "better than expected" Gallic grub; chatterboxes say "if you want to talk, it's always quiet."

La Rivista ●
19 | 17 | 19 | $46

313 W. 46th St. (bet. 8th & 9th Aves.), 212-245-1707

■ Broadway babies "running late" for the theater nip into this "convenient" Restaurant Row Italian not just for its "better-than-average" food and "prompt" service – the bonus "discount voucher for the parking lot" also comes in handy.

La Taza de Oro ●≠
19 | 7 | 15 | $15

96 Eighth Ave. (bet. 14th & 15th Sts.), 212-243-9946

■ You can "beef up your Spanish" at this "scruffy" Chelsea Puerto Rican where the "ultra-cheap" chow comes accompanied by extra-"strong" cups of Joe; just "don't be scared off" by the "divey" digs – thousands of "taxi drivers can't be wrong."

La Tour S
18 | 17 | 18 | $40

1319 Third Ave. (bet. 75th & 76th Sts.), 212-472-7578

■ "Now available every day", the "fantastic" $15 all-you-can-eat mussels-and-frites deal at this Upper East Side French bistro is the hands-down favorite; living up to its Gallic aspirations, it's "frequented by many French" people – "even the smoke is authentic."

Lattanzi ●
22 | 19 | 21 | $48

361 W. 46th St. (bet. 8th & 9th Aves.), 212-315-0980

■ Still "one of the best in the Theater District", this "classy" Restaurant Row Italian, run by the family of the same name, impresses with "efficient service", a "picturesque garden" and an "excellent" Roman-influenced menu; the "fabulous fried artichokes" regularly bring down the house.

Lavagna S
23 | 17 | 19 | $34

545 E. Fifth St. (bet. Aves. A & B), 212-979-1005

■ A "great find that too many people have found", this "intimate" Alphabet City Mediterranean gets "crowded for good reason": a frequently "changing menu" offering lots of "intriguing flavors"; better yet, "bargain prices" rule the day here.

Layla S
19 | 21 | 19 | $48

211 W. Broadway (Franklin St.), 212-431-0700

■ "Glitz and shimmer" are the watchwords at this "over-the-top" TriBeCa Med-Mideastern from Drew Nieporent and Robert De Niro, where you can "channel Marrakech" while feasting on "unique", flavorful fare in colorful surroundings; still, some say it "lays la egg" and find the "pricey" "food secondary to the belly dancer."

Le Beaujolais S
19 | 14 | 19 | $39

364 W. 46th St. (bet. 8th & 9th Aves.), 212-974-7464

■ "Plenty of choices" on the "reasonable" prix fixe menu lure "Wednesday matinee"-goers to this "small" Theater District French bistro; in spite of the name, "you don't come here for the wine."

| F | D | S | C |

LE BERNARDIN
| 28 | 27 | 27 | $84 |

155 W. 51st St. (bet. 6th & 7th Aves.), 212-489-1515

■ "Superlatives do not suffice" to describe Maguy LeCoze's French "seafood extravaganza", yet "hooked" fans try anyway, lauding chef Eric Ripert's "flawless" food, a "sumptuous" setting offering that "most precious NY commodity – space" – and service that's "attentive but non-intrusive" (voted No. 1 in this *Survey*); granted, pricing is equally "extravagant" but worth it for the "*ne plus ultra*" of fine "dining from start to finish" (prix fixe only: $45 lunch, $77 dinner).

Le Bilboquet S
| 21 | 17 | 16 | $49 |

25 E. 63rd St. (bet. Madison & Park Aves.), 212-751-3036

☏ "Double kisses" "for the owner" may land you a table at this "trendy" East Side French mini-bistro, but usually the rule here is "beauty before reservations"; though the food's fine, the scene is its raison d'être.

Le Boeuf à la Mode S
| 22 | 20 | 22 | $50 |

539 E. 81st St. (bet. East End & York Aves.), 212-249-1473

■ An "old friend" "after all these years", this Upper East Side French bistro welcomes its "quiet", "middle-aged crowd" with "attentive service", "delicious" cooking and a "great prix fixe"; an "off-the-beaten-track" address supplies some "secret-location" frisson.

Le Charlot ●S
| 19 | 16 | 16 | $48 |

19 E. 69th St. (bet. Madison & Park Aves.), 212-794-1628

☏ It's "quite the scene" at this "crowded" East Side bistro that's a hazy mix of "smoke, wine, Euros and good food" at rather "*cher*" prices; you'll be "treated like royalty" "if you're a regular", but if irregular, the staff can be "a bit snippy."

LE CIRQUE 2000 S
| 26 | 27 | 26 | $82 |

NY Palace Hotel, 455 Madison Ave. (bet. 50th & 51st Sts.), 212-303-7788

■ "In a class by itself", "over the top in every way" and a "Manhattan happening" – all apply to ringmaster Sirio Maccioni's Midtown French "landmark"; it's a "high-wire act" that balances a kitchen "at the top of its game" with a "clairvoyant" staff and enough colorful "circus wonderland" decor to create "sensory overload"; despite the presence of tourists on the scene, this is still the place for NYers to flash "their Harry Winston jewels" and "impress" the hell out of someone.

L'Ecole
| 24 | 19 | 22 | $42 |

French Culinary Institute, 462 Broadway (Grand St.), 212-219-3300

■ Graduate to dining cum laude at this SoHo FCI cooking school where promising pupils prepare pantastic food at "giveaway prices" ($29.95 five-course tasting menu); delighted "guinea pigs" declare "these students can practice on me anytime."

Le Colonial S
| 22 | 23 | 20 | $50 |

149 E. 57th St. (bet. Lexington & 3rd Aves.), 212-752-0808

■ "Loaded with tropical atmosphere", this East Side Vietnamese makes you feel like you're "eating in pre-war Saigon" and is "so sexy you'll crave a cigarette" afterward; besides a "hip bar upstairs", there's a "comfortable" dining room below that offers "clean and pure tasting" "aromatic dishes" – especially those "divine" spring rolls.

Le Gamin ●S
| 18 | 16 | 12 | $21 |

183 Ninth Ave. (21st St.), 212-243-8864
27 Bedford St. (Downing St.), 212-243-2846
50 MacDougal St. (bet. Houston & Prince Sts.), 212-254-4678
536 E. Fifth St. (bet. Aves. A & B), 212-254-8409

☏ When "crêpe cravings" erupt, try these French cafes where the style is "Left Bank" and the mood is wired (thanks to the "rocket-fuel

| F | D | S | C |

café au lait"); though it seems "you can sit forever" waiting for service, it eventually "comes with a cute accent."

Le Garrick S | 19 | 17 | 18 | $42
Mayfair Hotel, 242 W. 49th St. (bet. B'way & 8th Ave.), 212-489-8600

■ "One of the delights of the Theater District", this "reliable" hotel dining room serves "comfortingly old-fashioned" French fare in a "clubby", "am-I-in-London?" setting – however, when it gets "crowded", the "staff needs some prompting."

Le Gigot S | 23 | 19 | 21 | $44
18 Cornelia St. (bet. Bleecker & W. 4th Sts.), 212-627-3737

■ "Play kneesies with someone you love" at this "atmospheric" West Village bistro that's "big in every way except size", from its "delicious" French cuisine to the "exceptionally friendly staff"; fans say the "Village was invented" for this kind of place.

Le Jardin Bistro S | 21 | 20 | 19 | $39
25 Cleveland Pl. (bet. Kenmare & Spring Sts.), 212-343-9599

■ In cool weather, this SoHo French bistro evokes "lace-curtain Paris", while in warmer months the action moves to its "transporting garden" "roofed with so many grapevines" that it's "practically a vineyard"; year-round, there's "pleasant", "reliable" fare to be had at modest prices.

Le Madeleine S | 20 | 19 | 19 | $41
403 W. 43rd St. (bet. 9th & 10th Aves.), 212-246-2993

■ For a "lovely overture to a theater evening", drop by this veteran Hell's Kitchen French bistro offering "consistent" cooking and an "inviting" indoor garden; "hardly Proustian" pre-curtain (try "hectic" and "noisy"), it's more of an "oasis" after ticket-holders head out.

Le Madri S | 22 | 21 | 21 | $54
168 W. 18th St. (bet. 6th & 7th Aves.), 212-727-8022

■ Longtime followers of restaurateur Pino Luongo cheer "keep it up", knowing they'll always "eat well" at this "festive" Chelsea Tuscan, whether in the handsome dining room or on the cute deck out back; expect cooking with "flair", but at a high enough cost that some only "go on payday."

Le Marais S | 21 | 16 | 17 | $45
150 W. 46th St. (bet. 6th & 7th Aves.), 212-869-0900 ●
15 John St. (bet. B'way & Nassau St.), 212-285-8585

■ "All are welcome" at this "convivial" kosher French steakhouse in the Theater District, but "religious people" worship this "savior", since the meat is the "primest of prime"; expect "canned, faux-bistro decor" and some "jostling" during prime times; N.B. the Downtown branch serves American fare.

Lemon, The ● | 14 | 16 | 13 | $34
230 Park Ave. S. (bet. 18th & 19th Sts.), 212-614-1200

■ When it comes to "martinis and a date" with a liberal garnish of "people-watching", this "sexy", high-ceilinged Union Square American turns the trick, but the "drinks are better than the food", and service runs the gamut from "inattentive" to "sloppy."

Le Monde ●S | 17 | 17 | 14 | $28
2885 Broadway (bet. 112th & 113th Sts.), 212-531-3939

■ "Captive audience" Columbia students are divided on this good-looking French brasserie: fans claim it brings "quality cooking" to Morningside Heights, but foes find it a "charming envelope with nothing inside", except "poor service" that's particularly galling.

F	D	S	C

Lemongrass Grill S
17 | 13 | 15 | $23

2534 Broadway (bet. 94th & 95th Sts.), 212-666-0888 ●
138 E. 34th St. (bet. Lexington & 3rd Aves.), 212-213-3317
80 University Pl. (11th St.), 212-604-9870
37 Barrow St. (7th Ave. S.), 212-242-0606
53 Ave. A (4th St.), 212-674-3538 ●
110 Liberty St. (Church St.), 212-962-1370
61A Seventh Ave. (bet. Berkeley & Lincoln Pls.), Brooklyn, 718-399-7100

■ This "handy", "populist" Thai chain "does the job" for "cheap, tasty" eats – "and nothing more"; despite a "stay-as-long-as-you-wish attitude", "awful lighting" and "lackluster" service lead many to opt for takeout.

Lenox S
21 | 21 | 20 | $54

1278 Third Ave. (bet. 73rd & 74th Sts.), 212-772-0404

■ "The magic continues" at this "civilized" East Side New American (fka The Lenox Room) that's "fresh from a renovation", oozing even more svelte East 70s "sophistication"; though amateur psychologists say it's "without identity", diehards dub it a "solid classic" and credit "charming" owner Tony Fortuna, who makes sure all "works well" here.

Lentini ●S
▽ 21 | 20 | 19 | $51

1562 Second Ave. (81st St.), 212-628-3131

■ Giuseppe Lentini (ex Elio's) has moved a few blocks south on the Upper East Side to unveil this "promising" new Italian; though they're "still working out the kinks", early reports tell of a "pretty" setting, "quite good" cooking and "expensive" tabs.

L'Entrecote
19 | 16 | 20 | $46

1057 First Ave. (bet. 57th & 58th Sts.), 212-755-0080

■ There's "lots of charm" (if not lots of space) at this "cozy" Sutton Place "so-French" bistro known for its namesake steak; though "smoking is permitted" and it's had the "same menu for 30 years", loyalists insist "every neighborhood should have one."

Leopard, The
21 | 22 | 23 | $60

253 E. 50th St. (bet. 2nd & 3rd Aves.), 212-759-3735

■ "Nothing beats" the "unlimited wine" $55 dinner prix fixe and private party rooms at this East Midtown French-Continental that's also lauded for its "townhouse" setting and "secluded, quiet" air; critics label both the menu and decor "faded", and even some fans admit it's "coasting – but from a very great height."

Le Pain Quotidien S≠
20 | 17 | 15 | $22

1131 Madison Ave. (bet. 84th & 85th Sts.), 212-327-4900
1336 First Ave. (bet. 71st & 72nd Sts.), 212-717-4800
833 Lexington Ave. (bet. 63rd & 64th Sts.), 212-755-5810
50 W. 72nd St. (bet. Central Park W. & Columbus Ave.), 212-712-9700
ABC Carpet & Home, 38 E. 19th St. (bet. B'way & Park Ave. S.), 212-673-7900
100 Grand St. (bet. Greene & Mercer Sts.), 212-625-9009

■ "Quintessential" Belgian bakery/cafe chain that draws "beautiful people with fat wallets" and a yen for "unbelievable bread and pastries"; lonely hearts say their "brilliant" "community tables" are "like having a meal at a Hamptons summer share."

Le Père Pinard ●S
▽ 20 | 18 | 18 | $31

175 Ludlow St. (Houston St.), 212-777-4917

■ Say *au revoir* to NY and *bonjour* to France at this "cute" "Country French" bistro brimming with "young" Lower Eastsiders; everything's "authentic" here, including the "hearty, traditional" fare, "well-rounded wine list", "cramped", "smoky, noisy", "shabby-chic" interior and "erratic service."

		F	D	S	C

Le Perigord S
25 | 23 | 25 | $69

405 E. 52nd St. (bet. FDR Dr. & 1st Ave.), 212-755-6244
■ "Consistently" "marvelous" French cuisine, "legendary hospitality" and loads of "elegant", "old-world charm" are the keys to the longevity of this Sutton Place "grande dame" that's guaranteed to "make you feel special"; evidence of its continuing vitality – including the arrival of "excellent new chef" Jacque Qualin and the addition of a private dining room – leaves the "AARP crowd" crowing; dinner is $62 prix fixe.

Le Pescadou ●S
20 | 16 | 18 | $45

18 King St. (6th Ave.), 212-924-3434
☐ "You'll feel like family" (thanks to "congenial" host-owner Chuck) at this French seafooder serving "delish fish" in a bistro-style setting complete with "great outdoor seating" perfect for taking in the "lively" SoHo scene; penny-pinchers warn "Le Pesca-don't."

Le Petit Hulot S
18 | 17 | 18 | $43

973 Lexington Ave. (bet. 70th & 71st Sts.), 212-794-9800
■ A "nice place to linger" for an "après Frick" meal, this "cozy" East Side French bistro offers a $26 prix fixe "treat"; if its "charming" space "needs a little paint", there's always the "gorgeous" back garden.

Le Refuge S
23 | 21 | 21 | $52

166 E. 82nd St. (bet. Lexington & 3rd Aves.), 212-861-4505
■ "The name says it all" at this "calming", "quiet" East Side bistro "loaded with charm" that dishes out "delightful" "French country-style" meals perfect after hitting the Met; though prix fixe deals help "make it more affordable", otherwise it's pretty "expensive."

Le Refuge Inn (Bronx) S
▽ 23 | 24 | 24 | $51

Le Refuge Inn, 620 City Island Ave. (Sutherland St.), 718-885-2478
■ A "haven from the kitsch of City Island", this morsel of "Provence in the Bronx" specializes in French "culinary escapes" that can be extended into "romantic" "getaways" by "including a sleepover" in one of the upstairs bedrooms.

Le Rivage S
20 | 16 | 20 | $41

340 W. 46th St. (bet. 8th & 9th Aves.), 212-765-7374
☐ Considered "a cut above" many on Restaurant Row, this French "standby" provides one of the "best buys" in the area with its four-course prix fixe dinner for under $26; while critics complain that the fare is "pedestrian", theatergoers give thanks for the speedy staff that "gets you to the show on time."

Les Deux Gamins ●S
19 | 16 | 13 | $28

170 Waverly Pl. (Grove St.), 212-807-7357
☐ Complete with the "tight quarters" and "smoky" ambiance of its "Left Bank" counterparts, this "authentic" French bistro in the West Village cooks up "transportingly" tasty classics at "very reasonable" cost; if the service is "non-caring", at least it's "like being ignored in France."

Les Halles ●S
21 | 16 | 17 | $44

411 Park Ave. S. (bet. 28th & 29th Sts.), 212-679-4111
■ "If you need a beef fix" or a "cheap vacation to Paris", this "rowdy" French bistro/butcher shop fills the bill, though given its "deafening" frites; never at a loss for customers, this "carnivore's delight" is more "packed" than ever after the release of chef Anthony Bourdain's tell-all tome, *Kitchen Confidential.*

Leshko's ●S
16 | 17 | 15 | $25

111 Ave. A (7th St.), 212-777-2111
☐ "Mike Brady meets George Jetson" at this "fab", "retro-futuristic" New American in an East Village "reinvented coffee shop" sporting a

F	D	S	C

"gay-friendly" vibe and a "hip" clientele; while "trendy" types tag it an affordable "winner", others say they "preferred the old dive to this yupscale version."

Le Singe Vert ●S   18 | 17 | 17 | $35
160 Seventh Ave. (bet. 19th & 20th Sts.), 212-366-4100
■ With all the hallmarks of a "Parisian street cafe" – air thick with "cigarette smoke and French accents", a "cramped", "hustle-and-bustle" feel and "hearty, flavorful" food – this French bistro in Chelsea has the added allure of "super" live jazz; its service seems to be improving too.

Le Souk ●S   ∇ 19 | 21 | 17 | $32
47 Ave. B (bet. 3rd & 4th Sts.), 212-777-5454
☒ "Belly dancers, hookahs" wafting "scented tobacco", "cool", souk-inspired decor and a "hip" young crowd make this Alphabet City North African newcomer "fun and festive"; add tasty tagines, a "family-like staff" and "good value", and you'll understand why surveyors say "it's worth the schlep."

LESPINASSE   27 | 28 | 27 | $90
St. Regis Hotel, 2 E. 55th St. (bet. 5th & Madison Aves.), 212-339-6719
■ "Well near perfect" "in every regard", this "magnificent" Midtown French "treat for the senses" provides "elegance and grandeur like no place else", from the "gilded" Louis XV dining room out of the "good old days of real luxury", to "top-of-his-game" chef Christian Delouvrier's "sublime" cuisine, to the "discreet", "cosseting" formal service; but just "be prepared" to "mortgage the house" because naturally such "memorable experiences" don't come cheap; N.B. dinner only.

Les Routiers S   20 | 16 | 19 | $43
568 Amsterdam Ave. (bet. 87th & 88th Sts.), 212-874-2742
■ "It's ours" declare locals wary of "letting the secret out" about this "Westside gem" of a French bistro; given the "delicious", "good-value" fare, "warm" service and "homey" atmosphere (the "nicest truck stop in NY"), it's no wonder the neighbors are possessive.

Le Tableau S   23 | 17 | 20 | $36
511 E. Fifth St. (bet. Aves. A & B), 212-260-1333
■ If you "can't hear the person across from you" at this "tiny", "impossibly noisy" East Village French bistro, that's all the better for "paying attention to the exquisite food in front of you"; while it's a "tight squeeze at prime time", "great prices" and a "charming" staff take the edge off.

Letizia Amore Restaurant S   – | – | – | M
1374 First Ave. (bet. 73rd & 74th Sts.), 212-517-2244
For a cozy, traditional Italian meal replete with Sinatra, Marilyn and Kennedy photos, you could do worse than consider this new Eastsider; the pastas and other standards are joined by less typical game dishes like pheasant and rabbit.

Levana S   21 | 18 | 20 | $51
141 W. 69th St. (bet. B'way & Columbus Aves.), 212-877-8457
☒ "Who said [glatt] kosher can't be sophisticated?" marvel admirers of this "upscale" French–New American Westsider providing "outstanding", "beautifully presented" "gourmet" cuisine including prime steaks; most consider it among the "classiest" in its category, but a few grumble about "expensive" prices and "drab" decor.

Le Veau d'Or   18 | 14 | 18 | $47
129 E. 60th St. (bet. Lexington & Park Aves.), 212-838-8133
☒ A "Left Bank" throwback from the '30s, this French bistro near Bloomie's still has its loyalists, some of whom have "eaten here for 50

years"; the less "nostalgic" suggest it "needs to revamp", warning "trips down memory lane" here lead to "disappointment."

Lexi's [S] – | – | – | I

90 W. Third St. (bet. Sullivan & Thompson Sts.), 212-674-2547

NYU students have a new option for dirt-cheap Mexican eats in this diminutive Village newcomer; while its decor is decidedly hole-in-the-wall, its fiesta colors are cheerful, the staff's friendly and the guacamole's homemade.

L'Express [S] 18 | 16 | 15 | $27

249 Park Ave. S. (20th St.), 212-254-5858

◪ "More authentic than the usual faux brasserie", this 24/7 Flatiron French bistro is still "really hopping at 4 AM" with a "noisy", "young" crowd that squeezes in for "decent" eats; passengers disgruntled with the "inconsistent service" quip "take the local" instead.

Le Zie 2000 ◐[S]⊄ 22 | 16 | 20 | $35

172 Seventh Ave. (bet. 20th & 21st Sts.), 212-206-8686

■ Chelseans craving a dose of "auntie's cooking" with a "touch of Venice" tout this "unassuming" Northern Italian, now slightly larger than a "gondola" following an expansion; its "tasty, fresh, no-nonsense" classics, "warm" service and "inexpensive" tabs ensure a loyal following.

Le Zinc ◐[S] 20 | 18 | 20 | $40

139 Duane St. (bet. Church St. & W. B'way), 212-513-0001

◪ Chanterelle's new "casual" cousin has "hit the ground running" in TriBeCa with a roster of "superior" French "bistro comfort food" and a mostly "on-top-of-it" staff; though critics complain that it's "too loud" and "spare" ("great gallery posters" notwithstanding), it has been "a scene" from the get-go, particularly at the "beautiful" zinc bar that often stays "crowded" until the kitchen closes at 4 AM.

Le Zoo [S] 20 | 17 | 18 | $39

314 W. 11th St. (Greenwich St.), 212-620-0393

◪ "Always packed" and for good reason, this "tiny gem" of a West Village date place offers "tasty", "affordable" French bistro food and usually "pleasing" service from a "handsome" staff; however, popularity, tight space and a no-reservations policy produce "crowding" and "high decibel levels", especially on weekends.

Lili's Noodle Shop & Grill [S] 18 | 15 | 16 | $22

1500 Third Ave. (bet. 84th & 85th Sts.), 212-639-1313
102 North End Ave. (bet. Murray & Vesey Sts.), 212-786-1300

■ "Fun for a fast bite", this Upper East Side Chinese and its new Downtown sibling ladle out "wide choices" of "belly-filling soups" that amount to "bargains in a bowl"; given the "bright, cheerful" decor, slurpers say it's a "notch above" the typical noodle house.

Limoncello [S] 21 | 19 | 20 | $48

Michelangelo Hotel, 777 Seventh Ave. (51st St.), 212-582-7932

■ "Lots of businesspeople" "escape from the hustle and bustle of Broadway" by lunching at this "relaxing" Theater District Italian, which in the evening becomes a "good option" for pre- or post-show dining; those who wince at the "sky-high" tabs seek out more casual nibbles in the "cellar" Grotto.

Lipstick Cafe 17 | 15 | 16 | $26

Lipstick Bldg., 885 Third Ave. (bet. 53rd & 54th Sts.), 212-486-8664

■ "Workaholics" and other Midtown types "pucker up" for "quick", "light and unpretentious" Eclectic breakfasts and lunches served in the Lipstick Building's "booming" lobby; evening office lingerers wish they'd "open for dinner."

		F	D	S	C

Liquors (Brooklyn) ●S
▽ 20 | 15 | 17 | $31

219 DeKalb Ave. (bet. Adelphi St. & Clermont Ave.), 718-488-7700
■ Since it was once a liquor store, it's no surprise that this "treasure" amidst Fort Greene's "ever-expanding" dining scene mixes delightful drinks to wash down its "creative" International fare; the regulars who fill its "sparse but cozy" interior enthuse it just "gets better and better."

Little Basil S
21 | 15 | 17 | $28

39 Greenwich Ave. (Charles St.), 212-645-8965
■ "Very tasty Thai" classics "with zip" look pretty on the plate at this "cute, little" West Village Holy Basil sibling; if there are a few complaints, the "low prices prevent any indigestion" over "small portions" (think "nouvelle") and undistinguished, "cramped quarters."

Little Havana ●S
▽ 19 | 14 | 16 | $27

30 Cornelia St. (bet. Bleecker & W. 4th Sts.), 212-255-2212
☑ Anything larger than a "big appetite" won't fit into this 19-seat "Village hideaway" where "wonderful" Cuban cooking has locals "lining up in the street"; still, contras call it "too basic to be interesting."

Little Italy Pizza
20 | 8 | 14 | $10

1 E. 43rd St. (bet. 5th & Madison Aves.), 212-687-3660
72 W. 45th St. (bet. 5th & 6th Aves.), 212-730-7575
182A Varick St. (bet. Charlton & King Sts.), 212-366-5566
11 Park Pl. (bet. B'way & Church St.), 212-227-7077
☑ "Authentic, basic slices" – "crust, sauce, cheese and grease" – make for a "cheap", "quick" meal at these decidedly "no-frills" pizzerias around town; they're "a mob scene at lunch", but the "endless lines" move fast thanks to "abrupt" but efficient service.

Lobster Box (Bronx) S
18 | 15 | 16 | $42

34 City Island Ave. (Belden St.), 718-885-1952
☑ "As close to Cape Cod as you get in the Bronx", this City Island stalwart is a "favorite" of "large families" and "tourists" who go as much for the "nice water view" as the "big lobsters" and "so-so" "fried seafood"; critics may crab it's "overpriced" and "living in the past", but its "tremendous popularity" speaks for itself.

Locanda Vini & Olii (Brooklyn) S
▽ 22 | 24 | 21 | $39

129 Gates Ave. (Cambridge Pl.), 718-622-9202
■ Located in a "restored old pharmacy" in Clinton Hill, this newcomer "retains its past decor" while its kitchen (shoehorned behind the druggist's counter) dispenses "unusual" Northern Italian fare; patients cite "stingy portions", but there's an Rx: "order more antipasti."

Lola S
20 | 19 | 18 | $45

30 W. 22nd St. (bet. 5th & 6th Aves.), 212-675-6700
☑ "Always a party", this Flatiron Southern–New American is known for its "crammin', jammin' bar", "jazzy" live music and popular "hand-clappin'" Sunday gospel brunch ("make reservations"); while devotees cheer "fun, fun, fun", the unconverted complain it's "overpriced" and over-"crowded."

Lola's Buena Vista ●S
– | – | – | M

244 E. 79th St. (bet. 2nd & 3rd Aves.), 212-737-7777
By itself on a quiet stretch of East 79th Street, this festive South American boasts semi-exotic cuisine, deep-red walls and guitar music, all of which help transport Eastsiders to warmer Latin climes.

Lombardi's S⊄
24 | 12 | 15 | $21

32 Spring St. (bet. Mott & Mulberry Sts.), 212-941-7994
■ "The best pizzas in Manhattan" (and a "close second" to Brooklyn's Grimaldi's) emerge from this "unassuming", "historic" SoHo Italian's

coal ovens, "crispy-crust" "beauties" that sustain fans through "daunting lines" and "tight quarters"; according to addicts, the trademark clam pie "will take your breath away."

Londel's Supper Club [S] ▽ 19 | 19 | 19 | $40

2620 Frederick Douglass Blvd. (bet. 139th & 140th Sts.), 212-234-6114

■ You can feel owner Londel Davis' "special touch" in the "friendly" atmosphere of his Harlem supper club, where the "Soul Food with sophistication" is "lip-smackingly delicious" and the live "jazz is great"; "reservations are a must" for the popular Sunday buffet brunch, and "if you leave hungry, it's really your fault."

London Lennie's (Queens) [S] 22 | 16 | 18 | $38

63-88 Woodhaven Blvd. (bet. Fleet Ct. & Penelope Ave.), 718-894-8084

■ A "godsend in Queens", this "unpretentious" Rego Park seafooder blessed with a "first-class raw bar" and "splendid" fresh fish reels in finicky fin fans by the boatload; the only "drag" is the "no-reservations policy", which spells "long waits", "especially on weekends."

Long Tan (Brooklyn) ◐ [S] – | – | – | M

196 Fifth Ave. (bet. Berkeley Pl. & Union St.), 718-622-8444

Full-tilt hipness hits Park Slope with this neo-Thai trendster; after satays and curries in the high-concept dining room (think a communal table and wide-open kitchen), chic sorts retire to the adjacent orange-lit bar, red-on-red lounge or petite garden to groove to a DJ's tunes over spicy ginger kamikazes.

L'Orange Bleue ◐ [S] 19 | 19 | 18 | $37

430 Broome St. (Crosby St.), 212-226-4999

■ A "lively SoHo scene" flourishes at this "exciting" French-Moroccan "surprise", where the "Euro"-heavy, French-speaking, Gauloise-smoking crowd likes to "let loose", particularly during "birthday serenades" and on Monday nights "with the belly dancer"; as for the "tasty" food, there's "something for everyone", and an equally "yummy" staff ("ooh-la-la").

Los Dos Molinos ▽ 20 | 14 | 17 | $30

119 E. 18th St. (bet. Irving Pl. & Park Ave. S.), 212-505-1574

■ Those who "like it hot" join the young "Banana Republic crowd" at this "festive" new Gramercy Park outpost of an Arizona chain; since the Southwestern kitchen really "lays on the spice", tender palates "call the fire department" while downing "gallon-size margaritas" to "temper the heat."

Lotfi's Moroccan Restaurant [S] 19 | 16 | 18 | $33

358 W. 46th St. (bet. 8th & 9th Aves.), 212-582-5850

■ "Genuine smiles" greet guests at this "family"-run "Moroccan oasis in the Theater District" that wins kudos for its couscous and other "consistently delectable", inexpensive dishes; still, the "intimate" setting becomes "cramped" when packed with pre-show diners.

Lot 61 ◐ 17 | 21 | 14 | $45

550 W. 21st St. (bet. 10th & 11th Aves.), 212-243-6555

◪ "Pretty young things linger by the bar" of this West Chelsea "hot spot" in a "cool" ex-"industrial" "warehouse", where "skinny" "Prada" types sip "fab martinis" and "poke at" "better-than-expected" (if "overpriced") International nibbles; snobs who spy "too many gold chains" suggest it's "not as hip as it used to be."

Lotus 19 | 22 | 18 | $59

409 W. 14th St. (bet. 9th Ave. & Washington St.), 212-243-4420

■ A "glammed-out", decidedly high-budget "non-Zen environment" awaits the "A-list" types and "wanna-bes" who get past the tough bouncers at this New American "scene" in the Meatpacking District;

sure, the "ok food" is served in "tiny portions" with "attitude galore", but then you're there "for the hype, not the meal."

Loui Loui ●S
16 | 14 | 16 | $34

1311 Third Ave. (75th St.), 212-717-4500
■ "One of the better neighborhood Italians" in the East 70s, this "cozy spot" with sidewalk seating and "reasonable prices" makes a "terrific" choice "for children as well as adults"; as for the "standard" fare, some call it "reliably delicious" and others merely "predictable."

Loulou (Brooklyn) S
▽ 23 | 21 | 23 | $38

222 DeKalb Ave. (bet. Adelphi St. & Clermont Ave.), 718-246-0633
■ Brittany comes to Brooklyn by way of this "great Fort Greene newcomer" whose "rustic", "cozy" interior feels so "very French"; the "honest", "authentic" Gallic coastal cuisine and "delightful" service have early visitors racing to return for more.

Luca S
21 | 16 | 19 | $38

1712 First Ave. (bet. 88th & 89th Sts.), 212-987-9260
■ It takes "lots of Luca to get a table" at this "noisy", jam-packed Upper East Side Northern Italian "neighborhood necessity", though it's easier now that they take reservations; once inside, diners feast on "abundant", first-rate food and are made to "feel at home" by "charming" owner Luca Marcato.

Lucien ●S
19 | 14 | 15 | $36

14 First Ave. (bet. 1st & 2nd Sts.), 212-260-6481
■ "A little slice of Paris" in the East Village, this "happening" Gallic transplant is "authentic" down to the "cramped" seating, "smoky", "convivial" atmosphere and "laid-back" French waiters; the crowning touch is "delicious" bistro fare that fits the "Left Bank" bill to a *oui*.

Lucky Cheng's S
12 | 17 | 16 | $36

24 First Ave. (bet. 1st & 2nd Sts.), 212-473-0516
☒ "It's all about the drag queens" at this East Village Asian-Eclectic "hoot" where "vulgar", "absolutely hilarious" "transvestite" waiters reign over a throng of "birthday and bachelorette parties", "tourists" and "embarrassed coworkers"; there's "nothing lucky" about the edibles, but of course, eating's not the point.

Lucky Strike ●S
16 | 16 | 15 | $31

59 Grand St. (bet. W. B'way & Wooster St.), 212-941-0479
■ "Still lit after all these years", this "reasonably priced" SoHo "classic" French bistro is noteworthy for its "late-night" hours; once trendy, these days it's more a "local" spot, which is fine with regulars who like its "killer" cocktails and "smoke-anywhere policy."

Luke's Bar & Grill ●S∅
17 | 14 | 17 | $26

1394 Third Ave. (bet. 79th & 80th Sts.), 212-249-7070
■ "Great pub grub" makes this East 70s "staple" a "favorite" of the "burger-and-brew" crew, who claim every neighborhood should have a "casual", "comfortable", "kid-friendly" place like it.

L'Ulivo Focacceria ●S∅
– | – | – | M

184 Spring St. (Thompson St.), 212-343-1445
The laid-back ambiance at this SoHo Italian, especially in the sidewalk seating, makes diners feel like they're on the streets of Rome – though neither lira nor credit cards work here; the focaccia, pizza and other no-nonsense dishes come at very affordable prices.

Lumi ●S
19 | 19 | 19 | $49

963 Lexington Ave. (70th St.), 212-570-2335
■ An "enchanting" East 70s townhouse is home to this "quiet", "classy" bi-level Italian, where the "cozy upstairs" room is especially

"charming"; pleasing pastas and other classics served with "European hospitality" endear it to card-carrying "neighborhood folks."

Luna Blu
▽ | 19 | 17 | 20 | $42

246 E. 44th St. (bet. 2nd & 3rd Aves.), 212-681-6541

■ "Doesn't get enough credit" say fans of this "pleasant" Italian "Midtown surprise", with virtues hard to find near Grand Central: "helpful service", tasty food and "pretty decor"; the unconvinced call it "good for what it is, but limited" and "too costly."

Luna Piena S
19 | 17 | 18 | $34

243 E. 53rd St. (bet. 2nd & 3rd Aves.), 212-308-8882

■ "Cheerful" and "no-frills", this Midtown Italian dishes out "hefty portions" of satisfying, "affordable" fare, but it's the "lovely courtyard" garden that makes it a summertime "neighborhood treasure."

Lundy Bros. S
16 | 16 | 15 | $39

Winter Garden Theater, 205 W. 50th St. (bet. B'way & 7th Ave.), 212-586-0022 ◐
1901 Emmons Ave. (Ocean Ave.), Brooklyn, 718-743-0022

■ This "revival" of the '30s Sheepshead Bay seafood landmark capitalizes on the "venerable" Lundy name; "nostalgists" say it's like "the old days", but less sentimental sorts lament "you can't go home again"; time will tell if the new Times Square outpost will make a splash.

Lupa ●S
24 | 19 | 21 | $42

170 Thompson St. (bet. Bleecker & Houston Sts.), 212-982-5089

■ Famously hard to get into ("even when you know someone"), this "bustling", "rustic" Village Italian induces "swoons" with its "mouthwatering" culinary feats; chalk it up as "another triumph" for the Batali-Bastianich-Denton team.

Lusardi's ●S
24 | 19 | 23 | $53

1494 Second Ave. (bet. 77th & 78th Sts.), 212-249-2020

■ Like visiting your "favorite restaurant in Firenze – without the jet lag", this "old faithful" East Side Northern Italian remains "hugely popular" with "sophisticated Italophiles" who never get enough of its "very fine" cuisine, "attentive" service and "calming atmosphere."

LUTÈCE
25 | 24 | 25 | $78

249 E. 50th St. (bet. 2nd & 3rd Aves.), 212-752-2225

■ No one will ever fill the shoes of Andre Soltner, but young French chef David Féau is producing his own "more contemporary" brand of "delicious food" that's "right up there with the best"; thanks to a successful rehab and continuing "excellent service", this "lovely" East Midtown townhouse deserves another try especially for the $38 "best value" lunch; for those diners who lament that "it's not the same as in the old days", think of it as Mantle replacing DiMaggio in center field.

Luxia ●S
18 | 16 | 17 | $39

315 W. 48th St. (bet. 8th & 9th Aves.), 212-957-0800

■ A "pretty little spot", this Theater District Italian-Eclectic "staple" offers a "limited but solid" "comfort food" menu best enjoyed in the "cozy", "quieter" back room or in the "secret" "back garden"; it may keep everyone "friendly."

Luzia's S
19 | 14 | 17 | $31

429 Amsterdam Ave. (bet. 80th & 81st Sts.), 212-595-2000

■ "Luzia herself is in the kitchen" at this "lusty, rustic" West Side "standby" that serves "hearty", "flavorful" Portuguese "home cooking" at "bargain" prices; fans advise forget the decor and go for the "glorious food" (especially the brunch).

		F	D	S	C

Macelleria ●🆂
▽ 20 | 19 | 18 | $45

48 Gansevoort St. (bet. Greenwich & Washington Sts.), 212-741-2555

◪ "Carnivores" convene at this "sleek" Meatpacking District Italian moohouse reminiscent of an old "butcher shop" (complete with "meet market" bar); the bullish ballyhoo its steaks "like butter", but bangers have beefs with "slow" service and call the eats "meaty-ocre."

Madiba (Brooklyn) ●🆂
▽ 19 | 22 | 19 | $32

195 DeKalb Ave. (bet. Adelphi St. & Carlton Ave.), 718-855-9190

■ "Step into another world" at this "memorable" South African eatery on Fort Greene's "new restaurant row", where appealing "shantytown" decor and an "energetic" ambiance are the pleasing backdrop for the menu's "exotic" dishes, each an "epicurean adventure"; a "sexy staff" rounds out this "must" dining experience.

Madison Bistro 🆂
19 | 17 | 19 | $44

238 Madison Ave. (37th St.), 212-447-1919

■ A "bit of Paris" in restaurant-starved Murray Hill, this "friendly" French bistro offers "well-served" "classic dishes" that are "faithful renditions" in every respect but one: "USA-size portions"; there's also a "lively bar scene" that gets "smoky" and "noisy" during happy hour.

Madras Cafe 🆂
▽ 21 | 12 | 16 | $22

79 Second Ave. (bet. 4th & 5th Sts.), 212-254-8002

■ "Go early or late" to this Indian vegetarian "sleeper" in the East Village, because "it's been discovered"; though there may be "no atmosphere" to speak of, its "cheap", "delish" cuisine ensures that even inveterate carnivores "always leave smiling."

Magnolia (Brooklyn) 🆂
▽ 19 | 19 | 20 | $29

486 Sixth Ave. (12th St.), 718-369-4814

■ A "wonderful addition" to Park Slope, this "very pretty", "candlelit" New American already "has found its stride" according to admirers of its "good 'n' plenty" "comfort food"; the "extensive menu" ensures "there's something for everyone."

Mai-Lin 🆂
– | – | – | M

205 E. 75th St. (bet. 2nd & 3rd Aves.), 212-517-7509

Tucked away just off Third Avenue in the space that used to house Orienta, this East 70s French-Vietnamese newcomer has a spare, calming, smallish dining room and a stylish menu boasting dishes like scallop-and-foie-gras tatin and ginger-accented onion soup.

Maison ●🆂
20 | 18 | 19 | $46

1477 Second Ave. (77th St.), 212-879-4824

◪ Life is a cabernet at this Upper East Side Franco-American that boasts an "amazing wine list" as well as "solid French cuisine" – and "they know how to put them together"; area denizens protective of their own little "burst of France" "hope it stays a hidden treasure."

Malaga 🆂
20 | 12 | 18 | $34

406 E. 73rd St. (bet. 1st & York Aves.), 212-737-7659

■ The "dumpy decor" seems like it "hasn't changed in 20 years", but this "friendly" Upper East Side Spaniard feels "like a party" because its "affordable", "tasty" classics and "best-ever sangria" continue to draw lots of "just-out-of-collegers" and other "tight-budget" types.

Malatesta Trattoria ●🆂⊘
21 | 17 | 18 | $29

649 Washington St. (Christopher St.), 212-741-1207

■ Though out-of-the-way, this way West Village Northern Italian is "dependable" and "inexpensive" enough to be worth seeking out; it's also a seriously "romantic" option, especially "when the French doors are open in summer."

| | | F | D | S | C |

Maloney & Porcelli ●S `22` `20` `21` `$56`
37 E. 50th St. (bet. Madison & Park Aves.), 212-750-2233
■ Everything's "gigantic" at this East Side "power" chophouse renowned for its "monster martinis" and "juicy steaks" in "*Flintstones*-esque" portions – with beefy "prices to match"; perhaps it's the "high testosterone levels" at this handsome "he-man joint", but the ambiance is as "crackling" as the "signature" "to-die-for" pork shank.

Mamá Mexico ●S `21` `17` `19` `$28`
2672 Broadway (bet. 101st & 102nd Sts.), 212-864-2323
■ "*Viva*" the "noisy fiesta" at this "big-hearted", always-"packed" West Side "haute Mexican", where "close tables", celebrated "guacamole made tableside" and "enthusiastic" "strolling musicians" (aka "maniacal child mariachis") all add to the *loco*-motion.

Mama's Food Shop ⊄ `22` `9` `12` `$13`
200 E. Third St. (bet. Aves. A & B), 212-777-4425
■ "Dirt-cheap home cookin'" draws "locals" to this Alphabet City "dive", where diners "feel like they're sitting on a porch in the South" as they chow down on "huge portions" of "wholesome" "comfort food" ("try the mac 'n' cheese") in a "self-service", "cafeteria-style" milieu; ardent fans implore mama "adopt me!"

Mamlouk S ▽ `21` `21` `19` `$38`
211 E. Fourth St. (bet. Aves. A & B), 212-529-3477
■ "Make sure you haven't eaten for days" before visiting this "sexy" "mini-Mideast" in Alphabet City, because the "delicious" six-course "chef's pleasure" tasting menu is the only option and it's always "very filling"; "relaxing" "Arabic music" and post-prandial "puffs on the hookah" add to the "transporting experience."

Mandarin Court S `20` `9` `12` `$21`
61 Mott St. (bet. Bayard & Canal Sts.), 212-608-3838
■ Dim sum devotees dive into the "delicious, diverse" selection of "tasty" "tidbits" at this "cheap", "reliable" Chinatown "standby"; it's "busy, loud" and "bland"-looking, with "smileless service", but those in-the-know "ignore the decor" and just "dig in."

Manducatis (Queens) `23` `14` `20` `$40`
13-27 Jackson Ave. (47th Ave.), 718-729-4602
■ "Don't be fooled by the run-down decor", because this moderately priced, "family-run" Long Island City "diamond in the rough" houses a "spectacular wine cellar" and "mouthwatering" red-sauce classics; "there really is an Italian grandma in the kitchen" – and "gifted" Ida Cerbone sure "can cook."

Mangia `20` `13` `13` `$20`
50 W. 57th St. (bet. 5th & 6th Aves.), 212-582-5554
16 E. 48th St. (bet. 5th & Madison Aves.), 212-754-0637
Trump Bldg., 40 Wall St. (bet. Broad & William Sts.), 212-425-4040
◪ These "crowded" Mediterranean "neo-cafeterias" elevate lowly lunch to a new level, thanks to a range of choices that make customers feel "like kids in a candy store"; whether for eat in or take out, they "redefine fast food" for the better, while still keeping it affordable for the average salaried Joe and Jane.

Mangia e Bevi ●S `17` `14` `16` `$30`
800 Ninth Ave. (53rd St.), 212-956-3976
◪ Despite the "so-so" eats at this West Side Italian, even the most curmudgeonly customers "begin to loosen up" "after joining the waiters in yet another round of *That's Amore*"; revelers rave it's "raucous and rewarding", while critics counter "dancing on tables with tambourines" "really isn't that much fun."

| F | D | S | C |

Mangiarini ⓢ ▽ 21 | 15 | 20 | $30
1593 Second Ave. (bet. 82nd & 83rd Sts.), 212-734-5500

■ "Unfortunately", it's "easy to miss" this "tiny", "special" Upper East Side Northern Italian where the "high-quality" cuisine at "real-deal" prices is matched by "very Zen", "minimalist" decor and "lovely service"; locals, insisting it "outstrips" other area trattorias, still want it to be their "neighborhood secret."

Manhattan Bistro ⓢ ▽ 19 | 18 | 17 | $39
129 Spring St. (bet. Greene & Wooster Sts.), 212-966-3459

◪ Steak frites the "*Parisienne*" way are the specialty of this "old-fashioned" French bistro that has managed to remain "low-key" and "not too trendy" despite its SoHo locale; though the blasé may find it "unremarkable", most sum it up in a word: "*bon.*"

Manhattan Chili Co. ⓢ 15 | 13 | 14 | $22
Ed Sullivan Theater, 1697 Broadway (bet 53rd & 54th Sts.), 212-246-6555 ●
1500 Broadway (43rd St.), 212-730-8666

◪ A "smorgasbord of chili options" meets Midtowners at this Southwestern duo slinging "quick, affordable eats" and "potent margaritas"; fans insist it's "hard to beat", but foes say it's "for tourists."

Manhattan Grille ⓢ 22 | 20 | 21 | $55
1161 First Ave. (bet. 63rd & 64th Sts.), 212-888-6556

■ "Meat lovers with class" favor this "old NY–style" chophouse on the far East Side that "caters to" a savvy "neighborhood crowd"; its first-rate steaks, "clubby", "civilized surroundings" and "gracious" staff lead loyalists to conclude it's "well worth" the "pricey" tab.

MANHATTAN OCEAN CLUB ⓢ 25 | 22 | 23 | $62
57 W. 58th St. (bet. 5th & 6th Aves.), 212-371-7777

■ "Caught fish aspire" to land on the "impeccable" menu at this Midtowner that's "as reliable as a Rolex" (and almost as "pricey"); with "beyond compare" seafood that's "as fresh as the last tide", a "refined", modern setting and "pampering" service, this "aptly named" club is definitely worth joining.

Man Ray ⓢ – | – | – | E
147 W. 15th St. (bet. 6th & 7th Aves.), 212-929-5000

A Far East–meets–flea market aesthetic seems a bizarre turn for über club owner Thierry Klemeniuk and his celeb-studded (Malkovich, Depp, Penn) band of backers, yet this vast new Asian-Fusion event in Chelsea has Buddha statuettes sharing space with musty banquettes and geisha-dressed waitresses clashing with American granny fixtures; just be sure to bring your gold card.

Maple Garden Duck House ⓢ ▽ 23 | 15 | 21 | $34
236 E. 53rd St. (bet. 2nd & 3rd Aves.), 212-759-8260

■ "Delectable" Peking duck has folks flocking to this Midtown Chinese where you can duck in when the mood strikes, since you "don't need to order it ahead"; granted, the "bland", "suburban" setting ruffles some feathers, but solid service and "reasonable prices" help smooth them.

Marbella (Queens) ●ⓢ ▽ 19 | 16 | 18 | $40
Ramada Inn, 220-33 Northern Blvd. (bet. 220th & 221st Sts.), 718-423-0100

◪ "Hidden" in a Bayside Ramada Inn, this "cozy" Spaniard flaunts a "stylish menu" and "old-world service"; however, critics of its "plastic decor" and "bland" grub say the only thing celestial is the harp player.

MARCH ⓢ 26 | 25 | 26 | $83
405 E. 58th St. (bet. 1st Ave. & Sutton Pl.), 212-754-6272

■ For "unforgettable splurging", this "flawless" New American in an "elegant" Sutton Place townhouse "marches to a higher culinary beat" thanks to a tasteful revamping and expansion and a $72 tasting menu from chef Wayne Nish; while most agree the meals are "heavenly", "heaven ain't cheap", so bring along an angel with "deep pockets."

Marchi's   20 | 18 | 20 | $49
251 E. 31st St. (bet. 2nd & 3rd Aves.), 212-679-2494
◪ "You make no decisions" at this Kip's Bay Italian septuagenarian that serves the same "menuless", "fixed-price banquet" (and "lots of it") every night; while some delight in this "no-thinking-required" approach and aren't surprised they've got it right after all these years, the "bored" say it "feels like eating in the '50s."

Marco Polo Ristorante (Brooklyn) S   21 | 18 | 20 | $42
345 Court St. (Union St.), 718-852-5015
◪ You can take a "trip to a bygone era" at this "classic Carroll Gardens Italian" "landmark" that habitués haunt for "dependable", midpriced cooking and "solicitous service" in a "*Sopranos*"-worthy setting; still, a few dissent: "seriously average", "past its prime."

Mardi Gras (Queens) ●S   21 | 20 | 19 | $30
70-20 Austin St. (bet. 70th Ave. & 70th Rd.), 718-261-8555
■ A "festive New Orleans atmosphere" and surprisingly good food lure a "fun, young crowd" to this "raging" Cajun-Creole in Forest Hills that feels "like carnival"; however, party-poopers dub the grub "spotty" and the service "slow."

Mare S⌿   ▽ 17 | 17 | 16 | $39
198 Eighth Ave. (20th St.), 212-675-7522
◪ Though perhaps "too early to tell", this new Chelsea Mediterranean has fans who claim it offers "well-prepared", "simple" seafood and foes who say it's just "ordinary"; one thing's certain: it's "cash only" – though an on-site ATM makes this less of a "pain."

Marichu Restaurant S   23 | 19 | 22 | $47
342 E. 46th St. (bet. 1st & 2nd Aves.), 212-370-1866
■ Rather than Basque in its own glory, this "tiny" "treasure" in the "no-man's-land" near the UN earns its kudos with a delicious, "different spin on Spanish" fare abetted by a "quiet" "garden oasis" out back; some of the "warmest service in town" assures that "everyone leaves happy."

Marika ●S   18 | 24 | 18 | $53
208 W. 70th St. (bet. Amsterdam & West End Aves.), 212-875-8600
◪ A much-reported "chef change" early on means this pricey West Side New American is "still a work in progress"; though so far many say its "snazzy" "*Architectural Digest*"–ready design "stands out more than the food", stalwarts swear it's "getting there"; stay tuned.

Marina Cafe (Staten Island) S   18 | 21 | 18 | $43
154 Mansion Ave. (Hillside Terr.), 718-967-3077
◪ Its "water" vistas may be a feast for the eyes, but this Staten Island seafooder garners mixed reviews on its eats, with the hooked labeling it "surprisingly inspired" and the unimpressed sighing "so-so"; "'70s decor" and "invisible service" are easily ignored given those "great sunsets."

Marinella S   ▽ 21 | 15 | 18 | $36
49 Carmine St. (Bedford St.), 212-807-7472
■ This "casual" Village Italian "charmer" is so "welcoming" it's "like eating with family, only the food is much better"; expect a "tiny", "old-fashioned" space complete with "blackboard" specials and "patrons speaking Italian" to the "attentive" servers.

Marion's Continental ●S   ▽ 18 | 20 | 18 | $31
354 Bowery (bet. 4th & Great Jones Sts.), 212-475-7621
■ Those venturing beyond the "great martini list" and "Goldfish crackers" say the American "comfort food" "has gotten better" at this "funky" Bowery "hoot"; others ask "who needs food?" when there's so much "atmosphere" – "kitsch like this you don't see every day!"

Mario's (Bronx) S   20 | 15 | 19 | $40
2342 Arthur Ave. (bet. 184th & 186th Sts.), 718-584-1188
◪ "*Numero uno* on Arthur Avenue" to some, this 83-year-old Bronx Italian "red-sauce heaven" is famed for its "can't-miss pizza"; contras contend it's a "shade of its former self", with only "ok food" and a "central casting" crowd heavy on the "bada-bing."

Mario's Seafood   ▽ 21 | 13 | 21 | $39
7 E. 30th St. (bet. 5th & Madison Aves.), 212-532-7787
◪ Ok, it "needs redecorating badly", but this Murray Hill vet (since 1962) "makes up for it" with "fresh", "really decent" fish, courtesy of "sweet" chef-owner Mario, who also earns "bravos" for being such a "gracious, charming host" and reasonable bill collector.

Maristella   ▽ 22 | 19 | 23 | $43
69 W. 55th St. (bet. 5th & 6th Aves.), 212-489-7655
■ Followers say it's "about time" this "overlooked", midpriced Midtown "gem" made it into the *Survey*; its "delicious" Northern Italian cooking draws nearby desk jockeys at lunchtime, and its slightly "formal" vibe is occasionally enlivened by a "waiter who bursts into song."

Maritime Restaurant   23 | 23 | 21 | $48
121 W. 49th St. (bet. 6th & 7th Aves.), 212-354-1717
■ This smoothly run, "high-concept", steamship-themed seafooder keeps Midtown's pseudo-seafarers smiling due to its "inspired menu" and "slick" yet "civilized setting"; though there's a bit of crabbing at the cost of steerage, satisfied surveyors suggest an early "return voyage."

MarkJoseph Steakhouse   ▽ 25 | 22 | 26 | $55
261 Water St. (off Peck Slip), 212-277-0020
■ An "exceptional" "new steakhouse on this side of the Brooklyn Bridge", this highly rated Downtown chop shop draws ardent applause for being "more convenient and friendly than Luger's"; despite just-the-facts-ma'am decor and "not cheap" pricing, fans are convinced it "will become a staple."

Mark's Restaurant and Bar S   24 | 25 | 24 | $63
The Mark Hotel, 25 E. 77th St. (bet. 5th & Madison Aves.), 212-879-1864
■ "Ladies and gentlemen" relax at this "aristocratic" Eastsider for "lap-of-luxury" dining in a "sublime refuge" reminiscent of a "private London club", while sampling new chef Andrew Chase's fine French-American cooking; P.S. "polished service" describes both the staff and the silverware at its "civilized" high tea.

Markt ●S   19 | 19 | 16 | $39
401 W. 14th St. (9th Ave.), 212-727-3314
■ "Mussel"-bound throngs convene at this "big, bawdy and brassy" Belgian brasserie in the Meatpacking District, whose "mile-long", "rich wood" bar is a perfect perch for "watching youthful NY in action"; while the myriad fans of this "happening" spot insist "there's good reason it's trendy", cynics consider it "overhyped" and "missing more than an 'e'."

Maroons S   ▽ 22 | 17 | 19 | $34
244 W. 16th St. (bet. 7th & 8th Aves.), 212-206-8640
■ Though you "sit on top of your neighbor" at this "tiny" Chelsea Caribbean-Southerner, no one minds much given the simpatico vibe,

modest prices and "friendly" staff; the "generous, roll-me-home portions" are "delicious" indeed, but they only add to the "tight fit"; P.S. the more casual lounge "feels like a friend's living room."

Mars 2112 S | 11 | 22 | 13 | $29 |

1633 Broadway (51st St.), 212-582-2112

At this futuristic Theater District "playland of a restaurant", you can "escape reality" via a spaceship ride to an "out-of-this-world experience"; "kids love it", but many adult earthlings are alienated by the "plastic" American eats and "hectic", commercial ambiance in which "all roads lead to the gift shop."

Marumi S | ∇ 23 | 13 | 16 | $28 |

546 La Guardia Pl. (bet. Bleecker & W. 3rd Sts.), 212-979-7055

The sushi queue at this "always-packed" Japanese "hole-in-the-wall" near NYU can get quite long, so show up early or "be prepared to wait" with the rest of 'em for the raw deal: "affordably priced", "fresh and tasty" rolls that "satisfy cravings to the fullest."

Maruzzella ●S | ∇ 19 | 16 | 18 | $35 |

1483 First Ave. (bet. 77th & 78th Sts.), 212-988-8877

Considered "the friendliest restaurant in the neighborhood" by the few frugal Eastsiders who know it, this "little" Northern Italian "find" elicits bravos for its "melt-in-your-mouth" dishes, "intimate setting" and "attentive staff" who won't keep you waiting.

Mary Ann's | 17 | 13 | 15 | $24 |

1503 Second Ave. (bet. 78th & 79th Sts.), 212-249-6165 ●
2452 Broadway (bet. 90th & 91st Sts.), 212-877-0132
116 Eighth Ave. (16th St.), 212-633-0877
80 Second Ave. (5th St.), 212-475-5939 ●

"Every day is Cinco de Mayo" at this "festive", "noisy" Tex-Mex mini-chain where the "killer margs" and "tasty", "generous portions" at "peso prices" ensure there's always a "crowd."

Marylou's Restaurant ●S | 19 | 18 | 19 | $44 |

21 W. Ninth St. (bet. 5th & 6th Aves.), 212-533-0012

A "time capsule" of old Greenwich Village, this "legendary" Continental seafooder continues to dish out "fine fish" fare to an ever-loyal clientele; the "romantic", "fireplaces-and-flowers" brownstone setting has enthusiasts insisting that this "landmark" is "still wonderful."

Mary's Fish Camp | 25 | 14 | 18 | $37 |

64 Charles St. (W. 4th St.), 646-486-2185

Lines "around the block" for this West Village take on a "New England lobster shack" confirm the view that a visit here is almost as good as a "trip to the Cape"; yes, the "wait is awful" and quarters "cramped", but "seafood lovers" swear the "succulent" shore fare and fair prices "make it all worthwhile."

Massimo al Ponte Vecchio S | ∇ 21 | 16 | 19 | $43 |

206 Thompson St. (bet. Bleecker & W. 3rd Sts.), 212-228-7701

It won't take you long to "become part of the family" at this "old-style" West Village Italian where the "fine" renderings of classic dishes are all the more "pleasant" thanks to the "warm" service; sidewalk tables make it particularly "worth visiting in summer."

Master Grill International (Queens) S | 18 | 14 | 17 | $31 |

34-09 College Point Blvd. (bet. 34th & 35th Aves.), 718-762-0300

It's easy to "gorge yourself silly" at this Flushing Brazilian "meat-lover's heaven" whose AYCE buffet boasts a "mind-boggling array" of international choices beyond grilled meat; it's a "gaudy", "cavernous" (1,000 seats) "circus" perfect for "taking the whole family", including cousins, and "eating until you have to be rolled out."

Mavalli Palace S

22 | 15 | 17 | $27

46 E. 29th St. (bet. Madison Ave. & Park Ave. S.), 212-679-5535

☑ "Delicious *dosai*" (stuffed crêpes) and other "top-notch", yet "cheap", Southern Indian dishes are the draw at this "superior", slightly "out-of-the-way" Curry Hill Vegetarian; the faithful call it a "serene" "little jewel", even if the decor's definitely on the "dull" side.

Max S≠

23 | 14 | 17 | $25

51 Ave. B (bet. 3rd & 4th Sts.), 212-539-0111 ●
1274 Amsterdam Ave. (123rd St.), 212-531-2221

■ "It doesn't get more authentic" than the "simple", "perfectly flavored carbs" and "delicious sauces" at this "teeny" East Village Southern Italian; it's "noisy", "smoky" and busier than rush hour on the subway, but "true paesano service" and "astoundingly inexpensive" prices compensate; N.B. there's a new branch in southern Harlem.

Max & Moritz (Brooklyn) S

22 | 18 | 20 | $37

426A Seventh Ave. (bet. 14th & 15th Sts.), 718-499-5557

■ The "imaginative" New American cuisine "cooked with care" at this "intimate" bistro with a French feel makes it a "Park Slope favorite", especially in summer, when the "very romantic garden" is a "must"; however, not everyone agrees: "just so-so."

Maya S

25 | 21 | 21 | $47

1191 First Ave. (bet. 64th & 65th Sts.), 212-585-1818

■ The "best Mexican in the city" – "manos down" – is this "adobe-like" Eastsider where "pretty people" savor "authentic", "artistically prepared" cuisine and "drop-dead margaritas"; despite a few grumbles about prices and "decibel levels", amigos advise "don't go to Mexico – this is better."

Mayrose S

15 | 12 | 13 | $21

920 Broadway (21st St.), 212-533-3663

☑ "Mac 'n' cheese that could tempt a supermodel" and other "tasty" "diner food for the *Sex and the City* crowd" is "served without pretense" at this often "mobbed" Flatiron "standby"; however, a few find this "glorified coffee shop" "too much of a scene", with "people more beautiful than the food."

Maz Mezcal S

21 | 18 | 20 | $34

316 E. 86th St. (bet. 1st & 2nd Aves.), 212-472-1599

■ Yorkvillers go "south-of-the-border" at this "dark", "mysterious" Mexican beloved for its "dependably" "delish" "gourmet" fare and "friendly owners"; their only regret is that this onetime "sleeper" has "been discovered" and it's now necessary to "call ahead."

McHales ●S≠

∇ 18 | 11 | 15 | $19

750 Eighth Ave. (46th St.), 212-997-8885

■ "You can feel your arteries start to close" when biting into the "enormous, tasty burgers" at this "hole-in-the-wall" Theater District pub; with "aspiring stars as waiters" and "stagehands" at the bar, it's easy to imagine that you're part of the show.

Medi S

– | – | – | VE

45 Rockefeller Plaza (50th St.), 212-399-8888

Practice your air-kissing before trying this new Rock Center Provençal-Tuscan from Bice's Roberto Ruggeri and legendary French chef Roger Vergé; its sunny interior awash with floral arrangements feels Mediterranean, and while the crowd tends to be touristy, it also draws plenty of power brokers and lovely lunching ladies; N.B. a more casual menu is available at the bar and on the outdoor 'piazza.'

Mediterraneo ◐ [S] — 19 | 15 | 16 | $35

1260 Second Ave. (66th St.), 212-734-7407

◪ "Sit outside (like in Rome)" and savor the "see-and-be-seen" scene at this East Side Italian that locals favor for its sidewalk tables and "light, crispy" brick-oven pizza; on the other hand, foes fault the staff's "herd-them-in-and-out" attitude.

Mee Noodle Shop [S] — – | – | – | I

922 Second Ave. (49th St.), 212-888-0027
795 Ninth Ave. (53rd St.), 212-765-2929 ◐
547 Second Ave. (bet. 30th & 31st Sts.), 212-779-1596
219 First Ave. (13th St.), 212-995-0333

Surveyors enthuse over this "consistent" quartet of Chinese "no-frills" shops ladling out "oodles of noodles" both "excellent and predictable"; they boast "zero decor", but then "you don't have to be fancy to be good."

Meigas — 24 | 19 | 22 | $55

350 Hudson St. (King St.), 212-627-5800

■ Amigos of this smoothly served SoHo Spaniard cheer "viva Barcelona!" citing "brilliant chef" Luis Bollo's "haute traditional" cuisine so "sublime" it verges on "art", though less cheerful are the "cavernous" space and "fierce din" when crowded; tabs run "many *pesetas*", but bargain-hunters "bring pals" and split the "top-notch tapas" at the bar.

Mekka ◐ [S] — ▽ 21 | 13 | 15 | $30

14 Ave. A (bet. Houston & 2nd Sts.), 212-475-8500

■ An "unexpected" slice of the "down-home" in Alphabet City, this Southern-Caribbean hybrid exudes a "bluesy" ambiance while cooking up "cheap", "hearty Soul Food" for a "hip, young" buppie clientele; if the seating inside is "a little close", there's always the "pretty" patio.

MeKong Restaurant [S] — 19 | 16 | 17 | $29

44 Prince St. (bet. Mott & Mulberry Sts.), 212-343-8169

■ "Post–gallery openings", this Vietnamese fills the bill with "reliably tasty" edibles, low prices and a "hip", "fun Downtown feel" best appreciated in the "outdoor seats"; never mind if "the place needs a decorator", just focus on the "cool crowd."

Meltemi [S] — 20 | 16 | 19 | $41

905 First Ave. (51st St.), 212-355-4040

◪ "Escape to the Aegean" via this "light" and "airy" Sutton Place Greek where the "traditional" seafood menu provides "no surprises" but the "fish is so fresh" it almost "swims to the table"; even if the decor "feels a little ancient", it's something of a "UN hangout."

Menchanko-tei ◐ [S] — 17 | 9 | 14 | $21

131 E. 45th St. (bet. Lexington & 3rd Aves.), 212-986-6805
43-45 W. 55th St. (bet. 5th & 6th Aves.), 212-247-1585

■ To "eat like the locals" do in Tokyo, try this "basic" but "authentic" noodle duo that's a "slurp heaven" thanks to its "fast", "super-cheap" and "ultra-satisfying" "meals in a bowl"; though not gourmet, it hits the spot "on a cold winter's day."

Mercer Kitchen, The ◐ [S] — 23 | 23 | 19 | $51

Mercer Hotel, 99 Prince St. (Mercer St.), 212-966-5454

◪ Fast becoming a "SoHo landmark", Jean-Georges Vongerichten's "ab fab" French–New American is "still a scene" supplying "star sightings galore" – even if the "sexy" "subterranean" setting is nearly "too dark

| F | D | S | C |

to see" who's at the next table; though costly, the "creative" cuisine always "delivers", as does the "hip" staff that "doubles as eye candy" and attitude exemplars.

Merchants, N.Y. ●S | 15 | 17 | 15 | $32 |
1608 First Ave. (bet. 83rd & 84th Sts.), 212-249-5924
1125 First Ave. (62nd St.), 212-832-1551
521 Columbus Ave. (bet. 85th & 86th Sts.), 212-721-3689
112 Seventh Ave. (bet. 16th & 17th Sts.), 212-366-7267

■ "Go for the cosmos", the "dark, cool atmosphere" and the "fun" "pickup scene" at these "lively" New Americans populated by "yuppie singles"; but remember, the "mediocre", "bargain-priced" eats are not a priority, and the staff is too "busy waiting for the next casting call" to be of much service.

Merge ●S | 20 | 17 | 18 | $41 |
142 W. 10th St. (bet. Greenwich Ave. & Waverly Pl.), 212-691-7757

■ "Boisterous but beautiful" to some, "bland"-looking and "loud" to others, this West Village New American offers "eclectic cuisine" that's "always interesting"; the popular Sunday night "*Sopranos*-style" prix fixe Italian dinner is a "hoot" – and a "great value."

MESA GRILL S | 24 | 21 | 21 | $50 |
102 Fifth Ave. (bet. 15th & 16th Sts.), 212-807-7400

■ Food Network romeo Bobby Flay's "always-crowded", sometimes-"frenzied" Flatiron Southwestern "fiesta" "should be declared a NYC landmark" because it's "still awesome after all these years" and has become something of "a mecca for fans" of the chef's TV show; "bring extra bucks", and "go for brunch" or just sip "great cactus margaritas" at the "hopping bar" – either way, you won't go wrong.

Meskerem ●S | 21 | 11 | 15 | $23 |
468 W. 47th St. (bet. 9th & 10th Aves.), 212-664-0520
124 MacDougal St. (bet. Bleecker & W. 3rd Sts.), 212-777-8111

■ "Go with someone you don't mind sharing food with" to this "dirt-cheap" Theater District–Village duo, because the "spicy Ethiopian" stews are literally "finger-lickin' good" ("no silverware allowed"); sure, the "slow service" grates and there's "no decor" to speak of, but for most it's a "fun" "adventure."

Métisse S | 22 | 17 | 21 | $39 |
239 W. 105th St. (bet. Amsterdam Ave. & B'way), 212-666-8825

■ "French style without French prices" is available "way up on the West Side" at this "cozy" "hideaway" "graciously" serving "bearded professors" "well-prepared, simple food" in "sedate" environs; fans call it the "perfect neighborhood bistro" and don't mind much if the "brick-walled interior" is "somewhat dingy."

Métrazur S | 19 | 22 | 17 | $47 |
Grand Central Terminal, East Balcony (42nd St. & Park Ave.), 212-687-4600

■ Perched over the "center of the universe" with a "gorgeous view" of the "best room in town – Grand Central", Charlie Palmer's New American makes a "great excuse to take a later train"; "most of the food is satisfying, and all of it pretty", though the service is "hit-or-miss" (maybe the staff is "watching the people too").

Metro Fish | 20 | 17 | 19 | $42 |
8 E. 36th St. (bet. 5th & Madison Aves.), 212-683-6444

■ You can order up "every fish imaginable, prepared any way you like" at this Murray Hill "seafood haven" where the service "makes you feel at home" and the "$22 prix fixe dinner" is "a great buy"; carpers call the angler-themed decor "diner-like" and warn of cost "creep."

| | | F | D | S | C |

Metro Grill S
▽ 19 | 17 | 18 | $37
Hotel Metro, 45 W. 35th St. (bet. 5th & 6th Aves.), 212-279-3535
■ "Close enough to Penn Station to catch the train back home after dinner", this New American "oasis" in a culinary "desert" provides "garmento gourmand" lunches for area fashionistas as well as "solid eating experiences" for the MSG crowd.

Metronome
19 | 22 | 18 | $42
915 Broadway (21st St.), 212-505-7400
■ "The ambiance is just right" at this "classy" deco Flatiron Med–New American, a "scene without attitude" where jazz fans sip "great cosmopolitans" and "watch the band playing above the bar"; hep cats call the food "nearly as tasty as the riffs and grooves", but those not in sync say "just ok."

Metropolitan Cafe ●S
16 | 16 | 17 | $34
959 First Ave. (bet. 52nd & 53rd Sts.), 212-759-5600
■ "Kid-friendly, standard and solid", this Sutton Place American "steady neighbor" offers "generous portions" at modest tabs, but the food's on the "ordinary" side, so stick to the "perfect salads" and "great brunch"; insiders tout the less-"hectic" garden or the "airy" atrium.

Metsovo ●S
20 | 20 | 19 | $40
65 W. 70th St. (bet. Columbus Ave. & CPW), 212-873-2300
■ "Ask for a seat by the fireplace" at this "cozy" Lincoln Center brownstone and feast on "unusual", "earthy" Greek seafood dishes; the service, though good, "isn't the greatest" and the room "could use better lighting", but it's easy to relax and "forget you're only steps away from the Columbus Avenue crowds."

Mexicana Mama S⌀
23 | 13 | 17 | $29
525 Hudson St. (bet. Charles & W. 10th Sts.), 212-924-4119
■ "No Tex-Mex" here: this "fun hole-in-the-wall" serves "excellent", "clever" "nouveau Mexican"; it's "claustrophobic" (only 21 seats), "drafty in winter" and "you share space with the kitchen", but "squeeze in" anyway, because you'll get a "big taste" for a small cost.

Mexican Radio ●S
19 | 15 | 16 | $25
19 Cleveland Pl. (bet. Kenmare & Spring Sts.), 212-343-0140
☑ "Don't touch that dial": in its new NoLita digs, this "above-average Mexican" finally has some elbow room, although it may be too dark to see; while nostalgists miss the old "charm", "killer margaritas" and "tasty" "grub" "cut through any static."

Mezzaluna ●S
19 | 15 | 17 | $41
1295 Third Ave. (bet. 74th & 75th Sts.), 212-535-9600
■ Fans insist this "tiny", "unpretentious" East Side Italian providing "solid pastas and pizzas" is "still great after all these years"; but even they admit you have to "shout to make yourself heard" by occasionally "rude" waiters – of course, that's just "like being in *Roma*."

Mezzogiorno ●S
20 | 17 | 18 | $40
195 Spring St. (Sullivan St.), 212-334-2112
■ "When in SoHo, you can't go wrong" at this "little restaurant with the big brick oven", where the classic eats are "wonderful", the crowd's "young and fun" and the sidewalk tables are "outstanding for celeb sightings"; so what if the staff is "slightly condescending?" – the place "never disappoints."

Mi ●
▽ 20 | 18 | 19 | $40
66 Madison Ave. (bet. 27th & 28th Sts.), 212-252-8888
☑ It's hard not to like the "attentive service", "pretty interior" and "great blend of Asian cuisines" at this newcomer in "restaurant-starved"

Midtown South with ex Match chef Gary Robins at the stove; however, "small portions" and not-so-small prices are less well received.

Michael Jordan's The Steak House NYC S
21 | 21 | 19 | $57

Grand Central Terminal, 23 Vanderbilt Ave. (bet. 43rd & 44th Sts.), 212-655-2300
■ "Business-y" types concur "his airness" "got game" at this "red-meat" palace, "a three-pointer" in Grand Central where the steaks and sides are always a "slam-dunk"; opponents deem it "noisy" and "expensive" and suggest that "difficult" waiters be fouled out.

Michael's
22 | 22 | 22 | $54

24 W. 55th St. (bet. 5th & 6th Aves.), 212-767-0555
■ You'll find "a little LA and a lot of NYC scene" at this Midtown palace of "California style" in a "gorgeous, sunny space" hung with "wonderful art" and delivering "sophisticated" "food to match" with "pleasant, easygoing service"; no wonder it's filled with "media moguls and fashionistas" making deals over breakfast and lunch.

Mickey Mantle's S
14 | 18 | 15 | $34

42 Central Park S. (bet. 5th & 6th Aves.), 212-688-7777
■ "Teenage boys of all ages" know this TV-centric CPS "shrine to the Mick" as a "field-of-dreams sports bar", but nonfans say it's merely a "decent" burger-and-beer joint that "strikes out" as often as No. 7 did – and "MIA service" hits into a "double play."

Mi Cocina S
22 | 15 | 17 | $36

57 Jane St. (Hudson St.), 212-627-8273
■ Freshly renovated and expanded, this "exuberant" West Villager turns out "non-clichéd" Mexican fare "fit for Montezuma", along with "extra-strength margaritas"; though "so-so" service detracts, the "price-to-taste exchange rate" is excellent.

Midway ●S
▽ 21 | 21 | 19 | $42

145 Charles St. (Washington St.), 212-352-1119
■ This "worthy reinvention of Waterloo" in the far West Village is as "chic" as ever and draws a younger following that says it's "worth a try" for "good" New American cooking at middling tabs; still, a few feel its "clean, open" space deserves "better eats."

Mignon (Brooklyn) S
23 | 17 | 19 | $39

394 Court St. (bet. Carroll St. & 1st Pl.), 718-222-8383
■ "Très magnifique" Carroll Gardens yearling providing the "flavors of France", served with "panache" and offered at pleasing "bistro prices"; since it's "not much to look at" and "crammed" at prime times, regulars escape the masses in its "lovely garden."

Mike & Tony's (Brooklyn) S
21 | 18 | 20 | $46

239 Fifth Ave. (Carroll St.), 718-857-2800
■ A Park Slope "class act", this Cucina sibling is a "top neighborhood joint", purveying "outstanding" steaks and other grilled Americana in a "cozy, library-like setting"; just plan on "Manhattan prices" – or "try the burger if on a budget."

MILOS, ESTIATORIO ●S
26 | 24 | 23 | $65

125 W. 55th St. (bet. 6th & 7th Aves.), 212-245-7400
■ Offering fish "fresh from the ocean to the table with a short kitchen detour", this "dramatic", high-ceilinged grill is the top "high-class Greek eatery in town", bar none, and many tout it as serving "NYC's best seafood", regardless of nationality; always fun with a group, it's a good value if you share appetizers or go for the $32 lunch or pre-theater prix fixe, but can get "deceptively expensive" if you order the main-course fish that's subject to "per pound pricing."

Minetta Tavern ◐ [S] 17 | 17 | 18 | $39

113 MacDougal St. (bet. Bleecker & W. 3rd Sts.), 212-475-3850

◪ "Not much has changed" since the '30s at this "vintage Village" "old-time Italian", specializing in "steady, basic fare" that's just the ticket for "pre–off-Broadway" dining; while some say it's "showing its age" and feels a tad "worn out", nostalgia buffs hope it "lasts forever."

Mingala Burmese Cuisine [S] 20 | 13 | 18 | $23

1393-B Second Ave. (bet. 72nd & 73rd Sts.), 212-744-8008

21-23 E. Seventh St. (bet. 2nd & 3rd Aves.), 212-529-3656

■ "Unusual", "exotic" Burmese cooking turns up at these East Side twins where the "low-budget", "thoughtful concoctions" are "fulfilling" and the service "sweet" – though the "total dive decor" leads many to opt "for takeout."

Minotaur Restaurant [S] – | – | – | E

44 W. 58th St. (bet. 5th & 6th Aves.), 212-759-0502

At this Midtown Greek newcomer, chef Stefanos Taktikos treats NYers to a diverse menu, mixing rare, ancient Hellenic dishes with more familiar modern ones; artistically presented plates meet their match in the room's grand murals of King Minos' throne room.

Miracle Grill ◐ [S] 20 | 17 | 17 | $32

112 First Ave. (bet. 6th & 7th Sts.), 212-254-2353

415 Bleecker St. (bet. Bank & W. 11th Sts.), 212-924-1900

■ "Affordable" East Side "miracles below 34th Street" famed for their "zesty" Southwestern fare and "mad margaritas"; despite "no-frills" decor and sometime "indifferent" service, the "irresistible" garden "oasis" at the East Village branch is a must-see – provided you can abide the "monthlong wait" to get in.

Mirchi ◐ [S] ▽ 22 | 19 | 18 | $34

29 Seventh Ave. S. (bet. Bedford & Morton Sts.), 212-414-0931

■ Some "like it hot", as this "inventive" West Village Indian proves – those "sweating bullets" warn "even the water's spicy" here; however, it "never fails to please, thanks to the cool "postmodern decor", open kitchen and outstandingly "diverse" menu that includes native street food.

Mishima [S] ▽ 20 | 11 | 17 | $29

164 Lexington Ave. (bet. 30th & 31st Sts.), 212-532-9596

■ You'd swear the "fish still wiggles" at this "reliable" Murray Hill Japanese where the "solid sushi" and "reasonable" prices (not the "neo-Nedick's" decor or "cramped" conditions) regularly produce a "full house."

Miss Mamie's/Miss Maude's [S] ▽ 20 | 9 | 14 | $21

366 W. 110th St. (bet. Columbus & Manhattan Aves.), 212-865-6744

547 Lenox Ave. (bet. 137th & 138th Sts.), 212-690-3100

■ On entering these "easygoing" Harlem Soul Food sisters, you'll feel you've been whisked away to the South, and the impression is confirmed by the "vast quantities" of "excellent" eats for "little money"; in short, despite some service issues, fans say these "true finds" "keep a smile on your face."

Miss Saigon [S] 19 | 12 | 16 | $27

1425 Third Ave. (bet. 80th & 81st Sts.), 212-988-8828

■ The "Broadway show's gone", but devotees doubt this "distinctive" Yorkville Vietnamese will ever shutter given its "flavorful" "bargain" fare that "deserves the crowds it draws"; though the food's "lovely", decor is "dismal", leading many to take the show on the road.

Miss Williamsburg Diner ▽ 21 | 16 | 18 | $32
(Brooklyn) ◐ [S] ⊄
206 Kent Ave. (bet. Metropolitan Ave. & N. 3rd St.), 718-963-0802
◪ Housed in a "funky '50s diner", this dinner-only, cash-only Williamsburg Italian is known for its "seedy flair", "flirty waitresses" and "creative" cooking; however, critics gripe about "small portions" and say it will never "win the Miss Congeniality title."

Mitali East ◐ [S] 19 | 14 | 17 | $27
334 E. Sixth St. (bet. 1st & 2nd Aves.), 212-533-2508
Mitali West ◐ [S]
296 Bleecker St. (7th Ave. S.), 212-989-1367
■ "Super-duper", separately managed Village Indians that are "classier than the Christmas lights places" thanks to "perfectly spiced food" and "not-as-touristy" crowds; though the Western outpost has "brighter ambiance" and a new chef, purists insist the just-redone Easterner is "still better."

Mme. Romaine de Lyon [S] 19 | 16 | 19 | $35
132 E. 61st St. (bet. Lexington & Park Aves.), 212-758-2422
◪ An "unchanging" East Side "landmark" hatched in 1938, this "civilized", egg-cellent French bistro specializes in salads and "amazing omelets" (over 500 varieties), with live "piano music" as an evening weekend bonus; skeptics say stick to breakfast and lunch, and try not to lay an egg when you get the tab.

Mo-Bay (Brooklyn) [S] – | – | – | I
112 DeKalb Ave. (bet. Ashland & Rockwell Pls.), 718-246-2800
Potted palms and small tables out front highlight this cheap, cheery, family-run Fort Greene Jamaican–Soul Food joint where you can dine in the ocher-walled, thatch-roofed matchbox interior, or out back by the burbling fountain; there's a bustling takeout biz too.

Mocca [S] ⊄ 18 | 10 | 16 | $26
1588 Second Ave. (bet. 82nd & 83rd Sts.), 212-734-6470
◪ Possibly the "last of its kind", this "old-world" Yorkville Hungarian serves "Mittel-Europa", "hungry-man" grub at "heartwarming" prices – but you'd best "eat all your food" or the "bossy" "waitresses who've been there since the beginning" may "scold you."

MOLYVOS ◐ [S] 23 | 21 | 21 | $49
871 Seventh Ave. (bet. 55th & 56th Sts.), 212-582-7500
■ Feast on "exquisite" Greek cuisine "fit for Zeus" at this West Side taverna near Carnegie Hall, where the fare's simultaneously "elegant and homey", the service "helpful" and the digs "handsome"; though usually "crowded" and "a tad pricey", it's "worth every damn drachma."

Mombar (Queens) [S] ⊄ ▽ 25 | 25 | 24 | $32
25-22 Steinway St. (bet. 25th & 28th Aves.), 718-726-2356
■ At this Astoria Southern Egyptian "wonderland", the eye-popping decor comes courtesy of multitasking chef-owner Moustafa El Sayed, who also "welcomes all guests" and can "cook a gourmet meal on a camp stove"; those who "can't get enough of this place" insist the experience is "sure to delight."

Monkey Bar [S] 21 | 22 | 20 | $53
Hotel Elysée, 60 E. 54th St. (bet. Madison & Park Aves.), 212-838-2600
■ "Luxe dining" is the draw at this "swanky" Midtown New American where the "'30s Warner Brothers" ambiance plays well against the "delightful" "21st-century flavor combinations"; you'll have to contend with a "bothersome", "jumping bar" scene up-front, but "once you're past the crush" the payoff is "high-class" grazing.

	F	D	S	C

Mon Petit Cafe S — 18 | 15 | 17 | $33
801 Lexington Ave. (62nd St.), 212-355-2233
◼ "Après Bloomie's", shoppers grab wine and quiche at this "sweet" bistro that's so "authentically French" it even supplies "aloof service"; skeptics detect "nothing spectacular" save the "reasonable prices."

Monsoon ●S — 19 | 14 | 16 | $28
435 Amsterdam Ave. (81st St.), 212-580-8686
◼ Contrary to the name, there's a "great weather forecast" at this "no-frills" Upper West Side Vietnamese offering "savory treats" and "fast service"; although a "makeover" has improved atmospheric conditions, some say it's become "more pricey" as a result.

Monster Sushi — 19 | 12 | 15 | $29
22 W. 46th St. (bet. 5th & 6th Aves.), 212-398-7707
158 W. 23rd St. (bet. 6th & 7th Aves.), 212-620-9131 S
535 Hudson St. (Charles St.), 646-336-1833 S
■ "Orca-size" sushi that you "eat with a forklift" turns up at these West Side Japanese triplets whose "name says it all"; "monstrous" decor and "clueless" service are "too much to swallow" for some, but it's definitely a "deal" and immensely "popular."

Mont Blanc — 18 | 14 | 19 | $37
306 W. 48th St. (bet. 8th & 9th Aves.), 212-582-9648
◼ This Hell's Kitchen Swiss-Austrian catering to "everyman" is a "throwback to another era" when they knew how to "bring on the fondue"; expect "kind service" and "comfy", if "shabby", surroundings.

Montebello — ▽ 22 | 20 | 23 | $47
120 E. 56th St. (bet. Lexington & Park Aves.), 212-753-1447
◼ "Consistency is the word" at this Midtown Northern Italian purveying "satisfying" classics in "intimate" digs; just right for a "business lunch", many file it under the "strictly expense-account" category.

Monte's S — 18 | 14 | 19 | $36
97 MacDougal St. (bet. Bleecker & W. 3rd Sts.), 212-228-9194
■ A "Village fixture" since 1918, this "traditional Italian" offers "steady", "old world" fare in the "red-sauce and baked clams" vein; despite "tired", "'50s" decor, loyalists insist this "reliable old friend" always offers a "warm welcome."

Monte's Italian (Brooklyn) S — 21 | 17 | 20 | $37
451 Carroll St. (bet. Nevins St. & 3rd Ave.), 718-624-8984
■ The "ghost of Sinatra salutes you from the bar" of this Carroll Gardens "old-time Italian" (since 1906) providing "great red sauce" that "you can't refuse" to a crowd that runs the gamut from "locals to big shots" – "Tony would love it."

Montparnasse ●S — ▽ 20 | 19 | 18 | $43
Pickwick Arms, 230 E. 51st St. (bet. 2nd & 3rd Aves.), 212-758-6633
◼ *Voilà*, a "real brasserie" on the East Side serving "very good" (if "basic") French fare in an "inviting" room; with a "discreet" staff and "nicely spaced" seating, the only flaw in its "authentic Parisian" act is that it's often "quieter than it should be."

MONTRACHET — 26 | 21 | 25 | $66
239 W. Broadway (bet. Walker & White Sts.), 212-219-2777
■ Ever a "model" for "gracious dining", this TriBeCa French "pioneer" is a "total pleasure" with "superior", "carefully orchestrated cuisine", a "terrific wine list" and "marvelous service"; the Friday $20 prix fixe lunch remains a "great deal", and despite hints that the "'80s" decor "needs sprucing up", most agree Drew Nieporent's beloved "baby never grows old."

	F	D	S	C

Moondance Seafood & Steak ●S | – | – | – | M |
613 Second Ave. (bet. 33rd & 34th Sts.), 212-889-4131
For a marvelous, moderately priced repast in Murray Hill, try this new little surf 'n' turfer featuring a cozy ambiance and a complimentary glass of wine with every entree; after a meal here, you may be dancing under the moon too.

Mooza ●S | – | – | – | M |
191 Orchard St. (bet. Houston & Stanton Sts.), 212-982-4770
Orchard Street continues to gentrify, as the adeptly prepared food at this new Med-Italian demonstrates; despite decor that madly mixes mosaic tile and leopard-skin prints, its prices satisfy Lower East Side budgets, while its garden is priceless.

Moran's Chelsea S | 19 | 20 | 19 | $42 |
146 10th Ave. (19th St.), 212-627-3030
☑ A "bit of Ireland in Chelsea", boasting the "best beer" and relics of "yesteryear" like "dark wood" and "Waterford crystal", plus "hospitality" "with a smile and a brogue"; though the "generous portions" of steaks and seafood hold "no surprises", you "gotta love" its "festive" flair.

Morrell Wine Bar & Cafe S | 19 | 19 | 18 | $43 |
1 Rockefeller Plaza (on 49th St., bet. 5th & 6th Aves.), 212-262-7700
■ "Stressfree wine tasting" is the grapevine report on this "spiffy" bi-level Rock Center cafe where a "savvy staff" pours vino from "every corner of the world"; it's fine for a glass or three paired with "good" American food, and there's a terrace for "sunny-day" people-watching.

Morton's of Chicago S | 24 | 20 | 22 | $60 |
551 Fifth Ave. (45th St.), 212-972-3315 ●
90 West St. (bet. Albany & Cedar Sts.), 212-732-5665
☑ These Chi-town "client-impresser" chain links run on "a formula, but the right one": "succulent slabs" of steak served in "heart attack"–size portions amid wood-paneled, "gentlemen's club" trappings; they're "expense-account" "staples" for a "noisy crowd" that seems undaunted by the "corny" preprandial "routine" of parading the "shrink-wrapped" "raw meat" before serving it.

Mosto ●S⌿ | – | – | – | M |
87 Second Ave. (5th St.), 212-228-9912
Look out for this new East Village Northern Italian, a crosstown sibling of Malatesta, which already is raising local eyebrows with well-executed, modestly priced Northern Italian fare from a bustling open kitchen; its simple brick room and helpful (if hard-to-understand) imported staff cement the old-country feel.

Moustache | 22 | 12 | 15 | $22 |
265 E. 10th St. (bet. Ave. A & 1st Ave.), 212-228-2022 ●S⌿
90 Bedford St. (bet. Barrow & Grove Sts.), 212-229-2220
■ "Pita fresh from the oven" is the hallmark of these "creative" "Middle Eastern meccas", where pilgrims endure "long lines" for the excellent "pitzas" and other "delights"; though "cramped and loud" as the "Casbah", they're "cheap, good and very Village."

Mr. Chow ●S | 22 | 22 | 20 | $61 |
324 E. 57th St. (bet. 1st & 2nd Aves.), 212-751-9030
☑ Proof that the "'80s aren't over", this East Side "gourmet Chinese" is coming back as a "place to be seen" against a "beautiful", "high-energy" deco backdrop flush with "'in'-crowd celebs"; do like "Puffy and company" and "let the waiter decide" for you, but remember to cash that residual check, since it's very – as in very – pricey (and not a little "pretentious").

	F	D	S	C

Mr. K's S   24 | 25 | 25 | $53
570 Lexington Ave. (51st St.), 212-583-1668
■ You enter a "different world" at this "first-class", top-priced East Side Chinese eye-catcher where the "elaborate", "flamingo-colored" room takes nothing away from the "excellent, creative" cooking; if a few find it "stuffy" and "overdone", those willing to "pay for it" can count on "star treatment."

Mughlai ⏺S   20 | 15 | 16 | $32
320 Columbus Ave. (75th St.), 212-724-6363
■ Known for "quality" and a location that's "not Downtown", this West Side "neighborhood" Indian is a "reliable" source of "respectable curry" and other "solid" subcontinental fare; admirers attest it's far "better than average" for the area.

Mugsy's Chow Chow ⏺   ▽ 21 | 18 | 17 | $29
31 Second Ave. (bet. 1st & 2nd Sts.), 212-460-9171
■ "Welcome to Fellini's kitchen", a "funky", "artistic" East Village Italian featuring "tasty", "homestyle" cooking from "one chef who does it all" in a very "tiny" space; sure, the "wait may kill ya" if the "close quarters" don't, but ultimately this one's "always fun", even when the bill arrives.

Muzy ⏺S≠   – | – | – | I
81 St. Marks Pl. (1st Ave.), 212-533-6876
An easy-to-miss sliver of a restaurant on a punky stretch of St. Mark's Place, this minimalist East Village newcomer's Korean menu showcases the usual suspects – bibimbop, mandoo, etc. – and fruity drinks to boot; perky, hip servers and low prices add to the appeal.

My Most Favorite Dessert Co. S   18 | 14 | 15 | $32
120 W. 45th St. (bet. B'way & 6th Ave.), 212-997-5130
◪ There's a "full menu" of "ok" kosher fare at this Theater District entry, but the "parve desserts" are so "remarkable" that a "backwards meal is best"; despite gripes about "pedestrian" surroundings and "inflated" prices, most maintain the sweet stuff is "worthy of the name."

Ñ ⏺S≠   18 | 18 | 14 | $27
33 Crosby St. (bet. Broome & Grand Sts.), 212-219-8856
◪ "Cute as a button", "closet"-size SoHo tapas bar that's "packed all the time" with Downtowners grazing happily; if lack of space and "absent service" get you down, clearly you need another drink to make it all seem "sexy."

Nadaman Hakubai S   ▽ 24 | 19 | 24 | $67
The Kitano New York, 66 Park Ave. (38th St.), 212-885-7111
■ "Traditional" types pronounce the multicourse kaiseki dinner at this Murray Hill hotel Japanese the "experience of a lifetime" and say the "great-tasting sushi", "beautiful presentation" and "very formal" service will make "you feel like you're in Japan" – unfortunately, the towering tab will too.

Nadine's ⏺S   17 | 15 | 17 | $32
99 Bank St. (Greenwich St.), 212-924-3165
◪ "Comfort food" at "fair prices" defines the "homey" style at this "relaxed" West Village American; if some snipe "so-so" and call for "a face-lift", it remains an amiable mainstay "jealously guarded by locals" who "adore it."

Namaskaar S   ▽ 22 | 17 | 20 | $29
337A W. Broadway (Grand St.), 212-625-1112
■ This SoHo Indian is something of a "find" for "thoughtfully prepared" fare "with just the right level of spice"; its "friendly staff" and

"reasonable prices" are most "welcome" in this high-stepping locale, leading some to wonder "why it's so quiet."

Nam Phuong S
▽ 20 | 11 | 16 | $22

19 Sixth Ave. (bet. Walker & White Sts.), 212-431-7715
■ TriBeCans tout the "healing soups" and other "fresh", "consistently good" dishes at this "authentic" Vietnamese; given the "sweet" staff and "cheap prices", any "fussing" over the plain decor "is not in order."

Nanni's
24 | 16 | 21 | $52

146 E. 46th St. (bet. Lexington & 3rd Aves.), 212-697-4161
■ "Nothing changes" at this Grand Central–area stalwart, from the first-rate "traditional" Northern Italian fare to the "old-school" "hospitality"; "everyone's made to feel special", so the "cramped quarters" and high cost are "soon forgotten."

Naples 45
17 | 15 | 15 | $31

MetLife Bldg., 200 Park Ave. (45th St.), 212-972-7001
☑ Commuters scarf "plentiful pastas" and thin-crust pizzas at this "loud", "cavernous" Italian in the MetLife Building; it's "tops" for "convenience" and "easy to get a table", even if skeptics say it has "spotty" service and "fast food at high prices."

Nation Restaurant & Bar
19 | 14 | 16 | $37

12 W. 45th St. (bet. 5th & 6th Aves.), 212-391-8053
■ "Hidden above a raucous bar", the "quiet" dining room of this Midtown New American is worth the "hike to the second floor" for "better-than-usual" fare at "decent prices"; it's big with "suits" who ignore the "dark, sterile decor" as they get into an "enjoyable" groove.

Neary's ●S
17 | 14 | 20 | $39

358 E. 57th St. (1st Ave.), 212-751-1434
■ A "real showman", Jimmy Neary, "makes you feel at home" at his "cheery" pub (or "club") frequented by "upscale" Eastsiders; so even if the "hearty" American fare seems "plain" and "you're young if you're under 50", all that "Irish charm" keeps the "loyal clientele" "in clover."

Negril ●S
20 | 17 | 16 | $31

362 W. 23rd St. (bet. 8th & 9th Aves.), 212-807-6411
■ "Ya mon", the "hot", "tasty Caribbean goodies" and "killer rum drinks" draw "cool" customers to this "happening" Chelsea spot; though "raucous and crowded" with a "boho" staff that operates on "island time", the "Jamaican vibe" is still "loads of fun"; N.B. at press time, a larger Village outpost is being readied.

Nellie's ●S
– | – | – | E

146 W. Houston St. (MacDougal St.), 212-375-1727
In the corner space that used to be Aggie's, this sleek, understated New American could be its quirky SoHo predecessor's polar opposite; in summer, its French doors open to the street, revealing a bar and cafe hopping with pretty young things.

Nello ●S
18 | 17 | 17 | $54

696 Madison Ave. (bet. 62nd & 63rd Sts.), 212-980-9099
475 W. Broadway (Houston St.), 212-677-7172
☑ "Bring your shades", because this East Side Northern Italian (with a new SoHo *sorella*) is "fabulous" for Eurocentric "people-watching and table-hopping"; there's also "good food", but critics carp it's "*molto* expensive", with limited service "if you're not a household name."

Nëo Sushi ●S
22 | 19 | 18 | $46

2298 Broadway (83rd St.), 212-769-1003
☑ Hailed as a "huge step forward" for the Upper West Side, this "Nobu-esque" Japanese newcomer arrives with "excellent" "nontraditional"

fare centered around "amazing sushi"; an as-yet unconvinced minority bemoans sizable tabs for "tiny portions" – "your stomach and wallet are empty an hour later."

New City Bar & Grill (Brooklyn) ▽ 22 | 16 | 16 | $46

25 Lafayette Ave. (bet. Ashland Pl. & Felix St.), 718-875-7197

◪ Admirers applaud this New American as "good accompaniment to BAM", citing its right-across-the-street location and "interesting", "delicious" menu for "pre- or post-"curtain dining; still, a few find the performance a bit "disorganized" and the set in need of redressing.

New Green Bo ●S⊅ ▽ 22 | 7 | 14 | $17

66 Bayard St. (bet. Elizabeth & Mott Sts.), 212-625-2359

■ This "no-frills Chinatown haunt" may be "low on atmosphere, but what a selection" it's got of "tasty, cheap Shanghai" specialties (notably "mouthwatering" soup dumplings); many rate it "one of the best", hence it's usually "crowded."

New Leaf Cafe S – | – | – | M

Fort Tryon Park, 1 Margaret Corbin Dr. (190th St.), 212-568-5323

Here's to Bette Midler and her NY Restoration Project for reclaiming gorgeous Fort Tryon Park; now, to pay for its upkeep, the Divine Miss M's group has opened this New American in a historic park building complete with flowering patio; try it for perfect post-Cloisters fueling.

New Pasteur S⊅ 21 | 8 | 15 | $17

85 Baxter St. (bet. Bayard & Canal Sts.), 212-608-3656

■ A "jury-duty favorite", this "Chinatown staple" courts favor with "knockout" Vietnamese cuisine; the judicious judge it "hard on the eyes" but "easy on the taste buds" and "too cheap to be true."

New Prospect Cafe (Brooklyn) S 19 | 13 | 17 | $28

393 Flatbush Ave. (bet. Plaza St. & Sterling Pl.), 718-638-2148

◪ Like an aging "hippie" on the Prospect Heights scene, this "venerable" "grassroots" Eclectic offers "high-quality", "healthy" eats, even if the room could stand a "redo" and whole-food foes say "too much tofu" makes for a "bland" trip.

Nha Trang S 23 | 8 | 15 | $18

87 Baxter St. (bet. Bayard & Canal Sts.), 212-233-5948 ⊅
148 Centre St. (bet. Walker & White Sts.), 212-941-9292

■ Despite the "cheesy decor", "dynamite Vietnamese" cooking, "great value" and "speedy service" make this "popular" C-towner the "best part of doing jury duty"; the newish Center Street addition means "less crowding", though purists "prefer the original."

Nice Restaurant S 19 | 10 | 13 | $26

35 E. Broadway (bet. Catherine & Market Sts.), 212-406-9510

◪ Join the "banquet" at this Chinatown "extravaganza", a "noisy, auditorium-like" space where "crowds of locals" feast on "elaborate" Cantonese and dim sum; there's an "endless wait" and decor is "completely lacking", but for "top-tier" eating, the "name says it all."

Nicholson ▽ 20 | 24 | 20 | $68

323 E. 58th St. (bet. 1st & 2nd Aves.), 212-355-6769

◪ A "romantic hideaway" on the East Side, this "class act" from chef-owner Patrick Woodside features "delightful" French food presented in an "exquisite room" adorned with "unique" tiled "mosaics"; it's a "swell" setting, but a few find it "too precious" in more ways than one.

Nick & Stef's Steakhouse 21 | 19 | 20 | $54

9 Penn Plaza (on 33rd St., bet. 7th & 8th Aves.), 212-563-4444

◪ All-star chef Joachim Splichal's LA-based meatery transplant, named after his twin sons, is "exactly what Madison Square Garden needed",

	F	D	S	C

and "not just for a game"; boosters claim it's a winner for "solid steaks" and other "robust" fare served in a "warm", "masculine" room, even if critics contend it's "rough around the edges."

Nick and Toni's Cafe S — 19 | 16 | 18 | $45
100 W. 67th St. (bet. B'way & Columbus Ave.), 212-496-4000
■ "If you can't get to the Hamptons", this "casual" LI import works for a "light meal" of "tasty", "wood-fired" Mediterranean fare; "handy to Lincoln Center", it's a "cozy, friendly", "see-and-be-seen place", though contras contend it's "plain" and "pricey" too.

Nick's Pizza (Queens) S⇗ — 24 | 13 | 17 | $21
108-26 Ascan Ave. (bet. Austin & Burns Sts.), 718-263-1126
■ "It's all good" enthuse fans of the "consistently perfect pizza", "gourmet toppings", "huge salads" and "fabulous cannoli" that make this pie palace "God's gift" to Forest Hills; the "decor's mediocre" and staff "attitude" may arise, but pie-eyed acolytes answer "who cares?"

Nicola Paone — 21 | 18 | 21 | $55
207 E. 34th St. (bet. 2nd & 3rd Aves.), 212-889-3239
■ Though perhaps "showing its age", this high-end Murray Hill Northern Italian still thrills with "delicious" food, a formidable "wine cellar" and "genial", "attentive" service; the room retains its "regal" bearing, even if it recalls the "set of a 1963 Sophia Loren movie."

Nicola's Restaurant ●S — 22 | 17 | 20 | $53
146 E. 84th St. (bet. Lexington & 3rd Aves.), 212-249-9850
■ "Upper East Side power brokers" gather at this "clubby" "favorite" for "simple" (but "pricey") "homestyle Italian" cooking that "doesn't disappoint"; though the room may "need a revamp", "dress well" and be polite, since regulars matter" here – "first-timers don't".

Nicole's S — ∇ 21 | 23 | 19 | $47
Nicole Farhi, 10 E. 60th St. (bet. 5th & Madison Aves.), 212-223-2288
■ "Civilized" shoppers and "Euro-trendy" lunchers descend to this "chic" basement Eclectic in the Nicole Fahri boutique for "wonderful" food with lots of "style" on the side; it's "oh so modern and slick", and fittingly dangles a "Gucci price tag."

Niederstein's (Queens) S — 18 | 16 | 18 | $34
69-16 Metropolitan Ave. (69th St.), 718-326-0717
■ Sited "next to the cemetery", this Middle Village "favorite" will "waken your spirits" with "stick-to-the-ribs" German "classics" served in a "faux Bavarian setting"; "around forever" (since 1889) and eternally "tacky", it's "good for parties" and "every birthday after 55."

Niko's Mediterranean Grill ●S — 19 | 12 | 16 | $27
2161 Broadway (76th St.), 212-873-7000
■ Boasting a "budget" menu that's "a mile long" and Greek-Med grub of "Olympian portions", this "hectic" West Side taverna is filled with "corny" floor-to-ceiling "clutter" ("behold the tchotchkes"); though service runs "hot and cold", regulars consider it one "big party."

92 ●S — – | – | – | E
45 E. 92nd St. (Madison Ave.), 212-828-5300
■ Well-prepped Upper Eastsiders "eagerly awaited" Ken Aretsky's brand-new brasserie with French looks but a New American comfort menu; their hopes have apparently been satisfied, since the neighbors have already dubbed it the "Uptown Odeon."

Nino's S — 23 | 20 | 22 | $54
1354 First Ave. (bet. 72nd & 73rd Sts.), 212-988-0002
■ "They spoil you" at this East Side Northern Italian "charmer" where amenities include "fabulous food", "gracious service", a "warm",

"wood-paneled" setting and "live piano music"; it caters to a "refined, older clientele" that swears it's "worth every dollar."

Nino's Positano S | 19 | 19 | 20 | $49
890 Second Ave. (bet. 47th & 48th Sts.), 212-355-5540

◪ Nino Selimaj's latest is a "real plus" for Midtown, offering "good" Southern Italian fare and "pleasant service" in a "pretty", "low-key" setting; some posit that it "doesn't match the original yet", though it does offer added prix fixe lunch and pre-theater "value."

Nippon | 23 | 18 | 22 | $53
155 E. 52nd St. (bet. Lexington & 3rd Aves.), 212-758-0226

■ Turning out "consistently excellent" sushi, tempura and soba, this Midtown Japanese standby is upmarket pricewise and a "little dated", but has "high standards" and "personal service" that make it an asset for "business" diners.

Nirvana ●S | 17 | 24 | 19 | $52
30 Central Park S. (bet. 5th & 6th Aves.), 212-486-5700

◪ The hard-to-beat combination of a "grand" Central Park view and an "Ali Baba's tent" interior at this penthouse Indian tends to distract from the "not-bad" food; few argue with the "scenery", though nonbelievers note it "tempers earthly pleasures by en-lightening your wallet."

Nisos ●S | ▽ 18 | 17 | 15 | $39
176 Eighth Ave. (19th St.), 646-336-8121

◪ "Hip but friendly" Chelsea Mediterranean newcomer with an "open-air feel" and "excellent", "could-be-on-Mykonos" fin fare; landlubbers lament the "average" food and "slow" service, but thanks to "good people-watching", they say "everything else is beside the point."

NL S | ▽ 20 | 17 | 17 | $47
169 Sullivan St. (bet. Bleecker & Houston Sts.), 212-387-8801

■ "Dutch treat" takes on a new meaning at this Village "curiosity" featuring "interesting" cookery via Holland and its spicier "former colonies" (mainly Indonesia); though the calling card–size space is "cramped", the "open kitchen puts on a brilliant show", turning out "small portions" at not-so small prices.

NOBU S | 28 | 25 | 25 | $70
105 Hudson St. (Franklin St.), 212-219-0500

■ It's next to impossible to get a seat (they don't always bother to pick up the phone) at Nobu Matsuhisa's Japanese-Peruvian "classic" in TriBeCa, where the "incredible" offerings prove "some things are worth the wait"; expect "dining as theater" in a "richly atmospheric" David Rockwell–designed setting "packed with celebs", but be prepared for "car payment"–worthy prices; P.S. those who "can't plan two months ahead" opt for Nobu's "gorgeous" Next Door sibling offering equally "brilliant food" for a "little less", without reservations.

Nocello S | 22 | 19 | 22 | $39
257 W. 55th St. (bet. B'way & 8th Ave.), 212-713-0224

■ A "quiet break from the Midtown rush", this "reasonably priced" trattoria is "serious about food", serving "satisfying" Northern Italian fare crafted from "fresh, homemade ingredients"; an "accommodating" staff and "cozy" digs compensate for the "lack of elbow room."

NoHo Star ●S | 18 | 15 | 16 | $28
330 Lafayette St. (Bleecker St.), 212-925-0070

◪ "Everyone can find something to eat" at this NoHo Asian-American putting forth three squares a day in a "luncheonette"-like setting; though perhaps "nothing earth-shattering" foodwise and a bit too "leisurely" servicewise, it's convenient "after the Angelika", and the price is right.

	F	D	S	C

Nonna ●S
– | – | – | M

504 La Guardia Pl. (bet. Bleecker & Houston Sts.), 212-420-0652
Located on an inauspicious NoHo block, this smallish Italian trattoria looks to dating NYUers and other locals to fill its sidewalk tables and midsize dining room; an open kitchen lends transparency to its interesting (if concise) midpriced menu.

Noodle Pudding (Brooklyn) S⇗
22 | 18 | 20 | $34

38 Henry St. (bet. Cranberry & Middagh Sts.), 718-625-3737
■ With "no sign", this Brooklyn Heights Italian is "hard to find", but its reasonably priced, "homestyle cooking" and overall "charisma" are worth sleuthing out; despite a "no reservations, no credit cards" policy and "limited seating", it's an "ideal neighborhood joint."

Noodles on 28 ●S
19 | 9 | 15 | $20

394 Third Ave. (28th St.), 212-679-2888
☑ "Dependable dumplings", "excellent noodles" and "fair everything else" sums up this Gramercy Chinese where locals opt for "lightning-quick" delivery since there's "not much decor" in sight; though "good for the 'hood", some shrug "not C-town quality."

Norma's S
24 | 21 | 20 | $34

Le Parker Meridien, 118 W. 57th St. (bet. 6th & 7th Aves.), 212-708-7460
■ The outstanding breakfasts are still the "most important meal of the day" at this "très chic" Midtown American where you can "lounge like a movie star" while you try to "make up your mind" what to sample from the "imaginative menu."

Notaro S
19 | 16 | 19 | $34

635 Second Ave. (bet. 34th & 35th Sts.), 212-686-3400
☑ For "pasta without pretense", this "adult" Murray Hill Northern Italian is a "delightful" "good value" (with an "unbelievable" prix fixe); the staff "can't do enough for you", and even if the room's a bit "drab", the fireplace lends a "romantic" air.

Novecento ●S
19 | 17 | 16 | $38

343 W. Broadway (bet. Broome & Grand Sts.), 212-925-4706
☑ "*Muy bueno*" is the verdict on this SoHo Argentine "meat bar/restaurant" that may be "smoky", "chaotic" and "beyond crowded", but makes for "sexy" "fun" thanks to its "oh-so-Euro" crowd and "feast-your-eyes staff."

Novitá S
23 | 20 | 21 | $48

102 E. 22nd St. (Park Ave. S.), 212-677-2222
■ "Beautiful people" patronize this "mildly trendy", "slightly snooty", plainly pricey Gramercy Northern Italian for its "perfect", "refined" food, service that's "friendly" "without fawning" and "simple yet tasteful" decor.

Nyonya ●S⇗
23 | 14 | 15 | $21

194 Grand St. (bet. Mott & Mulberry Sts.), 212-334-3669
5323 Eighth Ave. (54th St.), Brooklyn, 718-633-0808
☑ "You can't go wrong" at these bargain Malaysians, since everything's "exotic" and "delicious" as well as "hot and spicy"; forget the "forgettable decor", "so-so service" and "long lines" – the incredibly "cheap" bills make it all worthwhile.

Oak Room S
20 | 24 | 21 | $58

Plaza Hotel, 768 Fifth Ave. (Central Park S.), 212-546-5330
☑ Reflecting "olde NY" at its "sophisticated best", this "timeless" ode to oak in the Plaza is a "grown-up" steakhouse "where you still need to know which fork to use"; though a tad "overpriced", this "old money" "landmark" should be experienced at least "once in your lifetime."

	F	D	S	C

Obeca Li — 19 | 22 | 17 | $44
62 Thomas St. (bet. Church St. & W. B'way), 212-393-9887
■ Even though the Pan-Asian food's quite good, it is outshined by the "really modern" look of this "multi-level" TriBeCan; however, many appear to think that the "MIA" service is "just ridiculous."

OCEANA — 27 | 25 | 26 | $69
55 E. 54th St. (bet. Madison & Park Aves.), 212-759-5941
■ "Phenomenal phish" "leagues above the rest" defines this "opulent yacht" moored in landlocked Midtown that rises to the surface with "slick" "nautical decor" and "flawless service" directed by the "best captain in the city"; though priced way above the water (prix fixe only: $40 lunch, $65 dinner), this deep-sea "shrine" is "worth every last dime" – "you'll never want to go back on shore again."

Ocean Grill ●S — 23 | 21 | 21 | $47
384 Columbus Ave. (bet. 78th & 79th Sts.), 212-579-2300
■ Fans of Steve Hanson's "jumpin'" "seafood extravaganza" christen it a "godsend on the Upper West Side" for fish "so fresh" you can almost "feel the salt spray on your face"; toss in "knowledgeable service" and a "stylish" setting complete with "outdoor seating", and it's no wonder you "can't hear anyone talk."

Ocean Palace ●S — 21 | 12 | 16 | $26
5421-5423 Eighth Ave. (bet. 54th & 55th Sts.), Brooklyn, 718-871-8080
1414-1418 Ave. U (bet. E. 14th & 15th Sts.), Brooklyn, 718-376-3838
■ "Chinatown crosses the East River" at these Brooklyn twins that are so "huge" and "loud" "they should go into the bar mitzvah business"; "quality" Hong Kong–style dim sum and "moderate prices" are the lures, not the "overzealous service" or "run-down" looks.

Odeon, The ●S — 19 | 18 | 18 | $41
145 W. Broadway (bet. Duane & Thomas Sts.), 212-233-0507
■ "In a class all its own", this TriBeCa "legend" remains "forever hip" and "still relevant" thanks to enduring "good karma" matched by "steady" American-French fare; it's "at its best" "late night", when the "glorified" "diner decor" "looks better" – especially after the "celebs" and "arty" folk toddle in.

O.G. ●S — 22 | 15 | 18 | $31
507 E. Sixth St. (bet. Aves. A & B), 212-477-4649
■ "Très cool without 'tude", this "mellow" "Alphabet City winner" provides "excellent Pan-Asian" cooking that's "upscale" in taste yet "affordable" in price; a few say "the decor could use some help."

Oggi ●S — ▽ 19 | 18 | 17 | $34
211 Ave. A (13th St.), 212-979-7044
■ "Low-key, calming" East Village "hideout" that "no one seems to know about" despite "reasonably priced" Southern Italian dishes from a "small but tasty menu"; the decor is "rustic", service "friendly" and overall mood "inviting."

Ohta — – | – | – | M
168 Lexington Ave. (bet. 30th & 31st Sts.), 212-481-8088
Artfully presented sushi and quaintly named sakes ('Drunken Heart', 'Manly Mountain') served with free edamame give this simple Japanese a cutting edge over its Kips Bay neighbors; the slightly pricey menu also includes cooked classics like tempura and katsudon.

Oikawa ● — ▽ 20 | 17 | 18 | $41
805 Third Ave., 2nd fl. (50th St.), 212-980-1400
■ A "Nobu antidote" in the middle of Midtown, this "authentic" Japanese offers a "nifty Third Avenue view" from its "second-floor"

perch and "decent" food that's "a bit pricey"; still, what's "quiet" and "unpretentious" to some is "dead and slow" to others.

Old Homestead [S] 21 | 17 | 19 | $54

56 Ninth Ave. (bet. 14th & 15th Sts.), 212-242-9040

◪ "Clogging arteries for 130 years", this "original Meatpacking District" chophouse on the scene since 1868 is "still a contender" for "monster" portions of "big ol' steaks" at "Peter Luger prices"; skeptics say the dark, "dowdy" digs need a "revamp" (ditto the "old fogy" service) and opt to "moo-ve on", though at press time a revamp is in the works.

Old San Juan [S] 18 | 12 | 16 | $27

765 Ninth Ave. (bet. 51st & 52nd Sts.), 212-262-6761

◪ For "filling" "rice 'n' beans like grandma makes" at "dirt-cheap" tabs, this Hell's Kitchen Puerto Rican–Argentine does the job, however, foes feel it "misses" owing to "tired decor" and "glacial service."

Old Town Bar ◐ [S] 15 | 18 | 15 | $21

45 E. 18th St. (bet. B'way & Park Ave. S.), 212-529-6732

■ Stick to the "burgers and you can't go wrong" at this vintage 1892 Flatiron pub popular with "frat boys" for its "brewskies" and Luddites for its "no-cell-phone policy"; though "you can't beat the [turn-of-the-century] atmosphere", you must be patient: "they have both kinds of dumbwaiters here."

Oliva ◐ [S] 20 | 15 | 17 | $36

161 E. Houston St. (Allen St.), 212-228-4143

■ "Innovative" "modern Basque" cookery combines with a "cool, buzzing vibe" to make this Lower East Side "hole-in-the-wall" quite the "hip haven"; loyal subjects say "tapas reign", but the "high-volume", "energetic" "party scene" may dethrone it.

Olives [S] 23 | 21 | 20 | $50

W Union Square Hotel, 201 Park Ave. S. (E. 17th St.), 212-353-8345

■ Boston's Todd English is "Manhattan's best new citizen" with yet "another triumph" at this "trendy", high-energy Union Square Med where "inventive but tradition-rooted food" arrives in a "crowded", "mod" setting overlooking an "open kitchen"; both portions and price tags come "high", but overall the "fanfare is deserved" – "bravo."

Ollie's ◐ [S] 16 | 11 | 13 | $21

2315 Broadway (84th St.), 212-362-3712
1991 Broadway (bet. 67th & 68th Sts.), 212-595-8181
200B W. 44th St. (bet. B'way & 8th Ave.), 212-921-5988
2957 Broadway (116th St.), 212-932-3300

◪ This "no-frills" West Side Chinese quartet ladles out "bowls of noodles so big you could swim in them" at "easy-on-the-purse" prices; downsides are "cattle-call" ambiance and "soulless service" that's so "f-f-fast" you can have "dinner in under 10 minutes."

Omen ◐ [S] 24 | 20 | 21 | $48

113 Thompson St. (bet. Prince & Spring Sts.), 212-925-8923

■ For two decades, this SoHo Japanese has been among the "best and truest" of the genre, serving "delectable" "Kyoto-style" fare that many consider sheer "perfection"; "respectful service" and "tranquil" surroundings reinforce the "meditative" mood that is likely to continue after you pay the bill.

Omonia Cafe ◐ [S] 19 | 15 | 14 | $19

7612-14 Third Ave. (bet. 76th & 77th Sts.), Brooklyn, 718-491-1435
32-20 Broadway (33rd St.), Queens, 718-274-6650

■ "Forget the calories" – the "Greek pastries are addictive" at these brass 'n' glass, late night Astoria and Bay Ridge coffeehouses; ok, maybe they date back to "the age of the Greek gods" and suffer from cigarette "smog", but overall they "do Athens proud."

Once Upon a Tart S | 20 | 13 | 13 | $16

135 Sullivan St. (bet. Houston & Prince Sts.), 212-387-8869
☑ "Heavenly buttermilk scones" in the AM, "creative gourmet sandwiches" for lunch and "scrumptious" "sweet treats" all day long keep this "tiny", "no-glamour" SoHo cafe "busy"; the "aloof staff" also provides a "complimentary inferiority complex with every muffin."

O'Neals' ⏺S | 17 | 16 | 17 | $36

49 W. 64th St. (bet. B'way & CPW), 212-787-4663
☑ "Like an overstuffed easy chair", Michael O'Neal's "reliable" American pub near Lincoln Center, with several "cozy" seating areas, serves "hearty portions" of pleasing pub grub; though some sigh "bland", the "price is right" and they "get you to the curtain on time."

One C.P.S. ⏺S | 20 | 22 | 20 | $58

Plaza Hotel, 1 Central Park S. (59th St. & 5th Ave.), 212-583-1111
■ A "shot in the arm for the Plaza", this "bright" New American brasserie is quite the "transformation" from its "previous incarnation", purveying "well-served, delicious" fare that harmonizes with the Central Park views and "modernized splendor" of Adam Tihany's redesign (don't worry, the mega-red "lampshades will grow on you"); granted, "it ain't cheap", but it sure "shows promise."

ONE IF BY LAND, TIBS S | 25 | 27 | 25 | $68

17 Barrow St. (bet. 7th Ave. S. & W. 4th St.), 212-228-0822
■ There's a "reason why people fall in love" after a meal at this "romantic" Village New American townhouse where Aaron Burr once lived: its intoxicating blend of "fresh roses, piano music", the "best beef Wellington anywhere" and a "cuddle by the fireplace" is so swoonworthy, it "ought to be underwritten by the Romance Channel"; though you need to bring "big bucks" ($64 prix fixe only), "if you can't soften her up here, you're hopeless."

101 (Brooklyn) ⏺S | 20 | 17 | 17 | $33

10018 Fourth Ave. (bet. 100th & 101st Sts.), 718-833-1313
■ "Kick hack" with the rest of the "young vibrant crowd" at this "lively" Bay Ridge Italian-American where the food's reliably good, though some say it plays second fiddle to the "noisy" bar scene; "older" types "go early", then cede the joint to a "high-haired" "disco" crowd.

Onieal's Grand St. ⏺S | ▽ 18 | 22 | 20 | $41

174 Grand St. (bet. Centre & Mulberry Sts.), 212-941-9119
■ "Elegance without pretension" is the hallmark of this "undiscovered" Little Italy New American in a "landmark building" that's awash in dark wood and "romantic lighting"; "delicious food" and a "comfy bar" make it a more than "pleasant find."

Onigashima S | ▽ 18 | 12 | 15 | $30

43-45 W. 55th St., 2nd fl. (bet. 5th & 6th Aves.), 212-541-7145
■ Though located in "hectic Midtown", this "happily undiscovered", "authentic" Japanese supplies "delightful" eats "that are a steal for the quality"; regulars hope it remains a secret so they can keep the "magic things they do to tofu" all to themselves.

Oriental Garden ⏺S | ▽ 24 | 11 | 16 | $32

14 Elizabeth St. (bet. Bayard & Canal Sts.), 212-619-0085
■ "If it swims, they've got it" could be the motto of this all-white, fish tank–lined, Hong Kong–style seafood house in Chinatown; though usually crowded with C-town types, given the "excellent" quality and modest prices of its cuisine, it's surprising that so few of our seafood-savvy surveyors seem to have tried it.

	F	D	S	C

Oro Blu
▽ 20 | 18 | 20 | $39

333 Hudson St. (Charlton St.), 212-645-8004
■ A "standout" in the West SoHo "dining wasteland", this "open, airy" Italian is "lively" at lunch with neighboring "ad and printing" folk who praise its "above-average" food, "personable" service and "good food-to-dollar ratio."

Orsay ●S
19 | 21 | 16 | $56

1057 Lexington Ave. (75th St.), 212-517-6400
◪ This "very 'in'" East Side brasserie features the "best plastic surgery in town", sported by both its social "X-ray" crowd and the space itself (fka Mortimer's, nka "Balthazar Uptown"); though opinions diverge on the food ("innovative" vs. "overrated") and mood ("sophisticated" vs. "snobby"), it's very "popular" and consequently "noisy"; P.S. the "waiters don't have an attitude, they're just French."

Orso ●S
22 | 19 | 21 | $48

322 W. 46th St. (bet. 8th & 9th Aves.), 212-489-7212
■ You're likely to "sit next to the star of the show you've just seen" at this "comfortable" Italian standby that's garnering "standing ovations" for the "best pasta on Broadway"; since many deem it the "king of Restaurant Row", plan to reserve "a month ahead" and pray for luck.

Osaka (Brooklyn) S
▽ 22 | 18 | 19 | $29

272 Court St. (bet. DeGraw & Kane Sts.), 718-643-0044
■ Cobble Hill's "sushi snobs' paradise" slices up surprisingly affordable, "creative" raw fare that's served either in "tiny" indoor quarters where "tight seating dampens the mood", or outdoors in the mood-enhancing "peaceful garden."

Oscar's S
18 | 17 | 18 | $39

Waldorf-Astoria, 570 Lexington Ave. (50th St.), 212-872-4920
■ "Don't be intimidated" by its fancy hotel home: this "gentrified version of the old coffee shop" is "a good neighborhood joint"–cum–New American brasserie known for its "great lunch buffet"; in sum, "fine Waldorf dining in a less formal [and less expensive] setting."

Osso Buco S
17 | 16 | 17 | $33

1662 Third Ave. (93rd St.), 212-426-5422
88 University Pl. (bet. 11th & 12th Sts.), 212-645-4525
◪ "Humongous", "family-style" platters of "middle-of-the-road" food characterize these cheap, Carmine's-style Village and East Side Italians; while quality-minded surveyors find them "disappointing", realists plan to "eat there five days a week."

Osteria al Doge ●S
20 | 17 | 18 | $42

142 W. 44th St. (bet. B'way & 6th Ave.), 212-944-3643
■ "Sit upstairs" and "eat like a doge" at this "spirited" Venetian where the food's "interesting" and the ambiance almost "too charming for Times Square"; though it's a hassle "getting pre-theater reservations", it can be even tougher to "hail your waitress."

Osteria Laguna ●S
20 | 18 | 19 | $41

209 E. 42nd St. (bet. 2nd & 3rd Aves.), 212-557-0001
■ "Badly needed" in the "East Midtown wasteland", this "consistent" Northern Italian offers a "more spacious layout" than its Theater District sibling, but the same "satisfying" pasta and "designer pizza"; "too noisy" at lunch, it becomes more *intime* at dinner.

Otabe S
23 | 21 | 21 | $51

68 E. 56th St. (bet. Madison & Park Aves.), 212-223-7575
■ Split-personality Midtown Japanese offering "restful" dining up-front and a "fun" teppan grill in the rear reminiscent of a "deluxe

Benihana"; despite high marks all-around, it has never developed much of a following – perhaps the "high" prices are the reason.

Other Foods S ⊉ ▽ 23 | 17 | 17 | $24

47 E. 12th St. (bet. B'way & University Pl.), 212-358-0103
■ "When you need to feel cleansed and healthy", put this inexpensive organic Village cafe on your agenda; despite a somewhat "sterile" setting, "spotty service" and a "no credit card" policy, its food is "lovingly prepared" and "sinfully tasty."

Ouest S ▽ 24 | 21 | 21 | $54

2315 Broadway (84th St.), 212-580-8700
■ Chef Tom Valenti (ex Alison on Dominick, Butterfield 81) has "answered West Side gourmets' prayers" at this "exciting" New American showcasing a "clever menu" of "cutting-edge" fare; as a bonus, there are "wonderful" leather booths and an eye-grabbing "open kitchen", so it's no surprise that surveyors "can barely wait to return", regardless of the cost.

Our Place S 21 | 17 | 20 | $33

1444 Third Ave. (82nd St.), 212-288-4888
141 E. 55th St. (bet. Lexington & 3rd Aves.), 212-753-3900
■ "White tablecloths" and "upmarket menus" elevate these East Side siblings above "your average neighborhood Chinese", while "beautiful presentation" seals the bargain; though they're a "little more expensive", prices are "reasonable for the quality."

Outback Steakhouse S 16 | 14 | 16 | $30

23-48 Bell Blvd. (26th Ave.), Bayside, 718-819-0908
1475 86th St. (15th Ave.), Brooklyn, 718-837-7200
◪ There's "good eatin', mate" at these Brooklyn and Queens "family steakhouses" that "aren't bad for a chain" if you hanker for a low-budget "beef fix"; killjoys can't fathom why they're "always jammed", citing "prefab" fare that's "marginal at best."

Oyster Bar 22 | 18 | 17 | $43

Grand Central, lower level (42nd St. & Vanderbilt Ave.), 212-490-6650
■ This 1913 Grand Central "seafood tradition" is a "Damon Runyon"–esque "quintessential standard" that's *the* place for anything on the half-shell; despite "lousy acoustics", "grouchy" waiters and tabs that may run you a "lotta clams", it more than redeems itself with "wonderful" "fresh fish", a grand vaulted ceiling, lively counter seating and "chowder to dream about" – "if only the trains were this reliable."

Oyster Bar at the Plaza ● S 20 | 19 | 18 | $50

Plaza Hotel, 768 Fifth Ave. (enter on 58th St., bet. 5th & 6th Aves.), 212-546-5340
◪ "Delicious steamers" and other "essential seafood" surface in a "dark" "English pub" setting at this "old-world" Midtown haunt that's the most "casual" Plaza restaurant; still, the fin-icky fret it's "not exciting" and "pricier than ever."

Oznot's Dish (Brooklyn) ● S 22 | 20 | 18 | $29

79 Berry St. (N. 9th St.), 718-599-6596
■ "Wacky" Williamsburger giving out "good vibes" via "colorful" Eclectic cuisine with a Middle Eastern accent and a "great wine list" at a "reasonable" cost; the setting's as "quirky" as the crowd, but there's "no attitude" – no wonder it's "partially responsible for the gentrification" of the neighborhood.

Pad Thai S 19 | 15 | 17 | $26

114 Eighth Ave. (16th St.), 212-691-6226
■ The cooking is "hot" in both senses of the word at this "dark", "relaxed" Chelsea Thai known for its "great lunch specials"; though

you may "need patience" when it comes to service, "reasonable prices" are calming.

Paladar ⓢ⌀ ▽ 20 | 18 | 20 | $31
161 Ludlow St. (bet. Houston & Stanton Sts.), 212-473-3535
■ "Funky", wide-ranging Lower East Side Latino newcomer featuring "reliable Cuban dishes" accompanied by mojitos, caipirinhas and the like; the "cool" ambiance attracts correspondingly cool customers who dig the "cheap" tabs.

Palio 23 | 25 | 22 | $64
151 W. 51st St. (bet. 6th & 7th Aves.), 212-245-4850
◪ To "impress a client", try this Midtown Northern Italian that remains "high-end in all respects", from its "delicious" cooking and handsome, blond-wood setting to the "your-wish-is-their-command" service; detractors deriding "astronomical prices" claim the "best part" is the fantastic, four-wall Sandro Chia mural in the popular downstairs bar.

PALM 25 | 17 | 20 | $59
837 Second Ave. (bet. 44th & 45th Sts.), 212-687-2953
840 Second Ave. (bet. 44th & 45th Sts.), 212-697-5198 ⓢ
250 W. 50th St. (bet. B'way & 8th Ave.), 212-333-7256 ●ⓢ
◪ This "original" Jazz Age–era chop shop and its two spin-offs are right "out of a *New Yorker* story", with "rude waiters" serving "high rollers" "killer lobsters" and football-size filet mignon amid "flying sawdust" and floor-to-ceiling caricatures of famous clients; in spite of "national budget"-size tabs, the "high" energy here is "infectious."

Palma ⓢ – | – | – | M
28 Cornelia St. (bet. Bleecker & W. 4th Sts.), 212-691-2223
■ This mellow Italian newcomer on the Village's burgeoning Cornelia Street restaurant row offers "delicious" things from a menu that excels at seafood; the "charming owner and staff" keep the mood "friendly" enough to make some feel like they're "honeymooning on Capri."

Palm Court, The ●ⓢ 20 | 25 | 21 | $54
Plaza Hotel, 768 Fifth Ave. (Central Park S.), 212-546-5350
◪ Sitting under the Plaza's palms amidst "serenading violins" and "gilded splendor" enjoying high tea or Sunday brunch is sure to "wow your out-of-town guests" – unless they're ('ow') paying; for most, this is as close to dining in "Buckingham Palace" as they'll get.

Pamir ⓢ 20 | 17 | 19 | $34
1437 Second Ave. (bet. 74th & 75th Sts.), 212-734-3791
1065 First Ave. (58th St.), 212-644-9258
■ For "100 ways to serve lamb", you can count on these East Side Afghan kebab palaces that are "peaceful" "sanctuaries" for "change-of-pace" mavens; an "accommodating staff" and "reasonable" prices keep regulars regular.

Pampa ●ⓢ⌀ 20 | 16 | 16 | $32
768 Amsterdam Ave. (bet. 97th & 98th Sts.), 212-865-2929
■ "If you can't get to Buenos Aires", this Upper West Side Argentine provides a *muy bien* "meat orgy"; look for "bargain", "cash-only" tabs and "slow" service, though you can sustain yourself on its "wonderful aromas" while waiting.

Pam Real Thai Food ⓢ⌀ – | – | – | I
404 W. 49th St. (bet. 9th & 10th Aves.), 212-333-7500
You can test out your Thai at this unassuming, extremely authentic Hell's Kitchen taste of Bangkok proffering non-Westernized dishes such as *kaeng tai pla* (fish gut curry) and *nam phrik* (chili sauce with shrimp paste).

Pangea ◐[S] ▽ 19 | 18 | 17 | $29

178 Second Ave. (bet. 11th & 12th Sts.), 212-995-0900

◪ Its "thirtysomething" fan base likes this "dark, relaxed" Med for its "diverse menu" that's "always dependable" for "food with personality" at "old East Village prices"; its few critics consider it "uneven."

Pão! [S] 22 | 16 | 20 | $37

322 Spring St. (Greenwich St.), 212-334-5464

■ This "fun" Portuguese "haunt" parked in an "out-of-the-way" West SoHo nook has a "dark", "tight setting" counterbalanced by a menu of "bright, focused flavors"; loyalists tout its "authentic" atmosphere ("everybody smokes") and "inexpensive" tabs.

Paola's [S] 23 | 20 | 22 | $48

245 E. 84th St. (bet. 2nd & 3rd Aves.), 212-794-1890

■ Owner "Paola greets regulars like family" but "takes care of you no matter who you are" at this East Side "trattoria treasure" that's "many cuts above" the norm; purr-fectionists say it's the "cat's meow" for "upscale Italian" cooking in a "classy atmosphere."

Papaya King ≠ 19 | 6 | 11 | $9

179 E. 86th St. (3rd Ave.), 212-369-0648 [S]
255 W. 43rd St. (bet. 7th & 8th Aves.), 212-944-4594 [S]
121 W. 125th St. (bet. Lenox & 7th Aves.), 212-665-5732

■ For a "quick, cheap", "real NY experience", you can't do better than this "tube-steak" trio for its "uncannily good" hot dogs and "elixir-of-the-gods" fruit drinks; despite less-than-"no atmosphere", a standout stand-up meal here can be had for a "pittance" – and the theatrical cast of characters comes for free.

Paper Moon Milano 19 | 18 | 18 | $45

39 E. 58th St. (bet. Madison & Park Aves.), 212-758-8600

◪ Lunchtime volumes approach a "dull roar" at this Midtown Northern Italian that's always "crowded" with "business" folk savoring its "high-style" fare; dinner's quieter and better for "perusing Eurotrash", yet skeptics still say "ordinary" and "overpriced"; N.B. its Express siblings are cheaper and quicker.

Papillon ◐[S] ▽ 20 | 16 | 18 | $40

575 Hudson St. (bet. Bank & W. 11th Sts.), 646-638-2900

◪ "Admirably ambitious" West Village bistro with a schizophrenic side, since its "undiscovered" but "marvelous" French dining room is connected to a "busy", "trendy" Irish bar; though a few feel it "falls short" on setting and service, fans insist it's "just starting to buzz."

Paprika ◐[S]≠ ▽ 23 | 17 | 17 | $28

110 St. Marks Pl. (bet. Ave. A & 1st Ave.), 212-677-6563

■ "Inventive" Northern Italian cooking that will "make you feel like you're in Rome" transports diners at this East Village retooling of the former Pepe Rosso; though the menu's "small" and the room simple, service is "accommodating" and the prices even more so.

Paris Commune [S] 19 | 18 | 18 | $33

411 Bleecker St. (bet. Bank & W. 11th Sts.), 212-929-0509

■ "Ideal on cold rainy nights", this cozy West Village "standby" produces "old-fashioned" French bistro fare and a "moody", "romantic" mien; it's "always crowded" for brunch and especially favored by puffers, since it's "where the Euros go to smoke."

PARK, THE ◐[S] 19 | 25 | 16 | $47

118 10th Ave. (bet. 17th & 18th Sts.), 212-352-3313

◪ This "very hot" Way West Chelsea newcomer comes with divine "different rooms for different moods", including a "very LA" garden

F | D | S | C

and pulsating bar scene; be prepared for plenty of "beautiful beasts" and "celebs", plus a "surprisingly good" Mediterranean menu for a place this hip, but forget service – the staff's "too busy looking at their reflections in the plates."

Park Avalon ●S 20 | 21 | 19 | $40
225 Park Ave. S. (bet. 18th & 19th Sts.), 212-533-2500
■ With "remarkable staying power", this theatrical, candlelit Steve Hanson Park Avenue South "hot spot" continues to draw attractive, "high-energy" crowds with its well-prepared, well-priced New American "menu for all palates"; waits can be "long" and noise levels "loud", but there's always the "really nice", calmer Sunday jazz brunch as an option.

PARK AVENUE CAFE S 25 | 23 | 23 | $60
100 E. 63rd St. (bet. Lexington & Park Aves.), 212-644-1900
■ "All-American cooking goes Uptown" at this "top-rate" Eastsider where Neil Murphy's "clever" cooking is as much a "work of art" as the "folk art" decorating the room; ok, it's "très spendy", but from the "splendid bread basket to the opulent desserts", there are "no disappointments here."

Park Bistro S 22 | 18 | 20 | $48
414 Park Ave. S. (bet. 28th & 29th Sts.), 212-689-1360
■ A veteran that "should be landmarked", this "charming" Gramercy French bistro is "as Gallic as it gets" thanks to "classic" fare and "authentic" looks; just brace yourself for "lots of bumping" given the "very close quarters."

Park Side (Queens) ●S 24 | 20 | 21 | $42
107-01 Corona Ave. (51st Ave.), 718-271-9321
■ This authentic Corona Italian purveys "can't-miss food" that's almost as good as actually "being in Sicily"; but "book in advance", since it gets "crowded" on weekends, and "if you want quiet", request seats in the "Marilyn Monroe Room upstairs."

Parma ●S 21 | 15 | 20 | $49
1404 Third Ave. (bet. 79th & 80th Sts.), 212-535-3520
■ Dishing up "simply prepared", "traditional" fare, this 25-year-old "unpretentious" Upper East Side Northern Italian "never changes", and that's the way its "creatures-of-habit" crowd seems to like it; sure, it's "a bit expensive" and "needs a face-lift", but so do many of its well-heeled regulars.

Parsonage (Staten Island) S 21 | 23 | 20 | $44
74 Arthur Kill Rd. (Clarke Ave.), 718-351-7879
◪ Set in a "historic" parsonage on the grounds of the "Richmondtown restoration", this "romantic" Staten Island Continental boasts "excellent" fare that's "priced right"; though trendoids yawn "boring", traditionalists enjoy being "transported back" in time.

Pascalou S 21 | 15 | 18 | $38
1308 Madison Ave. (bet. 92nd & 93rd Sts.), 212-534-7522
■ Its "early-bird prix fixe is a huge bargain" and flavors are equally outsized at this unpretentious Carnegie Hill Eclectic-French bistro, but its space is another story ("diminutive", "lilliputian", "VW bug"– size, etc.); too bad its "increased popularity puts a strain on the help."

Pasha S 21 | 20 | 20 | $38
70 W. 71st St. (bet. Columbus Ave. & CPW), 212-579-8751
■ Even the "prices are right" at this "lush", "red-walled" "Turkish delight" where the "superb food" is "skillfully prepared" and conversations are blessedly "audible"; even better, this "interesting option" is "near Lincoln Center too."

Pasticcio [S] — 20 | 18 | 19 | $37

447 Third Ave. (bet. 30th & 31st Sts.), 212-679-2551

◪ Regulars report "solid food" and "superfriendly service" at this fresco-filled Murray Hiller that's the "neighborhood Italian of choice"; but a handful of spoilers say it's only "so-so", citing a "limited" menu and "pricey specials."

Pastis ☾ [S] — 20 | 21 | 17 | $42

9 Ninth Ave. (Little W. 12th St.), 212-929-4844

■ Keith McNally's "ultra"-hip, "high-energy" Meatpacking District take on a Paris bistro has lived up to all the "hoopla" thanks to its "great food", "wonderful Left Bank atmosphere", "outdoor seating" and celeb-centric clientele; despite "infinite waits" and "patronizing" service, the word is this "keeper" has "caught on because it deserves it."

Pastrami Queen [S] — 17 | 8 | 12 | $21

1269 Lexington Ave. (bet. 85th & 86th Sts.), 212-828-0007

◪ Having survived its "sex change" (fka Pastrami King), this East Side regent of "cholesterol" is "worth the heartburn" for "good kosher deli" eats; forget the "lousy" decor and "sloppy service" – and "go with the extra-lean" when ordering its eponymous specialty.

Patois (Brooklyn) [S] — 22 | 18 | 19 | $36

255 Smith St. (bet. DeGraw & Douglass Sts.), 718-855-1535

■ "Bistro perfection" thrives in Brooklyn at this "energetic" "Smith Street pioneer" serving "adventurous", "country-fresh" French fare courtesy of chef Alan Harding; its "lovely", renovated setting and "cute garden" are the backdrops for dining that's "satisfying to the palate, soul and wallet."

Patria [S] — 24 | 22 | 21 | $58

250 Park Ave. S. (20th St.), 212-777-6211

■ "Each dish is a head-turner", ditto many of the customers, at this Flatiron Nuevo Latino storefront that's still turning out "inventive, celebratory food" that's like "fireworks in your mouth"; the "undulating curves" of its "colorful" multi-level setting make diners "want to salsa", and though service may be "spotty" sometimes and prices "steep" at all times, there's "still no other restaurant like it."

Patsy's [S] — 20 | 16 | 19 | $45

236 W. 56th St. (bet B'way & 8th Ave.), 212-247-3491

◪ "They do it their way" at this Carnegie Hall–area "red-sauce" Southern Italian that once was a haunt of "Ol'-Blue-Eyes" and is "still living on his ghost"; expect lots of "good memories", but "indifferent" service and "long-in-the-tooth" decor.

Patsy's Pizzeria [S] 🚫💳 — 21 | 13 | 15 | $22

2287-91 First Ave. (bet. 117th & 118th Sts.), 212-534-9783 ☾
1312 Second Ave. (69th St.), 212-639-1000
61 W. 74th St. (bet. Columbus Ave. & CPW), 212-579-3000
509 Third Ave. (bet. 34th & 35th Sts.), 212-689-7500
318 W. 23rd St. (bet. 8th & 9th Aves.), 646-486-7400
67 University Pl. (bet. 10th & 11th Sts.), 212-533-3500

■ "Delicious thin-crust" pies make this mini-chain a "contender" for the best pizza crown, although "pushy service", "no credit cards" and "no delivery" are "bummers"; still, supporters say "cars are always double-parked" outside for a reason; N.B. the separately run East Harlem coal oven is still considered the best.

Paul & Jimmy's [S] — 19 | 16 | 20 | $40

123 E. 18th St. (bet. Irving Pl. & Park Ave. S.), 212-475-9540

■ "Old-world charm never goes out of style", and this "comfortable" Gramercy Park Italian has been offering a "nice family atmosphere" along with "reliable", "traditional" fare since 1950; longtimers like having "no surprises" but dislike prices that "keep climbing."

Payard Bistro | 24 | 21 | 20 | $48
1032 Lexington Ave. (bet. 73rd & 74th Sts.), 212-717-5252
■ François Payard's "divine pastries" join forces with Philippe Bertineau's "sensational" French fare at this East Side double-decker patisserie-cum-bistro (aka the "21st-century Schrafft's") where you can either "drool at the showcase" or head back for a "great meal"; every neighborhood should have one of these home-away-from-homes.

Peacock Alley S | 23 | 24 | 23 | $67
Waldorf-Astoria, 301 Park Ave. (bet. 49th & 50th Sts.), 212-872-4896
■ "Visiting pooh-bahs" flash their plumage at this "best-kept secret" in the Waldorf-Astoria, a "moveable feast" that's "no longer stuffy" thanks to Laurent Gras' "sublime" French cuisine; it's still "so quiet you find yourself whispering", but "maybe that's a good thing"; P.S. don't miss the "bacchanalian" "splurge" of a brunch.

Peanut Butter & Co. S | 20 | 14 | 16 | $13
240 Sullivan St. (bet. Bleecker & W. 3rd Sts.), 212-677-3995
☑ "Everything sticks to the roof of your mouth" at this "extreme comfort food" Village sandwich shop with "more variations on PB&J than you can imagine"; grinches groan it's all "fluff", citing "sloppy service" and minimal decor that even low prices can't butter over.

PEARL OYSTER BAR | 26 | 13 | 18 | $37
18 Cornelia St. (bet. Bleecker & W. 4th Sts.), 212-691-8211
■ Think "Maine on the Hudson" to get the gist of this Village "seafood luncheonette" where "superb" fish, lobster rolls and "fried oysters from heaven" translate into "lines that wrap around the block"; despite only 26 seats and "assembly-line" service, "you'll forget the squeeze" once you taste Rebecca Charles' "unbelievably good" cooking.

Pearls ●S | ∇ 18 | 16 | 18 | $22
796 Amsterdam Ave. (99th St.), 212-749-0300
■ Its "Shanghai specialties" lift this new Upper Westsider beyond "cookie-cutter Chinese" status, especially since its "quality" fare comes with "cheery service" and "affordable" tabs; hey, it just might "usurp the Szechuan empire!"

Pearson's Texas BBQ (Queens) S≠ | 24 | 7 | 13 | $20
71-04 35th Ave. (bet. 71st & 72nd Sts.), 718-779-7715
■ "Finger-lickin' good" BBQ and "kickin' sauces" turn up in the back of this "seedy", "hard-to-find" Jackson Heights joint; 'cue connoisseurs concur that the "ribs rock", but even they demand "new quarters" since the current "smoke-filled" "setup is abysmal."

Peasant ●S | 22 | 20 | 19 | $47
194 Elizabeth St. (bet. Prince & Spring Sts.), 212-965-9511
■ "Cool" NoLita open-kitchen Italian drawing "hip" types with "fabulous", "simple cooking" from its "wood-burning" oven; if there's "nothing peasant-like about the prices" and its "limited" menu could use "subtitles", they've managed to "control the noise level" without dampening its "fun", "friendly" feel.

Peking Duck House S | 22 | 14 | 16 | $32
28 Mott St. (bet. Chatham Sq. & Pell St.), 212-227-1810
☑ The "other dishes pale in comparison" to the "amazing" Peking duck at this Chinatown "classic" that's relocated and upgraded to mixed notices: new fans offer "kudos" to its "minimalist", "soothing" redo, but ex-fans "miss" its former "run-down" digs.

Pellegrino's [S] 22 | 17 | 20 | $38

138 Mulberry St. (bet. Grand & Hester Sts.), 212-226-3177

■ This "front-runner" stays a nose ahead of the Mulberry Street pack by serving "tasty", "fairly priced" pastas; though you can expect the "same old" "tacky" Little Italy decor, at least service is "fast and friendly" and it's "not overloaded with tourists."

Penang ◐[S] 19 | 17 | 16 | $29

1596 Second Ave. (83rd St.), 212-585-3838
240 Columbus Ave. (71st St.), 212-769-3988
64 Third Ave. (11th St.), 212-228-7888
109 Spring St. (bet. Greene & Mercer Sts.), 212-274-8883
38-04 Prince St. (Main St.), Queens, 718-321-2078 🚫

◪ These minimally priced, "marvelous Malaysian" "mainstays" come with "thatch-roofed", "bamboo-riot" decor and a "sarong"-wearing staff; some dub the grub "uneven" and "wish the noise level was lower", but you don't get this "packed" without being very popular; N.B. the Third Avenue branch is separately owned.

Pepe Giallo To Go [S] 22 | 11 | 14 | $17

253 10th Ave. (bet. 24th & 25th Sts.), 212-242-6055

Pepe Rosso To Go [S]🚫

149 Sullivan St. (bet. Houston & Prince Sts.), 212-677-4555

Pepe Verde To Go [S]🚫

559 Hudson St. (bet. Perry & W. 11th Sts.), 212-255-2221

Pepe Viola To Go [S]

200 Smith St. (Baltic St.), Brooklyn, 718-222-8279

◪ "Soul-satisfying", all-over-town Italians that dish out "cheap, tasty", "no-frills" fare in "zero atmosphere"; to avoid the "brusque service" and get "*paesano* treatment", "order in Italian."

Pepolino [S] 24 | 18 | 23 | $42

281 W. Broadway (bet. Canal & Lispenard Sts.), 212-966-9983

■ "Tuscany" comes to TriBeCa at this "terrific" trattoria that's relatively "unfound" despite the "consistency" of its "simple" yet "inventive" menu, and even better, there's "no pretense" at this "family-run spot."

Pergola des Artistes ∇ 21 | 15 | 21 | $32

252 W. 46th St. (bet. B'way & 8th Ave.), 212-302-7500

■ "*Grand-mère* cuisine" and "lots of it" is yours at this "homey" French bistro in the Theater District that's a "perfect overture" before curtains rise; it's a bit "anachronistic", but you "get your money's worth."

Periyali 25 | 22 | 23 | $53

35 W. 20th St. (bet. 5th & 6th Aves.), 212-463-7890

■ "Cancel the tickets to Athens" – this "haute" Flatiron Greek is much more convenient, offering "feasts worthy of the gods" delivered by a "caring" staff in "upscale" yet "low-key" digs; though prices can be as high as "Mount Olympus", the "grilled octopus alone is worth a trip" – no wonder it "keeps earning its high ratings."

Persepolis [S] 19 | 14 | 17 | $32

1423 Second Ave. (bet. 74th & 75th Sts.), 212-535-1100

■ Delightful dishes define the menu of this "comfortable" Upper Eastsider that's as "close to traditional Persian" cooking as you're likely to eat; though decor may be "limited", that "heavenly" sour cherry rice is "loved by all."

Pershing Square [S] 17 | 18 | 16 | $38

90 E. 42nd St. (Park Ave.), 212-286-9600

◪ Buzzy O'Keefe deserves bravos for having "recaptured" the space under the Park Avenue viaduct opposite Grand Central and turning it

		F	D	S	C

into a handsome American restaurant; however, except for the "fierce" "after-work" "bar scene", surveyors say he still has to work on improving the "average" cuisine and "glacial" service.

Pescatore ●S | 19 | 16 | 17 | $35 |
955 Second Ave. (bet. 50th & 51st Sts.), 212-752-7151
■ Appreciated both for its "terrific pastas" and seafood specialties, this "down-to-earth" Midtown "neighborhood" Italian also offers a "good bang for the buck" – no wonder "the suits love it here."

Petaluma ●S | 19 | 17 | 18 | $41 |
1356 First Ave. (73rd St.), 212-772-8800
■ The "Sotheby's crowd" finds this "bright, sunny" East Side Italian standby "lovely for lunch", and in the evenings it emits a "casual", "child-friendly" vibe; a few may find the eats just "ordinary" and "a bit overpriced", but they're easily outvoted by ardent admirers.

PETER LUGER STEAK HOUSE (Brooklyn) S | 27 | 15 | 20 | $59 |
178 Broadway (Driggs Ave.), 718-387-7400
■ "No one argues about" this one: "steak doesn't get any better" than at Williamsburg's "cash-only" "landmark", NY's No.1 red meatery for 18 years running; "carnivores consider it a "nostalgic" "pleasure to be mistreated by gruff, old-time waiters" and note its basic German beer hall decor is all the better for "concentrating on" the main event: porterhouse "like buttah" in "cow-and-a-half"-per-person portions – and "don't forget" the "oh-my-god" sides.

Pete's Downtown (Brooklyn) S | 20 | 18 | 19 | $35 |
2 Water St. (Cadman Plaza W.), 718-858-3510
■ "The River Cafe's less-expensive neighbor" has the same "supreme view of Manhattan"; it's "good Italian basics" seem almost beside the point when you're watching "the sun set behind Wall Street."

Pete's Tavern ●S | 14 | 15 | 15 | $30 |
129 E. 18th St. (Irving Pl.), 212-473-7676
◪ "O. Henry's hangout" is just "the way a tavern should be" – "smoky", "noisy", "dark and musty" – but this circa 1864 Gramercy "relic" may be "best for its history" since, except for its beer and burgers, most surveyors prefer to "eat elsewhere."

Petite Abeille S | 19 | 13 | 16 | $22 |
107 W. 18th St. (bet. 6th & 7th Aves.), 212-604-9350
400 W. 14th St. (9th Ave.), 212-727-1505
134 W. Broadway (Duane St.), 212-791-1360
466 Hudson St. (Barrow St.), 212-741-6479
■ Those craving a "fix" of "Brussels"-style "comfort food" make a beeline for these "bargain" "Tintin-themed" Belgians; service can be "slapdash", but their "rickety wooden tables" are always "packed."

Petrossian ●S | 24 | 24 | 24 | $66 |
182 W. 58th St. (7th Ave.), 212-245-2214
■ If you can afford it – and that's a big if – the "beluga overflows the plates" and the "champagne glasses are never empty" at this "tony" Franco-Russian near Carnegie Hall, where "exquisite cuisine" from new chef David Cunningham, "sumptuous" decor and "elegant service" can make one feel like "a czar" for the day; however, for those short on rubles, try the cafe down the block.

Pfiff ● | – | – | – | M |
35 Grand St. (Thompson St.), 212-334-6841
Set on a less-traveled corner of SoHo, this New American exudes a quiet-yet-cool vibe maximized by Orange Crush–colored banquettes

| F | D | S | C |

and a compact bar made for sipping sexy cocktails; seafood with tropical overtones stars on its stylish midpriced menu.

Philip Marie ●◐S | 20 | 18 | 19 | $38

569 Hudson St. (W. 11th St.), 212-242-6200
■ "Put it on your list" – this "cozy" and "relaxed" West Village New American bistro is run by a "charming husband-and-wife team" and has food that's always "well-prepared"; "fun" jazz nights cement its status as a local "find."

Pho Bang S | 19 | 7 | 12 | $16

6 Chatham Sq. (Mott St.), 212-587-0870
157 Mott St. (bet. Broome & Grand Sts.), 212-966-3797 ⌿
3 Pike St. (bet. Canal & Division Sts.), 212-233-3947 ⌿
82-90 Broadway (Elmhurst Ave.), Queens, 718-205-1500 ⌿
41-07 Kissena Blvd. (Main St.), Queens, 718-939-5520 ⌿
■ "Great to duck into" for a "fast" slurp, this "no-decor" Vietnamese noodle chain ladles out "big bowls of satisfying soup" at "lotsa locations" in Chinatown and Queens; plentiful portions and "dirt-cheap" prices add up to the best "bang pho the buck" going.

Phoenix Garden S⌿ | 22 | 10 | 15 | $28

242 E. 40th St. (bet. 2nd & 3rd Aves.), 212-983-6666
■ "Chinatown taste" close to the UN ensures this "cash-only" Tudor City Cantonese retains a "loyal" local following that happily overlook the "beyond-shabby" interior and "sassy"-at-best service in light of the "reasonable tabs" for great tastes enhanced by a BYO policy.

Pho Viet Huong S | 22 | 10 | 16 | $19

73 Mulberry St. (bet. Bayard & Canal Sts.), 212-233-8988
■ "You get more than you pay for" at this "supercheap" Chinatown Vietnamese maker of "marvelous noodle soups" catalogued on a menu that seems to "extend forever"; it may be "plain", but it's "clean and neat", and "perfect for those jury-duty lunches."

Piadina ●◐S⌿ | 19 | 17 | 16 | $32

57 W. 10th St. (bet. 5th & 6th Aves.), 212-460-8017
■ An "ab fab hole-in-the-wall", this "cave-like", "Tuscan-esque" West Villager tempts a "kind of trendy" crowd with "unpretentious" Northern Italian classics; puffers prefer "the back room" where they can "linger and smoke."

Piccola Venezia (Queens) S | 25 | 18 | 23 | $51

42-01 28th Ave. (42nd St.), 718-721-8470
■ "Still Queens' finest", this "back-to-the-'50s" Astoria "institution" makes you feel like "part of the family": order "sublime" "Italian with Continental flair" from the "exhaustive" menu, or make like it's "your own private kitchen" and have them whip up "whatever you want"; sure, the "marble" decor is "passé", the prices "Manhattan-style" and the "waits long", but loyalists agree it's all "worth it."

Piccolo Angolo S | 24 | 14 | 20 | $33

621 Hudson St. (Jane St.), 212-229-9177
■ You're in for "an eccentric night out" (after an "aggravating wait" to get in) at this "crowded", "noisy" West Village Italian where owner Renato Migliorini "recites the specials like an auctioneer"; the dishes arrive in "great, oversized portions", and luckily they're always good, because if you don't finish, you-know-who will want to know why.

PICHOLINE S | 27 | 24 | 25 | $69

35 W. 64th St. (bet. B'way & CPW), 212-724-8585
■ Proving that a "wonderful" restaurant can make it on the Upper West Side, Terry Brennan's "inventive", "comfortable" Lincoln Center

F **D** **S** **C**

Mediterranean "just keeps getting better", at least according to those who don't already consider it "impeccable"; if you can't get reservations at night, try it for the bargain prix fixe lunch, but at any meal leave room for the cheese course – unquestionably among "NY's best" – and let *fromager* Max McCalman explain them all to you.

Pico S | 23 | 22 | 21 | $61 |
349 Greenwich St. (bet. Harrison & Jay Sts.), 212-343-0700
☑ Ex JUdson Grill chef John Villa's "glorious" "take on" Portuguese cuisine at this TriBeCa "newcomer" has made it a fast "favorite" of foodies, while its "chic" space (the old Bazzini nut warehouse) has set "romantics" swooning; if a "disappointed" few deem it "over-hyped" and "overpriced", that's no surprise when expectations have been set so high.

Pierre au Tunnel S | 20 | 17 | 20 | $44 |
250 W. 47th St. (bet. B'way & 8th Ave.), 212-575-1220
☑ This Theater District "old-timer" has been belting out "French standards" to a full "pre-show" house since the days when "*The Pajama Game* and *My Fair Lady* were hits"; while it's a "nostalgic" "favorite" for many, critics contend that the kitchen's performance can be less than star quality.

Pierrot Bistro & Bar ●S | ▽ 19 | 19 | 18 | $32 |
28 Ave. B (bet. 2nd & 3rd Sts.), 212-673-1999
■ Have "Sunday brunch outside" on the patio at this "charming" Alphabet City bistro where the French-Eclectic menu is "good and inexpensive", the staff "kind and helpful" and the vibe "casual" – "great martinis" don't hurt, either.

Pier 25A (Queens) S | 17 | 15 | 16 | $36 |
215-16 Northern Blvd. (215th St.), 718-423-6395
☑ A faux "cruise ship" exterior and "nautically" themed interior say it all at this "old-fashioned" Bayside seafooder, where regulars order "nothing but fish" in portions sized to affordably satisfy the whole family; a mutinous minority, citing a "surly" crew serving "uninspired" eats, says this ship needs "deep-sixing."

Pietrasanta S | 20 | 15 | 18 | $32 |
683 Ninth Ave. (47th St.), 212-265-9471
■ As "unpretentious" as its Hell's Kitchen address, this Northern Italian storefront dispenses "warm welcomes" along with its "modestly priced" "homemade pastas"; it's no wonder "the TKTS crowd" jams in despite "seating so tight" they mustn't "eat too much."

Pietro's | 23 | 16 | 21 | $57 |
232 E. 43rd St. (bet. 2nd & 3rd Aves.), 212-682-9760
☑ At this "clubby" vintage Italian beef palace near Grand Central, "old-time waiters" who appear to have been there since it opened serve up "humongous steaks, perfectly done" and "amazing sides" to a clientele of "real guys"; though critics claim its "time has passed", loyal "carnivores" who're in on the "well-known secret" still consider it their meatery of choice.

Pig Heaven ●S | 18 | 14 | 17 | $32 |
1540 Second Ave. (bet. 80th & 81st Sts.), 212-744-4333
■ Even though this Chinese Eastsider serves more than just pork, the dishes from its menu's "porcine region" are "a cut above" the rest; if some longtime patrons are still adjusting to the "upscale" revamp a couple of years back, most say it "seems rejuvenated" and still provides priceless "pigging out."

F	D	S	C

Ping's Seafood ●S | 20 | 11 | 13 | $30 |
20 E. Broadway (bet. Catherine & Market Sts.), 212-965-0808
22 Mott St. (bet. Bayard & Pell Sts.), 212-602-9988
83-02 Queens Blvd. (Goldsmith St.), Queens, 718-396-1238
■ "Some of the freshest, subtlest food" in town can be had at this "Hong Kong–style" trio where the "exotic" seafood is "plucked from the tanks" and "artfully" prepared by "cooks who speak fluent delicious" – even if the servers suffer from "language barriers"; P.S. don't miss the "dynamite dim sum."

Pink Tea Cup ●S≠ | 18 | 12 | 15 | $22 |
42 Grove St. (bet. Bedford & Bleecker Sts.), 212-807-6755
■ "You'd better be hungry" when facing down this "cheap", "tiny", "trashy" West Village Soul Food institution's "terrific", "artery-clogging breakfasts" and fried chicken; naturally, "everything's pink" here, and whatever you did the night before, it's "perfect for the morning after."

Pinocchio S | ▽ 20 | 16 | 22 | $41 |
1748 First Ave. (bet. 90th & 91st Sts.), 212-828-5810
■ Recently "reincarnated" in a "lovely little" "storefront", this Upper East Side Italian's "tasty", "value"-priced fare and "friendly staff" are "as good as before"; the only trouble is, it's "very cramped" – "go early."

Pintaile's Pizza S | 18 | 8 | 12 | $15 |
26 E. 91st St. (bet. 5th & Madison Aves.), 212-722-1967
1577 York Ave. (bet. 83rd & 84th Sts.), 212-396-3479
1443 York Ave. (bet. 76th & 77th Sts.), 212-717-4990
1237 Second Ave. (bet. 64th & 65th Sts.), 212-752-6222
124 Fourth Ave. (bet. 12th & 13th Sts.), 212-475-4977
◪ The "healthy", "light-as-air" "designer" pizza at this popular takeout chain has "thin-crust" fans "raving", but even devotees dis the tiny Uptown outlets as barely "sit-down restaurants."

Pipa S | 21 | 22 | 18 | $39 |
ABC Carpet & Home, 38 E. 19th St. (bet. B'way & Park Ave S.), 212-677-2233
■ "Another winner for [ex-Patria chef] Douglas Rodriguez", this "dimly lit" Nuevo Spaniard inside the Flatiron's ABC Carpet & Home store peddles "tasty", "creative tapas" and "outstanding sangria" in a "sexy", "shabby-chic" setting (think "Miss Havisham's meets the bullring"); though the staff sometimes seems "lost", at these prices for this quality, hardly anyone is complaining.

Pisces ●S | 21 | 16 | 18 | $34 |
95 Ave. A (6th St.), 212-260-6660
■ It must've been born under a "delectable" sign, because this "nautically themed" East Village piscatorium is "damn good" at preparing "imaginative" seafood; it's also "just the right price", and if your table "has a view of" Avenue A, the "people-watching" "floor show" is free.

Pitchoune S | 19 | 14 | 16 | $40 |
226 Third Ave. (19th St.), 212-614-8641
■ "Cute" and "unassuming", this "tiny" Gramercy Park Med recently changed owners and got a new chef; now if only it could finesse a little "more breathing space" and some "fresh air", since it's like dining on "Paris' Left Bank", "complete with smokers."

Pizzeria Uno Chicago ●S | 15 | 12 | 13 | $20 |
220 E. 86th St. (bet. 2nd & 3rd Aves.), 212-472-5656
432 Columbus Ave. (81st St.), 212-595-4700
391 Sixth Ave. (bet. 8th St. & Waverly Pl.), 212-242-5230
55 Third Ave. (bet. 10th & 11th Sts.), 212-995-9668

(continued)

| F | D | S | C |

(continued)
Pizzeria Uno Chicago
South Street Seaport, 89 South St. (Pier 17), 212-791-7999
9201 Fourth Ave. (92nd St.), Brooklyn, 718-748-8667
39-02 Bell Blvd. (39th Ave.), Queens, 718-279-4900
107-16 70th Rd. (bet. Austin St. & Queens Blvd.), Queens, 718-793-6700

▨ It's "not gourmet", but this pizzeria chain is a "reliable standby" for "moms with kids" and others looking for "cheap" "group binges" on "huge" deep-dish pies sliced up in "laid-back", "bar-like" environs; skeptics scoff it's barely a "step above fast food."

P.J. Bernstein Deli S   17 | 9 | 14 | $23
1215 Third Ave. (bet. 70th & 71st Sts.), 212-879-0914

■ They offer "just what you'd expect" at this Upper East Side "local Jewish deli": "mouth-stretching", "high-cholesterol sandwiches" and "chicken soup with all the fat"; mind you, the food's "no Katz's", decor's at a minimum and service is "fast and perfunctory", but "when you gotta have pastrami", it'll do.

P.J. Clarke's ●S   15 | 14 | 14 | $29
915 Third Ave. (55th St.), 212-759-1650

▨ "Ratings may be low, but feelings run high" for this vintage 1890 Midtown "taste of old NY" that still "makes a damn fine burger" and remains the "kind of place every pub in America wishes it could be"; like Gotham itself, "if you love it, you forgive its shortcomings" ("grumpy waiters", "dingy" decor) "and enjoy it."

Place, The S   ▽ 22 | 22 | 21 | $42
310 W. Fourth St. (bet. Bank & W. 12th Sts.), 212-924-2711

■ "Snuggle in" for a "candlelit dinner" at this "intimate", subterranean West Village "den of romance", where "cute waiters" serve "serious" Mediterranean cuisine with a little "flirting" on the side; it gets "crowded", but the prices are "reasonable", and you "won't be rushed" as you gaze into each other's eyes.

Planet Hollywood ●S   12 | 17 | 13 | $29
1540 Broadway (45th St.), 212-333-7827

▨ This relocated-to-Times-Square chain link is among "the best of themes" and the worst of themes: applauded for its "fun" movie memorabilia and "clips playing on the monitors", it's hissed for "overpriced", "plastic"-tasting burger fare and "unpro" service; "kids and tourists" "love it", but others say "send it into orbit" – or at least to cooking school.

Planet Sushi ●S   18 | 13 | 17 | $29
380 Amsterdam Ave. (78th St.), 212-712-2162

■ It's "definitely not celestial", but this "bustling" West Side sushi joint is "a safe bet" for "giant", "satisfying" rolls and other Japanese standards at "affordable prices"; try to "sit outside" with the "young" crowd, because the "cheesy" interior looks "like a bad '70s movie."

Planet Thailand (Brooklyn) ●S≠   23 | 20 | 16 | $23
133 N. Seventh St. (Berry St.), 718-599-5758

■ "Funky, spicy and original", this "cool" Williamsburg "favorite" woks up "fab" Thai and Japanese fare at "phenomenal-value" prices; its "modern, spacious" and "loud" new space (with two bars and a DJ) still fills up at peak hours, so "go early – off the hipster schedule" – to avoid "long waits."

Plate 347 S   20 | 16 | 19 | $40
347 Second Ave. (bet. 20th & 21st Sts.), 212-388-0526

■ The "food wasteland" east of Gramercy Park "needed a place like this" French-American bistro boasting a "small menu" of "delicious

| F | D | S | C |

surprises" and a "friendly, efficient" staff; no one minds much if it's "cramped and smoky", since there's a "calming back garden" that's "heated in winter."

Pó S
24 | 17 | 20 | $45
31 Cornelia St. (bet. Bleecker & W. 4th Sts.), 212-645-2189
■ Under new chef Lee McGrath, this West Village Italian remains "a great little restaurant" with "no attitude", just "amazing, simple" cooking "that lives up to all the hype"; the $35 six-course tasting menu is "one of the last bargains" in the area, so even though the "tables are thisclosetogether", it's "worth the fight" for a reservation.

Pomodoro Rosso S
21 | 16 | 20 | $32
229 Columbus Ave. (bet. 70th & 71st Sts.), 212-721-3009
■ "One of the better choices" pre- or post–Lincoln Center, this "accommodating" West Side Italian proffers "simple, cheap" fare "done right"; as a result, it's often "packed" and "noisy", so "try for an outdoor seat" to better savor the "convivial" ambiance.

Pongal S
20 | 14 | 14 | $23
110 Lexington Ave. (bet. 27th & 28th Sts.), 212-696-9458
81 Lexington Ave. (26th St.), 212-696-5130
■ "Vegetarian Indian at its best" emerges from the kosher kitchen of this "cozy", "cheap" Curry Hill entry known for its "unbeatable" *dosai* and other "well-spiced" dishes, but not for its beatable decor and service; to handle the ever-present "line of people waiting", a twin location opened recently a block away.

Pongsri Thai S
20 | 12 | 17 | $24
244 W. 48th St. (bet. B'way & 8th Ave.), 212-582-3392
311 Second Ave. (18th St.), 212-477-4100 ●
■ They sure "aren't the fanciest places you'll ever eat", but these "fast" Gramercy and Theater District Thai bargains are forgiven given their "wonderful" cuisine, which is "just hot enough" to be "authentic" but not so "spicy" as to singe "American taste buds."

Ponticello (Queens) S
▽ 24 | 15 | 22 | $41
46-11 Broadway (bet. 46th & 47th Sts.), 718-278-4514
■ "Once people discover" this "old-world" Astoria Italian, "it becomes their favorite" according to fans of its "glorious" classic dishes (especially the "amazing osso buco"), "relaxed atmosphere" and "friendly staff"; never mind if it "could use a makeover."

Popover Cafe S
18 | 15 | 16 | $24
551 Amsterdam Ave. (bet. 86th & 87th Sts.), 212-595-8555
■ Eating "amidst the teddy bears" is "a little too cute" for some, but the "sublime popovers" baked at this West Side American ensure it's a "favorite" for most – hence the "long lines" for brunch; the rest of the time, the menu's just "average" and service "indifferent."

Porters New York S
▽ 20 | 21 | 19 | $44
216 Seventh Ave. (bet. 22nd & 23rd Sts.), 212-229-2878
■ "Undiscovered as yet", this "sophisticated" Chelsea New American is sure to pick up speed, say those who know its "civilized", art deco decor, "pleasing" cooking and "caring" staff; denizens hope the "expensive" tabs don't "outclass the neighborhood."

Porto Bello S
21 | 15 | 18 | $35
208 Thompson St. (bet. Bleecker & W. 3rd Sts.), 212-473-7794
◪ "*Bellissimo*" declare devotees of the "fabulous" pastas and grilled mushrooms that lend this longtime Village "old-world Italian" its name; gripers may grouse about "close quarters", but defenders deem it "reasonable, reliable and warm."

	F	D	S	C

Portofino Grille S   20 | 23 | 21 | $43
1162 First Ave. (bet. 63rd & 64th Sts.), 212-832-4141
■ Across from its "sister, Manhattan Grille", this newcomer – yet "another Italian on the Upper East Side" – "holds its own" thanks to "eye-poppingly" "pretty" decor, "pleasant" cuisine and "friendly staff"; even the tabs are competitive.

Positano Ristorante ●S   ▽ 20 | 16 | 18 | $35
122 Mulberry St. (bet. Canal & Hester Sts.), 212-334-9808
■ "A cut above" the "typical *turista* joints in Little Italy, this "old-school" Italian is reliable for "reasonably priced", "homey" pastas and other classics in "generous portions"; service is "attentive", but the "rustic" interior is nothing to write home about.

Post House S   23 | 20 | 22 | $63
Lowell Hotel, 28 E. 63rd St. (bet. Madison & Park Aves.), 212-935-2888
■ "Divine bovine" feasts accompanied by first-rate wines transpire in the wood-paneled, Americana-filled surroundings of this East Side "classic steakhouse for the well-heeled", where the staff "waits on everyone hand and foot" and the beef's "magnificent"; it's a "clubby" "power scene", yet a lot more "female-friendly" than most meateries.

Primavera ●S   24 | 21 | 23 | $61
1578 First Ave. (82nd St.), 212-861-8608
■ "Wonderful host" Nicola Civetta and his "attentive staff" create a "calming" haven of "understated elegance" for their necessarily well-heeled guests at this "jacket-required" Upper East Side Italian that feels miles "away from hectic Manhattan"; even more transporting are the "first-rate" cuisine and delicious wines not easily found elsewhere in NY.

Prime Grill S   ▽ 23 | 23 | 19 | $51
60 E. 49th St. (bet. Madison & Park Aves.), 212-692-9292
■ "Hats off (or on if you're Orthodox)" to this new Midtown steakhouse serving "excellent" beef "so good you forget it's kosher", and "delicious" sushi too; the dark-paneled look is "stylish" and the atmosphere "lively", so even if the "service could be better" and prices are steep, most say "*mazel tov*" – it's a "new star."

Primola S   23 | 17 | 21 | $52
1226 Second Ave. (bet. 64th & 65th Sts.), 212-758-1775
■ Meals at this "always-busy" East 60s Italian are "like eating at grandma's house" – that is if your grannie could seat you "between Woody and Barbra" and serve "everything from tripe to tiramisu"; once you're a regular "you get lots of attention", but service "can be frigid" for newcomers, which makes the pricey tab doubly hard to swallow.

Provence ●S   22 | 22 | 20 | $51
38 MacDougal St. (Prince St.), 212-475-7500
■ "Even in winter", this "romantic" SoHo bistro "transports" diners to sunnier climes with its "delightful" Provençal fare and "picturesque" interior with "windows for dreamers" up-front, "gorgeous flowers" everywhere and a "pretty" back garden "for kissing over *moules*"; "knowledgeable, friendly" service is icing on the cake.

Provence en Boite (Brooklyn) S   ▽ 23 | 19 | 19 | $39
8303 Third Ave. (bet. 83rd & 84th Sts.), 718-759-1515
■ "France comes to Bay Ridge at last" via this new "little" French bistro run by a "very friendly" husband-and-wife team (he's in the kitchen, she's out front); while it has yet to be discovered by most, locals-in-the-know call the food "very savory", the prices fair and the "touch-of-France" decor "cute."

	F	D	S	C

Prune ⓢ | 22 | 15 | 19 | $42

54 E. First St. (bet. 1st & 2nd Aves.), 212-677-6221

■ Not for "prudes", Gabrielle Hamilton's "inspired" East Village New American is strictly for those who "eat meat, smoke and drink" to their heart's content; "clever", "delicious" dishes are served by a "wacky, devoted staff" in "claustrophobic" quarters that may be "torture" for the plus-sized but suit its slim, "hipster" clientele just fine.

Psychic Cafe ⓢ | – | – | – | M

181 W. 10th St. (7th Ave. S.), 212-989-7059

Unless you go up to the main dining room, you'd never suspect the quirky charm of this West Village Italian; those who do are rewarded by offbeat vintage decor (e.g. a '30s-style animal-print couch) and a calm ambiance where between courses the resident psychic reads tarot cards.

Pump Energy Food, The | 19 | 7 | 14 | $14

40 W. 55th St. (bet. 5th & 6th Aves.), 212-246-6844
113 E. 31st St. (bet. Lexington Ave. & Park Ave. S.), 212-213-5733

■ "The fit and would-be fit" are "pumped" about these "hole-in-the-wall snack bars" serving "baked falafel" and other "creative", "low-fat" food "for carb-restrictors and carb-loaders" alike – amazingly, it "actually tastes good" and won't deflate your budget; P.S. "fast delivery" is part of the package.

Punch ⓢ | 20 | 18 | 18 | $34

913 Broadway (bet. 20th & 21st Sts.), 212-673-6333

■ With the "most eclectic" – and "linguistically challenging" – "menu in NY", this "inexpensive", "noisy" Flatiron New American (with an upstairs lounge) is cheered as "a knockout"; "insouciant" "circus-themed" decor paired with the "hottest staff" around means there's never a shortage of scenery.

Puttanesca ⓢ | 19 | 16 | 17 | $33

859 Ninth Ave. (56th St.), 212-581-4177

■ "Convenient to the theaters" and Lincoln Center, this Hell's Kitchen Italian can be counted on for "consistently" "enjoyable" pastas and other classics at "bargain-basement prices"; the "upbeat" ambiance becomes "harried" as curtain time approaches, so for "soothing" meals, "go after 8 PM."

Q, a Thai Bistro (Queens) ⓢ | 23 | 18 | 19 | $34

108-25 Ascan Ave. (bet. Austin & Burns Sts.), 718-261-6599

■ "In the wilds of Forest Hills", this "tiny" Thai "draws crowds" with its "creative" fare and "trendy", "Manhattan feel"; "the only problem" is it gets quite "cramped" ("any smaller, we'd be lap dancing").

Quartino ⓢ | ▽ 19 | 18 | 18 | $34

21 Peck Slip (Water St.), 212-349-4433

■ Modestly priced, "up-and-coming" South Street Seaport Northern Italian that's following an unusual approach: its "small menu" of "delicious" dishes is limited to light, heart-"healthy" choices (nothing fried or even sautéed), accompanied by "good wines" and served in "cute quartinos"; locals "hope the tourists don't discover it."

Quatorze Bis ●ⓢ | 21 | 18 | 19 | $49

323 E. 79th St. (bet. 1st & 2nd Aves.), 212-535-1414

■ This "pretty" bistro's "civilized clientele" would happily sup on its "terrific" French fare "every night" (that is, if it weren't quite so "pricey"); no one seems to mind that the "tables are crowded" and service "a little snooty" – it seems natural at this "bit of Paris on the East Side."

F	D	S	C

Quattro Gatti [S]

20	17	20	$41

205 E. 81st St. (bet. 2nd & 3rd Aves.), 212-570-1073

■ "Repeat customers" are "almost family" at this "reliable Italian" "tucked away" on an East 80s "side street", which "even cat-haters like" thanks to its "basic but delicious" standards; "moderate prices" make it a place locals "return to" often.

Queen (Brooklyn) [S]

24	14	20	$39

84 Court St. (bet. Livingston & Schermerhorn Sts.), 718-596-5955

■ It's "not much to look at, but boy, what food" sums up this "venerable" Brooklyn Heights Italian where the "excellent, authentic" edibles are "fit for a king" but the dining room resembles a "Midwestern Marriott"; never mind, just "close your eyes and eat."

Queen of Sheba ◐ [S]

▽ 20	15	18	$26

650 10th Ave. (bet. 45th & 46th Sts.), 212-397-0610

■ This new Hell's Kitchen Ethiopian serves "tangy", "cheap" traditional fare (mostly *berbere*-spiced meat stews and Vegetarian dishes) to be eaten with the hands or, rather, with the native injera bread; if the room is a tad "diner"-like, it suits the neighborhood fine.

Quilty's [S]

24	20	22	$54

177 Prince St. (bet. Sullivan & Thompson Sts.), 212-254-1260

■ The New American food at chef Katy Sparks' SoHo venue is "stylish, inventive" and, above all, "delicious", which is lucky since it's also "expensive"; the "lovely", if "spare", decor featuring butterfly collections makes for a "special, romantic" experience.

Quintessence [S]

▽ 21	16	18	$28

263 E. 10th St. (bet. Ave. A & 1st Ave.), 646-654-1823

◪ Some "feel very pure – almost holy" after eating at this East Village temple of uncooked, unprocessed, vegan cuisine, which acolytes consider the "best veggie place in the world"; however, the wholly unconverted counter "all raw, all the time – enough said."

Rachel's American Bistro ◐ [S]

20	15	18	$34

608 Ninth Ave. (bet. 43rd & 44th Sts.), 212-957-9050

■ Handily located "on the Theater District fringe", this "charming" bistro delivers "robust" American food in a "tiny", "homey" setting, though what's "cozy" for some can be "downright crowded" for others; "moderate" pricing and a popular Wednesday "matinee brunch" are bonuses.

Rafaella [S]

21	21	19	$36

381 Bleecker St. (bet. Charles & Perry Sts.), 212-229-9885

■ "Love is in the air" at this "dark" Village trattoria that "glows with romance"; the "delicious" Italian food further guarantees one "enchanted evening", and since it "actually seems underpriced", lotharios say "your date will think you spent a fortune."

Raffaele ◐

▽ 21	15	20	$45

1055 First Ave. (bet. 57th & 58th Sts.), 212-750-3232

◪ "First-rate food" and an "owner who really cares" make this Sutton Place Italian a bona fide "neighborhood find", yet those who label it "merely acceptable" complain that the so-so "decor doesn't warrant the pricey prices."

Rafina [S]

20	15	19	$37

1481 York Ave. (bet. 78th & 79th Sts.), 212-327-0950

■ A "great assortment" of "freshly prepared grilled fish" lures Eastsiders to this "inviting" Greek that follows through with "eager-to-please" service; "fair" prices, a "lovely" garden and "casual" mood make a meal here quite "pleasant" indeed.

		F	D	S	C

Raga S — 22 | 18 | 20 | $37
433 E. Sixth St. (bet. Ave. A & 1st Ave.), 212-388-0957
■ "Unusual" spices "enhance, not overwhelm" the "deft" fusion of Indian and French flavors at this "inventive" East Villager; add a "serene" setting, friendly" service and modest prices, and it's not surprising that it's fast become a local favorite.

Rain S — 21 | 21 | 19 | $38
1059 Third Ave. (bet. 62nd & 63rd Sts.), 212-223-3669
100 W. 82nd St. (bet. Amsterdam & Columbus Aves.), 212-501-0776
■ Despite the name, these "sexy" crosstown Pan-Asians are "all sunshine", offering "succulent" meals at "affordable", "Vong lite" tabs; though a few find fault with the service, most agree they're "very hot" in every meaning of the phrase.

RAINBOW ROOM S — 22 | 27 | 23 | VE
GE Bldg., 30 Rockefeller Plaza, 65th fl. (bet. 49th & 50th Sts.), 212-632-5100
■ Be prepared for an identity crisis at this sky-high Italian Midtown deco "landmark" where you'll "feel like Fred and Ginger" on the dance floor and Daddy Warbucks while supping, but more like Little Orphan Annie after paying the bill; though the Rainbow Room is only open to the public on "select" Fridays and Saturdays, the adjoining Grill is less grand, but almost as expensive, serving lunch and dinner daily.

Rao's ⌀ — 24 | 17 | 22 | $59
455 E. 114th St. (Pleasant Ave.), 212-722-6709
■ Taking reservations for 3002, this "cozy", "old-fashioned" East Harlem Southern Italian is the "toughest ticket in town" – about the only way to get in is to "go with a regular"; when you do, you'll sit between celebs and Sopranos in a charming, booth-lined room that looks like a *Goodfellas'* set, eat "surprisingly good" food and drink whatever bartender 'Nick the Vest' suggests; try to meet owner Franky 'No' Pellegrino – if he likes you, you may get in on your own next time; P.S. don't trip over the bodyguards out front.

Raoul's ●S — 23 | 20 | 19 | $49
180 Prince St. (bet. Sullivan & Thompson Sts.), 212-966-3518
■ "Perfect for a late-night rendezvous" and for "footsie under the table", this "timeless" SoHo French bistro is hard to beat; besides a "sultry, sexy" vibe, it offers "quality" cooking, especially the "must-have steak au poivre"; if you can arrange it, "sit outside on the patio."

Rasputin (Brooklyn) S — 20 | 22 | 20 | $65
2670 Coney Island Ave. (Ave. X), 718-332-8111
■ "Food is only part of the experience" at this vodka-fueled Brighton Beach Russian known for its "lavish", if "heavy-handed", cabaret "extravaganza" featuring the "best legs in Brooklyn"; for most, this "unforgettable experience" is a "riot", yet others find it all "too much" – as in noise, food and money.

Ratner's S — 16 | 10 | 13 | $25
138 Delancey St. (bet. Norfolk & Suffolk Sts.), 212-677-5588
■ "Not what it used to be", this longtime Lower East Side "dairy queen" is now "much smaller" and no longer strictly kosher, inspiring a chorus of "oy veys"; though the "great blintzes" and rude waiters remain, many say the redo "killed the character" – "some things shouldn't change."

Red/Bar S — 20 | 18 | 19 | $46
339 E. 75th St. (bet. 1st & 2nd Aves.), 212-472-7577
■ "They're trying hard" at this East Side New American "cloned from Southampton" that offers "surprisingly decent food" in "pleasant", if "tight", digs; those who feel the country cousin is "better" at least have the "pricey" tabs to remind them of their "Hamptons summers."

www.zagat.com

Red Cat ●S   22 | 19 | 20 | $46
227 10th Ave. (bet. 23rd & 24th Sts.), 212-242-1122
■ "Way out west" in Chelsea, this "stylish" Med–New American boasts a "sharp kitchen" that "takes food seriously"; it's "caught on fast" with a "who's who" of "hepcats" from the local art gallery scene, but given the price tags, it helps to be a "fat cat."

Redeye Grill ●S   21 | 19 | 19 | $47
890 Seventh Ave. (56th St.), 212-541-9000
■ For dining that hits the "bull's-eye", "showman" Shelly Fireman's "big and brassy" Carnegie Hall–area American brasserie is an on-target "crowd-pleaser", where the "dancing shrimp rock" and an "awesome raw bar" will make your head swim; sure, it's "loud" and "crowded", but the "din" is so "cheerful" you'll barely notice how "pricey" it is; P.S. check out the private party rooms.

Red Garlic ●S   21 | 13 | 17 | $28
916 Eighth Ave. (bet. 54th & 55th Sts.), 212-489-5237
■ "Undiscovered" Theater District Thai emphasizing "solid, tasty" seafood that's garnished with "garlic galore" and "won't burn a hole in your pocket"; "cheery", "high-energy" service gets you to the show on time, thus it's not too hard to "forget the decor."

Red Rail, The (Brooklyn) S   ▽ 18 | 15 | 18 | $24
502 Henry St. (Sackett St.), 718-875-1283
☒ "Locals meet and kibitz" at this "homey" Carroll Gardens Cal-American known for its $10 "bargain brunch" and "anything-goes kids policy" (including valet "stroller parking"); "funky" "garage-sale furnishings" and sometimes-"average" cooking that might be turnoffs at a more pricey place leave customers here "bemused."

Regency S   20 | 21 | 21 | $61
Regency Hotel, 540 Park Ave. (61st St.), 212-339-4050
■ "Big shots" "eat well and make things happen" over the ultimate "power breakfasts" at this "upbeat" Tisch-family East Side American where the "tables are well-spaced for biz talk" and the tabs are "quite affordable"; at night, it becomes Feinstein's at the Regency, arguably the swankiest cabaret in town.

Relish (Brooklyn) ●S   ▽ 22 | 21 | 19 | $28
225 Wythe Ave. (bet. Metropolitan Ave. & 3rd St.), 718-963-4546
■ Williamsburg "diner fans" dig this "picturesque" American housed in a "silver boxcar" for its "sophisticated" comfort chow, "moderate" prices and "hip yet unpretentious" air; though "flighty service" takes some flack, the "trendy" rear lounge and new garden space are highly acclaimed.

Remi ●S   23 | 23 | 21 | $53
145 W. 53rd St. (bet. 6th & 7th Aves.), 212-581-4242
■ "Wear your Armani" to this "swank" Midtown Northern Italian where Francesco Antonucci's "smashing" cooking and Adam Tihany's "sharp" design (the mural of Venice is alone worth a visit) make for always satisfying repasts; it's just the ticket for "romancing a business partner", and despite "tight" seating and "pricey" tabs, it certainly "lives up to its [stellar] reputation."

René Pujol   23 | 20 | 22 | $52
321 W. 51st St. (bet. 8th & 9th Aves.), 212-246-3023
■ "Dignified dining" devotees delight in the "old-fashioned goodness" of this Theater District French "standby" providing "excellent" food in a "comfortable", "not-too-highbrow" setting; its "well-timed", "Jeeves"-like service and "terrific prix fixe" strike some as "better than Paris", but watch out for its very Parisian à la carte prices.

Republic ⓢ   17 | 15 | 14 | $21
37 Union Sq. W. (bet. 16th & 17th Sts.), 212-627-7172
◪ "Always packed to the hilt", this mega-modern Union Square Pan-Asian gets a "big thumbs-up" for its "cheap, tasty" "meal-in-a-bowl" grub, though its "uncomfortable seating", "tiresome communal tables" and "rush 'em in, rush 'em out" service are another story.

Resto Léon ●ⓢ   ▽ 19 | 16 | 15 | $35
351 E. 12th St. (bet. 1st & 2nd Aves.), 212-375-8483
■ Its "cosmopolitan atmosphere" starts with "all those smokers" and wafts up to the "vaulted brick ceiling" at this East Village "micro" bistro where the French fare is "good all around", but the "waiters being trained on-the-job" leave some gasping "*mon dieu.*"

Rhône ●   18 | 21 | 17 | $47
63 Gansevoort St. (bet. Greenwich & Washington Sts.), 212-367-8440
◪ A "brilliant selection" of Rhône Valley wines is the "centerpiece" of this "trendy" Meatpacking District French, with a pricey menu that's either "surprisingly good" or "in need of a food sommelier"; surveyors similarly split on its "techno interior": "cool" and "sleek" vs. "cold" and "S&M"-ish.

Rialto ●ⓢ   19 | 20 | 18 | $37
265 Elizabeth St. (bet. Houston & Prince Sts.), 212-334-7900
◪ Cushy "red leather booths", "warm lighting" and a "romantic garden" make this "sexy" SoHo American very "hot date"–worthy, with food that's "pretty good" but really beside the point; still, the price is right and the "staff not nearly as pretentious as it could be."

Riazor ●ⓢ   ▽ 19 | 13 | 18 | $30
245 W. 16th St. (bet. 7th & 8th Aves.), 212-727-2132
■ "Neighborhoody" Chelsea Spaniard specializing in "copious portions" of "hearty" cooking that gets down to the real "nitty-gritty" for very "reasonable" tabs; the staff's refreshing "hospitality" compensates for the strictly "routine" decor.

Ribollita ⓢ   18 | 16 | 17 | $38
260 Park Ave. S. (bet. 20th & 21st Sts.), 212-982-0975
◪ For some "sanity" in the hyper-trendy Flatiron, low-key types turn to this "quiet, unassuming" Northern Italian for food that "tastes like Tuscany" in a room that "looks like Queens"; while "unpolished service" dulls the experience, "fair" pricing brightens it.

Rice ●ⓢ∌   19 | 14 | 14 | $18
227 Mott St. (bet. Prince & Spring Sts.), 212-226-5775
81 Washington St. (bet. Front & York Sts.), Brooklyn, 718-222-9880
■ Hipsters head for this "teeny" NoLita Eclectic (and its new DUMBO sibling) for "clever", "healthy" meals based around "just what the name says"; sure, it's "cramped", "dark" and "cash-only", but it's so "cheap" you could "recycle some cans" to pay the bill.

Rice 'n' Beans ⓢ   21 | 10 | 16 | $20
744 Ninth Ave. (bet. 50th & 51st Sts.), 212-265-4444
120 W. Third St. (bet. MacDougal St. & 6th Ave.), 212-375-1800
◪ These "postage stamp–size" Brazilians dish out "delish", "down-home" meals "cooked with love" that are more than "easy on your pocketbook", but not without some trade-offs: "zero decor" and "achingly slow service."

Rinconcito Peruano ⓢ∌   ▽ 19 | 6 | 14 | $17
803 Ninth Ave. (bet. 53rd & 54th Sts.), 212-333-5685
■ The "Incas would have been proud" of the "to-die-for food" at this "exotic" Hell's Kitchen Peruvian "adventure" where the decor is

"nonexistent", the prices "very cheap" and the seviche so "amazing" that supporters can only stutter "*sí, sí, sí.*"

Rincón de España S | 21 | 13 | 18 | $36
226 Thompson St. (bet. Bleecker & W. 3rd Sts.), 212-260-4950
■ After a few "strong margaritas" and some "delicious" chow at this longtime West Village Spaniard, fans cry "bring on the bulls"; but since the "small, dowdy" space gets so "crowded" that the "mariachi band has to stand on the tables to perform", "early arrival" and "reservations are suggested."

Rio Mar ●S | 17 | 12 | 15 | $29
7 Ninth Ave. (Little W. 12th St.), 212-242-1623
☒ This "weary"-looking remnant of the "original" (pre-Pastis) Meatpacking District comes alive with "hearty", "tasty" Spanish fare seasoned with "tons of garlic"; its "down-and-dirty" feel doesn't stop fans from "squeezing in" for some "mean paella" at "bargain" tabs.

Ristorante del Sogno S | ▽ 18 | 14 | 17 | $35
939 Eighth Ave. (bet. 55th & 56th Sts.), 212-262-5354
☒ For "Carnegie Hall events" and "City Center forays", this Northern Italian is geographically correct, turning out "solid, tasty" fare at "very appealing prices"; but naysayers find it "not special", citing service and decor "kinks."

Rive Gauche S | 18 | 16 | 15 | $31
560 Third Ave. (37th St.), 212-949-5400
☒ Alright, "it's not Paris", but this "bustling" French bistro tries to be "Murray Hill's answer to Balthazar" with "good" enough food at "decent" prices; the "outdoor dining" "distracts while you wait" for the "absent-minded" servers to remember you.

River S | 19 | 17 | 18 | $29
345 Amsterdam Ave. (bet. 76th & 77th Sts.), 212-579-1888
☒ This "bamboo"-bedecked West Side Viet-Thai distinguishes itself with "light, tasty" dishes "seasoned just right for an American palate" at more than "satisfactory" prices; but those who dub it a "trickling creek" cite "no surprises" and a "hut-like" atmosphere.

RIVER CAFE (Brooklyn) S | 25 | 27 | 24 | $70
1 Water St. (bet. Furman & Old Fulton Sts.), 718-522-5200
■ "All occasions are special ones" at this beautiful, barge-based Brooklyn waterside "escape", a "fabulous date place (even with your husband)" thanks to that "priceless view" that you "pay dearly for" (dinner $70 prix fixe only); its more-than-"memorable" American menu now comes courtesy of chef Brad Steelman, who joins an illustrious list of alumni – David Burke, Larry Forgione, Rick Laakkonen and Charlie Palmer – who all earned their stripes here.

Roberto's (Bronx) S | 25 | 17 | 19 | $39
632 E. 186th St. (Belmont Ave.), 718-733-9503
■ "Every Italian food fantasy is satisfied" at "sweetheart" chef Roberto Paciullo's Bronx fiefdom that's generally considered the "best on Arthur Avenue"; newly "renovated" digs, "very authentic" cooking with "no gimmicks" and service that makes you "feel like family" explain the "long weekend lines."

Roc ●S | ▽ 23 | 22 | 21 | $50
190A Duane St. (Greenwich St.), 212-625-3333
■ "Big spenders, celebs" and "neighborhood" folk rub shoulders at this "hip" TriBeCa Italian "rookie" offering "fresh", "honest" cooking that's as "solid" as a you-know-what; even skeptics who find it "noisy" and "overpriced" admit the service makes you feel like part of "*la famiglia.*"

	F	D	S	C

Rocco ⓢ   ▽ 21 | 16 | 20 | $34
181 Thompson St. (bet. Bleecker & Houston Sts.), 212-677-0590
◪ "Old Greenwich Village" is alive and well at this circa 1922 "traditional" Italian where the "inexpensive" "mama" meals are dispatched by a "hospitable" staff; "no ambiance" and an "ancient menu" sour modernists, but some of the "best pastries" around sweeten their mood.

Rock Center Café ⓢ   16 | 21 | 17 | $42
Rockefeller Ctr., 20 W. 50th St. (bet. 5th & 6th Aves.), 212-332-7620
◪ "Prettier and roomier since its renovation", this "stylish" Rock Center American offers "fabulous" views of the "ice rink" in the winter and enjoyable alfresco dining in summer; though some opt to skate past, saying it "should be better than it is", the presence of chef Theo Schoenegger in the kitchen is a good reason to glide on over.

Rocking Horse ⓢ   20 | 15 | 16 | $33
182 Eighth Ave. (bet. 19th & 20th Sts.), 212-463-9511
■ Chelsea's veteran "nouveau Mexican" "keeps reinventing itself", and the latest redo includes a name shortening, a "charming remodeling" and the arrival of a "new chef" with "haute ideas"; early word is the food is still "inexpensive" and "innovative", but service remains as "uninspired" as ever.

Roettele A.G. ⓢ   19 | 16 | 18 | $33
126 E. Seventh St. (bet. Ave. A & 1st Ave.), 212-674-4140
◪ East Village Swiss-German that's "heaven for heavy-food" lovers, with a "dirndl"- and "lederhosen"-clad staff thrown in for "kitsch" meisters; while the fondue, prices and garden are all wunderbar, a few find the experience too "quirky."

Rolf's ⓢ   18 | 19 | 16 | $34
281 Third Ave. (22nd St.), 212-477-4750
■ Year-round "Yuletide" decor "adds to the tacky charm" of this "cluttered" Gramercy German where "you'd better be hungry", since its "hearty" "comfort food" arrives in "plentiful" portions at hard-to-resist tabs; despite nonfestive service, this "Alpine hideaway" is a "must" for "Christmas orphans."

Roppongi ●ⓢ   20 | 17 | 18 | $32
434 Amsterdam Ave. (81st St.), 212-362-8182
■ "Damn good" sushi wins over Westsiders at this "affordable" Japanese that's "almost as good as Haru" across the street, with "shorter waits"; add "solicitous service" and a "calm, relaxing" ambiance and you have "all-around enjoyable dining."

ROSA MEXICANO ●ⓢ   23 | 21 | 20 | $45
1063 First Ave. (58th St.), 212-753-7407
61 Columbus Ave. (62nd St.), 212-977-7700
■ It's "fiesta city" every night at these "cheerful" "gourmet Mexicans" famed for their "fasten-your-seatbelt" pomegranate margaritas and "*muy excelente* guacamole" "made tableside"; though most amigos applaud the "showy" new West Side outpost (and its "fabulous" water wall), connoisseurs swear "East is better" – though both are equally "noisy" and "pricey."

Rose Water (Brooklyn) ⓢ   ▽ 24 | 19 | 23 | $35
787 Union St. (6th Ave.), 718-783-3800
■ "Park Slope scores" with this "worthy" Med-American "labor of love" offering "inspired", "delicately subtle" cooking at "affordable prices" plus "sidewalk" seating; while the "interior could be better" (and bigger), the "agile" staff keeps things "well run", though it doesn't hurt to "arrive early to avoid waits."

www.zagat.com

	F	D	S	C

Rossini's ◐S
21 | 19 | 21 | $50

108 E. 38th St. (bet. Lexington & Park Aves.), 212-683-0135

■ The waiters "wear tuxedos" at this "old-school", "upscale" Murray Hiller where "delectable" Northern Italian fare arrives accompanied by "opera singers on Saturday night"; though "not exactly cutting-edge", it's "reliable" to its "older crowd", albeit a bit "overpriced."

Rothmann's S
23 | 22 | 21 | $62

3 E. 54th St. (bet. 5th & Madison Aves.), 212-319-5500

■ NY's "steak wars" have a top new contender in this "handsome" Midtowner that stands apart from the crowd because "you don't get bullied by the staff" (indeed, they're unusually "delightful"); otherwise, its "generous servings" are "every bit as good" and just as "pricey" as its "high-end" rib-eyed rivals.

Roth's Westside Steak S
∇ 22 | 16 | 21 | $50

680 Columbus Ave. (93rd St.), 212-280-4103

■ A "star is born" at this new Upper West Side chop shop that's "truly needed" thanks to its "great combination" of "fine food" and "excellent" live jazz; a few find it "inconsistent", and more than a few gripe it's "too expensive for the neighborhood", but then again the neighborhood never had a good steakhouse before.

Royal Siam S
19 | 12 | 17 | $26

240 Eighth Ave. (bet. 22nd & 23rd Sts.), 212-741-1732

■ "Reliable" Thai fare cooked "with subtlety" and priced attractively is the draw at this Chelsea "neighborhood" venue; sure, it may be "dull" on looks, but it's "deliciously non-sceney", despite its trendy Eighth Avenue address.

Roy's New York S
24 | 20 | 21 | $51

Marriott Financial Ctr., 130 Washington St. (bet. Albany & Carlisle Sts.), 212-266-6262

■ "Paradise" comes to Lower Manhattan at this "original", if expensive, Asian seafooder from star Honolulu chef Roy Yamaguchi, whose "innovative" use of "exotic flavors" is "improving all the time"; its "airy" digs feel almost "as laid-back as Hawaii"; N.B. closed at press time.

RUBY FOO'S ◐S
19 | 22 | 18 | $40

2182 Broadway (77th St.), 212-724-6700
1626 Broadway (49th St.), 212-489-5600

☒ "Fu Manchu" fans flock to these "splashy" West Side and Times Square "lookers" delivering "showmanship" and "something-for-everyone" Pan-Asian fare; "deafening" "carnival atmosphere" and "tongue-in-cheek", "Murder on the Orient Express" decor lead "fooey"-sayers to shrug "all style, no substance", but it's tough to top when it comes to "sheer fun" and partying.

Rue 57 Brasserie ◐S
19 | 19 | 17 | $43

60 W. 57th St. (6th Ave.), 212-307-5656

☒ An "instant success", this high-energy brasserie in a "touristique" part of Midtown keeps the trade brisk with an "eclectic" bill of fare "avec sushi" and a "jumping bar" scene; though dissenters dis the "deafening" din, "schizophrenic" menu and "high prices", most call it a "welcome addition" to the neighborhood.

Rungsit Thai S
18 | 8 | 14 | $20

161 E. 23rd St. (bet. Lexington & 3rd Aves.), 212-260-0704
208 E. 34th St. (bet. 2nd & 3rd Aves.), 212-689-1029

■ "Addictive", "solid Thai" at "easy" tabs keeps this East Side duo popular; there are no complaints about the "remodeled" 34th Street outpost, but its southern cousin is primarily for "Thai on the fly", since the "decor screams takeout."

	F	D	S	C

Russian Samovar ●S | 21 | 18 | 19 | $45
256 W. 52nd St. (bet. B'way & 8th Ave.), 212-757-0168
■ Comrades commend this "folklore-ish" Theater District Russian for its "large portions" of "authentic", "pre-revolution" fare and vodka infused "20 different ways"; for "foot-stomping" "fun", come after 9 PM, when the "sing-along" pianist plays.

Russian Tea Room ●S | 19 | 25 | 21 | $62
150 W. 57th St. (bet. 6th & 7th Aves.), 212-974-2111
◪ The "comeback of the century" and a "dream come true" for some, "all smoke and mirrors" to others, this "gaudy" Midtown "red, red, red" Russian revived by the late, great Warner LeRoy splits voters: fans say the borscht and blintzes and "glittery", "Christmas"-like decor are "fit for a tsar", but foes insist the cooking's strictly "for rubes with rubles", ditto the "overdone" trimmings; granted, it's "as pricey as it looks", but the huge "glass bear aquarium" and "fine private dining" floors have most saying they're "glad it's back"; N.B. for a bargain taste of excess, try the $32 prix fixe.

Ruth's Chris Steak House ●S | 23 | 20 | 21 | $57
148 W. 51st St. (bet. 6th & 7th Aves.), 212-245-9600
◪ For "steak done right", "coated with a stick of butter", this Midtown link of the Louisiana-based chophouse chain is "uniformly excellent", with a bonus helping of "unrushed service" on the side; though "snooty purists" report a "formulaic", "suburb-y" vibe and tabs as "sizzling" as the beef, most find it hard to resist "licking the plate."

Sabor S | 20 | 16 | 18 | $36
462 Amsterdam Ave. (bet. 82nd & 83rd Sts.), 212-579-2929
◪ "Tops for tapas", this "vibrant" West Side Nuevo Latino features lots of "savory small dishes" that are a "terrific value", even if they come in "chihuahua-size" portions; given the "ear-shattering" indoor decibel level, those in-the-know opt to "linger over pitchers of sangria" at the sidewalk tables.

Sachi S | ▽ 22 | 13 | 18 | $37
1350 Madison Ave. (bet 94th & 95th Sts.), 212-534-5600
■ "Sushi for grown-ups" draws the Carnegie Hill crowd to this "low-key" Japanese offering dining "without the long waits of Downtown" joints; sure, it "needs better decor", but portions are "generous", "elegantly presented" and well-priced.

S'Agapo (Queens) ●S | ▽ 23 | 15 | 19 | $32
34-21 34th Ave. (35th St.), 718-626-0303
■ "Close your eyes and you're in Crete" at this Astoria Greek serving "fairly priced", "delicious fish" in "laid-back" but decor-challenged digs; for best results, the terrace is "perfect on a summer night."

Sag Harbor S | 20 | 18 | 18 | $37
356 W. 44th St. (bet. 8th & 9th Aves.), 212-445-0131
◪ There's "serene sailing" at this American seafood yearling that's a "safe harbor for superb fish" at "shockingly affordable" tabs for its Theater District locale; though a few critics cite "slow", "lost-at-sea" service, most say this lifesaver "tries hard to please" – and does.

Sahara (Brooklyn) ●S | 21 | 13 | 15 | $26
2337 Coney Island Ave. (bet. Aves. T & U), 718-376-8594
■ "Delicious kebabs" and other "tasty" "quick bites" at really "cheap" tabs keep this Gravesend Middle Eastern "bustling"; though the "barnlike" digs are a decor desert and service sometimes seems sunstroked, it's still "fun for the family" – and there's always takeout for those who find it too "hectic."

Saigon Fun [S] ▽ 21 | 11 | 17 | $19

772 Ninth Ave. (bet. 51st & 52nd Sts.), 212-581-3810

■ "Always-on-target" Hell's Kitchen Vietnamese that dishes out "wholly authentic" fare at "unbelievable-value" prices; despite no decor, service is so "friendly" that would-be "everyday" patrons say it "deserves a bigger following."

Saigon Grill ◐ [S] 22 | 8 | 16 | $21

1700 Second Ave. (88th St.), 212-996-4600
2381 Broadway (87th St.), 212-875-9072

◪ Regulars marvel at the "dazzling taste explosions" at these "embarrassingly cheap" crosstown Vietnamese siblings; however, "get 'em in, get 'em out service" and minimal "McSaigon" digs have surveyors suggesting "wear blinders" or get it delivered.

Sala ◐ [S] ▽ 18 | 20 | 16 | $32

344 Bowery (Great Jones St.), 212-979-6606

■ Seeking a "sexy setting" for a "sultry" supper, surveyors slip into this Bowery Spaniard offering a "hip tapas bar" and "sangria with a wicked punch"; there's a "cool downstairs lounge" too, though it's "too dark to see" very much.

Salaam Bombay [S] 21 | 18 | 18 | $35

317 Greenwich St. (bet. Duane & Reade Sts.), 212-226-9400

■ "Indian food done right" lures locals to this "terrific" TriBeCa "standby" where the "spicy" food comes accompanied by "live weekend sitar music"; the AYCE $12.95 lunch/brunch is not only an "impressive" spread, but a "bargain" too.

Salam Cafe & Restaurant [S] ▽ 22 | 17 | 18 | $32

104 W. 13th St. (bet. 6th & 7th Aves.), 212-741-0277

■ The "aromas alone" lure loyalists to this "cozy" West Villager known for its affordable, "delicious" Mideastern fare spiced with "subtle flair"; romancers love the low lights and the feeling that there's "no rush here."

Sal Anthony's [S] 17 | 16 | 18 | $38

55 Irving Pl. (bet. 17th & 18th Sts.), 212-982-9030

◪ This "old" Gramercy "standby" plays it "nice and simple", laying on the "Italian charm" with basic grub in "generous portions" that's "well-priced" to boot; however, an increasing cadre of detractors shrugs it's all too "predictable" and "living in the past."

Sal Anthony's S.P.Q.R. [S] 18 | 18 | 18 | $37

133 Mulberry St. (bet. Grand & Hester Sts.), 212-925-3120

◪ "Reliable" platefuls of "heavy-on-the-sauce" Italian fare and a sprawling setting keep this Little Italy vet popular with "large parties" requiring "lots of space"; sure, it can be "loud" and "touristy", but the cash-strapped claim the prix fixe makes it all "worth it."

Sala Thai ◐ [S] 21 | 13 | 18 | $29

1718 Second Ave. (bet. 89th & 90th Sts.), 212-410-5557

■ "Imaginative" cooking provides "excitement" at this "dependable", inexpensive Upper Eastsider that's "a cut above" the typical Thai; despite slightly "dowdy" digs, overall it's an "efficient" "neighborhood place" of "solid" standing.

Salmon River [S] – | – | – | M

Clarion Hotel Fifth Avenue, 3 E. 40th St. (bet. 5th & Madison Aves.), 212-481-7887

This amiable new Midtown seafood house is very conveniently located, especially if you're visiting the main library; with a large array of modestly priced fresh fish, it's a handy no-frills alternative to Gotham's growing number of pricey poisson palaces.

Saloon, The ◐ [S] 14 | 13 | 14 | $32

1920 Broadway (64th St.), 212-874-1500

◪ A "default" for Lincoln Center–goers in need of a "quick fix", this "energetic", modestly priced American supplies "reliable" bites from a "something-for-everyone" menu; but critics of the "just ok" food and "warehouse" setup call the "prime location" with sidewalk seating its "only asset."

Salute! [S] 18 | 17 | 16 | $37

101 W. 57th St. (6th Ave.), 212-445-0040
270 Madison Ave. (39th St.), 212-213-3440 ◐

◪ Whether for "business or pleasure", this Murray Hiller gives a "lively" salute to things Tuscan, serving fine "homemade pasta" at "reasonable" tabs; a "noisy", "busy lunch" hub, it's more "relaxed" at dinner, after the happy-hour "pickup" bar scene dies down; N.B. a Midtown branch opened at press time.

Sambuca [S] 19 | 16 | 18 | $32

20 W. 72nd St. (bet. Columbus Ave. & CPW), 212-787-5656

◪ "Go with a group" and an "appetite" to this West Side Southern Italian "garlic heaven" where "huge helpings" of "family-style" basics and an "accommodating staff" ensure "you get a lot for your money"; it's a "good alternative to Carmine's", i.e. "quieter" and "easier to get into."

Sammy's ◐ [S] 18 | 10 | 15 | $19

453 Sixth Ave. (11th St.), 212-924-6688
301-303 Sixth Ave. (Carmine St.), 212-337-9888

■ Noodle noshers note the "soups are a full meal" (and the "lunch special a steal") at this "budget-minded" Village Chinese twosome; given the "monstrous portions" served at a "lightning pace", not many even notice the "nondescript" decor.

Sammy's Roumanian [S] 19 | 10 | 16 | $47

157 Chrystie St. (Delancey St.), 212-673-0330

◪ This "unique" "museum of Jewish eating" is "worth the schlep" to the Lower East Side for its "enormous", "clog-the-arteries" servings of mittel-Europa classics accompanied by "chicken fat the way momachik used to make it"; one part rowdy "celebration", one part "nostalgia trip", it boasts a colorful staff and colorless "basement decor" – in sum, "go for the experience, stay for the heartburn."

Sam's Noodle Shop ◐ [S] 20 | 10 | 15 | $19

411 Third Ave. (29th St.), 212-213-2288

◪ Noted for "goodness and cheapness", this "reliable" Murray Hill Chinese slurp shop ladles out "better-than-average" grub in "portions that last all week"; though the service and decor are merely functional, "fast" takeout has fans playing it again and again.

Sandobe ◐ [S] ≠ 22 | 10 | 14 | $24

330 E. 11th St. (bet. 1st & 2nd Aves.), 212-780-0328

■ "Sushi for a song" results in "long lines" at this East Village Japanese "treasure" that's home to an "amazing assortment" of "succulent" specialties at "cut-rate", cash-only tabs; it's "packed every night" with "hard-core" sushiphiles who roll with the "spartan decor."

San Domenico [S] 23 | 22 | 22 | $65

240 Central Park S. (bet. B'way & 7th Ave.), 212-265-5959

■ Tony May's "class act" on Central Park South remains a "top-drawer" dining experience thanks to chef Odette Fada's "excellent" Nuovo Italiano cuisine, a "great wine list" and "splendid service"; though prices reflect the "high-toned" ambiance, its prix fixe lunches and $32 pre-theater dinner are "among the best values" in town.

		F	D	S	C

Sandro's   23 | 15 | 20 | $49
200 Ninth Ave. (bet. 22nd & 23rd Sts.), 212-633-8033
■ An "outstanding addition to Chelsea", this pricey, "high-energy" Northern Italian showcases repatriated chef Sandro Fioriti's "inventive", "lusty" cooking; admirers who are "glad he's back" say even the "bright yellow" room can't compete with his colorful culinary derring-do.

Sandwich Planet ≠   ∇ 20 | 8 | 12 | $13
534 Ninth Ave. (bet. 39th & 40th Sts.), 212-273-9768
■ "From old favorites to inspired combos", "everything you could want between two slices" gets stacked up at this "definitive" sandwich shop near the Port Authority; though the "huge selection" is a "revelation" to first-timers, the "cramped space" makes "takeout" the logical alternative.

San Giusto   ∇ 22 | 20 | 22 | $51
935 Second Ave. (bet. 49th & 50th Sts.), 212-319-0900
■ "Like an old friend", this "delightfully warm" East Side Italian is "special" and welcoming; it may be "a little expensive", but loyalists tout its "freshly prepared" Tuscaniana and "beyond-attentive" service, marveling that it's "not well known" after all these years.

San Pietro ●   24 | 21 | 23 | $63
18 E. 54th St. (bet. 5th & Madison Aves.), 212-753-9015
■ Plying "old-world charm in the middle of Midtown", this tony Italian is a bona fide "keeper" for "terrific" food and "fabulous service"; sure, it's "high-priced", but the "upscale" types who convene for its "noisy" "power lunch" and refined, romantic dinner say "life is beautiful" here.

Santa Fe ● S   19 | 19 | 19 | $38
72 W. 69th St. (bet. Columbus Ave. & CPW), 212-724-0822
■ This "mellow", "peach-toned" Southwesterner offers a hard-to-beat combination of "solid" standards and "frosty margaritas" at palatable prices; those who "don't expect innovation" "never tire" of the "pleasant" style, and it's "convenient to Lincoln Center" to boot.

Sant Ambroeus S   21 | 17 | 18 | $48
1000 Madison Ave. (bet. 77th & 78th Sts.), 212-570-2211
☒ "Art dealers" mix with "Europeans of a certain age" at this East Side Northern Italian cafe, a "pricey" purveyor of "authentic" bites and notable desserts ("awesome gelati", "cake good enough for a wedding"); still, the "stodgy", burial-casket decor has some grabbing the *dolci* and dashing out the door.

Sapore S≠   ∇ 21 | 11 | 17 | $21
55 Greenwich Ave. (Perry St.), 212-229-0551
☒ Ok, it's "so small you can't sneeze", but this "flavorful" West Village Italian "find" manages to turn out tasty "home cooking" at very "fair prices" (including "bargain" lunch specials); in clement weather, sidewalk seating relieves the "jam-packed" room.

Sapori d'Ischia (Queens)   – | – | – | M
55-15 37th Ave. (56th St.), 718-446-1500
Evening transforms this Italian import shop, incongruously set in industrial Woodside, into a lively, moderately tabbed trattoria where animated service, live music (opera on Thursdays) and bracing Neapolitan fare are the main attractions.

Sapphire Indian S   22 | 21 | 20 | $40
1845 Broadway (bet. 60th & 61st Sts.), 212-245-4444
■ A "delicious alternative" for Lincoln Center-goers, this Indian "jewel" "shines" with "quality" cuisine served in "exotic" environs;

F | D | S | C

although a tad "expensive" for dinner, rupee-pinchers find plenty of "value" in its $11.95 lunch buffet.

Sapporo East ●S   21 | 11 | 15 | $25
245 E. 10th St. (1st Ave.), 212-260-1330

◪ "Forget the decor" and focus on the "simple, satisfying" fare at this East Village Japanese "standby" that draws a "young crowd" thanks to its dirt "cheap sushi"; "go early" or gird yourself for "long waits."

Sarabeth's S   21 | 18 | 18 | $33
Hotel Wales, 1295 Madison Ave. (bet. 92nd & 93rd Sts.), 212-410-7335
Whitney Museum, 945 Madison Ave. (75th St.), 212-570-3670
423 Amsterdam Ave. (bet. 80th & 81st Sts.), 212-496-6280

■ Wear "comfortable shoes" since you're likely to wait in line at these "all-time favorite" breakfast/brunch scenes, a "cute" triple tribute to "Americana" known for "fresh", "wholesome" food; some say the "vanilla" ambiance comes with enough "chintz" to make "Martha" blush, but add that the Whitney branch is "less cutesy."

Sardi's ●S   16 | 19 | 18 | $48
234 W. 44th St. (bet. B'way & 8th Ave.), 212-221-8440

◪ The "legend" lives on at this über-"touristy" Times Square Continental, a "showbiz" survivor that's still a "place to stargaze" – even if it's only at the "caricatures on the walls"; some say it still has the "old pizzazz" and others warn "keep your expectations low", but most agree "you gotta go once."

Sarge's Deli ●S   17 | 9 | 14 | $23
548 Third Ave. (bet. 36th & 37th Sts.), 212-679-0442

◪ Maybe it's "no Katz's", but from the matzo ball soup to the "larger-than-life sandwiches", this 24/7 Murray Hill "local institution" remains a Jewish deli in the "true tradition"; given the "mess-hall" looks and typical, "less-than-amicable" deli service, most beat a hasty retreat and "get it delivered."

Saul (Brooklyn) S   24 | 17 | 20 | $42
140 Smith St. (bet. Bergen & Dean Sts.), 718-935-9844

■ A "top" talent in the "Smith Street renaissance", this "intimate", "friendly" Boerum Hill New American wins hearts and souls with chef-owner Saul Bolton's "serious", "sophisticated" cuisine; converts call it a "match for Manhattan" – at "half the price."

Savann S   19 | 14 | 17 | $41
414 Amsterdam Ave. (bet. 79th & 80th Sts.), 212-580-0202

■ "Surprisingly strong" cooking at "reasonable" tabs makes this "dependable" French "much-needed" on the Upper West Side; an increasingly discovered "find", it's more "tight-quartered" than ever: the "sleeper waketh."

Savore ●S   ▽ 21 | 18 | 20 | $43
200 Spring St. (Sullivan St.), 212-431-1212

■ SoHo's old guard "savors" this "traditional" "taste of Tuscany" where the "well-prepared" cooking comes in "comfortable", "rarely crowded" digs; it's also "affordable for the regular" diner – a "nice surprise" in this upmarket turf.

Savoy S   23 | 22 | 22 | $51
70 Prince St. (Crosby St.), 212-219-8570

■ "Romance personified", this SoHo Mediterranean presents "inventive", "beautifully thought-out" dishes in a "tasteful" duplex setting; though "pricey" (and prix fixe only upstairs), it's a "memorable" "date place" where "special occasions" are "really special."

Sazerac House [S] 17 | 16 | 18 | $30

533 Hudson St. (Charles St.), 212-989-0313

◪ Housed in an "old NY" building dating from 1826, this "pub-like" Cajun-American Villager is a "faithful standby" for jambalaya junkies; if it's "a bit tired", it never fails for "comfort food at comforting prices."

Scaletta [S] 21 | 19 | 22 | $48

50 W. 77th St. (bet. Columbus Ave. & CPW), 212-769-9191

■ "Unhurried dining" is all the rage at this "tranquil" Westsider where a "sedate, older crowd" convenes to "actually converse"; "above-average" Northern Italian food and a "hospitable" staff help maintain the "adult atmosphere."

Scalinatella ◐ [S] 24 | 18 | 21 | $63

201 E. 61st St. (3rd Ave.), 212-207-8280

■ "They spoil you from beginning to end" at the East Side's "favorite" subterranean "grotto" where the "sumptuous", "old-school Italian" cookery à la Capri ain't bad either; it packs plenty of "energy" into a "tight" space, though the lowdown on prices is "way high."

SCALINI FEDELI 26 | 25 | 25 | $71

165 Duane St. (bet. Greenwich & Hudson Sts.), 212-528-0400

■ A "bright star" transplanted from the Garden State, this "classic Italian" gives TriBeCa a taste of "what dining's all about" via Michael Cetrulo's "impeccably executed" cuisine; despite the "very expensive" price tag, the "gorgeous", "quietly elegant" room (that once housed Bouley) and always-"gracious" service cause customers to count this "masterpiece" among "NY's finest."

Scopa 22 | 18 | 20 | $41

79 Madison Ave. (28th St.), 212-686-8787

■ Vincent Scotto's "creative" steaks, pastas and pizzas are calculated to "please any palate" and most pocketbooks at this Gramercy Italian "winner", which, following a dramatic expansion, isn't so "understated" anymore and now boasts one of the longest bars in town; "warm" service completes the picture.

Screening Room, The [S] 20 | 19 | 19 | $38

54 Varick St. (Laight St.), 212-334-2100

■ "Dinner and a movie" is the "concept" at this "hip" TriBeCa New American–cum–screening room that earns "two thumbs up" for providing a first-rate "date idea" and an "inventive menu" that's "better than it needs to be"; have a drink in the "cozy lounge" for a "fun" triple feature.

Sea Grill 23 | 23 | 22 | $58

Rockefeller Ctr., 19 W. 49th St. (bet. 5th & 6th Aves.), 212-332-7610

◪ A "perfect" rinkside panorama and alfresco summer seating are major draws at this "rejuvenated" Rockefeller Center "seafood lovers' haven" where chef Ed Brown's "beautifully prepared" dishes are just as "polished" as the service; still, the cost is "a bit steep" and the "new look" evokes mixed emotions: "stunning" vs. "cold as ice."

SEA Thai [S] ▽ 21 | 18 | 18 | $21

75 Second Ave. (bet. 4th & 5th Sts.), 212-228-5505

■ Submerged below street level in "sleek" surroundings, this "cool" East Village Thai offers "dressed-up" versions of the "basics"; the "affordable prices" are producing waves of customers, so "go early."

Second Avenue Deli ◐ [S] 23 | 11 | 16 | $24

156 Second Ave. (10th St.), 212-677-0606

■ Most people's choice as "NY's best deli" – and hence "the world's best" – this East Village kosher veteran is "a little out-of-the-way, but well worth the trip" for "amazing" pastrami and corn beef, "cold-curing" matzo ball soup and "dare-you-to-find-better" chopped liver; not surprisingly, it's "always crowded", but "Abe Lebewohl would be proud to see it today" and "brother Jack has the knack" – "nobody does it better."

Seeda Thai S | 20 | 15 | 18 | $27

309 W. 50th St. (bet. 8th & 9th Aves.), 212-586-4040
■ This Theater District Siamese supplies "authentic", "flavorful" fare at "low prices" that compensate for its "simple" decor; though a few argue the Vietnamese dishes are even "better" than the Thai, there's consensus that it's "a valuable alternative" for the area.

Sekku S | ▽ 21 | 14 | 18 | $38

343 Lexington Ave. (bet. 39th & 40th Sts.), 212-697-9020
◪ "Longstanding", "reliable" Japanese catering to Grand Central–area wage slaves with "consistently fresh", "tasty" sushi; a "busy lunch rush" is the rule, but a few take exception to the "frazzled" staff and "predictable" fare.

Sen-ya ⇌ | – | – | – | M

174 Bleecker St. (bet. MacDougal & Sullivan Sts.), 212-228-1679
What sets this neatly appointed Village Japanese apart from dozens of other sushi joints is its tiny, startlingly tranquil back garden that's a relief after treading this hectic stretch of Bleecker Street.

Seo S | ▽ 24 | 19 | 21 | $45

249 E. 49th St. (bet. 2nd & 3rd Aves.), 212-355-7722
■ A "first-rate chef" slicing "very fresh" sushi and cooking "fantastic" classics elates Eastsiders at this UN-area Japanese yearling; despite a "therapeutic" "Zen interior", knowing naturalists naturally note that the "back garden" is a "must."

Seppi's ●S | ▽ 19 | 18 | 17 | $45

Le Parker Meridien, 123 W. 56th St. (bet. 6th & 7th Aves.), 212-708-7444
■ Raoul's "pleasant Midtown cousin", this "upscale" French bistro offers a "friendly" feel and food that's "surprisingly good"; insiders claim its "hidden" location in the Parker Meridien keeps it "quiet", giving them more room to spread out and enjoy its "late hours."

Serafina ●S | 19 | 17 | 16 | $37

1022 Madison Ave. (79th St.), 212-734-2676
29 E. 61st Street (bet. Madison & Park Aves.), 212-702-9898
393 Lafayette St. (E. 4th St.), 212-995-9595
◪ "Euro chic"-sters strike a pose at these "total scenes" that feature similarly stylish Italian menus of "light" pizzas, pastas and salads; there's a "breezy" roof deck at the Uptown outpost, but connoisseurs say the more "colorful" Downtowner is the "most fab."

Serendipity 3 ●S | 19 | 20 | 16 | $26

225 E. 60th St. (bet. 2nd & 3rd Aves.), 212-838-3531
■ "Willie Wonka" would envy this "unforgettable" East Side toy store/sweet shop's cachet among the "under-10" set, who go for its "unbelievable" "ice cream concoctions" (not to mention "calorific" burgers and foot-long dogs); grown-ups say the "landmark" frozen hot chocolate is "better than sex", but you pay for it with "steep" tabs and "l-o-n-g waits."

Seryna | 24 | 22 | 23 | $60

11 E. 53rd St. (bet. 5th & Madison Aves.), 212-980-9393
■ Build up "good karma" at this Midtown "Zen steakhouse" where diners savor beef charred on a "blazing hot rock right at your table" along with other "traditional" Japanese edibles; the "pastoral"

| F | D | S | C |

ambiance and "impeccable service" make it fine for "escaping", but would-be voyagers should "say sayonara" to their budgets.

Sette Mezzo ●S⊘ | 22 | 17 | 19 | $50 |
969 Lexington Ave. (bet. 70th & 71st Sts.), 212-472-0400
◪ Even fat cats are happy to "squeeze in" at this "cash-only" East Side Italian that proffers "fresh, tasty" "peasant food" in "private club"-like environs; though outsiders sniff "snooty" and "pricey", it's likely to be "packed" with lots of familiar faces.

Sette MoMA S | 18 | 20 | 18 | $43 |
Museum of Modern Art, 11 W. 53rd St. (bet. 5th & 6th Aves.), 212-708-9710
◪ This "artful" Italian affords a surprisingly "nice break" from the "hectic" MoMA galleries, even if the sculpture garden it overlooks is currently under construction; those who see the "larger picture" find the "pricey" food unusually "well-prepared" for what one would normally expect at a large institution.

Seven | ▽ 21 | 19 | 20 | $42 |
350 Seventh Ave. (bet. 29th & 30th Sts.), 212-967-1919
■ Everything's coming up sevens at this savory "seafood American-style" yearling that offers a break of good luck in its otherwise "arid" MSG neighborhood; providing "prompt pre-game attention", it's also "classy" enough for a good "business lunch."

71 CLINTON FRESH FOOD S | 27 | 17 | 22 | $53 |
71 Clinton St. (bet. Rivington & Stanton Sts.), 212-614-6960
■ All-out "enthusiasm" reigns at this "ultra-hip" Lower East Side storefront where chef Wylie Dufresne's "vibrant kitchen" is "hot" to the melting point, turning out "delectable", "highly imaginative" New American fare that elicits "wows"; despite "high-end" pricing, the "close" quarters and "star status" guarantee it's a "struggle to get in", at least until Dufresne moves to his new nearby restaurant, scheduled to open in the spring.

Sevilla ●S | 22 | 15 | 19 | $35 |
62 Charles St. (W. 4th St.), 212-929-3189
■ An "old-time favorite" with "tons of character", this West Village Spaniard is a "garlic lovers'" "heaven" pairing "excellent" paella and "fantastic green sauce" with pitchers of "to-die-for sangria"; the good "value" "never changes" – nor do the "killer" weekend waits; P.S. "bring Scope."

Shaan S | 22 | 21 | 20 | $37 |
Rockefeller Ctr., 57 W. 48th St. (bet. 5th & 6th Aves.), 212-977-8400
■ "Serene enough for business talk", this "tranquil" Rockefeller Center Indian is a subcontinental "standout" for its "rich" food, "unobtrusive service" and "spacious", "sumptuous" surroundings; it also draws applause for its "bountiful lunch buffet" and "high-style" pre-theater dinner.

Shabu-Shabu 70 S | 20 | 15 | 19 | $36 |
314 E. 70th St. (bet. 1st & 2nd Aves.), 212-861-5635
■ Something of a "secret", this "intimate", "unpretentious" East Side Japanese is a "good alternative" for "fresh sushi" and especially its signature shabu-shabu hot pots; "fast, attentive" service and "decent value" more than compensate for the "shabby-shabby decor."

Shabu-Tatsu | 20 | 14 | 17 | $32 |
1414 York Ave. (75th St.), 212-472-3322 S
216 E. 10th St. (bet. 1st & 2nd Aves.), 212-477-2972
■ For a "participatory" "change of pace", this "cook-your-own" BBQ duo offers an "eating experience" likened to "Japanese fondue";

			F	D	S	C

despite being decor-deprived, they're "steamy" "fun on a date" or with a group and a lot "cheaper than Japan."

Shaffer City Oyster Bar & Grill   23 | 17 | 21 | $45
5 W. 21st St. (bet. 5th & 6th Aves.), 212-255-9827
■ With one of the "best raw selections" around, this "bustling" Flatiron fish house is a "top-notch" choice for "impeccable" seafood and warm hospitality; though a bit on the "expensive" side, locals groan it's "getting popular – who told?"

Shallots NY S   ▽ 20 | 21 | 19 | $57
Sony Atrium, 550 Madison Ave. (bet. 55th & 56th Sts.), 212-833-7800
✉ "Finally, delicious kosher!" – so says the "Joe Lieberman crowd" at this "classy" Midtown venue with a "sophisticated", nondairy Mediterranean menu set up in "stylish", "spacious" surroundings; sure, service slips and "exorbitant" tabs take their toll, but overall it's "fine dining by any standard" and "worth" every shekel.

Shanghai Cuisine S≠   ▽ 21 | 14 | 16 | $23
89 Bayard St. (Mulberry St.), 212-732-8988
■ "Soup dumplings are a must" at this "step up from the typical Chinatown joint", offering "very authentic", very low-cost cooking; no wonder its "1930s Chiang Kai-shek"–style room is "always crowded" – despite Mao-style service.

Shangrila S   ▽ 18 | 19 | 20 | $24
129 Second Ave. (bet. 7th St. & St. Marks Pl.), 212-387-7908
■ Neophytes should bring a Sherpa to this aptly named, inexpensive East Village newcomer proffering a "wide range of Tibetan dishes" that reach their peak with especially "good *momos*" (crispy dumplings); a "gracious staff" and "Lhasa rural" decor highlight the ambiance.

Shark Bar ●S   20 | 16 | 16 | $35
307 Amsterdam Ave. (bet. 74th & 75th Sts.), 212-874-8500
■ Get your "chix-and-ribs" "fix" at this "happening" West Side "buppie hangout" where a "stylish" sports- and music-industry crowd gets down with "giant helpings" of "satisfying" Soul Food in "cramped" but "cool" digs; in one night here you're likely to "surpass your grease [and celebrity] quotient for the year."

Sharz Cafe & Wine Bar S   22 | 14 | 19 | $37
177 E. 90th St. (bet. Lexington & 3rd Aves.), 212-876-7282
■ A "welcoming" "gem" "convenient to the 92nd Street Y", this Med-Eclectic is a "rare find" for its reasonably priced food and "fantastic selection" of "wines by the glass"; the main downside is "uncomfortably small" digs that keep conversations from getting too "personal."

Shelly's New York ●S   19 | 20 | 20 | $49
104 W. 57th St. (bet. 6th & 7th Aves.), 212-245-2422
■ This "upbeat", multi-level Midtown American brasserie features a "date"-worthy "aphrodisiac raw bar", lots of private party space and conversation-starting "wonderful works of art" by Peter Max and LeRoy Neiman; a "most enjoyable" surf 'n' turf menu and "great martinis" keep the mood "cheery", though a few consider it kinda "costly" for "comfort food."

Sherwood Cafe (Brooklyn) S≠   – | – | – | M
195 Smith St. (bet. Baltic & Warren Sts.), 718-596-1609
At Smith Street's vintage housewares store, Robin des Bois, you can test the linoleum tables and chrome chairs by sitting down to a French nosh in the chockablock room, or out beneath the garden's apple tree; a salad or sandwich and a glass of wine makes for a fine refresher after a nearby flick.

	F	D	S	C

Shoebox Cafe 🆂
▽ 21 | 17 | 16 | $25

Grand Central Terminal, lower level (42nd St.), 212-986-5959
■ Connoisseurs of "true Southern cooking" for peanuts tout this great "little" "surprise" in Grand Central's basement, saying "if you gotta eat in a shoebox, this is the one"; even normally harried commuters can be spotted "grabbing some chicken" and biscuits "for the ride home."

Shun Lee ●🆂
24 | 22 | 21 | $47

43 W. 65th St. (bet. Columbus Ave. & CPW), 212-595-8895
■ "Tops" for "refinement", Michael Tong's "venerable" Lincoln Center "treasure" excites with a "plethora" of "dazzling", "high-end" Chinese choices concentrated under a "dramatic", "black-and-white", dragon-themed backdrop; for "gourmet" dining with "excellent", black-tie service, it's hard to do better on the West Side.

Shun Lee Cafe ●🆂
21 | 17 | 18 | $36

43 W. 65th St. (bet. Columbus Ave. & CPW), 212-769-3888
■ Rolling out "benchmark" dim sum, this "quick" Chinese is "handy" for a "pre–Lincoln Center" curtain-raiser; the stylish "checkerboard" decor and "delicious", cheap chow appeal to those out for "less fuss" and more "casual" "fun" than at its next-door sibling.

Shun Lee Palace ●🆂
24 | 22 | 22 | $50

155 E. 55th St. (bet. Lexington & 3rd Aves.), 212-371-8844
■ Michael Tong's "superior" East Midtown "grande dame" continues to set the NY "gold standard" for "sophisticated" Chinese dining; backed up by a clever, colorful Adam Tihany design and service that "never wavers" ("let them order for you"), it has a lock on the Sinophile market, since "one bite" transports patrons "worlds away."

Siam Inn ●🆂
20 | 14 | 18 | $28

854 Eighth Ave. (bet. 51st & 52nd Sts.), 212-757-4006
■ In the running as a "pre-theater haven", this "solid" West Side Thai delivers satays-faction with a "spicy" "variety" of "above-average" dishes at "reasonable prices"; though the "decor is wanting", sated showgoers will applaud the "good, quick" service.

Sichuan Palace 🆂
▽ 21 | 16 | 19 | $35

310 E. 44th St. (bet. 1st & 2nd Aves.), 212-972-7377
🗷 "China and the UN" are on the best of terms at this East Side "neighborhood resource" for "fine", "authentic" fare; though short of palatial ("nil decor"), it attracts a "loyal clientele" seeking a "quiet retreat" from practicing politics.

Silk Road Palace 🆂∌
19 | 9 | 17 | $20

447B Amsterdam Ave. (bet. 81st & 82nd Sts.), 212-580-6294
🗷 "Twentysomethings" lined up at this Westsider report "amazingly low prices" for "huge portions" of "decent" Chinese along with free "all-you-can-drink" wine and soda that's a "generous" plus; sure, it's "sparsely decorated" and "rushed", but the "more you drink", the less you care.

Silver Pond (Queens) ●🆂
20 | 10 | 14 | $27

56-50 Main St. (bet. Booth Memorial & 56th Aves.), 718-463-2888
🗷 A "dim sum expert" and purveyor of "authentic Hong Kong" deep-sea delicacies, this "busy" Flushing Chinese would be of note anywhere in town; just be ready for a language barrier and an ex-diner setting that might as well be underwater: "no atmosphere."

Sipan ●🆂
▽ 22 | 18 | 18 | $40

702 Amsterdam Ave. (94th St.), 212-665-9929
🗷 "Pleasant", moderately tabbed Upper West Side Peruvian yearling that specializes in "delicious", finely spiced dishes led by its specialty,

| F | D | S | C |

seafood seviche; it also offers the opportunity to sample the beer and wine that warms the Andes.

Sirabella's S 22 | 15 | 21 | $39
72 East End Ave. (bet. 82nd & 83rd Sts.), 212-988-6557
■ Known for its "hands-on owner", this "quiet, quaint" East Side Italian is "like dining at a close friend's", albeit one capable of "consistently delicious" cooking; since "there isn't any place to stand or move", claustrophobes opt for the "supremo" takeout.

Sirocco ●S – | – | – | M
199 Prince St. (bet. MacDougal & Sullivan Sts.), 212-254-4040
This SoHo Mediterranean newcomer offers a midpriced menu by ex Calle Ocho chef Alex Garcia as well as an extensive tapas selection available till 2 AM; tasting-menu samplers, a sidewalk cafe and two *intime* balcony tables make this look like an instant winner.

Sistina ●S 23 | 19 | 21 | $58
1555 Second Ave. (bet. 80th & 81st Sts.), 212-861-7660
■ Eastsiders confirm that this "dignified" Northern Italian standby is "still delivering the goods": "marvelous", "old-time cooking", "outstanding" wines and "gracious" service in "comfortable" surroundings; it's favored by "grown-ups" looking for a good – if "spendy" – time.

Slice of Harlem S ▽ 20 | 11 | 15 | $18
2527 Eighth Ave. (135th St.), 212-862-4089
308 Lenox Ave. (bet. 125th & 126th Sts.), 212-426-7400
■ A "breath of fresh air" in the Uptown culinary scene, this delicious deep-dish duo is building a rep with "made-to-order pizza" that may be "hands-down the best" anywhere, and yes, "you can buy a slice" as well; kudos also go to the "easygoing, friendly staff."

Smith & Wollensky ●S 23 | 18 | 20 | $58
797 Third Ave. (49th St.), 212-753-1530
■ "Carnivores in their element" hail Alan Stillman's "classic" Midtown steakhouse, a now-nationwide "tradition" for "tremendous" cuts of "mouthwatering" red meat consumed among "real men" (and "man-watching" women); the "hedonistic" duplex scene comes complete with "great wines", a "professional" staff, "lotsa noise and commotion" and tabs that encourage "meals on the client"; in sum, this is everything a great steakhouse should be, and a quintessential NY experience in the bargain.

Smith St. Kitchen (Brooklyn) S 23 | 16 | 21 | $39
174 Smith St. (bet. Warren & Wyckoff Sts.), 718-858-5359
■ "Fine, friendly dining" elevates this storefront seafooder to "star" status on Boerum Hill's restaurant row; the fin fare is "fresh and delicious", the staff "eager to please", and for the few who find the "minimalist" setting "cold", there's a "lovely garden" out back.

Snack S ▽ 23 | 14 | 18 | $18
105 Thompson St. (bet. Prince & Spring Sts.), 212-925-1040
■ Once a snack bar and still super-"cozy", this "unpretentious" SoHo Hellenic demonstrates how "delicious" (and inexpensive) "homemade" Greek dishes can be; despite the name, everyone "leaves full", and it's already so "cramped" (12 seats) that fans "hope more people don't discover it."

Soba-ya S 23 | 20 | 21 | $26
229 E. Ninth St. (bet. 2nd & 3rd Aves.), 212-533-6966
■ There's "no Americanizing" at this "mellow" East Village Japanese noodle shop that's frequented by "hip, young" things who salute its "superb" "handmade soba" and "perfect" soups; when you toss in

the "wonderful" sakes, "energetic servers" and "affordable" cost, it's no wonder many surveyors attain "Zen satisfaction."

Soho Steak S

20 | 16 | 17 | $38

90 Thompson St. (bet. Prince & Spring Sts.), 212-226-0602

Contented carnivores continually claim this "cheap, cheerful" "crowded" SoHo French-American bistro is a "fabulous deal" for "tasty", "no-frills" steak frites; though the "close" quarters draw brickbats, they can be a "plus" for "getting to know" the "trendy, pretty" folks at the surrounding tables.

Sol (Brooklyn) ● S

∇ 19 | 17 | 17 | $36

229 DeKalb Ave. (Clermont Ave.), 718-222-1510

"Up-and-coming" Fort Greene Nuevo Latino offering "hearty" cooking and quite the "bar scene"; though most say it has settled into the "right groove", a few fret it's in "trendy overdrive" and may be "overpriced for Brooklyn."

Solera

22 | 20 | 20 | $49

216 E. 53rd St. (bet. 2nd & 3rd Aves.), 212-644-1166

There's no need to "venture Downtown" for "top-notch" Spanish dining thanks to this "inviting" East Midtowner specializing in "tantalizing tapas" and other hard-to-find Iberian specialties; its "elegant" brownstone backdrop and "attentive" service are fit for a "special occasion", albeit a "pricey" one.

Soma Soup S

18 | 12 | 12 | $13

2067 Broadway (bet. 71st & 72nd Sts.), 212-721-7662

So "many choices" of "adventurous", "flavorful" soups have loyalists lauding this Westsider as a "great fast-food alternative" and "take-out staple"; still, as its ratings suggest, there's a spoonful of dissent over its decor and "poor" service.

Son Cubano ●

– | – | – | M

405 W. 14th St. (bet. 9th Ave. & Washington St.), 212-366-1640

Think Havana '59, then add a fresh batch of Meatpacking District thrill-seekers to get the idea behind this new Cuban/tapas joint; the longest bar in the city and live music lend to the festive feeling.

Sonora S

20 | 19 | 17 | $39

Eastgate Tower Hotel, 222 E. 39th St. (bet. 2nd & 3rd Aves.), 212-297-0280

An "open-air" alternative with "pleasant" "patio seating", this midpriced Murray Hill Nuevo Latino features "tasty", "inventive" fare from a "clever chef"; given the "uneven" service, carefree *compañeros* have "lots of time" to sip its "great sangria."

Sosa Borella S

∇ 20 | 17 | 19 | $32

460 Greenwich St. (bet. Desbrosses & Watts Sts.), 212-431-5093

Operating out of a "quiet" corner of TriBeCa, this "affordable" Italian-Argentine "find" works as an "unusual" lunch locus for "robust", "finger-licking" sandwiches or as an "undiscovered" dinner destination for "grilled meats"; either way, the "warm" staff keeps things "casual."

Soul Cafe S

19 | 18 | 17 | $39

444 W. 42nd St. (bet. 9th & 10th Aves.), 212-244-7685

Serving Soul Food in "hungry"-man portions, this "cool" West Side "neighborhood staple" is a fine "pre-theater choice" with a bonus "bar scene" and occasional "live jazz"; but dissatisfied souls say "spotty" service can be a spoiler.

Soul Fixins'

∇ 19 | 7 | 14 | $15

371 W. 34th St. (bet. 8th & 9th Aves.), 212-736-1345

"Good, greasy" "down-home" grub means this "basic" Soul Fooder near Penn Station fills a need as an "inexpensive" "pre-Garden" warm-

SOUP KITCHEN INTERNATIONAL, AL'S ⇗

27 | 5 | 9 | $14

259 W. 55th St. (bet. B'way & 8th Ave.), 212-757-7730
■ Immortalized on *Seinfeld* for his "amazingly hearty soups" and short fuse, Al Yeganeh "ladles on" at this Midtown "hole-in-the-wall"; so as not to annoy Al, regulars "practice their orders" while standing in line – but lament there's "'no soup for you' in summer", when Al gives it a rest.

South Shore Country Club (Staten Island)

▽ 20 | 24 | 19 | $50

200 Huguenot Ave. (W. Shore Expwy., exit 4), 718-356-7017
■ Praised for its "consistently good" French-Continental fare, this solid Staten Islander rises above the "routine" with a "beautiful setting" and a "marvelous" view of the local links; no surprise, it's a "favorite" for weddings and other special "occasions."

Spada S

▽ 20 | 19 | 19 | $35

1431 Third Ave. (81st St.), 212-650-0850
■ In an area where trattorias are "too numerous to count", this East Side "local Italian" distinguishes itself with fine "basic" fare at the "right price"; "inviting" sidewalk seating seals the deal.

SPARKS STEAK HOUSE

25 | 20 | 22 | $62

210 E. 46th St. (bet. 2nd & 3rd Aves.), 212-687-4855
■ Always a "cut above", this "cavernous" Midtown cow palace "makes life simple" with "massive", "melt-in-your-mouth" prime steaks and an "unbelievable wine list" that result in "extremely satisfying" "macho meals" for free-spending "financiers"; throw in "classic" "Diamond Jim Brady decor" and "no-nonsense professional" service, and even Luger loyalists wonder "why travel to Brooklyn?"

Spazzia ●S

18 | 15 | 17 | $37

366 Columbus Ave. (77th St.), 212-799-0150
◪ Backing the Museum of Natural History, this Westsider offsets "ordinary looks" with "tasty" pizza and other Med-Eclectic fare; though some snipe about "inexperienced, unpolished" service, budget-conscious locals consider it a "decent" enough "staple."

Spice S

19 | 15 | 16 | $23

1411 Second Ave. (bet. 73rd & 74th Sts.), 212-988-5348
199 Eighth Ave. (bet. 20th & 21st Sts.), 212-989-1116
60 University Pl. (10th St.), 212-982-3758
■ Despite the "simple" decor, the food's as "flavorful" "as the name" at these diminutive Thai "standouts"; "more-than-reasonable prices" and "quick-fix" delivery have devotees dreaming of one "on every corner."

Spirit Cruises S

13 | 21 | 16 | $56

Chelsea Piers, Pier 62 (W. 23rd St. & Hudson River), 212-727-2789
◪ Offering a "three-hour vacation" on the waters around Manhattan, this "floating catering hall" lays out an American buffet that's "no match" for the "amazing" skyline scenery; critics of the spiritless "basic" eats suggest you "bring a sandwich", yet the view alone is worth the tab.

Spring Street Natural ●S

19 | 17 | 17 | $26

62 Spring St. (Lafayette St.), 212-966-0290
■ This SoHo health food "tradition" keeps on "doing what comes naturally" with its "hearty" helpings of good organic grub (plus fish and fowl); despite an "amnesiac" staff, it's memorable as a "spacious", "cheap" alternative not limited to "seeds and weeds."

	F	D	S	C

Stage Deli ●S | 19 | 11 | 14 | $26 |
834 Seventh Ave. (bet. 53rd & 54th Sts.), 212-245-7850

☒ Ok, it's "less adored than the Carnegie", but this "old-style", tourist-centric Midtown deli should still be approached "on an empty stomach" to fully enjoy its "mile-high sandwiches"; old hands at "excess" report that this is where many out-of-towners learned the difference between the bagel and the lox – and discovered what real heartburn is like.

Stamatis ●S | 22 | 13 | 17 | $28 |
31-14 Broadway (bet. 31st & 32nd Sts.), Queens, 718-204-8964
29-12 23rd Ave. (bet. 29th & 30th Sts.), Queens, 718-932-8596

■ "Get over the kitsch" and into the "Greek-as-you-can-get" "homestyle cooking" at these "friendly" "neighborhood favorites"; for "down-to-earth" "family" dining, they're "definitely worth the trip to Astoria" – "in Manhattan they'd cost three times as much."

Starbucks S | 14 | 12 | 12 | $10 |
1642 Third Ave. (92nd St.), 212-360-0425
1117-1123 Lexington Ave. (78th St.), 212-517-8476
77 W. 125th St. (Lenox Ave.), 917-492-2454
152-154 Columbus Ave. (67th St.), 212-721-0470 ●
585 Second Ave. (32nd St.), 212-684-1299
684 Sixth Ave. (22nd St.), 212-691-1948
370 Seventh Ave. (31st St.), 212-967-8463
13-25 Astor Pl. (Lafayette St.), 212-982-3563 ●
141-143 Second Ave. (9th St.), 212-780-0024 ●
314 E. Fordham Rd. (Elm Pl.), Bronx, 718-329-9026
Plus other locations throughout the NY area

☒ Most "grudgingly" admit this "planetary ruler" brews up "damn good" "high-octane" java; even if boycotters berate the "bitter" brew as "totally overpriced", fans say "thanks a latte" for the "extra living room" – and easy access to Krispy Kremes.

Steak Frites ●S | 18 | 17 | 17 | $38 |
9 E. 16th St. (bet. 5th Ave. & Union Sq. W.), 212-463-7101

☒ The name "needs no translation" at this "casual", "reasonably priced" "oh-so"-French bistro off Union Square, where the eponymous house specialty is the dish of choice; though "a bit formulaic" with "so-so service", it still exudes enough "charm" to stay "packed."

Stella S | – | – | – | M |
58 MacDougal St. (bet. Houston & Prince Sts.), 212-674-4968

A charmer that makes everyone feel like a regular, this SoHo newcomer serves satisfying New American fare with a slight Gallic accent; the menu flirts with the unexpected (rosemary ice cream cone, anyone?), while raw brick walls, cozy window seats and rustic wooden tables make for an inviting setting.

Stella del Mare | 21 | 19 | 19 | $47 |
346 Lexington Ave. (bet. 39th & 40th Sts.), 212-687-4425

■ Catch some "consistently good seafood" in a "comfortable", cultivated setting at this Murray Hill Northern Italian, a "pleasant", if pricey, "haven" with a "great piano bar" downstairs; it's "not Esca", but it's certainly stella enough to be a "neighborhood favorite."

Stingy Lulu's ●S⌿ | 14 | 17 | 15 | $21 |
129 St. Marks Pl. (bet. Ave. A & 1st Ave.), 212-674-3545

☒ "Wigged-out" East Village American that gets away with merely "decent grub", since half its appeal is realizing "your waitress is really a man"; the "cheap" tabs, "killer" drinks and "late-night" "debauchery" are "still a trip", though a trip perhaps best taken while "under 25."

	F	D	S	C

St. Maggie's Cafe — 18 | 18 | 18 | $36
120 Wall St. (bet. Front & South Sts.), 212-943-9050
■ "Formal" Victorian decor and "reliable", if rather "run-of-the-mill", cooking make this Financial District American a "lunch mecca" and standby for "business occasions"; most agree its location closes the deal, given the "limited Downtown eating options."

St. Michel (Brooklyn) S — ▽ 23 | 20 | 21 | $49
7518 Third Ave. (bet. Bay Ridge Pkwy. & 76th St.), 718-748-4411
■ Francophiles just say "*oui*" to "Bordeaux à la Brooklyn" at this "quaint" Bay Ridge bistro, a "hideaway" for "fine" French fare and "romance" enhanced by "charming" service and "intimate" "live music"; more prosaic types say any romantic feelings are diminished when you pay the bill.

Stonewall Bistro S — – | – | – | M
113 Seventh Ave. S. (bet. Christopher & W. 10th St.), 917-661-1335
This pocket-size companion to the West Village's historic Stonewall offers a sit-down American dinner along with cabaret (after 9 PM); there's also a winsome Sunday brunch.

Strip House S — 22 | 20 | 20 | $58
13 E. 12th St. (bet. 5th Ave. & University Pl.), 212-328-0000
■ Just weaned, this Central Village steakhouse yearling steps up to the plate with "seriously good" meat and potatoes (including "luscious NY strips") served in the "sexiest room" around, a "blood-red" take on a "bordello" adorned with vintage "Follies nudes"; it's "chic" enough that "women love it", and service comes with "more tact" than traditional for the genre.

Sugar Bar S — ▽ 20 | 22 | 18 | $40
254 W. 72nd St. (bet. B'way & West End Ave.), 212-579-0222
◪ Owned by singer/songwriters Ashford and Simpson, this West Side African-Mediterranean draws a "random crowd" of yups and bups with an "artful", seafood-leaning menu and a "cool", recently renovated space; flat notes include "pricey" tabs and service that's "not solid as a rock."

Sugar Hill Bistro ●S — – | – | – | E
458 W. 145th St. (bet. Amsterdam & Convent Aves.), 212-491-5505
Near the beautiful brownstones of Harlem's highest hill, this newcomer spread over four floors and a back patio is drawing a bumper crop of buppies who savor its sophisticated Southern-Eclectic cuisine; live jazz keeps the joint jumping on weekend nights, and gospel singers serenade Sunday buffet brunchers.

SUGIYAMA — 26 | 20 | 24 | $83
251 W. 55th St. (bet. B'way & 8th Ave.), 212-956-0670
■ "Genius" chef Nao Sugiyama astounds at this "dazzling" West Midtowner featuring "sublime" kaiseki dinners akin to "metaphysical experiences" that tower like "Mt. Fuji" over ordinary Japanese fare; "spoiled" patrons are more than willing to "mortgage the house" for the "ultimate" meal, though a few wish it arrived in more spacious quarters; N.B. if money matters, go for lunch.

Sultan, The ●S — 21 | 14 | 20 | $32
1435 Second Ave. (bet. 74th & 75th Sts.), 212-861-0200
■ For a "tasty" intro to "Turkish delights", this "upbeat" Eastsider dispatches a "wonderful" selection with "cheerful" service as a bonus; though decor is "minimal", low prices let even the cash-strapped leave "feeling like the namesake."

Sung Chu Mei [S] ▽ 21 | 13 | 22 | $23

615 Hudson St. (bet. Jane & 12th Sts.), 212-675-0016

■ From outside it's "just a neighborhood place", but this Village Chinese wins strong indoor support with its "big menu" of "fresh" food along with "warm hospitality"; still, the homebound sing the praises of "fast delivery."

Supper Club, The 16 | 22 | 16 | $57

240 W. 47th St. (bet. Broadway & 8th Ave.), 212-921-1940

■ You'd "better have a date" at this "fantastic deco" Theater District "ballroom" that puts on a "great show" with a "big band" and "jumping" dance floor that "transport you back" to the '30s faster than you can say "Fred and Ginger"; the "ordinary" American menu "ain't bad" – it's just "incidental"; N.B. open Friday and Saturday only.

Supreme Macaroni Co. 18 | 15 | 17 | $28

511 Ninth Ave. (bet. 38th & 39th Sts.), 212-564-8074

◪ The "red sauce" works well with the "checkered tablecloths" at this truly "old-school" Italian "tucked away" behind a Hell's Kitchen grocery; as befits a joint known for serving "cheap wine" and pasta "like mama used to make", some "gotta love" it while others simply "cringe."

Sur (Brooklyn) [S] 20 | 17 | 17 | $35

232 Smith St. (bet. Butler & Douglass Sts.), 718-875-1716

■ "Those craving meat" in Carroll Gardens turn to this Argentinean steakhouse with a pampas "twist"; though the "rustic" room is usually "packed", throwing "service off", the carnivorous "fiesta" is as "enjoyable" and "affordable" as you'll find on Smith Street.

Surya [S] 20 | 18 | 16 | $40

302 Bleecker St. (bet. Grove St. & 7th Ave. S.), 212-807-7770

◪ "Imaginative" without straying "too far from authenticity", this "progressive" West Villager puts a "mod" spin on Indian dining with "delicate" flavors, a "fabulous garden" and "smooth" drinks garnished with "rose petals"; unfortunately, the staff's "attitude" is more sur-ly than ya.

Sushi a-go-go ◐ – | – | – | M

1900 Broadway (bet. 63rd & 64th Sts.), 212-724-7340

◪ Midtown go-getters tout this Japanese newcomer for a "quick" sushi fix, "fair non-sushi" dishes and "decent prices"; however, the format is "limited", and the overall word is just "ok."

Sushiden 24 | 18 | 20 | $47

19 E. 49th St. (bet. 5th & Madison Aves.), 212-758-2700

123 W. 49th St. (bet. 6th & 7th Aves.), 212-398-2800

■ "Execs trying to be healthy" "keep coming back" to these crosstown "business-lunch" dens for "fresh, fresh, fresh" sushi and "efficient service"; "crowded" conditions aside, they're "classier" than most rivals but a bit "overpriced in today's tough market."

Sushi Hana ◐ [S] 23 | 17 | 18 | $33

1501 Second Ave. (78th St.), 212-327-0582

■ Super servings of still-seaworthy sushi at sane prices ensure "huge lines" at this East Side Japanese; "bamboo hut" decor, "beautiful people" and the recent, around-the-corner addition of Sake Hana, a (rice) wine bar, can make it sometimes "chaotic."

Sushihatsu ◐ [S] 24 | 15 | 19 | $55

1143 First Ave. (bet. 62nd & 63rd Sts.), 212-371-0238

◪ Pay no mind to the "dull decor" at this Japanese Eastsider and focus instead on the "stunning" sushi; high rollers maintain it's worth the cost, and night owls like the "really late" hours.

			F	D	S	C

Sushi Jones S
| - | - | - | I |

17 E. 17th St. (bet. B'way & 5th Ave.), 646-230-0033

■ For a different spin on the basic Japanese model, this Flatiron newcomer offers classic sushi as well as some variations like grilled-portobello-and-goat-cheese rolls; the space-age setting and cafeteria-style setup work equally well for eating in or taking out.

SUSHI OF GARI S
| 26 | 14 | 19 | $50 |

402 E. 78th St. (1st Ave.), 212-517-5340

■ Sushi connoisseurs "hit it big" at this "tiny" East Side Japanese where "Mr. Gari himself" prepares the "amazing" "bite-size" delicacies; notwithstanding the "bleak space" and "platinum-card" pricing, reservations are a must, since it's usually "mobbed."

Sushi Rose
| 22 | 15 | 17 | $37 |

248 E. 52nd St., 2nd fl. (bet. 2nd & 3rd Aves.), 212-813-1800

■ Among the "most generous of Japanese", this Midtowner's "Saturday night half-off" deal is "worth waiting" for, and it rises to the occasion with "big pieces" of "fresh sushi and sashimi"; despite its "sterile environs", it's quite popular – "go early."

Sushi Samba ●S
| 23 | 22 | 18 | $43 |

245 Park Ave. S. (bet. 19th & 20th Sts.), 212-475-9377
87 Seventh Ave. S. (Barrow St.), 212-691-7885

■ "Hipper-than-thou" "*Sex and the City*" types pack this "really different" pair of Japanese-Latin hot spots for "killer drinks" and "fantastic combos" of "sushi with Brazilian flair" served to a "salsa beat"; putting cost aside, it's a "supercool" "party", particularly on the West Villager's rooftop terrace – "if you can get a table."

Sushisay
| 25 | 18 | 21 | $51 |

38 E. 51st St. (bet. Madison & Park Aves.), 212-755-1780

■ Ground zero for Midtown's "power–sushi lunch" scene, this "first-rate", blond-wood Japanese is among the "absolute best" in the eyes of "sushi pros" who say fresher fish "would still be swimming"; of course, this excellence comes at steep tabs, a fact of some importance to the "suits" on dwindling expense accounts.

Sushi Sen-nin
| 25 | 14 | 20 | $42 |

49 E. 34th St. (bet. Madison & Park Aves.), 212-889-2208

■ Though outwardly "unexciting" and relatively "undiscovered", this Murray Hill Japanese is "well known" among sushiphiles for the "outstanding", "ultra-fresh" quality of its "exotic rolls"; the "abundant" portions justify the prices.

Sushiya S
| 22 | 14 | 19 | $33 |

28 W. 56th St. (bet. 5th & 6th Aves.), 212-247-5760

▣ Midtowners say 'ya' to the "low prices" and "dependable" dishes, both "raw and cooked", at this "casual" Japanese "staple"; since it's "nothing exciting" lookswise, the "delicious, speedy takeout" is a popular option.

SUSHI YASUDA
| 27 | 23 | 23 | $61 |

204 E. 43rd St. (bet. 2nd & 3rd Aves.), 212-972-1001

■ "Melt-in-your-mouth" sushi and a "stylish", blond wood–lined interior make for "exquisite" (albeit "Tokyo-priced") dining at this UN-area Japanese "class act"; with "gracious" chef Maomichi Yasuda offering commentary, this is a "unique experience", no matter how you slice it.

Sushi Zen
| 25 | 17 | 20 | $47 |

57 W. 46th St. (bet. 5th & 6th Aves.), 212-302-0707

■ Though certainly "among the best", "expensive" price tags lead wags to dub this Theater District Japanese "Sushi Yen"; featuring "creative presentations" of "wonderful rolls", it can be a "spiritual experience" and you can "bring on the Zen" in its "relaxed" garden.

Sweet Melissa (Brooklyn) 🖪⇗ | 22 | 17 | 17 | $16 |
276 Court St. (bet. Butler & Douglass Sts.), 718-855-3410
■ "Couldn't be sweeter" pretty well sums up this "intimate" Cobble Hill patisserie that's perfect for a "dainty afternoon tea", "delicious desserts" or French-American light bites; the "charming garden" ices the cake.

Sweet-n-Tart ●🖪⇗ | 20 | 10 | 13 | $18 |
76 Mott St. (Canal St.), 212-334-8088
20 Mott St. (bet. Chatham Sq. & Pell Sts.), 212-964-0380
136-11 38th Ave. (Main St.), Queens, 718-661-3380
■ A "massive menu" of Chinese "snack foods" allows you to mix 'n' match at these "cheap, fast" Hong Kong–style "canteens" where the "unique" dim sum and *tong shui* (sweet soups "for what ails you") thankfully distract from the "tacky" surroundings and sometimes slam-bang, sometimes somnolent service.

Swifty's ●🖪 | 20 | 19 | 19 | $53 |
1007 Lexington Ave. (bet. 72nd & 73rd Sts.), 212-535-6000
■ "Fans of the old Mortimer's delight" in its revival at this "buzzy", "beautifully decorated" East Side American with a "polite" staff that still caters to its "regular" "A-list" clientele; yet this "transformation" offers a welcome difference: now there's "dependably" good food too – and they don't make newcomers feel like non-members.

Sylvia's 🖪 | 18 | 14 | 17 | $31 |
328 Lenox Ave. (bet. 126th & 127th Sts.), 212-996-0660
◪ Harlem's "queen of Soul Food" dishes out "lips-to-hips" "Deep South cooking" that attracts "cholesterol" lovers from far and wide ("where's Bill?"); its weekend jazz and gospel brunches are "lots of fun", though some rue the first coming of the "tour buses."

Syros Seafood (Queens) ●🖪 | ▽ 23 | 18 | 20 | $33 |
32-11 Broadway (bet. 32nd & 33rd Sts.), 718-278-1877
■ "Choose your dinner" from the iced display at this affordable recent arrival on the Astoria Greek scene; the "super" grilled fish blends well with the "comfortable" setting, though a few say "presidential elections have been decided in less time than it takes to be served" here.

TABLA 🖪 | 25 | 26 | 25 | $61 |
11 Madison Ave. (25th St.), 212-889-0667
■ "East meets West with delicious consequences" at Danny Meyer's "memorable" Madison Square New American where chef Floyd Cardoz's Indian-accented menu keeps your "imagination engaged" with "seriously subtle flavors", while "impeccable service" and a "gilded setting" also curry favor; if the $54 prix fixe dinner is too rich for your blood, lunch and the handsome ground-floor Bread Bar are more affordable.

Table d'Hôte 🖪 | 21 | 17 | 20 | $45 |
44 E. 92nd St. (bet. Madison & Park Aves.), 212-348-8125
■ Carnegie Hill cliff-dwellers hie themselves to this "sweet" French-American "nook" for "quality" cooking and a "can't-be-beat" $22.50 pre-theater prix fixe; the "closet-size space" is "like your apartment's dining room – only smaller" – though it's large on charm.

Tagine Dining Gallery ●🖪 | ▽ 19 | 14 | 16 | $32 |
537 Ninth Ave. (bet. 39th & 40th Sts.), 212-564-7292
◪ "Something different" in the "underserved" Port Authority area, this moderately priced Moroccan "outpost" purveys "beautifully prepared

| F | D | S | C |

Northern African" cuisine; though "weird decor" and languid service detract, weekend "belly dancers distract."

Tai Hong Lau S
▽ 20 | 11 | 12 | $23
70 Mott St. (bet. Bayard & Canal Sts.), 212-219-1431

◪ "Crowded" Cantonese offering "excellent" cooking and "good dim sum" "without pushcarts"; still, "communication is a problem", and both "decor and service aren't great – even by Chinatown standards."

TAKA ⚫S
25 | 14 | 19 | $40
61 Grove St. (bet. Bleecker St. & 7th Ave. S.), 212-242-3699

■ "Artistic" chef-owner Takako Yoneyama's top-of-the-line "inventive creations" range from her "aesthetically" assembled sushi to the "ceramic plates" and "pastels on the wall" at this "real McCoy" West Village Japanese; it's "tiny", however, so "long lines" are the norm.

Takahachi ⚫S
▽ 22 | 13 | 17 | $29
85 Ave. A (bet. 5th & 6th Sts.), 212-505-6524

■ East Village "hipsters" bop by this Japanese "treasure trove" for "reliably excellent" sushi and cooked items toted by "servers with Hello Kitty hairdos"; despite dour digs, "low" prices and "late" hours keep it "always crowded, and rightly so."

Tamarind ⚫S
24 | 25 | 21 | $44
41-43 E. 22nd St. (bet. B'way & Park Ave. S.), 212-674-7400

■ At this "brilliant" Flatiron "upscale Indian" newcomer, the "modern" cooking is so tempting even "Gandhi would have broken his fast"; though tabs run "high", it's hard to put a price on dining "nirvana."

Tangerine ⚫S
▽ 21 | 24 | 18 | $41
228 W. 10th St. (bet. Bleecker & Hudson Sts.), 212-463-8585

◪ The "orange" lacquered room echoes the name of this latest West Village "scene", a "Thai with a twist", where the great grub's as spicy "hot" as the crowd; still, "disorganized" service and "pricey" tabs lead some to adopt a "wait-and-see" approach.

Tang Pavilion S
22 | 18 | 20 | $36
65 W. 55th St. (bet. 5th & 6th Aves.), 212-956-6888

■ Far from the "roar of Chinatown", this "serene" Midtowner's "high-quality", "authentic Shanghai" cooking keeps the trade brisk; "warp-speed service" and "fair prices" are similarly satisfying at this "wonderful everyday" option.

Tanti Baci Caffé S
▽ 19 | 14 | 17 | $26
163 W. 10th St. (bet. 7th Ave. S. & Waverly Pl.), 212-647-9651
513 E. Sixth St. (bet. Aves. A & B), 212-979-8184

◪ "Good little finds" for "basic", "well-done" Italian fare, these crosstown Villagers may be on the "drab" side but compensate with "inexpensive" tabs; though "service leaves much to be desired", at least the "staff's rapidly learning English."

Tao ⚫S
21 | 26 | 18 | $50
42 E. 58th St. (bet. Madison & Park Aves.), 212-888-2288

◪ Bringing "drama" to East Midtown, this "trendy", theatrically exotic new Pan-Asian features a "hopping" bar scene and a crowded, cavernous dining room presided over by an enormous Buddha; though the "delicious" vittles surprise many, the downsides come as no surprise: "inept service", a "disco" decibel level, no-joke price tags and "waits, waits, waits" – "even with reservations."

Taormina ⚫S
20 | 17 | 19 | $42
147 Mulberry St. (bet. Grand & Hester Sts.), 212-219-1007

■ "Respectable food" arrives at "respectable prices" at this Little Italy "standby", formerly a John Gotti haunt that "now appeals to the tourist

| F | D | S | C |

crowd"; red sauce "to die for", "old Italian waiters" and interesting "people-watching" sum it up well.

Tappo ●🅂 ▽ 22 | 20 | 18 | $47
403 E. 12th St. (bet. Ave. A & 1st Ave.), 212-505-0001
■ A "great new addition to the East Village", this "friendly", midpriced Mediterranean has "got the basics down right": an "exciting", nightly changing menu, "good wine list" and rustic "farmhouse" setting complete with "communal tables."

Taqueria de Mexico 🅂 18 | 12 | 15 | $25
93 Greenwich Ave. (bet. Bank & W. 12th Sts.), 212-255-5212
◪ Alright, it "looks like a burrito joint", but this West Village Mexican "offshoot of Mi Cocina" rises to the occasion with "amazingly varied selections" that are easily "affordable"; given the "glacial service", it's a relief that "takeout travels well."

Tartine 🅂⌽ 22 | 15 | 17 | $26
253 W. 11th St. (W. 4th St.), 212-229-2611
◪ "Count on cooling your heels in line" (especially for weekend brunch) at this popular BYO West Village bistro that continues to boast an intense following for its "lovingly prepared" French fare; however, "curt service" and quarters that are "too small even for mice" put its popularity to the test.

Tasting Room ● 24 | 17 | 24 | $49
72 E. First St. (bet. 1st & 2nd Aves.), 212-358-7831
■ "Good things come in small packages" at this "excellent" but "expensive" East Village New American that's so "tiny" "it should be renamed the 'Tasting Closet'"; it's best known for "stellar service" and "earnest, focused" fare paired with an encyclopedic array of "well-chosen wines."

Tatany 🅂 22 | 14 | 18 | $33
250 E. 52nd St. (bet. 2nd & 3rd Aves.), 212-593-0203 ●
380 Third Ave. (bet. 27th & 28th Sts.), 212-686-1871
■ Ok, they may be "loud" with "simple" decor, but these East Side Japanese slice up "damned good sushi" at "very fair prices"; dissuaded by "packed houses", homebodies order in since "they don't skimp, even on delivery."

Taverna Kyclades (Queens) 🅂 ▽ 23 | 16 | 20 | $31
33-07 Ditmars Blvd. (bet. 33rd & 35th Sts.), 718-545-8666
■ For a "little bit of Greece" in Astoria, this "fantastic" seafooder is the "real article", offering "surprising quality" that's "excellent for the money"; sure, the "decor's simple" and the "overworked" staff is "prone to mistakes – but even the mistakes are good."

Taverna Vraka (Queens) ●🅂 ▽ 21 | 17 | 21 | $36
23-15 31st St. (bet. 23rd & 24th Aves.), 718-721-3007
■ "When the live music's playing", this "crowded" Astoria Greek is "lots of fun" and after the band's played out, the "authentic Cypriot" dishes are equally rousing; fair pricing pleases penny-pinchers, while aesthetes add the "service atones for the decorating sins."

TAVERN ON THE GREEN 🅂 17 | 25 | 18 | $57
Central Park West (bet. 66th & 67th Sts.), 212-873-3200
◪ The late Warner LeRoy's "breathtaking", "over-the-top" "glitz" "fantasyland" attracts tourists and locals alike with a choice of lovely rooms (especially the multi-chandeliered Crystal Room) and spacious gardens "perfect for parties"; while some find the American food "just average", far more say it's "improved" and "surprisingly good", especially for an alfresco meal; N.B. LeRoy's recent death leaves a void not just here but in the entire restaurant industry.

	F	D	S	C

Tazza 🚬
20 | 16 | 19 | $32

196 Eighth Ave. (20th St.), 212-633-6735
■ "You know you're in Chelsea" at this "campy" Mediterranean where the staff is a "hoot" and the "tasty" vittles are more than "worth the price"; it's a "good Joyce choice" geographically, though the straight-out-of-"Jersey" decor is off-the-map.

Tea Box
21 | 22 | 20 | $28

Takashimaya, 693 Fifth Ave. (bet. 54th & 55th Sts.), 212-350-0180
■ "Oh-so-civilized" Midtown Japanese-American tearoom tendering so much "tranquility" that you "forget how tired your feet are"; prices are "modern" (read: "expensive") and portions "tiny" ("men need a hot dog" afterward), but that's part of the "Zen experience."

Tello's 🚬
18 | 16 | 18 | $34

263 W. 19th St. (bet. 7th & 8th Aves.), 212-691-8696
■ "Red-sauce deluxe" dining at "reasonable" tabs makes this "tiny" Chelsea Med-Italian a magnet for "old-world" dining mavens, while its "romantic" "*Godfather* atmosphere" thrills amorous cineasts; a few say it's "still finding itself", but "packed" quarters suggest it has already been found.

Telly's Taverna (Queens) ●🚬∅
23 | 13 | 18 | $32

28-13 23rd Ave. (bet. 28th & 29th Sts.), 718-728-9056
■ "Eat your Greek heart out": this Astoria seafooder offers Hellenic "comfort food" so "fresh" and "inexpensive" that it's worth buying an "E-Z Pass" just to get back and forth to it; though the "kitschy decor is fun", the "smoke is not", so many opt to eat in its "great garden."

Ten Kai 🚬
21 | 14 | 18 | $37

20 W. 56th St. (bet. 5th & 6th Aves.), 212-956-0127
☑ "Plain-Jane" looks don't deter diners from this "solid" Midtown Japanese that's a "businessmen's haunt" at lunchtime, given always-"dependable" sushi at "reasonable" tabs; while the other offerings "could be better", "you can't beat the convenience."

Tennessee Mountain 🚬
16 | 12 | 15 | $29

143 Spring St. (Wooster St.), 212-431-3993
☑ It's "hard to believe" this "backwoods" BBQ has put down roots in SoHo, but "hillbilly" fans "pretend" they're in the hollow and "wallow" in "big ol' slabs of ribs"; critics contend that this "Jersey-esque approach", albeit inexpensive, is about as authentic as "New England clam chowder in Memphis."

Teodora 🚬
21 | 17 | 19 | $43

141 E. 57th St. (bet. Lexington & 3rd Aves.), 212-826-7101
■ One of the "best-kept secrets" in Midtown, this "real find" is an "unpretentious", "restful gem" purveying "well-prepared" Northern Italian cookery; though a bit "pricey" and "iffy" servicewise, it's still a "cozy" "destination" for those in-the-know.

Teresa's 🚬
18 | 11 | 15 | $20

103 First Ave. (bet. 6th & 7th Sts.), 212-228-0604
80 Montague St. (Hicks St.), Brooklyn, 718-797-3996
■ "Polish comfort food" "makes life worth living" at these "busy, bustling" coffee shops that seem to be "immune to gentrification" and thus "beloved neighborhood hangouts"; "back-to-the-'70s prices" are the "main draw", though "poor service" is off-putting.

Terrace in the Sky
23 | 26 | 23 | $60

400 W. 119th St. (bet. Amsterdam Ave. & Morningside Dr.), 212-666-9490
■ Known for its "spectacular skyline view", this "classy", terraced Morningside Heights rooftop "star in the sky" also provides "superb"

French-Med fare and "gracious service", while a harpist strikes the right chords; granted, it all comes at what seem like "splurge" prices this far Uptown, but you get "fantastic everything" in return.

Tevere S | 23 | 19 | 21 | $52 |
155 E. 84th St. (bet. Lexington & 3rd Aves.), 212-744-0210
■ "Don't ask for grated cheese", 'cause this East Side Italian is kosher, though you'd "never know it" given how "excellent" everything tastes; though it's a "pity it isn't larger", some wish the tabs were smaller.

T.G.I. Friday's | 11 | 11 | 12 | $24 |
604 Fifth Ave. (bet. 48th & 49th Sts.), 212-767-8335 S
47 E. 42nd St. (bet. Madison & Vanderbilt Aves.), 212-681-8458 S
1680 Broadway (bet. 52nd & 53rd Sts.), 212-767-8326 ● S
21 W. 51st St. (bet. 5th & 6th Aves.), 212-767-8352 S
761 Seventh Ave. (50th St.), 212-767-8350 S
1552 Broadway (46th St.), 212-944-7352 ● S
484 Eighth Ave. (34th St.), 212-630-0307 S
47 Broadway (Exchange Pl.), 212-483-8322
☒ For "fast" eating, this chain brew 'n' burger "tourist trap" is a step above "Mickey D's", but for most, it's a "last resort" offering "heartburn-on-a-plate" chow and "slower-than-a-snail service" at "expensive-for-what-it-is" tabs; in sum, "spare yourself."

Thai Cafe (Brooklyn) S⌀ | ▽ 23 | 14 | 16 | $21 |
925 Manhattan Ave. (Kent St.), 718-383-3562
☒ "Vibrant" Thai cooking bubbles up at this "original" Greenpoint standby where "spicy means spicy" and prices are "outrageously low"; still, "less-than-attentive service" and "nonexistent decor" lead some to earmark it "strictly for takeout."

Thai House Cafe ⌀ | 21 | 10 | 17 | $23 |
151 Hudson St. (Hubert St.), 212-334-1085
■ An "out-of-the-way location near the Holland Tunnel" doesn't keep those "stuck in traffic" away from this "killer" TriBeCa Thai and its "spicy kicks"; though the decor may be running on empty, pre-OPEC pricing allows for "affordable" fill-ups.

Thailand Restaurant S | 23 | 11 | 15 | $22 |
106 Bayard St. (bet. Baxter & Mulberry Sts.), 212-349-3132
■ Famed for its "court-crowd lunch" scene, this "popular" Chinatown Thai offers food so "amazing" that some "want to be called for jury duty" just for the proximity; though "disheveled" decor is a turnoff, "how-can-you-go-wrong?" prices are turn-ons.

Thalia Restaurant ● S | 20 | 21 | 19 | $49 |
828 Eighth Ave. (50th St.), 212-399-4444
☒ "Civilized" New American "contender" that "brings class" to the Theater District with a "soaring", "modernist" setting matched by "stylish cuisine"; dissenters say the "limited menu" "doesn't measure up to the hype", while the pricing exceeds expectations.

Thali Vegetarian S⌀ | 19 | 12 | 16 | $18 |
28 Greenwich Ave. (bet. Charles & W. 10th Sts.), 212-367-7411
■ "Indecisive" types like the "no-thinking" approach at this BYO Village Indian-Vegetarian that has "no menu", but rather a single, daily changing meal for a fixed $10 price; the trade-off is a "tiny", "hole-in-the-wall" setting, but this may be the "best value in NY."

3333 (Staten Island) S | ▽ 21 | 20 | 20 | $50 |
3333 Hylan Blvd. (bet. Hopkins & Spratt Aves.), 718-667-9333
☒ "Artfully prepared" Mediterranean dishes grace the menu of this "roomy" Staten Islander with a "lively", "*Sopranos*-like feel"; but

	F	D	S	C

"out-of-sight" pricing for rather "average" eats leaves some sighing "once is enough."

Thom ●◐S — — — E
60 Thompson Hotel, 60 Thompson St. (bet. Broome & Spring Sts.), 212-219-2000
On the ground floor of the new 60 Thompson Hotel, this SoHo stunner from the owners of Bond Street and Indochine seamlessly fuses the familiar with the exotic, adding vibrant Asian flavors (lemongrass, tamarind) to a seafood-focused American-Eclectic menu; it's sleek and seductive, from the low-lit, loungey interior to the eye-candy staff and leggy, Manolo-shod clientele.

Tibetan Yak (Queens) S ▽ 22 | 15 | 22 | $17
72-20 Roosevelt Ave. (72nd St.), 718-779-1119
■ "Unique" Tibetan cuisine alights in Jackson Heights at this "simply stated" but "vastly underrated" venue wedged under the elevated train tracks; though the food's "very satisfying" and service "sweet", the decor's somewhat of a "drag."

Tibet on Houston S — | — | — | M
136 W. Houston St. (bet. MacDougal & Sullivan Sts.), 212-995-5884
Airy and cheerful, with French doors open to the street in summer, this SoHo eatery is among the city's few Tibetan options; it speaks to the cuisine's authenticity that the crowd savoring tasty beef dishes here consists largely of Tibetan expats.

Tierras Colombianas S≠ ▽ 20 | 12 | 17 | $21
33-01 Broadway (33rd St.), Queens, 718-956-3012
82-18 Roosevelt Ave. (83rd St.), Queens, 718-426-8868
■ "Bring your Berlitz" to work with the "patient staff" at this pair of "popular Latin American family places" in Queens; ok, there's "little ambiance", yet the "great big portions" of "starchy but interesting" Colombiana "will fill the hungriest stomach."

Tiger Blossom ●S — | — | — | E
324 Bowery (bet. Bleecker & Bond Sts.), 212-673-3020
Joining the Pan-Asian invasion while it's still hot, this tiny, brick-lined Bowery newcomer features an interesting menu running the gamut of Far East cuisines; it's minimalist to a tee, with red lanterns above the sleek bar completing the hipness equation.

Time Cafe ●S 16 | 15 | 15 | $29
2330 Broadway (85th St.), 212-579-5100
380 Lafayette St. (Great Jones St.), 212-533-7000
☑ "Once trendy" New American eateries that appear to have morphed into "casual" "neighborhood diners" with "no-surprises" grub served by a "lost-in-space" staff; their Moroccan bar adjuncts are still timely when it comes to "hip people-watching."

Tino's ●S ▽ 19 | 16 | 16 | $46
40 W. 56th St. (bet. 5th & 6th Aves.), 212-262-9300
■ "Solid" Northern Italian via restaurateur Tino Scarpa with a "pleasant" enough atmosphere that's especially "good for a date" "pre-Carnegie Hall", but even if you're ticketless, a staff with a "wonderful sense of humor" provides entertainment.

Tinto (Brooklyn) S ▽ 18 | 18 | 16 | $30
60 Henry St. (Cranberry St.), 718-243-2010
☑ "Tapas come to Brooklyn Heights" at this Spanish yearling that's "much-appreciated in the neighborhood", since there's "plenty of room to relax"; some think it "just misses", pointing to "hit-or-miss" cooking and advising neophytes to "choose carefully."

	F	D	S	C

Tio Pepe ●S
19 | 17 | 19 | $31
168 W. Fourth St. (bet. 6th Ave. & 7th Ave. S.), 212-242-9338
■ This "Greenwich Village classic" is known for its "festive, year-round Christmas" vibe, "adorable" skylit garden room and "amazing" cocktails; but surveyors split on the Spanish-Mexican grub ("top-notch" vs. "disappointing"), though there sure is "lots of it."

Tír na nóg ●S
19 | 18 | 19 | $31
5 Penn Plaza (bet. 33rd & 34th Sts.), 212-630-0249
■ Parked near Penn Station, this Celtic-American goes beyond Guinness to offer "simply grand Irish fare" as well as live traditional Irish music; conversationalists find it "ok for lunch" but almost "impossible" at suppertime – unless you're a "noisemaker" too.

Titou S
21 | 18 | 19 | $34
259 W. Fourth St. (bet. Charles & Perry Sts.), 212-691-9359
■ "Cute, cozy" Village French bistro (and Tartine sibling) that lures fresh-air fans to its "popular" sidewalk cafe and keeps them there with "honest" home cooking that comes with "just-right" service and prices.

Tja! ●S
∇ 20 | 21 | 17 | $45
301 Church St. (Walker St.), 212-226-8900
■ The name "sounds strange" but the "food's tasty" at this TriBeCa fusion of Scandinavian and Asian cuisine – yes, that's right – that also offers the "unique" option of "ordering the entire menu in appetizer sizes"; more to the point, there's a raging, "flavor-of-the-month" "bar scene" overseen by "hot hostesses with an attitude."

Tocqueville S
24 | 20 | 22 | $58
15 E. 15th St. (bet. 5th Ave. & Union Sq. W.), 212-647-1515
■ Surveyors give a "tip of the toque" to this diminutive New American "beauty" with a pronounced French accent, giving it high marks for its "stylish, serious" cooking and "intimate" (if "underdecorated") setting just west of Union Square; dot-goners, however, may want to take out a loan first, since the "bill may floor you."

Toledo
22 | 21 | 23 | $49
6 E. 36th St. (bet. 5th & Madison Aves.), 212-696-5036
■ "Spanish flair" is alive and well at this Murray Hill standby that will "carry you away" with its olé-worthy mix of "high-quality" food, "old-world decor" and "gracious service" – still, all this doesn't come cheap.

Tommaso's (Brooklyn) S
23 | 19 | 21 | $45
1464 86th St. (bet. 14th & 15th Aves.), 718-236-9883
■ At this "friendly", "old-fashioned" red-sauce Bensonhurst Italian, the meals are "just like mama used to make" and the arias performed by the owner "even better"; ok, it's "loud and busy", and mama didn't charge for her solos.

TOMOE SUSHI
27 | 10 | 16 | $35
172 Thompson St. (bet. Bleecker & Houston Sts.), 212-777-9346
☑ "Something fishy" is going on at this West Villager: "mind-boggling" "pristine sushi at bargain prices" that's among the "city's best"; the trade-off is a "rinky-dink", "postage stamp–size" setting translating into "long lines" that look like "open casting calls", making the "need to expand *urgent.*"

Tomo Sushi & Sake Bar ●S
19 | 16 | 17 | $25
2850 Broadway (bet. 110th & 111th Sts.), 212-665-2916
☑ Given its low prices and lack of local competition, it's not surprising that this Morningside Heights Japanese is "always crowded"; despite nondescript decor and "rushed service", they sure know how to slice.

	F	D	S	C

Tom's (Brooklyn) ⇗   ▽ 20 | 18 | 23 | $16
782 Washington Ave. (Sterling Pl.), 718-636-9738

■ They treat you like "long-lost family" at this "ideal" Prospect Heights luncheonette that's been doling out good "old-fashioned breakfasts" and "special fountain-fare lunches" (but no dinner) since 1936; "unbelievably inexpensive" tabs cement the time-warp experience.

Tonic, The   22 | 21 | 20 | $53
108 W. 18th St. (bet. 6th & 7th Aves.), 212-929-9755

■ "Peaceful and elegant" in its "lovely" dining room and buzzing at the "terrific" front bar, this Chelsea New American expense-accounter offers the best of both worlds; it has "changed chefs" and "may require re-evaluation", but it's still a definite "contender" whether you prefer "high-quality" "adult" dining or would rather "let your hair down a little."

Tony's Di Napoli ●S   18 | 14 | 17 | $32
1606 Second Ave. (83rd St.), 212-861-8686

◪ "Portions big enough to make grandma proud" at "modest prices" draw "busloads" to this "family-style" Italian that's aka "Carmine's for Upper Eastsiders"; calling it "hectic is an understatement", what with the "feed-your-whole-building", "party atmosphere."

Topaz Thai S   21 | 13 | 16 | $27
127 W. 56th St. (bet. 6th & 7th Aves.), 212-957-8020

◪ "When you're on your own nickel", this "terrific Thai" near Carnegie Hall is more than "affordable", even if the "zealous" staff is sometimes "too rushed" and the "tiny" digs too "cramped"; ultimately, the "lines out the door say everything."

Top of the Tower S   18 | 26 | 19 | $49
Beekman Tower, 3 Mitchell Pl. (1st Ave. & 49th St.), 212-980-4796

■ The piano "music is a nice touch", but the "amazing", 360-degree skyline vistas and cool cocktails are the hooks at this romantic Beekman penthouse aerie, not the "middling", "expensive", American-Continental menu; overall, it's a "great place to wow a date" – but "phone ahead", as it's often booked for "private parties."

Toraya   ▽ 22 | 24 | 21 | $27
17 E. 71st St. (bet. 5th & Madison Aves.), 212-861-1700

■ Spent shopaholics can't say enough about this "minimalist" East Side Japanese tearoom that's a "calm, meditative" respite after punishing the sidewalks of Madison Avenue; the traditional sweets and tea cakes made with bean paste are "almost too attractive to eat."

Torch ●S   20 | 23 | 18 | $42
137 Ludlow St. (bet. Rivington & Stanton Sts.), 212-228-5151

■ This "smoldering" Lower East Side take on a "'40s nightclub" feels like a cross between a swank "dinner party and an awards show"; look for "solid" French–South American fare, live music ranging from jazz to "accordion players" and a "Downtown swingers" crowd – and remember that "pushy", "arrogant" service comes with the territory.

Torre di Pisa   19 | 22 | 19 | $49
19 W. 44th St. (bet. 5th & 6th Aves.), 212-398-4400

◪ The "colorful", "off-kilter" David Rockwell design steals the show at this Midtown Northern Italian where the food, though "tasty" enough, is "secondary in importance"; calculators call it "Fendi expensive" but admit it "will impress a client."

Tortilla Flats ●S   17 | 17 | 16 | $24
767 Washington St. (W. 12th St.), 212-243-1053

■ At this intentionally "tacky" West Village Tex-Mex hot spot, "hula-hooping frat guys" and "bingo"-mad bachelorettes down "dangerous" margaritas and bypass the bypass-inducing food; come "have some laughs", but just "make sure you don't have to work the next day."

Tossed
19 | 10 | 13 | $15

30 Rockefeller Plaza Concourse (bet. 49th & 50th Sts.), 212-218-2525
295 Park Ave. S. (bet. 22nd & 23rd Sts.), 212-674-6700 S
■ It's easy being green at these "damn good", mix 'n' match "salad heavens" known for their "fresh ingredients and innovative dressings"; most "feel healthier just by walking in", yet others feel they've discovered roughage after being exposed to the decor and service here.

Totonno Pizzeria Napolitano S
22 | 11 | 14 | $21

1544 Second Ave. (bet. 80th & 81st Sts.), 212-327-2800
1524 Neptune Ave. (bet. W. 15th & W. 16th Sts.), Brooklyn, 718-372-8606
☒ As much of a "Coney Island treasure as the Cyclone", the "original" Brooklyn branch of this pizzeria duo is renowned for "classic", "crispy thin-crust" pies that are clearly "better" than the fancier Manhattan offshoot's; nonpizza items are strictly "off the assembly line."

Tout Va Bien ●S
19 | 14 | 19 | $39

311 W. 51st St. (bet. 8th & 9th Aves.), 212-974-9051
■ Since 1947, this "unassuming" Theater District bistro has been a "pre-theater bargain" and continues to offer "tasty", "simple French cooking" that's "always reliable"; those feeling "*rien va bien*" say it's "bordering on shabby" and in need of a "face-lift."

TOWN S
25 | 26 | 22 | $63

Chambers Hotel, 15 W. 56th St. (bet. 5th & 6th Aves.), 212-582-4445
■ "Look out, gourmands" – this New American newcomer with a sexy upstairs bar scene in Midtown's Chambers Hotel is a "serious" destination for "inventive yet recognizable" cuisine from standout chef Geoffrey Zakarian (ex 44, Patroon); with a well-edited, almost minimalist menu enhanced by a "wonderful", "soaring" space, this "bright star" is pretty near "perfection", except perhaps for the price.

Trata S
22 | 17 | 18 | $50

1331 Second Ave. (bet. 70th & 71st Sts.), 212-535-3800
■ "Impeccably fresh, out-of-the-ordinary seafood" makes for transporting dining at this attractive East Side Greek where the "only things missing are the grapevines and Mediterranean view"; though far from cheap, it's enough of a success that the room's been "expanded" to handle overflow crowds.

Trattoria Alba
20 | 18 | 20 | $39

233 E. 34th St. (bet. 2nd & 3rd Aves.), 212-689-3200
☒ At this "reliable", if "sleepy", Murray Hill Northern Italian, you'll find "generous portions" of well-priced, well-cooked "classical dishes" served by an "attentive staff"; its "nicely-dressed older crowd" calls it "good for the neighborhood" but would have second thoughts about traveling to it.

Trattoria Chianti S
20 | 17 | 19 | $42

1043 Second Ave. (55th St.), 212-980-8686
☒ "My friend loves this place, but I think 'ho-hum'" sums up the mixed reports on this East Midtown Italian that boosters call a "neighborhood favorite" for an "elegant", "solid" midpriced meal; on the contrary, critics cry "much ado about nothing", claiming it's no more than a "fancy" pasta joint.

Trattoria Dell'Arte ●S
22 | 21 | 20 | $49

900 Seventh Ave. (bet. 56th & 57th Sts.), 212-245-9800
■ "Still immensely popular", this long-running Italian opposite Carnegie Hall keeps on humming with its "incredible antipasti bar" and "superb

pizza", while "whimsical" "body-parts" artwork "adds pizzazz"; given the "hectic atmosphere", it might not work for "good conversation or love trysts", but otherwise this "cheery" spot "never disappoints."

Trattoria Dopo Teatro ◐[S] 17 | 16 | 17 | $39

125 W. 44th St. (bet. B'way & 6th Ave.), 212-869-2849

◪ Showgoers looking for a "quick" bite troop into this Times Square Italian for reliably "decent food" at "reasonable" tabs; still, its "here's-your-hat, what's-your-hurry?" service is a bit too breezy for some.

Trattoria L'incontro (Queens) [S] ▽ 25 | 20 | 22 | $39

21-76 31st St. (Ditmars Blvd.), 718-721-3532

■ Imagine a "top-notch SoHo trattoria airlifted into Astoria" – that's the feel at this "imaginative" Italian where "the list of specials is longer than the menu"; it "isn't going to be a sleeper for long", so many advise reserving ahead, especially on weekends.

Trattoria Pesce & Pasta [S] 20 | 14 | 17 | $30

1562 Third Ave. (bet. 87th & 88th Sts.), 212-987-4696
1079 First Ave. (59th St.), 212-888-7884 ◐
625 Columbus Ave. (bet. 90th & 91st Sts.), 212-579-7970
262 Bleecker St. (bet. 6th Ave. & 7th Ave. S.), 212-645-2993 ◐

■ Praised for its "great value" and "hearty", "lick-the-bowl" cooking, this "dependable" Italian quartet is not known for its ambiance; still, dreamers "wish it could be cloned" to their neighborhoods.

Trattoria Romana (Staten Island) [S] ▽ 25 | 17 | 22 | $39

1476 Hylan Blvd. (Benton Ave.), 718-980-3113

■ Don't forget to "bring your appetite" along to this Staten Island storefront, since its "flavorful" Italian fare comes in "oversized portions"; though recently expanded, it still doesn't take reservations and has lines so long you can develop an appetite while waiting.

Trattoria Rustica [S] 20 | 16 | 19 | $36

343 E. 85th St. (bet. 1st & 2nd Aves.), 212-744-1227

■ This "homey" "little hideaway" in Yorkville is a local favorite for "delicious Italian fare" at "very neighborly prices"; if a bit "uneven" and "thin on variety", the consensus seems to be "absolutely charming."

Trattoria Spaghetto ◐[S]≠ 19 | 14 | 16 | $25

232 Bleecker St. (Carmine St.), 212-255-6752

■ "One of the best deals in the Village", this "tasty" Italian "hits the spot" for "affordable" eating, and regulars report its sidewalk cafe "is best"; just "go to the ATM" beforehand, as it's "cash only."

Tre Pomodori [S] 19 | 14 | 18 | $26

1742 Second Ave. (bet. 90th & 91st Sts.), 212-831-8167
210 E. 34th St. (bet. 2nd & 3rd Aves.), 212-545-7266

◪ "Wonderful little finds" for "homey" cooking, these East Side Italians may be "cheap", yet critics find "nothing to knock your socks off" and complain the setups are "so small that large people walk in sideways."

Triangolo ◐[S]≠ 21 | 16 | 20 | $35

345 E. 83rd St. (bet. 1st & 2nd Aves.), 212-472-4488

■ "Flirty", "funny" waiters who are "happy to see you" serve "delicious fresh pasta" at this "hidden" Yorkville Italian that "hits all the bases"; the only "annoying" drawback: they "don't take credit cards."

Tribeca Grill [S] 22 | 21 | 21 | $53

375 Greenwich St. (Franklin St.), 212-941-3900

◪ "You're in good hands" at Robert De Niro and Drew Nieporent's "creative" New American veteran in TriBeCa that's "still flying" when it comes to "glorious food" in a handsome, "high-ceilinged" setting; conversationalists complain it's so "loud" that you should "go with someone to whom you have nothing to say", or just join the jumping bar scene.

Triomphe | 24 | 22 | 22 | $58

Iroquois Hotel, 49 W. 44th St. (bet. 5th & 6th Aves.), 212-840-3080
■ The "name says it all" at this "peaceful" French Eclectic yearling in the Theater District's Iroquois Hotel; despite its "limited space" and hefty tabs, the "superb" cooking is enough of a "surprise" that advocates "talk it up" for both business and romance.

Triple Eight Palace S | 19 | 11 | 13 | $23

88 E. Broadway (bet. Division & Market Sts.), 212-941-8886
■ "Be adventurous and you'll be rewarded" at this cheap, "massive" Chinatown "feast palace" specializing in Hong Kong–style dim sum; be prepared for "garish" decor and "long lines" – and "bring a local or the best carts will pass you by."

Trois Marches | 20 | 17 | 19 | $41

306 E. 81st St. (bet. 1st & 2nd Aves.), 212-639-1900
◪ An "undiscovered" Yorkville "treasure", this "cozy" Asian-accented New French "should be packed every night", since its "delish" dishes are such a "good value" (especially the "wallet-friendly early-bird"); but pickier eaters say this "valiant effort" "doesn't always hit the mark."

Tropica | 22 | 19 | 19 | $49

Metlife Bldg., 200 Park Ave. (45th St. & Lexington Ave.), 212-867-6767
■ "For business or pleasure or whatever", this "reliably excellent" Key West–style seafooder is a "commuter's dream" given its location above Grand Central, coupled with a "sure hand with fresh fish"; sure, it can be a "zoo at lunch", but it's perfect for a "quiet dinner" during the week; N.B. it's closed on weekends.

T Salon & T Emporium S | 18 | 20 | 16 | $25

11 E. 20th St. (bet. B'way & 5th Ave.), 212-358-0506
◪ Made for "girlfriend-bonding lunches" or "bridal showers", this "quaint" Flatiron "tea-lovers' haven" offers one of "the best selections in NY" in "atmospheric" environs; the only drawback is "spotty" service that doesn't jibe with the "tranquil environment."

Tsampa ●S | 21 | 21 | 19 | $26

212 E. Ninth St. (bet. 2nd & 3rd Aves.), 212-614-3226
■ Some say "yum", others chant "om" at this "atmospheric" East Village Tibetan offering "meditative", "escape-from-NY" meals akin to "religious experiences"; while the "tranquil decor" soothes "frayed nerves", "calming" prices make for wallet "nirvana."

Tse Yang S | 24 | 24 | 23 | $57

34 E. 51st St. (bet. Madison & Park Aves.), 212-688-5447
■ "As inspiring as the Great Wall", this Midtown "haute Chinese" presents "serious", "meticulously prepared" fare (the "best Peking duck in NY, hands-down") in "handsome" surroundings that the "emperor himself would feel at home in"; naturally, prices are princely, but it's "worth every penny", particularly if you want to "wow" someone.

Tudor Grill | – | – | – | M

45 Tudor City Pl. (bet. 1st & 2nd Aves.), 212-922-0002
Way off everyone's radar screen on a forgotten block of Tudor City, this New American turns out surprisingly tasty fare in civilized, if bland, surroundings; usually underpopulated, it's got illicit rendezvous written all over it.

	F	D	S	C

Tupelo Grill — 20 | 19 | 19 | $45
1 Penn Plaza (33rd St., bet. 7th & 8th Aves.), 212-760-2700
■ "Not just for those with testosterone", this surf 'n' turfer near MSG also draws "those with other hormones" with its fairly priced, "better-than-average" food and "airy" setting; given the "lack of competition" nearby, it morphs into "expense-account territory" at lunchtime.

Turkish Kitchen S — 21 | 19 | 19 | $38
386 Third Ave. (bet. 27th & 28th Sts.), 212-679-6633
■ A "red-carpet ride from start to finish", this "exotic" Gramercy Turk provides a "boisterous" trip to the Bosphorus via "richly seasoned", pasha-worthy dishes served in "bordello-ish", ruby-red digs; finish off with the "best baklava anywhere" and you'll leave flying high.

Turkuaz S — 20 | 21 | 19 | $32
2637 Broadway (100th St.), 212-665-9541
◪ "Tented rooms" set the "fantasy" mood at this atmospheric Upper West Side Turk that "evokes the Ottoman empire" with its "subtly spiced, perfectly executed" cooking; though the staff's "hokey" costumes draw jeers, the weekend belly dancers win cheers.

Tuscan Square — 19 | 20 | 18 | $42
16 W. 51st St. (bet. 5th & 6th Aves.), 212-977-7777
■ Jettisoning the market that was part of the original concept, Pino Luongo's Rockefeller Center Tuscan is now all dining and much less "cramped", pleasing fans of its "hearty, rustic" fare; though "tourist-prone" with a slightly pricey "exchange rate", it certainly deserves another visit.

Tuscan Steak ●S — 20 | 22 | 18 | $55
622 Third Ave. (40th St.), 212-404-1700
◪ Size matters at Jeffrey Chodorow's "enormous" steakhouse where "family-style" means "you *need* a family to finish just one portion"; the "jazzy" decor and "hot bar" scene are pluses, but "slow service", "marathon waits" and "off-the-planet" pricing get demerits.

Tuscany Grill (Brooklyn) S — 23 | 18 | 20 | $44
8620 Third Ave. (bet. 86th & 87th Sts.), 718-921-5633
■ "No reservation" = "no table" at this popular Bay Ridge "treasure", since the "consistent" Tuscan cooking is "comparable to Manhattan" and better priced to boot; granted, its "shoebox" space can get "crowded", but at least there's no need to "go to Firenze" – this "comfortable standby" "never disappoints."

12th St. Bar & Grill (Brooklyn) S — 22 | 19 | 20 | $36
1123 Eighth Ave. (12th St.), 718-965-9526
■ "Tiny" but "friendly" New American that's "Park Slope defined" thanks to its "reliably great" cooking and a "Manhattan atmosphere" – "minus the price inflation"; it works for both a "date" and "impressing visiting parents" because it "just feels right."

'21' CLUB — 22 | 23 | 23 | $65
21 W. 52nd St. (bet. 5th & 6th Aves.), 212-582-7200
■ "A timeless NY classic that's still going strong", this Midtown townhouse "landmark" has "improved with age", offering "handsome" men's club quarters, seamless black-tie service, a "happening" "see-and-be-seen" power scene and "better-than-ever" American food from chef Erik Blauberg; in addition, there are numerous private party rooms – don't miss the wine cellar – and bargain prix fixe menus at lunch ($29) and pre-theater ($33) that allow you to "feel like a master of the universe" for a day-trader tab; N.B. jackets and ties are required, of course.

27 Sunrise Seafood ●S   _|_|_| M
27 Division St. (bet. Bowery & Market St.), 212-219-8498
Huge tanks in the window swimming with eels, lobsters and other sea creatures beckon one to this Chinatown seafood palace; the typical banquet-hall setting may not separate it from the competition, but the cooked-to-your-preference, ultra-fresh seafood does.

26 Seats ●S   ▽ 22 | 17 | 22 | $29
168 Ave. B (bet. 10th & 11th Sts.), 212-677-4787
■ New owners have 86'd the American menu and gone Gallic, but the number of seats remains the same at this "quirky" East Village French where everything's mismatched from the chairs to the plates; though "barely big enough for those who have discovered it", some still find it surprisingly "empty."

Two Boots S   19 | 11 | 13 | $15
Grand Central, lower level (42nd St. & Lexington Ave.), 212-557-7992
201 W. 11th St. (7th Ave. S.), 212-633-9096 ●
74 Bleecker St. (B'way), 212-777-1033 ●
37 Ave. A (bet. 2nd & 3rd Sts.), 212-505-2276 ●
42 Ave. A (3rd St.), 212-254-1919 ●
514 Second St. (bet. 7th & 8th Aves.), Brooklyn, 718-499-3253
30 Rockefeller Plaza, downstairs (bet. 49th & 50th Sts.), 212-332-8800
■ "Exotic" Cajun toppings, "cornmeal crusts" and "fun" entree names separate this "rocking" mini-chain from the pizzeria pack; despite the "adult menus", they're ultra-"kid friendly", leading "quiet-dining" mavens to "call for delivery."

212 Restaurant & Bar ●S   18 | 17 | 17 | $45
133 E. 65th St. (bet. Lexington & Park Aves.), 212-249-6565
■ Despite a "Euro-Hamptons" bar scene right out of *Sex and the City*, this East Side American turns out "surprisingly good chow"; there's no truth to the "rumor they're opening a street cart called 917."

Two Toms (Brooklyn) ⊅   22 | 9 | 16 | $32
255 Third Ave. (bet. President & Union Sts.), 718-875-8689
◪ "They tell you what you want to eat – and they're right" at this menuless Boerum Hill vet that's been dishing out "big portions" of bona fide Italian "home cooking" to garrulous groups for over 50 years; regulars remain "rapturous", oblivious to the cash-only policy and "nil decor", though irregulars yawn the "novelty's worn thin."

Two Two Two S   23 | 21 | 22 | $62
222 W. 79th St. (bet. Amsterdam Ave. & B'way), 212-799-0400
◪ West Side Continental–New American that's "not too, too, too hard to take" given its "sublime food", "eager-to-please" staff and "charming" townhouse setting; still, foes fret about its "precious", "tchotchke"-laden decor (complete with a "Barbie doll" collection) and "out-of-hand prices" – except for the $29 pre-theater prix.

Ubol's Kitchen (Queens) S   ▽ 23 | 11 | 20 | $25
24-42 Steinway St. (bet. Astoria Blvd. & 25th Ave.), 718-545-2874
■ A "star" in Astoria for "glorious" Thai cooking, this "bare-bones" venue may "look like a fast-food joint from the outside" but offers "beautifully presented food" that's "not too expensive" inside.

Uguale ●S   22 | 20 | 20 | $38
396 West St. (W. 10th St.), 212-229-0606
■ Ok, "it's a hike to get there", since it's "so far west", but this Village Italian-French is "worth the trek" for "affordable", "top-notch" fare; "sunset" seekers note that though it faces the Hudson, the view is mainly "West Side Highway."

	F	D	S	C

Ukrainian East Village S 🚭 — 17 | 10 | 15 | $21
140 Second Ave. (bet. 9th St. & St. Marks Pl.), 212-529-5024
■ "Tasty Ukrainian standards" fill out the "utilitarian menu" of this East Villager that offers "few frills" but is a "fun way to get your carbs" via "big portions" of blintzes, pierogi and the like; the decor's so "dingy" you'll feel "overdressed", but "hey, it's cheap enough."

Ulrika's S — 22 | 19 | 21 | $43
115 E. 60th St. (bet. Lexington & Park Aves.), 212-355-7069
■ For the "best thing from Sweden since blonds", try this "almost-Stockholm" Midtown Scandinavian offering "robust" cooking in a "calming" setting straight out of the "Ikea catalog"; though there's debate over the cost ("pricey" vs. "reasonable"), there's consensus that it "should be better known."

Uncle George's (Queens) ● S 🚭 — 20 | 9 | 14 | $22
33-19 Broadway (34th St.), 718-626-0593
■ "Dirt cheap" "authentic" Hellenic dishes keep this 24/7 Astoria Greek taverna "always mobbed", even if some protest "typical" eats, "brusque service" and "low-class" "diner" looks.

Uncle Jack's Steakhouse (Queens) S — ▽ 24 | 19 | 21 | $58
39-40 Bell Blvd. (40th Ave.), 718-229-1100
■ "Mouthwatering" "steaks worthy of Manhattan" (including Kobe beef) are served by a "friendly", "tuxedoed" staff at this upscale Bayside surf 'n' turfer that's a "true gem for Queens"; contrarians say it "belongs in Midtown with those prices."

Uncle Nick's S — 20 | 12 | 16 | $29
747 9th Ave. (bet. 50th & 51st Sts.), 212-245-7992
749 9th Ave. (bet. 50th & 51st Sts.), 212-397-2892 ●
■ "Justifiably popular" Hell's Kitchen Greek that's known for "excellent quality" eats "on the cheap", although "dicey service" and a "crazed atmosphere" may come with the territory; check out the "little-known back patio", or for "great tapas"-size servings, go next door to their late-night Ouzaria.

Uncle Pho (Brooklyn) S — 18 | 17 | 17 | $31
263 Smith St. (DeGraw St.), 718-855-8737
■ "Upper-class" Carroll Gardens Vietnamese in a "hip, happening Smith Street setting" that presents "innovative", affordable cooking amidst "funky" decor; still, some grumble "all style, no substance."

UNION PACIFIC — 26 | 26 | 25 | $70
111 E. 22nd St. (bet. Lexington Ave. & Park Ave. S.), 212-995-8500
■ "Knockout dining" leaves fans breathless at this Gramercy New American "paragon" where "rock star" chef Rocco DiSpirito produces "sublime", "synergistic" dishes that more than "meet expectations"; service is equally "flawless", the "waterfall"-equipped setting "therapeutic", and though the "bottom line" is "platinum card"–worthy, it's hard to put a price on a "guaranteed magical evening."

UNION SQUARE CAFE S — 27 | 24 | 26 | $60
21 E. 16th St. (bet. 5th Ave. & Union Sq. W.), 212-243-4020
■ What alchemy keeps Danny Meyer's original Cafe NYers' No. 1 favorite for the sixth year in a row?; the answer is an "appealing amalgam of three different, muraled dining areas", an "urbane", "comfortably casual" ambiance, genuinely "friendly" service and "good value" for chef Michael Romano's "always fresh, wonderfully prepared" "regular American food"; other restaurants may beat USC in specific areas, but no one "makes it seem so easy."

	F	D	S	C

Üsküdar S — 21 | 12 | 18 | $32
1405 Second Ave. (bet. 73rd & 74th Sts.), 212-988-2641
■ The "vest-pocket" size of this East Side Turk "doesn't matter", since the food's so "savory" and the tabs such a "bargain"; some suspect that the name is "Turkish for 'world's smallest bathroom.'"

Utsav S — 22 | 22 | 20 | $36
1185 Sixth Ave. (enter on 46th or 47th St., bet. 6th & 7th Aves.), 212-575-2525
■ "Ambitious Indian" food arrives in Midtown at this "sophisticated" yearling serving "sumptuous" dishes in "spacious", "pretty" environs; though nearly "impossible to find" (given the misleading Sixth Avenue address), bargain hunters happily sleuth it out for its $20 pre-theater prix fixe "steal."

Va Bene S — 22 | 19 | 20 | $44
1589 Second Ave. (bet. 82nd & 83rd Sts.), 212-517-4448
■ Say 'shalom Rome' at this "attractive", "upscale" kosher Italian that's an "interesting change" for the Upper East Side; adherents say "everything's good" here – except perhaps the price.

V&T Restaurant ●S — 18 | 9 | 12 | $18
1024 Amsterdam Ave. (bet. 110th & 111th Sts.), 212-666-8051
◪ For a slice of history, try this circa 1945 Morningside Heights "stalwart" for "delicious, gooey pizza" priced for a Columbia "student's budget"; despite digs that "have never been decorated", it's "worth a visit if only for nostalgia's sake."

Vatan S — 22 | 23 | 21 | $30
409 Third Ave. (29th St.), 212-689-5666
■ At this "all-you-can-eat Indian-Vegetarian", patrons feast on a "lovely" $21.95 buffet amid a "Disney World"–like setting that beautifully recreates a small Indian village; regulars recommend reservations and "clean socks", since you'll "take off your shoes and stay a while."

Va Tutto! S — 19 | 18 | 17 | $38
23 Cleveland Pl. (bet. Kenmare & Spring Sts.), 212-941-0286
◪ "Cut-above-average" SoHo Northern Italian known for its "tranquil" garden, "delightful" fare and "affordable" tabs; though some call it the "coziest in the city", others lament a chef shift and say "service is slower than a trip to Rome."

Vaux Bistro (Brooklyn) S — 21 | 20 | 21 | $40
278 Fifth Ave. (bet. 1st St. & Garfield Pl.), 718-499-1433
■ Fka just plain Vaux, this Park Slope venue has been "reconceived" as a French-American bistro and has "moderated" its prices accordingly (a "great improvement"); the food's just as "inventive" and "delicious" as before, ditto the "lovely" room and "gracious" staff.

Vegetarian Paradise S — 20 | 11 | 15 | $18
144 W. Fourth St. (bet. MacDougal St. & 6th Ave.), 212-260-7130
33-35 Mott St. (Canal St.), 212-406-6988
◪ "Perfect imitations of meat" rendered in tofu ("faux chicken", "fake duck") "please the eye and palate" at these separately owned Chinese-Vegetarians; although "cheap", the "atmosphere's not that good", so many "get it to go."

Veniero's ●S — 23 | 14 | 14 | $16
342 E. 11th St. (bet. 1st & 2nd Aves.), 212-674-7070
◪ Purveying "confectionery perfection" since 1894, this East Village "dessert lover's paradise" is venerated for its "holy cannolis" and

"sinful pastries"; though sourpusses sigh about "sugar shock", a visit will make you "postpone that diet."

Vera Cruz (Brooklyn) ●S
▽ 18 | 17 | 16 | $23
195 Bedford Ave. (bet. N. 6th & N. 7th Sts.), 718-599-7914
■ Though it "looks like a hole-in-the-wall", this "intimate" Mexican is "fast becoming a landmark" on Williamsburg's "Bedford Avenue strip" thanks to its "huge portions" of "authentic" chow at "small prices"; "hip" habitués hiding from the crowd head for the "nice garden."

Verbena S
24 | 22 | 22 | $58
54 Irving Pl. (bet. 17th & 18th Sts.), 212-260-5454
■ "Attention to detail" and "perfection in presentation" make you feel "well cared for" at this "civilized" Gramercy New American where the "creative menu" is reflected in "intelligent service" and a "cool as a cucumber" garden; though costly, it's worth revisiting, since both the decor and menu have been remade following the recent marriage of chef-owners Diane Forley and Michael Otsuka – congratulations, guys!

VERITAS S
27 | 23 | 25 | $75
43 E. 20th St. (bet. B'way & Park Ave. S.), 212-353-3700
■ A "mind-boggling" number of "treasures in the cellar" make this Flatiron New American an oenophile's fantasy, but chef Scott Bryan's "symphonic" fare provides such a "lovely chorus" that some conclude "in food, veritas"; true, it's "expensive" ($68 prix fixe dinner only), but worth it for "luxurious" dining that "deserves all the accolades."

Vermicelli S
21 | 18 | 18 | $30
1492 Second Ave. (bet. 77th & 78th Sts.), 212-288-8868
■ Alright, it's "a funny name for a Vietnamese restaurant", but this "Yorkville knockout" is serious about its "scrumptious", modestly priced fare; even better, its "classy lunch box" is one of the "best deals in town."

Veronica ⊄
▽ 19 | 8 | 12 | $18
240 W. 38th St. (bet. 7th & 8th Aves.), 212-764-4770
◪ There's "so much variety" at this "hectic" Garment Center Italian "cafeteria-style" "institution" that "you can go every day" for its "cheap" and "tasty high-caloric lunches" and bountiful breakfasts; P.S. it's "not open" for dinner or on weekends.

Veselka ●S
19 | 12 | 14 | $18
144 Second Ave. (9th St.), 212-228-9682
■ Loosen your borscht belt for the "gut-filling" "Eastern European soul food" at this 24/7 "East Village staple" that's known for its "dirt cheap" tabs; despite "cavalier service", it's "always packed" with "students planning revolutions or new art movements."

Via Brasil S
20 | 17 | 20 | $35
34 W. 46th St. (bet. 5th & 6th Aves.), 212-997-1158
■ "Reassuringly solid" fare comes at prices that "won't have you mortgaging" the casa at this Midtown Brazilian that's an "old favorite" of ravenous carnivores; music lovers note that its "festive" live melodies are more "bossa nova cool than samba hot."

Viand S
16 | 9 | 15 | $18
300 E. 86th St. (2nd Ave.), 212-879-9425 ●
1011 Madison Ave. (78th St.), 212-249-8250
673 Madison Ave. (bet. 61st & 62nd Sts.), 212-751-6622 ⊄
◪ These separately owned East Side coffee shops whip up typical "luncheonette food" highlighted by the "best turkey sandwich"; though "not places to sit" and linger, they're "convenient" "bargains", even if "you [only] get what you pay for."

Via Oreto [S] — 22 | 17 | 20 | $42

1121-1123 First Ave. (bet. 61st & 62nd Sts.), 212-308-0828

■ "Old-fashioned service" from "such nice people" makes you feel like "part of the family" at this "top-notch" East Side Sicilian; though it's "noisier" since it "expanded", the "solid", midpriced "mama" cooking is as good as ever.

Via Quadronno [S] — ▽ 22 | 17 | 18 | $32

25 E. 73rd St. (bet. 5th & Madison Aves.), 212-650-9880

■ Expats pounce on the super soups, salads and sandwiches at this "small" but "authentic" East Side paninoteca where "more Italian than English" is spoken; there's definitely an "escape-to-Milan" vibe here – right down to the "$5 per bite" pricing.

Viareggio [S] — ▽ 20 | 16 | 17 | $37

1347 Second Ave. (71st St.), 212-585-2900

◪ "Affordable", "better-than-average" pasta turns up at this new East Side Italian that boasts handsome "floor-to-ceiling windows"; but critics suggest the "lax service" needs to "get up to speed" to match the "*molto bene*" grub.

ViceVersa — 22 | 22 | 21 | $47

325 W. 51st St. (bet. 8th & 9th Aves.), 212-399-9291

■ What the "waiters promise, the kitchen delivers" at this "highly innovative" Italian "standout" on an "unassuming block" in Hell's Kitchen's burgeoning restaurant district; "reasonable" tabs, a "sleek" interior and an "exquisite" outdoor garden make this one a "real winner."

Vico ◑ [S] ≠ — 20 | 15 | 18 | $49

1302 Madison Ave. (bet. 92nd & 93rd Sts.), 212-876-2222

◪ It boasts "all the mannerisms of a good restaurant" – "terrific" cuisine, "glamorous" patrons, a "clubby" ambiance – but this Carnegie Hill Italian misses the mark with service that's "sycophantic" to regulars and "indifferent" to newcomers; those in the know recommend "carry tons of cash", since it's "expensive" and "allergic to credit cards."

Victor's Cafe ◑ [S] — 21 | 18 | 19 | $42

236 W. 52nd St. (bet. B'way & 8th Ave.), 212-586-7714

■ "Bring on the beans" cry amigos of this Theater District "landmark" known for its "'50s Cuban" "fare with flair", which goes down well with the "incredible homemade sangria"; though it's getting "pricey" and a bit "rough around the edges", "live music" lends a "festive" mood that recalls "old Havana."

Vietnam [S] — 22 | 8 | 15 | $20

11-13 Doyers St. (bet. Bowery & Pell St.), 212-693-0725

■ "Stellar" dishes "bursting with flavor" await the "courageous" connoisseurs who're willing to brave this Chinatown Vietnamese's "spotty service" and "dingy", "subterranean" locale; though "far short of fine dining", an "epic menu" at "bargain prices" is compensation enough for most.

View, The [S] — 19 | 26 | 20 | $54

Marriott Marquis Hotel, 1535 Broadway (bet. 45th & 46th Sts.), 212-704-8900

■ "Not just for tourists", this surprisingly impressive rotating rooftop Continental in the Times Square Marriott (NY's only revolving dining room) rewards sphere-seekers with "spectacular", "360-degree" metropolitan vistas; though a few might find it a bit pricey for "eating in circles", undeniably, it's very convenient before or after the theater.

			F	D	S	C

Villa Berulia S — 22 | 19 | 23 | $47
107 E. 34th St. (bet. Lexington & Park Aves.), 212-689-1970
■ Murray Hill locals "feel at home" at this "welcoming Northern Italian" that's like "having dinner at a relative's house"; sure, it could use "a bit of sprucing up", but the "aim-to-please" service is fine as is.

Village ●S — 19 | 19 | 18 | $42
62 W. Ninth St. (bet. 5th & 6th Aves.), 212-505-3355
◪ "Good food, great karma" and an "Odeon-ish" vibe make this Village yearling a magnet for French-American food groupies; despite jeers about "subpar" eats, there's applause for its spiffy townhouse setting.

Villa Mosconi — 21 | 17 | 21 | $41
69 MacDougal St. (bet. Bleecker & Houston Sts.), 212-673-0390
■ This "venerable" Villager dishes out "solid" Italian fare at "time-capsule" prices in a setting right out of a "Francis Ford Coppola film"; despite a "no-surprises" menu, it's a "steady favorite" of addicts craving a "red-sauce" fix along with "endless jugs of wine."

Vince and Eddie's S — 19 | 16 | 18 | $44
70 W. 68th St. (bet. Columbus Ave. & CPW), 212-721-0068
◪ At times, this West Side American could pass for a "country" inn, what with its hearty, "basic" chow, "cozy" fireplace and "nice garden"; but when the Lincoln Center pre-curtain crowds invade, it gets so "tight" that "only anorexics" can "squeeze in."

Vine — 23 | 21 | 20 | $52
25 Broad St. (enter on Exchange Pl.), 212-344-8463
■ The "food's di-Vine" at this Wall Street–area New American with an equally heavenly setting overlooking the NYSE; even more noteworthy are the blue-chip "private dining spaces" set in subterranean, refurbished "bank vaults."

Vinnie's Pizza ●S≠ — 21 | 7 | 14 | $11
285 Amsterdam Ave. (bet. 73rd & 74th Sts.), 212-874-4382
◪ You'll be "full for hours" after just "one slice" of the "delicious", thick-crusted cheesy pies at this West Side pizzeria, but since the "decor leaves much to be desired", most reserve it solely for "takeout."

Virgil's Real BBQ S — 20 | 14 | 16 | $29
152 W. 44th St. (bet. B'way & 6th Ave.), 212-921-9494
◪ "Loosen your belt", "stuff yourself silly" and call your cardiologist later is the routine at this "Dixie meets Times Square" BBQ that's "as good as it gets in NY"; to cope with the "tacky atmosphere", "poor service" and "killer crowds" (that "put the 'din' in din-din"), veterans offer two words of advice: "Alka-Seltzer."

Virot S — ▽ 25 | 24 | 24 | $70
Dylan Hotel, 52 E. 41st St. (bet. Madison & Park Aves.), 646-658-0266
■ "If you can find" this Midtown newcomer – housed in the back of the "old Chemists' Club" building, nka the Dylan Hotel – you're in for some "imaginative" French food that "will knock your socks off" from "talented" chef-owner Didier Virot; there are quibbles about the "expensive" tabs and debate about the ambiance ("beautiful" vs. "dead"), yet most believe this one will "only get better with time."

Vittorio Cucina ●S — ▽ 22 | 17 | 21 | $38
308-310 Bleecker St. (bet. Grove St. & 7th Ave. S.), 212-463-0730
■ Look for "great regional" dishes at this Village Italian stalwart where "warm, welcoming" service and a "lovely" outdoor garden make for "priceless" dining that's not too pricey; P.S. the "pasta served in a cheese wheel" is "truly amazing."

| F | D | S | C |

Vivolo ●S
20 | 19 | 20 | $45

140 E. 74th St. (bet. Lexington & Park Aves.), 212-737-3533
■ The "emphasis is on relaxation" at this "charming" duplex East Side townhouse luring "sophisticated, older" types; the "always good" Italian cuisine arrives in a setting oozing such "discreet elegance" that it's a natural for "clandestine" fireside rendezvous.

Volare
▽ 22 | 19 | 24 | $42

147 W. Fourth St. (bet. MacDougal St. & 6th Ave.), 212-777-2849
■ Its "old-fashioned" setting may be why this 25-year-old Italian is "often overlooked", but the food's tasty and it "could give other restaurants a lesson in service"; though a few shrug "ordinary", for many it's a good reason to "live in the Village."

VONG S
25 | 25 | 23 | $60

200 E. 54th St. (3rd Ave.), 212-486-9592
☑ French-Thai fusion followers "long for Vong", Jean-Georges Vongerichten's "sultry" "original" that "hits on all cylinders" with "luscious", "feast-for-the-eyes" edibles served in "exotic", "celeb"-studded digs; although "dainty portions" and "blisteringly expensive" tabs give some pause, the $38 pre-theater deal is one way "Sadie Thompson" wanna-bes can experience "cloud nine in Midtown."

Vynl S
17 | 16 | 17 | $21

824 Ninth Ave. (54th St.), 212-974-2003
■ "Kitschy but tasty twists on diner favorites" surface at this "arty" Hell's Kitchen American-Thai featuring conversation-starting "record sleeve menus" that echo its "retro" looks; "low prices" make it a "great pre-theater" option, despite occasionally "laughable service."

Walker's ●S
20 | 17 | 17 | $26

16 N. Moore St. (Varick St.), 212-941-0142
■ TriBeCans savor "what's left of the old neighborhood" at this "trend-proof", circa 1890 "old NY" tavern where "superior bar food" comes at rock-bottom tabs; though some are "underwhelmed" by the "chirpy" service, the "low-key" vibe is hard to beat.

Wallsé S
23 | 19 | 20 | $57

344 W. 11th St. (Washington St.), 212-352-2300
■ "Inspired", "light as a feather" Viennese fare and "hard-to-find" Austrian wines share top billing at Kurt Gutenbrunner's "hip" West Villager with a "stark", "minimalist design" and "cordial, efficient" service; though some picky eaters "can't get too excited about Wiener schnitzel", folks who "still hope to send their kids to Harvard" say this "poor man's Danube" is "worth a return visit."

Wasabi S
▽ 20 | 16 | 19 | $31

213 Smith St. (bet. Baltic & Butler Sts.), Brooklyn, 718-243-2028
205 Bedford Ave. (bet. N. 5th & N. 6th Sts.), Brooklyn, 718-302-2035 ●
☑ Hep locations (in Williamsburg and Carroll Gardens' Smith Street) plus "bang for the buck" pricing lure lots of "students" to these Japanese sushi specialists, although some say their quality leaves "much to be desired."

Water Club, The S
22 | 25 | 22 | $59

500 E. 30th St. (bet. East River & 30th St., enter via E. 34th St.), 212-683-3333
■ It's "all view" all the time at this "civilized" East River barge where the "vibrant" American vittles are almost on a par with the "location, location, location"; canny Casanovas confide that "drinks on the upper deck are a great seduction tool" and sidestep the "top-of-the-line" prices by ordering the money-saving prix fixes.

	F	D	S	C

WATER'S EDGE (Queens) | 23 | 26 | 23 | $60
44th Dr. & East River (Vernon Blvd.), 718-482-0033
■ For a "literally transporting dining experience", take a free ferry to this "smart-looking" Long Island City American where the "high-quality" cooking "matches" the "drop-dead" "Big Apple skyline" vistas; it's the perfect setting to "take your sweetheart" and pop the question – but "eat before you propose", since it's kind of spendy.

West Bank Cafe ●S | 19 | 16 | 19 | $35
Manhattan Plaza, 407 W. 42nd St. (bet. 9th & 10th Aves.), 212-695-6909
■ "Immensely popular" Theater District American (aka the "off-B'way Sardi's") providing "surprisingly good" food at "affordable" tabs; ignore the "noise" and "plain decor", and "eavesdrop on Broadway career conversations" instead.

West 63rd Street Steakhouse | 21 | 21 | 20 | $60
Empire Hotel, 44 W. 63rd St. (bet. B'way & Columbus Ave.), 212-246-6363
■ "Perfect for Lincoln Center", this West Side "diamond in the rough" meatery offers both "honest steaks" and "bartenders who know their martinis"; despite "daunting prices", its handsome, "clubby" setting compensates with "plenty of elbow room" and "calm" that's hard to find at other steak places.

White Horse Tavern ●S⊄ | 13 | 15 | 13 | $21
567 Hudson St. (11th St.), 212-989-3956
☒ "What better place to drown your sorrows" than this "historically mandatory", circa 1880 West Village pub where the "cheap", burger-oriented menu is beside the point; most prefer to tip a lid to "Dylan Thomas' ghost" from the "popular" sidewalk seats.

Willow S | 20 | 20 | 19 | $46
1022 Lexington Ave. (73rd St.), 212-717-0703
■ This "genteel" French-American set in a duplex East Side townhouse works best for an "intimate" tête-à-tête on its "cozy" second floor; though some say it's "a bit old-fashioned", most of its "polite", "moneyed" crowd says "that's not bad."

Wo Hop ●S⊄ | 20 | 7 | 13 | $17
17 Mott St. (Canal St.), 212-267-2536
■ This 24/7 Chinatown "slumming" "classic" has been dishing out "dependable" eats since LaGuardia was mayor; sure, it's a "crowded" "dump" and dubious for "delicate digestive systems", so "close your eyes" and think of the "ridiculously low prices" instead.

Wolf & Lamb S | 19 | 14 | 16 | $33
10 E. 48th St. (bet. 5th & Madison Aves.), 212-317-1950
☒ For "a quick, not fancy meal", this modestly priced Midtown kosher deli/steakhouse should be on your list; "no atmosphere" detracts, but fans say this "work in progress" is "worth a try."

Wolf's ●S | 16 | 13 | 14 | $26
41 W. 57th St. (bet. 5th & 6th Aves.), 212-888-4100
☒ "Upscale" Midtown deli that stacks up a "sandwich that can feed a family of three" at "decent prices"; though the clean, modern decor's a "vast improvement" over the old Wolf's, the waiters are as reassuringly "surly" as ever.

Wollensky's Grill ●S | 22 | 17 | 19 | $46
205 E. 49th St. (3rd Ave.), 212-753-0444
■ "More informal" than Smith & Wollensky's, this next-door annex purveys "standout steaks" and "excellent burgers" at "easier-on-the-wallet" prices; later hours, sidewalk seating and a "jumping" bar scene make it "just as satisfying as the main establishment."

www.zagat.com

	F	D	S	C

Wondee Siam ⓈØ
▽ 22 | 5 | 16 | $16

792 Ninth Ave. (bet. 52nd & 53rd Sts.), 212-459-9057

■ It may "look like a laundromat" from the street, but this itty-bitty West Side "hole-in-the-wall" is no washout when it comes to "delicious" Thai at "what-a-deal" prices; until they "dim the lights", "takeout" is touted.

Wong Kee ⓈØ
23 | 7 | 12 | $17

113 Mott St. (bet. Canal & Hester Sts.), 212-966-1160

■ The good news is that this "fantastic" Chinatown Cantonese delivers "superb food" at "bargain basement" "'70s prices", but not so good are a "grumpy" staff and "zero atmosphere" where "everything's Formica"; diehards insist "don't look", just eat.

Won Jo ●Ⓢ
21 | 12 | 14 | $27

23 W. 32nd St. (bet. B'way & 5th Ave.), 212-695-5815

☑ "Home cooking" on your own "personal grill" draws do-it-yourselfers to this Midtown Korean BBQ that's "authentic", "reasonably priced" and "open 24 hours"; despite a staff in a "big rush", most tag this one a "keeper."

Woo Chon ●Ⓢ
21 | 13 | 14 | $31

8-10 W. 36th St. (bet. 5th & 6th Aves.), 212-695-0676
41-19 Kissena Blvd. (Main St.), Queens, 718-463-0803

■ "Bustling" Korean duo known for their "amazing bulgoki", kimchi and BBQ, not the "erratic service"; aficionados rate the smaller Queens location "better", though both are great "last resorts when working late", given their 24/7 open-door policies.

Woo Lae Oak Ⓢ
22 | 21 | 19 | $43

148 Mercer St. (bet. Houston & Prince Sts.), 212-925-8200

☑ Given the "chic", "slick" surroundings, this SoHo Korean just may be the "hippest" of its genre; purists protest its "timid" menu and not-so-timid prices but agree the "trendy" bar scene can be amusing.

World Yacht Ⓢ
15 | 22 | 17 | $67

Pier 81, W. 41st St. & Hudson River (12th Ave.), 212-630-8100

☑ "Memorable moments" abound on this dinner cruise whose raison d'être is its "breathtaking" "sunset views" of lower Manhattan; as for the food, opinion runs the gamut from "pretty darn good" to "edible."

Wu Liang Ye Ⓢ
21 | 12 | 15 | $27

215 E. 86th St. (bet. 2nd & 3rd Aves.), 212-534-8899
36 W. 48th St. (bet. 5th & 6th Aves.), 212-398-2308
338 Lexington Ave. (bet. 39th & 40th Sts.), 212-370-9648

■ "Bring some tissues – it's well worth sniffling" over the spicy hot chow at these Szechuan triplets whose "ample" menus "blend the traditional with the exotic"; sure, they're "nothing fancy" and service is "rushed", but their "authenticity" is on a par with the best of C-town.

WWF New York Ⓢ
11 | 15 | 12 | $28

1501 Broadway (43rd St.), 212-398-2563

☑ "Heaven for wrestling fans, hell for the rest of us", this new multi-screen Times Square themery strikes critics as "cheesy enough to cushion a body slam" with food that "tasted better at XFL games"; however, there are enough "adrenaline-pumped" fans around to keep the place "crowded", "loud" and even "fun" on the right fight night.

Wyanoka ●
▽ 23 | 20 | 21 | $41

173½ Mott St. (bet. Broome & Grand Sts.), 212-941-8757

■ Way "out of the way" in Little Italy lies this hepcat-friendly New American–Eclectic; "if you can find it", expect a "funky" crowd, "hip music", a "charming" staff and "inventive", "wonderful food" that runs a "close second to the great vibe."

XO Kitchen [S] ≠ ▽ 19 | 11 | 14 | $18

148 Hester St. (bet. Bowery & Elizabeth St.), 212-965-8645

An off-the-beaten-path, quirky Chinatown find, this funky, "always-crowded", Hong Kong–style joint resembles a dingy rec room; its adventurous menu offers "great variety", which can be a problem, since some find it "hard to figure out what's good" and what's simply strange.

Xunta [S] 20 | 14 | 14 | $25

174 First Ave. (bet. 10th & 11th Sts.), 212-614-0620

■ "Damn good sangria" and "cheap", "tasty tapas" meet cute at this "hip" East Villager that draws "loud gringos" in search of "festive" times; "awful waits" and "no elbow room" are the norm, while tables made from "giant kegs" are conversation starters.

YAMA 25 | 13 | 16 | $35

122 E. 17th St. (Irving Pl.), 212-475-0969

92 W. Houston St. (bet. La Guardia Pl. & Thompson St.), 212-674-0935 ◐ [S]

38-40 Carmine St. (bet. Bedford & Bleecker Sts.), 212-989-9330 [S]

■ "Glistening", "mammoth" sushi makes this Japanese trio the "gold standard" for deep sea diners, and "decent pricing" makes them insanely "popular"; to get around the "crazy" waits, savvy surveyors suggest "Carmine Street", as it's the only one that takes reservations.

Ye Waverly Inn [S] 17 | 21 | 18 | $38

16 Bank St. (Waverly Pl.), 212-929-4377

◪ "New management is reviving" this longtime Village shrine to pre–Revolutionary War NY; now the menu's gone "upscale", fusing American and French fare, though some complain it's "lost its funk" and "gotten expensive."

York Grill [S] 21 | 20 | 20 | $42

1690 York Ave. (bet. 88th & 89th Sts.), 212-772-0261

■ This American "gem" in the Yorkville "culinary wasteland" attracts "young and old alike" with its "consistently fine" food; selfish types are "thankful it's out of the way or everybody would be eating here."

Yuka [S] – | – | – | I

1557 Second Ave. (bet. 80th & 81st Sts.), 212-772-9675

"You can't beat all-you-can-eat for $18" at this "first-rate sushi and sashimi" Eastsider; despite the "tacky decor", given the current economy, it's no wonder they "can no longer seat the crowds."

Yura & Co. [S] 19 | 12 | 15 | $24

1645 Third Ave. (92nd St.), 212-860-8060

1292 Madison Ave. (92nd St.), 212-860-8060

◪ Upper East Side "country cafe" Americans that draw crowds for their "terrific baked goods" and "wonderful take-out" sandwiches; too many "strollers" and not enough service are the downsides.

Zarela [S] 22 | 17 | 17 | $40

953 Second Ave. (bet. 50th & 51st Sts.), 212-644-6740

■ "Scary margaritas" so strong they "double as truth serum" make for interesting conversations at the "sizzling" bar of Zarela Martinez's "colorful" East Side Mexican; those seeking a "quieter scene" head upstairs where the "super-authentic" cuisine is oh-so-"delicious."

Zenith Vegetarian Cuisine [S] 19 | 16 | 18 | $25

888 Eighth Ave. (52nd St.), 212-262-8080

◪ "Even carnivores have a good time" at this Theater District Vegetarian, since they can "feel noble" grazing on "quality" fare at "reasonable" tabs; still, some say the grub "all tastes the same", opting to "talk to their plants" rather than eat them.

Zen Palate [S] 20 | 18 | 17 | $26

2170 Broadway (bet. 76th & 77th Sts.), 212-501-7768
663 Ninth Ave. (46th St.), 212-582-1669
34 Union Sq. E. (16th St.), 212-614-9291

◪ "Sinfully healthy" Vegetarian threesome where "calming" decor rendered in the "same color as the food" complements a "guilt-free" menu that tastes much "better than it sounds"; the "unadventurous" say the "skimpy portions" of "twigs and gravel" leave them "still hungry" but admit it's "light on the wallet."

Zócalo [S] 20 | 17 | 17 | $36

174 E. 82nd St. (bet. Lexington & 3rd Aves.), 212-717-7772
Grand Central Terminal (42nd St. & Vanderbilt Ave.), 212-687-5666

■ "It's always a party" at this "happening" East Side cantina (and its "quick bite" Grand Central sibling) known for "creative", "untypical" Mexicana; a mind-boggling array of tequilas anchors the margarita-centric bar, though the "can't-hear-yourself-drink" decibel level can probably be "heard at the border."

Zoë [S] 22 | 20 | 20 | $47

90 Prince St. (bet. B'way & Mercer St.), 212-966-6722

■ Long a "SoHo standard", this "polished", open-kitchen New American is "still cranking", turning out "fresh, crisp" fare paired with a "seriously good" all-American wine list in "airy", "California-style" digs; though "kind of expensive", there's "never a dull moment" here.

Zum Stammtisch (Queens) [S] 23 | 19 | 20 | $33

69-46 Myrtle Ave. (Cooper Ave.), 718-386-3014

■ Nobody ever "leaves hungry" from this "gemütlich" Glendale German where the "hearty" chow (you can "consume your body weight in Jaegerschnitzel") is more than a "fair value"; "year-round Oktoberfest" decor that's like "eating inside a cuckoo clock" adds authenticity, even if the waitresses "don't look like the St. Pauli Girl."

Zuni ◐ [S] 19 | 14 | 17 | $31

598 Ninth Ave. (43rd St.), 212-765-7626

◪ "Interesting combinations" of "zippy" eats for "surprisingly little money" make this Hell's Kitchen New American a "reliable" pre-theater option; some deem it "terminally average" and disparage its "dowdy" looks, but overall, it's a "cozy" "hangout."

Zutto [S] 21 | 17 | 17 | $36

62 Greenwich Ave. (bet. 7th Ave. S. & W. 11th St.), 212-229-1796
77 Hudson St. (Harrison St.), 212-233-3287

◪ "Primo sushi" "without the hassle" of fancier raw fisheries is yours at this Downtown Japanese duo that are local "best-kept secrets"; however, they may not be for long, as more and more boosters tout their "serene settings" and "rare affordability."

Indexes

CUISINES
LOCATIONS
SPECIAL FEATURES

Indexes list the best of many within each category.

Cuisine Index

CUISINES

(Restaurant name followed by Food Rating and neighborhood; dash denotes restaurant is unrated.)

Afghan
Afghan Kebab Hse./*17/Multi. Loc.*
Kabul Cafe/*19/W 50s*
Pamir/*20/Multi. Loc.*

African
Sugar Bar/*20/W 70s*

American (New)
Abajour/*18/E 60s*
Abigael's/*19/Garment*
Above/*20/W 40s*
Aesop's Tables/*22/Staten Is.*
Aleutia/*19/Flatiron*
Alley's End/*19/Chelsea*
Alva/*19/Flatiron*
Ambassador Grill/*20/E 40s*
An American Pl./*21/E 50s*
Annisa/*25/Village*
Archer's/*23/E 80s*
Archives/*18/Dtown Bklyn*
Atlas/*24/W 50s*
Aureole/*27/E 60s*
Avalon Bar-Grill/*20/Murray Hill*
AZ/*23/Flatiron*
Bateaux NY/*18/Chelsea*
B B&G/*14/NoHo*
Beacon/*23/W 50s*
Bid/-/*E 70s*
Blue Hill/*25/Village*
Blue Ribbon/*25/Multi. Loc.*
Blue Water Grill/*24/Union Sq.*
Boat House/*17/E 70s*
Boerum Hill Food/*21/Boerum Hill*
Boughalem, Rest./*21/Village*
Bridge Cafe/*21/Dtown*
Brooklyn Grill/*21/Boerum Hill*
Butterfield 81/*21/E 80s*
Cafe Alyss/*19/Village*
Cafe Colonial/*20/SoHo*
Cafe S.F.A./*19/E 40s*
Canal House/*20/SoHo*
Candela/*19/Union Sq.*
Canteen/*18/SoHo*
Caviar Russe/*25/E 50s*
Chameleon/*21/Murray Hill*
Charlotte/*19/W 40s*
Chop't Creative Salad/*21/Flatiron*
Cibi Cibi/Yellowfingers/*15/E 60s*
Cibo/*21/E 40s*
City Eatery/*19/NoHo*
Clove/-/*E 80s*
Coconut Grill/*16/E 70s*
Commune/*18/Flatiron*
Cooke's Corner/*21/W 90s*
Cornelia St. Cafe/*19/Village*
Coup/*21/E Vil*
Craft/*25/Flatiron*
Cub Room/*21/SoHo*
Della Femina/*20/E 50s*
Dining Room/*22/E 70s*
District/*20/W 40s*
Druids/*18/W 50s*
Duane Park Cafe/*24/TriBeCa*
Eatery/*18/W 50s*
Eleven Madison Pk./*25/Gramercy*
Essex/*21/Low E Side*
Etats-Unis/*23/E 80s*
Eugene/*17/Flatiron.*
55 Wall/*20/Dtown*
Fifty Seven Fifty Seven/*24/E 50s*
First/*21/E Vil*
Five Points/*21/NoHo*
44 & X Hell's Kit./*23/W 40s*
Fressen/*19/Meatpacking*
Garage/*19/Village*
Garden Cafe/*25/Prospect Hts.*
Giorgio's/Gramercy/*21/Flatiron*
Globe/-/*Gramercy*
good/*20/Village*
Gotham B&G/*27/Central Vil*
Grace/*18/TriBeCa*
Gramercy Tavern/*27/Flatiron*
Grocery/*25/Carroll Gdns.*
Grove/*19/Village*
Halcyon/*21/W 50s*
Harbour Lights/*17/Dtown*
Heartbeat/*20/E 40s*
Heartland Brewery/*14/Multi. Loc.*
Heights Cafe/*17/Bklyn Hts.*
Henry's/*18/W 90s*
Henry's End/*23/Bklyn Hts.*
Herban Kitchen/*20/SoHo*
Icon/*22/Murray Hill/E 30s*
Ilo/-/*W 40s*
Inside/*20/Village*
Irving on Irving/*19/Gramercy*
Isabella's/*20/W 70s*
Jane/-/*Village*
Josephina/*19/W 60s*
Josie's/*22/Multi. Loc.*
JUdson Grill/*23/W 50s*
Judy's Chelsea/*17/Chelsea*
Julian's/*20/W 50s*
Juniper Café/*20/TriBeCa*
Lenox/*21/E 70s*
Leshko's/*16/E Vil*
Levana/*21/W 60s*

Cuisine Index

Lola/20/Flatiron
Lotus/19/Meatpacking
Magnolia/19/Park Slope
Maison/20/E 70s
Man Ray/-/Chelsea
March/26/E 50s
Marika/18/W 70s
Mark's/24/E 70s
Max & Moritz/22/Park Slope
Mercer Kitchen/23/SoHo
Merchants, N.Y./15/Multi. Loc.
Merge/20/Village
Métrazur/19/E 40s
Metro Grill/19/Garment
Metronome/19/Flatiron
Midway/21/Village
Mike & Tony's/21/Park Slope
Monkey Bar/21/E 50s
Morrell Wine Bar/19/W 40s
Nation/19/W 40s
Nellie's/-/Village
New City B&G/22/Dtown Bkln
New Leaf Cafe/-/Wash. Hts. & Up
92/-/E 90s
NoHo Star/18/NoHo
Norma's/24/W 50s
Oceana/27/E 50s
One C.P.S./20/W 50s
One if by Land/25/Village
101/20/Bay Ridge
Onieal's Grand St./18/Little Italy
Oscar's/18/E 50s
Ouest/24/W 80s
Park Avalon/20/Flatiron
Park Ave. Cafe/25/E 60s
Pfiff/-/SoHo
Philip Marie/20/Village
Plate 347/20/Gramercy
Porters NY/20/Chelsea
Prune/22/E Vil
Punch/20/Flatiron
Quilty's/24/SoHo
Rachel's/20/W 40s
Red/Bar/20/E 70s
Red Cat/22/Chelsea
Redeye Grill/21/W 50s
Regency/20/E 60s
Relish/22/Williamsburg
Rialto/19/SoHo
River Cafe/25/Bklyn Hts.
Rose Water/24/Park Slope
Sag Harbor/20/W 40s
Saul/24/Boerum Hill
Screening Room/20/TriBeCa
Seven/21/Chelsea
71 Clinton/27/Low E Side
Shelly's NY/19/W 50s
Stella/-/SoHo
Stingy Lulu's/14/E Vil

Tabla/25/Gramercy
Table d'Hôte/21/E 90s
Tasting Room/24/E Vil
Tavern on Green/17/W 60s
Tea Box/21/E 50s
Thalia/20/W 50s
Thom/-/SoHo
Time Cafe/16/Multi. Loc.
Tocqueville/24/Union Sq.
Tonic/22/Chelsea
Town/25/W 50s
Tribeca Grill/22/TriBeCa
Tudor Grill/-/E 40s
12th St. B&G/22/Park Slope
212/18/E 60s
Two Two Two/23/W 70s
Union Pacific/26/Gramercy
Union Sq. Cafe/27/Union Sq.
Vaux Bistro/21/Park Slope
Verbena/24/Gramercy
Veritas/27/Flatiron
Village/19/Village
Vine/23/Dtown
Vynl/17/W 50s
Water's Edge/23/LIC
West Bank Cafe/19/W 40s
Willow/20/E 70s
World Yacht/15/W 40s
Wyanoka/23/Little Italy
York Grill/21/E 80s
Zoë/22/SoHo
Zuni/19/W 40s

American (Regional)
Acme B&G/15/NoHo
America/14/Flatiron
An American Pl./21/E 50s
Anglers & Writers/16/Village
Brother Jimmy's/15/Multi. Loc.
Cooking with Jazz/24/Whitestone
Delta Grill/19/W 40s
Grange Hall/20/Village
Harvest/17/Cobble Hill
Home/21/Village
Hudson River Club/23/Dtown
Mary's Fish Camp/25/Village
Mesa Grill/24/Flatiron
Michael's/22/W 50s
Pearl Oyster Bar/26/Village
Red Rail/18/Carroll Gdns.
Tropica/22/E 40s

American (Traditional)
AKA Cafe/-/Low E Side
Algonquin Hotel/16/W 40s
America/14/Flatiron
American Grill/-/Staten Is.
American Park/19/Dtown
Amy's Bread/23/Multi. Loc.
Anglers & Writers/16/Village

Cuisine Index

Annie's/16/E 70s
Archer's/23/E 80s
Avenue/20/W 80s
Bar 89/16/SoHo
Barking Dog/16/Multi. Loc.
Bar Odeon/18/TriBeCa
Bayard's/24/Dtown
Bendix Diner/15/Multi. Loc.
Billy's/16/E 50s
B.K. Sweeney's/17/Douglaston
Blue Elephant/-/E 70s
Brooklyn Diner USA/16/Multi. Loc.
Broome St. Bar/16/SoHo
Bryant Park Grill/Cafe/17/W 40s
Bubby's/19/TriBeCa
Cafe Nosidam/18/E 60s
Cafeteria/17/Chelsea
Chadwick's/20/Bay Ridge
Charley O's/13/W 40s
Chat n' Chew/17/Flatiron
Chelsea Grill/18/Chelsea
City Bakery/23/Flatiron
City Crab/19/Flatiron
City Grill/16/W 70s
City Hall/21/TriBeCa
Coffee Shop/16/Union Sq.
Comfort Diner/15/Multi. Loc.
Corner Bistro/23/Village
Diner/22/Williamsburg
Dizzy's/-/Park Slope
DuMont/-/Williamsburg
Edison Cafe/16/W 40s
EJ's Luncheonette/16/Multi. Loc.
Elephant & Castle/18/Village
Ellen's Stardust/13/W 50s
Empire Diner/15/Chelsea
ESPN Zone/13/W 40s
Fairway Cafe/18/W 70s
Fanelli Cafe/15/SoHo
Fred's/18/Multi. Loc.
Friend of a Farmer/17/Gramercy
Good Enough to Eat/20/W 80s
Grill Room/21/Dtown
Hard Rock Cafe/13/W 50s
Harley Davidson Cafe/12/W 50s
Houlihan's/11/Multi. Loc.
Hourglass Tavern/17/W 40s
Houston's/20/Multi. Loc.
Hudson Cafeteria/17/W 50s
ike/-/E Vil
Independent/18/TriBeCa
Jackson Hole/16/Multi. Loc.
Jekyll & Hyde/12/W 50s
Jerry's/17/SoHo
J.G. Melon/18/E 70s
Joe Allen/17/W 40s
Johnny Rockets/15/Central Vil
King Cole Bar/20/E 50s
Kitchenette/20/TriBeCa
Lemon/14/Flatiron
Maloney & Porcelli/22/E 50s
Mama's Food Shop/22/E Vil
Manhattan Grille/22/E 60s
Marion's/18/NoHo
Mars 2112/11/W 50s
Mayrose/15/Flatiron
McHales/18/W 40s
Metropolitan Cafe/16/E 50s
Mickey Mantle's/14/W 50s
Nadine's/17/Village
Neary's/17/E 50s
Odeon/19/TriBeCa
Old Town Bar/15/Flatiron
O'Neals'/17/W 60s
Pershing Sq./17/E 40s
Pete's Tavern/14/Gramercy
P.J. Clarke's/15/E 50s
Planet Hollywood/12/W 40s
Popover Cafe/18/W 80s
Rock Center Café/16/W 50s
Saloon/14/W 60s
Sarabeth's/21/Multi. Loc.
Sazerac Hse./17/Village
Soho Steak/20/SoHo
Spirit Cruises/13/Chelsea
St. Maggie's Cafe/18/Dtown
Stonewall Bistro/-/Village
Supper Club/16/W 40s
Swifty's/20/E 70s
T.G.I. Friday's/11/Multi. Loc.
Tír na nóg/19/Garment
Top of Tower/18/E 40s
T Salon/18/Flatiron
'21' Club/22/W 50s
Vince & Eddie's/19/W 60s
Walker's/20/TriBeCa
Water Club, The/22/E 30s
White Horse/13/Village
Wollensky's Grill/22/E 40s
WWF NY/11/W 40s
Ye Waverly Inn/17/Village
Yura & Co./19/Multi. Loc.

Argentinean

Campo/18/W 80s
Chimichurri Grill/21/W 40s
Novecento/19/SoHo
Old San Juan/18/W 50s
Pampa/20/W 90s
Sosa Borella/20/TriBeCa
Sur/20/Carroll Gdns.

Asian

Afghan Kebab Hse./17/Multi. Loc.
Aleutia/19/Flatiron
Asia de Cuba/24/Murray Hill
AZ/23/Flatiron
Bright Food Shop/19/Chelsea
Cafe Asean/20/Village

Cuisine Index

Cendrillon/*21/SoHo*
China Grill/*23/W 50s*
Chow Bar/*21/Village*
Daily Chow/*18/E Vil*
Faan/*-/Carroll Gdns.*
Forbidden City/*21/E Vil*
Friend House/*-/E Vil*
Kelley & Ping/*18/SoHo*
Komodo/*23/E Vil*
Lucky Cheng's/*12/E Vil*
Man Ray/*-/Chelsea*
Mi/*20/Gramercy*
NoHo Star/*18/NoHo*
Obeca Li/*19/TriBeCa*
O.G./*22/E Vil*
Rain/*21/Multi. Loc.*
Republic/*17/Union Sq.*
Roy's NY/*24/Dtown*
Ruby Foo's/*19/Multi. Loc.*
Tao/*21/E 50s*
Tiger Blossom/*-/Central Vil*
Tja!/*20/TriBeCa*

Australian
Eight Mile Creek/*21/SoHo*

Austrian
Cafe Steinhof/*-/Park Slope*
Danube/*26/TriBeCa*
Mont Blanc/*18/W 40s*
Wallsé/*23/Village*

Bakeries
Blue Ribbon Bakery/*23/Village*
City Bakery/*23/Flatiron*
Columbus Bakery/*19/Multi. Loc.*
Cupcake Cafe/*22/Garment*
La Bergamote/*22/Chelsea*
Le Pain Quotidien/*20/Multi. Loc.*
My Most Favorite/*18/W 40s*
Omonia Cafe/*19/Multi. Loc.*
Once Upon a Tart/*20/SoHo*
Payard Bistro/*24/E 70s*
Sweet Melissa/*22/Cobble Hill*

Barbecue
Acme B&G/*15/NoHo*
Brother Jimmy's/*15/Multi. Loc.*
Brothers BBQ/*16/Village*
Cowgirl Hall of Fame/*15/Village*
Daily Chow/*18/E Vil*
Dallas BBQ/*15/Multi. Loc.*
Do Hwa/*21/Village*
Duke's/*17/Gramercy*
Emily's/*18/E 90s*
Green Field Churr./*19/Corona*
Hog Pit BBQ/*17/Meatpacking*
Kang Suh/*21/Garment/W 30s*
Kum Gang San/*22/Multi. Loc.*
Master Grill/*18/Flushing*

Pearson's/*24/Jackson Hts.*
Tennessee Mtn./*16/SoHo*
Virgil's/*20/W 40s*

Belgian
Café de Bruxelles/*21/Village*
Le Pain Quotidien/*20/Multi. Loc.*
Markt/*19/Meatpacking*
Petite Abeille/*19/Multi. Loc.*

Brasserie
Artisanal/*23/Murray Hill*
Balthazar/*23/SoHo*
Brasserie/*20/E 50s*
Brasserie 8½/*20/W 50s*
Brasserie Julien/*19/E 80s*
Cafe Centro/*19/E 40s*
City Hall/*21/TriBeCa*
Gaby Brasserie/*20/W 40s*
Globe/*-/Gramercy*
Guastavino, Downstairs/*18/E 50s*
Jacques/*19/E 80s*
La Bicyclette/*17/W 80s*
L'Absinthe/*22/E 60s*
L'Actuel/*19/E 50s*
Le Monde/*17/Columbia*
Les Halles/*21/Gramercy*
Markt/*19/Meatpacking*
Montparnasse/*20/E 50s*
92/*-/E 90s*
One C.P.S./*20/W 50s*
Orsay/*19/E 70s*
Oscar's/*18/E 50s*
Pastis/*20/Meatpacking*
Redeye Grill/*21/W 50s*
Rue 57 Brasserie/*19/W 50s*
Shelly's NY/*19/W 50s*

Brazilian
Cabana Carioca/*17/W 40s*
Cafe Colonial/*20/SoHo*
Casa/*23/Village*
Churrascaria Plataforma/*22/W 40s*
Circus/*20/E 60s*
Green Field Churr./*19/Corona*
Ipanema/*19/W 40s*
Master Grill/*18/Flushing*
Rice 'n' Beans/*21/Multi. Loc.*
Via Brasil/*20/W 40s*

Burmese
Mingala/*20/Multi. Loc.*

Cajun/Creole
Acme B&G/*15/Central Vil/NoHo*
Bayou/*21/Harlem*
Cooking with Jazz/*24/Whitestone*
Delta Grill/*19/W 40s*
Great Jones Cafe/*19/NoHo*
La Belle Epoque/*17/Central Vil*

www.zagat.com

Cuisine Index

Mardi Gras/*21/Forest Hills*
Sazerac Hse./*17/Village*

Californian
California Pizza/*15/Multi. Loc.*
Michael's/*22/W 50s*
Red Rail/*18/Carroll Gdns.*

Cambodian
Cambodian Cuisine/*21/Ft. Greene*

Caribbean
A/*-/W 90s*
Bambou/*20/E Vil*
Bistro Latino/*18/W 50s*
Brawta Caribbean/*19/Boerum Hill*
Cabana Nuevo/*21/Multi. Loc.*
Cafe Con Leche/*17/Multi. Loc.*
Island Spice/*20/W 40s*
Justin's/*17/Flatiron*
Maroons/*22/Chelsea*
Mekka/*21/E Vil*
Negril/*20/Chelsea*

Chinese
Au Mandarin/*20/Dtown*
Big Wong/*21/Ctown*
Bill Hong's/*21/E 50s*
Canton/*25/Ctown*
Chef Ho's/*19/E 80s*
Chiam Chinese/*22/E 40s*
China Fun/*15/Multi. Loc.*
Chinam 28/*19/E 80s*
Chin Chin/*23/E 40s*
Chinoiserie/*17/Gramercy*
Dim Sum Go Go/*19/Ctown*
Dish of Salt/*20/W 40s*
East Lake/*20/Flushing*
Empire Szechuan/*16/Multi. Loc.*
Evergreen Shanghai/*18/Multi. Loc.*
Excellent Dumpling/*19/Ctown*
Flor de Mayo/*19/Multi. Loc.*
Friend House/*-/E Vil*
Funky Broome/*19/SoHo*
Golden Unicorn/*20/Ctown*
Goody's/*20/Ctown*
Grand Sichuan/*23/Multi. Loc.*
Great NY Noodle/*22/Ctown*
Henry's Evergreen/*22/E 60s*
HSF/*19/Ctown*
Hunan Park/*17/Multi. Loc.*
Ivy's Cafe/*19/W 70s*
Jade Palace/*21/Flushing*
Jade Plaza/*22/Sunset Pk.*
Jimmy Sung's/*19/E 40s*
Joe's Shanghai/*22/Multi. Loc.*
Kam Chueh/*24/Ctown*
K.B. Garden/*20/Flushing*
Keewah Yen/*20/W 50s*
La Caridad 78/*16/W 70s*

Lili's Noodle/*18/Multi. Loc.*
Mandarin Court/*20/Ctown*
Maple Garden/*23/E 50s*
Mee Noodle/*-/Multi. Loc.*
Mr. Chow/*22/E 50s*
Mr. K's/*24/E 50s*
New Green Bo/*22/Ctown*
Nice Restaurant/*19/Ctown*
Noodles on 28/*19/Gramercy*
Ocean Palace/*21/Multi. Loc.*
Ollie's/*16/Multi. Loc.*
Oriental Garden/*24/Ctown*
Our Place/*21/Multi. Loc.*
Pearls/*18/W 90s*
Peking Duck Hse./*22/Ctown*
Phoenix Garden/*22/E 40s*
Pig Heaven/*18/E 80s*
Ping's Seafood/*20/Multi. Loc.*
Sammy's/*18/Multi. Loc.*
Sam's Noodle Shop/*20/Gramercy*
Shanghai Cuisine/*21/Ctown*
Shun Lee/*24/W 60s*
Shun Lee Cafe/*21/W 60s*
Shun Lee Palace/*24/E 50s*
Sichuan Palace/*21/E 40s*
Silk Road Palace/*19/W 80s*
Silver Pond/*20/Flushing*
Sung Chu Mei/*21/Village*
Sweet-n-Tart/*20/Multi. Loc.*
Tai Hong Lau/*20/Ctown*
Tang Pavilion/*22/W 50s*
Triple Eight/*19/Ctown*
Tse Yang/*24/E 50s*
27 Sunrise Seafood/*-/Ctown*
Veg. Paradise/*20/Multi. Loc.*
Wo Hop/*20/Ctown*
Wong Kee/*23/Ctown*
Wu Liang Ye/*21/Multi. Loc.*
XO Kitchen/*19/Ctown*

Coffeehouses/Desserts
Cafe Lalo/*20/W 80s*
Cupcake Cafe/*22/Garment*
DT•UT/*17/E 80s*
Edgar's Cafe/*18/W 80s*
Emack & Bolio's/*24/Multi. Loc.*
Ferrara/*20/Multi. Loc.*
Grey Dog's Coffee/*20/Village*
Krispy Kreme/*22/Multi. Loc.*
Lady Mendl's/*22/Gramercy*
La Lanterna/*18/Village*
Le Pain Quotidien/*20/Multi. Loc.*
Omonia Cafe/*19/Multi. Loc.*
Once Upon a Tart/*20/SoHo*
Sant Ambroeus/*21/E 70s*
Serendipity 3/*19/E 60s*
Starbucks/*14/Multi. Loc.*
Sweet Melissa/*22/Cobble Hill*
Veniero's/*23/E Vil*

Cuisine Index

Coffee Shops/Diners
Artie's Deli/15/W 80s
Bendix Diner/15/Multi. Loc.
Bonnie's Grill/20/Park Slope
Broadway Diner/14/Multi. Loc.
Brooklyn Diner USA/16/Multi. Loc.
Burger Heaven/15/Multi. Loc.
Caffe Reggio/17/Village
Chat n' Chew/17/Flatiron
Christine's/16/E Vil
Comfort Diner/15/Multi. Loc.
Edison Cafe/16/W 40s
Eighteenth & Eighth/17/Chelsea
Eisenberg Sandwich/19/Flatiron
EJ's Luncheonette/16/Multi. Loc.
Ellen's Stardust/13/W 50s
Empire Diner/15/Chelsea
Florent/19/Meatpacking
Googie's/16/E 70s
Home Sweet Harlem Café/–/Harlem
Junior's/18/Multi. Loc.
Mayrose/15/Flatiron
Tom's/20/Prospect Hts.
Uncle George's/20/Astoria
Viand/16/Multi. Loc.

Colombian
Tierras Colombianas/20/Multi. Loc.

Continental
Cafe du Pont/19/E 50s
Cal's/19/Flatiron
Carlyle/24/E 70s
Four Seasons/27/E 50s
Historic Old Bermuda/18/Staten Is.
Kings' Carriage/21/E 80s
Leopard, The/21/E 50s
Marylou's/19/Village
Palm Court/20/W 50s
Parsonage/21/Staten Is.
Petrossian/24/W 50s
Piccola Venezia/25/Astoria
Sardi's/16/W 40s
South Shore Country Club/20/Staten Is.
Top of Tower/18/E 40s
Two Two Two/23/W 70s
View/19/W 40s

Cuban
Asia de Cuba/24/Murray Hill
Bistro Latino/18/W 50s
Cabana Nuevo/21/Multi. Loc.
Cafe Con Leche/17/Multi. Loc.
Café Habana/20/SoHo
Calle Ocho/22/W 80s
Cuba Libre/20/Chelsea
Havana Chelsea/20/Chelsea
Isla/19/Village
La Caridad 78/16/W 70s
Little Havana/19/Village
Paladar/20/Low E Side
Son Cubano/–/Meatpacking
Victor's Cafe/21/W 50s

Delis/Sandwich Shops
Artie's Deli/15/W 80s
Barney Greengrass/23/W 80s
Ben's Kosher Deli/18/Multi. Loc.
Carnegie Deli/21/W 50s
Columbus Bakery/19/Multi. Loc.
Cosi/18/Multi. Loc.
E.A.T./20/E 80s
Eisenberg Sandwich/19/Flatiron
Emerald Planet/17/Multi. Loc.
Ess-a-Bagel/21/Multi. Loc.
Fine & Schapiro/16/W 70s
Grey Dog's Coffee/20/Village
Grilled Cheese NYC/23/Low E Side
Hampton Chutney/–/SoHo
Katz's Deli/21/Low E Side
Pastrami Queen/17/E 80s
Peanut Butter & Co./20/Village
P.J. Bernstein/17/E 70s
Sandwich Planet/20/Garment
Sarge's Deli/17/Murray Hill
Second Ave. Deli/23/E Vil
Stage Deli/19/W 50s
Via Quadronno/22/E 70s
Wolf & Lamb/19/E 40s
Wolf's/16/W 50s

Dim Sum
Chiam Chinese/22/E 40s
China Fun/15/Multi. Loc.
Chin Chin/23/E 40s
Dim Sum Go Go/19/Ctown
East Lake/20/Flushing
Forbidden City/21/E Vil
Golden Unicorn/20/Ctown
Henry's Evergreen/22/E 60s
HSF/19/Ctown
Jade Palace/21/Flushing
Jade Plaza/22/Sunset Pk.
K.B. Garden/20/Flushing
Mandarin Court/20/Ctown
Nice Restaurant/19/Ctown
Ocean Palace/21/Multi. Loc.
Oriental Garden/24/Ctown
Pearls/18/W 90s
Ping's Seafood/20/Multi. Loc.
Ruby Foo's/19/Multi. Loc.
Shun Lee/24/W 60s
Shun Lee Cafe/21/W 60s
Silver Pond/20/Flushing
Tai Hong Lau/20/Ctown
Triple Eight/19/Ctown
27 Sunrise Seafood/–/Ctown

Cuisine Index

Dominican
Cafe Con Leche/*17/Multi. Loc.*

Dutch
NL/*20/Village*

Eclectic/International
Anton's/*20/Village*
Barrio/*21/Low E Side*
Blue Elephant/*-/E 70s*
Blue Ribbon/*25/Multi. Loc.*
Blue Ribbon Bakery/*23/Village*
B. Smith's/*19/W 40s*
Café Boulud/*27/E 70s*
Carol's Cafe/*25/Staten Is.*
Chelsea Grill/*18/Chelsea*
China Grill/*23/W 50s*
Cupping Room Cafe/*17/SoHo*
Delegates' Din. Rm./*21/E 40s*
Dinerbar/*-/E 100s*
Dishes/*21/E 40s*
Druids/*18/W 50s*
East of Eighth/*17/Chelsea*
Eli's/*20/E 80s*
Eli's Vinegar Fact./*20/E 90s*
F & B/*19/Chelsea*
Global 33/*19/E Vil*
Guastavino, Downstairs/*18/E 50s*
Ivy's Bistro/*21/TriBeCa*
Kitchen Club/*22/SoHo*
Lipstick Cafe/*17/E 50s*
Liquors/*20/Ft. Greene*
Lot 61/*17/Chelsea*
Lucky Cheng's/*12/E Vil*
Luxia/*18/W 40s*
Mangia/*20/Multi. Loc.*
New Prospect Cafe/*19/Pr. Hts.*
Nicole's/*21/E 60s*
Oznot's Dish/*22/Williamsburg*
Pascalou/*21/E 90s*
Pierrot Bistro/*19/E Vil*
Rice/*19/Multi. Loc.*
Roy's NY/*24/Dtown*
Rue 57 Brasserie/*19/W 50s*
Sharz Cafe/*22/E 90s*
Spazzia/*18/W 70s*
Sugar Hill Bistro/*-/Harlem*
Thom/*-/SoHo*
Triomphe/*24/W 40s*
Wyanoka/*23/Little Italy*

Egyptian
Casa La Femme/*17/SoHo*
Mombar/*25/Astoria*

English
Chip Shop/*19/Park Slope*
Lady Mendl's/*22/Gramercy*
Landmark Tavern/*16/W 40s*

Eritrean
Adulis/*20/Flatiron*

Ethiopian
Ghenet/*20/SoHo*
Meskerem/*21/Multi. Loc.*
Queen of Sheba/*20/W 40s*

Filipino
Cendrillon/*21/SoHo*

Fish 'n' Chips
Chip Shop/*19/Park Slope*

French
Alain Ducasse/*26/W 50s*
Bayard's/*24/Dtown*
Bouterin/*22/E 50s*
Box Tree/*23/E 40s*
Brasserie Julien/*19/E 80s*
Café Botanica/*22/W 50s*
Café Boulud/*27/E 70s*
Café des Artistes/*24/W 60s*
Café Pierre/*23/E 60s*
Carlyle/*24/E 70s*
Chanterelle/*28/TriBeCa*
Chez Es Saada/*19/E Vil*
Chez Oskar/*20/Ft. Greene*
Chez Suzette/*17/W 40s*
Daniel/*28/E 60s*
Demarchelier/*17/E 80s*
Gaby Brasserie/*20/W 40s*
Gascogne/*22/Chelsea*
Guastavino, Upstairs/*21/E 50s*
Indochine/*21/Central Vil*
Jean Georges/*28/W 60s*
La Baraka/*22/Little Neck*
La Belle Epoque/*17/Central Vil*
La Bergamote/*22/Chelsea*
La Bicyclette/*17/W 80s*
L'Absinthe/*22/E 60s*
La Caravelle/*26/W 50s*
La Côte Basque/*26/W 50s*
La Grenouille/*27/E 50s*
La Metairie/*21/Village*
La Mirabelle/*22/W 80s*
Le Bernardin/*28/W 50s*
Le Cirque 2000/*26/E 50s*
L'Ecole/*24/SoHo*
Le Gamin/*18/Multi. Loc.*
Le Garrick/*19/W 40s*
Leopard, The/*21/E 50s*
Le Refuge/*23/E 80s*
Le Refuge Inn/*23/Bronx*
Le Rivage/*20/W 40s*
Lespinasse/*27/E 50s*
Levana/*21/W 60s*
L'Orange Bleue/*19/SoHo*
Loulou/*23/Ft. Greene*
Lutèce/*25/E 50s*

Cuisine Index

Mai-Lin/-/E 70s
Mark's/24/E 70s
Mercer Kitchen/23/SoHo
Métisse/22/W 100s
Montparnasse/20/E 50s
Montrachet/26/TriBeCa
Peacock Alley/23/E 40s
René Pujol/23/W 50s
Rhône/18/Meatpacking
Savann/19/W 70s
Sherwood Cafe/-/Cobble Hill
South Shore Country Club/20/ Staten Is.
Table d'Hôte/21/E 90s
Terrace in Sky/23/Columbia
Tocqueville/24/Union Sq.
Torch/20/Low E Side
Triomphe/24/W 40s
26 Seats/22/E Vil
Uguale/22/Village
Village/19/Village
Vong/25/E 50s
Willow/20/E 70s
Ye Waverly Inn/17/Village

French (Bistro)

A/-/W 100s
Abajour/18/E 60s
Alison on Dominick/24/SoHo
Alouette/21/W 90s
Artisanal/23/Murray Hill
À Table/19/Ft. Greene
Avenue/20/W 80s
Balthazar/23/SoHo
Banania Cafe/20/Carroll Gdns.
Bandol Bistro/19/E 70s
Bar Odeon/18/TriBeCa
Bar Six/16/Village
BarTabac/17/Boerum Hill
Belmondo/-/E Vil
Bienvenue/19/Murray Hill
Bistro du Nord/19/E 90s
Bistro Les Amis/20/SoHo
Bistro Le Steak/18/E 70s
Bistro St. Mark's/-/Park Slope
Bistrot Margot/19/SoHo
Bouchon/22/Village
Brasserie Julien/19/E 80s
Café Crocodile/21/E 70s
Café de Paris/19/E 40s
Cafe Deville/23/E Vil
Cafe du Pont/19/E 50s
Cafe Joul/21/E 50s
Cafe Loup/19/Village
Cafe Luluc/-/Carroll Gdns.
Cafe Luxembourg/21/W 70s
Cafe Petite Crevette/20/Bklyn Hts.
Cafe Un Deux Trois/16/W 40s
Capsouto Frères/24/TriBeCa
Casimir/21/E Vil
Chazal Bistro/19/Gramercy
Chelsea Bistro/22/Chelsea
Chez Bernard/19/Ctown
Chez Brigitte/18/Village
Chez Jacqueline/21/Village
Chez Ma Tante/19/Village
Chez Michallet/23/Village
Chez Napoléon/20/W 50s
Coq Hardi/20/Bklyn Hts.
Cornelia St. Cafe/19/Village
Country Cafe/21/SoHo
Danal/21/Central Vil
D'Artagnan/21/E 40s
db Bistro Moderne/-/W 40s
Deux Amis/19/E 50s
Elephant/22/E Vil
Félix/17/SoHo
Ferrier Bistro/19/E 60s
Flea Mkt. Cafe/19/E Vil
Florent/19/Meatpacking
French Roast/15/Multi. Loc.
Frère Jacques/18/Murray Hill
Grove/19/Village
Jarnac/23/Village
Jean Claude/23/SoHo
Jean-Luc/-/W 80s
Jo Jo/25/E 60s
Jubilee/23/E 50s
Jules/19/E Vil
La Belle Vie/19/Chelsea
La Boite en Bois/21/W 60s
La Bonne Soupe/17/W 50s
La Bouchée/17/Bklyn Hts.
La Bouillabaisse/23/Bklyn Hts.
L'Acajou/20/Flatiron
La Goulue/20/E 60s
La Lunchonette/21/Chelsea
La Mangeoire/20/E 50s
La Mediterranée/19/E 50s
La Petite Auberge/20/Gramercy
L'Ardoise/18/E 60s
La Ripaille/20/Village
La Tour/18/E 70s
Le Beaujolais/19/W 40s
Le Bilboquet/21/E 60s
Le Boeuf à la Mode/22/E 80s
Le Charlot/19/E 60s
Le Gigot/23/Village
Le Jardin Bistro/21/SoHo
Le Madeleine/20/W 40s
Le Marais/21/Multi. Loc.
L'Entrecote/19/E 50s
Le Père Pinard/20/Low E Side
Le Perigord/25/E 50s
Le Pescadou/20/SoHo
Le Petit Hulot/18/E 70s
Les Deux Gamins/19/Village
Les Halles/21/Gramercy

Cuisine Index

Le Singe Vert/*18/Chelsea*
Les Routiers/*20/W 80s*
Le Tableau/*23/E Vil*
Le Veau d'Or/*18/E 60s*
L'Express/*18/Flatiron*
Le Zinc/*20/TriBeCa*
Le Zoo/*20/Village*
Lucien/*19/E Vil*
Lucky Strike/*16/SoHo*
Madison Bistro/*19/Murray Hill*
Maison/*20/E 70s*
Manhattan Bistro/*19/SoHo*
Mignon/*23/Carroll Gdns.*
Mme. Romaine/*19/E 60s*
Mon Petit Cafe/*18/E 60s*
Odeon/*19/TriBeCa*
Orsay/*19/E 70s*
Papillon/*20/Village*
Paris Commune/*19/Village*
Park Bistro/*22/Gramercy*
Pascalou/*21/E 90s*
Pastis/*20/Meatpacking*
Patois/*22/Carroll Gdns.*
Payard Bistro/*24/E 70s*
Pergola/Artistes/*21/W 40s*
Pierre au Tunnel/*20/W 40s*
Pierrot Bistro/*19/E Vil*
Plate 347/*20/Gramercy*
Provence/*22/SoHo*
Provence en Boite/*23/Bay Ridge*
Quatorze Bis/*21/E 70s*
Raoul's/*23/SoHo*
Resto Léon/*19/E Vil*
Rive Gauche/*18/Murray Hill*
Seppi's/*19/W 50s*
Soho Steak/*20/SoHo*
Steak Frites/*18/Union Sq.*
St. Michel/*23/Bay Ridge*
Tartine/*22/Village*
Titou/*21/Village*
Tout Va Bien/*19/W 50s*
Vaux Bistro/*21/Park Slope*

French (New)

Adrienne/*23/W 50s*
Alouette/*21/W 90s*
Arabelle/*-/E 60s*
Banania Cafe/*20/Carroll Gdns.*
Bouley Bakery/*27/TriBeCa*
Cafe Alyss/*19/Village*
Café Pierre/*23/E 60s*
Cello/*26/E 70s*
Chez Josephine/*20/W 40s*
Chinoiserie/*17/Gramercy*
Destinée/*23/E 60s*
Fleur de Sel/*24/Flatiron*
14 Wall St./*20/Dtown*
Jacques/*19/E 80s*
Le Monde/*17/Columbia*
Medi/*-/W 50s*
Nicholson/*20/E 50s*
Petrossian/*24/W 50s*
Trois Marches/*20/E 80s*
Virot/*25/E 40s*

German

Gebhardt's/*20/Glendale*
Hallo Berlin/*18/Multi. Loc.*
Heidelberg/*18/E 80s*
Killmeyer's/*21/Staten Is.*
Niederstein's/*18/Middle Village, Qns*
Roettele A.G./*19/E Vil*
Rolf's/*18/Gramercy*
Zum Stammtisch/*23/Glendale*

Greek

Avra Estiatorio/*23/E 40s*
Briam/*20/E Vil*
Cafe Greco/*18/E 70s*
Christos Hasapo/*21/Astoria*
Eliá/*25/Bay Ridge*
Elias Corner/*24/Astoria*
Esperides/*22/Astoria*
Estia/*21/E 80s*
Gus' Place/*21/Village*
Ithaka/*23/Village*
It's Greek to Me/*-/E Vil*
Karyatis/*23/Astoria*
Kyma/*21/W 40s*
Meltemi/*20/E 50s*
Metsovo/*20/W 70s*
Milos/*26/W 50s*
Minotaur/*-/W 50s*
Molyvos/*23/W 50s*
Niko's/*19/W 70s*
Periyali/*25/Flatiron*
Rafina/*20/E 70s*
S'Agapo/*23/Astoria*
Snack/*23/SoHo*
Stamatis/*22/Multi. Loc.*
Syros Seafood/*23/Astoria*
Taverna Kyclades/*23/Astoria*
Taverna Vraka/*21/Astoria*
Telly's Taverna/*23/Astoria*
Trata/*22/E 70s*
Uncle George's/*20/Astoria*
Uncle Nick's/*20/Multi. Loc.*

Hamburgers

Big Nick's/*17/W 70s*
Bonnie's Grill/*20/Park Slope*
Broome St. Bar/*16/SoHo*
Burger Heaven/*15/Multi. Loc.*
Cal's/*19/Flatiron*
Charley O's/*13/W 40s*
Chelsea Grill/*18/Chelsea*
City Hall/*21/TriBeCa*
Corner Bistro/*23/Village*
Dallas BBQ/*15/Multi. Loc.*

Cuisine Index

Elephant & Castle/*18/Village*
Fanelli Cafe/*15/SoHo*
Hard Rock Cafe/*13/W 50s*
Harley Davidson Cafe/*12/W 50s*
Heartland Brewery/*14/Multi. Loc.*
Houlihan's/*11/Multi. Loc.*
Houston's/*20/Multi. Loc.*
Island Burgers/*21/W 50s*
Jackson Hole/*16/Multi. Loc.*
J.G. Melon/*18/E 70s*
Johnny Rockets/*15/Central Vil*
Luke's B&G/*17/E 70s*
McHales/*18/W 40s*
Old Town Bar/*15/Flatiron*
P.J. Clarke's/*15/E 50s*
Sandwich Planet/*20/Garment*
'21' Club/*22/W 50s*
White Horse/*13/Village*
Wollensky's Grill/*22/E 40s*

Health Food
Chop't Creative Salad/*21/Flatiron*
Dojo/*15/Multi. Loc.*
Emerald Planet/*17/Multi. Loc.*
Good Health Cafe/*-/E 80s*
Heartbeat/*20/E 40s*
Herban Kitchen/*20/SoHo*
Josie's/*22/Multi. Loc.*
Other Foods/*23/Central Vil*
Pump/*19/Multi. Loc.*
Quintessence/*21/E Vil*
Spring St. Natural/*19/SoHo*
Tossed/*19/Multi. Loc.*

Hot Dogs
F & B/*19/Chelsea*
Gray's Papaya/*19/Multi. Loc.*
Papaya King/*19/Multi. Loc.*
Serendipity 3/*19/E 60s*

Hungarian
Mocca/*18/E 80s*

Indian
Adä/*20/E 50s*
Baluchi's/*18/Multi. Loc.*
Banjara/*23/E Vil*
Bay Leaf/*21/W 50s*
Bombay Palace/*19/W 50s*
Bread Bar at Tabla/*24/Gramercy*
Bukhara Grill/*23/E 40s*
Cafe Spice/*20/Multi. Loc.*
Chola/*22/E 50s*
Curry Leaf/*19/Gramercy*
Dakshin/*20/Multi. Loc.*
Dawat/*23/E 50s*
Delhi Palace/*21/Jackson Hts.*
Diwan Grill/*21/E 40s*
Diwan's Curry Hse./*20/W 70s*
Hampton Chutney/*-/SoHo*
Haveli/*21/E Vil*
India Grill/*19/E 80s*
Jackson Diner/*23/Jackson Hts.*
Jewel of India/*21/W 40s*
Madras Cafe/*21/E Vil*
Mavalli Palace/*22/Gramercy*
Mirchi/*22/Village*
Mitali West/*19/Multi. Loc.*
Mughlai/*20/W 70s*
Namaskaar/*22/SoHo*
Nirvana/*17/W 50s*
Pamir/*20/Multi. Loc.*
Pongal/*20/Multi. Loc.*
Raga/*22/E Vil*
Salaam Bombay/*21/TriBeCa*
Sapphire/*22/W 60s*
Shaan/*22/W 40s*
Surya/*20/Village*
Tabla/*25/Gramercy*
Tamarind/*24/Flatiron*
Thali Vegetarian/*19/Village*
Utsav/*22/W 40s*
Vatan/*22/Gramercy*

Indonesian
Bali Nusa Indah/*18/W 40s*

Irish
Landmark Tavern/*16/W 40s*
Moran's Chelsea/*19/Chelsea*
Neary's/*17/E 50s*
Tír na nóg/*19/Garment*

Israeli
Azuri Cafe/*23/W 50s*

Italian
(N=Northern; S=Southern;
N&S=Includes both)
Acappella (N)/*23/TriBeCa*
Al Di La (N)/*23/Park Slope*
Alfredo of Rome (N&S)/*18/W 40s*
Amarone (N&S)/*19/W 40s*
Amici Amore I (N)/*21/Astoria*
Anche Vivolo (N&S)/*19/E 50s*
Angelina's (N&S)/*22/Staten Is.*
Angelo's/Mulberry (S)/*20/Lit. Italy*
Angelo's Pizzeria (S)/*20/W 50s*
Angels (N&S)/*17/E 60s*
Anton's (N&S)/*20/Village*
Areo (N&S)/*24/Bay Ridge*
Arezzo (N&S)/*-/Flatiron*
Arqua (N)/*23/TriBeCa*
Arté (N)/*18/Central Vil*
Arturo's Pizzeria (S)/*20/Village*
Artusi (N)/*19/W 50s*
Assaggio (N&S)/*-/W 80s*
Babbo (N&S)/*26/Village*
Bacco (N&S)/*20/SoHo*
Baci (N&S)/*18/W 70s*

www.zagat.com

Cuisine Index

Baci Italian (N&S)/*22/Bay Ridge*
Baldoria (N&S)/*20/W 40s*
Bamonte's (S)/*22/Williamsburg*
Baraonda (N)/*17/E 70s*
Barbaresco (N)/*18/E 60s*
Barbetta (N)/*20/W 40s*
Bardolino (N&S)/*18/E 70s*
Barolo (N)/*19/SoHo*
Bar Pitti (N)/*21/Village*
Basta Pasta (N&S)/*19/Flatiron*
Becco (N)/*20/W 40s*
Bella Blu (N)/*18/E 70s*
Bella Donna (N&S)/*17/Multi. Loc.*
Bella Luna (N)/*17/W 80s*
Bellavista Cafe (N&S)/*19/Bronx*
Bellini (N&S)/*22/E 50s*
Bello (N)/*21/W 50s*
Belluno (N)/*22/Murray Hill*
Beppe (N)/*21/Flatiron*
Bice (N)/*20/E 50s*
Biricchino (N)/*20/Chelsea*
Bondi Ristorante (S)/*21/Flatiron*
Borgo Antico (N&S)/*18/Central Vil*
Bot (N)/*17/SoHo*
Bottino (N)/*19/Chelsea*
Bravo Gianni (N)/*22/E 60s*
Bricco (S)/*19/W 50s*
Brio (N)/*19/E 60s*
Brunelli (N)/*19/E 70s*
Bruno (N&S)/*23/E 50s*
Bussola (S)/*20/Central Vil*
Cafe Fiorello (N&S)/*20/W 60s*
Cafe Nosidam (N&S)/*18/E 60s*
Cafe Picasso (N&S)/*20/Village*
Cafe Trevi (N)/*23/E 80s*
Caffe Cielo (N)/*19/W 50s*
Caffe Grazie (N&S)/*19/E 80s*
Caffe Linda (N&S)/*21/E 40s*
Caffé on Green (N&S)/*22/Bayside*
Caffe Rafaella (N)/*18/Village*
Caffe Reggio (N&S)/*17/Village*
Caffe Rosso (N&S)/*20/Village*
Campagna (N)/*24/Flatiron*
Campagnola (N&S)/*24/E 70s*
Canaletto (N)/*22/E 60s*
Candido Pizza (S)/*20/E 80s*
Cara Mia (N)/*20/W 40s*
Carino (S)/*21/E 80s*
Carmaya (N&S)/-/*Williamsburg*
Carmine's (S)/*20/Multi. Loc.*
Casa Mia (N&S)/*20/Gramercy*
Cascina (N&S)/-/*W 40s*
Castellano (N)/*20/W 50s*
Cellini (N)/*22/E 50s*
Cent'Anni (N)/*22/Village*
Centolire (N)/*19/E 80s*
Chelsea Rist. (N)/*20/Chelsea*
Chianti (N&S)/*20/Bay Ridge*
Chinghalle (N&S)/*18/Meatpacking*

Ciao (S)/-/*Village*
Ciao Europa (N&S)/*19/W 50s*
Cibo (N)/*21/E 40s*
Cinquanta (N&S)/*22/E 50s*
Cinque Terre (N)/*21/Murray Hill*
Circo (N)/*22/W 50s*
Coco Marina (N)/*17/Dtown*
Coco Pazzo (N)/*21/Multi. Loc.*
Cola's (N&S)/*19/Chelsea*
Col Legno (N)/*20/E Vil*
Coppola's (N&S)/*19/Multi. Loc.*
Cucina (N)/*24/Park Slope*
Cucina di Pesce (N&S)/*19/E Vil*
Da Andrea (N&S)/*22/Village*
Da Antonio (N&S)/*21/E 50s*
Da Ciro (N&S)/*21/Murray Hill*
Da Filippo (N)/*21/E 60s*
Da Nico (N&S)/*21/Little Italy*
Daniella (N&S)/*23/Chelsea*
Da Silvano (N)/*22/Village*
Da Tommaso (N)/*21/W 50s*
Da Umberto (N)/*24/Chelsea*
DeGrezia (N)/*23/E 50s*
Divino (N)/*19/E 80s*
Domani (N&S)/*23/E 80s*
Dominick's (S)/*22/Bronx*
Don Giovanni (N&S)/*18/Multi. Loc.*
Don Peppe (N)/*24/Ozone Pk.*
Due (N)/*21/E 70s*
East Post (N&S)/*22/E Vil*
East River Cafe (N)/*19/E 60s*
Ecco (N&S)/*21/TriBeCa*
Ecco-la (N&S)/*18/E 90s*
Elaine's (N&S)/*14/E 80s*
Elio's (N&S)/*23/E 80s*
Ennio & Michael (N&S)/*21/Central Vil*
Enoteca i Trulli (S)/*23/Gramercy*
Enzo's (N&S)/*23/Bronx*
Erminia (N)/*24/E 80s*
Ernie's (N&S)/*16/W 70s*
Esca (S)/*23/W 40s*
Felidia (N&S)/*25/E 50s*
Ferdinando's (S)/*21/Carroll Gdns.*
Ferrara (N&S)/*20/Multi. Loc.*
F.illi Ponte (N&S)/*22/TriBeCa*
Fino (N)/*20/Murray Hill/E 30s*
Fiorentino's (N&S)/*20/Gravesend*
Firenze (N)/*21/E 80s*
Frank (N&S)/*23/E Vil*
Frank's (N&S)/*21/Meatpacking*
Fred's at Barneys (N)/*19/E 60s*
Fresco by Scotto (N)/*23/E 50s*
Fresco on the Go (N)/*20/E 50s*
Frutti di Mare (N&S)/*18/E Vil*
Gabriel's (N)/*23/W 60s*
Gargiulo's (S)/*22/Coney Is.*
Gene's (N&S)/*19/Village*
Gennaro (N&S)/*25/W 90s*
Giambelli (N)/*21/E 50s*

Cuisine Index

Gigino Trattoria (N)/*21/TriBeCa*
Gigino/Wagner Pk. (S)/*19/Dtown*
Gino (S)/*20/E 60s*
Giovanni (N)/*20/W 50s*
Giovanni Venticinque (N)/*21/E 80s*
Girasole (N&S)/*21/E 80s*
Gnocco Caffe (N&S)/*21/E Vil*
Grace's Trattoria (N&S)/*18/E 70s*
Gradisca (N)/*19/Village*
Grano Trattoria (N&S)/*18/Village*
Grappa Café (N&S)/*20/Bklyn Hts.*
Grifone (N)/*23/E 40s*
Harry Cipriani (N)/*22/E 50s*
I Coppi (N)/*22/E Vil*
Il Bagatto (N&S)/*23/E Vil*
Il Buco (N&S)/*22/NoHo*
Il Cantinori (N)/*23/Central Vil*
Il Corallo (N&S)/*21/Little Italy*
Il Cortile (N&S)/*23/Little Italy*
Il Covo dell'Est (N)/*20/E Vil*
Il Fornaio (N)/*22/Little Italy*
Il Gatto/La Volpe (N)/*21/E 60s*
Il Giglio (N)/*25/Dtown*
Il Menestrello (N&S)/*21/E 50s*
Il Monello (N)/*-/E 70s*
Il Mulino (N)/*27/Village*
Il Nido (N)/*24/E 50s*
Il Palazzo (N)/*23/Little Italy*
Il Postino (N&S)/*23/E 40s*
Il Riccio (S)/*21/E 70s*
Il Tinello (N)/*24/W 50s*
Il Vagabondo (N)/*18/E 60s*
Il Valentino (N)/*21/E 50s*
'ino (N&S)/*22/Village*
Intermezzo (N&S)/*19/Chelsea*
Isola (N&S)/*19/W 80s*
I Tre Merli (N)/*17/SoHo*
I Trulli (S)/*23/Gramercy*
Joanna's (N)/*18/E 90s*
John's of 12th St. (N&S)/*20/E Vil*
John's Pizzeria (N&S)/*21/Multi. Loc.*
La Cantina (S)/*25/Village*
La Giara (N&S)/*19/Murray Hill*
La Gioconda (N)/*21/E 50s*
La Grolla, Rist. (N)/*20/Multi. Loc.*
La Houppa (N)/*18/E 60s*
La Locanda (N)/*20/W 40s*
La Mela (N&S)/*19/Little Italy*
La Nonna (N)/*19/Village*
Lanza (N)/*17/E Vil*
La Pizza Fresca (N)/*21/Flatiron*
La Rivista (N)/*19/W 40s*
Lattanzi (N)/*22/W 40s*
Le Madri (N)/*22/Chelsea*
Lentini (N&S)/*21/E 80s*
Letizia Amore (N&S)/*-/E 70s*
Le Zie 2000 (N)/*22/Chelsea*
Limoncello (N&S)/*21/W 50s*
Locanda Vini (N)/*22/Clinton Hill*

Loui Loui (N&S)/*16/E 70s*
Luca (N)/*21/E 80s*
L'Ulivo Focacceria (N&S)/*-/SoHo*
Lumi (N&S)/*19/E 70s*
Luna Blu (N&S)/*19/E 40s*
Luna Piena (N&S)/*19/E 50s*
Lupa (N&S)/*24/Village*
Lusardi's (N)/*24/E 70s*
Luxia (N)/*18/W 40s*
Macelleria (N)/*20/Meatpacking*
Malatesta Trattoria (N)/*21/Village*
Manducatis (S)/*23/LIC*
Mangia e Bevi (S)/*17/W 50s*
Mangiarini (N)/*21/E 80s*
Marchi's (N)/*20/Murray Hill*
Marco Polo (N)/*21/Carroll Gdns.*
Marinella (N&S)/*21/Village*
Mario's (S)/*20/Bronx*
Maristella (N)/*22/W 50s*
Maruzzella (N)/*19/E 70s*
Massimo/Ponte (N&S)/*21/Village*
Max (S)/*23/Multi. Loc.*
Medi (N)/*-/W 50s*
Mediterraneo (N)/*19/E 60s*
Mezzaluna (N&S)/*19/E 70s*
Mezzogiorno (N&S)/*20/SoHo*
Minetta Tavern (N&S)/*17/Village*
Miss Williamsburg (N&S)/*21/W'burg*
Montebello (N)/*22/E 50s*
Monte's (N)/*18/Village*
Monte's (S)/*21/Carroll Gdns.*
Mooza (N)/*-/Low E Side*
Mosto (N)/*-/E Vil*
Mugsy's Chow (N&S)/*21/E Vil*
Nanni's (N)/*24/E 40s*
Naples 45 (S)/*17/E 40s*
Nello (N)/*18/Multi. Loc.*
Nicola Paone (N)/*21/Murray Hill*
Nicola's (N)/*22/E 80s*
Nino's (N)/*23/E 70s*
Nino's Positano (S)/*19/E 40s*
Nocello (N)/*22/W 50s*
Nonna (N&S)/*-/Village*
Noodle Pudding (N&S)/*22/Bklyn Hts.*
Notaro (N)/*19/Murray Hill*
Novitá (N)/*23/Gramercy*
Oggi (S)/*19/E Vil*
101 (N&S)/*20/Bay Ridge*
Oro Blu (N&S)/*20/SoHo*
Orso (N)/*22/W 40s*
Osso Buco (N)/*17/Multi. Loc.*
Osteria al Doge (N)/*20/W 40s*
Osteria Laguna (N)/*20/E 40s*
Palio (N)/*23/W 50s*
Palma (N&S)/*-/Village*
Paola's (N&S)/*23/E 80s*
Paper Moon Milano (N)/*19/E 50s*
Paprika (N)/*23/E Vil*

www.zagat.com 229

Cuisine Index

Park Side (N&S)/*24/Corona*
Parma (N)/*21/E 70s*
Pasticcio (N&S)/*20/Murray Hill*
Patsy's (S)/*20/W 50s*
Paul & Jimmy's (N&S)/*19/Gramercy*
Peasant (N&S)/*22/SoHo*
Pellegrino's (N&S)/*22/Little Italy*
Pepe Giallo (N&S)/*22/Multi. Loc.*
Pepolino (N)/*24/TriBeCa*
Pescatore (N&S)/*19/E 50s*
Petaluma (N&S)/*19/E 70s*
Pete's D'town (N&S)/*20/Bklyn Hts.*
Piadina (N)/*19/Village*
Piccola Venezia (N&S)/*25/Astoria*
Piccolo Angolo (N)/*24/Village*
Pietrasanta (N)/*20/W 40s*
Pietro's (N)/*23/E 40s*
Pinocchio (N&S)/*20/E 90s*
Pó (N&S)/*24/Village*
Pomodoro Rosso (N&S)/*21/W 70s*
Ponticello (N)/*24/Astoria*
Porto Bello (N&S)/*21/Village*
Portofino Grille (N&S)/*20/E 60s*
Positano (S)/*20/Little Italy*
Primavera (N)/*24/E 80s*
Primola (N&S)/*23/E 60s*
Psychic Cafe (N&S)/*-/Village*
Puttanesca (N&S)/*19/W 50s*
Quartino (N)/*19/Dtown*
Quattro Gatti (N&S)/*20/E 80s*
Queen (N&S)/*24/Bklyn Hts.*
Rafaella (N)/*21/Village*
Raffaele (N)/*21/E 50s*
Rainbow Room (N)/*22/W 40s*
Rao's (S)/*24/E 100s*
Remi (N)/*23/W 50s*
Ribollita (N)/*18/Flatiron*
Rist. del Sogno (N)/*18/W 50s*
Roberto's (N)/*25/Bronx*
Roc (N&S)/*23/TriBeCa*
Rocco (N&S)/*21/Village*
Rossini's (N)/*21/Murray Hill*
Sal Anthony's (N&S)/*17/Gramercy*
Sal Anthony SPQR (N&S)/*18/Lit. Italy*
Salute! (N)/*18/Multi. Loc.*
Sambuca (S)/*19/W 70s*
San Domenico (N&S)/*23/W 50s*
Sandro's (N)/*23/Chelsea*
San Giusto (N)/*22/E 40s*
San Pietro (S)/*24/E 50s*
Sant Ambroeus (N)/*21/E 70s*
Sapore (N&S)/*21/Village*
Sapori d'Ischia (S)/*-/Woodside*
Savore (N)/*21/SoHo*
Scaletta (N)/*21/W 70s*
Scalinatella (N&S)/*24/E 60s*
Scalini Fedeli (N)/*26/TriBeCa*
Scopa (N&S)/*22/Gramercy*
Serafina (N&S)/*19/Multi. Loc.*
Sette Mezzo (N&S)/*22/E 70s*
Sette MoMA (N&S)/*18/W 50s*
Sirabella's (N)/*22/E 80s*
Sistina (N)/*23/E 80s*
Sosa Borella (N)/*20/TriBeCa*
Spada (N)/*20/E 80s*
Stella del Mare (N)/*21/Murray Hill*
Supreme Mac. (N&S)/*18/Garment*
Tanti Baci (N&S)/*19/Multi. Loc.*
Taormina (N&S)/*20/Little Italy*
Tello's (N&S)/*18/Chelsea*
Teodora (N)/*21/E 50s*
Tevere (N&S)/*23/E 80s*
Tino's (N)/*19/W 50s*
Tommaso's (N&S)/*23/Bensonhurst*
Tony's Di Napoli (S)/*18/E 80s*
Torre di Pisa (N)/*19/W 40s*
Tratt. Alba (N)/*20/Murray Hill*
Tratt. Dopo Teatro (N&S)/*17/W 40s*
Tratt. L'incontro (N&S)/*25/Astoria*
Trattoria Chianti (N&S)/*20/E 50s*
Trattoria Dell'Arte (N&S)/*22/W 50s*
Tratt. Pesce/Pasta (N&S)/*20/Multi.*
Tratt. Romana (N&S)/*25/Staten Is.*
Tratt. Rustica (N&S)/*20/E 60s*
Tratt. Spaghetto (N&S)/*19/Village*
Tre Pomodori (N&S)/*19/Multi. Loc.*
Triangolo (N&S)/*21/E 80s*
Tuscan Sq. (N&S)/*19/W 50s*
Tuscan Steak (N)/*20/E 40s*
Tuscany Grill (N)/*23/Bay Ridge*
Two Toms (S)/*22/Boerum Hill*
Uguale (N&S)/*22/Village*
Va Bene (N&S)/*22/E 80s*
Va Tutto! (N)/*19/SoHo*
Veniero's (N&S)/*23/E Vil*
Veronica (N&S)/*19/Garment*
Via Oreto (S)/*22/E 60s*
Via Quadronno (N)/*22/E 70s*
Viareggio (N&S)/*20/E 70s*
ViceVersa (N&S)/*22/W 50s*
Vico (N&S)/*20/E 90s*
Villa Berulia (N)/*22/Murray Hill*
Villa Mosconi (N)/*21/Village*
Vittorio Cucina (N)/*22/Village*
Vivolo (N&S)/*20/E 70s*
Volare (N&S)/*22/Village*

Jamaican

Brawta Caribbean/*19/Boerum Hill*
Maroons/*22/Chelsea*
Mo-Bay/*-/Ft. Greene*
Negril/*20/Chelsea*

Japanese

Ajisen Noodle/*-/Ctown*
Aki Sushi/*18/E 70s*
Basta Pasta/*19/Flatiron*
Benihana/*17/Multi. Loc.*
Blue Ribbon Sushi/*26/SoHo*

Cuisine Index

Bond Street/25/NoHo
Chikubu/22/E 40s
Choshi/19/Gramercy
Donguri/26/E 80s
East/-/Multi. Loc.
Empire Szechuan/16/Multi. Loc.
Friend House/-/E Vil
Fujiyama Mama/20/W 80s
Gingko Leaf Cafe/-/Park Slope
Go Sushi/-/Multi. Loc.
Haikara Grill/21/E 50s
Hakata Grill/-/W 40s
Hamachi/21/Flatiron
Haru/23/Multi. Loc.
Hasaki/25/E Vil
Hatsuhana/25/Multi. Loc.
Honmura An/25/SoHo
Ikeno Hana/20/E 70s
Inagiku/24/E 40s
Iso/24/E Vil
Ivy's Cafe/19/W 70s
Japonica/23/Central Vil
Jeollado/20/E Vil
Jewel Bako/-/E Vil
Jimmy Sung's/19/E 40s
Junno's/21/Village
Katsuhama/21/E 40s
Kazusa/-/E 70s
Kiiroi-Hana/19/W 50s
Kitchen Club/22/E Vil
Kodama Sushi/19/Multi. Loc.
Kotobuki Bistro/-/Carroll Gdns
Kuruma Zushi/27/E 40s
Lan/23/E Vil
Marumi/23/Central Vil
Menchanko-tei/17/Multi. Loc.
Mishima/20/Murray Hill
Monster Sushi/19/Multi. Loc.
Nadaman Hakubai/24/Murray Hill
Nëo Sushi/22/W 80s
Nippon/23/E 50s
Nobu/28/TriBeCa
Obeca Li/19/TriBeCa
Ohta/-/Murray Hill
Oikawa/20/E 50s
Omen/24/SoHo
Onigashima/19/W 50s
Osaka/22/Cobble Hill
Otabe/23/E 50s
Planet Sushi/18/W 70s
Planet Thailand/23/Williamsburg
Roppongi/20/W 80s
Sachi/22/E 90s
Sandobe/22/E Vil
Sapporo East/21/E Vil
Sekku/21/Murray Hill/E 30s
Sen-ya/-/Village
Seo/24/E 40s
Seryna/24/E 50s
Shabu-Shabu 70/20/E 70s
Shabu-Tatsu/20/Multi. Loc.
Soba-ya/23/E Vil
Sugiyama/26/W 50s
Sushi a-go-go/-/W 60s
Sushiden/24/Multi. Loc.
Sushi Hana/23/E 70s
Sushihatsu/24/E 60s
Sushi Jones/-/Flatiron
Sushi of Gari/26/E 70s
Sushi Rose/22/E 50s
Sushi Samba/23/Multi. Loc.
Sushisay/25/E 50s
Sushi Sen-nin/25/Murray Hill
Sushiya/22/W 50s
Sushi Yasuda/27/E 40s
Sushi Zen/25/W 40s
Taka/25/Village
Takahachi/22/E Vil
Tatany/22/Multi. Loc.
Tea Box/21/E 50s
Ten Kai/21/W 50s
Tomoe Sushi/27/Village
Tomo Sushi/19/Columbia
Toraya/22/E 70s
Wasabi/20/Multi. Loc.
Yama/25/Multi. Loc.
Yuka/-/E 80s
Zutto/21/Multi. Loc.

Jewish

Artie's Deli/15/W 80s
Barney Greengrass/23/W 80s
Ben's Kosher Deli/18/Multi. Loc.
E.A.T./20/E 80s
Ess-a-Bagel/21/Multi. Loc.
Essex/21/Low E Side
Fine & Schapiro/16/W 70s
Katz's Deli/21/Low E Side
Ratner's/16/Low E Side
Sammy's Roumanian/19/Low E Side
Sarge's Deli/17/Murray Hill/E 30s
Second Ave. Deli/23/E Vil
Stage Deli/19/W 50s
Wolf's/16/W 50s

Korean

Cho Dang Gol/23/Garment/W 30s
Clay/19/SoHo
Do Hwa/21/Village
Dok Suni's/21/E Vil
Emo's/19/E 80s
Gam Mee Ok/21/Garment
Hangawi/24/Murray Hill
Jeollado/20/E Vil
Kang Suh/21/Garment
Korea Palace/18/E 50s
Kori/19/Dtown
Kum Gang San/22/Multi. Loc.
Muzy/-/E Vil

Cuisine Index

Won Jo/*21/Garment*
Woo Chon/*21/Multi. Loc.*
Woo Lae Oak/*22/SoHo*

Lebanese
Al Bustan/*19/E 50s*

Malaysian
Ba Ba Malaysian/*21/Ctown*
Nyonya/*23/Multi. Loc.*
Penang/*19/Multi. Loc.*

Mediterranean
Acquario/*20/NoHo*
Adulis/*20/Flatiron*
Aesop's Tables/*22/Staten Is.*
Amaranth/*16/E 60s*
Bouterin/*22/E 50s*
Briam/*20/E Vil*
Café Botanica/*22/W 50s*
Cafe Centro/*19/E 40s*
Café Crocodile/*21/E 70s*
Cafe Greco/*18/E 70s*
Cafe Mogador/*21/E Vil*
Cafe Noir/*17/SoHo*
Cal's/*19/Flatiron*
Cola's/*19/Chelsea*
Convivium Osteria/*25/Park Slope*
Coq Hardi/*20/Bklyn Hts.*
Epices du Traiteur/*19/W 70s*
Figs/*19/Flushing*
Five Points/*21/NoHo*
Gus' Figs/*20/Chelsea*
Gus' Place/*21/Village*
Il Buco/*22/NoHo*
Isabella's/*20/W 70s*
Jarnac/*23/Village*
Julian's/*20/W 50s*
La Corniche/-/*E 60s*
La Houppa/*18/E 60s*
Lavagna/*23/E Vil*
Layla/*19/TriBeCa*
Mangia/*20/Multi. Loc.*
Mare/*17/Chelsea*
Metronome/*19/Flatiron*
Mignon/*23/Carroll Gdns.*
Mooza/-/*Low E Side*
Nick & Toni's/*19/W 60s*
Niko's/*19/W 70s*
Nisos/*18/Chelsea*
Olives/*23/Union Sq.*
Pangea/*19/E Vil*
Park, The/*19/Chelsea*
Picholine/*27/W 60s*
Pitchoune/*19/Gramercy*
Place/*22/Village*
Red Cat/*22/Chelsea*
Rose Water/*24/Park Slope*
Savoy/*23/SoHo*
Shallots NY/*20/E 50s*
Sharz Cafe/*22/E 90s*
Sirocco/-/*SoHo*
Spazzia/*18/W 70s*
Sugar Bar/*20/W 70s*
Tappo/*22/E Vil*
Tazza/*20/Chelsea*
Terrace in Sky/*23/Morningside*
3333/*21/Staten Is.*
Verbena/*24/Gramercy*

Mexican/Tex-Mex
Baby Bo's/-/*Murray Hill*
Benny's Burritos/*17/Multi. Loc.*
Bright Food Shop/*19/Chelsea*
Burritoville/*16/Multi. Loc.*
Café Frida/*18/W 70s*
Café Habana/*20/SoHo*
Casa Mexicana/*20/Low E Side*
Cosmic Cantina/-/*E Vil*
Danzón/-/*Gramercy*
El Parador/*20/Murray Hill*
El Rio Grande/*17/Murray Hill*
El Teddy's/*17/TriBeCa*
Gabriela's/*18/Multi. Loc.*
Hell's Kitchen/*23/W 40s*
Komodo/*23/E Vil*
La Cocina/*19/Multi. Loc.*
La Flor Bakery/-/*Woodside*
La Palapa/*23/E Vil*
Lexi's/-/*Village*
Los Dos Molinos/*20/Gramercy*
Mamá Mexico/*21/W 100s*
Mary Ann's/*17/Multi. Loc.*
Maya/*25/E 60s*
Maz Mezcal/*21/E 80s*
Mexicana Mama/*23/Village*
Mexican Radio/*19/SoHo*
Mi Cocina/*22/Village*
Rocking Horse/*20/Chelsea*
Rosa Mexicano/*23/Multi. Loc.*
Taqueria de Mexico/*18/Village*
Tio Pepe/*19/Village*
Tortilla Flats/*17/Village*
Vera Cruz/*18/Williamsburg*
Zarela/*22/E 50s*
Zócalo/*20/Multi. Loc.*

Middle Eastern
Al Bustan/*19/E 50s*
Azuri Cafe/*23/W 50s*
Cafe Mogador/*21/E Vil*
Layla/*19/TriBeCa*
Mamlouk/*21/E Vil*
Moustache/*22/Multi. Loc.*
Oznot's Dish/*22/Williamsburg*
Sahara/*21/Gravesend*
Salam Cafe/*22/Village*

Cuisine Index

Moroccan
Al Baraka/*19/E 80s*
Bar Six/*16/Village*
Chez Es Saada/*19/E Vil*
Cookies & Couscous/*19/Village*
Country Cafe/*21/SoHo*
Darna/*22/W 80s*
Le Souk/*19/E Vil*
L'Orange Bleue/*19/SoHo*
Lotfi's/*19/W 40s*
Tagine Dining/*19/Garment*

Noodle Shops
Ajisen Noodle/*-/Ctown*
Big Wong/*21/Ctown*
Bo-Ky/*20/Ctown*
Great NY Noodle/*22/Ctown*
Honmura An/*25/SoHo*
Kelley & Ping/*18/SoHo*
Lili's Noodle/*18/Multi. Loc.*
Mee Noodle/*-/Multi. Loc.*
Menchanko-tei/*17/Multi. Loc.*
Noodles on 28/*19/Gramercy*
Ollie's/*16/Multi. Loc.*
Pho Bang/*19/Multi. Loc.*
Pho Viet Huong/*22/Ctown*
Republic/*17/Union Sq.*
Sammy's/*18/Multi. Loc.*
Sam's Noodle Shop/*20/Gramercy*
Soba-ya/*23/E Vil*
Sweet-n-Tart/*20/Multi. Loc.*

Nuevo Latino
Babalu/*20/W 40s*
Beso/*20/Park Slope*
Cabana Nuevo/*21/Multi. Loc.*
Esperanto/*21/E Vil*
Jimmy's Bronx Cafe/*19/Bronx*
Jimmy's Uptown/*21/Harlem*
Patria/*24/Flatiron*
Sabor/*20/W 80s*
Sol/*19/Ft. Greene*
Sonora/*20/Murray Hill*

Persian
Persepolis/*19/E 70s*

Peruvian
Cocina Cuzco/*20/Multi. Loc.*
Coco Roco/*21/Park Slope*
Flor de Mayo/*19/Multi. Loc.*
Rinconcito Peruano/*19/W 50s*
Sipan/*22/W 90s*

Pizza
Angelo's Pizzeria/*20/W 50s*
Arturo's Pizzeria/*20/Village*
Bella Blu/*18/E 70s*
Bella Donna/*17/Multi. Loc.*
Bellavista Cafe/*19/Bronx*
Cafe Picasso/*20/Village*
California Pizza/*15/Multi. Loc.*
Candido Pizza/*20/E 80s*
Chelsea Rist./*20/Chelsea*
Denino's Pizzeria/*23/Staten Is.*
Don Giovanni/*18/Multi. Loc.*
Grimaldi's/*26/Bklyn Hts.*
Joe's Pizza/*22/Multi. Loc.*
John's Pizzeria/*21/Multi. Loc.*
La Pizza Fresca/*21/Flatiron*
Little Italy Pizza/*20/Multi. Loc.*
Lombardi's/*24/SoHo*
Mediterraneo/*19/E 60s*
Moustache/*22/Multi. Loc.*
Naples 45/*17/E 40s*
Nick's Pizza/*24/Forest Hills*
Patsy's Pizzeria/*21/Multi. Loc.*
Pintaile's Pizza/*18/Multi. Loc.*
Pizzeria Uno/*15/Multi. Loc.*
Slice of Harlem/*20/Multi. Loc.*
Totonno Pizzeria/*22/Multi. Loc.*
Two Boots/*19/Multi. Loc.*
V&T/*18/Columbia*
Vinnie's Pizza/*21/W 70s*

Polish
Christine's/*16/E Vil*
Teresa's/*18/Multi. Loc.*

Portuguese
Alfama/*20/Village*
Alphabet Kitchen/*21/E Vil*
Luzia's/*19/W 80s*
Pão!/*22/SoHo*
Pico/*23/TriBeCa*

Puerto Rican
La Taza de Oro/*19/Chelsea*
Old San Juan/*18/W 50s*

Russian
Caviarteria/*22/E 50s*
FireBird/*21/W 40s*
Petrossian/*24/W 50s*
Rasputin/*20/Brighton Bch.*
Russian Samovar/*21/W 50s*
Russian Tea Rm./*19/W 50s*

Scandinavian
Aquavit/*26/W 50s*
Christer's/*22/W 50s*
Good World B&G/*19/Low E Side*
Tja!/*20/TriBeCa*
Ulrika's/*22/E 60s*

Seafood
Acquario/*20/NoHo*
American Park/*19/Dtown*
Aquagrill/*25/SoHo*
Aquavit/*26/W 50s*

Cuisine Index

Atlantic Grill/*22/E 70s*
Barney Greengrass/*23/W 80s*
Blue Water Grill/*24/Union Sq.*
Cafe Petite Crevette/*20/Bklyn Hts.*
Captain's Table/*18/E 40s*
Cello/*26/E 70s*
Christer's/*22/W 50s*
Citarella/-/*W 40s*
City Crab/*19/Flatiron*
Dalga Seafood/*23/E 60s*
Docks Oyster/*21/Multi. Loc.*
Dolphins/*19/Central Vil*
Elias Corner/*24/Astoria*
Esca/*23/W 40s*
Esperides/*22/Astoria*
Estia/*21/E 80s*
Fifth Ave. Seafood/-/*Harlem*
Fish/*21/Village*
Fish/*19/W 100s*
Foley's Fish Hse./*20/W 40s*
Frutti di Mare/*18/E Vil*
Gage & Tollner/*22/Bklyn Hts.*
Harry's/Hanover Sq./*18/Dtown*
Jack Rose/*17/W 40s*
Jade Plaza/*22/Sunset Pk.*
Kam Chueh/*24/Ctown*
La Bouillabaisse/*23/Bklyn Hts.*
Lansky Lounge/*18/Low E Side*
Le Bernardin/*28/W 50s*
Le Pescadou/*20/SoHo*
Lobster Box/*18/Bronx*
London Lennie's/*22/Rego Pk.*
Lundy Bros./*16/Multi. Loc.*
Manhattan Ocean/*25/W 50s*
Mare/*17/Chelsea*
Marina Cafe/*18/Staten Is.*
Mario's Seafood/*21/Murray Hill*
Maritime/*23/W 40s*
Marylou's/*19/Village*
Mary's Fish Camp/*25/Village*
Meltemi/*20/E 50s*
Metro Fish/*20/Murray Hill*
Metsovo/*20/W 70s*
Milos/*26/W 50s*
Moondance/-/*Murray Hill*
Moran's Chelsea/*19/Chelsea*
Oceana/*27/E 50s*
Ocean Grill/*23/W 70s*
Oriental Garden/*24/Ctown*
Oyster Bar/*22/E 40s*
Oyster Bar/Plaza/*20/W 50s*
Pearl Oyster Bar/*26/Village*
Pescatore/*19/E 50s*
Pier 25A/*17/Bayside*
Ping's Seafood/*20/Multi. Loc.*
Pisces/*21/E Vil*
Red Garlic/*21/W 50s*
Roy's NY/*24/Dtown*
Sag Harbor/*20/W 40s*
Salmon River/-/*E 40s*
Sea Grill/*23/W 40s*
Seven/*21/Chelsea*
Shaffer City Oyster/*23/Flatiron*
Silver Pond/*20/Flushing*
Smith St. Kitchen/*23/Boerum Hill*
Stella del Mare/*21/Murray Hill*
Taverna Kyclades/*23/Astoria*
Telly's Taverna/*23/Astoria*
Trata/*22/E 70s*
Tropica/*22/E 40s*
Tupelo Grill/*20/Garment*
27 Sunrise Seafood/-/*Ctown*

Soups

Daily Soup/*18/Multi. Loc.*
Hale & Hearty Soups/*20/Multi. Loc.*
Soma Soup/*18/W 70s*
Soup Kitchen Int'l/*27/W 50s*

South African

Madiba/*19/Ft. Greene*

South American

Bistro Latino/*18/W 50s*
Boca Chica/*19/E Vil*
Cabana Nuevo/*21/Multi. Loc.*
Calle Ocho/*22/W 80s*
Campo/*18/W 80s*
Chicama/*22/Flatiron*
Chimichurri Grill/*21/W 40s*
Churrascaria Plataforma/*22/W 40s*
Coco Roco/*21/Park Slope*
Coffee Shop/*16/Union Sq.*
Flor's Kitchen/*19/E Vil*
good/*20/Village*
Ideya/*20/SoHo*
Lola's Buena Vista/-/*E 70s*
Paladar/*20/Low E Side*
Patria/*24/Flatiron*
Sabor/*20/W 80s*
Sonora/*20/Murray Hill*
Sushi Samba/*23/Multi. Loc.*
Torch/*20/Low E Side*

Southern/Soul

Acme B&G/*15/NoHo*
Amy Ruth's/*21/Harlem*
Brother Jimmy's/*15/Multi. Loc.*
Brothers BBQ/*16/Village*
Bubby's/*19/TriBeCa/Dtown*
Charles' Southern/*27/Harlem*
Copeland's/*19/Harlem*
Duke's/*17/Gramercy*
Emily's/*18/E 110s*
Fifth Ave. Seafood/-/*Harlem*
Great Jones Cafe/*19/NoHo*
Harvest/*17/Cobble Hill*
Jezebel/*20/W 40s*

Cuisine Index

Jimmy's Uptown/21/*Harlem*
Justin's/17/*Flatiron*
Lola/20/*Flatiron*
Londel's/19/*Harlem*
Mardi Gras/21/*Forest Hills*
Maroons/22/*Chelsea*
Mekka/21/*E Vil*
Miss Mamie's/Maude's/20/*Multi.*
Mo-Bay/-/*Ft. Greene*
Pink Tea Cup/18/*Village*
Shark Bar/20/*W 70s*
Shoebox Cafe/21/*E 40s*
Soul Cafe/19/*W 40s*
Soul Fixins'/19/*Garment*
Sugar Hill Bistro/-/*Harlem*
Sylvia's/18/*Harlem*

Southwestern

Arizona 206/18/*E 60s*
Canyon Rd. Grill/20/*E 70s*
Cilantro/18/*Multi. Loc.*
Citrus B&G/18/*W 70s*
Cowgirl Hall of Fame/15/*Village*
Los Dos Molinos/21/*Gramercy*
Manhattan Chili/15/*Multi. Loc.*
Mesa Grill/24/*Union Sq.*
Miracle Grill/20/*Multi. Loc.*
Santa Fe/19/*W 60s*

Spanish

AKA Cafe/-/*Low E Side*
Allioli/-/*Williamsburg*
Alphabet Kitchen/21/*E Vil*
Bolo/23/*Flatiron*
Cafe Español/19/*Multi. Loc.*
Don Luca/-/*Carroll Gdns.*
El Charro Español/20/*Village*
El Cid/22/*Chelsea*
El Faro/21/*Village*
El Pote/22/*Murray Hill*
El Quijote/20/*Chelsea*
Flor de Sol/20/*TriBeCa*
1492 Food/21/*Low E Side*
Francisco's Centro/22/*Chelsea*
La Paella/21/*E Vil*
Malaga/20/*E 70s*
Marbella/19/*Bayside*
Marichu/23/*E 40s*
Meigas/24/*SoHo*
Ñ/18/*SoHo*
Oliva/20/*Low E Side*
Pipa/21/*Flatiron*
Riazor/19/*Chelsea*
Rincón de España/21/*Village*
Rio Mar/17/*Meatpacking*
Sala/18/*NoHo*
Sevilla/22/*Village*
Solera/22/*E 50s*
Tinto/18/*Bklyn Hts.*
Tio Pepe/19/*Village*
Toledo/22/*Murray Hill*
Xunta/20/*E Vil*

Steakhouses

Angelo & Maxie's/21/*Multi. Loc.*
Ben Benson's/23/*W 50s*
Benihana/17/*Multi. Loc.*
Billy's/16/*E 50s*
Bobby Van's/22/*E 40s*
Bull & Bear/19/*E 40s*
Chadwick's/20/*Bay Ridge*
Chimichurri Grill/21/*W 40s*
Christos Hasapo/21/*Astoria*
Churrascaria Plataforma/22/*W 40s*
Cité/22/*W 50s*
Cité Grill/21/*W 50s*
Dan Maxwell's/18/*E 80s*
Del Frisco's/22/*W 40s*
Delmonico's/20/*Dtown*
Dylan Prime/22/*TriBeCa*
Embers/22/*Bay Ridge*
Frankie & Johnnie's/21/*W 40s*
Frank's/21/*Meatpacking*
Gage & Tollner/22/*Bklyn Hts.*
Gallagher's/21/*W 50s*
Harry's/Hanover Sq./18/*Dtown*
Jack Rose/17/*W 40s*
Jackson Ave. Steak/21/*LIC*
J. W.'s Steakhouse/21/*W 40s*
Keens Steak/21/*Garment*
Knickerbocker/20/*Central Vil*
Lansky Lounge/18/*Low E Side*
Le Marais/21/*Multi. Loc.*
Les Halles/21/*Gramercy*
Macelleria/20/*Meatpacking*
Maloney & Porcelli/22/*E 50s*
Manhattan Grille/22/*E 60s*
MarkJoseph Steak/25/*Dtown*
Michael Jordan's/21/*E 40s*
Moondance/-/*Murray Hill*
Moran's Chelsea/19/*Chelsea*
Morton's/24/*Multi. Loc.*
Nick & Stef's Steak/21/*Garment*
Oak Room/20/*W 50s*
Old Homestead/21/*Meatpacking*
Otabe/23/*E 50s*
Outback Steak/16/*Multi. Loc.*
Palm/25/*Multi. Loc.*
Peter Luger/27/*Williamsburg*
Pietro's/23/*E 40s*
Post House/23/*E 60s*
Prime Grill/23/*E 40s*
Rothmann's/23/*E 50s*
Roth's Westside Steak/22/*W 90s*
Ruth's Chris/23/*W 50s*
Smith & Wollensky/23/*E 40s*
Soho Steak/20/*SoHo*
Sparks Steak/25/*E 40s*

www.zagat.com

Cuisine Index

Strip House/*22*/*Central Vil*
Tupelo Grill/*20*/*Garment*
Tuscan Steak/*20*/*E 40s*
Uncle Jack's Steak/*24*/*Bayside*
West 63rd Steak/*21*/*W 60s*
Wolf & Lamb/*19*/*E 40s*
Wollensky's Grill/*22*/*E 40s*

Swedish
Good World B&G/*19*/*Low E Side*

Swiss
Mont Blanc/*18*/*W 40s*
Roettele A.G./*19*/*E Vil*

Tapas
Cafe Español/*19*/*Multi. Loc.*
Cafe Noir/*17*/*SoHo*
El Cid/*22*/*Chelsea*
Flor de Sol/*20*/*TriBeCa*
1492 Food/*21*/*Low E Side*
La Paella/*21*/*E Vil*
Meigas/*24*/*SoHo*
Ñ/*18*/*SoHo*
Oliva/*20*/*Low E Side*
Pipa/*21*/*Flatiron*
Rio Mar/*17*/*Meatpacking*
Sabor/*20*/*W 80s*
Sala/*18*/*NoHo*
Solera/*22*/*E 50s*
Son Cubano/*-*/*Meatpacking*
Tinto/*18*/*Bklyn Hts.*
Xunta/*20*/*E Vil*

Thai
Bangkok Cafe/*18*/*Flatiron*
Bangkok Cuisine/*19*/*W 50s*
Bann Thai/*19*/*Forest Hills*
Bendix Diner/*15*/*Multi. Loc.*
Chanpen Thai/*20*/*W 50s*
Elephant/*22*/*E Vil*
Holy Basil/*22*/*E Vil*
Jai Ya Thai/*21*/*Multi. Loc.*
Jasmine/*21*/*E 80s*
Joya/*23*/*Cobble Hill*
Kin Khao/*21*/*SoHo*
Kotobuki Bistro/*-*/*Carroll Gdns*
Lemongrass Grill/*17*/*Multi. Loc.*
Little Basil/*21*/*Village*
Long Tan/*-*/*Park Slope*
Pad Thai/*19*/*Chelsea*
Pam Real Thai/*-*/*W 40s*
Planet Thailand/*23*/*Williamsburg*
Pongsri/*20*/*Multi. Loc.*
Q, a Thai Bistro/*23*/*Forest Hills*
Red Garlic/*21*/*W 50s*
River/*19*/*W 70s*
Royal Siam/*19*/*Chelsea*
Rungsit Thai/*18*/*Multi. Loc.*
Sala Thai/*21*/*E 80s*
SEA Thai/*21*/*E Vil*
Seeda Thai/*20*/*W 50s*
Siam Inn/*20*/*W 50s*
Spice/*19*/*Multi. Loc.*
Tangerine/*21*/*Village*
Thai Cafe/*23*/*Greenpoint*
Thai House/*21*/*TriBeCa*
Thailand Rest./*23*/*Ctown*
Topaz Thai/*21*/*W 50s*
Ubol's Kitchen/*23*/*Astoria*
Vong/*25*/*E 50s*
Vynl/*17*/*W 50s*
Wondee Siam/*22*/*W 50s*

Tibetan
Shangrila/*18*/*E Vil*
Tibetan Yak/*22*/*Jackson Hts.*
Tibet on Houston/*-*/*Village*
Tsampa/*21*/*E Vil*

Tunisian
Epices du Traiteur/*19*/*W 70s*
La Baraka/*22*/*Little Neck*

Turkish
Bereket/*21*/*Low E Side*
Dalga Seafood/*23*/*E 60s*
Dervish Turkish/*21*/*W 40s*
Kazan/*21*/*Rego Pk.*
Pasha/*21*/*W 70s*
Sultan/*21*/*E 70s*
Turkish Kitchen/*21*/*Gramercy*
Turkuaz/*20*/*W 90s*
Üsküdar/*21*/*E 70s*

Ukrainian
Ukrainian E. Vil./*17*/*E Vil*
Veselka/*19*/*E Vil*

Vegetarian
Angelica Kitchen/*21*/*E Vil*
Candle Cafe/*20*/*E 70s*
Dojo/*15*/*Multi. Loc.*
Good Health Cafe/*-*/*E 80s*
Grilled Cheese NYC/*23*/*Low E Side*
Hangawi/*24*/*Murray Hill/E 30s*
Herban Kitchen/*20*/*SoHo*
Madras Cafe/*21*/*E Vil*
Mavalli Palace/*22*/*Gramercy*
Other Foods/*23*/*Central Vil*
Pongal/*20*/*Multi. Loc.*
Quintessence/*21*/*E Vil*
Rice 'n' Beans/*21*/*Multi. Loc.*
Thali Vegetarian/*19*/*Village*
Vatan/*22*/*Gramercy*
Veg. Paradise/*20*/*Multi. Loc.*
Zenith Vegetarian/*19*/*W 50s*
Zen Palate/*20*/*Multi. Loc.*

Cuisine Index

Venezuelan
Flor's Kitchen/*19/E Vil*

Vietnamese
Blue Velvet/*20/E Vil*
Bo-Ky/*20/Ctown*
Chinam 28/*19/E 80s*
Cyclo/*20/E Vil*
Indochine/*21/Central Vil*
L'Annam/*20/Gramercy*
Le Colonial/*22/E 50s*
Mai-Lin/*-/E 70s*
MeKong/*19/SoHo*
Miss Saigon/*19/E 80s*
Monsoon/*19/W 80s*
Nam Phuong/*20/TriBeCa*
New Pasteur/*21/Ctown*
Nha Trang/*23/Multi. Loc.*
Pho Bang/*19/Multi. Loc.*
Pho Viet Huong/*22/Ctown*
River/*19/W 70s*
Saigon Fun/*21/W 50s*
Saigon Grill/*22/Multi. Loc.*
Seeda Thai/*20/W 50s*
Uncle Pho/*18/Carroll Gdns.*
Vermicelli/*21/E 70s*
Vietnam/*22/Ctown*

Location Index

LOCATIONS

(Restaurant name followed by its street location.
A=Avenue, s=Street, e.g. 1A/116s=First Ave. at 116th St.;
3A/82-3s=Third Ave. between 82nd & 83rd Sts.)

Central Village/NoHo
(14th to Houston Sts.,
Fifth to Third Aves.)
Acme B&G *Gr. Jones/Bway-Lafayette*
Acquario *Bleecker/Bowery-Elizabeth*
Arté *9s/5A-University Pl.*
B B&G *4s/Bowery-Lafayette*
Bond Street *Bond/Bway-Lafayette*
Borgo Antico *13s/5A-University Pl.*
Bussola *4A/9-10s*
Cafe Spice *University Pl./10-11s*
City Eatery *Bowery/Bleecker*
Cosi *Bway/13s*
Dallas BBQ *University Pl./8s*
Danal *10s/3-4A*
Dojo *4s/Mercer*
Dolphins *Cooper Sq./5-6s*
Emerald Planet *Gr. Jones/Bway-Laf.*
Ennio & Michael *La Guardia Pl./
 Bleecker-3s*
Evergreen Shanghai *Bway/10s*
Five Points *Gr. Jones/Lafayette*
Gotham B&G *12s/5A-University Pl.*
Great Jones Cafe *Gr. Jones/Bowery*
Il Buco *Bond/Bowery-Lafayette*
Il Cantinori *10s/Bway-University Pl.*
Indochine *Lafayette/Astor Pl.-4s*
Japonica *University Pl./12s*
Johnny Rockets *8s/Bway-Univ. Pl.*
Knickerbocker *University Pl./9s*
La Belle Epoque *Bway/12-3s*
Lemongrass Grill *University Pl./11s*
Marion's *Bowery/4s-Gr. Jones*
Marumi *La Guardia Pl./Bleecker-3s*
NoHo Star *Lafayette/Bleecker*
Osso Buco *University Pl./11-2s*
Other Foods *12s/Bway-University Pl.*
Patsy's Pizzeria *University Pl./10-11s*
Pintaile's Pizza *4A/12-3s*
Sala *Bowery/Gr. Jones*
Serafina *Lafayette/4s*
Spice *University Pl./10s*
Starbucks *Astor Pl./Lafayette*
Strip House *12s/5A-University Pl.*
Tiger Blossom *Bowery/Bl.-Bond*
Time Cafe *Lafayette/Gr. Jones*
Two Boots *Bleecker/Bway*

Chelsea
(30th to 24th Sts., west of Fifth
Ave., and 24th to 14th Sts.,
west of Sixth Ave.)
Alley's End *17s/8-9A*
Amy's Bread *9A/15-6s*
Bateaux NY *23s/Hudson River*
Bendix Diner *8A/21s*
Biricchino *29s/8A*
Bottino *10A/24-5s*
Bright Food Shop *8A/21s*
Burritoville *23s/7-8A*
Cafeteria *7A/17s*
Chelsea Bistro *23s/8-9A*
Chelsea Grill *8A/16-7s*
Chelsea Rist. *8A/15-6s*
Cola's *8A/17-8s*
Cuba Libre *8A/20-1s*
Daniella *8A/26s*
Da Umberto *17s/6-7A*
Don Giovanni *10A/22-3s*
East of Eighth *23s/7-8A*
Eighteenth & Eighth *8A/18s*
El Cid *15s/8-9A*
El Quijote *23s/7-8A*
Empire Diner *10A/22s*
F & B *23s/7-8A*
Francisco's Centro *23s/-6-7A*
Gascogne *8A/17-8s*
Grand Sichuan *9A/24s*
Gus' Figs *27s/7-8A*
Hale & Hearty Soups *9A/15-6s*
Havana Chelsea *8A/19-20s*
Intermezzo *8A/20-1s*
Judy's Chelsea *8A/18-9s*
Krispy Kreme *23s/7-8A*
La Belle Vie *8A/19-20s*
La Bergamote *9A/20s*
La Lunchonette *10A/18s*
La Taza de Oro *8A/14-5s*
Le Gamin *9A/21s*
Le Madri *18s/6-7A*
Le Singe Vert *7A/19-20s*
Le Zie 2000 *7A/20-1s*
Lot 61 *21s/10-11A*
Man Ray *15s/6-7A*
Mare *8A/20s*
Maroons *16s/7-8A*
Mary Ann's *8A/16s*
Merchants, N.Y. *7A/16-7s*
Monster Sushi *23s/6-7A*
Moran's Chelsea *10A/19s*
Negril *23s/8-9A*
Nisos *8A/19s*
Pad Thai *8A/16s*
Park, The *10A/17-8s*
Patsy's Pizzeria *23s/8-9A*
Pepe Giallo *10A/24-5s*
Petite Abeille *18s/6-7A*

Location Index

Porters NY *7A/22-3s*
Red Cat *10A/23-4s*
Riazor *16s/7-8A*
Rocking Horse *8A/19-20s*
Royal Siam *8A/22-3s*
Sandro's *9A/22-3s*
Seven *7A/29-30s*
Spice *8A/20-1s*
Spirit Cruises *23s/Hudson River*
Tazza *8A/20s*
Tello's *19s/7-8A*
Tonic *18s/6-7A*

Chinatown

(South of Hester St.,
east of Lafayette St.;
west of Allen & Pike Sts.)

Ajisen *Mott/Chatham Sq.-Pell*
Ba Ba *Bayard/Bowery-Mott*
Big Wong *Mott/Bayard-Canal*
Bo-Ky *Bayard/Mott-Mulberry*
Canton *Division/Bowery-Market*
Dim Sum Go Go *E. Bway/Chatham*
Evergreen Sh. *Mott/Bayard-Canal*
Exc. Dumpling *Lafayette/Canal-Walker*
Golden Unicorn *E. Bway/Catherine*
Goody's *E. Bway/Catherine-Oliver*
Grand Sichuan *Canal/Bowery*
Great NY Noodle *Bowery/Bayard*
HSF *Bowery/Bayard-Canal*
Joe's Shanghai *Pell/Bowery-Mott*
Kam Chueh *Bowery/Bayard-Canal*
Mandarin Court *Mott/Bayard-Canal*
New Green Bo *Bayard/Eliz.-Mott*
New Pasteur *Baxter/Bayard-Canal*
Nha Trang *Baxter/Bayard-Canal; Centre/Walker-White*
Nice *E. Bway/Catherine-Market*
Oriental Garden *Eliz./Bayard-Canal*
Peking Duck *Mott/Chatham Sq.-Pell*
Pho Bang *Chatham Sq./Mott; Pike/Canal-Division*
Pho Viet Huong *Mulberry/Canal*
Ping's Seafood *E. Bway/Catherine-Market; Mott/Bayard-Pell*
Shanghai Cuisine *Bayard/Mulberry*
Sweet-n-Tart *Mott/Canal; Mott/Chatham Sq.-Pell*
Tai Hong Lau *Mott/Bayard-Canal*
Thailand *Bayard/Baxter-Mulberry*
Triple Eight *E. Bway/Division-Market*
27 Sunrise Seafood *Division/Bowery-Market*
Veg. Paradise *Mott/Pell*
Vietnam *Doyers/Bowery-Pell*
Wo Hop *Mott/Canal*
Wong Kee *Mott/Canal-Hester*
XO Kitchen *Hester/Bowery-Elizabeth*

East 40s

(East of Fifth Ave.)

Ambassador Grill *UN Plaza/1-2A*
Avra Estiatorio *48s/Lex-3A*
Bobby Van's *Park/46s*
Box Tree *49s/2-3A*
Bukhara Grill *49s/2-3A*
Bull & Bear *Lex/49s*
Burger Heaven *49s/5A-Mad; Mad/40-1s*
Cafe Centro *45s/Vanderbilt*
Café de Paris *2A/49s*
Cafe S.F.A. *5A/49-50s*
Cafe Spice *42s/Lex*
Caffe Linda *49s/Lex-3A*
Captain's Table *2A/46s*
Chiam Chinese *48s/Lex-3A*
Chikubu *44s/5A-Mad*
Chin Chin *49s/2-3A*
Cibo *2A/41s*
Comfort Diner *45s/2-3A*
Cosi *3A/43-4s; 45s/Mad-Vanderbilt*
Daily Soup *3A/48-9s; 43s/Lex-3A*
D'Artagnan *46s/Lex-3A*
Delegates' Din. Rm. *1A/45s*
Dishes *44s/Mad-Vanderbilt*
Diwan Grill *48s/Lex-3A*
Docks Oyster *3A/40s*
East *44s/2-3A*
Ferrara *Mad/45-6s*
Grifone *46s/2-3A*
Hale & Hearty Soups *3A/43-4s; 47s/5A-Mad*
Haru *48s/Mad-Park*
Hatsuhana *48s/Mad-Park; 46s/Lex-Park*
Heartbeat *49s/Lex-3A*
Houlihan's *Lex/42s*
Il Postino *49s/1-2A*
Inagiku *48s/Lex-Park*
Jimmy Sung's *44s/2-3A*
Junior's *42s/Park*
Katsuhama *47s/5A-Mad*
Kuruma Zushi *47s/5A-Mad*
Little Italy Pizza *43s/5A-Mad*
Luna Blu *44s/2-3A*
Mangia *48s/5A-Mad*
Marichu *46s/1-2A*
Mee Noodle *2A/49s*
Menchanko-tei *45s/Lex-3A*
Métrazur *42s/Park*
Michael Jordan's *Vanderbilt/43-4s*
Morton's *5A/45s*
Nanni's *46s/Lex-3A*
Naples 45 *45s/Lex-Vanderbilt*
Nino's Positano *2A/47-8s*
Osteria Laguna *42s/2-3A*
Oyster Bar *42s/Vanderbilt*
Palm *2A/44-5s*
Peacock Alley *Park/49-50s*

Location Index

Pershing Sq. *42s/Park*
Phoenix Garden *40s/2-3A*
Pietro's *43s/2-3A*
Prime Grill *49s/Mad-Park*
Salmon River *40s/5A-Mad*
San Giusto *2A/49-50s*
Seo *49s/2-3A*
Shoebox Cafe *42s/Park*
Sichuan Palace *44s/1-2A*
Smith & Wollensky *3A/49s*
Sparks Steak *46s/2-3A*
Sushiden *49s/5A-Mad*
Sushi Yasuda *43s/2-3A*
T.G.I. Friday's *5A/48-9s; 42s/Mad-Vanderbilt*
Top of Tower *Mitchell Pl.:1A/49s*
Tropica *45s/Lex*
Tudor Grill *Tudor City Pl./1-2A*
Tuscan Steak *3A/40s*
Two Boots *42s/Lex*
Virot *41s/Mad-Park*
Wolf & Lamb *48s/5A-Mad*
Wollensky's Grill *49s/3A*
Zócalo *42s/Vanderbilt*

East 50s
(East of Fifth Ave.)

Adä *58s/2-3A*
Al Bustan *3A/50-1s*
An American Pl. *Lex/50-1s*
Anche Vivolo *58s/2-3A*
Bellini *52s/2-3A*
Benihana *56s/Lex-Park*
Bice *54s/5A-Mad*
Bill Hong's *56s/2-3A*
Billy's *1A/52-3s*
Bouterin *59s/1A-Sutton Pl.*
Brasserie *53s/Lex-Park*
Broadway Diner *Lex/52s*
Bruno *58s/2-3A*
Burger Heaven *53s/5A-Mad; Mad/54-5s*
Burritoville *3A/52s*
Cafe du Pont *1A/56-7s*
Cafe Joul *1A/58-9s*
Caviar Russe *Mad/54-5s*
Caviarteria *Park/59s*
Cellini *54s/Mad-Park*
Chola *58s/2-3A*
Cinquanta *50s/Mad-Park*
Columbus Bakery *1A/52-3s*
Cosi *52s/Lex-3A; 56s/Mad-Park*
Da Antonio *55s/Lex-3A*
Dawat *58s/2-3A*
DeGrezia *50s/2-3A*
Della Femina *54s/Lex-Park*
Deux Amis *51s/1-2A*
Ess-a-Bagel *3A/50-1s*
Felidia *58s/2-3A*
Fifty Seven Fifty Seven *57s/Mad-Park*

Four Seasons *52s/Lex-Park*
Fresco by Scotto *52s/Mad-Park*
Fresco on the Go *52s/Mad-Park*
Giambelli *50s/Mad-Park*
Go Sushi *2A/52s*
Guastavino, Down. *59s/1A-York*
Guastavino, Upstairs *59s/1A-York*
Haikara Grill *2A/53-4s*
Harry Cipriani *5A/59-60s*
Houlihan's *Lex/56s*
Houston's *54s/3A*
Il Menestrello *52s/Mad-Park*
Il Nido *53s/2-3A*
Il Valentino *56s/1-2A*
Jubilee *54s/1-2A*
King Cole Bar *55s/5A-Mad*
Korea Palace *54s/Lex-Park*
L'Actuel *50s/Lex-3A*
La Gioconda *53s/2-3A*
La Grenouille *52s/5A-Mad*
La Mangeoire *2A/53-4s*
La Mediterranée *2A/50-1s*
Le Cirque 2000 *Mad/50-1s*
Le Colonial *57s/Lex-3A*
L'Entrecote *1A/57-8s*
Leopard, The *50s/2-3A*
Le Perigord *52s/1A-FDR Dr.*
Lespinasse *55s/5A-Mad*
Lipstick Cafe *3A/53-4s*
Luna Piena *53s/2-3A*
Lutèce *50s/2-3A*
Maloney & Porcelli *50s/Mad-Park*
Maple Garden *53s/2-3A*
March *58s/1A-Sutton Pl.*
Meltemi *1A/51s*
Metropolitan Cafe *1A/52-3s*
Monkey Bar *54s/Mad-Park*
Montebello *56s/Lex-Park*
Montparnasse *51s/2-3A*
Mr. Chow *57s/1-2A*
Mr. K's *Lex/51s*
Neary's *57s/1A*
Nicholson *58s/1-2A*
Nippon *52s/Lex-3A*
Oceana *54s/Mad-Park*
Oikawa *3A/50s*
Oscar's *Lex/50s*
Otabe *56s/Mad-Park*
Our Place *55s/Lex-3A*
Pamir *1A/58s*
Paper Moon Milano *58s/Mad-Park*
Pescatore *2A/50-1s*
P.J. Clarke's *3A/55s*
Raffaele *1A/57-8s*
Rosa Mexicano *1A/58s*
Rothmann's *54s/5A-Mad*
San Pietro *54s/5A-Mad*
Seryna *53s/5A-Mad*
Shallots NY *Mad/55-6s*

Location Index

Shun Lee Palace *55s/Lex-3A*
Solera *53s/2-3A*
Sushi Rose *52s/2-3A*
Sushisay *51s/Mad-Park*
Tao *58s/Mad-Park*
Tatany *52s/2-3A*
Tea Box *5A/54-5s*
Teodora *57s/Lex-3A*
Trattoria Chianti *2A/55s*
Tratt. Pesce & Pasta *1A/59s*
Tse Yang *51s/Mad-Park*
Vong *54s/3A*
Zarela *2A/50-1s*

East 60s
(East of Fifth Ave.)
Abajour *1A/62-3s*
Amaranth *62s/5A-Mad*
Angels *1A/62-3s*
Arabelle *64s/Mad-Park*
Arizona 206 *60s/2-3A*
Aureole *61s/Mad-Park*
Baluchi's *1A/63s*
Barbaresco *Lex/64-5s*
Bravo Gianni *63s/2-3A*
Brio *Lex/61s*
Brooklyn Diner USA *3A/63-4s*
Cabana Nuevo *3A/60-1s*
Cafe Nosidam *Mad/66s*
Café Pierre *61s/5A*
California Pizza *60s/2-3A*
Canaletto *60s/2-3A*
China Fun *2A/64s*
Cibi Cibi/Yellowfingers *60s/3A*
Circus *Lex/62-3s*
Da Filippo *2A/69-70s*
Dalga Seafood *62s/1A-York*
Daniel *65s/Mad-Park*
Destinée *61s/Lex-Park*
East *66s/1-2A*
East River Cafe *1A/61s*
Ferrier Bistro *65s/Mad-Park*
Fred's at Barneys *Mad/60s*
Gino *Lex/60-1s*
Hale & Hearty Soups *Lex/64-5s*
Henry's Evergreen *1A/69-70s*
Il Gatto/La Volpe *1A/63-4s*
Il Vagabondo *62s/1-2A*
Jackson Hole *64s/2-3A*
John's Pizzeria *64s/1A-York*
Jo Jo *64s/Lex-3A*
L'Absinthe *67s/2-3A*
La Corniche *64s/Lex-3A*
La Goulue *Mad/64-5s*
La Houppa *64s/5A-Mad*
L'Ardoise *1A/65-6s*
Le Bilboquet *63s/Mad-Park*
Le Charlot *69s/Mad-Park*
Le Pain Quotidien *Lex/63-4s*

Le Veau d'Or *60s/Lex-Park*
Manhattan Grille *1A/63-4s*
Maya *1A/64-5s*
Mediterraneo *2A/66s*
Merchants, N.Y. *1A/62s*
Mme. Romaine *61s/Lex-Park*
Mon Petit Cafe *Lex/62s*
Nello *Mad/62-3s*
Nicole's *60s/5A-Mad*
Park Ave. Cafe *63s/Lex-Park*
Patsy's Pizzeria *2A/69s*
Pintaile's Pizza *2A/64-5s*
Portofino Grille *1A/63-4s*
Post House *63s/Mad-Park*
Primola *2A/64-5s*
Rain *3A/62-3s*
Regency *Park/61s*
Scalinatella *61s/3A*
Serafina *61s/Mad-Park*
Serendipity 3 *60s/2-3A*
Sushihatsu *1A/62-3s*
212 *65s/Lex-Park*
Ulrika's *60s/Lex-Park*
Viand *Mad/61-2s*
Via Oreto *1A/61-2s*

East 70s
(East of Fifth Ave.)
Afghan Kebab Hse. *2A/70-1s*
Aki Sushi *York/75-6s*
Amy's Bread *Lex/70-1s*
Annie's *3A/78-9s*
Atlantic Grill *3A/76-7s*
Bandol Bistro *78s/Lex-3A*
Baraonda *2A/75s*
Bardolino *2A/77-8s*
Barking Dog *York/77s*
Bella Blu *Lex/70-1s*
Bella Donna *77s/1-2A*
Bid *York/71s*
Bistro Le Steak *3A/75s*
Blue Elephant *2A/73-4s*
Boat House *72s/Park Dr. N.*
Brother Jimmy's *2A/77-8s*
Brunelli *York/75s*
Burritoville *1A/77-8s*
Café Boulud *76s/5A-Mad*
Café Crocodile *74s/1-2A*
Cafe Greco *2A/71-2s*
Campagnola *1A/73-4s*
Candle Cafe *3A/74-5s*
Canyon Rd. Grill *1A/76-7s*
Carlyle *76s/Mad*
Cello *77s/Mad-Park*
Cilantro *1A/71s*
Coconut Grill *2A/77s*
Coco Pazzo *74s/5A-Mad*
Dallas BBQ *3A/72-3s*
Dining Room *79s/Lex-3A*
Due *3A/79-80s*

Location Index

EJ's Luncheonette *3A/73s*
Evergreen Shanghai *3A/78-9s*
Googie's *2A/78s*
Grace's Trattoria *71s/2-3A*
Haru *3A/76s*
Ikeno Hana *Lex/72-3s*
Il Monello *2A/76-7s*
Il Riccio *79s/Lex-3A*
J.G. Melon *3A/74s*
Kazusa *2A/72-3s*
La Tour *3A/75-6s*
Lenox *3A/73-4s*
Le Pain Quotidien *1A/71-2s*
Le Petit Hulot *Lex/70-1s*
Letizia Amore *1A/73-4s*
Lola's Buena Vista *79s/2-3A*
Loui Loui *3A/75s*
Luke's B&G *3A/79-80s*
Lumi *Lex/70s*
Lusardi's *2A/77-8s*
Mai-Lin *73s/2-3A*
Maison *2A/77s*
Malaga *73s/1A-York*
Mark's *77s/5A-Mad*
Maruzzella *1A/77-8s*
Mary Ann's *2A/78-9s*
Mezzaluna *3A/74-5s*
Mingala *2A/72-3s*
Nino's *1A/72-3s*
Orsay *Lex/75s*
Pamir *2A/74-5s*
Parma *3A/79-80s*
Payard Bistro *Lex/73-4s*
Persepolis *2A/74-5s*
Petaluma *1A/73s*
Pintaile's Pizza *York/76-7s*
P.J. Bernstein *3A/70-1s*
Quatorze Bis *79s/1-2A*
Rafina *York/78-79s*
Red/Bar *75s/1-2A*
Sant Ambroeus *Mad/77-8s*
Sarabeth's *Mad/75s*
Serafina *Mad/79s*
Sette Mezzo *Lex/70-1s*
Shabu-Shabu 70 *70s/1-2A*
Shabu-Tatsu *York/75s*
Spice *2A/73-74s*
Starbucks *Lex/78s*
Sultan *2A/74-5s*
Sushi Hana *2A/78s*
Sushi of Gari *78s/1A*
Swifty's *Lex/72-3s*
Toraya *71s/5A-Mad*
Trata *2A/70-1s*
Üsküdar *2A/73-4s*
Vermicelli *2A/77-8s*
Viand *Mad/78s*
Via Quadronno *73s/5A-Mad*
Viareggio *2A/71s*
Vivolo *74s/Lex-Park*
Willow *Lex/73s*

East 80s
(East of Fifth Ave.)

Al Baraka *2A/83-4s*
Archer's *1A/85-6s*
Baluchi's *2A/81-2s*
Bella Donna *1A/86-7s*
Brasserie Julien *3A/80-1s*
Butterfield 81 *81s/Lex-3A*
Cafe Trevi *1A/81-2s*
Caffe Grazie *84s/5A-Mad*
Candido Pizza *1A/83-4s*
Carino *2A/88-9s*
Centolire *Mad/85-6s*
Chef Ho's *2A/89-90s*
Chinam 28 *2A/85-6s*
Cilantro *2A/88-9s*
Clove *80s/5A-Mad*
Comfort Diner *86s/Lex*
Dakshin *1A/88-9s*
Dan Maxwell's *2A/88-9s*
Demarchelier *86s/Mad-Park*
Divino *2A/80-1s*
Domani *1A/82-3s*
Donguri *83s/1-2A*
DT•UT *2A/84-5s*
E.A.T. *Mad/80-1s*
Elaine's *2A/88-9s*
Elio's *2A/84-5s*
Eli's *3A/80s*
Emo's *2A/81-2s*
Erminia *83s/2-3A*
Estia *86s/1-2A*
Etats-Unis *81s/2-3A*
Firenze *2A/82-3s*
Giovanni Venticinque *83s/5A-Mad*
Girasole *82s/Lex-3A*
Good Health Cafe *86s/1-2A*
Heidelberg *2A/85-6s*
India Grill *81s/2-3A*
Jackson Hole *2A/83-4s*
Jacques *85s/2-3A*
Jasmine *2A/84s*
Kings' Carriage *82s/2-3A*
Kodama Sushi *3A/82-3s*
Krispy Kreme *3A/84-5s*
Le Boeuf à la Mode *81s/E. End-York*
Lentini *2A/81s*
Le Pain Quotidien *Mad/84-5s*
Le Refuge *82s/Lex-3A*
Lili's Noodle *3A/84-5s*
Luca *1A/88-9s*
Mangiarini *2A/82-3s*
Maz Mezcal *86s/1-2A*
Merchants, N.Y. *1A/83-4s*
Miss Saigon *3A/80-1s*
Mocca *2A/82-3s*
Nicola's *84s/Lex-3A*
Our Place *3A/82s*
Paola's *84s/2-3A*
Papaya King *86s/3A*
Pastrami Queen *Lex/85-6s*

Location Index

Penang *2A/83s*
Pig Heaven *2A/80-1s*
Pintaile's Pizza *York/83-4s*
Pizzeria Uno *86s/2-3A*
Primavera *1A/82s*
Quattro Gatti *81s/2-3A*
Saigon Grill *2A/88s*
Sala Thai *2A/89-90s*
Sirabella's *E. End/82-3s*
Sistina *2A/80-1s*
Spada *3A/81s*
Tevere *84s/Lex-3A*
Tony's Di Napoli *2A/83s*
Totonno Pizzeria *2A/80-1s*
Tratt. Pesce & Pasta *3A/87-8s*
Tratt. Rustica *85s/1-2A*
Triangolo *83s/1-2A*
Trois Marches *81s/1-2A*
Va Bene *2A/82-3s*
Viand *86s/2A*
Wu Liang Ye *86s/2-3A*
York Grill *York/88-9s*
Yuka *2A/80-1s*
Zócalo *82s/Lex-3A*

East 90s & Up
(East of Fifth Ave.)
Barking Dog *3A/94s*
Bistro du Nord *Mad/93s*
Brother Jimmy's *3A/92s*
Burritoville *3A/90-1s*
Dinerbar *Lex/100-1s*
Ecco-la *3A/93s*
Eli's Vinegar Fact. *91s/1A-York*
Emily's *5/111-2s*
Fred's *3A/92-3s*
Jackson Hole *Mad/91s*
Joanna's *92s/5A-Mad*
92 *92s/Mad*
Osso Buco *3A/93s*
Pascalou *Mad/92-3s*
Patsy's Pizzeria *1A/117-8s*
Pinocchio *1A/90-1s*
Pintaile's Pizza *91s/5A-Mad*
Rao's *114s/Pleasant*
Sachi *Mad/94-5s*
Sarabeth's *Mad/92-3s*
Sharz Cafe *90s/Lex-3A*
Starbucks *3A/92s*
Table d'Hôte *92s/Mad-Park*
Tre Pomodori *2A/90-1s*
Vico *Mad/92-3s*
Yura & Co. *3A/92s; Mad/92s*

East Village
(14th to Houston Sts., east of Third Ave.)
Alphabet Kitchen *Ave. A/10-11s*
Angelica Kitchen *12s/1-2A*
Baluchi's *2A/6-7s*
Bambou *14s/2-3A*
Banjara *1A/6s*
Belmondo *Ave. B/6-7s*
Bendix Diner *1A/10-11s*
Benny's Burritos *Ave. A/6s*
Blue Velvet *1A/13-4s*
Boca Chica *1A/1s*
Briam *14s/1-2A*
Burritoville *2A/8-9s*
Cafe Deville *3A/13s*
Cafe Mogador *St. Marks/Ave. A-1A*
Casimir *Ave. B/6-7s*
Chez Es Saada *1s/1-2A*
Christine's *1A/12-3s*
Cocina Cuzco *Ave. A/4s*
Col Legno *9s/2-3A*
Cosmic Cantina *3A/13s*
Coup *6s/Aves. A-B*
Cucina di Pesce *4s/Bowery-2A*
Cyclo *1A/12-3s*
Daily Chow *2s/Bowery*
Dallas BBQ *2A/St. Marks Pl.*
Dojo *St. Marks Pl./2-3A*
Dok Suni's *1A/7s-St. Marks Pl.*
East Post *2A/5-6s*
Elephant *1s/1-2A*
Esperanto *Ave. C/9s*
First *1A/5-6s*
Flea Mkt. Cafe *Ave. A/9s-St. Marks*
Flor's Kitchen *1A/9-10s*
Forbidden City *Ave. A/13-4s*
Frank *2A/5-6s*
Friend House *3A/12-3s*
Frutti di Mare *4s/2A*
Global 33 *2A/5-6s*
Gnocco Caffe *10s/Aves. A-B*
Hasaki *9s/2-3A*
Haveli *2A/5-6s*
Holy Basil *2A/9-10s*
I Coppi *9s/Ave. A-1A*
ike *2A/6s*
Il Bagatto *2s/Aves. A-B*
Il Covo dell'Est *Ave. A/13s*
Iso *2A/11s*
It's Greek to Me *7s/Ave. A-1A*
Jeollado *4s/1-2A*
Jewel Bako *5s/2-3A*
John's of 12th St. *12s/2A*
Jules *St. Marks Pl./1-2A*
Komodo *Ave. A/12s*
Lan *3A/10-11s*
Lanza *1A/10-11s*
La Paella *9s/2-3A*
La Palapa *St. Marks Pl./1-2A*
Lavagna *5s/Aves. A-B*
Le Gamin *5s/Aves. A-B*
Lemongrass Grill *Ave. A/4s*
Leshko's *Ave. A/7s*
Le Souk *Ave. B/3-4s*
Le Tableau *5s/Aves. A-B*

Location Index

Lucien *1A/1-2s*
Lucky Cheng's *1A/1-2s*
Madras Cafe *2A/4-5s*
Mama's Food Shop *3s/Aves. A-B*
Mamlouk *4s/Aves. A-B*
Mary Ann's *2A/5s*
Max *Ave. B/3-4s*
Mee Noodle *1A/13s*
Mekka *Ave. A/Houston-2s*
Mingala *7s/2-3A*
Miracle Grill *1A/6-7s*
Mitali East *6s/1-2A*
Mosto *2A/5s*
Moustache *10s/Ave. A-1A*
Mugsy's Chow Chow *2A/1-2s*
Muzy *St. Marks Pl./1A*
O.G. *6s/Aves. A-B*
Oggi *Ave. A/13s*
Pangea *2A/11-2s*
Paprika *St. Marks Pl.-Ave. A-1A*
Penang *3A/11s*
Pierrot Bistro *Ave. B/2-3s*
Pisces *Ave. A/6s*
Pizzeria Uno *3A/10-11s*
Prune *1s/1-2A*
Quintessence *10s/Ave. A-1A*
Raga *6s/Ave. A-1A*
Resto Léon *12s/1-2A*
Roettele A.G. *7s/Ave. A-1A*
Sandobe *11s/1-2A*
Sapporo East *10s/1A*
SEA Thai *2A/4-5s*
Second Ave. Deli *2A/10s*
Shabu-Tatsu *10s/1-2A*
Shangrila *2A/7s-St. Marks Pl.*
Soba-ya *9s/2-3A*
Starbucks *2A/9s*
Stingy Lulu's *St. Marks Pl./Ave. A-1A*
Takahachi *Ave. A/5-6s*
Tanti Baci *6s/Aves. A-B*
Tappo *12s/Ave. A-1A*
Tasting Room *1s/1-2A*
Teresa's *1A/6-7s*
Tsampa *9s/2-3A*
26 Seats *Ave. B/10-11s*
Two Boots *Ave. A/2-3s; Ave. A/3s*
Ukrainian E. Vil. *2A/9s-St. Marks Pl.*
Veniero's *11s/1-2A*
Veselka *2A/9s*
Xunta *1A/10-11s*

Flatiron District/Union Square

(Between Chelsea & Gramercy Park, bounded by 24th and 14th Sts., between 6th Ave. and Park Ave. S.)

Adulis *19s/Bway-Park S.*
Aleutia *Park S./18s*
Alva *22s/Bway-Park S.*
America *18s/Bway-5A*
Angelo & Maxie's *Park S./19s*
Arezzo *22s/5-6A*
AZ *17s/5-6A*
Bangkok Cafe *20s/Bway-Park S.*
Basta Pasta *17s/5-6A*
Bella Donna *23s/Mad*
Beppe *22s/Bway-Park S.*
Blue Water Grill *Union Sq. W./16s*
Bolo *22s/Bway-Park S.*
Bondi Ristorante *20s/5-6A*
Cal's *21s/5-6A*
Campagna *21s/Bway-Park S.*
Candela *16s/Irving Pl.-Park S.*
Chat n' Chew *16s/5A-Union Sq. W.*
Chicama *18s/Bway-Park S.*
Chop't Creative Salad *17s/Bway-5A*
City Bakery *18s/5-6A*
City Crab *Park S./19s*
Coffee Shop *Union Sq. W./16s*
Commune *22s/Bway-Park S.*
Cosi *17s/Bway-5A*
Craft *19s/Bway-Park S.*
Eisenberg Sandwich *5A/22-3s*
Eugene *24s/5-6A*
Fleur de Sel *20s/Bway-5A*
Giorgio's *21s/Bway-Park S.*
Gramercy Tavern *20s/Bway-Park S.*
Hamachi *20s/Bway-Park S.*
Heartland Brew. *Union Sq. W./16-7s*
Justin's *21s/5-6A*
L'Acajou *19s/5-6A*
La Pizza Fresca *20s/Bway-Park S.*
Lemon *Park S./18-9s*
Le Pain Quotidien *19s/Bway-Park S.*
L'Express *Park S./20s*
Lola *22s/5-6A*
Mayrose *Bway/21s*
Mesa Grill *5A/15-6s*
Metronome *Bway/21s*
Old Town Bar *18s/Bway-Park S.*
Olives *Park S./17s*
Park Avalon *Park S./18-9s*
Patria *Park S./20s*
Periyali *20s/5-6A*
Pipa *19s/Bway-Park S.*
Punch *Bway/20-1s*
Republic *Union Sq. W./16-7s*
Ribollita *Park S./20-1s*
Shaffer City Oyster *21s/5-6A*
Starbucks *6A/22s*
Steak Frites *16s/5A-Union Sq. W.*
Sushi Jones *17s/Bway-5A*
Sushi Samba *Park S./19-20s*
Tamarind *22s/Bway-Park S.*
Tocqueville *15s/5A-Union Sq. W.*
Tossed *Park S./22-3s*
T Salon *20s/Bway-5A*

Location Index

Union Sq. Cafe *16s/5A-Union Sq. W.*
Veritas *20s/Bway-Park S.*
Zen Palate *Union Sq. E./16s*

Garment District/West 30s
(40th to 30th Sts., west of Fifth Ave.)

Abigael's *Bway/38-9s*
Ben's Kosher Deli *38s/7A*
Burritoville *39s/9A*
Cho Dang Gol *35s/5-6A*
Cosi *36s/7-8A*
Cupcake Cafe *9A/39s*
Emack & Bolio's *34s/Herald Sq.*
Gam Mee Ok *32s/Bway-5A*
Gray's Papaya *8A/37s*
Hale & Hearty Soups *7A/35-6s*
Houlihan's *Penn Plaza/33s*
Kang Suh *Bway/32s*
Keens Steak *36s/5-6A*
Krispy Kreme *Penn Plaza/33s*
Kum Gang San *32s/Bway-5A*
Metro Grill *35s/5-6A*
Nick & Stef's Steak *33s/7-8A*
Sandwich Planet *9A/39-40s*
Soul Fixins' *34s/8-9A*
Starbucks *7A/31s*
Supreme Macaroni *9A/38-9s*
Tagine Dining *9A/39-40s*
T.G.I. Friday's *8A/34s*
Tír na nóg *8A/33-4s*
Tupelo Grill *33s/7-8A*
Veronica *38s/7-8A*
Won Jo *32s/Bway-5A*
Woo Chon *36s/5-6A*

Gramercy Park
(30th to 24th Sts., east of Fifth Ave., and 24th to 14th Sts., east of Park Ave. S.)

Bread Bar at Tabla *Mad/25s*
Casa Mia *24s/2-3A*
Chazal Bistro *Mad/26s*
Chinoiserie *Park S./26s*
Choshi *Irving Pl./19s*
Coppola's *3A/27-8s*
Curry Leaf *Lex/27s*
Daily Soup *Park S./24-5s*
Danzón *28s/Lex-Park S.*
Duke's *19s/Irving Pl.-Park S.*
East *3A/26-7s*
Eleven Madison Pk. *Mad/24s*
Empire Szechuan *3A/27-8s*
Enoteca i Trulli *27s/Lex-Park S.*
Ess-a-Bagel *1A/21s*
Friend of a Farmer *Irving Pl./18-9s*
Globe *Park S./26-7s*
Houston's *Park S./27s*
Irving on Irving *Irving Pl./17s*
I Trulli *27s/Lex-Park S.*
Jai Ya Thai *3A/28-9s*
Lady Mendl's *Irving Pl./17-8s*
L'Annam *3A/28s*
La Petite Auberge *Lex/27-8s*
Les Halles *Park S./28-9s*
Los Dos Molinos *18s/Irv.-Park S.*
Mavalli Palace *29s/Mad-Park S.*
Mi *Mad/27-8s*
Noodles on 28 *3A/28s*
Novitá *22s/Park S.*
Park Bistro *Park S./28-9s*
Paul & Jimmy's *18s/Irv.-Park S.*
Pete's Tavern *18s/Irving Pl.*
Pitchoune *3A/19s*
Plate 347 *2A/20-1s*
Pongal *Lex/26s; Lex/27-8s*
Pongsri *2A/18s*
Rolf's *3A/22s*
Rungsit Thai *23s/Lex-3A*
Sal Anthony's *Irving Pl./17-8s*
Sam's Noodle Shop *3A/29s*
Scopa *Mad/28s*
Tabla *Mad/25s*
Tatany *3A/27-8s*
Turkish Kitchen *3A/27-8s*
Union Pacific *22s/Lex-Park S.*
Vatan *3A/29s*
Verbena *Irving Pl./17-8s*
Yama *17s/Irving Pl.*

Greenwich Village
(14th to Houston Sts., west of Fifth Ave.)

Alfama *Hudson/Perry*
Anglers & Writers *Hudson/St. Luke's*
Annisa *Barrow/7A S.-4s*
Anton's *4s/Perry*
Arturo's Pizzeria *Houston/Thompson*
Babbo *Waverly/MacDougal-6A*
Baluchi's *6A/Washington Pl.-4s*
Bar Pitti *6A/Bleecker-Houston*
Bar Six *6A/12-3s*
Benny's Burritos *Greenwich A/Jane*
Blue Hill *Wash. Pl./6A-Wash. Sq.*
Blue Ribbon Bak. *Downing/Bedford*
Bouchon *Greenwich A/Charles-Perry*
Boughalem *Bedford/Downing*
Brothers BBQ *Varick/Clarkson*
Burritoville *Bleecker/7A S.*
Cafe Alyss *Thompson/Bleecker-3s*
Cafe Asean *10s/Greenwich A-6A*
Café de Bruxelles *Greenwich A/13s*
Café Español *Bleecker/MacDougal-Sullivan; Carmine/7s*
Cafe Loup *13s/6-7A*
Cafe Picasso *Bleecker/Charles-10s*
Caffe Rafaella *7A S./Charles-10s*
Caffe Reggio *MacDougal/Bleecker*

Location Index

Caffe Rosso *12s/4s*
Casa *Bedford/Commerce*
Cent'Anni *Carmine/Bedford-Bl.*
Chez Brigitte *Greenwich A/Bank-7A*
Chez Jacqueline *MacDougal/Bl.-Houston*
Chez Ma Tante *10s/Bleecker-4s*
Chez Michallet *Bedford/Grove*
Chow Bar *4s/10s*
Ciao *Bleecker/MacDougal*
Cookies & Couscous *Thompson/Bl.-4s*
Cornelia St. Cafe *Cornelia/Bl.-4s*
Corner Bistro *4s/Jane*
Cowgirl Hall of Fame *Hudson/10s*
Da Andrea *Hudson/Perry-11s*
Da Silvano *6A/Bleecker-Houston*
Do Hwa *Carmine/Bedford-7A S.*
EJ's Luncheonette *6A/9-10s*
El Charro *Charles/Greenwich A-7A S.*
Elephant Castle *Greenwich A/6-7A*
El Faro *Greenwich s/Horatio*
Emack & Bolio's *7A/13-4s*
Empire Szechuan *7A S./Perry-11s; Greenwich A/6A-10s*
Fish *Bleecker/Jones*
French Roast *11s/6A*
Garage *7A S./Barrow-Grove*
Gene's *11s/5-6A*
good *Greenwich A/Bank-12s*
Go Sushi *Greenwich A/6A*
Gradisca *13s/6-7A*
Grange Hall *Commerce/Barrow*
Grano Trattoria *Greenwich A/10s*
Gray's Papaya *6A/8s*
Grey Dog's *Carmine/Bedford-Bleecker*
Grove *Bleecker/Grove*
Gus' Place *Waverly/6A*
Home *Cornelia/Bleecker-4s*
Il Mulino *3s/Sullivan-Thompson*
'ino *Bedford/Downing-6A*
Inside *Jones/Bleecker-4s*
Isla *Downing/Bedford-Varick*
Ithaka *Barrow/Bedford-Bleecker*
Jane *Houston/La Guardia-Thompson*
Jarnac *12s/Greenwich s*
Joe's Pizza *Bl./Carmine; Carmine/6A*
John's Pizzeria *Bleecker/6A-7A S.*
Junno's *Downing/Bedford-Varick*
La Cantina *8A/Jane*
La Lanterna *MacDougal/3-4s*
La Metairie *10s/4s*
La Nonna *13s/6-7A*
La Ripaille *Hudson/Bethune-12s*
Le Gamin *Bedford/Downing*
Le Gigot *Cornelia/Bleecker-4s*
Lemongrass Grill *Barrow/7A S.*
Les Deux Gamins *Waverly/Grove*
Lexi's *3s/Sullivan-Thompson*
Le Zoo *11s/Greenwich s*

Little Basil *Greenwich A/Charles*
Little Havana *Cornelia/Bleecker-4s*
Lupa *Thompson/Bleecker-Houston*
Malatesta *Washington/Christopher*
Marinella *Carmine/Bedford*
Marylou's *9s/5-6A*
Mary's Fish Camp *Charles/4s*
Massimo *Thompson/Bleecker-3s*
Merge *10s/Greenwich A-Waverly*
Meskerem *MacDougal/Bleecker-3s*
Mexicana Mama *Hudson/Charles*
Mi Cocina *Jane/Hudson*
Midway *Charles/Washington*
Minetta Tavern *MacDougal/Bl.-3s*
Miracle Grill *Bleecker/Bank-11s*
Mirchi *7A S./Bedford-Morton*
Mitali West *Bleecker/7A S.*
Monster Sushi *Hudson/Charles*
Monte's *MacDougal/Bleecker-3s*
Moustache *Bedford/Barrow-Grove*
Nadine's *Bank/Greenwich s*
Nellie's *Houston/MacDougal*
NL *Sullivan/Bleecker-Houston*
Nonna *La Guardia/Bleecker-Houston*
One if by Land *Barrow/7A S.-4s*
Palma *Cornelia/Bleecker-4s*
Papillon *Hudson/Bank-11s*
Paris Commune *Bleecker/Bank-11s*
Peanut Butter *Sullivan/Bl.-3s*
Pearl Oyster Bar *Cornelia/Bl.-4s*
Pepe Verde *Hudson/Perry-11s*
Petite Abeille *Hudson/Barrow*
Philip Marie *Hudson/11s*
Piadina *10s/5-6A*
Piccolo Angolo *Hudson/Jane*
Pink Tea Cup *Grove/Bedford-Bl.*
Pizzeria Uno *6A/8s-Waverly*
Place *4s/Bank-12s*
Pó *Cornelia/Bleecker-4s*
Porto Bello *Thompson/Bleecker-3s*
Psychic Cafe *10s/7A S.*
Rafaella *Bleecker/Charles-Perry*
Rice 'n' Beans *3s/MacDougal-6A*
Rinçon España *Thompson/Bl.-3s*
Rocco *Thompson/Bleecker-Houston*
Salam Cafe *13s/6-7A*
Sammy's *6A/11s; 6A/Carmine*
Sapore *Greenwich A/Perry*
Sazerac Hse. *Hudson/Charles*
Sen-ya *Bleecker/MacDougal-Sullivan*
Sevilla *Charles/4s*
Stonewall Bistro *7A S./Christopher*
Sung Chu Mei *Hudson/Jane-12s*
Surya *Bleecker/Grove-7A S.*
Sushi Samba *7A S./Barrow*
Taka *Grove/Bleecker-7A S.*
Tangerine *10s/Bleecker-Hudson*
Tanti Baci *10s/7A S.-Waverly*
Taq. de Mexico *Greenwich A/Bank-12s*

Location Index

Tartine *11s/4s*
Thali *Greenwich A/Charles-10s*
Tibet on Houston *Houston/MacDougal*
Tio Pepe *4s/6A-7A S.*
Titou *4s/Charles-Perry*
Tomoe Sushi *Thompson/Bl.-Houston*
Tortilla Flats *Washington/12s*
Tratt. Pesce & Pasta *Bl./6A-7A S.*
Tratt. Spaghetto *Bleecker/Carmine*
Two Boots *11s/7A S.*
Uguale *West St./10s*
Veg. Paradise *4s/MacDougal-6A*
Village *9s/5-6A*
Villa Mosconi *MacDougal/Bl.-Houston*
Vittorio Cucina *Bl./Grove-7A S.*
Volare *4s/MacDougal-6A*
Wallsé *11s/Washington*
White Horse *Hudson/11s*
Yama *Carmine/Bedford-Bleecker; Houston/La Guardia-Thompson*
Ye Waverly Inn *Bank/Waverly Pl.*
Zutto *Greenwich A/7A S.-11s*

Harlem
(West of Fifth Ave., from W. 110th–W. 157th Sts.; east of Morningside Ave./St. Nicholas Ave. up to W. 125th St.)
Amy Ruth's *116s/Lenox-7A*
Bayou *Lenox/125-6s*
Charles' Southern *8A/151-2s*
Copeland's *145s/Amst.-Bway*
Fifth Ave. Seafood *5A/125s*
Home Sweet Harlem *135s/7-8A*
Jimmy's Uptown *7A/130-1s*
Krispy Kreme *125s/8A*
Londel's *8A/139-140s*
Max *Amst./123s*
Miss Mamie's *110s/Col.-Manh. A*
Miss Maude's *Lenox/137-8s*
Papaya King *125s/Lenox-7A*
Slice of Harlem *8A/135s; Lenox/125-6s*
Starbucks *125s/Lenox*
Sugar Hill *145s/Amst.-Convent*
Sylvia's *Lenox/126-7s*

Lower East Side
(Houston to Canal Sts., east of Bowery)
AKA Cafe *Clinton/Rivington-Stanton*
Barrio *Stanton/Ludlow-Orchard*
Bereket *Houston/Orchard*
Casa Mexicana *Ludlow/Rivington*
Essex *Essex/Rivington*
1492 Food *Clinton/Rivington-Stanton*
Good World B&G *Orchard/Division*
Grilled Cheese NYC *Ludlow/Stanton*
Katz's Deli *Houston/Ludlow*
Lansky Lounge *Norfolk/Rivington*
Le Père Pinard *Ludlow/Houston*
Mooza *Orchard/Houston-Stanton*
Oliva *Houston/Allen*
Paladar *Ludlow/Houston-Stanton*
Ratner's *Delancey/Norfolk-Suffolk*
Sammy's Rouman. *Chrystie/Delancey*
71 Clinton *Clinton/Rivington-Stanton*
Torch *Ludlow/Rivington-Stanton*

Meatpacking District
(Gansevoort St. to W. 15th St., west of Ninth Ave.)
Chinghalle *Gansevoort/Greenw. s*
Florent *Gansevoort/Greenw. s-Wash.*
Frank's *10A/15s*
Fressen *13s/9A-Washington*
Hog Pit BBQ *9A/13s*
Lotus *14s/9-Washington*
Macelleria *Gansevoort/Greenw. s*
Markt *14s/9A*
Old Homestead *9A/14-5s*
Pastis *9A/Little W. 12s*
Petite Abeille *14s/9A*
Rhône *Gansevoort/Greenw. s-Wash.*
Rio Mar *9A/Little W. 12s*
Son Cubano *14s/9A-Washington*

Morningside Heights/ Columbia U.
(West of Morningside Ave., from W. 110th–W. 125th Sts.)
Le Monde *Bway/112-3s*
Ollie's *Bway/116s*
Terrace in Sky *119s/Amst.-Morning. Dr.*
Tomo Sushi *Bway/110-1s*
V&T *Amst./110-1s*

Murray Hill/East 30s
(40th to 30th Sts., east of Fifth Ave.)
Artisanal *Park/32s*
Asia de Cuba *Mad/37-8s*
Avalon Bar-Grill *32s/5A-Mad*
Baby Bo's *2A/34-5s*
Belluno *Lex/39-40s*
Bienvenue *36s/5A-Mad*
Chameleon *39s/Lex-Park*
Cinque Terre *38s/Mad-Park*
Da Ciro *Lex/33-4s*
East *38s/5A-Mad*
El Parador *34s/1-2A*
El Pote *2A/38-9s*
El Rio Grande *38s/Lex-3A*
Evergreen Shanghai *38s/5A-Mad*
Fino *36s/5A-Mad*
Frère Jacques *37s/5A-Mad*
Go Sushi *3A/34-5s*
Hangawi *32s/5A-Mad*
Houlihan's *5A/34s*

www.zagat.com 247

Location Index

Icon *39s/Lex*
Jackson Hole *3A/35s*
Josie's *3A/37s*
La Cocina *3A/30s*
La Giara *3A/33-4s*
Lemongrass Grill *34s/Lex-3A*
Madison Bistro *Mad/37s*
Marchi's *31s/2-3A*
Mario's Seafood *30s/5A-Mad*
Mee Noodle *2A/30-1s*
Metro Fish *36s/5A-Mad*
Mishima *Lex/30-1s*
Moondance *2A/33-4s*
Nadaman Hakubai *Park/38s*
Nicola Paone *34s/2-3A*
Notaro *2A/34-5s*
Ohta *Lex/30-1s*
Pasticcio *3A/30-1s*
Patsy's Pizzeria *3A/34-5s*
Pump *31s/Lex-Park S.*
Rive Gauche *3A/37s*
Rossini's *38s/Lex-Park*
Rungsit Thai *34s/2-3A*
Salute! *Mad/39s*
Sarge's Deli *3A/36-7s*
Sekku *Lex/39-40s*
Sonora *39s/2-3A*
Starbucks *2A/32s*
Stella del Mare *Lex/39-40s*
Sushi Sen-nin *34s/Mad-Park*
Toledo *36s/5A-Mad*
Tratt. Alba *34s/2-3A*
Tre Pomodori *34s/2-3A*
Villa Berulia *34s/Lex-Park*
Water Club, The *30s/East River*
Wu Liang Ye *Lex/39-40s*

SoHo – Little Italy
(Houston to Canal Sts., west of Bowery)

Alison *Dominick/Hudson-Varick*
Angelo's *Mulberry/Grand-Hester*
Aquagrill *Spring/6A*
Bacco *Spring/W. Bway-Wooster*
Balthazar *Spring/Bway-Crosby*
Baluchi's *Spring/Sullivan-Thompson*
Bar 89 *Mercer/Broome-Spring*
Barolo *W. Bway/Broome-Spring*
Bistro Les Amis *Spring/Thompson*
Bistrot Margot *Prince/Eliz.-Mott*
Blue Ribbon *Sullivan/Prince-Spring*
Blue Ribbon Sushi *Sullivan/Prince*
Bot *Mott/Prince-Spring*
Broome St. Bar *W. Bway/Broome*
Cafe Colonial *Elizabeth/Houston*
Café Habana *Prince/Elizabeth*
Cafe Noir *Grand/Thomspon*
Canal House *W. Bway/Canal-Grand*
Canteen *Mercer/Prince*
Casa La Femme *Wooster/Prince*
Cendrillon *Mercer/Broome-Grand*
Chez Bernard *W. Bway/Canal-Grand*
Clay *Mott/Kenmare-Spring*
Country Cafe *Thomp./Broome-Spring*
Cub Room *Sullivan/Prince*
Cupping Room Cafe *W. Bway/Broome*
Da Nico *Mulberry/Broome-Grand*
Eight Mile *Mulberry/Prince-Spring*
Fanelli Cafe *Prince/Mercer*
Félix *W. Bway/Grand*
Ferrara *Grand/Mott-Mulberry*
Funky Broome *Mott/Broome*
Ghenet *Mulberry/Houston-Prince*
Hampton Chutney *Prince/Bway*
Herban Kit. *Hudson/Dominick-Spring*
Honmura An *Mercer/Houston-Prince*
Ideya *W. Bway/Broome-Grand*
Il Corallo *Prince/Sullivan-Thompson*
Il Cortile *Mulberry/Canal-Hester*
Il Fornaio *Mulberry/Grand-Hester*
Il Palazzo *Mulberry/Grand-Hester*
I Tre Merli *W. Bway/Houston-Prince*
Jean Claude *Sullivan/Houston-Prince*
Jerry's *Prince/Greene-Mercer*
Kelley & Ping *Greene/Houston-Prince*
Kin Khao *Spring/Thompson-W. Bway*
Kitchen Club *Prince/Mott*
La Mela *Mulberry/Broome-Grand*
L'Ecole *Bway/Grand*
Le Gamin *MacDougal/Houston-Prince*
Le Jardin *Cleve. Pl./Kenmare-Spring*
Le Pain Quotidien *Grand/Mercer*
Le Pescadou *King/6A*
Little Italy Pizza *Varick/Charlton-King*
Lombardi's *Spring/Mott-Mulberry*
L'Orange Bleue *Broome/Crosby*
Lucky Strike *Grand/W. Bway-Wooster*
L'Ulivo *Spring/Thompson*
Manhattan Bistro *Spring/Greene*
Meigas *Hudson/King*
MeKong *Prince/Mott-Mulberry*
Mercer Kitchen *Prince/Mercer*
Mex. Radio *Cleve. Pl./Kenmare*
Mezzogiorno *Spring/Sullivan*
Ñ *Crosby/Broome-Grand*
Namaskaar *W. Bway/Grand*
Nello *W. Bway/Houston*
Novecento *W. Bway/Broome-Grand*
Nyonya *Grand/Mott-Mulberry*
Omen *Thompson/Prince-Spring*
Once Upon a Tart *Sullivan/Prince*
Onieal's *Grand/Centre-Mulberry*
Oro Blu *Hudson/Charlton*
Pão! *Spring/Greenwich s*
Peasant *Elizabeth/Prince-Spring*
Pellegrino's *Mulberry/Grand-Hester*
Penang *Spring/Greene-Mercer*
Pepe Rosso *Sullivan/Houston-Prince*

Location Index

Pfiff *Grand/Thompson*
Pho Bang *Mott/Broome-Grand*
Positano *Mulberry/Canal-Hester*
Provence *MacDougal/Prince*
Quilty's *Prince/Sullivan-Thompson*
Raoul's *Prince/Sullivan-Thompson*
Rialto *Elizabeth/Houston-Prince*
Rice *Mott/Prince-Spring*
Sal A's SPQR *Mulberry/Grand-Hester*
Savore *Spring/Sullivan*
Savoy *Prince/Crosby*
Sirocco *Prince/MacDougal-Sullivan*
Snack *Thompson/Prince-Spring*
Soho Steak *Thompson/Prince-Spring*
Spring St. Natural *Spring/Lafayette*
Stella *MacDougal/Houston-Prince*
Taormina *Mulberry/Grand-Hester*
Tennessee Mtn. *Spring/Wooster*
Thom *Thompson/Broome-Spring*
Va Tutto! *Cleve. Pl./Kenmare-Spring*
Woo Lae Oak *Mercer/Prince*
Wyanoka *Mott/Broome-Grand*
Zoë *Prince/Bway-Mercer*

TriBeCa – Downtown
(South of Canal St., including Wall St. area)

Acappella *Hudson/Chambers*
American Park *Battery Park/State*
Arqua *Church/White*
Au Mandarin *Vesey/West*
Bar Odeon *W. Bway/Duane-Thomas*
Bayard's *Hanover Sq./Pearl-Stone*
Bouley Bakery *W. Bway/Duane*
Bridge Cafe *Water/Dover*
Bubby's *Hudson/N. Moore*
Cabana Nuevo *Seaport/Fulton-John*
Capsouto Frères *Washington/Watts*
Chanterelle *Harrison/Hudson*
City Hall *Duane/Church-W. Bway*
Coco Marina *WFC/Liberty-Vesey*
Daily Soup *Broad/Beaver; John/Dutch-Nassau; Rector/Trinity Pl.*
Danube *Hudson/Duane-Reade*
Delmonico's *Beaver/S. William*
Duane Park *Duane/Hudson-W. Bway*
Dylan Prime *Laight/Greenwich s*
Ecco *Chambers/Church-W. Bway*
El Teddy's *W. Bway/Franklin-White*
55 Wall *Wall/Hanover-William*
F.illi Ponte *Debrosses/W. Side Hwy.*
Flor de Sol *Greenwich s/Harrison*
14 Wall St. *Wall/Broad-Bway*
Gigino *Greenwich s/Duane-Reade*
Gigino/Wagner Pk. *Battery Pl./West*
Grace *Franklin/Church-W. Bway*
Grill Room *Liberty/West*
Harbour Lights *Seaport/Fulton*
Harry's *Hanover Sq./Pearl-Stone*
Houlihan's *Bway/Fulton-John*
Hudson River Club *WFC/West St.*
Il Giglio *Warren/Greenwich s*
Independent *W. Bway/Leonard*
Ivy's Bistro *Greenwich s/N. Moore*
Juniper Café *Duane/Greenwich s*
Kitchenette *W. Bway/Warren*
Kori *Church/Franklin-Leonard*
Layla *W. Bway/Franklin*
Le Marais *John/Bway-Nassau*
Lemongrass Grill *Liberty/Church*
Le Zinc *Duane/Church-W. Bway*
Lili's Noodle *North End/Murray*
Little Italy *Park Pl./Bway-Church*
Mangia *Wall/Broad-William*
MarkJoseph Steak *Water/Peck Slip*
Montrachet *W. Bway/Walker-White*
Morton's *West/Albany-Cedar*
Nam Phuong *6A/Walker-White*
Nobu *Hudson/Franklin*
Obeca Li *Thomas/Church-W. Bway*
Odeon *W. Bway/Duane*
Pepolino *W. Bway/Canal-Lispenard*
Petite Abeille *W. Bway/Duane*
Pico *Greenwich s/Harrison-Jay*
Pizzeria Uno *Seaport/Pier 17*
Quartino *Peck Slip/Water*
Roc *Duane/Greenwich s*
Roy's NY *Washington/Albany-Carlisle*
Salaam Bombay *Greenwich s/Duane*
Scalini Fedeli *Duane/Greenwich s*
Screening Room *Varick/Laight*
Sosa Borella *Greenwich s/Watts*
St. Maggie's Cafe *Wall/Front-South*
T.G.I. Friday's *Bway/Exchange Pl.*
Thai House *Hudson/Hubert*
Tja! *Church/Walker*
Tribeca Grill *Greenwich s/Franklin*
Vine *Broad/Exchange Pl.*
Walker's *N. Moore/Varick*
Zutto *Hudson/Harrison*

Washington Hts. & Up
(North of W. 157th St.)

Dallas BBQ *Bway/166s*
New Leaf Cafe *M. Corbin/190s*

West 40s
(West of Fifth Ave., including Theater District)

Above *42s/7-8A*
Afghan Kebab Hse. *46s/6-7A*
Alfredo of Rome *49s/5-6A*
Algonquin Hotel *44s/5-6A*
Amarone *9A/47-8s*
Amy's Bread *9A/46-7s*
Babalu *44s/8-9A*
Baldoria *49s/Bway-8A*
Bali Nusa Indah *9A/45-6s*
Barbetta *46s/8-9A*
Becco *46s/8-9A*

Location Index

Bryant Park Grill/Cafe 40s/5-6A
B. Smith's 46s/8-9A
Burritoville 9A/44s
Cabana Carioca 45s/6-7A
Cafe Un Deux Trois 44s/Bway-6A
California Pizza 42s/7-8A
Cara Mia 9A/45-6s
Carmine's 44s/Bway-8A
Cascina 9A/45-6s
Charley O's 45s/Bway-8A
Charlotte 44s/Bway-6A
Chez Josephine 42s/9-10A
Chez Suzette 9A/46-7s
Chimichurri Grill 9A/43-44s
Citarella 6A/49s
Coco Pazzo 49s/Bway-8A
Cosi 42s/5-6A; 48s/5-6A
Dallas BBQ 43s/Bway-6A
db Bistro Moderne 44s/5-6A
Del Frisco's 6A/49s
Delta Grill 9A/48s
Dervish Turkish 47s/6-7A
Dish of Salt 47s/6-7A
District 46s/6-7A
Don Giovanni 44s/8-9A
Edison Cafe 47s/Bway-8A
Emerald Planet Rock Plz./49-50s
Esca 43s/9A
ESPN Zone Bway/42s
FireBird 46s/8-9A
Foley's Fish Hse. 7A/47-8s
44 & X Hell's Kit. 10A/44s
Frankie & Johnnie's 45s/Bway-8A
Gaby Brasserie 45s/5-6A
Hakata Grill 48s/Bway-8A
Hale & Hearty Soups 42s/5-6A
Hallo Berlin 10A/44-5s
Haru 43s/Bway-8A
Heartland Brewery 43s/Bway-6A
Hell's Kitchen 9A/46-7s
Houlihan's 7A/49s
Hourglass Tavern 46s/8-9A
Ilo 40s/5-6A
Ipanema 46s/5-6A
Island Spice 44s/9-10A
Jack Rose 8A/47s
Jewel of India 44s/5-6A
Jezebel 9A/45s
Joe Allen 46s/8-9A
John's Pizzeria 44s/Bway-8A
J. W.'s Steakhouse Bway/45-6s
Kodama Sushi 45s/8-9A
Krispy Kreme 8A/40-1s
Kyma 46s/8A
La Cocina 8A/46-7s
La Locanda 9A/49-50s
Landmark Tavern 11A/46s
La Rivista 46s/8-9A
Lattanzi 46s/8-9A
Le Beaujolais 46s/8-9A
Le Garrick 49s/Bway-8A
Le Madeleine 43s/9-10A
Le Marais 46s/6-7A
Le Rivage 46s/8-9A
Little Italy Pizza 45s/5-6A
Lotfi's 46s/8-9A
Luxia 48s/8-9A
Manhattan Chili Bway/43s
Maritime 49s/6-7A
McHales 8A/46s
Meskerem 47s/9-10A
Monster Sushi 46s/5-6A
Mont Blanc 48s/8-9A
Morrell Wine Bar 49s/5-6A
My Most Favorite 45s/Bway-6A
Nation 45s/5-6A
Ollie's 44s/Bway-8A
Orso 46s/8-9A
Osteria al Doge 44s/Bway-6A
Pam Real Thai 49s/9-10A
Papaya King 43s/7-8A
Pergola/Artistes 46s/Bway-8A
Pierre au Tunnel 47s/Bway-8A
Pietrasanta 9A/47s
Planet Hollywood Bway/45s
Pongsri 48s/Bway-8A
Queen of Sheba 10A/45-6s
Rachel's 9A/43-44s
Rainbow Room Rock Plz./49-50s
Ruby Foo's Bway/49s
Sag Harbor 48s/8-9A
Sardi's 44s/Bway-8A
Sea Grill 49s/5-6A
Shaan 48s/5-6A
Soul Cafe 42s/9-10A
Supper Club 47s/Bway-8A
Sushiden 49s/6-7A
Sushi Zen 46s/5-6A
T.G.I. Friday's Bway/46s
Torre di Pisa 44s/5-6A
Tossed Rock Plz./49-50s
Tratt. Dopo Teatro 44s/Bway-6A
Triomphe 44s/5-6A
Two Boots Rock Plz./49-50s
Utsav 6A/46-7s
Via Brasil 46s/5-6A
View Bway/45-6s
Virgil's 44s/Bway-6A
West Bank Cafe 42s/9-10A
World Yacht 41s/12A
Wu Liang Ye 48s/5-6A
WWF NY Bway/43s
Zen Palate 9A/46s
Zuni 9A/43s

West 50s
(West of Fifth Ave.)
Adrienne 5A/55s
Afghan Kebab Hse. 9A/51-2s
Alain Ducasse 58s/6-7A
Angelo & Maxie's 6A/52s

Location Index

Angelo's Pizzeria *57s/6-7A*
Aquavit *54s/5-6A*
Artusi *52s/5-6A*
Atlas *CPS/5-6A*
Azuri Cafe *51s/9-10A*
Baluchi's *56s/Bway-8A*
Bangkok Cuisine *8A/52-3s*
Bay Leaf *56s/5-6A*
Beacon *56s/5-6A*
Bello *9A/56s*
Ben Benson's *52s/6-7A*
Benihana *56s/5-6A*
Bistro Latino *Bway/54s*
Bombay Palace *52s/5-6A*
Brasserie 8½ *57s/5-6A*
Bricco *56s/8-9A*
Broadway Diner *Bway/55s*
Brooklyn Diner USA *57s/Bway-7A*
Café Botanica *CPS/6-7A*
Caffe Cielo *8A/52-3s*
Carnegie Deli *7A/55s*
Castellano *55s/6-7A*
Chanpen Thai *9A/51s*
Chez Napoléon *50s/8-9A*
China Fun *Bway/51-2s*
China Grill *53s/5-6A*
Christer's *55s/6-7A*
Ciao Europa *54s/5-6A*
Circo *55s/6-7A*
Cité *51s/6-7A*
Cité Grill *51s/6-7A*
Cosi *Bway/51s*
Daily Soup *54s/Bway-8A*
Dakshin *9A/50s*
Da Tommaso *9A/53-4s*
Druids *10A/50 1s*
East *55s/Bway-8A*
Eatery *9A/53s*
Ellen's Stardust *Bway/51s*
Gallagher's *52s/Bway-8A*
Giovanni *55s/5-6A*
Go Sushi *9A/50s*
Grand Sichuan *9A/50-1s*
Halcyon *54s/6-7A*
Hale & Hearty Soups *56s/5-6A*
Hallo Berlin *51s/9A*
Hard Rock Cafe *57s/Bway-7A*
Harley Davidson Cafe *6A/56s*
Heartland Brewery *51s/6-7A*
Hudson Cafeteria *58s/8-9A*
Il Tinello *56s/5-6A*
Island Burgers *9A/51-2s*
Jekyll & Hyde *6A/57-8s*
Joe's Shanghai *56s/5-6A*
JUdson Grill *52s/6-7A*
Julian's *9A/53-4s*
Kabul Cafe *54s/Bway-8A*
Keewah Yen *56s/5-6A*
Kiiroi-Hana *56s/5-6A*
La Bonne Soupe *55s/5-6A*
La Caravelle *55s/5-6A*
La Côte Basque *55s/5-6A*
Le Bernardin *51s/6-7A*
Limoncello *7A/51s*
Lundy Bros. *50s/Bway-7A*
Mangia *57s/5-6A*
Mangia e Bevi *9A/53s*
Manhattan Chili *Bway/53-4s*
Manhattan Ocean *58s/5-6A*
Maristella *55s/5-6A*
Mars 2112 *Bway/51s*
Medi *Rock Plz./50s*
Mee Noodle *9A/53s*
Menchanko-tei *55s/5-6A*
Michael's *55s/5-6A*
Mickey Mantle's *CPS/5-6A*
Milos *55s/6-7A*
Minotaur *58s/5-6A*
Molyvos *7A/55-6s*
Nirvana *CPS/5-6A*
Nocello *55s/Bway-8A*
Norma's *57s/6-7A*
Oak Room *5A/CPS*
Old San Juan *9A/51-2s*
One C.P.S. *CPS/5A*
Onigashima *55s/5-6A*
Oyster Bar/Plaza *58s/5-6A*
Palio *51s/6-7A*
Palm *50s/Bway-8A*
Palm Court *5A/CPS*
Patsy's *56s/Bway-8A*
Petrossian *58s/7A*
Pump *55s/5-6A*
Puttanesca *9A/56s*
Redeye Grill *7A/56s*
Red Garlic *8A/54-5s*
Remi *53s/6-7A*
René Pujol *51s/8-9A*
Rice 'n' Beans *9A/50-1s*
Rinconcito Peruano *9A/53-4s*
Rist. del Sogno *8A/55-6s*
Rock Center Café *55s/5-6A*
Rue 57 Brasserie *57s/6A*
Russian Samovar *52s/Bway-8A*
Russian Tea Rm. *57s/6-7A*
Ruth's Chris *51s/6-7A*
Saigon Fun *9A/51-2s*
Salute! *57s/6A*
San Domenico *CPS/Bway-7A*
Seeda Thai *50s/8-9A*
Seppi's *56s/6-7A*
Sette MoMA *53s/5-6A*
Shelly's NY *57s/6-7A*
Siam Inn *8A/51-2s*
Soup Kitchen Int'l *55s/Bway-8A*
Stage Deli *7A/53-4s*
Sugiyama *55s/Bway-8A*
Sushiya *56s/5-6A*
Tang Pavilion *55s/5-6A*
Ten Kai *56s/5-6A*
T.G.I. Friday's *51s/5-6A; 7A/50s; Bway/52-3s*

Location Index

Thalia *8A/50s*
Tino's *56s/5-6A*
Topaz Thai *56s/6-7A*
Tout Va Bien *51s/8-9A*
Town *56s/5-6A*
Trattoria Dell'Arte *7A/57s*
Tuscan Sq. *51s/5-6A*
'21' Club *52s/5-6A*
Uncle Nick's *9A/50-1s*
ViceVersa *51s/8-9A*
Victor's Cafe *52s/Bway-8A*
Vynl *9A/54s*
Wolf's *57s/5-6A*
Wondee Siam *9A/52-3s*
Zenith Vegetarian *8A/52s*

West 60s
(West of Fifth Ave.)
Café des Artistes *67s/Col.-CPW*
Cafe Fiorello *Bway/63-4s*
Empire Szechuan *Col./68-9s*
Gabriel's *60s/Bway-Col.*
Houlihan's *Bway/63s*
Jean Georges *CPW/60-1s*
John's Pizzeria *65s/Col.-CPW*
Josephina *Bway/63-4s*
La Boite en Bois *68s/Col.-CPW*
Levana *69s/Bway-Col.*
Nick & Toni's *67s/Bway-Col.*
Ollie's *Bway/67-8s*
O'Neals' *64s/Bway-CPW*
Picholine *64s/Bway-CPW*
Rosa Mexicano *Col./62s*
Saloon *Bway/64s*
Santa Fe *69s/Col.-CPW*
Sapphire *Bway/60-1s*
Shun Lee *65s/Col.-CPW*
Shun Lee Cafe *65s/Col.-CPW*
Starbucks *Col./67s*
Sushi a-go-go *Bway/63-4s*
Tavern on Green *CPW/66-7s*
Vince & Eddie's *68s/Col.-CPW*
West 63rd Steak *63s/Bway-Col.*

West 70s
(West of Central Park)
Baci *Amst./79-80s*
Baluchi's *Col./73-4s*
Big Nick's *Bway/76-7s*
Burritoville *72s/Amst.-Col*
Café Frida *Col./77-8s*
Cafe Luxembourg *70s/Amst.-W. End*
China Fun *Col./71-2s*
Citrus B&G *Amst./75s*
City Grill *Col./72-3s*
Coppola's *79s/Amst.-Bway*
Dallas BBQ *72s/Col.-CPW*
Diwan's Curry Hse. *Col./74-5s*
Emack & Bolio's *Amst./78-9s*
Empire Szechuan *72s/Bway-W. End*
Epices du Traiteur *70s/Bway-Col.*
Ernie's *Bway/75-6s*
Fairway Cafe *Bway/74s*
Fine & Schapiro *72s/Bway-Col.*
Gabriela's *Amst./75s*
Gray's Papaya *Bway/72s*
Hunan Park *Col./70-1s*
Isabella's *Col./77s*
Ivy's Cafe *72s/Bway-Col.*
Josie's *Amst./74s*
Krispy Kreme *72s/Bway-Col.*
La Caridad 78 *Bway/78s*
La Grolla, Rist. *Amst./79-80s*
Le Pain Quotidien *72s/Col.-CPW*
Marika *70s/Amst.-W. End*
Metsovo *70s/Col.-CPW*
Mughlai *Col./75s*
Niko's *Bway/76s*
Ocean Grill *Col./78-9s*
Pasha *71s/Col.-CPW*
Patsy's Pizzeria *74s/Col.-CPW*
Penang *Col./71s*
Planet Sushi *Amst./78s*
Pomodoro Rosso *Col./70-1s*
River *Amst./76-7s*
Ruby Foo's *Bway/77s*
Sambuca *72s/Col.-CPW*
Savann *Amst./79-80s*
Scaletta *77s/Col.-CPW*
Shark Bar *Amst./74-5s*
Soma Soup *Bway/71-2s*
Spazzia *Col./77s*
Sugar Bar *72s/Bway-W. End*
Two Two Two *79s/Amst.-Bway*
Vinnie's Pizza *Amst./73-4s*
Zen Palate *Bway/76-7s*

West 80s
(West of Central Park)
Artie's Deli *Bway/82-3s*
Assaggio *Col./82-3s*
Avenue
Barney Greengrass *Amst./86-7s*
Bella Luna *Col./88-9s*
Brother Jimmy's *Amst./80-1s*
Burritoville *Amst./81-2s*
Cafe Con Leche *Amst./80-1s*
Cafe Lalo *83s/Amst.-Bway*
Calle Ocho *Col./81-2s*
Campo *Amst./84-5s*
Columbus Bakery *Col./82-3s*
Darna *Col./89s*
Docks Oyster *Bway/89-90s*
Edgar's Cafe *84s/Bway-W. End*
EJ's Luncheonette *Amst./81-2s*
Flor de Mayo *Amst./83-4s*
Fred's *Amst./83s*
French Roast *Bway/85s*
Fujiyama Mama *Col./82-3s*
Good Enough to Eat *Amst./83-4s*
Haru *Amst./80-1s*
Isola *Col./83-4s*
Jackson Hole *Col./85s*

Location Index

Jean-Luc *Col./84-5s*
La Bicyclette *Col./85s*
La Cocina *85s/Amst.-Bway*
La Mirabelle *86s/Amst.-Col.*
Les Routiers *Amst./87-8s*
Luzia's *Amst./80-1s*
Merchants, N.Y. *Col./85-6s*
Monsoon *Amst./81s*
Nëo Sushi *Bway/83s*
Ollie's *Bway/84s*
Ouest *Bway/84s*
Pizzeria Uno *Col./81s*
Popover Cafe *Amst./86-7s*
Rain *82s/Amst.-Col.*
Roppongi *Amst./81s*
Sabor *Amst./82-3s*
Saigon Grill *Bway/87s*
Sarabeth's *Amst./80-1s*
Silk Road Palace *Amst./81-2s*
Time Cafe *Bway/85s*

West 90s & 100s
(West of Fifth Ave.)
A *Col./106-7s*
Afghan Kebab Hse. *Bway/102s*
Alouette *Bway/97-8s*
Cafe Con Leche *Amst./95-6s*
Carmine's *Bway/90-1s*
Cooke's Corner *Amst./90s*
Empire Szechuan *Bway/100s; Bway/97s; Bway/170-1s*
Fish *Bway/108s*
Flor de Mayo *Bway/101s*
Gabriela's *Amst./93s*
Gennaro *Amst./92-3s*
Henry's *Bway/105s*
Hunan Park *Col./95s*
La Cocina *Bway/98-9s*
Lemongrass Grill *Bway/94-5s*
Mamá Mexico *Bway/101-2s*
Mary Ann's *Bway/90-1s*
Métisse *105s/Amst.-Bway*
Pampa *Amst./97-8s*
Pearls *Amst./99s*
Roth's Westside Steak *Col./93s*
Sipan *Amst./94s*
Tratt. Pesce & Pasta *Col./90-1s*
Turkuaz *Bway/100s*

BRONX

Bellavista Cafe *235s/Johnson*
Dominick's *Arthur/Crescent-187s*
Enzo's *Williamsbridge/Neill*
Jimmy's *W. Fordham/Mjr. Deegan*
Le Refuge Inn *City Is./Sutherland*
Lobster Box *City Is./Belden*
Mario's *Arthur/184-186s*
Roberto's *186s/Belmont*
Starbucks *E. Fordham/Elm Pl.*

BROOKLYN

Bay Ridge
Areo *3A/85s*
Baci Italian *3A/71-2s*
Chadwick's *3A/89s*
Chianti *3A/86s*
Eliá *3A/86-7s*
Embers *3A/95-6s*
Omonia Cafe *3A/76-7s*
101 *4A/100-1s*
Pizzeria Uno *4A/92s*
Provence en Boite *3A/83-4s*
St. Michel *3A/76s*
Tuscany Grill *3A/86-7s*

Bensonhurst
Tommaso's *86s/14-5A*

Boerum Hill
BarTabac *Smith/Dean*
Boerum Hill *Smith/Bergen-Dean*
Brawta Caribbean *Atlantic/Hoyt*
Brooklyn Grill *Atlantic/Hoyt-Smith*
Saul *Smith/Bergen-Dean*
Smith St. Kitchen *Smith/Warren*
Two Toms *3A/President-Union*

Brighton Beach
Rasputin *Coney Island/Ave. X*

Brooklyn Hts./DUMBO
Cafe Petite Crevette *Atlantic/Henry*
Coq Hardi *Montague/Clinton-Henry*
Gage & Tollner *Fulton/Jay*
Grappa Café *Court/State*
Grimaldi's *Old Fulton/Front-Water*
Hale & Hearty Soups *Court/Remsen*
Heights Cafe *Montague/Hicks*
Henry's End *Henry/Cranberry*
La Bouchée *Montague/Clinton*
La Bouillabaisse *Atlantic/Clinton*
Noodle Pudding *Henry/Middagh*
Pete's Dtwn. *Water/Cadman Plaza W.*
Queen *Court/Livingston-Schermerhorn*
Rice *Washington/Front-York*
River Cafe *Water/Furman-Old Fulton*
Teresa's *Montague/Hicks*
Tinto *Henry/Cranberry*

Carroll Gardens
Banania Cafe *Smith/Douglass*
Cafe Luluc *Smith/Baltic*
Don Luca *Smith/Baltic-Butler*

Location Index

Faan *Smith/Baltic*
Ferdinando's *Union/Columbia-Hicks*
Grocery *Smith/Sackett-Union*
Kotobuki Bistro *Columbia/DeGraw-Sackett*
Marco Polo *Court/Union*
Mignon *Court/Carroll-1 Pl.*
Monte's *Carroll/Nevins-3A*
Patois *Smith/DeGraw-Douglass*
Pepe Viola *Smith/Baltic*
Red Rail *Henry/Sackett*
Sur *Smith/Butler-Douglass*
Uncle Pho *Smith/DeGraw*
Wasabi *Smith/Baltic-Butler*

Clinton Hill
Locanda Vini *Gates/Cambridge Pl.*

Cobble Hill
Harvest *Court/Warren*
Joya *Court/Warren*
Osaka *Court/DeGraw-Kane*
Sherwood Cafe *Smith/Baltic*
Sweet Melissa *Court/Butler*

Coney Island
Gargiulo's *15s/Mermaid-Surf*
Totonno Pizzeria *Neptune/15-6s*

Downtown
Archives *Adams/Willoughby*
Junior's *Flatbush Ext./DeKalb*
New City *Lafayette/Ashland Pl.*

Dyker Heights
Outback Steak *86s/15A*

Fort Greene
À Table *Lafayette/Adelphi*
Cambodian Cuis. *S. Elliot/Fulton*
Chez Oskar *DeKalb/Adelphi*
Liquors *DeKalb/Adelphi-Clermont*
Loulou *DeKalb/Adelphi-Clermont*
Madiba *DeKalb/Adelphi-Carlton*
Mo-Bay *DeKalb/Ashland-Rockwell*
Sol *DeKalb/Clermont*

Gravesend
Fiorentino's *Ave. U/McDonald-West*
Sahara *Coney Island Ave./Aves. T-U*

Greenpoint
Thai Cafe *Manhattan/Kent*

Ocean Parkway
Ocean Palace *Ave. U/14-5s*

Park Slope
Al Di La *5A/Carroll*
Beso *5A/Union*
Bistro St. Mark's *St. Mark's/Flatbush*
Blue Ribbon *5A/1s-Garfield Pl.*
Bonnie's Grill *5A/1s-Garfield Pl.*
Cafe Steinhof *7A/14s*
Chip Shop *5A/6-7s*
Cocina Cuzco *7A/3s*
Coco Roco *5A/6-7s*
Convivium *5A/Bergen-St. Mark's*
Cucina *5A/Carroll-Garfield Pl.*
Dizzy's *9s/8A*
Gingko Leaf Cafe *Union/6-7A*
Lemongrass *7A/Berkeley-Lincoln Pls.*
Long Tan *5A/Berkeley Pl.-Union*
Magnolia *6A/12s*
Max & Moritz *7A/14-5s*
Mike & Tony's *5A/Carroll*
Rose Water *Union/6A*
12th St. B&G *8A/12s*
Two Boots *2s/7-8A*
Vaux Bistro *5A/1s-Garfield Pl.*

Prospect Heights
Garden Cafe *Vanderbilt/Prospect Pl.*
New Prospect Cafe *Flatbush/Plaza*
Tom's *Washington/Sterling Pl.*

Sheepshead Bay
Lundy Bros. *Emmons/Ocean A*

Sunset Park
Jade Plaza *8A/60-1s*
Nyonya *8A/54s*
Ocean Palace *8A/54-5s*

Williamsburg
Allioli *Grand/Havemeyer-Roebling*
Bamonte's *Withers/Lorimer-Union*
Carmaya *6s/Bedford*
Diner *Bway/Berry*
DuMont *Union/Devoe-Metropolitan*
Miss Williamsburg *Kent/3s*
Oznot's Dish *Berry/9s*
Peter Luger *Bway/Driggs*
Planet Thailand *7s/Berry*
Relish *Wythe/Metropolitan-3s*
Vera Cruz *Bedford/6-7s*
Wasabi *Bedford/5-6s*

QUEENS

Astoria
Amici Amore I *Newton/30s*
Christos Hasapo *23A/41s*
Elias Corner *31s/24A*
Esperides *30A/37s*
Karyatis *Bway/35-6s*
Mombar *Steinway/25-28A*
Omonia Cafe *Bway/33s*
Piccola Venezia *28A/42s*
Ponticello *Bway/46-7s*
S'Agapo *34A/35s*
Stamatis *23A/29-30s; Bway/31-32s*
Syros Seafood *Bway/32-3s*
Taverna Kyclades *Ditmars/33-35s*

Location Index

Taverna Vraka *31s/23-4A*
Telly's Taverna *23A/28-9s*
Tierras Colombianas *Bway/33s*
Tratt. L'incontro *31s/Ditmars*
Ubol's Kitchen *Steinway/Astoria-25A*
Uncle George's *Bway/34s*

Bayside
Ben's Kosher Deli *26A/Bell*
Caffé on the Green *Cross Is. Pkwy*
Jackson Hole *Bell/35A*
Marbella *Northern/220-1s*
Outback Steak *Bell/26A*
Pier 25A *Northern/215s*
Pizzeria Uno *Bell/39A*
Uncle Jack's Steak *Bell/40A*

Corona
Green Field Churr. *Northern/108s*
Park Side *Corona/51A*

Douglaston
B.K. Sweeney's *235s/RR Station*

Elmhurst
Jai Ya Thai *Bway/81-2s*
Joe's Shanghai *Bway/45A-Whitney*
Pho Bang *Bway/Elmhurst*
Ping's Seafood *Queens/Goldsmith*

Flushing
East Lake *Main/Franklin*
Figs *La Guardia Airport*
Jade Palace *38A/Main*
Joe's Shanghai *37A/Main-Union*
K.B. Garden *39A/Main-Union*
Kum Gang San *Northern/Main-Union*
Master Grill *College Point/34-5A*
Penang *Prince/Main*
Pho Bang *Kissena/Main*
Silver Pond *Main/56A*
Sweet-n-Tart *38A/Main*
Woo Chon *Kissena/Main*

Forest Hills
Baluchi's *Queens/76 Rd.*
Bann Thai *Austin/Yellowstone*
Cabana *70 Rd./Austin-Queens*
Mardi Gras *Austin/70A-70 Rd.*
Nick's Pizza *Ascan/Austin-Burns*
Pizzeria Uno *70 Rd./Austin-Queens*
Q, a Thai Bistro *Ascan/Austin-Burns*

Glendale
Gebhardt's *Myrtle/65 Pl.-65s*
Zum Stammtisch *Myrtle/Cooper*

Jackson Heights
Afghan Kebab Hse. *37A/74-5s*
Delhi Palace *74s/Roosevelt-37A*
Jackson Diner *74s/Roosevelt-37A*
Jackson Hole *Astoria/70s*
Pearson's *35A/71-2s*
Tibetan Yak *Roosevelt/72s*
Tierras Colombianas *Roosevelt/83s*

Little Neck
La Baraka *Northern/Little Neck Pkwy.*

Long Island City
Jackson Ave. Steak *Jackson/47 Rd.*
Manducatis *Jackson/47A*
Water's Edge *44 Dr. & East River*

Middle Village
Niederstein's *Metropolitan/69s*

Ozone Park
Don Peppe *Lefferts/149A*

Rego Park
Kazan *Queens/63A-63 Dr.*
London Lennie's *Woodhaven/Fleet*

Whitestone
Cooking with Jazz *154s/12A*

Woodside
La Flor Bakery *Roosevelt/53s-43A*
Sapori d'Ischia *37A/56s*

STATEN ISLAND

Aesop's Tables *Bay/Maryland*
American Grill *Forest/Bard-Hart*
Angelina's *Jefferson/Annadale*
Carol's Cafe *Richmond/Four Corners*
Denino's *Pt. Richmond/Hooker*
Hist. Old Bermuda *Arthur Kill/St. Lukes*
Killmeyer's *Arthur Kill/Sharrotts*
Marina Cafe *Mansion/Hillside*
Parsonage *Arthur Kill/Clarke*
South Shore Country Club *Huguenot/Shore Expy.*
3333 *Hylan/Hopkins-Spratt*
Tratt. Romana *Hylan/Benton*

Special Features

(Restaurants followed by a † may not offer that feature at every location.)

All You Can Eat
(Call ahead for times and prices)
Bangkok Cuisine (Wed-Fri lunch)
Bay Leaf
Becco
Bombay Palace
Brother Jimmy's (Sun–Mon, Wed)†
Bukhara Grill
Charles' Southern
Chola
Churrascaria Plataforma
Green Field Churr.
Killmeyer's (Mon-Tue)
La Tour (mussels)
Master Grill
Shaan
Tennessee Mtn. (Mon–Tues)
Utsav
Yuka

Bathrooms to Visit
Bar 89
Bateaux NY
Beacon
Blue Hill
Brasserie
Café Botanica
Cello
Daniel
Danube
ESPN Zone
Guastavino
Jean Georges
Marika
Ñ
Pastis
Picholine
P.J. Clarke's
Rainbow Room
Rock Center Café
Sea Grill
Tao
Town

Breakfast
(All hotels and the following standouts)
An American Pl.
Anglers & Writers
Avenue
Balthazar
Barney Greengrass
Bendix Diner
Brasserie 8½
Broadway Diner†
Brooklyn Diner USA†
Bubby's
Café Botanica
Cafe Con Leche
Cafeteria
Carlyle
City Bakery
Columbus Bakery
Comfort Diner
Copeland's
Cupping Room Cafe
E.A.T.
EJ's Luncheonette
Empire Diner
Florent
French Roast
Friend of a Farmer
Good Enough to Eat
Googie's
Home
Jean Georges
Jerry's
Junior's†
Katz's Deli
Kitchenette
La Bergamote
Le Pain Quotidien†
L'Express
Mayrose
Michael's
Norma's
Once Upon a Tart
Pastis
Payard Bistro
Pershing Sq.
Pink Tea Cup
Popover Cafe
Ratner's
Red Rail
Regency
Rock Center Café
Sant Ambroeus
Sarabeth's†
Second Ave. Deli
Tartine
Teresa's
Tom's
Veselka
Viand
Yura & Co.

Special Feature Index

Brunch
Ambassador Grill
America
Anglers & Writers
Aquagrill
Aquavit
Artisanal
Avenue
Balthazar
Blue Water Grill
Box Tree
Butterfield 81
Café Botanica
Café de Bruxelles
Café des Artistes
Cafe Luxembourg
Candela
Capsouto Frères
Carlyle
Charlotte
Chez Michallet
Copeland's
Cornelia St. Cafe
Danal
Dolphins
Eli's Vinegar Fact.
Ferrier Bistro
First
Five Points
Friend of a Farmer
Gascogne
Grange Hall
Grove
Gus' Place
Halcyon
Harbour Lights
Independent
Isabella's
Jubilee
Jules
La Belle Epoque
La Belle Vie
L'Absinthe
La Goulue
Landmark Tavern
Le Jardin Bistro
Le Singe Vert
Lola
Londel's
L'Orange Bleue
Manhattan Grille
Marion's
Mark's
Markt
Metropolitan Cafe
Nadine's
New Prospect Cafe
Odeon
Palm Court
Park Avalon
Park Ave. Cafe
Pastis
Patois
Provence
Quilty's
River Cafe
Rocking Horse
Rose Water
Shark Bar
Sur
Sylvia's
Tavern on Green
Time Cafe
Trata
Tribeca Grill
Verbena
View
Walker's
Water Club, The
Zoë

Buffet Served
(Nearly all Indians, plus the following)
Adrienne
Al Baraka
Ambassador Grill
Aquavit
Arabelle
Café Botanica
Carlyle
Casimir
Charlotte
Chazal Bistro
Flea Mkt. Cafe
Gabriela's†
Halcyon
Historic Old Bermuda
Jimmy's Uptown
La Belle Epoque
Lavagna
Londel's
Mekka
Palm Court
Peacock Alley
Roy's NY
Sahara
Shark Bar
Soul Cafe
Sugar Bar
View
Water Club, The
World Yacht

Business Dining
Al Bustan
Alfredo of Rome
Aquavit

Special Feature Index

Artisanal
Aureole
Bayard's
Ben Benson's
Beppe
Bouley Bakery
Bukhara Grill
Chiam Chinese
China Grill
Chin Chin
Citarella
City Hall
Craft
Daniel
Da Umberto
Dawat
db Bistro Moderne
Del Frisco's
District
Duane Park Cafe
Eleven Madison Pk.
FireBird
Four Seasons
14 Wall St.
Fresco by Scotto
Gabriel's
Gage & Tollner
Gotham B&G
Haikara Grill
Hudson River Club
Il Menestrello
Il Nido
Ilo
Il Postino
Jean Georges
Kuruma Zushi
La Caravelle
La Côte Basque
Le Bernardin
Le Cirque 2000
Le Marais
Manhattan Ocean
MarkJoseph Steak
Michael's
Milos
Morton's
Oceana
Orso
Palm
Periyali
Petrossian
Redeye Grill
River Cafe
San Domenico
San Pietro
Shaan
Shun Lee Palace
Smith & Wollensky
Sparks Steak
Sugiyama
Sushisay
Town
Trattoria Dell'Arte
Tropica
Tse Yang
'21' Club
Union Pacific
Union Sq. Cafe
Vine
Virot
Vong
Zarela

Celebrity Chefs

(Most celeb chefs travel often and don't actually cook even when on-premises)

Alain Ducasse, *Alain Ducasse*
An American Pl., *Larry Forgione*
Annisa, *Anita Lo*
Aquavit, *Marcus Samuelsson*
Arezzo, *Margherita Aloi*
Artisanal, *Terry Brennan*
Atlas, *David Coleman*
AZ, *Patricia Yeo*
Babbo, *Mario Batali*
Bayard's, *Eberhard Mueller*
Beacon, *Waldy Malouf*
Beppe, *Cesare Casella*
Bouley Bakery, *David Bouley*
Campagna, *Mark Strausman*
Cello, *Laurent Tourondel*
Chanterelle, *David Waltuck*
Chicama, *Douglas Rodriguez*
Christer's, *Christer Larsson*
Craft, *Tom Colicchio*
Daniel, *Daniel Boulud*
Danube, *David Bouley*
Destinée, *Jean-Yves Schillinger*
Felidia, *Lidia Bastianich*
Fleur de Sel, *Cyril Renaud*
Four Seasons, *Christian Albin*
Gotham B&G, *Alfred Portale*
Gramercy Tavern, *Tom Colicchio*
Ilo, *Rick Laakkonen*
Jean Georges, *Jean-Georges Vongerichten*
JUdson Grill, *Bill Telepan*
La Côte Basque, *Jean-Jacques Rachou*
Le Bernardin, *Eric Ripert*
Le Cirque 2000, *Pierre Schaedelin*
L'Ecole, *Alain Sailhac*
Les Halles, *Anthony Bourdain*
Lespinasse, *Christian Delouvrier*
Lutèce, *David Féau*
March, *Wayne Nish*
Mesa Grill, *Bobby Flay*
Mi, *Gary Robins*
Monkey Bar, *David Walzog*

Special Feature Index

Nobu, *Nobu Matsuhisa*
Oceana, *Rick Moonen*
Olives, *Todd English*
One C.P.S., *David Burke*
Ouest, *Tom Valenti*
Payard, *F. Payard, P. Bertineau*
Peacock Alley, *Laurent Gras*
Picholine, *Terry Brennan*
Quilty's, *Katy Sparks*
River Cafe, *Brad Steelman*
San Domenico, *Odette Fada*
Sandro's, *Sandro Fioriti*
Scopa, *Vincent Scotto*
Sea Grill, *Ed Brown*
71 Clinton, *Wylie Dufresne*
Soup Kitchen Int'l, *Al Yeganeh*
Town, *Geoffrey Zakarian*
Union Pacific, *Rocco DiSpirito*
Union Sq. Cafe, *Michael Romano*
Verbena, *Diane Forley & Michael Otsuka*
Veritas, *Scott Bryan*
Zarela, *Zarela Martinez*

Cheese Trays

Alain Ducasse
Alva
Artisanal
Aureole
Babbo
Brasserie 8½
Cafe Steinhof
Cello
Chanterelle
Circo
Commune
Eleven Madison Pk.
Fred's at Barneys
Gramercy Tavern
Guastavino
Herban Kitchen
I Trulli
Jean Georges
JUdson Grill
La Caravelle
La Grenouille
Lespinasse
Milos
One C.P.S.
Picholine
Solera
Veritas

Child-Friendly

(Besides the normal fast-food places; * indicates children's menu available)
America*
Amy Ruth's*
Anglers & Writers*
Avenue*
Barking Dog†
Bateaux NY
B B&G*
Benihana
B.K. Sweeney's*
Brooklyn Diner USA†
Brother Jimmy's*
Bryant Park Grill/Cafe
Cafe Un Deux Trois
Campagna*
Carmine's
Carnegie Deli
Centolire*
Charles' Southern
Churrascaria Plataforma
City Hall*
Comfort Diner*
Copeland's
Cowgirl Hall of Fame*
Dallas BBQ†
EJ's Luncheonette*
Ellen's Stardust*
Empire Szechuan†
Ernie's*
ESPN Zone*
Figs*
Friend of a Farmer*
Gabriela's*
Gebhardt's*
Good Enough to Eat*
Googie's*
Green Field Churr.*
Guastavino, Downstairs*
Hard Rock Cafe*
Harbour Lights*
Harley Davidson Cafe*
Harvest*
Heartland Brewery*
Historic Old Bermuda*
Houston's†
Il Cortile*
Isabella's
Jack Rose*
Jackson Hole*
Johnny Rockets*
John's Pizzeria
Junior's*
Juniper Café*
Katz's Deli
La Bonne Soupe*
Lobster Box*
Lundy Bros.*
Manhattan Chili*
Mars 2112*
Mary Ann's*
Mezzaluna*
Mickey Mantle's*
Niko's*
92*

Special Feature Index

Nirvana
Norma's*
Odeon*
O'Neals'*
Outback Steak*
Patsy's Pizzeria†
Peanut Butter & Co.*
Pizzeria Uno*
Popover Cafe*
Red Rail*
Rock Center Café*
Saloon*
Sarabeth's
Second Ave. Deli
Serendipity 3
Spazzia*
Stage Deli*
Sylvia's*
Tavern on Green*
Tennessee Mtn.*
Tony's Di Napoli*
Tortilla Flats*
Tribeca Grill*
Two Boots*
Virgil's
Walker's*
WWF NY*
Zum Stammtisch*

Delivery/Takeout

(Nearly all Asians, coffee shops, delis, diners and pizzerias deliver or do takeout; here are some best bets that do both; call to check range and charges, if any)
Amy Ruth's
Artisanal
Barney Greengrass
Bayou
Broadway Diner
Brother Jimmy's
Burritoville
Carmine's
Carnegie Deli
Chin Chin
Columbus Bakery
Cooke's Corner
Copeland's
Cupping Room Cafe
Daily Soup
Dallas BBQ
D'Artagnan
Dawat
Dim Sum Go Go
E.A.T.
Eisenberg Sandwich
EJ's Luncheonette
Emerald Planet
Fred's
Fresco on the Go
Gabriela's
good
Isola
Kodama Sushi
Lentini
Les Halles
Levana
Lombardi's
Lusardi's
Mangia
Manhattan Grille
Mi
Miss Mamie's/Maude's
Monsoon
Moran's Chelsea
Mr. Chow
Old San Juan
Osso Buco
Our Place
Pamir
Paola's
Park Bistro
Pastis
Q, a Thai Bistro
Quartino
Remi
Sant Ambroeus
Scopa
Shoebox Cafe
Snack
Tanti Baci
Tír na nóg
Tomo Sushi
Trattoria Dell'Arte
212
Ubol's Kitchen
Uncle Jack's Steak
Viand
Vince & Eddie's
Vine
Virgil's
Wondee Siam
Zarela

Dining Alone

(Other than hotels, coffee shops, sushi bars and places with counter service)
Alphabet Kitchen
Amy's Bread†
Anglers & Writers
Aquagrill
Aquavit
Artisanal
Big Nick's

Special Feature Index

Bouterin
Brasserie
Café Botanica
Café de Bruxelles
Cafe S.F.A.
Carlyle
Carnegie Deli
Caviar Russe
Christine's
City Hall
Cosi†
EJ's Luncheonette
Elephant & Castle
Eleven Madison Pk.
Fairway Cafe
FireBird
Fred's at Barneys
Good Enough to Eat
Gotham B&G
Gramercy Tavern
Gray's Papaya†
Gus' Place
Hudson Cafeteria
Hudson River Club
Il Monello
Jackson Hole
JUdson Grill
La Caravelle
Le Pain Quotidien†
Lespinasse
Mangia
Mark's
Mme. Romaine
Naples 45
Neary's
Nick & Toni's
Oceana
Ollie's
O'Neals'
Oyster Bar
Oyster Bar/Plaza
Pearl Oyster Bar
Petite Abeille†
Petrossian
Ratner's
Republic
Sant Ambroeus
Sarabeth's
Sette MoMA
Soup Kitchen Int'l
Sushisay
Sushiya
Tabla
Tuscan Sq.
Union Sq. Cafe
Veselka
Vinnie's Pizza
Wolf's
Zen Palate

Entertainment
(Check days, times and performers for entertainment; see *Zagat NYC Nightlife Survey*)
Algonquin Hotel (cabaret)
Allioli (Flamingo)
Belmondo (DJ)
Blue Water Grill (jazz)
B. Smith's (Jazz, R&B)
Café Pierre (piano player/singer)
Chez Es Saada (DJ/belly dancer)
Chez Josephine (jazz)
Cooking with Jazz (jazz)
Delta Grill (blues/jazz)
Dinerbar (DJ)
Emily's (jazz/pop)
FireBird (harpist/piano)
Flor de Sol (flamenco)
Garage (jazz)
Hard Rock Cafe (varies)
Home Sweet Harlem Café (poetry)
Jimmy's Bronx Cafe (Latin bands)
Jules (jazz)
Karyatis (guitar/piano/singing)
Knickerbocker (jazz)
La Lunchonette (singer)
La Mediterranée (piano)
Layla (belly dancer)
Le Singe Vert (jazz)
Letizia Amore (singer)
Lola (funk/Motown/R&B)
Londel's (jazz/pop/R&B)
Lucky Cheng's (drag shows)
Madiba (South African cabaret)
Manhattan Grille (jazz)
Mardi Gras (blues/jazz)
Medi (Latino)
Metronome (jazz/Latin)
Metropolitan Cafe (jazz)
Mosto (jazz)
Ñ (flamenco)
One if by Land (piano)
Pam Real Thai (karaoke)
Psychic Cafe (jazz)
Rainbow Room (orchestra)
Rasputin (cabaret/international)
River Cafe (piano)
Russian Samovar (vocals)
Russian Tea Rm. (violin)
Son Cubano (Cuban band)
Soul Cafe (gospel/jazz/R&B)
Spirit Cruises (DJ)
Stella del Mare (piano/vocals)
Sugar Bar (blues/jazz/R&B)
Sugar Hill Bistro (jazz)
Supper Club (big band/swing)
Sylvia's (gospel/jazz)
Tommaso's (piano/singers)
Top of Tower (piano)

Special Feature Index

Torch (ballads/jazz)
Tudor Grill (piano)
Walker's (jazz)
World Yacht (bands)

Entertainment/Dancing
(See *Zagat NYC Nightlife Survey*)
Allioli
Babalu
Bateaux NY
Bistro Latino
Eugene
Garage
Jack Rose
Jimmy's Bronx Cafe
Jimmy's Uptown
La Belle Epoque
Lotus
Rainbow Room
Rasputin
South Shore Country Club
Spirit Cruises
Supper Club
Tavern on Green
World Yacht

Family-Style
Asia de Cuba
Becco
Brother Jimmy's†
Campagna
Canton
Carino
Carmine's
Chiam Chinese
Chianti
China Grill
Chin Chin
Churrascaria Plataforma
Copeland's
Dawat
Don Peppe
Green Field Churr.
Jackson Diner
John's Pizzeria
Kum Gang San
Le Colonial
Marchi's
Master Grill
Oriental Garden
Osso Buco
Penang
Rao's
Siam Inn
Tasting Room
Tony's Di Napoli
Ulrika's

Fireplaces
Adä
Asia de Cuba
Barbetta
Box Tree
Cafe Centro
Chelsea Bistro
Christer's
Circus
Cornelia St. Cafe
Gage & Tollner
Heartbeat
I Trulli
Keens Steak
La Lanterna
Landmark Tavern
Lot 61
March
Marylou's
Moran's Chelsea
O'Neals'
One if by Land
Paris Commune
Park, The
Patois
René Pujol
Savoy
Shaffer City Oyster
Vivolo
Water Club, The
Water's Edge
Ye Waverly Inn

Game in Season
Acappella
Aesop's Tables
Alain Ducasse
An American Pl.
Annisa
Atlas
Aureole
Babbo
Barbetta
Bayard's
Beacon
Beppe
Borgo Antico
Café Boulud
Café Crocodile
Café des Artistes
Craft
Cub Room
Daniel
Danube
Da Umberto
Eight Mile Creek
Felidia
Four Seasons
Gabriel's

Special Feature Index

Gramercy Tavern
Guastavino, Upstairs
Hell's Kitchen
Henry's End
I Trulli
Jean Georges
Keens Steak
L'Absinthe
La Caravelle
La Grenouille
La Nonna
Le Perigord
March
Massimo/Ponte
Minotaur
Picholine
Pó
San Domenico
San Pietro
Swifty's
Terrace in Sky
Tudor Grill
Two Two Two
Union Pacific
Union Sq. Cafe
Veritas

Historic Places

(50+ yrs.; year opened;
* building only)
1726 One if by Land*
1794 Bridge Cafe*
1826 Sazerac Hse.*
1853 Moran's Chelsea*
1855 Parsonage*
1863 City Hall*
1864 Pete's Tavern
1868 Landmark Tavern
1868 Old Homestead
1870 Billy's
1875 Harry's/Hanover Sq.
1875 Vivolo*
1879 Gage & Tollner
1880 White Horse
1885 Keens Steak
1887 Peter Luger
1888 Katz's Deli
1889 Niederstein's
1889 Tonic*
1890 P.J. Clarke's
1890 Walker's
1891 Delmonico's
1892 Ferrara†
1892 Old Town Bar
1894 Veniero's
1896 Rao's
1900 Bamonte's
1902 Algonquin Hotel
1904 Ferdinando's
1904 Lanza
1905 Ratner's
1906 Barbetta
1906 Monte's (Bklyn)
1907 Gargiulo's
1907 Oak Room
1907 Palm Court
1907 One C.P.S.*
1908 Barney Greengrass
1908 John's of 12th St.
1913 Oyster Bar (Gr. Cent.)
1917 Café des Artistes
1918 Monte's (Manh)
1919 Gene's
1919 Mario's
1919 Caffé on the Green*
1920 Ye Waverly Inn
1921 Sardi's
1922 Fanelli Cafe
1922 Rocco
1924 Totonno Pizzeria
1925 El Charro Español
1926 Frankie & Johnnie's
1926 Palm†
1927 El Faro
1927 Fine & Schapiro
1927 Gallagher's
1929 Eisenberg Sandwich
1929 John's Pizzeria†
1929 '21' Club
1930 El Quijote
1930 Marchi's
1931 Café Pierre
1931 Peacock Alley
1932 Patsy's Pizzeria (E. Harlem)
1932 Pietro's
1933 Gebhardt's
1934 Papaya King†
1934 Rainbow Room
1934 Tavern on Green
1936 Tom's
1937 Carnegie Deli
1937 Le Veau d'Or
1937 Minetta Tavern
1937 Stage Deli
1938 Wo Hop
1939 Heidelberg
1941 Sevilla
1944 Patsy's
1945 Gino
1945 V&T
1946 Lobster Box
1947 Delegates' Din. Rm.
1947 Supreme Macaroni
1949 King Cole Bar
1949 Tout Va Bien
1949 Two Toms
1950 Junior's
1950 Marion's

Special Feature Index

1950 McHales
1950 Paul & Jimmy's
1950 Pierre au Tunnel

Hotel Dining

Algonquin Hotel
  Algonquin Hotel
Beekman Tower
  Top of Tower
Belvedere Hotel
  Churrascaria Plataforma
Benjamin Hotel
  An American Pl.
Box Tree
  Box Tree
Bryant Park Hotel
  Ilo
Carlyle Hotel
  Carlyle
Chambers Hotel
  Town
City Club Hotel
  db Bistro Moderne
Clarion Hotel Fifth Ave.
  Salmon River
Delmonico Hotel
  Caviarteria
Dylan Hotel
  Virot
Eastgate Tower Hotel
  Sonora
Embassy Suites Hotel
  Lili's Noodle
Empire Hotel
  West 63rd Steak
Essex House
  Alain Ducasse
  Café Botanica
Four Seasons Hotel
  Fifty Seven Fifty Seven
Hilton Times Square
  Above
Hotel Avalon
  Avalon Bar-Grill
Hotel Edison
  Edison Cafe
Hotel Elysée
  Monkey Bar
Hotel Giraffe
  Chinoiserie
Hotel Metro
  Metro Grill
Hotel Plaza Athénée
  Arabelle
Hotel Wales
  Sarabeth's
Hudson Hotel
  Hudson Cafeteria
Inn at Irving Place
  Lady Mendl's
Iroquois Hotel
  Triomphe
Kitano Hotel
  Nadaman Hakubai
Le Refuge Inn
  Le Refuge Inn
Lowell Hotel
  Post House
Lucerne Hotel
  Baci
Mark Hotel
  Mark's
Marriott Financial Center
  Roy's NY
Marriott Marquis Hotel
  J. W.'s Steakhouse
  View
Mayfair Hotel
  Le Garrick
Mercer Hotel
  Mercer Kitchen
Michelangelo Hotel
  Limoncello
Millennium Broadway Hotel
  Charlotte
Morgans Hotel
  Asia de Cuba
Muse Hotel
  District
NY Marriott Brooklyn
  Archives
NY Palace Hotel
  Le Cirque 2000
Parker Meridien
  Norma's
  Seppi's
Peninsula Hotel
  Adrienne
Pierre Hotel
  Café Pierre
Plaza Hotel
  Oak Room
  One C.P.S.
  Oyster Bar/Plaza
  Palm Court
Ramada Inn (Queens)
  Marbella
Regency Hotel
  Regency
Renaissance NY Hotel
  Foley's Fish Hse.
Rihga Royal Hotel
  Halcyon
Roosevelt Hotel
  Ferrara
60 Thompson Hotel
  Thom

Special Feature Index

Sofitel
   Gaby Brasserie
SoHo Grand Hotel
   Canal House
St. Regis Hotel
   King Cole Bar
   Lespinasse
Sutton Hotel
   Il Valentino
Time Hotel
   Coco Pazzo†
Trump Int'l Hotel
   Jean Georges
UN Plaza Hotel
   Ambassador Grill
W Court Hotel
   Icon
W New York
   Heartbeat
W Union Square
   Olives
Waldorf-Astoria
   Bull & Bear
   Inagiku
   Oscar's
   Peacock Alley
Warwick Hotel
   Ciao Europa

"In" Places

Annisa
Artisanal
Asia de Cuba
Atlas
AZ
Babbo
Balthazar
Beppe
Blue Hill
Blue Ribbon†
Blue Water Grill
Bond Street
Bot
Cafeteria
Calle Ocho
Chez Es Saada
Chez Josephine
Craft
Cuba Libre
db Bistro Moderne
Esca
Gabriel's
Gramercy Tavern
Guastavino, Downstairs
Guastavino, Upstairs
Hudson Cafeteria
Indochine
Jean Georges
Junno's
La Grenouille
Le Cirque 2000
Le Colonial
Le Zinc
Lot 61
Lotus
Man Ray
Markt
Mary's Fish Camp
Mercer Kitchen
Milos
Molyvos
Nello†
Nobu
Odeon
Olives
Orsay
Ouest
Park, The
Pastis
Patois
Rao's
Red/Bar
Red Cat
Rhône
71 Clinton
Son Cubano
Strip House
Sushi Samba†
Sushi Yasuda
Tabla
Tamarind
Tao
Tasting Room
Tja!
Town
Tuscan Steak
Union Pacific
Veritas

Jacket Required

(* Tie also required)
Acappella*
Alain Ducasse*
Algonquin Hotel
Aquavit
Aureole
Avalon Bar-Grill
Bambou
Bouley Bakery
Bouterin
Box Tree*
Café des Artistes
Café Pierre
Carlyle
Cello*
Chanterelle
Daniel
Danube

Special Feature Index

Delegates' Din. Rm.
Destinée
Erminia
Felidia
Four Seasons
Fresco by Scotto
Giovanni Venticinque
Harry Cipriani*
Il Mulino
Il Tinello
Jean Georges
Jimmy Sung's
Joanna's
King Cole Bar
Kings' Carriage
L'Absinthe
La Caravelle
La Côte Basque
La Grenouille*
Le Bernardin
Le Cirque 2000*
Le Colonial
Leopard, The
Le Perigord*
Le Refuge Inn
Lespinasse
Lutèce
March
Oak Room*
One if by Land
Palio
Peacock Alley
Picholine
Primavera
Rainbow Room*
Rasputin
River Cafe
San Domenico
San Giusto
San Pietro
Supper Club
Sushisay
Terrace in Sky
Top of Tower
'21' Club*
World Yacht

Jury Duty
(Near the courthouses)
Arqua
Bo-Ky
Bouley Bakery
Bridge Cafe
City Hall
Da Nico
Danube
Duane Park Cafe
Ecco
Great NY Noodle
Il Cortile
Il Fornaio
Il Palazzo
Joe's Shanghai
Kitchenette
L'Ecole
Nam Phuong
New Green Bo
New Pasteur
Nha Trang†
Nobu
Odeon
Oriental Garden
Pho Viet Huong
Queen
Roc
Sal Anthony's S.P.Q.R.
Sweet-n-Tart
Taormina
Thailand Rest.
Vietnam
Wo Hop
Wong Kee

Kosher
Abigael's
Ben's Kosher Deli
Darna
Domani
Fine & Schapiro
Haikara Grill
Le Marais
Levana
Madras Cafe
My Most Favorite
Pastrami Queen
Pongal
Prime Grill
Second Ave. Deli
Shallots NY
Tevere
Va Bene
Wolf & Lamb

Late Dining
(Weekday closing hour)
Alva (2 AM)
Balthazar (1:30 AM)
Bar 89 (1 AM)
Barrio (24 hrs.)
Bar Six (2 AM)
BarTabac (1 AM)
Bereket (24 hrs.)
Big Nick's (24 hrs.)
Blue Elephant (1 AM)
Blue Ribbon (4 AM)
Blue Ribbon Sushi (2 AM)
Brasserie (1 AM)
Broome St. Bar (1:30 AM)

Special Feature Index

Cafe Deville (4 AM)
Cafe Lalo (2 AM)
Cafe Noir (4 AM)
Cafeteria (24 hrs.)
Caffe Reggio (2 AM)
Carnegie Deli (4 AM)
Casa La Femme (1 AM)
Chez Josephine (1 AM)
Chinoiserie (2 AM)
Churrascaria Plataforma (1 AM)
Coffee Shop (2 AM)
Corner Bistro (4 AM)
Edgar's Cafe (2:45 AM)
Elaine's (2 AM)
Empire Diner (24 hrs.)
Fanelli Cafe (1 AM)
Ferrier Bistro (2 AM)
First (2 AM)
Florent (5 AM; 24 hrs. wkends)
Forbidden City (4 AM)
Frank (1 AM)
French Roast (24 hrs.)
Garage (1 AM)
Good World B&G (1 AM)
Grace (4 AM)
Gray's Papaya (24 hrs.)
Great NY Noodle (4 AM)
Hudson Cafeteria (1 AM)
'ino (2 AM)
J.G. Melon (2:30 AM)
Jimmy's Bronx Cafe (2 AM)
Jules (1 AM)
Kam Chueh (4 AM)
Kang Suh (24 hrs.)
Knickerbocker (1 AM)
Kum Gang San (24 hrs)
La Lanterna (3 AM)
L'Express (24 hrs.)
Le Zinc (4 AM)
Long Tan (2 AM)
L'Orange Bleue (1 AM)
Lot 61 (3 AM)
Lucien (2 AM)
Lucky Strike (3 AM)
Luke's B&G (2 AM)
Markt (1 AM)
Mezzogiorno (1 AM)
Ñ (1:30 AM)
Neary's (1:30 AM)
Odeon (2 AM)
Omonia Cafe (3:30 AM)
Park, The (1 AM)
Pastis (2 AM)
P.J. Clarke's (4 AM)
Planet Thailand (1 AM)
Rio Mar (1:15 AM)
Sahara (1:30 AM)
Sirocco (2 AM)
Smith & Wollensky (2 AM)
Stage Deli (1 AM)
Stingy Lulu's (4 AM)
Tio Pepe (1 AM)
Torch (1 AM)
Uncle George's (24 hrs.)
Veselka (24 hrs.)
Walker's (1 AM)
Wo Hop (24 hrs.)
Wollensky's Grill (2 AM)

Meet for a Drink

(Most hotels and the following standouts)
Aleutia
Alva
Amaranth
Artisanal
Bacco
Balthazar
Bar Six
BarTabac
Boat House
Brasserie 8½
Bread Bar at Tabla
Carlyle
Charley O's
Chez Josephine
Circo
City Hall
Cub Room
db Bistro Moderne
Eleven Madison Pk.
Forbidden City
Four Seasons
Fressen
Globe
Gotham B&G
Gramercy Tavern
Heartland Brewery†
ike
Jean Georges
JUdson Grill
Junno's
Keens Steak
Landmark Tavern
Le Cirque 2000
Le Colonial
Lot 61
Mark's
Markt
Merchants, N.Y.†
Michael Jordan's
Monkey Bar
Nisos
Old Town Bar
Pastis
Pershing Sq.
Pete's Tavern
Petrossian

Special Feature Index

P.J. Clarke's
Punch
Red/Bar
Red Cat
Rhône
Shark Bar
Shelly's NY
Soul Cafe
Strip House
Tonic
Vong

Natural/Organic
(Most places cook to order to meet any dietary request; call in advance to check; almost all Chinese, Indian and other ethnics have health-conscious meals, as do the following)
Angelica Kitchen
Avalon Bar-Grill
Candle Cafe
Cho Dang Gol
Chop't Creative Salad
Fressen
Good Health Cafe
Heartbeat
Herban Kitchen
Josie's
L'Annam
Other Foods
Popover Cafe
Pump
Quintessence
Soma Soup
Toraya
Tossed†
T Salon
Zenith Vegetarian
Zen Palate†

Noteworthy Newcomers (221)
(Name, *cuisine*; * not open at press time, but looks promising)
A, *French/Carib.*
Adä, *Indian*
Ajisen Noodle, *Japanese*
AKA Cafe, *American*
Al Baraka, *Moroccan*
Aleutia, *American*
Alias*, *American*
Alfredo of Rome, *Italian*
Allioli, *Spanish*
Alphabet Kitchen, *Spanish/Port.*
American Grill, *American*
Amici Amore I, *Italian*
Arabelle, *French*
Arezzo, *Italian*
Artisanal, *French Brasserie*
Assaggio, *Italian*
@SQC*, *American*
Azalea*, *Italian/Continental*
Banjara, *Indian*
Bann Thai, *Thai*
BarTabac, *French*
Belmondo, *French*
Beppe, *Italian*
Bid, *American*
Bistro Olivia*, *Mediterranean*
Bistro St. Mark's, *French*
B.K. Sweeney's, *American*
Blue Door*, *French*
Blue Elephant, *American*
Blue Fin*, *Seafood*
Blue Grotto*, *Mediterranean*
Blue Smoke*, *Barbecue*
Bot, *Italian*
Buddha Bar*, *Asian*
Butter*, *Asian*
Cafe Alyss, *French/American*
Cafe Charbon*, *French*
Cafe Deville, *French Brasserie*
Cafe Luluc, *French*
Café Sabarsky*, *Austrian*
Cafe Steinhof, *Austrian*
Caffe Linda, *Italian*
Cantinetta I*, *Italian*
Carmaya, *Italian*
Cascina, *Italian*
Catch*, *Seafood*
Centolire, *Italian*
Chinghalle, *Italian*
Chinoiserie, *French/Chinese*
Chip Shop, *British*
Chop't Creative Salad, *Salads*
Ciao, *Italian*
Cipriani Dolci*, *Italian*
Citarella, *Seafood*
Clove, *American*
Coconut Grove*, *South Asian*
Commissary NY*, *American*
Convivium Osteria, *Med., Amer.*
Cooke's Corner, *European*
Coq Hardi, *French/Med.*
Cosmic Cantina, *Tex-Mex*
Craft, *American*
Cuba*, *Cuban*
Curry Leaf, *Indian*
Dalga Seafood, *Turkish Seafood*
Danzón, *Mexican*
D'Artagnan, *French*
db Bistro Moderne, *French*
Dinerbar, *American*
District, *American*
Django*, *French*

Special Feature Index

Domicile*, *French/Italian*
Don Luca, *Spanish*
Dosaria*, *Indian*
DuMont, *American*
East Post, *Italian*
Emo's, *Korean*
Essex, *Eclectic*
Equivico*, *Latin American*
Faan, *Asian Fusion*
Falucka*, *Moroccan*
Fiamma Osteria*, *Italian*
Figs, *Mediterranean*
Fleur de Sel, *French*
Forbidden City, *Asian*
44 & X Hell's Kit., *American*
1492 Food, *Spanish*
Fraunces Tavern*, *American*
Friend House, *Chinese/Japan.*
Gingko Leaf Cafe, *Japanese*
Gradisca, *Italian*
Hakata Grill, *Asian*
Harrison, The*, *Mediterranean*
Home Sweet Harlem Café, *Deli*
ike, *American*
Il Gattopardo*, *Italian*
Ilo, *American*
Inside, *American*
Irving on Irving, *American*
It's Greek to Me, *Greek*
Jane, *American*
Jean-Luc, *French*
Jewel Bako, *Japanese*
Jimmy's Downtown*, *Nuevo Latino*
Jimmy's Uptown, *Latin/Soul*
Joya, *Thai*
Kazusa, *Japanese*
Kotobuki Bistro, *Japanese*
Kyma, *Greek Seafood*
La Bouchée, *French*
La Corniche, *Mediterranean*
La Flor Bakery, *Mexican*
La Palapa, *Mexican*
Lenox, *American*
Lentini, *Italian*
Le Souk, *North African*
Letizia Amore, *Italian*
Lexi's, *Mexican*
Le Zinc, *French*
Locanda Vini, *Italian*
Lola's Buena Vista, *S. American*
Long Tan, *Thai*
Los Dos Molinos, *Mexican/Southwest*
Louis BBQ*, *Barbecue*
Loulou, *French*
Lo Zoo*, *Chinese*
Luce*, *Italian*
Lure NYC*, *Seafood*
Mai-Lin, *French/Vietnamese*
Man Ray, *French/Asian*
Mare, *Med./Seafood*
Marika, *American*
Marissa's*, *American*
MarkJoseph Steak, *Steakhouse*
Mary's Fish Camp, *Seafood*
Marseille*, *French/Med.*
Medi, *Mediterranean*
Meet*, *Mediterranean*
Midway, *American*
Minnow*, *Seafood*
Minotaur, *Greek*
Mo-Bay, *Jamaican/Soul*
Moda*, *American*
Moondance, *Seafood/Steakhse.*
Mooza, *Med./Italian*
Morimoto*, *Japanese*
Mosto, *Italian*
Muzy, *Korean*
Nellie's, *American*
Nëo Sushi, *Japanese*
Nessa*, *Italian*
New Leaf Cafe, *American*
92, *American*
Nisos, *Mediterranean*
NL, *Dutch*
Nonna, *Italian*
Ohta, *Japanese*
Olives, *American/Med.*
Opia*, *Int'l*
Ouest, *American*
Paladar, *Latin American*
Palma, *Italian/French*
Pam Real Thai, *Thai*
Pangaea*, *Asian*
Paradou*, *French*
Park, The, *Mediterranean*
Patang*, *Indian*
Pfiff, *American*
Pico, *Portuguese*
Pigalle*, *French*
Pipa, *Spanish*
Plumeri*, *Italian*
Portofino Grille, *Italian*
Prime Grill, *Kosher Steakhouse*
Provence en Boite, *French*
Providence*, *Mediterranean*
Psychic Cafe, *Italian*
Quartino, *Italian*
Queen of Sheba, *Ethiopian*
Red/Bar, *American*
Red Square*, *Int'l*
Roth's Westside, *Steakhouse*
R.S.V.P.*, *American*
Sahara, *Middle Eastern*
Salmon River, *Seafood*
Sen-ya, *Japanese*
Shangrila, *Tibetan*
Sherwood Cafe, *American*
Sho*, *Japanese*

Special Feature Index

Shoebox Cafe, *Southern*
Sipan, *Peruvian*
Sirocco, *Med./Spanish*
Son Cubano, *Cuban*
Spice Market*, *Asian*
Stella, *American*
Stonewall Bistro, *American*
Suba*, *Latin/French*
Sugar Hill Bistro, *Southern/Ecl.*
Sushi a-go-go, *Japanese*
Sushi Jones, *Japanese*
Tamarind, *Indian*
TanDa*, *Southeast Asian*
Tangerine, *Thai*
Tao, *Asian*
Tappo, *Mediterranean*
Theo*, *American/Continental*
Thom, *Seafood*
Tibetan Yak, *Tibetan*
Tiger Blossom, *Asian Fusion*
Touché*, *Asian*
Town, *American*
Tuscan Steak, *Italian Steakhouse*
27 Sunrise Seafood, *Chinese*
Vicala*, *Vietnamese*
Virot, *French*
Vitoune*, *Moroccan*
Wasabi, *Japanese*
Washington Park*, *American*
Wei*, *Vietnamese*
Wyanoka, *American/Ecl.*
Zebu Grill*, *South American*

Noteworthy Closings (80)

Acacia
Acadia Parish
Aggie's
Aqua
Armani Cafe
Askew
Belgo Nieuw York
Bellew
Biryani
Bodega
Bossa Nova's
Brasserie Americaine
BrasserieBit
Cafe Margaux
Cafe O
Cafe Word of Mouth
Chelsea Lobster Co.
Chiado de Portugal
Clementine
Cuisine de Saigon
EQ, Restaurant
Fernicola Osteria
Fireman's of Brooklyn
Florentine
Follonico
Frontière
Grand Ticino
Great Shanghai
Gubbio
Jin Dal Lae
Joanie's
Kalio
Kiev
La Soirée d'Asie
Le Gans
Le Quercy
Le Régence
Les Pyrénées
Little Dove
Little Pho
Lobster Club
Longacre Square
L-Ray
Malevo
Maratti
Marco Polo Cafe (Manh.)
Mary's
Match Uptown
Matthew's
Mesopotamia
Mike's American Bar & Grill
Montana Steak & Grill
Moomba
Orienta
Palladin
Passage to India
Peccavi
Placido Domingo
Provi Provi
Puccini
Quake
Quince
RBG Grill
Revel
Rustic
Sans Souci
Sono
Spartina
Sweet Mamas
Tano
Tapika
Times Square Brewery
Tin Room Cafe
27 Standard
Violino Rosso
Viva Brasil
Vox
Waterloo Brasserie
Wild Blue
Windows on the World

Special Feature Index

Outdoor Dining
(G=garden; P=patio;
S=sidewalk; T=terrace)
Aesop's Tables (G)
Allioli (G)
Alphabet Kitchen (G)
American Park (P,T)
Aquagrill (T)
Atlas (S)
Aureole (G)
AZ (G)
Barbetta (G)
Barolo (G)
Ben Benson's (S,T)
Blue Hill (G)
Blue Water Grill (P,S)
Boat House (T)
Bottino (G)
Bread Bar at Tabla (P)
Bryant Park Grill/Cafe (G,T)
Cafe Centro (G,S)
Cafe Fiorello (S)
Caffe Rafaella (S)
Carmaya (G)
Chelsea Grill (G)
Chez Ma Tante (S)
Circo (P)
Commune (P,S)
Da Silvano (S)
Demarchelier (P)
Dolphins (G)
Druids (G)
East of Eighth (G)
Ennio & Michael (P)
Esca (P)
55 Wall (T)
Friend of a Farmer (S)
Gascogne (G)
Gigino/Wagner Pk. (P)
Grove (G)
Guastavino, Downstairs (G,T)
Harbour Lights (T)
Home (G)
I Coppi (G)
Il Cortile (P,S)
Il Palazzo (G,S)
Isabella's (S)
I Trulli (G)
Jean Georges (T)
Julian's (S,T)
La Belle Vie (S)
La Nonna (G)
Lanza (G)
Lattanzi (G)
Le Jardin Bistro (G)
Le Madri (S)
Le Refuge (P)
Les Deux Gamins (S)
Le Zie 2000 (S)
March (T)
Markt (S,T)
Massimo/Ponte (S)
Medi (P)
Metropolitan Cafe (G)
Mezzogiorno (S)
Mickey Mantle's (S)
Midway (S)
Mignon (G)
Milos (T)
Miracle Grill†
Mooza (G)
Morrell Wine Bar (P)
Naples 45 (G)
Nick & Stef's Steak (T)
Ocean Grill (S)
Orsay (T)
Park, The (G)
Pisces (S)
Place (T)
Plate 347 (G)
Porters NY (G)
Porto Bello (S)
Provence (G)
Rock Center Café (G)
Rose Water (P)
Sahara (G)
Saloon (S)
Sea Grill (G)
Surya (G)
Sushi Samba†
Tavern on Green (G)
Terrace in Sky (T)
Time Cafe (T)
Tratt. Spaghetto (S)
Va Tutto! (G)
Verbena (G,P)
ViceVersa (G,P)
Vittorio Cucina (G)
Water Club, The (P)
Water's Edge (P,T)
White Horse (S)
Wollensky's Grill (S)

Parkside Views
American Park
Atlas
Boat House
Bread Bar at Tabla
Bryant Park Grill/Cafe
Café Botanica
Eleven Madison Pk.
Gigino/Wagner Pk.
Jean Georges
Mickey Mantle's
Nirvana
One C.P.S.
Park Side (Queens)
San Domenico
Tabla

Special Feature Index

People-Watching
Artisanal
Asia de Cuba
Atlas
Babbo
Balthazar
Bar Pitti
Bar Six
Bice
Blue Hill
Blue Ribbon†
Blue Water Grill
Bond Street
Cafe Luxembourg
Cafe Nosidam
Campagna
Canteen
Casa La Femme
Chez Es Saada
China Grill
Coffee Shop
Danube
Da Silvano
Eight Mile Creek
Elio's
Ferrier Bistro
Fresco by Scotto
Gabriel's
Gotham B&G
Guastavino, Downstairs
Harry Cipriani
Hudson Cafeteria
Il Valentino
Indochine
La Grenouille
Le Bernardin
Le Charlot
Le Cirque 2000
Le Colonial
Lot 61
Lotus
Man Ray
March
Markt
Mercer Kitchen
Monkey Bar
Mr. Chow
Nello†
Nicole's
Nino's
Nobu
Odeon
Orsay
Park, The
Park Avalon
Pastis
Rain
Russian Tea Rm.
Saloon
Sardi's
Time Cafe
Tja!
Town
Union Sq. Cafe
Veritas
Vong

Power Scenes
Aquavit
Artisanal
Atlas
Aureole
Bayard's
Ben Benson's
Café Boulud
Carlyle
Cello
Chanterelle
Daniel
Da Silvano
Del Frisco's
Della Femina
Eleven Madison Pk.
Felidia
Four Seasons (lunch)
Fresco by Scotto
Gabriel's
Gotham B&G
Harry Cipriani
Harry's/Hanover Sq.
Hudson River Club
Il Mulino
Il Nido
Jean Georges
JUdson Grill
La Caravelle
La Côte Basque
La Grenouille
Le Bernardin
Le Cirque 2000
Lespinasse
Michael's
Milos
Morton's
Oceana
Palm
Park Ave. Cafe
Peter Luger
Petrossian
Picholine
Post House
Rao's
Regency (breakfast)
Smith & Wollensky
Trattoria Dell'Arte
'21' Club

Special Feature Index

Pre-Theater/Prix Fixe Menus
(See pages 21–22, plus the following good bets; call to check prices and times; B=brunch, L=lunch, D=dinner, * means dinner prix fixe is pre-theater only)
Anche Vivolo (L,D*)
Au Mandarin (L)
Bangkok Cafe (L,D)
Bardolino (L,D)
Biricchino (L,D)
Café de Paris (L,D)
Chameleon (L,D)
Cinquanta (L,D)
Cité (D)
Cité Grill (D)
Cucina di Pesce (D*)
Four Seasons (D*)
Gramercy Tavern (65)
Green Field Churr. (L,D)
Hourglass Tavern (D)
Intermezzo (L,D)
Jewel of India (L,D)
La Grenouille (L,D)
Lanza (L,D)
Le Beaujolais (D)
Le Bernardin (L,D)
Le Cirque 2000 (L,D)
Le Petit Hulot (D)
Le Refuge Inn (B,D)
Le Rivage (L,D)
Le Tableau (D*)
Le Veau d'Or (L,D)
L'Orange Bleue (D)
Lotus (D)
Mamlouk (D)
March (D)
Master Grill (L,D)
Mr. Chow (D)
Notaro (L,D)
Oceana (L,D)
One if by Land (D)
Parsonage (D)
Pascalou (D*)
Pergola/Artistes (D*)
Pierre au Tunnel (L,D)
Pó (L,D)
Primola (L,D)
René Pujol (L,D)
Roettele A.G. (D)
Scalini Fedeli (D)
Spirit Cruises (L,D)
Torch (D)
Tse Yang (L,D)
'21' Club (L,D)
Veritas (D)
View (D)
World Yacht (B,D)

Private Rooms for Parties
(See *Zagat NYC Marketplace Survey* for room capacities & additional locations)
Avra Estiatorio
AZ
Barbetta
Bayard's
Becco
Beppe
Blue Water Grill
Bond Street
Bouley Bakery
Box Tree
Brasserie 8½
Bruno
Cellini
Cello
Chelsea Bistro
Chez Josephine
Chin Chin
Citarella
City Hall
Daniel
Danube
Del Frisco's
Eleven Madison Pk.
ESPN Zone
Felidia
FireBird
Four Seasons
14 Wall St.
Fresco by Scotto
Fressen
Gramercy Tavern
Guastavino, Downstairs
Guastavino, Upstairs
Il Buco
Il Monello
Ilo
Independent
Jimmy Sung's
Keens Steak
La Côte Basque
La Grenouille
La Petite Auberge
Le Bernardin
Le Cirque 2000
Le Perigord
Lola
Lot 61
Lotus
Lupa
Lutèce
Maloney & Porcelli
Manhattan Ocean

Special Feature Index

Man Ray
Marika
Marylou's
Metronome
Metropolitan Cafe
Milos
Moran's Chelsea
Morton's
Obeca Li
Oceana
Old Homestead
O'Neals'
One C.P.S.
Park, The
Park Ave. Cafe
Philip Marie
Picholine
Quilty's
Remi
River Cafe
Russian Tea Rm.
Ruth's Chris
Sammy's Roumanian
San Domenico
Sardi's
Scopa
Screening Room
Sea Grill
Shelly's NY
Tao
Tavern on Green
Terrace in Sky
Toledo
Tonic
Tribeca Grill
Tuscan Steak
'21' Club
212
Union Pacific
Vine
Water Club, The
Water's Edge
West 63rd Steak
WWF NY

Pubs/Bars/ Microbreweries

(See *Zagat NYC Nightlife Survey* for more listings)
Bar Six
B.K. Sweeney's
Broome St. Bar
Charley O's
Corner Bistro
Druids
Fanelli Cafe
Ferrier Bistro
Gramercy Tavern
Heartland Brewery†
J.G. Melon
Joe Allen
Keens Steak
Killmeyer's
King Cole Bar
Knickerbocker
Landmark Tavern
Luke's B&G
Mark's
Markt
Monkey Bar
Moran's Chelsea
Neary's
Old Town Bar
O'Neals'
Onieal's Grand St.
Palio (bar)
Pete's Tavern
P.J. Clarke's
Shark Bar
T.G.I. Friday's
Tír na nóg
Walker's
White Horse
Wollensky's Grill

Quick Bites

Ajisen Noodle
Baby Bo's
Bereket
Burritoville
Caffe Linda
Chez Brigitte
Chip Shop
Chop't Creative Salad
Cosi
Cosmic Cantina
Daily Soup
Dishes
Emerald Planet
F & B
Figs
Fresco on the Go
Good Enough to Eat
Go Sushi
Gray's Papaya
Grilled Cheese NYC
Hale & Hearty Soups
Hampton Chutney
'ino
Mee Noodle
Mexicana Mama
Oyster Bar
Papaya King
Pump
Second Ave. Deli
Snack
Tossed

Special Feature Index

Quiet Conversation
Alain Ducasse
Arqua
Atlas
Barbetta
Belluno
Box Tree
Café Botanica
Café Boulud
Café Pierre
Carlyle
Caviar Russe
Chanterelle
Chez Michallet
Danal
Daniel
Danube
Destinée
Eleven Madison Pk.
FireBird
Fleur de Sel
Four Seasons
Gramercy Tavern
Halcyon
Il Monello
Il Tinello
Jean Georges
La Caravelle
Lady Mendl's
La Grenouille
Le Bernardin
Lespinasse
Loulou
Lutèce
March
Mark's
Montrachet
Mr. K's
Oak Room
One if by Land
Peacock Alley
Petrossian
Picholine
Primavera
Provence
San Domenico
Seryna
Tea Box
Terrace in Sky
Thalia
Tocqueville
Toraya
Tse Yang
Union Pacific
Verbena
Vine
Virot
Water's Edge
West 63rd Steak

Raw Bars
Aquagrill
Artisanal
Atlantic Grill
Avenue
Balthazar
Blue Ribbon
Blue Water Grill
City Hall
Cooking with Jazz
Docks Oyster
Fish
Harbour Lights
Independent
London Lennie's
Lundy Bros.
Man Ray
Marika
Markt
Mercer Kitchen
Ocean Grill
Ohta
Oyster Bar
Oyster Bar/Plaza
Pisces
Redeye Grill
Rue 57 Brasserie
Sea Grill
Shaffer City Oyster
Shelly's NY

Romantic Places
Alain Ducasse
Alison on Dominick
Atlas
Aureole
AZ
Bambou
Barbetta
Bateaux NY
Box Tree
Café des Artistes
Candela
Capsouto Frères
Casa La Femme
Cello
Chelsea Bistro
Chez Es Saada
Chez Josephine
Chez Michallet
Danal
Danube
Erminia
FireBird
Gascogne
Il Buco
Jezebel
King Cole Bar
Kings' Carriage

Special Feature Index

La Belle Epoque
L'Absinthe
La Caravelle
La Côte Basque
Lady Mendl's
La Grenouille
La Lanterna
Le Cirque 2000
Le Colonial
Le Refuge
Le Refuge Inn
March
Mark's
Mr. K's
Nicholson
One if by Land
Place
Primavera
Provence
Rafaella
Rainbow Room
River Cafe
Sirocco
Spirit Cruises
Tavern on Green
Terrace in Sky
Top of Tower
Torch
Two Two Two
Water's Edge
World Yacht

Saturday – Best Bets

(B=brunch; L=lunch)
Anglers & Writers (B,L)
Artisanal (L)
Atlas (B,L)
Balthazar (B)
Barbetta (L)
Bice (L)
Blue Ribbon Bakery (B,L)
Blue Water Grill (L)
Bouley Bakery (L)
Café Botanica (B)
Café Boulud (L)
Café de Bruxelles (B)
Café des Artistes (B)
Cafe Luxembourg (B)
Cafeteria (B,L)
Cal's (L)
Capsouto Frères (B,L)
Carnegie Deli (B,L)
Cello (L)
Chanterelle (L)
Circo (L)
Daniel (L)
Danube (L)
Da Silvano (L)
Dawat (L)

Demarchelier (L)
Eleven Madison Pk. (L)
Esca (L)
FireBird (L)
First (L)
Fleur de Sel (L)
Gramercy Tavern (L)
Houston's (L)
Il Nido (L)
Ilo (B)
Japonica (L)
L'Absinthe (B)
La Côte Basque (L)
La Goulue (L)
La Grenouille (L)
La Lunchonette (B,L)
Le Cirque 2000 (L)
Le Refuge (B,L)
Lupa (L)
Madiba (B,L)
Maloney & Porcelli (B,L)
Marika (B,L)
Markt (B)
Mercer Kitchen (B,L)
Mesa Grill (B,L)
Miracle Grill (B)
Odeon (B,L)
Old Homestead (L)
O'Neals' (B,L)
Orsay (L)
Park, The (L)
Park Ave. Cafe (B,L)
Payard Bistro (L)
Pershing Sq. (B,L)
Petaluma (B,L)
Petrossian (B)
Picholine (L)
Pico (L)
Pipa (B)
Prune (B)
Quatorze Bis (B,L)
Quilty's (B,L)
Rachel's (B,L)
Redeye Grill (B)
Red Rail (B,L)
René Pujol (L)
River Cafe (L)
Russian Tea Rm. (B)
Sarabeth's (B)
Second Ave. Deli (B,L)
Shelly's NY (B,L)
Swifty's (L)
Sylvia's (B,L)
Tamarind (L)
Tavern on Green (B,L)
Terrace in Sky (L)
Thom (B,L)
Tonic (L)
Town (B)

Special Feature Index

Trattoria Dell'Arte (B)
212 (B,L)
Union Sq. Cafe (L)
Verbena (L)
Water Club, The (L)

Sunday – Best Bets

(All places open on Sunday have an S after their names in the directory; also see hotels and most Asians; B=brunch; L=lunch; D=dinner)

Aleutia (B,D)
Alphabet Kitchen (B,D)
Ambassador Grill (B,L,D)
America (B,L,D)
Amy Ruth's (L,D)
Anglers & Writers (B,L,D)
Aquagrill (B,D)
Aquavit (B,D)
Artisanal (L,D)
Atlantic Grill (B,D)
Atlas (B,L,D)
Avenue (B,L,D)
AZ (D)
Babbo (D)
Balthazar (B,D)
Barbetta (L,D)
Ben Benson's (D)
Blue Hill (D)
Blue Ribbon (D)
Blue Ribbon Bakery (B,L,D)
Blue Water Grill (B,D)
Boat House (B,L,D)
Bouley Bakery (L,D)
Brasserie (B,L,D)
Bravo Gianni (D)
B. Smith's (B,L,D)
Café Botanica (B,D)
Café de Bruxelles (B,D)
Café des Artistes (B,D)
Cafe Deville (B,D)
Cafe Luxembourg (B,D)
Café Pierre (B,D)
Calle Ocho (B,D)
Campagna (D)
Capsouto Frères (B,L,D)
Carlyle (B,L,D)
Carnegie Deli (B,L,D)
Chez Michallet (B,D)
Chiam Chinese (L,D)
Chicama (D)
China Grill (D)
Chin Chin (D)
Circo (D)
Craft (D)
Danube (L,D)
Da Silvano (L,D)
Dawat (D)
Dominick's (L,D)
Eleven Madison Pk. (D)
Etats-Unis (D)
Fifty Seven Fifty Seven (B,L,D)
FireBird (D)
Fred's (B,D)
Gabriela's (B,D)
Gotham B&G (D)
Gramercy Tavern (L,D)
Guastavino, Downstairs (B,D)
Guastavino, Upstairs (D)
Gus' Place (B,L,D)
Houston's (L,D)
Il Cortile (L,D)
Il Monello (L,D)
Ilo (B,D)
Independent (B,D)
Isabella's (B,D)
Jean Georges (B,D)
Jimmy's Bronx Cafe (L,D)
Josie's (B,D)
Jubilee (B,D)
L'Absinthe (B,D)
La Côte Basque (D)
La Lunchonette (B,L,D)
La Mediterranée (B,L,D)
Le Bilboquet (L,D)
Le Cirque 2000 (D)
Le Colonial (D)
Le Perigord (L,D)
Le Refuge (B,L,D)
Les Halles (B,L,D)
Levana (L,D)
Le Zinc (B,D)
L'Orange Bleue (B,L,D)
Lumi (B,L,D)
Lupa (L,D)
Madiba (B,L,D)
Maloney & Porcelli (B,L,D)
Manhattan Grille (B,D)
Manhattan Ocean (D)
March (D)
Marika (B,L,D)
Mark's (B,L,D)
Markt (B,D)
Maya (D)
Mercer Kitchen (B,L,D)
Mesa Grill (B,L,D)
Milos (D)
Miracle Grill (B,D)
Molyvos (L,D)
Nello (L,D)
92 (B,D)
Nobu (D)
Ocean Grill (B,D)
Odeon (B,L,D)
Olives (B,D)
One if by Land (D)
Orsay (B,D)

Special Feature Index

Ouest (B,D)
Park, The (L,D)
Park Ave. Cafe (B,L,D)
Park Bistro (B,D)
Pastis (B,L,D)
Patria (D)
Pershing Sq. (B,L,D)
Peter Luger (L,D)
Petrossian (B,D)
Piccola Venezia (D)
Picholine (D)
Pico (D)
Pipa (B,D)
Plate 347 (B,D)
Portofino Grille (D)
Provence (B,L,D)
Remi (D)
Rosa Mexicano (B,D)
Rose Water (B,D)
Russian Tea Rm. (B,D)
Salaam Bombay (B,L,D)
San Domenico (D)
Shun Lee Palace (L,D)
Smith & Wollensky (L,D)
Spring St. Natural (B,L,D)
Sylvia's (B,L,D)
Table d'Hôte (B,D)
Tao (D)
Tartine (B,D)
Tavern on Green (B,L,D)
Town (B,D)
Trattoria Dell'Arte (B,D)
212 (B,L,D)
Two Two Two (D)
Union Sq. Cafe (D)
Va Bene (D)
Va Tutto! (B,D)
Verbena (B,D)
Veritas (D)
Vong (D)
Water Club, The (B,D)
Zarela (D)
Zoë (B,D)

Senior Appeal

Ambassador Grill
Aureole
Barbetta
Box Tree
Café Botanica
Café des Artistes
Cafe Greco
Carlyle
Castellano
Daniel
Danube
Destinée
Duane Park Cafe
Eleven Madison Pk.
Felidia
FireBird
Fleur de Sel
Four Seasons
Gallagher's
Gus' Figs
Halcyon
Heartbeat
Historic Old Bermuda
Hudson River Club
Il Cortile
Il Monello
Il Nido
Il Tinello
Jean Georges
La Caravelle
La Côte Basque
La Grenouille
La Petite Auberge
Lattanzi
Le Bernardin
Le Cirque 2000
Le Perigord
Lespinasse
Lusardi's
Lutèce
March
Mark's
Mme. Romaine
Mr. K's
Nicola Paone
Nippon
Oak Room
Oceana
Palm†
Palm Court
Peacock Alley
Peter Luger
Picholine
Primavera
Rainbow Room
Remi
Rossini's
Russian Samovar
Russian Tea Rm.
Sea Grill
Shun Lee
Shun Lee Palace
Sushisay
Tavern on Green
Tse Yang
Two Two Two
Union Sq. Cafe
Virot
West 63rd Steak
World Yacht

Special Feature Index

Singles Scenes
(See *Zagat NYC Nightlife Survey*)
Amaranth
Angelo & Maxie's†
Artisanal
Atlantic Grill
Balthazar
Bar Six
Blue Water Grill
Boca Chica
Bread Bar at Tabla
Charley O's
Chez Es Saada
Chinoiserie
City Hall
Coconut Grill
Cub Room
DT•UT
Ernie's
Ferrier Bistro
First
Guastavino, Downstairs
Heartland Brewery†
Hudson Cafeteria
Independent
Isabella's
JUdson Grill
La Goulue
Man Ray
Marion's
Markt
Merchants, N.Y.†
Monkey Bar
Ocean Grill
Park Avalon
Pastis
Pershing Sq.
Pete's Tavern
P.J. Clarke's
Ruby Foo's†
Shark Bar
Tao
Tja!
Tortilla Flats
Town
Tribeca Grill
Zarela

Sleepers
(Good to excellent food, but little known)
Bonnie's Grill
Casa
Charles' Southern
Convivium Osteria
Dalga Seafood
East Post
Enzo's
1492 Food
Gaby Brasserie
Grilled Cheese NYC
Kam Chueh
La Bergamote
La Cantina
Le Père Pinard
Liquors
Locanda Vini
Massimo/Ponte
Miss Mamie's/Maude's
Nadaman Hakubai
Namaskaar
Oikawa
Oro Blu
Other Foods
Palma
Paprika
Quintessence
Roth's Westside Steak
Sachi
Seo
Sipan
Slice of Harlem
Snack
Tangerine
Tibetan Yak
26 Seats
Vittorio Cucina
Wondee Siam
Wyanoka

Teflons
(Get lots of business, despite so-so food, i.e. they have other attractions that prevent criticism from sticking)
America
Broadway Diner
Elaine's
Ellen's Stardust
ESPN Zone
Hard Rock Cafe
Harley Davidson Cafe
Heartland Brewery†
Houlihan's
Jekyll & Hyde
Lemon
Lucky Cheng's
Mars 2112
Mickey Mantle's
Pete's Tavern
Planet Hollywood
Saloon
Starbucks
T.G.I. Friday's
White Horse

Special Feature Index

Tasting Menus
Alain Ducasse ($160 & up)
Aquavit ($85)
Atlas ($140 & up)
Aureole ($85)
Bid ($70)
Blue Hill ($65)
Bouley Bakery ($75)
Cello ($97 & up)
Chanterelle ($95)
Citarella ($75 & up)
Craft ($68)
Cub Room ($65)
Daniel ($110 & up)
Danube ($80)
Della Femina ($69)
Eleven Madison Pk. ($75)
Felidia ($105)
Four Seasons ($125)
Gramercy Tavern ($90)
Guastavino, Upstairs ($95 & up)
Ilo ($90 & up)
Jean Georges ($115)
L'Absinthe ($70)
La Caravelle ($90 & up)
La Côte Basque ($80)
La Grenouille ($115)
Le Bernardin ($125)
Lespinasse ($125)
Lotus ($75)
Lutèce ($135)
Montrachet ($78)
Nobu ($80 & up)
Oceana ($90)
One if by Land ($78)
Peacock Alley ($89)
Picholine ($75 & up)
Pico ($100)
Pó ($35)
San Domenico ($70)
Savoy ($52)
Scalini Fedeli ($75)
Sea Grill ($150)
Solera ($70)
Sugiyama ($60)
Sushisay ($80 & up)
Sushi Zen ($70)
Tabla ($75 & up)
Terrace in Sky ($110)
Tocqueville ($75)
Tonic ($73)
'21' Club ($70)
Union Pacific ($115 & up)
Virot ($75)
Vong ($72)
Wallsé ($60)

Tea Service
(See also *Hotels*)
Al Baraka
Algonquin Hotel
Anglers & Writers
Box Tree
Café Botanica
Cafe Lalo
Café Pierre
Cafe S.F.A.
Carlyle
Caviar Russe
Danal
Ferrier Bistro
55 Wall
Heartbeat
Hudson Cafeteria
Jean Georges
Kings' Carriage
Lady Mendl's
La Lanterna
Limoncello
Mark's
Nicole's
Orsay
Palm Court
Payard Bistro
Russian Samovar
Russian Tea Rm.
Sarabeth's†
Sweet Melissa
Tea Box
Toraya
T Salon

Theme Restaurants
Babalu
Brooklyn Diner USA†
Ellen's Stardust
ESPN Zone
Hard Rock Cafe
Harley Davidson Cafe
Jekyll & Hyde
Johnny Rockets
Lucky Cheng's
Mars 2112
Mickey Mantle's
Planet Hollywood
WWF NY

Transporting Experiences
Alain Ducasse
Anglers & Writers
Aquavit
AZ
Balthazar
Bambou
Bateaux NY
Box Tree

Special Feature Index

Café des Artistes
Casa La Femme
Chez Es Saada
Chez Josephine
FireBird
Gramercy Tavern
Guastavino, Upstairs
Heidelberg
Il Buco
Jezebel
La Belle Epoque
La Côte Basque
La Grenouille
Landmark Tavern
Le Colonial
Le Refuge
Le Refuge Inn
Mars 2112
Nicholson
Nirvana
Nobu
Oyster Bar (Gr. Cent.)
Rao's
Russian Tea Rm.
Sylvia's
Tabla
Tavern on Green
Vatan
Vong
World Yacht

Visitors on Expense Account

Alain Ducasse
Aquavit
Atlas
Aureole
Baldoria
Bateaux NY
Bayard's
Café des Artistes
Café Pierre
Caviar Russe
Cello
Craft
Daniel
Danube
Del Frisco's
Felidia
Four Seasons
Gotham B&G
Gramercy Tavern
Guastavino, Upstairs
Harry Cipriani
Il Cantinori
Il Mulino
Il Nido
Ilo
Il Postino

Jean Georges
Kuruma Zushi
La Caravelle
La Côte Basque
La Grenouille
Le Bernardin
Le Cirque 2000
Lutèce
March
Medi
Milos
Mr. K's
Nobu
Oceana
One if by Land
Peter Luger
Petrossian
Post House
Remi
River Cafe
Rothmann's
San Domenico
Scalini Fedeli
Shun Lee Palace
Smith & Wollensky
Sushisay
Tavern on Green
Terrace in Sky
Two Two Two
Veritas
Vong
Water's Edge

Winning Wine Lists

Alain Ducasse
Alison on Dominick
Aquagrill
Aquavit
Artisanal
Atlantic Grill
Aureole
AZ
Babbo
Balthazar
Barbetta
Barolo
Bayard's
Becco
Ben Benson's
Blue Water Grill
Bouley Bakery
Bull & Bear
Capsouto Frères
Carlyle
Cello
Chanterelle
Chiam Chinese
Cité
City Hall

Special Feature Index

Craft
Cub Room
Daniel
Del Frisco's
Eleven Madison Pk.
Enoteca i Trulli
Felidia
F.illi Ponte
Four Seasons
Fresco by Scotto
Gabriel's
Gotham B&G
Gramercy Tavern
Harry's/Hanover Sq.
Henry's Evergreen
Il Monello
Il Mulino
Ilo
I Trulli
Jean Georges
JUdson Grill
La Caravelle
La Côte Basque
La Grenouille
Le Bernardin
Le Cirque 2000
L'Ecole
Le Perigord
Lespinasse
Lutèce
Maloney & Porcelli
Manhattan Ocean
March
Mark's
Métrazur
Michael Jordan's
Michael's
Milos
Monkey Bar
Montrachet
Morrell Wine Bar
Ñ
Nick & Stef's Steak
Nicola Paone
Oceana
Ocean Grill
One C.P.S.
One if by Land
Oyster Bar (Gr. Cent.)
Park Ave. Cafe
Patria
Peacock Alley
Piccola Venezia
Picholine
Post House
Remi
René Pujol
Rhône
River Cafe
Rothmann's
Ruby Foo's†
San Domenico
San Pietro
Scalini Fedeli
Sea Grill
Sharz Cafe
Sistina
Smith & Wollensky
Sparks Steak
Strip House
Tabla
Tasting Room
Tavern on Green
Terrace in Sky
Tommaso's
Tribeca Grill
Tropica
Union Pacific
Union Sq. Cafe
Verbena
Veritas
Water Club, The
Zoë

Wine Vintage Chart 1985–2000

This chart is designed to help you select wine to go with your meal. It is based on the same 0 to 30 scale used throughout this *Survey*. The ratings (prepared by our friend **Howard Stravitz**, a law professor at the University of South Carolina) reflect both the quality of the vintage and the wine's readiness for present consumption. Thus, if a wine is not fully mature or is over the hill, its rating has been reduced. We do not include 1987, 1991–1993 vintages because they are not especially recommended for most areas.

	'85	'86	'88	'89	'90	'94	'95	'96	'97	'98	'99	'00
WHITES												
French:												
Alsace	24	18	22	28	28	26	25	23	23	25	23	25
Burgundy	24	24	18	26	21	22	27	28	25	24	25	–
Loire Valley	–	–	–	26	25	22	24	26	23	22	24	–
Champagne	28	25	24	26	29	–	24	27	24	24	–	–
Sauternes	22	28	29	25	27	–	22	23	24	24	–	20
California:												
Chardonnay	–	–	–	–	–	21	26	22	25	24	25	–
REDS												
French:												
Bordeaux	26	27	25	28	29	24	26	25	23	24	22	25
Burgundy	23	–	22	26	29	20	26	27	25	23	26	–
Rhône	25	19	26	29	28	23	25	22	24	28	26	–
Beaujolais	–	–	–	–	–	–	22	20	24	22	24	–
California:												
Cab./Merlot	26	26	–	21	28	27	26	24	28	23	26	–
Zinfandel	–	–	–	–	–	26	24	25	23	24	25	–
Italian:												
Tuscany	26	–	24	–	26	23	25	19	28	24	25	–
Piedmont	25	–	25	28	28	–	24	26	28	26	25	–

So, where are you going *after* dinner?

Check out the new 2002 Zagat Survey New York City Nightlife guide. 1,100 bars, clubs and lounges rated and reviewed by more than 3,200 night crawlin' New Yorkers.

Available at booksellers everywhere, at zagat.com or by calling toll-free 800-333-3421.